Music and Consciousness

Music and Consciousness

Philosophical, Psychological, and Cultural Perspectives

Edited by

David Clarke

Eric Clarke

OXFORD
UNIVERSITY PRESS

OXFORD
UNIVERSITY PRESS

Great Clarendon Street, Oxford ox2 6DP

Oxford University Press is a department of the University of Oxford.
It furthers the University's objective of excellence in research, scholarship,
and education by publishing worldwide in

Oxford New York

Auckland Cape Town Dar es Salaam Hong Kong Karachi
Kuala Lumpur Madrid Melbourne Mexico City Nairobi
New Delhi Shanghai Taipei Toronto

With offices in

Argentina Austria Brazil Chile Czech Republic France Greece
Guatemala Hungary Italy Japan Poland Portugal Singapore
South Korea Switzerland Thailand Turkey Ukraine Vietnam

Oxford is a registered trade mark of Oxford University Press
in the UK and in certain other countries

Published in the United States
by Oxford University Press Inc., New York

© Oxford University Press, 2011

The moral rights of the author have been asserted
Database right Oxford University Press (maker)

First published 2011

British Library Cataloguing in Publication Data
Data available

Library of Congress Cataloging in Publication Data
Music and consciousness : philosophical, psychological, and cultural perspectives/
edited by David Clarke, Eric Clarke.
     p. cm.
  Includes index.
  ISBN 978–0–19–955379–2
  1. Music—Psychological aspects. 2. Music—Philosophy and aesthetics.
  3. Consciousness. I. Clarke, David (David Ian) II. Clarke, Eric F.
  ML3830.M963 2011
  781'.11—dc23
                              2011021170

Typeset in Minion by Glyph International, Bangalore, India
Printed in Great Britain
on acid-free paper by
CPI Antony Rowe, Chippenham, Wiltshire

ISBN 978–0–19–955379–2

10 9 8 7 6 5 4 3 2 1

Contents

Contributors

Alicia Peñalba Acitores is a lecturer in the Didactics of Music department at Valladolid University (Spain) where she teaches Music Therapy, Musical Expression, Music Evaluation, and History of Music. Her research interests include music and embodied mind, music and ecological theory, proprioception in music, music controllers, and music therapy. This research, funded by grants from the Spanish Ministry of Education, included periods of time as a visiting researcher at Sheffield University (UK), Université René Descartes, CNRS, Paris (France), McGill University, Montreal (Canada), and University of Genova (Italy). She was awarded her PhD in 2008, with a thesis on the body in music performance. Recent publications include 'New gestural relationships in the performance of digital instruments' (*Transcultural Music Review* 2010); 'Music therapy and ADHD' (*Revista Musical Catalana*, 2010); 'Interactive dance in children with cerebral palsy' (AELFA, 2010); and 'Body, music, proprioception and experience' (*Etno-Folk*, 2009). She has been editor of *Transcultural Music Review* since 2005, and is a member of the Renaissance dance group 'Il buon tempo'.

Meurig Beynon is an Emeritus Reader in Computer Science at the University of Warwick, UK. Over his career, he has made research contributions to mathematics, theoretical computer science, and Empirical Modelling, a new research area that he established and has developed in collaboration with colleagues and research students over many years. Empirical Modelling offers an alternative conceptual framework for computing with applications to human–computer interaction, computer graphics and computer-aided design, software development, decision-support, educational technology, and humanities computing. Meurig has had a lifelong interest in music as a pianist who particularly enjoys playing chamber music and accompanying singers in lieder and opera. His publications relating to the themes of consciousness and music include: 'Empirical modelling and the foundations of artificial intelligence' (1999), 'Liberating the computer arts' (2001), 'Radical empiricism, empirical modelling and the nature of knowing' (2005), 'Mathematics and music—models and morals' (2006), and 'Human computing: modelling with meaning' (2006) (co-authored with Steve Russ and Willard McCarty).

Ian Biddle is a musicologist and theorist based at Newcastle University. His work ranges from the cultural history of music and masculinity, through to theorizing music's intervention in communities and subjectivities. He has interests in German music 1800–1945, musics of Eastern Europe 1877–1945, traditional musics of Spain and Portugal, especially Flamenco and Fado, and Anglo-American popular music traditions. He is co-founder and co-ordinating editor (with Richard Middleton) of the journal *Radical Musicology*. He is author of *Music, Masculinity and the Claims of History* (Ashgate, 2011), and co-editor, with Kirsten Gibson, of *Masculinity* *and Western Musical Practice* (Ashgate, 2009) and, with Vanessa Knights, of *Music, National Identity and the Politics of Location: Between the Global and the Local* (Ashgate, 2006).

Ansuman Biswas was born in India and now has an international practice incorporating music, moving image, live art, installation, writing, and theatre. He is interested in interdisciplinary, transdisciplinary, and cross-cultural approaches to consciousness and embodiment. This interest has been underpinned for the last 25 years by the practice of vipassana meditation. He is a board member of Arts Catalyst, the science–art agency, and of Studio Upstairs, working on mental health through the arts. He has been an Arts Council International Fellow and has worked at Hewlett-Packard's research labs in Bangalore, The National Institute of Medical Research, and CRiSAP (Creative Research into Sound Arts Practice). Ansuman has shown visual art at galleries throughout the world and, while maintaining strong foundations in Indian classical music, he has also worked in free improvisation and sound art. He has performed as an orchestral soloist and as a jazz percussionist, and he has been commissioned to compose music for theatre and dance companies.

David Clarke is Professor of Music at Newcastle University, UK. He is a music theorist in the broadest sense, interested in analytical, philosophical, cultural, and semiological approaches to music. Underlying these several approaches and a wide-ranging corpus of published work is a concern with musical meaning. This can be seen in his many writings on the composer Michael Tippett—including *The Music and Thought of Michael Tippett: Modern Times and Metaphysics* (Cambridge University Press, 2001). And it is also reflected in his work on the aesthetics of musical modernism and post-modernism, on music and language, and on music and cultural pluralism. Writings from this last project include 'Elvis and Darmstadt' (*twentieth-century music*, 2007) and 'Beyond the global imaginary: decoding BBC Radio 3's *Late Junction*' (*Radical Musicology*, 2007). His fascination with cultural plurality is also reflected in his activities as a musical practitioner: he is a violinist, an orchestral conductor, and, more recently, a vocalist in the North Indian khyāl tradition.

Eric Clarke is Heather Professor of Music at Oxford, and a Professorial Fellow of Wadham College. He has published widely on various issues in the psychology of music, musical meaning, and the analysis of pop music, including *Empirical Musicology* (Oxford University Press, 2004, co-edited with Nicholas Cook), *Ways of Listening* (Oxford University Press, 2005), *The Cambridge Companion to Recorded Music* (Cambridge University Press, 2009, co-edited with Nicholas Cook, Daniel Leech-Wilkinson, and John Rink) and *Music and Mind in Everyday Life* (Oxford University Press, 2010, co-authored with Nicola Dibben and Stephanie Pitts). He was an Associate Director of the AHRC Research Centre for the History and Analysis of Recorded Music, and is an Associate Director of the successor Centre for Musical Performance as Creative Practice (2009–14). He is on a number of editorial boards, and was elected a Fellow of the British Academy in 2010.

Tia DeNora is Professor of Music Sociology at the University of Exeter. Her scholarly interests include aesthetic politics, music, science and social differentiation, and music, health, and wellbeing. From 1999 to 2001 she was Founding Chair of the European

Sociological Association's Network on Sociology of the Arts. She is author of *Beethoven and the Construction of Genius* (University of California Press, 1995/Fayard, 1998), *Music in Everyday Life* (Cambridge University Press, 2000), *After Adorno* (Cambridge University Press, 2003), which received honourable mention for the American Sociological Association's Culture Book Prize in 2005, and *Music in Action: Essays in Sonic Ecology* (Ashgate, 2011). In collaboration with Gary Ansdell of the Nordoff Robbins Centre for Music Therapy, she has recently completed a five year longitudinal study of music and mental health. She and Ansdell are preparing a three volume based upon their research *(Music, Health and Wellbeing: Ecological Perspectives)* to be published by Ashgate in 2013.

Richard Elliott is based at Newcastle University's International Centre for Music Studies, where he teaches courses on popular and world musics, recorded sound, cultural theory, and the politics of authenticity. His research interests are in the roles played by loss, memory, nostalgia, and revolution in popular music. His work in these areas is heavily influenced by theories of place and spatiality and he is particularly interested in the ways in which music creates or evokes 'memory places' that take on significance for individuals and communities. In addition to Anglophone popular musics he works on Portuguese fado, Latin American nueva canción, and musics of the African diaspora. He is the author of the book *Fado and the Place of Longing: Loss, Memory and the City* (Ashgate, 2010), as well as of articles and reviews covering a wide variety of subjects. His book on Nina Simone is forthcoming in Equinox's 'Icons of Popular Music' series and he is currently working on a co-written book on ritual, remembrance, and recorded sound. He is Associate Editor of the journal *Radical Musicology*.

Jörg Fachner is Senior Research Fellow at the music therapy unit of the Finnish Centre of Excellence in Interdisciplinary Music Research at the University of Jyväskylä, Finland. He studied music and social and education science, and did his PhD in Medicine with EEG research on cannabis and music perception. He researches the social pharmacology of music, i.e. how internal and external neuropharmacological agents and their corresponding brain reward processes influence music perception, production, and creativity. His publications include *Music and Altered States* (Jessica Kingsley Publishers, 2006), *Music Therapy and Addictions* (Jessica Kingsley Publishers, 2010), and *Cannabis und Musikwahrnehmung* (SVH, 2010). He is has published numerous articles and book chapters on music, youth, and drug culture; on drugs in healing rituals and consciousness alteration; and on music therapy and medication interaction. His current EEG research in music therapy focuses on music perception in depressive states.

Michael Gallope is a Harper & Schmidt Fellow at the University of Chicago, where he is also a Collegiate Assistant Professor of the Humanities. In 2011 he completed his PhD thesis in Historical Musicology at New York University while also earning an Advanced Certificate in Poetics and Theory. His research focuses on the philosophy and intellectual history of music, with specific attention to practices of philosophical self-justification both in the tradition of continental musical thought (Schopenhauer, Nietzsche, Bloch, Adorno, Jankélévitch, Deleuze) and in vernacular practices of musical modernism (punk, no wave, hip-hop, indie rock). His work has been published or is forthcoming in *The Journal of the American Musicological Society*, *The Journal of Music Theory*, *Perspectives of New Music*, *Contemporary Music Review*, *Current Musicology* and two edited volumes.

Rolf Inge Godøy is Professor of Music Theory at the Department of Musicology, University of Oslo. His main interest is in phenomenological approaches to music theory, meaning taking subjective impressions of musical sound as the point of departure for music theory, and trying both to explore the content of these mental images and to correlate them with the acoustic substrate of the sound. This work has led to an edited book (with Harald Jørgensen), *Elements of Musical Imagery* (Swets & Zeitlinger, 2001) and a number of papers on different aspects of this topic. This work on musical imagery has been expanded to explore music-related body movement, and as a result Godøy directed the Musical Gestures Project (2004–7) at the University of Oslo, and participated in various European research projects leading to a number of publications within this area including *Musical Gestures: Sound, Movement, and Meaning*, edited with colleague Marc Leman (Routledge, 2010). Godøy is presently directing an interdisciplinary research project, the Sensing Music-Related Actions Project (2008–12), using various conceptual and technological tools to explore the relationships between sound and body movement in the experience of music.

Ruth Herbert is an Associate Lecturer in Music for the Open University, and was formerly head of performance at Dartington College of Arts. Her research interests include music and altered states of consciousness, evolutionary psychology, ethology, music in everyday life, and music education. She is the author of *Everyday Listening: Absorption, Dissociation and Trancing* (Ashgate, 2011), plus several articles concerning consciousness transformation, musical involvement, and the phenomenology of everyday listening.

Bennett Hogg is a composer, improviser, and cultural theorist who teaches at Newcastle University. Much of his creative work has been in the field of electroacoustic composition, and he is also involved in a series of environmental sound art projects. His academic research is focused around ideas of embodiment and technology in music from the perspectives of phenomenology and consciousness studies, the intellectual and creative legacies of surrealism and other 'modernisms', and psychoanalytical perspectives on voice and vocality. He is co-editor of an issue of *Contemporary Music Review* on 'resistant materials' with long-time academic collaborator Sally Jane Norman, director of the Attenborough Centre for the Creative Arts at Sussex University. He is committed to Small's idea of 'musicking'—music as verb rather than noun—and to Varela's 'enactive consciousness', taking the view that music and consciousness are things we do, not things we have.

Tara Kini is an independent consultant in Education and Music. She has trained in Hindustani classical vocal music since the age of six under great masters and musicologists. She continues to train in the khyāl genre from Lalit J. Rao and also learns about the dhrupad genre at the Gundecha Brothers' gurukul in Bhopal. She has taught primary school music and high school physics in Mallya Aditi International School for 20 years. After a MA in Education from Oxford Brookes University, she specialized in training teachers and curriculum development at Srishti School of Art, Design and

Technology, Bangalore. Tara has composed music for theatre, and conceptualized and directed music shows that make classical music accessible to the lay listener. She has conducted extensive research on the music and poetry of Kabir and directed a new media performance related to this research at the ARS Electronica Festival in Linz, Austria in 2005. She taught a course on the Music and Religion of India at Stanford University, California along with Dr Linda Hess in 2004 and 2010.

Jeffrey Kurtzman is Professor of Music at Washington University in St. Louis, Missouri, USA. A specialist in sixteenth and seventeenth century Italian music, he has published books and articles on Claudio Monteverdi and other Italian composers, as well as numerous scholarly editions of music by Monteverdi and others from the same period. Together with Anne Schnoebelen of Rice University in Houston, Texas, he has recently completed a detailed catalogue of some 2000 mass, office, and Holy Week music prints published in Italy between 1516 and 1770. He was the founder of the international Society for Seventeenth-Century Music, has served as the Reviews Editor of the Society's Journal, and is a member of the editorial boards of the Journal and the Society's *Web Library of Seventeenth-Century Music*. His research and teaching interests also include performance practices, music aesthetics and criticism, and the psychology of Carl Gustav Jung.

Bethany Lowe is a Lecturer in Music at Newcastle University. Her research interests include the music of Sibelius and the relationship between music analysis and perform-ance. These concerns variously combine in her publications on the symphonic music of Sibelius in *Indiana Theory Review* (2003), *The Cambridge Companion to Sibelius* (2004), and *Music Analysis* (2010). She has been a practising Buddhist since 1996, studying in the Zen, Western, and Tibetan traditions. Her research in this field has been dissemi-nated as at such interdisciplinary occasions as the Third International Conference on Consciousness, Theatre, Literature and the Arts (University of Lincoln, 2009) and the 2010 Spirituality, Theology and Mental Health Conference (Durham University). She is active as a conductor and performer, teaches the history and analysis of Western music, and, as Pastoral Tutor at Newcastle University's Music Department, has an emerging role in developing the student experience of music in higher education.

Andy McGuiness holds a PhD from the Open University, UK, and an MPhil in Electronic arts from the Centre for New Media Art, Australian National University. His research interests are interdisciplinary and combine aspects of music aesthetics with music cognition and philosophy of mind. Research topics include the experience of music performance (from both the performer's and the listener's perspective), the nature and sources of responses to music, and the psychological and neurobiological underpinnings of rhythm. Forthcoming publications include 'Performance and shame' in *Experience and Meaning in Music Performance*, edited by Martin Clayton, Byron Dueck, and Laura Leante (Oxford University Press).

Eugene Montague is an Assistant Professor of Music at the George Washington University in Washington, DC. His research focuses on the interaction of music and movement, including theories of performance, and links between musical experience and human consciousness. Current projects include the development of a systematic approach to the analysis of productive bodily movements in musical performance, and the exploration of embodiment in piano performance through a study of the well-known finger exercises by Hanon. Montague received his PhD in Music from the University of Pennsylvania, studying with Christopher Hasty, Cristle Collins Judd, and Eugene Narmour. Recent publications include an essay on the role of the compass as metaphor in Luciano Berio's *Sequenza VIII* for solo violin, and a study of the appropriation of garage rock by the Clash. Montague was born and grew up in Ireland, and studied piano at the Royal Irish Academy of Music, where he earned advanced diplomas in both performance and teaching.

Katie Overy is a Senior Lecturer in Music at the University of Edinburgh, where she is Director of the MSc in Music in the Community, and Co-director of the Institute for Music in Human Development. Her research interests revolve around musical learning, with a specific interest in rhythm, and a strong emphasis on bringing together theory, research, and practice across disciplines including music neuroscience, music psychology, music therapy, and music education. Her PhD research into the use of rhythm games as a phonological remediation tool for dyslexic children was awarded a Psychological Corporation Postgraduate Award in 2001. After further postgraduate study at the Zoltán Kodály Pedagogical Institute of Music, she conducted her postdoctoral research at Harvard Medical School, where she designed music fMRI research stimuli and protocols for young children and aphasic stroke patients. Her recent publications include an edited special issue of *Cortex* entitled *The Rhythmic Brain* (Overy and Turner 2009), and she is currently the UK partner in the EU PhD training network EBRAMUS (Europe, Brain and Music).

Benny Shanon is currently a chaired Professor in the Department of Psychology of the Hebrew University of Jerusalem, where he has been since 1976. His academic studies were pursued at Tel Aviv University and Stanford University. He has taught at MIT, Cornell University, and Swarthmore College. He has held visiting appointments at Harvard University, Princeton University, the Center for Advanced Studies in Bellagio, Italy, the École Polytechnique in Paris, France, and the Center for Interdisciplinary Research in Bielefeld, Germany. Nowadays his research focuses on the phenomenology of human consciousness and on philosophical issues pertaining to contemporary cognitive psychology. Over the years he has also worked on the semantics and pragmatics of natural language, discourse processes, bilingualism, and the philosophy of mind. Among his publications are two monographs: *The Representational and the Presentational* (Havester Wheatsheaf, 1993; a revised and expanded edition appeared in 2009), and *The Antipodes of the Mind* (Oxford University Press, 2003), which was awarded the Polonsky Prize for Creativity and Originality by the Hebrew University of Jerusalem.

Lawrence M. Zbikowski is an Associate Professor in the Department of Music at the University of Chicago. His research focuses on the application of recent work in cognitive science to various problems confronted by music scholars, including the nature of musical syntax, text–music relations, the relationship between music and movement, and the structure of theories of music. He is the author of *Conceptualizing Music: Cognitive Structure, Theory, and Analysis* (Oxford University Press, 2002), and has contributed chapters to *The Cambridge Handbook of Metaphor and Thought*

(Cambridge University Press, 2008), *Communication in Eighteenth Century Music* (Cambridge University Press, 2008), and *New Perspectives on Music and Gesture* (Ashgate, 2011), as well as reviews and articles to *Music Humana, Musicæ Scientiæ,* and *Music Analysis.* In the spring of 2011 he was *Muziektheoreticus in residentie* for the Dutch-Flemish Society for Music Theory, the Orpheus Institute Ghent, the Universities of Leuven and Amsterdam, and the Conservatory of Amsterdam.

Conventions used in this book

Quotations and emphasis

In all quoted matter, emphasis (shown with italics) is as given in the original text unless otherwise indicated.

Pitch

Where necessary, specific registers of musical pitches are shown using the scientific pitch notation of the Acoustical Society of America—where C4 is middle C, C3 the C an octave lower, C5 the C an octave higher, and so on.

Preface

Contexts

As if 'consciousness' itself weren't already a problematic enough concept, here is a book that conjoins it with another elusive term: 'music'. Does this encounter promise stimulating new debates and insights, or will it simply open up a Pandora's box of further complication and disagreement? While consciousness studies has become recognized as a legitimate academic discipline (evidenced by the establishment of such bodies as the University of Arizona's Center for Consciousness Studies and the Association for the Scientific Study of Consciousness), it is one that is marked, perhaps even defined, by a remarkable degree of non-consensus. The jury seems still to be out regarding even a basic definition of the term (to which fact a special issue of *Journal of Consciousness Studies* entitled 'Defining consciousness' (Nunn 2009) bears witness). Does consciousness mean something more than mere awareness? Does it connote an awareness of self in the process (being aware of being aware), and therefore should it be seen as distinct from sub-, non-, or unconscious mental activity? Is it simply an attribute of mind, or is its material embodiment the thing that really matters? More radically, does consciousness as we think we know it actually exist in conformity with our most cherished intuitions about it? Given these unresolved debates, could it be that our experience and understandings of music might offer some timely contribution to them—possibly even be suggestive of ways to reorientate them? And might thinking about consciousness also suggest new ways of thinking about music?

There would be a certain irony if the role of the arts and humanities in these debates were merely to react to an agenda set by the scientific study of consciousness, since the empirical sciences have been the most recent to arrive at the table. Nevertheless, developments in the latter field have undoubtedly been responsible for the recent resurgence of scholarly (and indeed popular) preoccupation with the subject, which has then stimulated its growth as a major area of interdisciplinary study—this at a time of increasing numbers of initiatives bent on exploring possible interfaces between the arts and sciences. There is, then, a backstory here, one that broadly defines the historical conjuncture from which the present, musically orientated, project emerges, and one that is worth briefly rehearsing as a way of understanding that project's potential pertinence.

Where to pick up this story remains moot, but Güven Güzeldere (1997: 11–21) helpfully indicates some milestones in the history of the term consciousness in Western philosophy and psychology. Descartes's early modern account of mind as something distinct from body (*res cogitans* as opposed to *res extensa*) could be viewed as foundational for modern formulations of consciousness, and for their vicissitudes. William James's radical-empiricist writings on consciousness around the turn of the twentieth century, including his questioning of the concept—as in his 1904 essay, 'Does consciousness exist?' (published as James 1912)—would be another touchstone.

A further salient historical moment could be located in the early 1960s around the demise of behaviourism's embargo on the category of the mental, as something known only as private, subjective experience, and therefore not amenable to scientific inquiry. Developments in cognitive psychology (both before and definitely after behaviourism's ascendancy) demonstrated the possibility and necessity of writing subjective experience back into the scientific study of the mind, establishing experimental methods and theoretical models by which to understand the hidden mental apparatus of human perception, cognition, and action (e.g. Miller *et al.* 1960; Neisser 1976). Thus it became possible to talk legitimately about consciousness within a scientific framework. Advances in neuroscience have marked another turn in the consciousness debate. Through technical developments in scanning (positron emission tomography (PET), functional magnetic resonance imaging (fMRI), magnetoencephalography (MEG)), we now know rather more about how the brain works; and among other things it has become possible to observe what goes on in an individual's brain as they actually have an experience. With this comes the notion that it may be possible to describe the neural conditions that are coterminous with conscious experience—the so-called neural correlates of consciousness.

Realizing such an aspiration depends not only on the technical challenges of capturing the appropriate data, but also on developing an appropriate epistemological framework through which to interpret them. Not least among the existing theoretical problems that neuroscientific explanations have made even more urgent is how to resolve the dualism of brain and mind. Models variously put forward by philosophically informed neuroscientists and psychologists (and neuroscientifically and psychologically informed philosophers) such as Daniel Dennett, Antonio Damasio, and Jeffrey Gray have posed important challenges to received assumptions about both the status of consciousness and of the self that allegedly experiences it. Not all have found these explanations persuasive or palatable; that even some at the harder end of the scientific spectrum (e.g. Popper and Eccles 1977) have been reluctant to relinquish versions of dualistic thinking demonstrates that you don't have to be a mysterian to believe that explanations of consciousness cannot be reduced to accounts of neural processes alone.

Viewing these matters from a different discursive space, a cultural historian might see them as pointing to a late phase in a crisis around materialism (or physicalism) that has been on the cards at least since the Enlightenment. To paraphrase John Searle (1984) and others, what is alluring about studying the mind (and consciousness in particular) is exactly the qualitative discrepancy between the squishy grey matter of the brain and the fact this supports human lived experience in its infinite variety—including, of course, the many modes of enjoyment offered by music. But this dichotomy is also a source of anxiety—on all sides. For the rigorous empiricist, any explanation of mind that is not grounded in matter would smack of metaphysics: there must be nothing more. For others, any explanation of mind that limits the richness of lived experience—knowable as such only from a first-person, subjective perspective—to description in purely neurophysiological terms would be unthinkably reductionist: there must something more. The anxiety, then, revolves around the question of whether consciousness—the very thing in which our being as human subjects would seem to inhere—can be considered in the same way as any other material object of investigation in the world. Can we treat the apparent source of our selfhood in this way without losing the very concept of what it is to be human? Moreover, should brains and minds in any case be the only, or even the key, terms of reference as we seek to understand consciousness?

Music, culture, and consciousness

What if we were to approach these problems from another perspective—one that encompassed collective human experiences of doing, making, and signifying, and their associated states of consciousness? This would be the space of culture, a space of activity and production (of doing and making) as real and material as any other facet of our world. What if we refused to consider consciousness as existing outside these conditions, and therefore chose to roll them into the inquiry? This would mean a refusal of the reductionist path, without necessarily cutting loose from a materialist account—but invoking a more extended, more humanizing understanding of materialism. More radically still, this might move the terms of the debate beyond the binary opposition of physicalism versus Idealism, perhaps deconstructing it, perhaps even prompting the revaluation of notions repressed under the sign of Western post-Enlightenment Reason—especially if this also meant an openness to cultural formations other than Western. It is from this space that those working in the arts and humanities have much to offer the study of consciousness.

If this were true of culture(s) in general, what is it that music in particular has to offer in this context? Another way to ask the question might be: Does music simply offer *an* insight into consciousness—in principle no better or worse than a whole range of other human activities and interests (e.g. gardening or golf), though certainly of interest to musicians—or does it have a special claim in this respect that may be of broader significance? Those seeking to advance the latter, strong claim might choose to emphasize music's ontological grounding in sound and time. Invoking just such a premise, Laird Addis (1999) has argued that sound uniquely shares with consciousness the essential properties of being both temporally based and non-reliant on change; and from this premise he has argued that 'music represents possible states of consciousness' (69). While the second of these attributions—that neither sound nor consciousness is ontologically dependent on change—is contentious, Addis's point about the temporal determination of both suggests a salutary corrective to the habitual preoccupation with non-temporal visual perception in certain quarters of consciousness studies (most notoriously the fixation on the colour red in the qualia debate) that has perhaps generated as much heat as light. Paying due attention to the structured temporality of music, then, might help bring a much needed focus to the key dimension of time in the constitution of consciousness.

Music might have further grounds for its claim to a strong relationship to consciousness—based on the way that it combines social, conceptual, technical, emotional, perceptual, and motor attributes; the way that it is distributed in/around societies; the high value that is placed upon it in at least some (perhaps many) cultures; the fact that it seems *not* to be the official medium of communication in any culture—and therefore perhaps escapes formalized social controls, arguably remaining closer to a less obviously ideologically regulated imprint/reflection of 'what it is like to be a human' (in the spirit of Thomas Nagel's (1974) essay, 'What is it like to be a bat?'). Moreover, philosophers, psychologists, and musicologists from many very different perspectives have argued that music has the capacity both to reflect human subjectivity and to be a powerful element in constituting it. These points indicate a *prima facie* case for music as offering significant insights into consciousness—with a further important complementary perspective on that relationship. If music has a special relationship to consciousness, we might also ask: What can we discover or claim about the specific nature of musical consciousness? What kinds of musical consciousness are there? How do they come about? What do they mean—what is their significance? Is there even such a thing as 'musical consciousness'?

The scope of this book

This, then, begins to mark out some of the terrain that would define the study of music and consciousness. It was with just such an intent that we convened the first International Conference on Music and Consciousness in July 2006. Jointly organized by Sheffield University Music Department and Newcastle University's International Centre for Music Studies, the event proved to be an energetic dialogue between an eclectic range of positions; in many ways a model of the kind of inter- (or multi-) disciplinarity that consciousness studies promises. As editors of the present volume we have sought to represent this situation by including a number of papers from the conference, asking contributors to develop their ideas further, and also inviting additional perspectives from other authors. To the best of our knowledge, this represents the first book-length collaboration devoted solely to such a wide-ranging enquiry into music and consciousness. Considered as a whole, the collection both acknowledges and contributes to debates in consciousness studies at large, but it also maps out areas that could be seen as peculiar to music and consciousness. Some of the larger issues discussed above are addressed, others remain relatively unexplored (and hence particularly open to future discussion), while yet further questions are raised.

In a collection of essays by separate individuals with different priorities and agendas, it would be specious to claim a single overarching narrative. Even more than is usually the case, the present book is the convergence of a wide range of disciplinary, subdisciplinary, and personal concerns. Our volume's subtitle, 'Philosophical, Psychological, and Cultural Perspectives', announces the broad conceptual categories into which our authors' contributions fall. While our original intention had been to divide the volume into three sections corresponding to those categories, it eventually became clear that almost every author explored territory that combined at least two, and sometimes all three, domains. Our response, therefore, has been to look beyond the original idea of separate sections and opt instead for a continuous sequence of chapters, in which the chapter-to-chapter links create something that is more like a continuous narrative, while the shape of original schema remains discernible behind it.

The initial chapters perhaps represent those most overtly informed by notions from philosophy and its more recent relatives, cultural and critical theory. Given the intensity of debates around first-person experience in consciousness studies, and with this a resurgence of interest in phenomenology, it is appropriate that Edmund Husserl figures at the outset (and indeed makes several subsequent appearances). He is in the foreground of the opening pair of chapters, in which David Clarke and Eugene Montague offer complementary takes on temporality as a fundamental and recurrent link between music and consciousness. Montague points out that music has its own version of the so-called 'hard problem' of consciousness that has loomed large in recent philosophical and scientific studies—the relationship between subjective and objective perspectives on experience. Montague explores the physical gestures of the performer, and embodied cognition in general, as a fruitful way to approach that 'hard problem'. David Clarke examines the complex relationship between phenomenological and semiological understandings of music and consciousness through the window of time. He also explores the polar tension between Husserl's phenomenology and Derrida's critique of it, considering what the experience of music might have to offer in response to the critical question of what is most primordial or essential to consciousness: the unceasing, differential movement of meaning, or some pure flow of subjectivity that underpins all our experience. These core epistemological issues are also at the heart of Michael Gallope's deconstructivist approach to the phenomenology of consciousness. Invoking both Derrida and Bernard Stiegler, Gallope takes 'technicity' as his central concept—a synthesis of technology and inscription that puts the history and materiality of music in the critical spotlight and that articulates a decidedly post-Husserlian, and arguably post-humanist, position. In related fashion, Ian Biddle critiques phenomenological approaches for the assumptions they bring to listening—not least under the Husserl-inspired notion of 'reduced listening' propounded by Pierre Schaeffer. Drawing on a track by Madonna, and the writing of Lacan and Žižek, Biddle casts doubt on the idea of 'pure' consciousness and the apparently universalizing assumptions behind it, as well as the eclipse of the particular, and indeed the vernacular, that this has historically entailed. Bennett Hogg also argues for consciousness as culturally and historically situated, and for 'sonic intertexuality' as operative at every moment in the practice of musical improvisation. Derrida is again invoked here in a critique of those attitudes that assume improvisation to emerge from some originary, 'natural' or pre-cultural space. If Hogg in effect still argues for the pertinence of phenomenology, this is a phenomenology construed, after Francisco Varela and others, as thoroughly enactive—consciousness as something we do, rather than have.

That notion—of consciousness in practice—also lies at the heart of the three succeeding chapters, by Ansuman Biswas, Bethany Lowe, and David Clarke and Tara Kini, which consider music and consciousness from Eastern perspectives. From the standpoints of their respective Buddhist traditions, Lowe and Biswas underscore how meditation is above all a practical pathway for developing consciousness. From his particular standpoint as a multidisciplinary artist, and not least as a musical improviser (like Hogg), Biswas offers a richly personal account of music and consciousness that is at every stage informed by the practice and principles of vipassana meditation. Lowe's chapter details further some of the key aspects of Buddhist thought, especially the place of sound and music in its accounts of consciousness, from which she goes on to consider the place of Buddhist notions of consciousness in the work of a number of Western composers. In complementary fashion, but this time within a Hindu philosophical framework, Clarke and Kini take an ethnographic and philosophical approach to Dhrupad, showing how this North Indian vocal tradition both emanates from and is able to instil deep states of consciousness. While all these studies might seem to foreground cultural perspectives on music and consciousness, we should beware of falling prey to ethnocentricity; their perspectives are no more or less 'cultural' than any other chapter in this book, and they make as strong a claim as any to its philosophical strand. Not least, they confront Western mind–body dualisms with altogether different formulations of the relationship between matter, mind, and consciousness. Moreover, by insisting on philosophy as at once an intellectual and practical activity (readily absorbable into all aspects of life, including musical life), these traditions make it possible to recover notions of the spiritual as a legitimate topic of inquiry.

The critical scrutiny of conventional dualisms—as well as a concern for the experiential dimension of performance—connects these chapters to Meurig Beynon's discussion of music, consciousness, and computing. Here the philosophical tenor shifts to the American pragmatic tradition, and in particular James's radical empiricism. Beynon draws on 'Empirical Modelling' techniques from computer science to explore issues in the modelling of musical consciousness, and in doing so makes a link to a run of chapters that focus on broadly psychological perspectives. Lawrence Zbikowski considers a variety of ways in which the kind of consciousness that is associated with attending to music differs from the kind of consciousness associated with attending to language, focusing on questions of corporeality and memory structure. Eric Clarke's chapter uses ideas from James Gibson's ecological approach to perception, Gerald Edelman's distinction between primary and higher-order consciousness, and Daniel Dennett's 'multiple drafts' model, to explore the consequences for consciousness of the reciprocal relationship between musical materials and perceptual processes. Chapters by Alicia Peñalba Acitores, Rolf Inge Godøy, and Andy McGuiness and Katie Overy take a variety of approaches to a central question for both music and consciousness: the embodied character of human experience, and the function of embodied cognition—of which music is a prime example—in the constitution of consciousness. These accounts, which further deconstruct entrenched mind–body dualisms, draw upon studies ranging from aesthetics, phenomenology, and the philosophy of mind to neuroscience. Completing this run of broadly psychological perspectives are three chapters that explore people's experiences of music in more and less 'extraordinary' and 'ordinary' states of consciousness: strikingly altered states of musical experience induced by drugs, as discussed in chapters by Jörg Fachner and Benny Shanon; and an entire gamut of conscious states found in the experience of music in people's everyday lives, as discussed with great vividness by Ruth Herbert.

One of music's strongest claims to a voice in the more general field of consciousness studies is its extraordinary reach and cultural diversity, of which the last three chapters of the volume explore what is inevitably only a tiny slice. In a chapter of considerable conceptual breadth, Tia DeNora focuses on consciousness formation in the pragmatic circumstances of a mental health context in which music plays a seminal role, presenting musical consciousness as a medium for social relation, regulation, and self-presentation. Taking the social context of Latin American political song, Richard Elliott adapts ideas from Lacanian psychoanalysis to explain how music can articulate a collective consciousness in moments of socio-political trauma. In the process he draws attention to the claim (arguably under-explored in scientific and philosophical studies) that consciousness (at least its distinctively human form) has a strongly public dimension—a perspective that connects his analysis with that of DeNora. Analogously, Jeffrey Kurtzman's chapter offers a corrective to 'presentist' tendencies, by showing us how, as far back as the early seventeenth century, a work such as Striggio and Monteverdi's opera *L'Orfeo* offered an aesthetic exploration of the relationship between conscious and unconscious levels of the human psyche. Kurtzman's deployment of early twentieth-century Jungian concepts in a discussion of early seventeenth-century music and drama reminds us not only that history entails a dialogue between past and present, but also that psychoanalysis (itself an historically occasioned and conditioned movement) offers yet further models for understanding consciousness.

These are some of the threads that link the chapters into some kind of developing sequence. But just as striking are themes that recur across the span of the whole volume. One such is the relationship between listening and consciousness, represented in chapters by Biddle, Biswas, D. Clarke, Clarke and Kini, E. Clarke, Gallope, Herbert, and Lowe. A second, represented particularly in chapters by DeNora, Elliott, Godøy, McGuiness and Overy, and Peñalba might be encapsulated in the question Where is consciousness? Should it only be identified with a narrow and brain-bound notion of mind, or might we imagine consciousness as a more extended, and in some sense public, agency of our own and others' bodies, artefacts, and performances—in short as a distributed property of brain/mind, body, and world? A third theme, running through many of the chapters—but particularly those by D. Clarke, Montague, and Fachner—picks up the central question of the relationship between temporality and consciousness. And a fourth articulates the ways in which music makes manifest different levels and modes of consciousness: primary (or 'core') and higher order (E. Clarke, Zbikowski, Peñalba); retentional and recollective (D. Clarke, Gallope, Godøy, McGuiness and Overy, Montague); everyday and beyond/behind the everyday (DeNora, Elliott, Fachner, Herbert, Lowe, Shanon); captured-in-language and evading language (Biddle, Zbikowski).

Consciousness as discourse

On the one hand, then, this overview demonstrates continuities and connections between our authors' contributions. On the other hand, it also lays bare the sheer discursive multiplicity generated by considering music and consciousness in conjunction. If this makes it impossible to distil any single thesis from the book's contents, it might instead point to epistemic diversity as one of the volume's more salutary implications. Among the things critical and cultural theory offers consciousness studies is the insight that the instability of a term's meaning is something that might be embraced—reflexively absorbed into its usage. 'Consciousness' (and for that matter 'music') is a sign whose referent is not a pre-ordained, already delimited object in the world waiting to have a label stuck onto it; whatever we understand it as comes into being in the very act of signifying it. And the ways we choose to signify it, the ways in which we relate this signifier to other signifiers and other discursive networks, are (*pace* Saussure) far from arbitrary. Slavoj Žižek (1989: 87–8) makes an analogous point with reference to the signifier 'democracy': although, theoretically speaking, the signifier might exist in a 'pre-ideological' moment, when it circulates in a free-floating discursive network, the moment any group (e.g. liberals, socialists, communists) actually uses it for an interested purpose it becomes pinned down, in the process fixing an ideological field around its own nodal point. So too with consciousness. Each discipline (or subdiscipline) will want to stitch 'consciousness' into its own discursive quilt of signifiers, each producing its own ideological field.

This plurality of definitions, and hence ideologies, is a condition of multidisciplinarity, and our aspiration for the volume is not to resolve these manifold perspectives into some kind of unified account, but to allow them to speak to one another and to open up still further dialogues with other constituencies. On the one hand, then, this book is an invitation to other disciplines across the arts, humanities, and sciences. On the other, it perhaps also represents an inner multidisciplinarity, pointing to new possibilities for conversations within musicology, broadly defined. If by bringing music into discourse with the study of consciousness we have not miraculously clinched any definitive solution to the latter's problems, we might nevertheless claim to have generated for the moment a new intellectual formation around them, in which music studies, looking across and beyond its own boundaries, makes a significant contribution.

David Clarke and Eric Clarke

References

Addis, L. (1999). *Of Mind and Music* (Ithaca, NY: Cornell University Press).

Güzeldere, G. (1997). The many faces of consciousness: a field guide, in N. Block, O. Flanagan and G. Güzeldere (eds.) (1997). *The Nature of Consciousness: Philosophical Debates*, 1–67 (Cambridge, MA: MIT Press).

James, W. (1912). Does consciousness exist? in *Essays in Radical Empiricism*, 1–38 (New York, NY: Longmans, Green, and Co.).

Miller, G., Galanter, E., and Pribram, K. (1960). *Plans and the Structure of Behavior* (New York, NY: Holt, Rinehart and Winston).

Nagel, T. (1974). What is it like to be a bat? *Philosophical Review*, 83, 435–50.

Neisser, U. (1976). *Cognition and Reality* (San Francisco, CA: W.H. Freeman).

Nunn, C. (ed.) (2009). *Defining Consciousness*, special issue of *Journal of Consciousness Studies*, 16(5).

Popper, K. and Eccles, J. (1977). *The Self and its Brain* (Berlin: Springer International).

Searle, J. (1984). *Minds, Brains and Science: The 1984 Reith Lectures* (London: BBC).

Žižek, S. (1989). *The Sublime Object of Ideology* (London: Verso).

Chapter 1

Music, phenomenology, time consciousness: meditations after Husserl

David Clarke

Introduction

If music has any special claim in debates about consciousness this might reside in two of its most essential attributes (so intimately related as to be almost one). First, music models, moulds, and makes audible the flow of our inner, subjective life—the sense of our being-in-the-world, 'the pattern, or logical form, of sentience', as Susanne Langer (1953: 27) famously put it. Secondly, these processes and their musical analogues are by definition *temporalities*. To be conscious is to know one's being from one moment to the next and to generate some apprehension of unity—an enduring self, an enduring world (whether 'real' or illusory)—out of the experience.[1] And while much in the everyday business of human doing furnishes such conditions for consciousness, the making of music might be argued as distinctive in these respects, since 'musicking' captures in its very temporal essence the temporality that is essential to the knowing of being—i.e. consciousness.[2]

This is a position that resonates strongly with the philosophy of Edmund Husserl (1859–1938). Husserl is significant for the study of consciousness because he held consciousness to be the very grounding condition of our knowledge of the world, with the consequence that philosophy must understand the world as it appears to consciousness, that is, to us as subjects. This phenomenological orientation, whose roots are in the earlier part of the twentieth century, has seen a resurgence as a major strand in present-day consciousness studies, one that has strongly argued for first-person (subject orientated) approaches to the study of consciousness. On a related front, Husserl also anticipated a vital strand in today's debates on consciousness by positing it as *intentional*—meaning that we are conscious because we are conscious *of something*; that consciousness is a result of our intentions towards the world—including our selves.

Temporality lies at the foundation of Husserl's phenomenology: 'All constitution, of every type and level of existence, is a temporalizing', as he aphoristically puts it (Husserl 1970: 169; as quoted by Klaus Held 2003b: 46). The nub of what Husserl meant by this is outlined by Held:

> Consciousness is a stream of lived experiences, in other words, a flowing manifold. But these many different types of lived experiences are known to me as 'my experiences'.

> Through their all belonging to 'me', these experiences all belong together, and thus they form a unity. This synthetic unity of the diversity of the *stream of lived experiences* is, according to Husserl, temporality. Temporality makes up the form of how consciousness exists, and, strangely enough, it does this in such a way that consciousness simultaneously innerly 'knows' this as its own form. This is 'inner time-consciousness'. (43)

These notions are explored in depth by Husserl in the corpus of writings collected as Volume X of *Husserliana* and known in translation as *On the Phenomenology of the Consciousness of Internal Time (1893–1917)* (Husserl 1991). In the *Phenomenology* we see the growth and maturation of his thinking on time consciousness through an extensive series of writings, comprising lectures, notes, and fragments. Also significant is that, unusually among philosophers, Husserl makes music a recurring focus of his reflections. Or, more precisely, he repeatedly considers two particular types of musical phenomenon as pertinent to an understanding of temporal perception: a single tone, in its various phases; and melody, which is apprehended as something more than an unsynthesized succession of notes.

Husserl's consideration of musical elements is, unsurprisingly, in the interests of exploring phenomenology rather than vice versa. His inquiry proceeds in abstract philosophical terms, and since he never tells us specifically which melody, or even what kind of melody, he has in mind, his discussion is prone to a certain universalizing tendency.[3] One might argue that Husserl is simply being consistent with his own principles of 'bracketing out' the particularities of history and culture in order to reach the essence (in this case, the temporal essence) of the phenomenon under consideration. Yet whether this goal is even in principle possible or desirable—whether there is anything left once the historically and culturally contingent traces of meaning have been suspended under the phenomenological reduction—has been a point of critique for subsequent generations of theorists and philosophers, among the most trenchant of which has been Jacques Derrida's deconstruction of the very notion of unmediated temporal experience (discussed below; see also Michael Gallope, Chapter 3 of this volume).

Precisely because of these unresolved polemics, Husserl's phenomenology in general and his study of time consciousness in particular retain currency in present-day thought, not least for consciousness studies.[4] Therefore, and also because of its recurring references to music, it promises a productive place from which to launch an inquiry into music and consciousness.[5] My stance here is to use Husserl's rich insights to draw out the possibilities that music and consciousness offer for a reciprocal understanding, while at the same time not being oblivious to the various lacunae and (productive) theoretical contradictions of the *Phenomenology*. Because it was not Husserl's intention to consider music for music's sake, I will need to offer a somewhat fuller and more particularized discussion of music than he does. My analysis is conducted through three musico-philosophical meditations, each identifying a different standpoint from which to consider Husserl. In the first I will draw on the 'microgenetic' theory of Jason Brown; in the second the structural linguistics of Ferdinand de Saussure and Roman Jakobson; and in the third Derrida's seminal critique of Husserl. These meditations are to a degree autonomous; each pursues its own line of argument to its own conclusion, and tends to unfold as an essay in its own right. Yet, while my intention is not to create a higher synthesis between these three studies, there are connections between them, and their effect is cumulative. First, however, in order to set the scene, I turn in the following two sections to some of Husserl's key terms of reference.

Husserl and memory: retention and its others

At the outset of the *Phenomenology* Husserl asserts that his concern is not with an objective modality of time, but with time as it is given to us, subjectively, in consciousness. While time may be measured with instruments and modelled mathematically within sciences such as physics or cosmology, 'the time [phenomenologists] assume is the *immanent time* of the flow of consciousness' (Husserl 1991: 5); it is only from this experience that an objective time can be known. Hence, while any given moment can be mathematically modelled as a theoretically durationless point on a line, our actual experience of 'now', our consciousness of the present (consciousness being nowhere else present than in—or as—the present), is an altogether different matter.

As early as 1904, Husserl noted:

> *any state or condition that intuits time* is possible only as *extended*, and . . . *the intuiting of a time-point* is possible only *within a nexus*. I see with evidence that the consciousness of a time itself requires time; the consciousness of a duration, duration; and the consciousness of a succession, succession. (198)

These observations resonate strongly with ideas published in 1892 by William James, whom Husserl greatly—and unrequitedly—admired (see Bailey 1999: 142 n. 2). In particular, James upheld psychologist E.R. Clay's notion of the *specious present*, in which the present is understood not as a theoretical, durationless point in time, but as

> a sort of saddle-back of time with a certain length of its own, on which we sit perched, and from which we look in two directions into time. The unit of composition of our perception of time is a *duration*, with a bow and stern, as it were—a rearward- and a forward-looking end. It is only as parts of this *duration-block* that the relation of *succession* of one end to the other is perceived . . . The experience is from the outset a synthetic datum . . . (James 1905: 280)

Husserl pursues an analysis of just this kind of present, a present that paradoxically extends beyond the immediacy of 'now' into its own past.[6] His recurring example of the kind of object that is congruent with our immanent temporal world is melody. In Husserl's parlance, a melody is a *unitary temporal object*: even though its notes are given one at a time—i.e. in a succession—we also come to intend it as a whole (Husserl 1991: 21–5). As he puts it:

> the extension of the melody is not only given point by point in the extension of the act of perceiving, but the unity of the intentional consciousness still 'holds on to' the elapsed tones themselves in consciousness and progressively brings about the unity of the consciousness that is related to the unitary temporal object, to the melody. (40)

This is no parochial observation. The process Husserl describes for a melody epitomizes our very ability to put the manifold of temporally constituted objects of the world together into a coherent unity of consciousness. One of the crucial enabling capacities in this process is alluded to when Husserl speaks above of '"hold[ing] on to" the elapsed tones'; this is the capacity—the mode of intentionality—he came to term *retention*.[7]

Retention would seem a straightforward enough concept to grasp. To paraphrase from Husserl's account, if I hear a note A followed by a note B, at the moment B sounds (becomes present) A does not disappear from consciousness even though it is no longer present as a sensory percept. What I hear is a *succession* A–B; not A, then (as if in some disjointed space) B. In other words, even though no longer physically sounding, A persists as a retention, still doing its work in temporally structured relation to B. Retention, then, is a kind of memory—in Husserl's parlance, *primary memory*. Without it, what I would hear is not an emerging melody, but just a meaningless concatenation of notes (and maybe not even a concatenation).

For Husserl, retention is a critical concept for understanding the present as it appears to consciousness, which is in turn crucial for understanding consciousness per se, and hence for his entire phenomenological project. And, on the face of it, the notion squares with everyday experience. For example, we perform an act of retention every time we apprehend a sentence—keeping the sense of just-perceived words alive, relating these to ones just being uttered, and so grasping, i.e. synthesizing, the meaning of the sentence as a whole (in principle the same process as for a melody). But its complexities preoccupy Husserl for a sizeable portion of the *Phenomenology*. These unfold as he seeks to define the concept differentially, along two fronts.[8]

On the first front Husserl wants to distinguish retention, or primary memory, from what one is apprehending immediately 'now'—what he termed the *primal impression* or *primary sensation*. This latter term is equated with the act of perception proper: 'perception would be the phase of consciousness that constitutes the pure now, and memory would be every other phase of the continuity' (42). Nevertheless (and to adumbrate my eventual engagement with Derrida), Husserl's writing reveals the strain of upholding such a distinction—of trying to maintain the identity of the primal impression as precisely a real phenomenological datum (as opposed to an abstract notion) that can be kept distinct from retention or primary memory. For example, in the following passage Husserl takes his description of the primal impression to a point of overdetermination (including the italics, present in the original) in order to convey it as something in lived experience, only subsequently to concede it as something of an altogether different nature: 'First of all', he writes, 'we have the *primal sensation-consciousness*, the *absolutely original* consciousness, in which the actual tone-point stands before us "in person", as present itself, as now'; but soon after he states, 'Primal sensation is something *abstract*' (338). In short, primal sensation, the 'pure now', is an ideal construct; we can only actually experience it through what is other than it, through its retention:

> In the ideal sense, then, perception (impression) would be the phase of consciousness that constitutes the pure now, and memory would be every other phase of the continuity. But the now is precisely only an ideal limit, something abstract, which can be nothing by itself. Moreover it remains to be said that this ideal now is not something *toto coelo* different from the not-now but is continuously mediated with it. And to this corresponds the continuous transition into primary [i.e. retentional] memory. (42)

On the second front, Husserl differentiates retention from *recollection*. Although retention is a kind of memory, it involves not an active recalling of, or reflection on, just-elapsed perceptions; more a simple, unconsidered holding of them as a presence: 'retention itself is not a looking-back that makes the elapsed phase into an object' (122). By contrast, recollection involves actual rehearsal of what has 'elapsed as whole' (122), it is 'a re-presented present' (38), the repetition of an already presented temporal object (see 113). As I listen to a song, for example, I apprehend it subjectively as it 'runs off' as a temporal object in a continuum of retentions. But after the song is over I may choose to recall all or parts of it. This would be an act of recollection: the melody is not given of itself, I make it present to myself of my own volition (see Husserl 1991: 42–3, 49–50). Hence for Husserl, while retention or primary memory is *presentation* (German, *Gegenwärtingung*, *Vorstellung*), recollection or secondary memory is *re-presentation* (*Vergegenwärtingung*, *Re-Präsentation*).

There is one other other of retention in Husserl's scheme that merits consideration: its future-orientated counterpart *protention*. As retention refers to what is just past, so protention refers to the fringe of expectation where what is just about to happen colours our experience of now. Like retention, then, it determines our consciousness of the present, and is thus ostensibly no less essential a mode of intentionality. Yet, curiously, Husserl devotes dramatically less wordage to it (and is even more reticent about *anticipation*, the future-equivalent term to recollection). He seems content to posit protention as merely symmetrically equivalent to retention, and therefore implicitly covered by anything he says about the latter. Yet phenomenologically speaking, past and future perspectives are radically asymmetrical. What might better explain Husserl's predilection for modes of past-orientated intentionality is perhaps his apparently foundational intuition that the present, phenomenologically speaking, is a form(ation) of *memory*—a point which I consider from various perspectives in what follows.

From temporal schematics to musical particulars

Husserl's earlier writings in the *Phenomenology* are marked by his attempt to treat temporality schematically, and, not infrequently, graphically. Differences aside, Husserl's graphics have as their common theme the modelling of retention as a process of 'running off' into the past. One such example is the pair of diagrams given here as Figure 1.1. In the upper diagram the horizontal axis charts the continuity of successive 'now-points' as a temporal object such as a melody extends across time. This axis considers the temporal *object* as just that: a transcendent object-to-be-perceived.[9] Conversely, the vertical and diagonal axes represent the object's passage into memory; in other words, they consider the object as subjectively apprehended, as an *immanent* object. Under this process, each given now-point, for example P, 'runs off' or 'sinks' into the past, succeeded by further nows (Husserl 1991: 29–30). Hence, the axes differentiate between what Husserl called the 'concrete continuity' of a temporal object (376), on the one hand, and its accumulation in memory as a continuum of retentions, on the other. For example, the primal impression at E is fused with a retention compounded of all the immediately preceding now-points. This shows us how each now contains, and is conditioned by, its own immediate past. Finally, in the

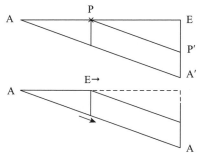

AE – The series of now-points.

AA′ – Sinking into the past.

EA′ – Continuum of phases (now-point with horizon of the past).

E→ – The series of nows perhaps filled with other objects.

Fig. 1.1 'The diagram of time'. Reprinted from Husserl, E., *On the Phenomenology of the Consciousness of Internal Time (1893–1917)*, 1991, p.29, with kind permission from Springer Science + Business Media B.V.

lower diagram, Husserl demonstrates (28–9) how the entire duration A–E itself eventually sinks even deeper into the past as it is supplanted by a new series of nows following E.

As discussed above, such modellings are highly abstract. So let us now consider how their attendant understandings of temporality could inform and be informed by reflection on an actual temporal object, specifically an actual melody. Example 1.1 quotes the opening bars of the first movement of Mozart's *Eine kleine Nachtmusik*, K. 525 (1787). The work's classic status means that it is an epitome of its kind, which makes it suitable as a case study to illustrate several key points in the ensuing discussion.

Other than the harmonization of the first note with the tonic chord of G major, the quoted melody is presented with only doublings one, two, and three octaves lower, which allows us to focus on its melodic characteristics. But even with this simplification, we can already note a first point of difference in principle from Husserl's schematic, which simply represents temporal objects as a set of equidistant points.

Example 1.1 Mozart, *Eine kleine Nachtmusik*, K. 525: opening of first movement.

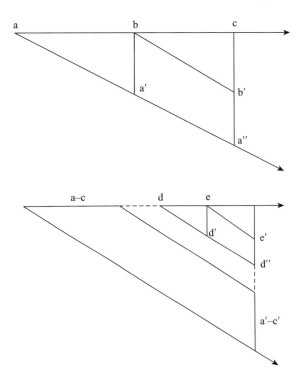

Fig. 1.2 Temporal modelling, after Husserl, of the opening of *Eine kleine Nachtmusik*.

Here instead we a have a phenomenon that is given to us as already structured. The eight-bar melody falls into two four-bar phrases—antecedent and consequent. These in turn are formed from—and cognized as—a series of motivic segments, whose discreteness is underwritten by the rests between them. The labels *a–f* applied to these motifs in Example 1.1 are intended to indicate, for the time being, only their serial order, not any other form of interrelatedness. And this temporal relationship can be modelled along Husserlian lines, as in Figure 1.2.

What does such a modelling tell us? The upper diagram, which considers the antecedent phrase, shows how as each motif is successively given in consciousness we do not apprehend it in isolation. Its meaning is not only determined by the retention of motifs that preceded it, but is in turn modified by those that succeed it. Hence at motif *b*'s place (time) on the horizontal axis motif *a* is running off into primary memory, and conditions the feel of *b*. And when *c* is presented, not only is our apprehension of it coloured by the just-elapsed *b*, but the meaning of *b* is also reciprocally modified in turn (and is hence notated as *b'*). Moreover *c* is conditioned not merely by *b'* alone, but by the running off of *a* and *b* together (*a''–b'*). This cumulative property becomes even more apparent in the lower diagram, which considers both phrases. The dotted portion of the horizontal axis indicates how at the point *d*, when the consequent phrase begins to sound, the entire antecedent phrase is 'cut loose', and 'sinks' into the past as a retention still intended against the new phrase that has displaced it.

So far, so Husserlian. But the translation of Mozart's musical particulars into the abstraction of Husserl's schematics entails glossing over two important—indeed 'essential'—points. First, the graphology does not address the fact that the 'nows' labelled *a–e* are anything but the absolute now-points associated with the 'primal impression'—especially evident in the temporally rather extended motifs *c* and *e*. Secondly, the exclusive concern with seriality ignores a set of interconnections based on similarity between the motifs, which causes them to function as musical signs. While this connective network is of a different order from the serial one, it is arguably no less essential to consciousness. These lacunae, then, point to areas of inquiry left underplayed, unaddressed, or unresolved by Husserl, and prompt me now to embark upon my musico-philosophical meditations. The first two of these address in turn the two issues just raised, while the third, in an encounter with Derrida, further explores the question of just how 'primordial' the differential role of the signifier may or may not be to consciousness.

Meditation I: when is now?

As noted above, considering the particulars of an actual melody problematizes the idea of an absolute immediate present, or now-point. With which dimension of the temporal phenomenon music are we meant to associate this notion? And, in doing so, how do we make a robust distinction between the moment of perception and the beginnings of memory? Husserl was as alive as anyone to the ambiguities. In the following we see him acknowledge that the application of these categories to a melody (including, presumably, ones like our Mozart example) is entirely mutable:

> If the intentional act of meaning is aimed at the melody, at the whole object, then we have nothing but perception. But if it is aimed at the single tone all by itself or at a measure by itself, then we have perception precisely as long as what is meant is perceived and sheer retention as soon as it is past. With respect to objectivity, the measure then no longer appears as 'present' but as 'past'. But the whole melody appears as present as long as it still sounds, as long as tones belonging to it and meant in *one* nexus of apprehension still sound. It is past only after the final tone is gone. (1991: 40)

So, the ambit of 'now', of the present, would seem subjectively variable, depending on where 'the intentional act of meaning is aimed';[10] and the present can be dilated for as long as it is possible to hold a temporal object in a single 'nexus of apprehension' (a notion akin to the Jamesian specious present). Further, the present ceases to be the present 'only after the final tone is gone'—hence when the melody (or any of its components) is registered as having attained closure.

Again we see Husserl allowing himself licence to blur perception as an analytical category, since if it is to apply equally to a melody as to a brief isolated note it must already incorporate acts of retention. (Indeed this conclusion is reached in the passage quoted earlier, where Husserl concedes that 'this ideal now is not something *toto coelo* different from the not-now but is continuously mediated with it' (42).) Moreover, even the said brief isolated note does not escape the ambiguity of where 'now' lies (and its attendant ambiguity of how perception is differentiated from retention); for, as Husserl puts it, 'this relativity carries over to the *individual* tones. Each tone becomes constituted in a continuity of tone-data; and at any given time, only one punctual phase is present as now, while the others are attached as a retentional tail' (40).

Following Husserl into the temporal life of a single musical note[11] (which, as we intend the note, is also *our* temporal life) only intensifies the paradoxes. As an example, let us consider the opening G of *Eine kleine Nachtmusik*, which we might safely say pins down a 'now', fixes a present. To ask, When does it do so? would seem to lead to a perversely circular answer: it presents a now, now. But the paradox in the tautology is that in the case of a sonic object as brief as this, its presentation of the now is only apprehended as such when it terminates—that is, when it attains the status of being immediately past (hence, 'then').

To elaborate this point, let us view the note from another perspective—one that relates to the kind of real-life interpretative decisions a performer might make. Consider the various ways in which Mozart's opening G could be articulated (perhaps stretching the parameters of actual performance styles a little, for argument's sake). Among other things, the note could be shortened with a *staccato* or lengthened through a *tenuto*. How, or, more pertinently, when would a listener know for sure which? Answer: when the note is over—sooner in the case of the former, later in the case of the latter. But sooner and later are terms of (conscious) cognitive judgement that are only formulated retrospectively. For all its brevity, the note remains a process (this is its inner life), and in the earlier phases of the *staccato* version of the note we would not yet know that it is destined to take a *staccato* identity: the performer might change his or her mind and make it a *tenuto* note after all. Theoretically, in these earlier phases both possibilities (or others along the continuum between them) are potentially available—perhaps in the manner of Schrödinger's cat.[12] But at the point where it is clocked in consciousness the note and its *staccato*-ness appear as one and the same thing: we do not seem to be consciously aware of other durations the note might have been going to take at the time those possibilities were still open. In this sense, the time of those possibilities—the time defined, animated, by those possibilities—was not a time as such (was not a time at the time); that is, was not a time in an immanent, phenomenal sense.

This points to something very un-Husserlian (although entirely commensurate with his blurring of perception and memory): the notion that essential to our consciousness of time—the consciousness which is supposedly the essence of consciousness itself—is an undertow of non- or un-consciousness. At the moment we become consciously aware of it, the opening G of *Eine kleine Nachtmusik* is known to us as both an object—it is a 'thing' with an identity, for example a *staccato* note—and as a (completed) process. Without our having unconsciously partaken of the note's temporal phases no duration could be attributed to it at all—we must have had the measure of the note in our lived experience; but until those phases are over and the note has appeared to us in consciousness as an object, there is no thing to attribute duration to. The fact that we recognize the note as *staccato* and not *tenuto* is a conscious judgement on what just a moment ago we were experiencing unconsciously.

Husserl would nonetheless strenuously deny such a scenario—'It is just nonsense to talk about unconscious content that would only subsequently become conscious', he writes (123). Yet this very premise is intriguingly explored by Jason Brown in his theories of 'microgenesis' (see, for example, Brown 1999, 2010). Brown's acknowledged influences include Alfred North Whitehead and Henri Bergson, and his 'cognitive metaphysics' is strongly informed by a background in neuroscience (see Brown 1998). Yet the philosophical bent of his thought and his particular interest in time perception bring him to territory that is both resonant with, and productively different from, Husserl's mode of inquiry.

The resonances are implicit in the way Brown formulates the problem of how we perceive events in a series (a formulation in which short-term or working memory might be construed as an approximate empirical counterpart to retention):

> To hear language or music supposes that temporal-order in memory accounts for time-order in perception. The usual idea is that the order is first perceived and then transferred to short-term or working memory. But, since an 'instant' no longer exists when the next occurs, working memory is merely a technical term to mask explanation. What does it mean for something to be held in memory if the immediate past no longer exists in actuality? (2010: 10)

Brown's answer involves an inversion of the conventional wisdom of much empirical psychology of memory. Whereas the latter would hold that events are first perceived (in a sequence) and subsequently transferred to short-term and then long-term memory, Brown argues for the reverse: that '*instead of perception laying down memory, memory lays down perception*' (12). Congruently with this (and in contradistinction to Husserl as just quoted), he argues that '[f]or microgenetic theory a memorial unconscious underlies and is *antecedent* to conscious experience' (11).[13]

Brown models the movement from unconscious memory to conscious perception as a 'phase-transition', using schematics such as that reproduced as Figure 1.3. To paraphrase the contents of Brown's caption for the figure (12): This transition is a 'process of becoming', originating in an unconscious core self determined by long-term memory. Sensation, an aspect of the external world (represented by the horizontal arrow in the schematic), acts on visual and verbal imagery ('including conceptual and intentional feeling') arising out of long-term into short-term memory, in order 'to externalize and adapt the state to the physical world'. This stabilizes in the conscious perception of an object. The whole process might be summarized in an aphorism Brown invokes from Maurice Merleau-Ponty, namely that 'we remember events into perception' (21).

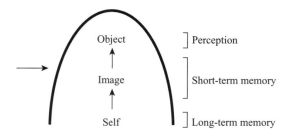

Fig. 1.3 'Phase-transition', from core self to perception; as modelled by Jason Brown. Figure from Brown, J.W. (2010). Simultaneity and serial order. *Journal of Consciousness Studies*, **17**(5–6), 7–40, © Imprint Academic, reproduced by permission.

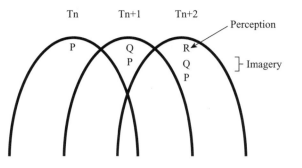

Fig. 1.4 Overlapping phase-transitions as a basis for perceptual stability. Figure from Brown, J.W. (2010). Simultaneity and serial order. *Journal of Consciousness Studies*, **17**(5–6), 7–40, © Imprint Academic, reproduced by permission.

Phase-transitions are momentary but dynamic mental states (lasting a fraction of a second). The curve with which Brown represents them models consciousness as an *actualization* followed by a *decay*, since along with their 'potential for activation', memories may also be 'destined to be forgotten' (28). What allows a perception to persist is its revival across a sequence of discrete but overlapping transitions—see Figure 1.4. Similarities to, and differences from Husserl are both evident here. Like Husserl, Brown models successive moments as an accumulation of memories—or in Brown's parlance 'images'—of preceding perceptions (here labelled as P, Q, and R, at the time points Tn, Tn+1, and Tn+2). But whereas Husserl depicts the retained moments as points sinking ever further into the past, Brown shows perceptions as pulsations whose decay is overlapped by ever-new (and ever-renewing) arisings.[14]

Brown terms such an overlapping succession of phase-transitions an *epoch*. And it is only within an epoch, rather than a single phase, that a temporal object is actualized:

> Entities have a temporal extensibility over which they become what they are. In mind, late phases are not the outputs of early ones which, having been traversed, disappear, but rather early phases are embedded in late ones and all phases actualize together on completion of the final phase. (15)

Hence, on Brown's view, the opening G of *Eine kleine Nachtmusik* would actualize and decay in every moment of its microgenesis; but over an epoch of phase-transitions the perception would be sustained above the threshold of consciousness and be cumulatively enriched with images embedded from successive earlier phases (thus perhaps conveying something of the granularity of the note—slight wobbles of intonation, the fluctuation of vibrato, and so on). But the note would only be actualized as such—i.e. become the *entity* it is—as the final phase is completed (an event presumably determined by the cessation of the note as a sensation from the external world).

Thus, an entity in the process of becoming finally comes to be at the moment when all the transitional phases 'actualize together'. And for Brown an entity thus realized has the character of a *simultaneity*: 'Simultaneity . . . encloses, in a spatial epoch, the duration or temporal extensibility of the process through which the entity becomes what it is' (11). As in Husserl, there is a paradox here, but one that Brown seems more willing to acknowledge. For it is only as a simultaneity that the seriality that determines an entity can be apprehended as such.[15] Indeed, in a gesture that also acknowledges Freud among others, Brown views the unconscious (from whence all perceptions arise) as characterized by *non-temporality* or simultaneity, as the prior stage in 'a transition from timelessness to the temporal order' (11).

Concluding this meditation, we can draw two key points from Brown that offer alternative takes on Husserl. First, as just noted, seriality, whose essence is temporal, is utterly implicated in simultaneity, the spatialization—and hence de-temporalization—of time. Secondly, to repeat an earlier quotation, 'a memorial unconscious underlies and is *antecedent* to conscious experience' (11). 'Unconscious', of course, could be a cipher for many types of thing (defined not least by one's own epistemic persuasion): actual (non-)remembered objects and experiences, unacknowledged ideologies, unarticulated aesthetic preferences, unrecognized conditions of possibility, and so on. Many unconscious factors may yield images that lie just beneath, our conscious perception of the opening G of *Eine kleine Nachtmusik*: the connotations of the timbre of the classical string ensemble playing it, the concept of what a note is, the notion of a kind of music (i.e. composed in Western classical sonata form) that has a rhetorical beginning of this kind and that has certain possibilities for continuation (and not others), even a notion of what music is—all factors of culture and meaning absent from the high abstraction of Husserl's phenomenological account,[16] that nonetheless bear on consciousness. If these elements are important contextual determinants informing musical consciousness, there is yet another dimension of memory that, in a piece such as our Mozart example, is mobilized within and by the work itself, that has no less a bearing on consciousness, and has further implications for our reading of Husserl.

Meditation II: equivalence and recollection

To identify this further memorial dimension we need to revisit the complete opening theme of *Eine kleine Nachtmusik* (Example 1.1) and its graphical modelling as a series of retentions (Figure 1.2). In keeping with Husserl, the graphics portray the immanent temporal apprehension of the musical object in question *as a pure sequence*. The meaning supplied to each now by its forebears is that of its relationship to the latter as part of a series. What this mode of diagramming does not capture (the additional dimension that is my concern in this meditation) is the fact that the two main phrases of the opening theme, for example, are bonded not only through their temporal contiguity but also through their similarity. That is to say, they are also associated through *equivalence*—as can be seen from the vertical realignment of the melody in Example 1.2.

The equivalence between the phrases is determined by a similarity of form, including the identical duration and sequence of their constituent motifs. Example 1.2 highlights this aspect of similarity by supplementing the motivic labels of the second phrase with their equivalents from the first; hence d is also labelled as a^1, e also as b^1, f also as c^1 (this last also presenting an elegant symmetry of trajectory between the

Example 1.2 Mozart, K. 525 opening, showing equivalences between phrases.

equivalent terms). To underline the difference between this principle and that of sequentiality, let us imagine (however painfully) an alternative version of Mozart's second phrase—say, with the motifs of the second phrase in reverse order. Despite this modification, there would be no significant change in the Husserlian diagram. Even the letters would not need to change, since the alphabetic sequence models a temporal one—the seriality per se of events and not their content. In other words, the diagram's architecture would be just the same: it would still show one phrase as a retention sinking into the past as a new phrase is intended. Yet, in our imaginary modified version of the theme, the originally strong rhythmic similarity between the two phrases is dismembered: we have gone some way to destroying the equivalence that originally obtained between them, with a consequent loss of at least one aspect of the music's meaning. What this thought experiment reveals, then, is both the significance of the principle of equivalence, and its absence from the Husserlian scheme of things.

The term 'principle of equivalence' comes from Roman Jakobson's article 'Linguistics and poetics' (1960)—a classic of mid-twentieth-century structuralism, strongly influenced by the semiology and linguistics of Saussure (see Saussure 1974), which in turn dates from around the first decade of the century (i.e. roughly coincident with the time Husserl was theorizing his phenomenology of time consciousness).[17] What Jakobson takes from Saussure is the notion that language operates simultaneously along two axes (Jakobson 1960: 358; Saussure 1974: 122–7). One of these is, in Saussurian parlance, the *syntagmatic* axis (depicted horizontally), along which linguistic terms are chained together in a linear sequence. The most obvious example would be the ordering of words in a sentence, and broadly speaking this corresponds to the temporal axis with which Husserl is preoccupied. Saussure terms the other linguistic axis the *associative* axis (depicted vertically), on which lie terms cognate to those actually uttered, for example synonyms and words with similar sonic properties.[18] These are terms that might equally well have been chosen to go into a sentence, and which nonetheless condition *in absentia* the meaning (or linguistic *value*) of the terms that do appear.[19] Jakobson's point is first to remind us that the absent terms are related to any given present one (and to one another) under some form of equivalence; and then to assert that the *poetic function* of language transpires when this principle of equivalence is projected into the utterance itself (1960: 358). Many an advertising slogan (e.g. 'Beanz Meanz Heinz') demonstrates that the poetic function is not the province of poets alone.[20]

Nor indeed of language alone. As we have begun to see, a version of the principle whereby 'equivalence is promoted to the constitutive device of the sequence' also obtains for music[21]—clearly so in the case of our Mozart example. Returning to the opening of *Eine kleine Nachtmusik* (Example 1.2), we can note that equivalence is audible not only between the antecedent and consequent phrases but also within them. The bond between motifs *a* and *b* is partly forged by equivalence based on pitch, as the second note of *b* lands back on the same note (G) that constituted *a*. Motif *c*'s entry into our consciousness is formed by first replicating, then compounding, and finally extending the trajectory of the two notes of motif *b*. There is also a proportional equivalence: motif *c* is as long as *a* and *b* combined. Even within the relatively short duration of this musical opening, then, we can detect the principle of equivalence operating on several levels. And listening beyond the quoted opening we would also hear equivalence operating within the medium-scale phrase structure and the large-scale formal structure. Thus, as the piece unfurls along its temporal axis, these equivalences activate a complex and multi-levelled network of internal associations—sometimes contiguous, sometimes discontiguous—based on similarity in various parameters.

Such a rich associative network is of course a feature of the eighteenth-century classical style, based as it is on a principle of balanced phrases that affords a play of symmetry and thus equivalence. More generally still, the equivalence principle is definitive for the cultural form we call a tune, which obtains as strongly in popular as in classical music. But this principle *is* culturally and historically specific—a point to posit against the universalizing assumptions of Husserl's account. In other words, we may not find equivalence in as pronounced or essential a way in music composed in other times or places, or with other aesthetic dispositions.

This becomes apparent on listening to a piece such as Orlando Lassus's motet *Vide homo* (1594), whose opening is quoted in Example 1.3.[22] While the piece is certainly not devoid of a gentle teleological impetus (fuelled by phrase accumulation and decay, cadential implication and deferral), what is most obviously different from the Mozart example is the lack of an articulated, question–answer style of phrase structure that allows listeners to ingest the music in bite-sized chunks and intuitively to grasp the equivalences between elements through their symmetry. Nor is there any single privileged melody that stands out from an accompanying texture. Instead we have an apparently seamless interweaving of overlapping voices, in which the flowing phrases envelop and occlude what little thematic imitation there is, and often well exceed what we can hold in our consciousness in a single stretch (i.e. extend beyond the specious present).

Paradoxically, even though sixteenth-century polyphony probably wasn't what Husserl had in mind when he spoke of melody, the temporal flow here seems to correspond more closely than in Mozart's case to the principle of the running-off of temporal continua that Husserl sought to diagram. Particularly salient here is another variant of his graphical archetype, shown in Figure 1.5. To apply Husserl's annotation

Example 1.3 Lassus, motet, *Vide homo*, opening.

at the top of this figure, our experience of the Lassus motet is one of 'ever new [musical] life'—ever new content flowing into the present and then sinking into the past. Husserl's description of this latter phase as a 'march of death' sounds a little melodramatic, but it does contain a whiff of truth. For as each now of the music is superseded by the next, the continuum of what we have just heard flows away into a kind of oblivion. Because the motet eschews any extensive principle of repetition, once any given material has slipped away beyond a certain point into the past its precise content seems to have dissolved. Retention here would seem to mean savouring for a little while what appears in the seeming immediacy of consciousness, and then letting go;

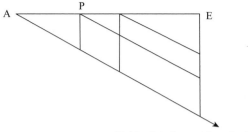

The series of nows (ever new life)

Sinking into the past (march of death)

Fig. 1.5 Further version of Husserl's temporal schematic. Reprinted from Husserl, E., *On the Phenomenology of the Consciousness of Internal Time (1893–1917)*, 1991, with kind permission from Springer Science + Business Media B.V.

retention dissipates into forgetting. In fact, the overlapping arches of Brown's phase-transition model (Figure 1.4) would, writ large, make as eloquent a paradigm as any for the temporal flow of polyphony of this kind; in both music and model each phase is a moment of actualization into consciousness followed by a decay back into unconsciousness.[23]

'Retention produces no enduring objectivities', writes Husserl (1991: 38); and this point is certainly consistent with the temporality of the Lassus motet. But Husserl does not explicitly draw the inference that this has for his retentional diagrams: that they cannot be extended indefinitely. Indeed if there are no enduring objectivities in retention, then the diagrams ought not to be symmetrically constructed, with the contents of the horizontal (objective) axis being unproblematically reproduced along the diagonal (intentional) axis. For this suggests retention as a kind of mental tape recording of the objective musical contents—the immanent object as simply a duplicate of the transcendental object it intends. If one were to extend a Husserlian retentional graph beyond a few instants (something Husserl never attempted in the *Phenomenology*), this would, in the case of a work such as Lassus's, need to model differently the dissolution into forgetting or unconsciousness that is the destiny of temporally more remote intentions—perhaps using dotted lines rather than solid ones, and then abandoning neat straight lines altogether to show the dissipation of these retentions.

If forgetting is actually an essential, and rather beautiful, aspect of the phenomenology of the Lassus piece (and others like it), the articulate network of equivalences that we find in the Mozart work (and others like it) foregrounds the opposite phenomenological disposition: remembering. But this is remembering according to the Husserlian modality of memory that is other to retention, namely *recollection*. This, let us recollect, is a more active process of recall; and in music like Mozart's it is triggered at just about every moment and across all magnitudes of temporal extension. Recollection is effected each time a motif is repeated (be it contiguously or discontiguously, in modified or unmodified form)—a process deployed particularly intensively in sonata form development sections. But perhaps the most graphic instance of recollection in such movements is at their recapitulation. Example 1.4, which quotes the retransition into

Recapitulation

Example 1.4 Mozart, *Eine kleine Nachtmusik*, K. 525, first movement: recapitulation.

the recapitulation of the first movement of *Eine kleine Nachtmusik*, illustrates how, some considerable time after the movement's opening, the opening is re-presented, i.e. made present again.

This is a formal gesture entirely typical of the eighteenth-century classical style, and quite unlike anything in the polyphony of Lassus's era. The equivalence between recapitulation and opening radically expands the temporal depth of field: recollection here functions actively to pull the elapsed music back into the present and to recharge the past—to bring it back to consciousness and to life. Importantly, this gesture of re-presentation does not supplant retention: the very reason the moment of recapitulation feels different from the opening it recapitulates is that it is imbued with the cumulative, ongoing presence of all of the elapsed piece behind it, and this profoundly conditions the moment's meaning. (Just as we unconsciously retain the measure of a single note and are thus able to identify it as long or short, so we retain a sense, however far below consciousness, of the content and duration of what has elapsed on a much larger scale between these two moments.) It is the interaction of retention and re-presentation that we need to underline here. While recollection had a secondary status for Husserl, and equivalence, its constitutive mechanism in music, is ignored in his invocation of melody, the re-presentational agency of recollection is no less essential a determinant of musical consciousness. Indeed it becomes a fundamental support for memory in the apprehension of such large-scale musical objects as sonata form movements. In their constant revitalization of retentions that have sunk below the threshold of consciousness, such movements themselves perform virtual acts of memory, which we re-create or realize as we intend them. They share with us the labour of remembering.

Meditation III: Derrida and Husserl

In suggesting that retention and recollection might function as symbiotic informants of consciousness, I venture (again) towards territory explored by Derrida. His scrutiny of these categories is therefore as good a place as any from which to launch a by now timely exploration of his critique of Husserl's phenomenology. Derrida's larger inquiry is set out across several works, but the fifth chapter of his 1967 essay *Speech and Phenomena* (1973) is where he specifically addresses Husserl's phenomenology of time consciousness. At the end of the previous meditation I considered a convergence in music of the categories of retention and recollection; but Derrida goes further, arguing for a deconstruction of these modes of intentionality. Their difference, he claims, 'is not the radical difference Husserl wanted between perception and nonperception; it is rather a difference between two modifications of nonperception' (1973: 65).

To grasp the full portent of this assertion, we need first to recall that for Husserl perception is a category synonymous with primordiality and presence; it is 'the phase of consciousness that constitutes the pure now' (1991: 42). But, as we have seen, and as Derrida relentlessly argues, we are never able to intend this absolute now-point of perception as such—never able to be utterly present with the present—since, on Husserl's own account, we can only grasp it as it slips into the past, i.e. in retention (or as it emerges into being, i.e. in protention). Nonetheless, Husserl hesitates to classify retention under the category of non-perception, since he regards it also as partaking in 'the primordial character of the living now' (Derrida 1973: 67). As Derrida argues, Husserl finds it necessary

> to keep retention in the sphere of primoridial certitude and to shift the frontier between the primordial and the nonprimoridal. The frontier must pass not between the pure present and the nonpresent, i.e., between the actuality and inactuality of a living now, but rather between two forms of the re-turn or re-stitution of the present: re-tention and re-presentation. (67)

Thus, for Husserl the umbrella of perception extends beyond the primal impression of the living now to cover retention (primary memory); while recollection (secondary memory) re-presents what is no longer perception ('nonperception'), and no longer present ('nonpresence'). But Derrida wants to drive home the point that '[w]hatever the phenomenological difference between these two modifications [of the now] may be . . . it only serves to separate two ways of relating to the irreducible nonpresence of another now' (65). As against Husserl's extended investment in the presence of 'the living now', Derrida argues for 'an irreducible nonpresence as having a constituting value, and with it a nonlife, a nonpresence or nonself-belonging of the living present, an ineradicable nonprimordiality' (6–7). In other words, he moves Husserl's frontier back to the absolute now-point, and extends the dominion of non-presence (and its cognate terms—non-life, non-perception, etc.) to both retention and re-presentation.

More than a minor boundary dispute, this signals a radical reorientation of how we construe consciousness (and music, for that matter).

How much is at stake in Derrida's redrawing of the line of primordiality? Among other things it opposes Husserl's notion of the present as the source of our self-presence, and hence of consciousness as a self-constituting flow. On Derrida's view, we are never present at the 'living now'; we are always just behind or just ahead of it. We can only know presence through non-presence, the life of the now through what is no longer living (indeed Husserl's varying metaphors for retention—on the one hand a 'comet's tail' emanating from the now, on the other a 'march of death'—betray his own equivocation in this matter).[24] For Derrida, the dislocation between self and now is a matter of not merely difference but *différance*—an admixture of delay and deferral, in which, as Martin Hägglund puts it, '[t]he delay is marked by the retentional awareness of being *too late* (in relation to what is no longer), while the deferral is marked by the protentional awareness of being *too early* (in relation to what is not yet)' (2008: 70).

Différance, the movement of *alterity*, is thus the concept that encapsulates the fundamental agency of non-presence with which Derrida would deconstruct Husserl's model of time consciousness. Not least among Derrida's targets is a 'metaphysics of presence', which he detects alive and well within Husserl's account, notwithstanding Husserl's claims to have excluded metaphysical adventure from his phenomenology (see Derrida 1973: 6). But there is more. By supplanting presence with *différance* Derrida seeks to eliminate any notion of a transcendent self as the constituting core of consciousness; consciousness is now constituted from a different place. The habitat of *différance* is language: it is the mechanism of the linguistic signifier, whose character on Derrida's account (and contrary to that of Saussure) is to deny meaning any final resting place in a stable signified, and instead to render it as a ceaseless movement of difference-cum-deferral from signifier to signifier. It is *this* process and not one of self-present presence through which Derrida reinterprets Husserl's unstable—and on Derrida's view unstabilizable—frontier between primal impression, retention, and protention. And *différance* is in turn an attribute of a still more all-embracing Derridian concept: *arche-writing*. As Hägglund points out:

> Arche-writing should not be confused with the empirical concept of writing. Rather, Derrida's argument is that a number of traits associated with empirical writing—such as the structure of representation, intrinsic finitude, and the relation to an irreducible exteriority—reinforce the conditions of possibility for experience and life in general, which is thus characterized by an arche-writing. (2008: 51)

Derrida's intention, then, is not to demolish Husserl's account of consciousness (which would be a misunderstanding of 'deconstruction') but to apply to it the linguistic turn of his poststructuralist brand of philosophy. But in the process he does radically deconstruct cherished, humanist notions of consciousness founded on the immediacy of autoaffection (a subject's feeling directly present to itself),[25] and shifts its locus instead to the ideality, the de-subjectivized 'technicity', of arche-writing.[26] Unsurprisingly, Derrida's arguments have elicited some equally weighty counter-critiques from phenomenologists,[27] such that it is probably true to say that these

matters are as yet far from resolved. I will attempt in the last part of this essay to contribute some perspectives from the purview of music.

My previous meditation ended with the observation that, at least in the example of
eighteenth-century music, retention and recollection interact. Given the preceding
discussion of Derrida, the stakes are now dramatically raised, since, if the qualitative
distinction between these two modes of memory is seen to be upheld in this interaction, it may be possible to claim that in music's case (which is as real as any other)
this is something more than simply 'a difference between two modifications of
nonperception' (Derrida 1973: 65).

On the face of it, the principles are as distinct as they are mutually entailing.
As observed in Meditation II, Mozart's recapitulation (Example 1.4) is on the one
hand an unequivocal gesture of re-presentation—a modification of what had ceased
to be perceived (the opening of the work)—and on the other hand the source of a new
emanation of retentions within its own timeframe. Those new retentions are crucial
for prolonging the moment of the recapitulation as a presence, which in turn is essential for its character as a recollection of the opening to be identified as such: the
re-presentational function is clocked not at the absolute first instant of the first note
(which would not be enough to establish a thematic equivalence with the opening),
but during the course of the ensuing thematic contents, intended within the retention
of that moment. Retention thus becomes a necessary condition for re-presentation, in
a moment whose very essence is the transformation of non-presence into presence.
Here we have the music's own performance (in the virtual sense discussed earlier) of
two distinct modalities of memory, where performativity itself is (by definition) an act
of presentation that thus renders the essence of one of those modalities transparent,
and transparently different from non-presence.

So, retention can here be seen supporting recollection without rescinding presence.
What if we considered the reverse possibility? Might it also be the case that retentions
are never intended without a re-presentation, and thus might after all depend for their
essence on non-presence?

Of the works we have considered here, it is Lassus's which might best enable us to
falsify this argument (and so provide us with the stronger case in favour of it if we fail
to do so). As we have seen, the musical material of *Vide homo* is significantly less
dependent than in Mozart's case on actual or modified repetition of musical ideas, a
principal basis for equivalence and hence re-presentation. Nor are there significant
principles of formal equivalence—no articulated phrases, no development or recapitulation that rehearse the events of an exposition. But might there be other bases for
equivalence? Perhaps we ought to attend instead to more generalized kinds of event in
the motet that might qualify: vocal entries in the polyphonic texture that could be
heard as repetitions of a generic gesture of inception; a recurring quasi-antiphonal
exchange between sub-choirs; unexpected chord changes that loosely parallel one
another; occasional melodic turns that remind one of something similar heard a little
earlier. Extending this logic more radically, there is a palpable tactus, which might
suggest that each beat be heard to invoke the ones accumulated before it, or the ones
yet to come. And if such features—which in one sense all involve invocations or modifications of the non-present—obtain for music of Lassus's era, then they, or their

counterparts, might obtain for many forms of music, and hence evidence a wider principle whereby each moment allegedly based on presence is in fact underscored by its other.

But this will not do. The problem is that these more generic features are by definition not *thematized*—to use a term fortuitously musical and phenomenological. For Husserl, an unthematized appearance is one where our attention is not directed to its manner-of-givenness; such an appearance functions 'as a medium through which we relate to the object that exists for us', but not as an object itself (Held 2003a: 20). Retention is one example of an unthematic mode of givenness (Held 2003b: 45); to recall Husserl, 'retention . . . produces no enduring objectivities';[28] whereas recollection, 'in union with [retentions] constitutes (or rather: re-constitutes) an immanent or transcendent enduring objectivity' (Husserl 1991: 38). And this is the point about the equivalences surmised in the Lassus motet. Tone, constantly revived in the melodic flow; pulse unceasingly generated by the tactus; voices entering and re-entering: these form a medium or framework for musical meaning, a generalized happening-ness that floods retention; but they are not objects of meaning in their own right.

It is worth noting here a possible connection, but also difference, between Husserl's notion of 'enduring objectivity' and what Brown terms an 'entity' (as discussed in Meditation I). For Brown, an entity is the crystallization of a process of becoming: the actualization of all its earlier phases. However, as we have noted, a single note may fall into this category; whereas, as we have just observed with the Lassus work, this will not necessarily count as an 'objectivity' in the Husserlian sense. Nor will the mere repetition of a tone necessarily count as a recollection, the action necessary for it to appear as an enduring object (one might say, to bring it over a certain threshold of consciousness). So some additional factor must be necessary to thematize it into objectivity. One obvious musical candidate for this function of phenomenological thematization is—thematization(!). What we have seen manifested much more strongly in Mozart than Lassus is that process whereby distinctive configurations of melodic, and/or intervallic, and/or durational elements are sufficiently preserved under repetition to appear as recollections of their forebears. But we might also say that what makes them thematic is that they transcend their first moment of presence and endure as signs. Motives, themes, musical ideas become objectivities by dint of signalling a connection between a present moment and a non-present one.

This observation looks set to shift the balance in the dialogue of Husserlian and Derridian positions. On the one hand, we have seen how music is a locus of experience where a meaningful distinction between retention and recollection can be upheld, and with this a distinction between presence and non-presence (Husserl's original boundary of primordiality). On the other hand, we have seen how the intending of objects also entails registering those objects as signs. This principle conceded, the floodgates open. For sonic presence can be thematized into objectivity not only as a recollection of what has already happened in the piece (intratextual signification) but also through a whole repository of cultural memories structured by such mechanisms as connotative and intertextual signification.[29] This entire picture points to another structuring principle of consciousness, one based on semiology or (for the poststructurally inclined) *différance*.

For Derrida, such structures of signification or *différance* would be aspects of arche-writing. The concept extends beyond the empirical mode of writing embodied, say, by musical scores. Arche-writing might refer to any production of a trace resulting from transactions with phenomena; such a trace renders phenomena into ideality (they can now be considered—remembered, repeated, reworked—without being physically present); the trace thus structures our relationship with the world in a different (or *différant*) kind of way. One particular consequence is that phenomena become de- or trans-temporalized; and this is indeed what happens as a result of the thematization of musical material. When thematized, musical material extends its essence beyond the immediacy of any local retention: material becomes idea, and a musical idea is not reducible to any one instant of a piece. This supratemporal, idealist transformation also makes it possible to reflect on and talk about music as if it were a text, transcending any real-time, living performance (a discourse pursued most formally in the activity of music analysis). At the opposite pole of our argument, then, it would seem that non-presence, non-life, and non-self might indeed, as Derrida argues, claim a prominent place in the equation of consciousness.

The question, then, is not that of eliminating one side of the equation or the other, but of how their relationship is to be construed, and indeed whether the equation can, or should, be made to add up or balance. Shaun Gallagher appears to incline towards addition: 'Derrida . . . does not set out to show that Husserl's analysis is wrong; rather, he attempts to show that it holds within itself conclusions that Husserl failed to draw' (1998: 80). It is true that Derrida pays his dues to Husserl,[30] but he also characterizes his stance towards him as a 'dialectic' (Derrida 1973: 69). Derrida does not deny the experience of the present, nor the life that inheres in perception; rather he wants to assert that these aspects themselves rely on an 'irreducible nonpresence' (65). Both the equivocation and endgame of this dialectic emerge when he writes:

> this relation to nonpresence neither befalls, surrounds, nor conceals the presence of the primordial impression, rather it makes possible its ever renewed upsurge and virginity. However [NB], it radically destroys any possibility of simple self-identity . . .
>
> The fact that nonpresence and otherness are internal to presence strikes at the very root of the argument for the uselessness of signs in the self-relation. (65–6)

The status of the sign, of language, of arche-writing lies at the heart of what is in fact Derrida's agon with Husserl. For Husserl, consciousness is its own ultimate principle, an absolute, self-present flow; as the condition of possibility for everything else, it is transcendental, and hence prior to language. Derrida wants to overturn this primacy, and supplant it with the trace of arche-writing that is 'more "primordial" than what is phenomenologically primordial' (67). This, then, is a struggle (perhaps an oedipal one) for who has the correct transcendent principle.

The question is whether there is anything left of consciousness when we have subtracted all the features of signification that constitute a phenomenon (which would in effect be to perform a phenomenological reduction). Husserl argues not only that there is—the flow of pure consciousness—but that this is foundational. Derrida does not deny consciousness, but does deny its foundational status, arguing that the signifier cannot be stripped from it; on his view, the experience of presence arises from the differential movement between signifiers of presence apprehended just as they become non-present.

The belief in consciousness as an ultimate transcendent principle is not of course confined to phenomenology or indeed Western philosophy. Various Eastern meditative practices aim at a quietening of the mind, the ceasing of linguistic activity and thought—a cessation of *différance*, one might say—to arrive at a consciousness of pure being in which the difference between self and object falls away (see Chapters 6 and 7, this volume). Such experiences, if authentic, might support Husserl's claims for a foundational consciousness that can be known to itself through a self-appearing flow (see, for example Husserl 1991: 393). Such a consciousness might be approached via musical routes—in Indian classical music, for example, in the practice of intoning 'sā', and, related to this, the achievement of *samādhi* states (totally focused consciousness) in a *rāga* performance (see Chapter 8, this volume); or, in Western music, in the reduced sensory input of minimalism, or the radically passive intending of sound promoted by Cage (again, see Chapter 7), and the inward trajectory that follows on from attending to silence (again, see Chapter 6).

These are clearly not the everyday conditions of musical experience; and it would be derelict to deny the worldly vitality and significance that music brings precisely through its manifold possibilities of signification. Yet neither should we deny that— even in more quotidian modes of experience—it is the *temporalization* of these signs, the immanence of their being experienced in the flow of consciousness, that renders them vital, and indeed as *musical* signs rather than as, say, literary or linguistic ones.

On one hand, then, this is to suggest both semiology (whether in structuralist or poststructuralist flavour) and phenomenology as essential dimensions in the study of consciousness, and that perhaps we should not get too hung up on claims for the transcendency of one or other principle. On the other hand, this is not to say that the Husserlian and Derridian approaches are simply complementary; or that—whatever the dialectics involved—they can be sublated into a higher synthesis. Derrida does not cancel Husserl. Rather, the aporia between their accounts creates a space which the study of consciousness (musical or otherwise) can most profitably inhabit.

In this spirit I would like to make a closing speculative gesture, which invokes both Derrida and Husserl, but begins by recapitulating Brown. Brown's microgenetic model of consciousness arising from an array of overlapping pulsations, or phase-transitions (see Figure 1.4), would seem consistent with accounts in the brain sciences of the oscillatory firing of neurons (see, for example, Gray 2004: 211). But this might also model the microgenetic life of *différance* and (depending how one looks at it) the self-appearing flow of consciousness. If each individual phase-transition in Brown's model represents a brain state, then this would presumably include networks of neurons that in turn model the network of signs intended in an object—such as a musical one—in that proto-moment. But, we might surmise, our consciousness arises not from such neuronal arrays themselves, but from the (temporalized) *renewal* of those states as one phase-transition overlaps another. The ceaseless displacement and renewal of Brown's transitions could be seen to exemplify Derridian *différance*, or arche-(re-)writing in action, and hence support the case for this principle as the fundamental basis for consciousness. The question might be whether there is any still-prior, 'ultratranscendental' principle. This would be the question, What drives the pulsations in Brown's model, and hence, What motivates *différance*? What, in Dylan Thomas's words, is the source of 'the force that through the green fuse drives the flower'?

Husserl wrestled ceaselessly with this problem (especially clearly in §54 of the *Phenomenology*). And his conclusion (arguably not incongruent with Derrida's) would seem to be that there is no further level of transcendence. The flow of consciousness is its own transcendental principle, known to itself in its own self-appearance:

> the flow itself must necessarily be apprehensible in the flowing. The self-appearance of the flow does not require a second flow; on the contrary, it constitutes itself as a phenomenon in itself. The constituting and the constituted coincide . . . (Husserl 1991: 393)

And also:

> It is *absolute subjectivity* and has the absolute properties of something to be designated *metaphorically* as 'flow'; the absolute property of a point of actuality, of the primal source-point 'now', and a continuity of moments of reverberation. For all of this, we have no names. (382)

Here, then, we see Husserl not only asserting these principles as an absolute, but also showing a salutary awareness that discourse about them pushes at the very limits of what is linguistically tractable. His recognition of the metaphoricity of the venture interestingly includes not only the metaphor of flow, but also, appropriately to Brown's model, that of reverberation. And if, '[f]or all of this we have no names', we do still have another invaluable source through which to approach these problems; a source that, like language, is implicated in signification, but that, unlike language, is concerned with something other than the conceptual; a source that, more deeply than language, traces the flowing and knowing of our being. This source is: music.

Acknowledgements

I should like to thank Paul Fleet and Bethany Lowe who offered helpful feedback on earlier versions of this chapter. I have also drawn inspiration from Michael Gallope, Eugene Montague, and other contributors to this volume who explore aspects of Husserlian phenomenology; in particular, Gallope's deconstructionist approach to music and consciousness was dialectically instrumental in generating the third meditation of my own account.

References

Bailey, A.R. (1999). Beyond the fringe: William James and the transitional parts of the stream of consciousness, in F.J. Varela and J. Shear (eds.), *The View from Within: First-Person Approaches to the Study of Consciousness*, 141–53 (Bowling Green, OH: Imprint Academic).

Brown, J.W. (1998). Foundations of cognitive metaphysics. *Process Studies*, **27**, 79–92.

Brown, J.W. (1999). Microgenesis and Buddhism: the concept of momentariness. *Philosophy East and West*, **3**, 261–77.

Brown, J.W. (2010). Simultaneity and serial order. *Journal of Consciousness Studies*, **17**(5–6), 7–40.

Clarke, D. (1989). Structural, cognitive and semiotic aspects of the musical present. *Contemporary Music Review*, **3**, 111–31.

Clarke, D. (1996a). Language games: is music like language? what makes a musical discourse? *The Musical Times*, **137**(1835), 5–10.

Clarke, D. (1996b). Speaking for itself: how does music become autonomous? *The Musical Times*, **137**(1836), 14–18.

Cleobury, S. (dir.) (2006). Motet: Vide homo, performed by Collegium Regale. Lassus: *Lamentationes Jeremiæ Prophetæ*. CD (Signum Records, SIGCD).

Derrida, J. (1973). *Speech and Phenomena, and Other Essays on Husserl's Theory of Signs*, trans. D.B. Allison (Evanston, IL: Northwestern University Press).

Fleet, P.W. (2009). *Ferruccio Busoni: A Phenomenological Approach to his Music and Aesthetics* (Saarbrücken: Lambert Academic Publishing).

Gallagher, S. (1998). *The Inordinance of Time* (Evanston, IL: Northwestern University Press).

Gray, J. (2004). *Consciousness: Creeping up on the Hard Problem* (Oxford: Oxford University Press).

Hägglund, M. (2008). *Radical Atheism: Derrida and the Time of Life* (Stanford, CA: Stanford University Press).

Held, K. (2003a). Husserl's phenomenological method, trans. L. Rodemeyer, in D. Welton (ed.) *The New Husserl: A Critical Reader*, 3–31 (Bloomington, IN: Indiana University Press).

Held, K. (2003b). Husserl's phenomenology of the life-world, trans. L. Rodemeyer, in D. Welton (ed.) *The New Husserl: A Critical Reader*, 32–64 (Bloomington, IN: Indiana University Press).

Husserl E. (1970). *The Crisis of European Sciences and Transcendental Phenomenology: An Introduction to Phenomenological Philosophy*, trans. D. Carr (Evanston, IL: Northwestern University Press).

Husserl, E. (1991). *On the Phenomenology of the Consciousness of Internal Time (1893–1917)*, trans. J.B. Brough (Dordrecht: Kluwer Academic Publishers).

Ihde, D. (2007). *Listening and Voice: Phenomenologies of Sound*, 2nd edn (Albany, NY: State University of New York Press).

Jakobson. R. (1960). Closing statement: linguistics and poetics, in T.A. Sebeok (ed.), *Style in Language*, 350–77 (New York and London: MIT Press/John Wiley and Sons).

James, W. (1905). *Psychology: Briefer Course* (London: Macmillan and Co.).

Langer, S. (1953). *Feeling and Form* (London: Routledge and Kegan Paul).

Saussure, F. de. (1974). *Course in General Linguistics*, ed. C. Bally and A. Sechehaye, with A. Reidlinger; trans. W. Baskin. Revised edn (London: Fontana/Collins).

Small, C. (1998). *Musicking: The Meanings of Performing and Listening* (Middletown, CT: Wesleyan University Press).

Varela, F.J. (1999). Present-time consciousness, in F.J. Varela and J. Shear (eds.), *The View from Within: First-Person Approaches to the Study of Consciousness*, 111–40 (Bowling Green, OH: Imprint Academic).

Varela, F.J. and Shear, J. (eds.) (1999). *The View from Within: First-Person Approaches to the Study of Consciousness* (Bowling Green, OH: Imprint Academic). Special issue of *Journal of Consciousness Studies*, **6**(2–3).

Welton, D. (ed.) (2003). *The New Husserl: A Critical Reader* (Bloomington, IN: Indiana University Press).

Notes

1. As I will presently be drawing attention to the problems of insouciant universalizing, I had better acknowledge that the conditions of consciousness I portray here probably have a Western bias. In Chapter 8 Tara Kini and I discuss rather different notions of consciousness in Hinduism, in which such an image of the self would be considered illusory, and not an essential criterion of consciousness (see also Chapter 7 for consciousness in Buddhism).

2. The term 'musicking' is broadly intended in the sense coined for it by Christopher Small (1998), to mean activity around music—performing, composing, and listening in their many contexts, public and private. There is perhaps a certain irony in using the term in the present chapter, which will soon shift its focus towards matters other than the embodied, social experience of music that Small is concerned to privilege. I would, however, want to endorse those levels of experience as germane to musical consciousness, and they are indeed tackled by many other contributors to this book (for example, Eric Clarke, Tia DeNora, Ruth Herbert, Bennett Hogg, and Alicia Peñalba Acitores). My own contribution here is to contemplate the very core (and in that sense metaphysical) conditions of musical consciousness on which everything else depends—or at least to test out what such a conceit implies.

3. Ian Biddle, this volume, associates the 'the charm of the universal' with, among other things, the Idealist philosophical tradition of Husserl's forebears.

4. Don Welton's *The New Husserl* (2003), and Francisco Varela and Jonathan Shear's *The View from Within* (1999) are paradigmatic collections in this respect. Within the latter, Varela's article, 'Present-time consciousness' reflects a longstanding concern to combine neuroscientific and phenomenological perspectives—in short a 'neurophenomenology'.

5. In making Husserl the starting point of this inquiry I am in certain respects repeating a gesture made in substantial accounts of music and phenomenology by Don Ihde (2007) and Paul Fleet (2009), just as Shaun Gallagher (1998) has made Husserl the touchstone for his philosophical inquiry—all of which testifies to the enduring fascination and significance of this founding father of phenomenology. These studies nonetheless follow rather different trajectories. In my own case, one motivation has been to return to some long-unfinished business around temporality, semiology, and subjective experience (Clarke 1989) that (I now realize) adumbrates notions in Husserl. Another, related motivation—expounded in Meditation II, below—has been to pursue the idea that phenomenology might be the complementary perspective of a semiological orientation developed in Clarke (1996a, 1996b).

6. At one point in the *Phenomenology* (1991: 42) Husserl talks of 'the "rough" now', a notion similar to the specious present. Nonetheless, there are fundamental differences between James's and Husserl's notions of an extended present. As Gallagher (1998: Ch. 3) points out, whereas for James the specious present was the solution to a problem, for Husserl it was a problem to which the notions of retention and protention offered a solution, and from which his entire phenomenology of time consciousness develops. Martin Hägglund (2008: 61–3) also judges Husserl's formulation to have the critical edge over that of James.

7. Rudolf Boehm, editor of *Husserliana* Volume X, surmises that the term first appears around 1904 in Husserl's manuscripts (see Husserl 1991: 281 n. 26).

8. Difference is precisely the textual strategy onto which Derrida will fasten in his critique of Husserl, so it is worth underlining that Husserl couches his framework in explicitly differential terms—see, for example, Husserl (1991: 41).

9. On the notion of transcendent, as opposed to immanent, objects, see Held (2003b: 34):

> Objects exist 'in themselves', that is, they are more than, or are not exhausted by, that which is momentarily given as situationally relative to the subject. The object strikes me as something that has existence beyond this manifold of momentary manners of givenness; in this sense, the object *transcends* such multiplicity.

10. Ihde (2007: 80–91) uses the term 'temporal focus' in discussing this mutability of the intentionality of listening.

11. See, for example, Husserl (1991: 383–4).

12. This figure was famously used by Erwin Schrödinger to dramatize the more bizarre corollaries of quantum physics. Jeffrey Gray (2004: 242) paraphrases as follows:

> Place a cat in a box with a vial of poison. Outside the box, a quantum event—for instance, the passage/not passage of a single photon through a half-silvered mirror—is causally connected to the release of the poison inside the box. Since the photon both passes and does not pass through the mirror, the poison is both triggered and not triggered. Therefore . . . the cat must be both dead and alive until the box is opened and the cat observed. At that moment . . . the system chooses either dead cat or live cat; thus, the conscious observation essentially selects reality.

While I invoke the conditions of this thought experiment as a passing simile for the kinds of decision made during a musical performance, this nonetheless prompts me to speculate on the possibility that the dynamics of 'musicking' (the often split-second decisions that underpin acts of performance, improvisation, and composition, and that raise significant questions about the processes of free will) might offer rich material for investigations of consciousness informed by quantum physics. The pioneers in this field are Roger Penrose and Stuart Hameroff, whose account Gray paraphrases in the passage from which I quote above.

13. Nonetheless, there are apparent variances in Husserl's position. He does, for example, talk of 'an ultimate consciousness, which would necessarily be an "unconscious" consciousness; as ultimate intentionality it cannot be an object of attention . . ., and therefore it can never become conscious in this particular sense' (1991: 394)—a formulation not so remote from that being proposed by Brown here.

14. For a further account of this and other aspects of Brown's microgenetic model, see Brown (1999), which also explores points of similarity and difference between his theories and Buddhist philosophy.

15. In the middle of a dense passage that seeks to uphold the distinction between the 'two ensembles' of simultaneity and succession, Husserl writes, 'it is also the case that simultaneity is nothing without temporal succession and temporal succession is nothing without simultaneity, and consequently simultaneity and temporal succession must become constituted correlatively and inseparably' (1991: 82). This could be seen as yet another aspect of Husserl's wrestling with the implication of the non-temporal in the temporal that would become the focal point of Derrida's critique (discussed in Meditation III, below).

16. As Gallope (Chapter 3) points out in his account of listening to Fela Kuti, these are all the kinds of factor that would be 'bracketed out' under a Husserlian phenomenological reduction.

17. In fact the synchrony between Husserl and Saussure may be anything but coincidental. Their ideologies share an introversive focus—Husserl's on the inner reaches of subjectivity, Saussure's on the internal organization of a linguistic system. Saussure's 'synchronic' linguistics might itself be seen to perform a reduction, bracketing out the historical, 'diachronic' dimension of language as a determinant of meaning for any actual linguistic community. In both cases this may reflect an apotheosis of principles of subjective and structural autonomy emergent in post-Enlightenment Idealist philosophy and the scientistic mores of the day.

18. Jakobson uses the terms *axis of combination* and *axis of selection* as respective counterparts to Saussure's syntagmatic and associative axes.

19. Saussure characterizes the abode of these unuttered terms as an 'inner storehouse' (1974: 123). In Brown's microgenetic model this might correspond to the 'memorial unconscious' which forms the core self and which by analogy supplies the imagery (in this case verbal) that informs objects (linguistic signs) sustained in consciousness.

20. Jakobson (1960: 357) also gives a vernacular example of poetic function: the political electioneering slogan 'I like Ike'. He also underlines the fact that equivalence can obtain between many aspects of an utterance—'word stress is assumed to equal word stress, as unstress equals unstress; prosodic long is matched with long, and short with short; word boundary equals word boundary, no boundary equals no boundary; syntactic pause equals syntactic pause, no pause equals no pause' (358).

21. Jakobson (1960: 358)—where, significantly, he also writes: 'Measure of sequences is a device which, outside of poetic function, finds no application in language. Only in poetry with its regular reiteration of equivalent units is the time of the speech flow experienced, as it is—to cite another semiotic pattern—with musical time.'

22. I have rendered this passage at the pitch of the CD recording by Collegium Regale (Cleobury 2006). The following commentary is based primarily on my aural encounter with this recording rather than on an extensive analytical interpretation of the score itself, a sample of which is included here more as a proxy for the sonic experience than as the main object of inquiry.

23. Perhaps it could be said that protention is the more prominent mode of intending such polyphony: given that past contents and phases are not explicitly reinvoked, each present moment is less tied to the past and thus allows a stronger orientation towards the musical future.

24. Compare Husserl (1991: 389, 376).

25. Hägglund (2008: 66) glosses the term as follows: 'Traditionally autoaffection has been understood as a mode of interiority where there is no distance or difference between the one who affects and the one who is affected. In autoaffection, then, the subject would be so close to itself that any kind of mediation is excluded.'

26. See Gallope's discussion of these terms, this volume.

27. These include Rudolf Bernet, Daniel Birnbaum, John Brough, Richard Cobb-Stevens, Leonard Lawlor, Paul Ricoeur, and Dan Zahavi—all variously discussed or mentioned in Chapter 2 of Hägglund (2008).

28. Cf. also Husserl (1991: 346): '*Retention* . . . is an expression used to designate the intentional relation . . . of phase of consciousness to phase of consciousness; and in this case the phases of consciousness and continuities of consciousness must not be regarded as temporal objects themselves.'

29. Cf. also the above discussion of Brown's schema (Figure 1.3), where 'images' (signs?) act as a mediating agency for the passage from memorial unconscious to consciously perceived objects.

30. From a deconstructive perspective, Derrida's explicit acknowledgements of admiration for the *Phenomenology* are less interesting than the signs within his own text (often smuggled away into sub-clauses) of an equivocal recognition of the significance of the very differences he wants to deconstruct: 'without reducing the abyss *which may indeed separate retention from re-presentation* . . .'; 'whatever the phenomenological differences between these two modifications may be, and despite . . . *the necessity of taking them into account* . . .' (Derrida 1973: 65, 67; emphases added; see also p. 7).

Chapter 2

Phenomenology and the 'hard problem' of consciousness and music

Eugene Montague

Introduction

In this chapter I compare what is termed 'the hard problem' in the study of consciousness with a similar issue in music scholarship. The grounds for this comparison are difficulties common to both disciplines, to do with the incorporation of subjective experience within an objective explanatory framework. In highlighting these common difficulties I suggest that they may be open to similar solutions. In particular, I argue that musicology would do well to revisit theoretical perspectives that reject a fundamental opposition between objective and subjective, such as the (European) Continental tradition of phenomenology, since such perspectives have proved useful in meeting challenges posed in the study of consciousness. In this vein, I undertake a fresh look at Edmund Husserl's well-known analysis of time consciousness, using this analysis to provide a theoretical framework within which to understand the objectivity of a musical piece through the subjective experience of the performing body. Such an understanding can, I believe, provide a resolution to the difficulties that underlie the hard problem of music, and, in conclusion, I demonstrate this through a brief analytical engagement with a Chopin étude.

Hard problems in consciousness and music

In 1996 David Chalmers' book *The Conscious Mind* created a stir in the interdisciplinary nexus surrounding cognitive science, neurology, and philosophy of mind. Chalmers argued that the model of mind prevalent in most scientific research was incapable of explaining the human experience of consciousness in any satisfactory way. For Chalmers, this model was predicated on an empirical functionalism that understands the mind solely as the psychological cause of human behaviour. Although he admitted that such a functionalist view of the human mind had underpinned many advances in cognitive science over the preceding decades, Chalmers maintained that the functionalist model's disregard of phenomenal experience was a mistake. In particular, this left the 'biggest mystery' intractable: the question, 'Why are we conscious?' (Chalmers 1996: 7–22). Chalmers called for new directions in cognitive science and neurobiology in order to deal with what he famously dubbed the 'hard problem' of consciousness (xii–xiii).

This was far from a new argument, as Chalmers readily admitted. The problem of the relation between internal experiences and the external world has roots in Western philosophy that go back at least as far as Plato. Chalmers' argument also echoed questions raised by more recent philosophers, such as Thomas Nagel in his seminal essay 'What is it like to be a bat?' (1974). Nagel was the first of a series of Anglo-American philosophers to express dissatisfaction with the materialist account of mind that underpinned cognitive science, of whom John Searle has been perhaps the most prominent (Searle 1984, 2002, 2004; Searle *et al.* 1997). Nonetheless, if Chalmers' book was not entirely novel, it attracted considerable attention due to its considered and sympathetic treatment of the achievements of cognitive science, and to its vivid characterization of the central problem. *The Conscious Mind* both encouraged and benefited from a growing interest among neuroscientists in developing a secure experiential basis for their observations, which in turn generated a fresh assessment of the question of consciousness among analytic philosophers. A scholarly journal came into being, international conferences on consciousness were held and an association founded, and books by distinguished scientists such as Alain Berthoz and Antonio Damasio put a recognizable face on the quest of neuroscience to include subjective experience (Berthoz 2000; Damasio 1999).[1] Chalmers' book contributed in no small way to this outburst of enthusiasm, and his pithy phrase, 'the hard problem of consciousness', became a touchstone for the new academic discipline.[2]

Given the centrality of consciousness to all human experience, it is unsurprising that an issue that arises within this discipline can be related to other fields of academic inquiry. The hard problem of the relationship between subjective experience and objective, functional analysis has particular resonance for the study of music in two ways. First, there is a trope—familiar to both consciousness and music studies—concerning the resistance of experience to verbal explanation: How can an apparently ineffable experience be rendered in words without losing that which makes it particular? Secondly, there is in the fields of consciousness and music a shared engagement with the problems of temporal experience and, therefore, a common difficulty in using atemporal categories and terms to illuminate experience that is in its essence defined in time. As a rough example of this difficulty, if my seeing red now is functionally indistinguishable from my seeing red yesterday (i.e. the same neurons are firing), then how can the undeniable differences between the experiences be understood? Running through both of these questions is a difficulty in harmonizing the demands of objectivity with the recognition of subjective experience.

Such a difficulty may sometimes seem to strengthen the power of both consciousness and music, even while frustrating researchers. Of consciousness, Chalmers writes admiringly that it is 'startlingly intense . . . [and] frustratingly diaphanous . . . so intangible that even [a] limited attempt at a definition could be disputed' (1996: 3). A similar sentiment is present in many sayings that celebrate the opacity of music and its resistance to words, such as the oft-cited aphorism, 'Writing about music is like dancing about architecture',[3] and the statement by novelist Aldous Huxley: 'After silence, that which comes nearest to expressing the inexpressible is music' (1931: 17).

For both consciousness and music, then, common modes of explanation and analysis do not seem to capture what is central to the experience of the subject. As Chalmers has it: 'for every functional explanation, there remains a further question, "why is the performance of the function associated with conscious experience?"' (1997: 5). Thus, an explanation of the experience of 'seeing red' that limits itself to a description of the firing of certain neurons in the brain does not begin to address the *experience* of seeing red: there seems to be a fundamental mismatch between the terms of explanation and what it is like to have the experience. Such a criticism might be levelled with equal justice at purely functional accounts of musical structure. For example, the closing 29 bars of the last movement of Beethoven's Symphony No. 5 might quite accurately by explained in terms of harmonic function as 'a prolongation of the tonic chord'. However, these terms, which represent a formalist interpretation of these musical events, do not offer much connection to the experience of attending to this music. Worse, the terminology of the explanation itself seems to cut off further investigation into such experience. If the question here is 'What are listeners experiencing when they hear this music?', then the response 'a prolongation' seems almost as irrelevant as the answer 'the firing of neurons in the cortex' is to the question 'What are viewers experiencing when they see red?'. One benefit of solving the hard problem of music, then, would be to connect functional analytical explanations to the totality of musical experience, and thus to make the analyses themselves more meaningful.[4]

As already mentioned, a second connection between the twin hard problems is their common sensitivity to time. More precisely, the temporal qualities of musical experience seem close to those of conscious experience. It is generally accepted that time is of central importance in the experience of consciousness; thus philosopher Brian O'Shaughnessy argues that: 'a direct confrontation with time is constitutive of consciousness as such' (2000: 51). This means not only that the condition of being conscious is a temporal state, but also that the ability to create a series of events in a temporal sequence, or to experience a single event as continuous, is in some sense constitutive of consciousness itself. As William James put it

> Consciousness . . . does not appear to itself chopped up in bits . . . It is nothing jointed; it flows. A 'river' or a 'stream' are the metaphors by which it is most naturally described. *In talking of it hereafter, let us call it the stream of thought, of consciousness, or of subjective life.* (1890: 239)

If all conscious experiences are temporal, then music most closely approximates this quality of flow, more so, for example, than literature or figurative art. Music both takes place in time and moulds time in its passing; listening to music demands attention in the immediate present (now) or the opportunity is lost. Moreover, on a pragmatic level, temporal issues are a core concern for musicians of all genres. The need to play together in time is manifested by the presence of a conductor for a classical ensemble, or by the centrality of the rhythm section in a rock or jazz band. Even when practising solo, musicians regularly pay homage to the importance of exact temporal synchronicity through the use of a metronome. Music, like consciousness, must confront time, and thus discussion of music must find ways to acknowledge the centrality of time.

Given these structural similarities, it might be objected that a hard problem of music is not really a distinct problem: the experience of music, as conscious experience, is merely one aspect of consciousness, and thus the hard problem of music will be solved whenever the hard problem of consciousness is. In one sense it is true that musical experience is part of the general problem of consciousness: thus, Chalmers argues that solving the latter is the all-encompassing problem, as aesthetic questions 'do not pose metaphysical and explanatory problems comparable to those posed by conscious experience' (1996: 84). Yet, in a disciplinary sense, the hard problem of music is conceptually distinct. For the language of formal music analysis is sufficiently removed from so many of the varied ranges of musical experience that even if we were to have a satisfactory theory of consciousness tomorrow, this would not by itself suffice to connect musical experience and analytic discourse. We might imagine a satisfactory explanation as to why a particular neurological event is accompanied by a particular sensation—for example why I experience sadness when a particular collection of neurons fire. Such an explanation, however, would have no immediate purchase on the language and vocabulary of musical analysis, and it would be a quite separate task to map these findings on to music. The two problems are similar in type, but do not admit of the same solution.

Nonetheless, approaches to one hard problem may well have relevance for the other; therefore, in approaching music's problem it is useful to consider consciousness studies. Responses to Chalmers have been many and varied, ranging from the denial that such a problem exists, to the belief that the problem is inherently unanswerable. The very existence of the debate, however, has increased interest in approaches that value subjective experience, and among these is the European phenomenological tradition. Chalmers himself, with a background in Anglo-American analytic philosophy, argues that a phenomenological approach 'must be absolutely central to an adequate science of consciousness: after all, it is our own phenomenology that provides the data that need to be explained!' (1997: 35). From the other side of the analytic/Continental divide, philosophers from the phenomenological tradition have been attracted to the increasing emphasis on consciousness, as well as the ongoing successes of cognitive science, and many phenomenologists have worked to bring their discipline into a constructive dialogue with natural science. The fruits of this growing intersection of interests can be found in the burgeoning literature on embodied cognition.[5]

This *rapprochement* between the two traditions is not without its oddities. In strict phenomenological terms the hard problem does not exist but is simply the result of a misguided emphasis on empirical objectivity, as there is, at base, no external/internal divide in perception. Thus, most phenomenologists initially answered Chalmers' dilemma by redirecting the question to the mode of inquiry, demanding close and detailed attention to the data of our experiences.[6] Informed by the work of philosophers such as Maurice Merleau-Ponty on the role of the physical body in perception, scholars such as Varela and Gallagher worked to incorporate cognitive science, placing the body at the centre of subjective experience and its investigation. I believe that similar phenomenological approaches to musical experience, incorporating the physicality of the body, hold promise for the hard problem of music. To demonstrate this, I turn to a key inquiry in early Continental phenomenology, which provides a suggestive methodology: Husserl's analysis of time consciousness.

Husserl, music, and time consciousness

Husserl's concern with issues of time and consciousness began in his lectures of 1905. These lectures were published later, and became the best-known source for his views, but he continued to write on these topics throughout his career, making several important revisions to his earlier positions. Thus, the lectures are most usefully read as part of an ongoing engagement with the temporality of consciousness, which is how they appear in John Brough's translation in *On the Phenomenology of the Consciousness of Internal Time (1893–1917)* (Husserl 1991). It is in the 1905 lectures that Husserl first uses the experience of perceiving a melody to answer a number of questions about time and human consciousness. These questions stem from what Husserl thought of as a primary task of phenomenology: to explain how the objects we perceive through what he termed the 'natural attitude' come to be objectified as such. In other words: How do the processes of our perception work to create the persistent, three-dimensional objects that we see, touch, and use in everyday life, given that we are never able to perceive such an object in all of its dimensions at once? To use a common spatial example, how is it that we see a table as a four-sided object, even though we only see it from one side at any one time? For Husserl, the answer lies in the relationship between the raw data that we perceive and our objectifying, in-the-world, consciousness.[7] In further investigating the workings of this consciousness, Husserl chooses the apprehension of a melody as a model example of how any object is temporally constituted. Therefore, he undertakes a phenomenological analysis, putting to one side ('bracketing') our initial perception of a melody as such, in order to analyse the structures involved in the apprehension of any melody.

Through this analysis, Husserl argues that certain temporal mechanisms of consciousness form the conditions for the creation of objects, whether in sound (as in a melody) or in sight (as in a table). In hearing a melody, we do not in fact hear merely one note at a time, just as we do not see merely one side of a table at a time. Rather we perceive both aural object and visual object as continua, structured by the immediate past and anticipated future.[8] The mechanisms that create such continua he called, respectively, *retention*, the incorporation of past experience into the present, and *protention*, the effect of future events on current experience. These twin devices of time consciousness allow a melody to exist as an object and to be conceptualized as such.

As mentioned above, Husserl revisited the relationship of time and consciousness many times over the years following the 1905 lectures. He generally used diagrams to illustrate his insights, and Figure 2.1 shows such a diagram, reproduced from the unpublished Bernauer manuscripts (1917–18). It appears in a re-assessment of Husserl's ideas on time by the philosopher Lanei Rodemeyer, to whose insightful analysis I am indebted (see Rodemeyer 2003: 130).

Using Husserl's own example of a melody, we might interpret the first element on the left, E_1, as a single perceived event—the hearing of an individual pitch is perhaps

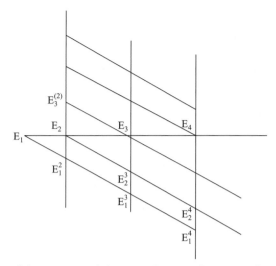

Fig. 2.1 Diagram of the structure of time-consciousness from Husserl's unpublished papers. Adapted from Rodemeyer, L. (2003). Developments in the theory of time-consciousness: an analysis of protention, in D. Welton (ed.), *The New Husserl: A Critical Reader,* 125–56 Copyright ©, Indiana University Press. Reprinted with permission of Indiana University Press.

the most convenient example. The diagonal line extending down from E_1 then illustrates the consciousness of this pitch in the time following its sounding as it becomes ever more distant, a phenomenon that Husserl variously called 'running-off' or 'slipping away'. Each sub- or superscripted number in the diagram indicates, respectively, past or future experiences within the current present, or 'phase' of consciousness. Thus the point E_1^2 found on the diagonal line, represents the retention of the musical event that occurred at E_1 as it is experienced in the phase of E_2. The retention of E_1 cannot be detached or set apart from the experience of E_2: it is a fundamental aspect of the latter phase. Similarly, protention also structures the experience of each phase: $E_3^{(2)}$ indicates how the coming of E_3 is intuited in prescience as part of the experience of E_2. Finally, the vertical lines on the diagram illustrate the connectedness of this experience, showing how the various retentions and protentions not only join to the 'now' phase, but constitute it.

The mechanisms of retention and protention are therefore fundamental to the formation of time consciousness. However, as Rodemeyer suggests, these mechanisms do not operate on or in a pre-existing temporal flux: the continuum represented by the horizontal line in the diagram is the *last* thing to emerge, and it does so only as the product of retention and protention. Time, therefore, is not a series of now-points upon which retention and protention act. Rather, it is the pushing together of protentions and retentions that forms temporal continuity. Thus, if Figure 2.1 were to be animated, E_1 would first appear, together with the ongoing retention of this sound illustrated by the diagonal line downwards. As E_2 occurs, so too would the first vertical line appear, since it is the perceived relationship between the retention E_1^2 and the new sound E_2 that in part constitutes the now point (the relevant protentions also, of course, play their part). Then, and only then, would the horizontal line connecting E_1 to E_2 appear, as the temporal continuum emerges out of the retentional–protentional mechanisms.[9]

Husserl uses his deliberations on melodic perception as a way into a discussion of consciousness. He argues that this analysis illustrates 'the phenomenon of time-constituting consciousness, of the consciousness in which temporal objects with their temporal determinations become constituted' (Husserl 1991: 28). Thus, Husserl suggests that not just one but every example of a melody *qua* object is constructed through retention and protention, and, further, that this method of constructing time consciousness is itself a universal law of all acts of consciousness.[10] In this reading, the temporality he discovers becomes the foundation of consciousness: a synthesis of diverse lived experiences into a stream that determines how consciousness exists.

Despite the emphasis on musical experience in Husserl's account, it has largely been ignored by music scholars. In part, this may be due to its apparent lack of detail: the seemingly vague references to 'a melody' give little in the way of musical crumbs to follow. Those few scholars who have approached music from a phenomenological perspective have certainly been influenced by Husserl's analysis, yet have taken it as a general account of time consciousness in which the specific role of music tends to fall out of view.[11] Even F.J. Smith's (1973) evaluation of Husserl's ideas, which is exceptional in the extent of its attention to Husserl's writing, tends to focus less on the details of Husserl's analysis of time and more on its larger philosophical contexts. The result is that the finer points of Husserl's analysis of time consciousness have not been discussed in the context of studies of rhythm and musical temporality.

This situation is unfortunate, for in Husserl's suggestion that the formation of musical objects depends on details of perception is the kernel of a solution for music's hard problem. In what Husserl would call the 'natural attitude' of discourse about music, we commonly and fruitfully talk about objects such as melodies, chords, harmonies, textures, timbres, and indeed prolongations, among many others. Such musical 'things' are, of course, the stuff of analysis. If Husserl's account of temporal consciousness is correct, such objects depend for their existence on the details of phenomenological experience. Thus, there is a clear interrelation between the emergence of musical objects of analysis and subjective experience, a connection that promises a path toward a solution for music's hard problem.

Temporal continuity and the performing body

To realize this promise, two further questions must be addressed. Husserl's account explains how musical objects appear, but who is the listener who hears these objects? And, can we assume that such perceptions are shared by all who hear music? Shaun Gallagher has argued for a negative answer to the second question. In particular, he takes Husserl to task for ignoring the diverse temporal possibilities in the act of listening, finding that his analysis is so inflexible in its serial temporality that 'one almost begins to wonder whether Husserl ever listened to music' (Gallagher 1998: 97). For Gallagher, Husserl's apparent ignorance of non-serial forms of temporal experience that are made possible through listening renders his account quite insufficient.

However, Gallagher's criticisms may miss the intention of Husserl's account. Klaus Held has remarked that 'All Husserlian constitutive analyses are guided by the basic goal of explaining how objectivity . . . arises for consciousness' (2003: 43). Thus, as argued above, Husserl chooses a melody because it is the best, and simplest, example of a temporal *object*. He does not attempt to describe a set of general conditions for listening to music because his goal is more limited: an investigation into how the musical object 'melody' emerges into consciousness as part of our natural attitude, and how this object itself conditions temporal experience. In one sense, of course, this very limitation proves Gallagher's wider point: Husserl's analysis is indeed quite flawed if considered as a general account of the phenomenology of music. We cannot assume that all listeners hear such objects or that they are constrained by the temporality of objectivity. This has been something of a problem for music analysis as it seeks to locate a perspective from which to discuss its object. Often analysts find recourse in the figure of 'the listener', assumed or explicit: an all-attentive, all-purpose recipient of the aural stimulus, who faithfully follows the chronological course of the music in its entirety. Yet this recourse is ultimately unsatisfactory from a methodological standpoint, not only because it tends to deprive the analysis of any specific links to subjective experience but also because, as Gallagher argues above, there is no real ground for the notion that listeners must be following the temporal *flux* of the music in a serial fashion.

However, if listeners as a general category do not necessarily hear complete musical objects, there remains a sub-category of more specialist listeners who, by virtue of the conditions under which they engage with music, hear and understand it as a set of objects (melodies, phrases, harmonies) that unfold in a serial fashion. This sub-category of listeners, who might therefore more closely operate under the conditions described by Husserl, includes performers. A performer who uses his or her body to produce sound through the medium of an instrument will need to know through physical gesture exactly 'what comes next' and 'what has just been'; and this knowledge, contained in the body, will rely on the experience of the melody as a serial temporal succession.[12] David Sudnow's account of practising jazz is revealing in this regard: 'I specifically recall playing one day and finding . . . that I'd expressly aimed for the sounds of these next particular notes, that the sounds seemed to creep up into my fingers . . . [realizing] a specific sound I'd gone there to make' (2001: 40). Sudnow speaks of bodily knowledge, implying that his fingers are themselves agents. Such agency creates a particularly concentrated relationship with time as a series of events.[13] When I am playing, my body is playing *now*, in a focused, committed engagement with time. One gesture follows another in necessary succession, and only when I finish, or stop suddenly, will this temporality end. In a common phrase with a very apposite double meaning, when playing music, it is of decisive importance that I play *in time*. Both the time in which I play and the objects which are fashioned through my playing are created through the interaction of protentions and retentions.

This is not to say that the subjective experience of temporality in performance is exclusively serial; far from it. However, due to the intense engagement with time that is a requirement of musical performance, the body's activity in playing music creates, of necessity, a series of gestures. These gestures exist for the performer's body as musical objects, realized on and through an instrument. And these objects, in their seriality, imply the existence of a temporal continuum, just as the perception of a melody as a musical object implies the temporal flux described by Husserl.

If performers create, and therefore rely on, a temporal continuum, this kind of time is also important for another type of listener: musical analysts. In the undertaking of any analysis, there is an acceptance of, and commitment to, some sort of objectivity: without this there is no "object" to investigate. Listeners such as Gallagher may indeed wish to emphasize non-serial forms of temporality. Analysts, however, cannot be so quick to dismiss the objectifying qualities of a temporal continuum, as discussed by Husserl. Indeed, as noted above, many insightful studies of musical pieces and experiences rely on an all-purpose listener who functions as a receptacle for the sounds in the order of performance, thus guaranteeing the objectivity of the music. A problem with such methodological sleight-of-hand is that it risks departing from subjective experience: the hard problem already discussed. Against this, the physical gestures of a performer offer an alternative purchase on serial temporality in music, and thus an opportunity to discuss the experience of music as a continuous event, structured in a Husserlian sense by the interactions of protention and retention.[14] Insofar as the body relies on this time, then, musical analysis based on this understanding of seriality will succeed in presenting one aspect of subjective experience. This aspect, to paraphrase Nagel, will be one part of what it is like to be a performer.[15] Such analysis should speak to the hard problem of music in bringing together subjective experience and the creation of musical objects.[16]

The performing body and its objects: a brief analysis

I close this chapter with a brief analytical investigation of bodily movement in performance. I have chosen a piece, Chopin's Étude in A flat major, Op. 25 No. 1, in which the physical movements required of the performer are limited, given that the player must repeat a similar gesture (defined by a spreading of the fingers, and a lateral movement of the forearm) through almost the entire course of the music. This economy of gesture is typical of the musical genre of the étude, and the consequent straightforward quality of this music in relation to movement makes an analysis of bodily action attractive. In this analysis, then, the object is not principally the sound considered in isolation, but the sound reflected through the demands on the performer's body in performance. This approach creates an ontological link between the analytic object and the performer's physical actions, thus connecting the subjective experience of movement with the objective quality of the music in its temporal continuity.

In common with most pieces of Western art music, this étude is traditionally communicated through a score, and my analysis begins from that text, using the score as a way to draw inferences about a performer's movements. As a score provides the pitches to be played, and the relative times to play them, it also constitutes a reservoir of information about the performative gestures necessary to the piece.[17] These gestures are subjective, experienced by the performer at the time of performance. Thus, they are comparable to the hardness or redness that might be an initial tactile or visual impressions of a table. Likewise, following Husserl's analysis of a melody, the initial subjective impressions characterized by gestures become part of a protentional–retentional network, and part of the musical object—the temporal continuity—that is the piece.

It is the performer's absorption of his or her gestures into the temporal continuity of performance that allows the piece, as object, to emerge. When I begin to play this étude one of the central tasks for my body is to create a temporal flow through the piece, and I create this through an ordered succession of gestures. Within this flow, each past gesture influences how I approach the next, and the need to make future gestures equally determines my current movements. Which is to say that my gestures, interacting through retention and protention, constitute a serial temporality like that described by Husserl: these gestures (with which I create *this* music) are analogous to the 'phases' that constitute time consciousness.[18] The consequent serial organization of my gestures is motivated by sound, but independent of it, for the organization is created through the activity of playing the music alone: thus, performance on a dummy keyboard would create the same serial order, even if the music did not sound.

Example 2.1 maps Husserl's diagram onto the opening bar of the étude to show how phases relate to each other, forming retentions and protentions. The nature of the performer's gesture suggests that each current phase begins with the E♭5 played

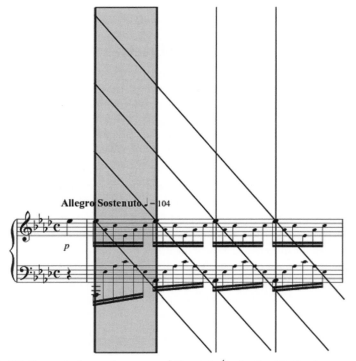

Example 2.1 Phases in the performance of Chopin's Étude, Op. 25 No. 1.

by the right hand, and then, as suggested by the diagonal line, recedes as part of the 'running off' characteristic of retention. The initial shaded area implies that the first phase consists in the duration of the six-note gesture in both right and left hands; this is also true of each successive phase, though the shading is discontinued in the example for practical purposes. As these phases form the piece in performance, they generate retentions and protentions and thus create the temporal continuum. However, unlike in Husserl's sketches, there is no horizontal line here, for the score itself stands in as the visual presentation of temporal continuity.

As I play, my knowledge of the music arises through a network of retentions and protentions as defined through bodily gesture. Such a network is flexible; it is not based on a mathematically fixed unit, and the duration of a gesture may vary without disturbing its place as a phase in the musical flux. As a rough example, I might respond to the spaciousness of the low A♭1 at the start by playing the opening gesture some-what more slowly, then speeding up over the course of the next three gestures. This is arguably an unsubtle performance, but it remains a performance of 'the' piece none-theless, at least in part because I maintain a retentional–protentional relationship between my gestures.[19] Indeed, the very regularity of the repeating gesture makes fluctuations in its duration an important characteristic of the piece. The score implies such fluctuations through its detailing of the span of successive notes, and hence its implications for their fingering. These details become physical experiences of expan-sion and contraction for the performer, experiences that are objectified within the network of protentions and retentions. This process defines two particularly impor-tant moments later in the music: a sequential passage in bb. 7–9 and a modulation to A major in bb. 22–24.

In b. 7 a B♭ dominant seventh resolves onto an E♭ harmony; this in turn becomes a dominant seventh that resolves onto A♭ at the start of b. 9 (see Example 2.2). The sequential aspect of this harmonic progression is explored in the figuration of the chords: b. 8 is an almost exact copy of b. 7, transposed down a perfect fifth. Almost, but not exactly. As Example 2.2 shows, the left hand figuration in b. 8 includes three pitches that are not exact transpositions of b. 7, leading to an intervallic expan-sion in the first arpeggio. Such small changes do not alter the harmonic character of the chord: they might well pass unremarked by a silent and static listener, and many traditional analytic approaches would ignore them. Yet, they necessarily change the experience of performing the piece. In terms of physical gesture, the first arpeggio in

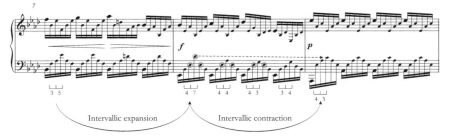

Example 2.2 Broadening of left hand gesture, bb. 7–9.

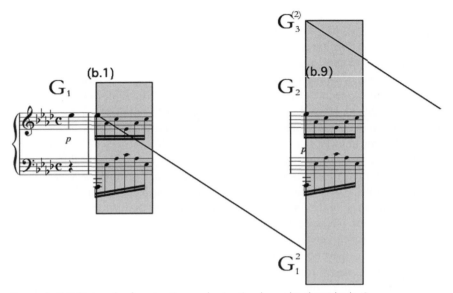

Example 2.3 Network of protention and retention brought about by b. 9.

the left hand in b. 8 demands an unusually wide span, making increased demands on the pianist's speed of movement. Thus, the performance becomes somewhat more difficult, and literally, broader, a change which both justifies and motivates, in phenomenal terms, the *forte* at this bar. The physical experience of broadening thus becomes part of the experience of playing this bar.

The resolution onto the tonic in b. 9 brings an easing of this stretch, with its return to the gestural organization and sound of the opening music; and with this return comes an intensification of temporal relationships. As shown in Example 2.3, this repeat of the opening music creates a retentional marking-point, with the quality of hearing the same object (the opening arpeggio) at a different temporal moment. In this example I have marked the phases with letters, as Husserl did in his diagram, using 'G' to stand for gesture. As with the construction of a melody for Husserl's listener, a player does not need to actively *remember* the opening at this time for the retention to come into effect: it is simply a facet of the emerging object that is the piece (just as seeing the same table from a different angle will, intentionally or not, inform our understanding of the table object). Moreover, as the retention emerges, a protention comes into effect, again shown in Example 2.3, presenting the potential for this music to return again. The interactions of temporal structures intensify the effect of temporal continuity, just as in Husserl's discussion of his melody. In turn, this continuity supports the nature of the piece as an object, created through the retentional–protentional network.

This network is available in sound, and thus may be heard by a listener, including any performer of the piece. However, given the potential freedom of the listener from the constraints of objectivity, it is certainly possible that a listener may not hear b. 9 as a return of the opening: for such a listener the retentional structure shown in Example 2.3 will not come to pass, and this aspect of the piece as object will not emerge. For the performer, however, the retention is also a matter of physical reality, given the necessity to repeat the opening gesture. Therefore, the temporal continuity shown in Example 2.3 is defined through gesture, not sound.

A further temporal subtlety thickens the quality of b. 9 for the performer. As shown by the dotted line in Example 2.2, the Db4 in the left hand arpeggio of b. 8, which demanded the broadened gesture, can be heard and felt to move to the C4 of b. 9, through the voice-leading resolution, but also through the physical sensation of keyboard proximity in the left hand thumb. Such temporal relations enrich the emerging object of the piece for the performer, allowing the subjective experience of expansion and contraction to become inextricably entangled with the properties of the object. In this sense, the analytic qualities of both a formal return and a resolution of a chordal seventh exist within and through the subjective experience of the performer; and, from a phenomenological perspective, it is this mode of existence that casts permanent doubt on the utility of maintaining a split between the subjective and the objective.

A similar wrinkle in the fabric of performance occurs in bb. 22–24, this time created in a chromatic modulation to A major, and involving a movement of the right hand 'inwards' from white to black keys on the piano keyboard (see Example 2.4). In bb. 22–3 the right hand moves from a chord of C major through a diminished seventh to E major, while maintaining a position over the white keys of the piano: the melody E–D–F–E played by the fifth finger and the thumb is based on all white notes, as shown in the circled pitches in Example 2.4. Despite the move to A major in b. 24, this hand position does not alter until the third beat, when the melody changes to F♮ on the third note. This shift necessitates moving the right hand inward towards the piano as well as a wider leap from the D before it and to the E following (D–F♮–E replaces

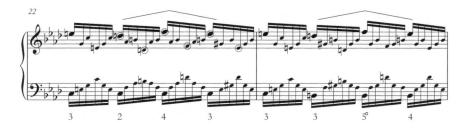

Example 2.4 Enlarged gesture in a modulation to A major, bb. 22–4.

D–F–E, as shown by the angled braces in Example 2.4). The change here is not dramatic, but is nonetheless quite marked in the limited context of the gestures of this piece, so that the physical sensation of moving 'wider' and 'inward' are central elements in the experience of playing this passage. The *ritenuto* marked above the score pays tribute to this experience, the 'holding back' of the tempo motivated by the physical conditions of the phrase.

The objective qualities of these measures are again a product of retention and protention, in at least two related ways. First, as shown in Example 2.4, there is the local context for the right hand's F♮: it is only when set against the repeated E–F–E of bb. 22–23 that the whole step to F♮ gains effect. This context includes dissonant harmonic intervals between the melodic F and the bass in b. 22 (a fourth) and again in b. 23 (a diminished fifth), as shown by the numbers below the stave in Example 2.4. Thus, the shift to F♮ brings both physical and harmonic expansion, as the interval changes to a sixth. Both these gestural and intervallic qualities emerge only through the situating of the F♮ within a retentional context, allowing it to attain objective status. The second way in which retention affects this moment in the music is more wide-ranging, coming in the resolution to A major in b. 25. This resolution brings a momentary return to the layout of the opening arpeggio, with the exception that the first note in the left hand is played in a higher register. As with the A♭ major arpeggio in b. 9, then, this return is marked by retention, now involving both b. 1 and b. 9. Such retention, once more, may not be available through listening alone, but it is unavoidably contained within the physical gestures of the player, thus forging the temporal continuity of the piece. Yet, this retention also brings an element of comparison: the 'return' is not quite right, because the hand position has now shifted one key to the right, since the tonality has modulated to A major, even as it invokes a similar gesture of gestural expansion to that found in bb. 7–9. Thus, much as with the events of bb. 7–9, the specific experience of gesture in b. 24 acquires both a local and a long-range context through the structures of retention and protention. And these structures, creating the piece as object, also become imbued with the experience of playing, so that the performance of this F♮, in the context of this piece, becomes a moment of particular poignancy.

Conclusion

In these two brief examinations of moments in this étude, I have argued that the physical experiences of the performer create musical objects through the activity of protentional and retentional mechanisms. The resultant objects are open to analytic investigation, and concepts of harmonic resolution, formal design, and voice leading can all be used productively in this context. In a mode of understanding that is faithful to phenomenological theory, objective explanation is inescapably linked to my subjective experience *qua* performer. Thus, analysis in such a manner provides an important connection to subjective experience, while retaining, and indeed depending on, the objective qualities of musical events.

In all cases, the human act of performing music generates the potential for a creation of temporal continuity through a network of protentions and retentions.

Such networks may be realized in several ways, which can include musical sound, the usual focus for analysis. However, if sound is considered through the lens of the physical gestures required to produce it, then it is clear that these gestures also create temporal continuity through a similar network. The special character of this continuity is that it is rooted in the body and the actions of the performer. While there may be uncertainty as to whether a listener hears continuity in sound, the player's gestures are a *sine qua non* of the performance. Therefore, such gestures—the shared bodily experiences of performers—offer objective bases for the explorations of analysis, as well as interesting phenomenal grounds for analytic judgements.

At the start of this chapter, I suggested that the hard problem of consciousness shared significant similarities with what I termed the hard problem of music, based on their common difficulties in resolving the claims of objective analysis with the realities of subjective experience. Following the lead of many scholars of consciousness and its related disciplines, I turned toward phenomenology, examining Husserl's account of objectivity and the role played by time consciousness. Based on the results of this examination, I argued that the temporal conditions for the formation of objects can be located, quite clearly, in the gestures of a performing musician, and that such gestures can be used productively as the basis for analysis.

This argument, unfortunately, cannot be directly extrapolated to the wider field of consciousness studies. More work on the relationship between performers' gestures and their conscious experience would be the minimum required before such connections could be drawn. However, in discussing the logic and meaning of physical gestures, this chapter brings concepts from the field of embodied cognition into the musicological arena, and thus advances the potential for further interdisciplinary work. Moreover, in providing one methodological solution to the hard problem of music, I propose an understanding of musical events that unites objective qualities and subjective experience. Such a proposal is at least suggestive for the more general study of consciousness, as it brings together the two poles of the hard problem. Any further investigation of the role of physical movement in creating performance and defining music should narrow the gap between subject and object and thus contribute to solutions for both hard problems, of music and of consciousness.

References

Adlington, R. (1997). Musical temporality: perspectives from Adorno and de Man. *Repercussions*, **6**, 5–60.

Bermúdez, J. (1998). *The Paradox of Self-Consciousness* (Cambridge, MA: MIT Press).

Bermúdez, J. (2003). *Thinking Without Words* (New York, NY: Oxford University Press).

Berthoz, A. (2000). *The Brain's Sense of Movement*, trans. G. Weiss (Cambridge, MA: Harvard University Press).

Chalmers, D. (1996). *The Conscious Mind: In Search of a Fundamental Theory* (New York, NY: Oxford University Press).

Chalmers, D. (1997). Moving forward on the problem of consciousness. *Journal of Consciousness Studies*, **4**, 3–46.

Clifton, T. (1983). *Music as Heard: A Study in Applied Phenomenology* (New Haven, CT: Yale University Press).

D'Ausilio, A., Altenmuller, E., Olivetti Belardinelli, M., and Lotze, M. (2006). Cross-modal plasticity of the motor cortex while listening to a rehearsed musical piece. *European Journal of Neuroscience*, **24**, 955–8.

Damasio, A. (1999). *The Feeling of What Happens: Body and Emotion in the Making of Consciousness* (New York, NY: Harcourt).

Gallagher, S. (1998). *The Inordinance of Time* (Evanston, IL: Northwestern University Press).

Gallagher, S. (2005a). *How the Body Shapes the Mind* (New York, NY: Clarendon Press, Oxford).

Gallagher, S. (2005b). Phenomenological contributions to a theory of social cognition. *Husserl Studies*, **21**, 95–110.

Held, K. (2003). Husserl's phenomenology of the life-world, in D. Welton (ed.), *The New Husserl: A Critical Reader*, 32–64 (Bloomington, IN: Indiana University Press).

Husserl, E. (1991). *On the Phenomenology of the Consciousness of Internal Time (1893–1917)*, trans. John Barnett Brough (Boston, MA: Kluwer Academic Press).

Huxley, A. (1931). *Music at Night and Other Essays* (London: Chatto and Windus).

James, W. (1890). *The Principles of Psychology*, Vol. 1 (New York, NY: Henry Holt).

Jeannerod, M. (2006a). Consciousness of action as an embodied consciousness, in S. Pockett, W.P. Banks, and S. Gallagher (eds.), *Does Consciousness Cause Behavior?* 25–38 (Cambridge, MA: MIT Press).

Jeannerod, M. (2006b). *Motor Cognition: What Actions Tell the Self* (Oxford: Oxford University Press).

Kerman, J. (1980). How we got into analysis, and how to get out. *Critical Inquiry*, **7**, 311–31.

Kramer, J. (1988). *The Time of Music: New Meanings, New Temporalities, New Listening Strategies* (New York, NY: Schirmer).

Lewin, D. (1986). Music theory, phenomenology, and modes of perception. *Music Perception*, **3**, 327–92.

Miller, I. (1984). *Husserl, Perception, and Temporal Awareness* (Cambridge, MA: MIT Press).

Nagel, T. (1974). What is it like to be a bat? *Philosophical Review*, **83**, 435–50.

O'Shaughnessy, B. (2000). *Consciousness and the World* (Oxford: Clarendon Press).

Petitot, J., Varela, F., Pachoud, B., and Roy, J.-M. (eds.) (1999). *Naturalizing Phenomenology: Issues in Contemporary Phenomenology and Cognitive Science* (Stanford, CA: Stanford University Press).

Rodemeyer, L. (2003). Developments in the theory of time-consciousness: an analysis of protention, in D. Welton (ed.), *The New Husserl: A Critical Reader*, 125–56 (Bloomington, IN: Indiana University Press).

Searle, J.R. (1984). *Minds, Brains and Science: The 1984 Reith Lectures* (London: BBC).

Searle, J.R. (2002). *Consciousness and Language* (New York, NY: Cambridge University Press).

Searle, J.R. (2004). *Mind: A Brief Introduction* (New York, NY: Oxford University Press).

Searle, J.R., Dennett, D.C., and Chalmers, D.J. (1997). *The Mystery of Consciousness* (New York, NY: New York Review of Books).

Shear, J. (1996). The hard problem: closing the empirical gap. *Journal of Consciousness Studies*, **3**(1), 54–68.

Smith, J. (1973). Musical sound as a model for Husserlian intuition and time-consciousness. *Journal of Phenomenological Psychology*, **4**(1), 271–96.

Sudnow, D. (2001). *Ways of the Hand: A Rewritten Account* (Cambridge, MA: MIT Press).

Varela, F. (1996). Neurophenomenology: a methodological remedy for the hard problem. *Journal of Consciousness Studies*, **3**(4), 330–49.

Notes

1. The *Journal of Consciousness Studies* was founded in 1993 (see http://www.imprint.co.uk/jcs.html). The Association for the Scientific Study of Consciousness was founded in 1996 (see http://assc.caltech.edu).

2. Chalmers self-deprecatingly acknowledged the importance of his phrase: 'Because of the unexpected influence of the "hard problem" formulation, I have occasionally received far more credit than I deserve . . . the reason the formulation has caught on is that everyone knew what the hard problem was all along' (1997: 4).

3. Definitive authorial attribution of this phrase remains elusive.

4. This hard problem, like that posited by Chalmers, is hardly new. The question is highlighted by many undergraduate textbooks that ask 'Why study music?', and suggest that the formal study of music enhances musical enjoyment. On a more advanced level, Joseph Kerman's (1980) celebrated attack on analysis as a disciplinary activity was in many ways a counterpart to Nagel's article: both scholars suggested that there were fundamental problems in the basic methods of a discipline, and both provoked numerous responses, both enthusiastic and critical.

5. An early and prime example of this literature is the collection of essays published as *Naturalizing Phenomenology* (Petitot *et al.* (eds.) 1999). Other relevant publications can be found in the work of José Bermúdez (1998, 2003), Shaun Gallagher (2005a, 2005b), Marc Jeannerod (2006a, 2006b), Francisco Varela (1996), and many others, including several mentioned in this chapter.

6. See, for example, the responses to Chalmers by Shear (1996) and Varela (1996).

7. This understanding of consciousness as fundamentally directed outside the self, and concerned with external objects rather than internal processes, is a distinctive contribution of Continental phenomenology, and marks a basic contrast to analytic accounts of consciousness as an internal state of the brain.

8. In this context, Husserl's choice of a melody as a model seems motivated by music's intimate relationship with temporal experience, as discussed above.

9. This point is missed in Itzhak Miller's computational account of Husserl's theory of time, as convincingly demonstrated by Shaun Gallagher (Gallagher 1998; Miller 1984). Miller's interpretation is important to musicology as his account directly influenced David Lewin's (1986) magisterial article on different modes of musical perception. While Lewin's paper is full of musical insight, its theoretical reliance on independently existing now-points runs counter to most accepted readings of Husserl's concept of time consciousness.

10. This is reading consciousness as *intentional* consciousness (i.e. consciousness *of* something)—in the accepted phenomenological sense.

11. Thus Thomas Clifton, author of what is arguably the most thorough English-language study on music and phenomenology (Clifton 1983), uses Husserl's analytic terms quite readily, without any detailed discussion of how they relate to, or stem from, musical experience.

12. Indeed, it is arguable that Husserl was not considering mere listening in his *Phenomenology*, but had in mind the kind of listening associated with performance. For example, he speaks in the lectures of the active reproduction of heard events, such as the transposition of a melody and the repetition of two tones (Husserl 1991: 14, 52). Such activities are impossible for someone 'just' listening, and are likewise inconceivable without an understanding of the melody as an object.

13. Many other activities, for example reading, writing, painting, or mowing the lawn, do not have this particular relationship with time.

14. Jonathan Kramer (1988) and Robert Adlington (1997) have presented compelling and lucid accounts of non-serial temporality in music. It is striking, however, that even in such writing, serial temporality is treated as a norm, the 'default' understanding of time, as it were. This suggests that there may be more to say about this sort of temporal experience, particularly since, as Husserl would argue, we cannot reduce it to a mere series of mathematical now-points.

15. At the time of performance this experience may not be conscious: a performer does not need, and indeed probably does not want, conscious control over every movement.

16. Recent work by philosophers and neurologists working both inside and outside the tradition of embodied cognition has illuminated the role of the body in determining conscious states and in affecting perceptual experience. Several empirical studies have addressed specifically the relationship between musical performance and listening. Of these, the most striking is that by D'Ausilio *et al.* (2006), which shows that the neurological activity of pianists listening to music will differ depending on whether or not they have practised the music. This suggests there may be a close link between bodily movements and listening experience.

17. This does not, of course, mean that the totality of every performer's experience can be deduced from the score. However, the common movements that are a necessity to the performance of the piece will provide a basic experience that is shared by all its performers.

18. My consciousness of the piece as a listener is, in theory, independent of this physical experience, though it is may be desirable that they interact with each other. David Sudnow, as quoted earlier, implies that his fingers have their own agency, but later in the same paragraph he argues that 'how the paths sounded to me was deeply linked to how I was making them. There wasn't one me listening, and another one playing along paths' (2001: 40).

19. A corollary of this view might be that a performance that does not maintain such a relationship—that is, a performance in which the gestures are not experienced as continuous will not be a performance of the piece. This is, I think, a defensible proposition, but such a defence would go well beyond the purview of this chapter.

Chapter 3

Technicity, consciousness, and musical objects

Michael Gallope

Introduction

The role that technology plays in mediating our musical practices seems to have transfixed music studies. In recent years, countless books and articles have appeared about the history of instruments, about printing technologies and notation systems, about analogue and digital editing devices, about circulation networks, mix tapes, online swapping, microphones and headphones, even about the large-scale effects of cultural policy and copyright law (for example, Ashby 2010; Brady 1999; Eisenberg 2005; Greene and Porcello 2005; Katz 2004; Kittler 1999; Rehding 2005; Sterne 2003). I would like to contribute to this discussion by considering the topics of music, consciousness, technique, and technology from the perspective of deconstruction.

A deconstructive philosophy of technology (informed variously by the work of Edmund Husserl, Martin Heidegger, Jacques Derrida, and Bernard Stiegler) complicates a phenomenological way of understanding conscious experiences of musical objects. In arguing that technology is not something that is exterior to humans, but is something that is intrinsic to life itself, this idea (which I call *constitutive technicity*) throws a sceptical light on any effort to secure a 'transcendental' or phenomenological description of what it means to experience music as an object. In fact, several arguments in this line of thinking go so far as to claim that a musical object may be, in a strict ontological sense, impossible. In this chapter I will attempt to sustain the logic of these ideas long enough for them to be understood clearly. Will this account offer any insights of empirical value?[1] Yes and no. While empirical inquiries into the correlation between consciousness and musical objects invariably confront the issues dealt with here, thinkers like Derrida and Stiegler can only offer a general sense of the complications such empirical inquiries confront. I hope that this is seen neither as a sign of inadequacy nor as an old fashioned attempt at universalism, but as a logical result of basic differences in methodology.

For my present purposes, I will use the word *technics* or *technicity* to unite the general properties shared by the terms *technology* (that is, a prosthesis of the living) and *technique* (which could be most broadly defined as any systematic, repeatable gesture by a living thing). This moves my usage away from the most problematic and insistent connotations carried by the English word *technology*, namely electronics, information, and communication technologies. When such connotations are intended, I will retain the use of the word technology, but otherwise I will adopt the more general term *technicity*. The first two sections of this chapter are exclusively philosophical, engaging in a demonstration of how thinkers in the tradition of deconstruction understand technology to be integral to life. Questions specifically relating to music and consciousness turn up in the following three sections, where I attempt to relate the idea of constitutive technicity to issues in the phenomenology of music.

Constitutive technicity

In what is arguably his most important book, *Of Grammatology* (1976), Derrida suggests that inscription is not simply a property of linguistic writing; it should instead be understood as a constitutive basis for all life. From the earliest inscriptions structuring the replication of DNA up through the complex algorithms that form the basis of electronic media, systems of writing and inscription (or the *'grammē'*) support every stage of the development and evolution of life. In the following passage, Derrida suggests that this broader understanding of inscription will allow us to call into question many distinctions we consider crucial to the definition of humanity—not only the distinction between human and animal, but instinct and intelligence, absence and presence of culture, and so on. His highly impersonal understanding of the evolution or 'movement' of life unfolds as a response to André Leroi-Gourhan's study of human origins, *Gesture and Speech* (1993). Derrida writes:

> Leroi-Gourhan no longer describes the unity of man and the human adventure thus by the simple possibility of the *graphie* in general; rather as a stage or an articulation in the history of life—of what I have called *différance*—as the history of the *grammē*. Instead of having recourse to the concepts that habitually serve to distinguish man from other living beings (instinct and intelligence, absence or presence of speech, of society, of economy, etc. etc.), the notion of *program* is invoked [by Leroi-Gourhan]. It must of course be understood in the cybernetic sense, but cybernetics is itself intelligible only in terms of a history of the possibilities of the trace as the unity of a double movement of protention [anticipation] and retention [somatic memory]. This movement goes far beyond the possibilities of the 'intentional consciousness'. . . . Since 'genetic inscription' and the 'short programmatic chains' regulating the behavior of the amoeba or the annelid up to the passage beyond alphabetic writing to the orders of the logos and of a certain *homo sapiens*, the possibility of the *grammē* structures the movement of its history according to rigorously original levels, types, and rhythms. . . . If the expression ventured by Leroi-Gourhan is accepted, one could speak of a 'liberation of memory', of an exteriorization always already begun but always larger than [that of] the trace which, beginning from the elementary programs of so-called 'instinctive' behavior up to the constitution of electronic card-indexes and reading machines, enlarges difference and the possibility for putting in reserve; it at once and in the same movement constitutes and effaces so-called conscious subjectivity, its logos, and its theological attributes. (1976: 84)

A deconstructive logic rejects the idea that technology is only an external prosthesis or tool that aids our otherwise non-technical lives; it instead says that all life is fundamentally constituted through the structures of prostheses, inscriptions, or programmable codes. This deconstructive grammatology holds that the *grammē* is an 'exteriorization' of life that has 'always already begun'. At every stage, life is structured by technical apparatuses that stretch from DNA replication to modern information and communications technology.

The evolutionary biologist Richard Dawkins also cites programmability as a 'fundamental unit' of all living things. In *The Selfish Gene*, he writes: 'The fundamental unit, the prime mover of all life, is the replicator. A replicator is anything in the universe of which copies are made' (Dawkins 1976: 264). That is, over three billion years ago little replicators, bits of matter, began to copy themselves according to programmatic chains. These genes survived and reproduced via another similar but distinct 'technology'—a 'gene machine,' for which technical components in the organism's body serve the ends of the genes themselves. Both primordial replicators and evolved gene machines must employ a minimal genetic or molecular code, or *grammē*, a program based in a form of inscription that enables life to survive and reproduce.

If an inscriptional or programmed technicity constitutes life's most basic properties (the security of homeostatic survival or self-maintenance and reproduction), deconstruction also emphasizes how survival and reproduction remain inherently risky endeavours.[2] This is due to the unpredictable character of time. Time dictates that everything is subject to the possibility of decay, just as it guarantees an undetermined future. So, according to Derrida, just as any written trace must remain available for misreading by a future reader, so too will any particular tool, program, inscription, gene, or organ run the risk of failure or self-destruction.

For Derrida, this is not a bad thing; in fact, we should think of the risk of failure as *constitutive* of what it means to live. Martin Hägglund calls this the deconstructive logic of 'survival,' a paradoxical way of understanding life that does not divide the survival of life from the risk of failure or death; it does not divide the security of programs, traces, or remains from the destructive or creative potential of time, but rather insists that these binaries be thought as co-constitutive. Hägglund (2008: 1) writes of how survival is grounded in the structure of the trace:

> The structure of the trace follows from the constitution of time, which makes it impossible for anything to be present *in itself*. Every now passes away as soon as it comes to be and must therefore be inscribed as a trace in order to be at all. The trace enables the past to be retained, since it is characterized by the ability to remain in spite of temporal succession. The trace is thus the minimal condition for life to resist death in a movement of survival. The trace can only live on, however, by being left for a future that may erase it.

Constitutive technicity means that the dynamism of life fully needs the inanimate program, the inorganic or 'dead' inscription, for its survival and reproduction. It is this idea that serves as an axiom for both Derrida and the work of French philosopher of technology Bernard Stiegler, although the two of them draw different conclusions about what kind of philosophy to write with it.

Derrida thinks of the co-constitution of the technical and temporal as embodying the structure of what he calls *différance*. While this term has many well-known definitions in literary studies and linguistics, for the purposes of this chapter, I propose a comparatively empirical definition. At one point in his article 'Différance', Derrida defines the term as 'the becoming-time of space and becoming-space of time' (Derrida 1982: 13).

Grafted on to the logic of technical life, this means that life is about survival and preservation in space, despite the eventual loss that comes with the passage of time. It could be represented as follows:

1 an organism takes up space, holding itself together (surviving) for an interval of time (the becoming-time of space);

2 the time of its development, reproduction, and movement take up space in the world (the becoming-space of time);

3 the organism creates *technical* remains, tools, or traces in space—dwellings, expressive creations (also the becoming-space of time);

4 these traces (including the body of the living thing itself, tools, writing, etc.) are subject to the inevitable process of temporal decay (the becoming-time of space).

According to the logic of *différance,* nothing can survive without the risk of decay, nothing can live without wanting to survive. One might say that life is matter that can convert time into space (through preservation, shelter, inscription of traces), and space into time (metabolism, dynamic movement, growth, but inevitable decay, and eventual annihilation). This is how we can understand technical life as a condition for living as such. And since living processes are essentially technical (or coextensive with the properties of technicity as such), we might say that to be constituted by technicity is to be constituted by *différance.* The origin of this whole process is senseless, unknowable, and unthinkable even as it forms the foundation for life itself. In an interview with Stiegler, Derrida says: 'The origin of sense makes no sense' and later, 'that which constitutes sense is senseless. This is a general structure' (Derrida and Stiegler 2002: 103).

All this generality notwithstanding, Derrida recognizes the possibility of other more empirical and historical approaches to constitutive technicity when he writes that: 'I will not be concerned, as I might have been, with describing a history [of *différance*] and narrating its stages, text by text, context by context, demonstrating the economy that each time imposed this graphic disorder; rather, I will be concerned with the *general system of this economy*' (Derrida 1982: 3). This 'text by text, context by context' history of *différance* is, in a sense, part of Bernard Stiegler's project. Stiegler uses *différance* as an explanatory model for specific epochs of technicity, so that it might serve as a foundation for a *history* of technical memory and its relationship to the living.[3] This leads him to a critical meditation on the empirical specificity of technological objects.

The history of life and the emergence of the world

What might such a technical 'history of life' according to the logic of *différance* look like? According to Darwin's principle of natural selection, as life forms evolved over three billion years, some developed neurological and functional complexity.[4] At some point, around 500 million years ago, a second form of technicity or memory began to emerge very slowly. In Stiegler's vocabulary, we can call this form of technicity *somatic* or *epigenetic* memory.[5] Like genetic memory before it, somatic memory conforms to the structure of technics in that it uses matter to 'write' something for future use, but its structure is different. Somatic memory sustains both the instinctive and learned 'programs' in the living creature itself. Even in primitive forms (flatworms, for example), these nervous systems are, in a sense, already coordinating responses to the organism's environment. Perhaps, in a very simple way, they could even be said to be 'reading' the outside world. As Stiegler says in his extensive commentary on the paleontology of Leroi-Gourhan:

> From the worm to the vertebrate a certain 'latitude of maneuver' of memory comes to the fore, witnessed by possibilities of conditioning and training. An individual memory is then constituted, registering past 'experience' (the adaptation of the individual), overdetermined by the non-species-related hereditary genetic capital responsible for the irregular efficiency of the various lineages of a species, the whole being subjected to the pressure of natural selection. (1998: 170)

Stiegler would argue that, insofar as these learned somatic traces remain for an appreciable length of time, and are stored in something more commonly called long-term memory, and insofar as these memories are integrated into the organism's behaviour, the creature may be said to begin to *anticipate* things in the world. This alone may seem unremarkable, but for Stiegler, techniques of genuine anticipation are crucial to a break in the evolution of life: the emergence of external technicity. According to Stiegler, as external supports arrive, tool-use drives the subsequent evolution of the human. He follows the theories ventured by Leroi-Gourhan here, which claim that the evolution of a hugely enlarged cortex is *materially* and *technically* driven by the presence of external *technical* supports—namely, stone flint (see Ingold 1999):

> Far from being simply determined by cortex evolution, the evolution of knapped flint determines in turn the process of corticalization. Such a hypothesis involves an attempt at elaborating a concept of artificial selection: the selection of mutations exerted at the cortical level in the context of a relation to the original milieu, mediated by the technical apparatus constituting the system of defense and predation . . . (Stiegler 1998: 176)

Derrida suggests this is the moment that makes the '*grammē* appear *as such*' (Derrida 1976: 84). At this point in the history of life the *grammē* no longer designates only the gene machine and its replicators, it now marks a minimal unit of external order that a life does not merely use, but experiences. It is an order that forms the basis of the totality of all potentially technical devices—akin to what Heidegger calls *world*. The appearance of the world to any living creature as containing traces of things past, as carrying significance, as having been written on before by something, will provide the material foundation for a substantially externalized technical order, one essential to life that anticipates and calculates the future.

For Stiegler, the cognitive technique of 'anticipation' reorganizes the temporality of life, such that self-perpetuating and evolving socio-technical systems can develop. The emergence of these technical systems enables two structural changes in technical life: first, the constitutive technicity of life is now *experienced* as such rather than merely used; and second, these technical experiences and anticipations are shared among ethnic groups rather than among the species as a whole, and are correspondingly transmitted from generation to generation along ethnic lines. Under the condition of external technicity, or what Stiegler calls 'epiphylogenetic memory', an individual can adopt tools and techniques from a generation whose experiences it did not live. This situation introduces an entirely new set of philosophical questions for life.

For example: if a technical device is the product of a cognitive technical anticipation, it could now be said to be an artefact of cognitive repetition. We might ask: why make a shovel? Only when we have a concept and a memory for what it means to dig holes over and over again, remembering how hard it is to do with our hands alone, would we decide to make, share, and hand down shovels. Here the shovel, the artefact, the technical object, becomes an artefactual repetition of digging holes. By consolidating the repetition of gestures in material form, life is explicitly pursued 'by means other than life' (Stiegler 1998: 17). Now, one might say, technical objects *remember* for us. For philosophy this presents a serious question. Philosophers are confronted with a form of technicity that is *so* exteriorized from our bodies that tools can now appear to us as prostheses, as an inheritance, a strange supplement to life, as something with a memory, with a past.[6]

For Heidegger, this is a characteristic existential predicament for humanity; in fact, our desire to make a world for ourselves by using techniques to preserve memories and tools is precisely what distinguishes us from animals. In *Being and Time*, Heidegger (1996) considers that the human being (or *Dasein*) *is* insofar as it *uses* things, through which, by a horizon of reference, or by a setting up of a world, it exists as *Dasein*, literally *being there* as a being-in-the-world. These useful things (or equipment—*Zeug* in German) are not simply invented: most must be inherited from already existing technical and referential systems. Since *Dasein* is made possible by this kind of inheritance, Heidegger does not describe it as a thinking subject external to its world. Rather, his philosophy explores an embedded self that is constituted by forms of external technical memory that can 'remember' outside the finite limitations of somatic memory.

For Heidegger, understanding an originary dependence upon shared tools, techniques, equipment, shelters, signs, and gestures is crucial for any philosophical description of existence. For if technicity *constitutes* us and we can *experience* this constitution, we can become profoundly aware of how our technical systems are more often than not quite concretely and even unconsciously a part of us. We are most of the time behaving towards these things in our world, in our finite technical milieu, as if we were *not necessarily conscious of them as objects*.

This is the basic disagreement Heidegger has with the phenomenology of Husserl: if Husserl argues that all consciousness is consciousness *of* something, Heidegger says such a meditative phenomenology is precisely what keeps us from understanding the true meaning of what it is to exist. He insists that existence is fundamentally built upon our everyday 'ontic' social, relational, linguistic, relationship to the world of our own technicity. It is from an ontic foundation that *Dasein* comes to understand itself as preoccupied with *ontological* questions—namely that of the meaning of Being. But these ontological questions remain contaminated by everyday ontic reality (not made transcendental through the presupposition of an a priori subjective foundation).[7]

The constitutive technicity thesis floated by Derrida and Stiegler takes this whole idea one step further by showing how it is not only external tools that structure existence, but the technicity of genetic and somatic memory that has developed over the course of evolution. This kind of thinking is radical enough to break down the distinction between human and animal, between conscious and unconscious life, in part because it reminds us that no transcendent or immaterial intervention arrived with the dawn of humanity. It says that no qualitatively new *substance* arrives to make life 'conscious', allowing us to fashion and adopt tools in sophisticated ways. In agreement with Darwin, a deconstructive logic would argue that all the materials for our life are already there in the technical history of life alone, in the vast archives of written traces—organic and inorganic, mechanical and expressive.

If we are right to follow Heidegger, Derrida, and Stiegler in thinking that our experiential technical world is substantially coextensive with properties immanent to the development of all living matter, we can now attempt to understand how this tradition might explain the ways in which our allegedly conscious experiences of musical objects are, at root, structured by an irreducible complexity of technical mediations. Specifically, I want to ask: How would the idea of constitutive technicity allow us to deconstruct the idealism behind a phenomenology of music? As I will argue, deconstruction can show how phenomenological efforts to isolate 'transcendental' experiences of musical objects (in the strict Husserlian sense) must suppress innumerable technical mediations (forms of musical writing and recording, unconscious or undetermined forms of memory, among others) that complicate (and structure) the very possibility of description.

The problem of musical time

In his lectures *On the Phenomenology of the Consciousness of Internal Time (1893–1917)* Husserl attempted to describe the conscious perception of melody by distinguishing two forms of retention (Husserl 1991):

1 primary memory—the *immediate retention* of something happening that fades like a comet's tail behind the continuous presence of experience;

2 secondary memory—the imaginary *recollection*, or the reproduction of the past, or the memory of the complete melody.

In the *Phenomenology*, an unspecified melodic musical object allegedly gives us a common experiential starting point for a phenomenological inquiry on the experience of time.[8] And it does this precisely because of its becoming: the flow of a melody isolates the flux that Husserl sees as the continuous perceptual 'now'. According to his thinking, if we can assume that the identity of a musical object has been agreed on and philosophically secured (in this case, a melodic sequence of notes), we can describe how a repeatable musico-temporal object can be synthesized through a conscious and intentional act (retention). The same melody can then be recalled, as a totality, in secondary memory (recollection). What Husserl calls the 'total memory' of the melody is an affirmed continuity between these two kinds of memory.[9]

The main issue Husserl must confront when describing the inner experience of time revolves around what is necessary for the synthesis of the melody to occur at all. Husserl alleges that a melody isolates the 'now', which requires a conscious subject not only to intentionally connect up the discrete sequence of notes into a continuous whole, but also to connect each phase of each note in itself so that each note is synthesized in its own right as a temporally extended individual sound.

For Husserl, both syntheses (that of each individual note in itself, and the sequence as a totality) reveal to the subject the way in which an originary perception of a melody fades into a retention (primary memory). Now, even if this is an adequate description of how we intentionally hear a melody, how do we know that describing the experience of time through the perception of a passing melody effectively isolates the 'now' as something distinct from secondary memory or recollection? For Derrida, Husserl steps on shaky ground when he solves this problem by rendering the distinction between primary and secondary memory as one between presence and non-presence. For Husserl, retention of the melody is present (attached to a continuous perceptual 'now' as the absolute origin of all memory), and the imaginary character of recollection (secondary memory) pertains to a non-present melody (stored for possible recollection).

Derrida argues that this distinction is untenable because *the sense input and synthesis of primary memory is nothing without a prior retention*; it is nothing without a cognitive technical program or an interpretive mechanism allowing consciousness to sense the outside world, binding these sense data into phenomena. In order to grasp the melody as a totality (if such an act is truly possible), secondary memory must constitute the act of listening at every point. Recollection is necessary for the perception of any melodic sequence. The deconstructive idea of constitutive technicity does not allow for an *atechnical* retention of music or 'living [musical] present' outside the cognitive techniques of recollection; rather, technicity continuously structures the temporality of the musical *now*.[10]

Moreover, according to a deconstructive logic, the ways in which recollection structures retention are undecidable. Let us specify a melody to make this point clear. Example 3.1 presents a transcription of the opening melody of the famous song 'Maar Dala' from the 2002 Bollywood film, *Devdas*, as sung by the Indian actress, Madhuri Dixit.[11] We could not simply say that knowing what Dixit's voice sounds like is a sufficient secondary memory for the perception of her voice singing a melody similar to the one above. Nor would remembered As, F♮s, C♮s, Ds, and Bs. Nor would intimate familiarity with the idiom of Bollywood songs, or formal elements such as common time and repeated, ornamented melodies. Deconstructively speaking, we cannot rigorously or transcendentally specify the preconditions for perception. This is because constitutive technicity, following the logic of *différance*, not only explains the way in which the temporality of the musical present is structured by memory, but argues that secondary memory cannot be understood to have *positive content*. A 'structure of delay', integral to *différance*, forbids it. In his 1895 essay, 'Project for a scientific

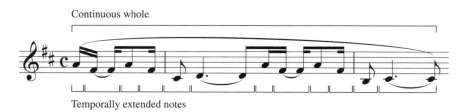

Example 3.1 Transcription of opening of 'Maar Dala' as sung by Madhuri Dixit, from *Devdas* (2002).

psychology' Freud called this phenomenon *Nachträglichkeit* (see Gay 1995). Derrida writes:

> The structure of delay (*Nachträglichkeit*) in effect forbids that one make of temporalization (temporization) a simple dialectical complication of the living present as an originary and unceasing synthesis—a synthesis constantly directed back on itself, gathered in on itself and gathering—of retentional traces and protentional openings. The alterity of the 'unconscious' makes us concerned not with horizons of modified—past or future—presents, but with a 'past' that has never been present, and which never will be, whose future to come will never be a *production* or a reproduction in the form of presence. (1982: 21)

From the standpoint of deconstruction, no phenomenology of music could be based on the naïve supposition that the brain has only one kind of memory that is always available to consciousness for synthetic acts of perception that compound primary with secondary memory. The repressed, the unconscious, an emotional memory, the seed of a trauma flushes the perceived temporality of music with alterity and unpredictability. This is not to say that listening adequately to a musical object is utterly impossible. Certainly, listening subjects have acquired skills based in musical knowledge that are necessary conditions for the perception of musico-temporal objects. The deconstructive logic merely reminds us that these skills cannot be *rigorously* specified (philosophically) in exactly the same way that notation can rigorously specify a sequence of pitches. This line of thinking would not deny that listening is possible in a pragmatic sense, it would only point to the general fabric of uncertainty inherent in the substance of living memory. If we agree with such a proposition, we might go on to conclude that the musical object cannot be rendered eidetic; it cannot be reduced to its identity in the act of perception since the retention that contaminates the passage of the musical object (the memory that is necessary for it to be 'grasped' at all) has neither positive nor secure content: it is subject to the unpredictability of the delay inherent in *Nachträglichkeit,* of the infinitely unknown *within* retention. Such is the logic of Derrida's notion of the trace: any memory of anything, musical or not, must remain open to the immanent possibility of distortion, effacement, or annihilation in order to remain at all.

Just as it is with secondary memory, so it is with external forms of musical technique and inscription, although the risk here is not only one of misreading or forgetting written musical traces: it is something that is inherent in any use of a tool. Deconstruction emphasizes that every instrument or technique must be *trusted* to be used. We do not know its past, who has used it when, and exactly how; we may not know how it was made. We may have a rough idea because we have seen how the instrument is used, but in acquiring any skill, in adopting any device we must negotiate an ontological uncertainty as to how to relate to a tool that is external to our body. In doing so, we must maintain a certain faith in the instrument—when picking up a hammer, a pencil, or even using a word, or making a gesture. We are never sure what is going to happen because we live under the condition of *adopting* techniques and tools that come from a past we did not live. The very character of technicity necessitates a kind of ontological faith at every moment of decision, anticipation, and timing. For Derrida, technical supplements 'produce no relief'; anticipation, necessary for the use of any tool, demands *some* uncertainty, whatever the reliability of our calculations

(Derrida 1976: 147). This faith is such that we pragmatically accept, trust, or use something whose history we *did not live*, only because it is left for us—it is our technical inheritance. Derrida follows the metaphysics of Immanuel Levinas when he calls this *trust* the mark of an *absolute past*: the unknowable past of a technical object, a technique, or a calculation for the future.

Returning to the passing melody: if constitutive technicity and all the uncertainty it entails is an ontological condition for life, then the intervention of such technical inheritances cannot be suspended for the duration of the musical object. *Contra* Husserl and his notion of the epoché, we do not stop inheriting to hear music, nor do the idioms, habits, techniques, and organizations of time we have inherited in the past stop for the musical object to be perceived as such. We cannot declare any form of musical mediation inessential to the act of listening. A deconstructive logic would argue that forms of entrainment or mediation cannot be subtracted out from listening, and that this is the source of an enduring dilemma in describing the experience of musico-temporal objects (or the experience of time in general, for that matter); we live through our inheritance of the musical world in an ex-stasis of time, through the perpetual birth of possibilities and anticipations, all made possible by the ontological enigma of the 'absolute past'. Technicity is constitutive of this existential predicament. Listening to music cannot suspend it through the act of a Husserlian *epoché*, by bracketing out the usual questions about what exists; technicity (and its uncertainties) must remain conditions of possibility for the act of listening at all.

So it is perhaps ironic to imagine that the one time Husserl wrote about music (in the arguments I just discussed in the *Phenomenology*), he also found himself revealing some of the deepest inconsistencies in his project—those of time and temporality, and of the complex ways in which our experience of a 'now' is structured by innumerable and highly complex mediations. For a phenomenology of music, where time and temporality are essential, this is a telling problem. Although Husserl never attempted a phenomenological reduction of any actual music, French electroacoustic composer Pierre Schaeffer did manage a version Husserl's project in the domain of music, attempting to hear music in the manner of a transcendental phenomenology, with attention to the conscious act of hearing alone.[12] As I will show in the next section, under the deconstructive lens, such a project cannot think of technicity as 'constitutive' of life, but will instead mark an evaluative distinction between 'good' and 'bad' technical mediations. Finally, I will show how deconstruction argues that these distinctions harbour metaphysical presuppositions.

Let us recap, briefly, two points. First: *constitutive technicity*. We can broaden the definition of technicity to encompass all forms of memory, from the replicator's material copies to information technology. Second: *irreducible alterity*. Following the logic of *différance*, we can affirm the ways in which these forms of memory cannot carry positive content due to an unconscious 'structure of delay', or because of the necessary uncertainty and faith one must have in every adopted technique. Now, if alterity is at work in technicity most generally (and we could probably show that mutation and genetic variation, for example, testify to the alterity at work in even the earliest forms of technicity), we can show that something like a Husserlian phenomenological description of a musical–temporal object runs into a fair bit of trouble accounting for the conditions of such an experience. Irreducible alterity, immanent to the structure of technicity as *différance*, produces an unreliable memory (somatic, technical) for the synthesis of musical objects in time. If, according to deconstruction, life is made up of technical formations from the beginning, then, for Derrida, no transcendental subject could be built on a metaphysical or vital substance external to techniques, external to the world. For this logic, it also follows that our musical objects cannot be simply synthesized through an intentional act, without recourse to the intervention of technical mediations. It is to the particularities of the musical object that I shall now turn.

The problem of musical technics

If Husserl used melody as a way to understand the experience of time, what if we attempted to look at a musical object in the face—as a Husserlian *intentional* object? The same issues can be framed differently here. If, in order to perceive a musical object, that object must have a minimally bounded identity, the phenomenologist begins by saying that this identity is not empirical; instead it is made by way of an intentional or transcendental description. Music theorist Brian Kane has accurately characterized and analysed the salient issues in Schaeffer's Husserlian approach to the musical object (in Schaeffer 1966), so for economy's sake, let us turn to his account. Kane (2007: 3) first summarizes the Husserlian intentional object as follows:

> This object of intentionality is not the same as the physically material object, which from a scientific perspective, causes my perceptions. Being the correlate of an act of synthesis on my part, the intentional object is no longer bound to any particular spatio-temporal adumbration. It is independent of any factual context—it has become an *essence*.

Now this 'essence,' which attempts to account transcendentally for the perception of an object, is simply a synthetic act of consciousness, whereby an undetermined sequence of 'adumbrations' or qualitatively different perspectives on the perceived object are brought together, bound into a constituted identity. The object is *made* by perception. This type of phenomenology, therefore, does not make recourse to empirical properties of the object (in the way that an acoustic or formalist analysis would for music). It focuses on the precise description of its objective constitution *by* consciousness.[13]

As Kane shows, Schaeffer makes a musical version of the intentional object through the technique of the 'acousmatic reduction'—drawn from Husserl's concept of the *epoché*. For Husserl, reducing perception through the *epoché* involves subtracting out an observer's relationship to the external, physical, and empirical world of causes and effects. Schaeffer proposes something extremely similar in his 'acousmatic reduction'. As Kane puts it: 'the first step is to bracket out the spatio-temporal causes, and distinguish them from what we are immanently hearing. What remains after the reduction is the *acousmatic*' (Kane 2007: 3).

Now suppose such an experience. A subject is listening to 20 seconds of music. It need not be notated, simple, or even particularly melodic—but suppose it is a 20-second fragment of an extended jam by Fela Kuti and his band Afrika '70 (e.g. from Kuti 2001). There is a riddle in getting at the acousmatic reduction here: in order to bracket anything out of the experience, negatively speaking, we have to first determine what the inessential spatio-temporal causes are. In the case of notated music, it may seem obvious to bracket out anything that is not reflected in the score. But is this immanent structure necessarily the default object? Certainly Schaeffer's method could emancipate sound from precisely this type of notated structure, and use phenomenology to develop a still more immanent musical alphabet. But in the case of something like a Fela Kuti record, for which the spatio-temporal cause may be obvious—because we know who he is, and we know the afrobeat idiom he pioneered—what are we left with once these causes are bracketed out? One can easily imagine the awkwardness of posing questions to Fela Kuti like: What are the notes? How do they fit together? Where do they lead? How are they being played? Even if a transcription were used to elicit phenomenological answers to these questions, we might be led astray by more pressing musical 'objects' that we determine as essential to the sound of afrobeat: What are the production techniques are for the recording? How have the musicians developed their skills? Who 'wrote' the structure of the song? Was it an improvisation that slowly got worked out and concretized over the course of several practices? Do some members dominate over others in the songwriting process? Were recordings of band practices used in the songwriting process? How? When? Were the vocals laid out separately? Complicating our effort to secure an essential objecthood for the music is the undeniable fact that answers to these questions relate only murkily to specific sounds. This could make isolating what happens in the listening experience harder. The amplification of all the material can make guitars bleed into keyboard sounds. Rhythm guitar can sound like percussion. The mix is punctuated by drumming. No doubt these empirical factors could radiate indefinitely.

But in our search for the essence of Fela Kuti and Afrika '70, let us not forget that 'the acousmatic experience reduces sounds to the field of hearing alone' (Kane 2007: 3). To do this, the subject must subtract *all* these empirical factors pertaining to the history of its musical life, each of which bears a technical implication, a mediation of some sort: a technique, a tool, an organization of time, a tradition, and so on. And suppose this subject could, through an act of sheer consciousness, leave Fela Kuti desiccated, without a musical past, allegedly *atechnical*, unmotivated, and without intention. Then what is minimally to bind the act of perception? How is the subject to know that 20 seconds of Fela Kuti is still happening? In other words, without any empirical or technical point of orientation for the listening experience, what would be the minimal condition of being able to listen at all, without these far stickier and more directed 'empirical' moments of listening I listed above?

We know that for the acousmatic logic, the Husserlian *epoché* teaches us to bracket out these empirical causes, to allegedly find nothing more than the sound itself. The obvious irony, of course, is that even as all possible empirical and technical questions radiate from our 20 seconds of Fela Kuti, we know they do not radiate *ex nihilo*. Minimally, they radiate from the technical mediation of sound recording. If the listening subject had somehow lost all points of binding orientation that gave her an empirical purchase on the musical object, the last thing left standing that binds the subject to the sound would be this minimally recorded substrate, a minimal inscription in the Derridian sense. Schaeffer is well aware of this. He points out how sound recording (among other modern audio technologies) makes it far easier to bracket a sound down to its essence; by recording sound only, it empirically subtracts sound from its original cause. For deconstruction, this is a symptomatic problem for both the *epoché* and the acousmatic reduction.[14]

The intentional object has to find its own immediacy within consciousness; otherwise it could not be an essence. Consequently, a musical object, taken as an intentional object after the acousmatic reduction, must remain absolutely *atechnical*. Any technicity would imply an empirical moment of mediation. But it is technicity that provides musical objects with an empirical or 'spatio-temporal' body in the first place. (For music, technicity could still be anything: instruments, techniques, notation, recordings, and so on; they are all forms of musical technicity—or musical 'writing' in Derrida's sense of *arche-writing* (see also Chapter 1)).

While deconstruction insists that we cannot do away with any technical medium (e.g. sound recording, writing) as an empirical component of the listening experience, we might say that the acousmatic reduction, like other metaphysical phenomenologies of music, manages to continue its reasoning by harbouring what could be something like a presupposition of an evaluative distinction between a good, or immediate, technicity, and other bad, or mediated technicities. For the modern acousmatic reduction the good immediacy is obviously a sound recording that enables an allegedly immediate abstraction of the listening act. The bad mediations would entail all the distracting empirical questions we asked in attempting to listen more closely to Fela Kuti.

But a deconstructive logic also goes on to point out that this qualitative distinction between 'good' musical immediacy and 'bad' technical mediation ends up being the very condition of music's metaphysical objecthood. That is, we can only conceive of the musical object as something transcendental via a hierarchical evaluation of different musical technicities. The immediate or 'good' technicity gives the music a proper objective foundation. If Schaeffer could be said to have elevated the waveform to a transcendental condition of sorts, it would not be difficult to show that there are many other paths to a metaphysical or objective immediacy for music. Innumerable musical media have been rendered immediate, essential, or metaphysical: notation over performance or technique, score over ornamentation, Roland Barthes's 'grain of the voice' over the musical work (Barthes 1978), background over foreground, performer over record producer, singer over backing band, structure over body, and so on.

From the perspective of constitutive technicity, we could do away with the evaluation of good and bad forms of musical technicity. This would render a claim to immediacy (as we see here with sound recording) as a mere symptom of the moment in phenomenology when the empirical refuses to leave behind the transcendental, and refuses to be bracketed off by an *epoché*.

Impossible musical objects

The deconstructive case against a phenomenology of music does not end there. Let us return to the problems with the temporal object. If our intentional Fela Kuti object could be constituted through the synthesis of different adumbrations, revealed via the acousmatic reduction (having successfully subtracted any empirical determination), we know these adumbrations still must unfold in a sequence or a succession. And it is the time taken up for this succession that is precisely at the root of the problem for the musical object: time is at once the condition for the possible synthesis of the musical object, but also (recalling Derrida's discussion of *Nachträglichkeit* and Stiegler's discussion of technical inheritance, recounted above) time is grounds for demonstrating the uncertainty immanent to any act of perception. Alterity or unpredictability is opened at the very moment that time, sound, and possible musical objects become in any way technically organized. If we take this idea seriously, are musical objects, according to the deconstructive logic, impossible?

If they are, it is because a constitutive definition of technicity challenges the experiential grounding for a transcendental description of music. The thesis shows how all mediations entail an irreducible alterity, contaminating the musical object with an uncertain correlation with consciousness, and it goes on to show that such transcendental descriptions of musical objects find their 'essence' impossible to achieve—in that they must bear the mark of an evaluative judgement about good and bad (immediate and mediated) forms of musical technicity, all of which, regardless of our attributed values, constitute listening. Inevitably, the effort to isolate a transcendental or invariant musical experience (either associated with the flux of the living present in the case of the temporal object, or something like Schaeffer's acousmatic reduction in the case of the intentional object) is haunted by its reliance on, and surreptitious prioritization of, the techniques and tools of the musical world. That is, insofar as we think that a phenomenological description of musical experience could proceed without reference to some technical musical medium, a format of musical technicity, or an agreed-upon system of immediate or good musical writing, we are led down a metaphysical path.

Or put otherwise: if transcendental musical objects were possible or actual for a subject (which one might imagine could be true for its transcendental describer) they would, in their essence, have to remain *atechnical*. The musical object could not be broken down into any smaller units of recognizable instruments, notes, gestures, motifs, styles, or recording techniques; it would have to somehow remain a sonorous sequence. And, for the deconstructive logic of time, this is precisely what is excluded as impossible. We can perhaps *imagine* such a pure sequence, and yet it seems that no pure sequence of sounds could ever be actually experienced or remembered without recourse to a technical unit, a code of repetition, a tradition of memory. For the very cognitive technique of binding sounds in a sequence at all is already resolutely technical, and based in the habits of our past. Even the minimal sequencing of sound is technical in its very successiveness.

Conclusion

If the philosophies of technicity developed by Heidegger, Derrida, and Stiegler have one common virtue, it is that they all develop concepts capable of explaining the relentless complexity of what it means for us to exist amidst incessant technical mediation (see also Nancy 2000). Knowing that a phenomenology of music must stabilize or presuppose both its subject and object in order to conduct its description, technicity as *différance* allows us to think the mutual contamination of subject and object along an essentially technical axis. In his *Technics and Time* volumes, Stiegler develops this question as a co-constitution of the *who* and the *what*. This co-constitution is central to the adoption of techniques: 'If the individual is organic organized matter, then its relation to its environment (to matter in general, organic or inorganic), when it is a question of a *who*, is mediated by the organized but inorganic matter of the *organon*, the tool with its instructive role (its role *qua* instrument), the *what*. It is in this sense that the *what* invents the *who* just as much as it is invented by it' (Stiegler 1998: 177).

Perhaps the most valuable question posed by constitutive technicity is ultimately not deconstructive, but genealogical. We might pose it in the form of a positive inquiry into the nature of musical writing. What might an empirical history of the musical object look like, outside of our experience of it? What technical properties of the musical object ensure its identical status across different repetitions? How do we know it is the same, say from one iteration to the next? We find one answer to this question when we consider the musical object as something that is irreducibly founded upon technical apparatuses. Specifically, we can consider a musical object as a form of musical writing before we assume it to be anything like an object for a conscious subject. That is, some form of sonorous inscription or memory must provide the basis for the musical object's existence.

Phenomenologies aside, it is worth nothing that an emphasis on inscription and mediation over the metaphysics of subjective experience and objective structure points us in a markedly different direction from certain constructions of musical practice that have still not shaken off nineteenth-century musicological tropes—such as the myth of the autodidactic genius who, by the standard narratives, manages his (usually male) creative feats thanks to the down-playing of any technological mediation or educational training. Such prejudices against the history of constitutive technicity tend to consider mediation only insofar as *new* technological devices (like the phonograph or the radio) supervene upon an originally created musical work or musical culture (setting into motion a crisis of authenticity, authorship, and so on). For deconstruction, however, the concept of musical writing entails something far more general. The logic asks us to consider *anything* that can remember or repeat music to constitute a form of technical mediation. This includes not only notation, but bodies, institutions and traditions that store and remember musical technique. What kind of histories might this logic produce? Friedrich Kittler's *Gramophone, Film, Typewriter* (1999) is a provocative exemplar, as it attempts a 'materialist' history of modern musical technicity, focused around impersonal and pre-subjective attributes of musical organization.

In any case, if it is obvious that deconstruction would dismantle any metaphysical attempt to say that music is, at its root, a transcendental becoming or presence, it may also yield positive projects both by signalling the complexity of music's empirical and technical determinations, and by reminding us how crucial alterity remains to the reality of any musical experience. Musical technicity or writing emerges when sound is anticipated and repeated, and in turn when instruments concretize this anticipation, and when future generations inherit the instrument and technique as a tradition. From this perspective, music is perhaps merely technical sound, perhaps a sonic exteriorization of creatures, subject to an uncertainty that exceeds the boundaries of a sentient consciousness.

References

Ashby, A. (2010). *Absolute Music, Mechanical Reproduction* (Berkeley, CA: University of California Press).

Barthes, R. (1978). The grain of the voice, in *Image–Music–Text*, trans. Stephen Heath, 179–89 (New York, NY: Hill and Wang).

Beardsworth, R. (1995). From a genealogy of matter to a politics of memory: Stiegler's thinking of technics. *Tekhnema: Technics and Finitude*, 2, 85–115.

Brady, E. (1999). *The Spiral Way: How the Phonograph Changed Ethnography* (Jackson, MS: University of Mississippi Press).

Dawkins R. (1976). *The Selfish Gene* (New York, NY: Oxford University Press).

Dennett, D. (1995). *Darwin's Dangerous Idea: Evolution and the Meanings of Life* (New York, NY: Simon and Schuster).

Derrida, J. (1976). *Of Grammatology*, trans. Gayatri Spivak (Baltimore, MD: Johns Hopkins University Press).

Derrida, J. (1982). Différance, in *Margins of Philosophy*, trans. Alan Bass, 1–29 (Chicago, IL: University of Chicago Press).

Derrida, J. and Stiegler, B. (2002). *Echographies of Television*, trans. Jennifer Bajorek (Cambridge, MA: Polity Press).

Eisenberg, E. (2005). *The Recording Angel: Music, Records, and Culture from Aristotle to Zappa* (New Haven, CT: Yale University Press).

Gay, P. (ed.) (1995). *The Freud Reader* (New York, NY: W.W. Norton and Co.).

Greene, P.D. and Porcello, T. (2005). *Wired for Sound: Engineering and Technologies in Sonic Cultures* (Middletown, CT: Wesleyan University Press).

Hägglund, M. (2008). *Radical Atheism: Derrida and the Time of Life* (Stanford, CA: Stanford University Press).

Heidegger, M. (1996). *Being and Time*, trans. Joan Stambaugh (Albany, NY: State University of New York Press).

Husserl, E. (1991). *On the Phenomenology of the Consciousness of Internal Time (1893–1917)*, trans. John Barnett Brough (Boston, MA: Kluwer Academic Press).

Ingold, T. (1999). 'Tools for the hand, language for the face': an appreciation of Leroi-Gourhan's *Gesture and Speech. Studies in History and Philosophy of Science Part C: Studies in History and Philosophy of Biological and Biomedical Sciences*, 30, 411–53.

Kane, B. (2007). L'Objet Sonore Maintenant: Pierre Schaeffer, sound objects and the phenomenological reduction. *Organized Sound*, 12, 15–24.

Katz, M. (2004). *Capturing Sound: How Technology Has Changed Music* (Berkeley, CA: University of California Press).

Kittler, F. (1999). *Gramophone, Film, Typewriter*, trans. Geoffrey Winthrop-Young (Stanford, CA: Stanford University Press).

Krims, A. (1998). Disciplining deconstruction (for music analysis). *19th-Century Music*, 21, 297–324.

Kuti, F. [Ransome-Kuti, O.O.O.] (2001 reissue, original 1976). *Ikoyi Blindness/Kalakuta Show.* CD (MCA, B00004XT1Z).

Leroi-Gourhan, A. (1993). *Gesture and Speech*, trans. Anna Bostock Berger (Cambridge, MA: MIT Press).

Mulhall, S. (1996). *Heidegger and Being and Time* (London: Routledge).

Nancy, J.L. (2000). *Being Singular Plural*, trans. R. Richardson and A. O'Byrne (Standford, CA: Stanford University Press).

Rehding, A. (2005). Wax cylinder revolutions. *The Musical Quarterly*, **88**, 123–60.

Schaeffer, P. (1966). *Traité des objets musicaux* (Paris: Éditions du Seuil).

Schneider, E.D. and Sagan, D. (2005). *Into The Cool: Energy, Flow, Thermodynamics, and Life* (Chicago, IL: University of Chicago Press).

Schrödinger, E. (1958). *What is Life? The Physical Aspect of the Living Cell* (Cambridge: Cambridge University Press).

Sterne, J. (2003). *The Audible Past* (Durham, NC: Duke University Press).

Stiegler, B. (1998). *Technics and Time, vol. 1: The Fault of Epimetheus*, trans. Richard Beardsworth and George Collins (Stanford, CA: Stanford University Press).

Stiegler, B. (2001). Derrida and technology: fidelity at the limits of deconstruction and the prosthesis of faith, in T. Cohen (ed.), *Jacques Derrida and the Humanities: A Critical Reader*, 238–70 (Cambridge: Cambridge University Press).

Stiegler, B. (2006). Anamnesis and hypomnesis: the memories of desire, in L. Armand and A. Bradley, (eds.), *Technicity*, 15–41 (Prague: Litteraria Pragensia).

Stiegler, B. (2008). *Technics and Time, vol. 2: Disorientation*, trans. Stephen Barker (Stanford, CA: Stanford University Press).

Zbikowski, L. (2008). Cognitive science, music theory, and music analysis, in J.P. Sprick, R. Bahr, and M. von Troschke (eds.), *Musiktheorie im Kontext: V. Kongress der Gesellschaft für Musiktheorie*, 447–63 (Berlin: Weidler Buchverlag).

Notes

1. One might also read this chapter as an alternative 'deconstruction' of music studies, one that explicitly attempts to avoid grafting deconstruction onto the analysis of musical scores, and instead attempts to return to the phenomenological roots of Derrida's thinking and relate them to enduring problems in the phenomenology of music. Earlier efforts at a deconstructive musical analysis are well-summarized and critiqued by Adam Krims (1998), who demonstrates how this generation of music scholars was highly influenced by a version of Derrida filtered through the deconstructive school of literary criticism of the 1970s (exemplified by Paul DeMan, Geoffrey Hartman, and J. Hillis Miller; and, later, Barbara Johnson, Jonathan Culler, and Avital Ronell).

2. See Schrödinger (1958) for a groundbreaking work on the homeostasis of life in relation to entropy, alongside a more recent study of the thermodynamics of life in Schneider and Sagan (2005).

3. The division between the two thinkers is elaborated in the transcription of Stiegler's interview with Derrida (Derrida and Stiegler 2002). Stiegler himself has published an enormous amount of untranslated French material, but for a quick and clear rundown of his philosophical position in English, see Stiegler (2006).

4. For a defence of the productive value embodied in the algorithmic simplicity of natural selection, see Dennett (1995).

5. Richard Beardsworth (1995) clearly delineates and explains the three kinds of memory instrumental for Stiegler: genetic, epigenetic/somatic, and epiphylogenetic, the last of which Stiegler defines as 'organized inorganic matter' or the exterior tools decisive for the evolution of the human.

6. A related point is made in Chapter 6 by Ansuman Biswas (this volume)—see the section entitled 'From tool as means to tool as object'.

7. Stephen Mulhall (1996: 4) characterizes the distinction between *ontic* and *ontological* as follows:

> such disciplines as physics and chemistry, biology and literary studies take as their central concern aspects of phenomena that remain implicit in our everyday dealings with them; and the specific theories that are produced as a result go to make up a body of what Heidegger would call *ontic* knowledge—knowledge pertaining to the distinctive nature of particular types of entity.
>
> However . . . those [ontic] foundations tend to remain unthematized by the discipline itself, until it finds itself in a state of crisis. Relativity theory precipitated such a crisis in physics . . . [The resulting] conceptual enquiries are not examples of theories that conform to the standards of the discipline, but rather explore that on the basis of which any such theory could be constructed, the *a priori* conditions for the possibility of such scientific theorizing. In Heideggerian language, what they reveal are the ontological presuppositions of ontic enquiry.

8. Husserl's phenomenology of time consciousness is also discussed in chapters in this volume by David Clarke (Chapter 1), Rolf Inge Godøy (Chapter 13), Andy McGuiness and Katie Overy (Chapter 14), and Eugene Montague (Chapter 2).

9. Derrida's arguments about Husserl's *Phenomenology*, are effectively discussed in Stiegler (2001: 242–5).

10. Stiegler (2008) develops another critique of the Husserlian temporal object.

11. As one might expect, many film clips featuring the song can be found on the website YouTube—for example, www.youtube.com/watch?v=fVg6Ehu1VXY.

12. Schaeffer's approach to listening is discussed in various chapters in the present volume, including those by Ian Biddle (Chapter 4), Eric Clarke (Chapter 11), Rolf Inge Godøy (Chapter 13), and Bennett Hogg (Chapter 5).

13. As a point of contrast, I draw the reader's attention to the fact that this is a *transcendental* synthesis of perception, and bears little resemblance to the music theory research associated with cognitive science. In the case of Lawrence Zbikowski's work—see, for example Zbikowski (2008)—the possibility of 'categorization' is retained as a kind of synthesis, but his analysis hinges on correlating possible perceptual categorizations with the empirical and spatio-temporal traces of notation, recordings, and so on. For Husserl the empirical and objective aspects of music are inessential to the synthesis of the intentional object.

14. Kane (2007: 8) is also sceptical about Schaeffer's relationship to modern technology: 'Schaeffer presents a picture of ahistorical, existential man discovering himself within a teleological horizon. What modern technology reveals for Schaeffer, aside from uncritically optimistic potential, is little more than an abstract glimpse into an ancient "originary experience"'.

Chapter 4

Listening, consciousness, and the charm of the universal: what it feels like for a Lacanian

Ian Biddle

> Consciousness in man is by essence a polar tension between an
> ego alienated from the subject and a perception which
> fundamentally escapes it, a pure *percipi*.
> (Lacan 1988: 117)

Introduction: consciousness, listening, and history

In this chapter I am interested in exploring some of the ways in which listening has been thought about, especially with regard to what might be termed quotidian listening, or listening in/to the everyday. I am also interested in asking what thinking about listening as a specific instance of consciousness might allow us to do. These two enquiries are intimately connected, not least because they are both implicated in interesting and contentious ways in the history of musicology itself as a discipline. The core analytical resource I draw on in this chapter is Lacanian: that set of tools designed to scrutinize the relationship between enjoyment and discipline. For, as we shall see, when it comes to musicology's construal of listening, discipline and enjoyment are inevitably bound together. One of the questions that has often been raised with regard to the work of Jacques Lacan, and one which will occupy me in this chapter, is the extent to which his analytical apparatus allows for what might be termed historicist thinking. Psychoanalysis (like psychology, neuroscience, and other 'harder' approaches to consciousness) has long been accused of universalizing or de-localizing human experience, and Lacan in particular has been accused (by feminists such as Julia Kristeva, Luce Irigaray, and Judith Butler, and by a whole range of historians, not least the so-called New Historicists of the late 1970s and 1980s) of seeking to install an inalienable male-centred monolithic model of subjectivity that obliterates the local. For those who read Lacan closely, however, it becomes clear very quickly that nothing could be further from the truth. As we shall see, it is his commitment to the notion that forms of consciousness are locally negotiated (and therefore historically delimited) that will distance him quite fundamentally from other more universalizing forms of knowledge about consciousness (see also Brennan 1993, especially 26–32).

Nonetheless, the Lacanian orientation will also inevitably raise questions about the very notion of consciousness itself since, for Lacan, consciousness is constituted around a tension (or negotiation) between, on the one hand, the subject's alienation from itself (a symptom of the woes of modernity) and, on the other, a supposition put in place to fill the gap of that alienation—what he terms a *percipi* (I will deal with the details of this argument later). While this chapter does not accept Lacan's assertion wholesale, it will take time in the final section to work through the challenges raised by Lacan's problematization of the term 'consciousness' more fully. With this in mind, I conceive of consciousness in the broadest possible terms while maintaining a focus on the discursive work of consciousness in discourses about listening. We might ask, first of all, to what extent the investigation of music and consciousness *ought* to be an investigation of the activity of listening. For many outside the fields of musicology and consciousness studies one's *listening* to music is understood as a constitutive part of the musical process, and yet a great deal of the scholarship we think of as addressing musical consciousness in the broadest sense (not only music psychology, but also the cultural theory of music, the sociology of music, ethnomusicology, historical musicology, and music analysis) has tended to sideline the listener (especially the 'non-specialist' listener) in favour of the avowedly poietic practices of playing, composing, performing, and so on. Hence, for me, any investigation of music and consciousness ought thereby to be, in part at least, about listening, about what we do when we listen, about how listening to music is different from other processes that go to make up what we have come to term 'consciousness'.

To think about listening and its relation to consciousness, then, is to think about the particular: listening is an instance, a materially focused *Sinnlichkeit* or 'sensed-ness'. And as such, it is susceptible, like all human activity, to what Antonio Gramsci (1971) famously termed 'articulation': it is susceptible, that is, to the transformational operation of ideology (different ways of seeing the world, different subject locations, and different symbolic systems). What this susceptibility points to is the *cultural and historical specificity* of listening. To understand something of the challenges raised by thinking about listening, we need, then, to include within the analytical trajectory an out-in-the-open encounter with the historical and cultural specificities of our—what Subotnik (1996: xlii) terms 'Western'—understanding of listening. How do our own 'articulations' of listening intervene in and shape the constitution of listening as a set of practices? What kinds of listening do our own historical locations and scholarly traditions make audible and, by implication, what kinds of listening do they silence?

Before proceeding to try to answer some of these questions, it is worth noting that listening represents for consciousness studies a set of specific challenges, not least because consciousness (as a way of thinking about humanity, identity, being in the world) is itself beholden to a certain disciplinary order. What I mean by this is that, in the arts and humanities disciplines in particular, especially in the West (to use the usual problematic shorthand), wherever the term 'consciousness' is deployed, a set of political, ideological, and epistemological assumptions is given reign: the term connects with a range of technologies for thinking about what in other discourses might have been termed subjectivity or selfhood. The term consciousness, then, is currency in a number of disciplines, from the 'hard' sciences of neuroscience and cognitive psychology through to a range of religious or metaphysical constructions of the self. What interests me is precisely the academy-mediated discourse that has followed in the wake of the 'harder' articulations of the term: in the last 20 years or so, especially in the 'softer' social scientific and humanities disciplines, 'consciousness' has come to stand for a collection of concerns that might be said to have fallen under the spell of what I am calling here *the charm of the universal*. This turning away from the particular (from the local, the contingent, the historical, and, in particular, the vernacular) has its roots firmly in the nineteenth-century Central and North European fascination with both Idealism and scientific materialism.

That turn is intimately connected to a way of thinking about the world as a kind of *an sich*, or an 'in-and-of-itself-ness', to use a phrase of which the Young Hegelians in German-speaking Europe such as Ludwig Feuerbach and Arnold Ruge were inordinately fond. Mid-nineteenth-century materialism, especially scientific materialism, went about 'freeing' the world of the differentiating effects of differentiated observation, putting in place a model of the universal (detached) observer that still remains largely in place. That observer (and, by implication, auditor) was a creature of the hegemonic institutions (such as the academy), and constitutes perhaps one of the clearest symptoms of the concerted effort in the second half of the nineteenth century to professionalize observation and audition (see Crary 1999: 147).

These changes implicate musicology in a set of socio-political relations that have since become hidden, in the manner of what Žižek has termed, after Hegel, a 'vanishing mediator' between the dreamy worlds of Hegelian metaphysics and the tough materialist discourse of the new scientism (Žižek 1991: 243). At that moment when musicology was first developing a self-awareness in the mid-nineteenth century, it was not the Hegelians (Young or Old) who were in the intellectual ascendancy. The doubt and structural prevarication at the heart of the fading (Old) Hegelian paradigm of, for example, A.B. Marx's *Die alte Musiklehre im Streit mit unserer Zeit* (1841) and his later *Beethoven* monograph (Marx 1857), are the result of his troubling encounter with the new highly popular work of scientific materialists such as Fechner (e.g. Fechner 1860) and Dorguth (an encounter that undoubtedly also impacted subsequently on his dark and gloomy *Das Ideal und die Gegenwart* of 1867). The pervasive counter-Idealism of these years, in which the primacy of the material or sensual world of *Sinnlichkeit* was advocated over the world of ideas and ideologies, was a direct challenge to the programme of Hegelian (Prussian) Idealism, and it is this presumptuous Oedipal challenge to the Prussian Academy that moves Karl Fortlage, an outspoken guardian of the (Old) Hegelian status quo, to speak in 1856 of materialism as a virus, a new infection for which there appeared to be no cure (Fortlage 1856: 541).

Marx was not alone among those mid-century professional music theorists in taking heed of the new order. The impact of German-language positivism on *Musikwissenschaft* as an academy-mediated discipline has been downplayed or sidelined in standard histories of the discipline in favour of the more usual Idealist narrative, of which Carl Dahlhaus himself was inordinately fond (Dahlhaus 1983). The (Hegelian) 'origins' of the discipline have been consistently foregrounded, I suggest, in a systematic attempt to tell the story of our discipline as completely consistent with the arts' and humanities' imagination of themselves as part of the humanist philosophical tradition.

That story of our discipline has tended to miss the very real impact of the material sciences on the way our discipline understands itself and imagines itself to function. In this regard, at least, any engagement with the notion of what might be termed 'musical consciousness' is also an engagement (however surreptitiously) with the history of the musicological discipline itself. The implications of this kernel of historicity at the heart of consciousness will become clear below but, for the moment, suffice it to say that historicizing tendencies in musicology have been almost uniformly opposed to its scientizing tendencies, and the two have been held apart in quite striking and unusually contentious ways since the very moment at which musicology sought to find a place for itself in the academy.

The regimes of fixated listening

For most musicologists 'listening' still embraces only a few highly disciplined modes of listening, which have been consistently connected to regimen, training, and acculturation. As we shall see, those canonic modes are quite rare outside the academy and are intimately connected to the historical origins of the discipline in which 'fixated' listening (a term I will elaborate below) is deemed normative and other forms of listening are deemed of lower value. And yet listening, as a particular instance of cognition, is not uniform; it cannot be captured from within the disciplinary demands of the work-centred paradigms of traditional musicology.

When Lars Iyer and I began thinking about a presentation on which the present chapter is partly based (Biddle and Iyer 2006), we were listening to Madonna. Allow me to re-create that originary moment, since it might be helpful to think about what is challenging about listening as an object of scrutiny. We were listening to the album version of 'What it feels like for a girl' (from *Music* 2000, produced by Madonna, Guy Sigsworth, and Mark Stent). The gentle high-pitched anacrusis of a sampled and reverbed guitar string pick (doubled by a wallowing reverbed sine-tone) on the fifth degree falls to the third and leads into a strangely squashed back texture. A 'wet' tick-tock-like foreground (a succession of opening and closing gate filters which sound like the initial 'click' of a guitar pick) is washed over with the to-and-fro of a further filter on the backfill chords. The mix is a little claustrophobic, squashed. A sample of Charlotte Gainsbourg speaking in Andrew Birkin's 1993 film adaptation of Ian McEwan's 1978 novel *The Cement Garden* is heard, outlining the differences between 'boys' and 'girls' and inviting boys to think about 'what it feels like' to be a girl, as a kind of gender incitement.[1]

A highly filtered 'slapped' bassline, hovering around the dominant pedal, slowly takes hold, and (at 0:36) Madonna's voice eventually arrives, just as the bassline settles for the first time onto a clear tonic. The intro, harmonically centred on the dominant, like a larger structural anacrusis, points to the arrival of Madonna's voice; it sets it up, calls for it, and marks her voice as a moment of structural gratification. We're listening closely. We pause, rewind, re-listen, over and over. What is that? How does that work? Our listening is fragmented, messy, disjointed. There is no 'event' of listening here, no song-unfolding, no in-the-whole encounter. In short, we're messing it up in the manner that only digital sound reproduction technology allows.

Often, as Anahid Kassabian suggests, listening has been articulated as 'active' and hearing as 'passive', and that distinction does something to many of those forms of listening we encounter in the everyday: it silences or downgrades them, making invisible some of the kinds of musical consciousness that attend our being-in-the-world (Kassabian, forthcoming). To put this another way, the challenge for musicology in thinking about listening is to make sense not just of the disciplinary specifics (that is, not just of 'disciplined' listening) but also of all the other ways in which we dally in the sonic vicinity of musical production. In our listening to Madonna's 'What it feels like', then, Lars and I were avowedly undisciplined. And yet the outcome we sought was disciplinary in some sense at least, in that we were seeking to understand the acoustic structures that constitute the object-song. It is not that our listening was transgressive or so maverick as to be fully excluded from the musicological terrain. What struck us both in those heady hours was the non-linearity of our relationship with the song object. Moving backwards and forwards within the song, shuttling between sonic-object-centred and form-hungry listening, laughing, chatting, singing along, and allowing any number of distractions to draw us away from the music. In short, the site of listening was a highly differentiated one, characterized by a multitude of modalities of listening, none of which could be said to have settled, despite every attempt we made to focus on the task at hand. In other words, there are some very important ways in which apparently undisciplined or more episodic and less uniform listening can still achieve quite complex analytical or descriptive ends, even when these modalities may not be sanctioned by the discipline (for example, Lars, a philosopher, would not want to make claims to being a trained musicologist, but his listening was by no means without very keen insight).

Within the disciplinary space of musicology, we have nonetheless tended to focus on the small and highly circumscribed set of listening practices that sits along the spectrum of what I come to call 'fixated listening' (Biddle, 2011). What I mean by this is those practices that require the listener to be in a state of diligent openness to the idea of the musical work, and thereby to be free from the distractions of the quotidian soundscape. I prefer the term 'fixated' here precisely because it captures something of the relation of 'charm' and 'concentration' (what mid-eighteenth-century German-language theorists of music variously termed *Anmut*, *Reiz*, or *Aufmerksamkeit*) in canonic models of listening. Along this disciplinary listening spectrum, then, lie a number of models of listening. Yet the spectrum is dominated by the two modalities, which Felix Salzer (1962) and Pierre Schaeffer (1966) have respectively termed 'structural hearing' and 'reduced listening'.[2]

Structural hearing, Salzer's famous stricture for the music analyst, involves being taken up completely by the conscious plotting of the flow of forms. It is, to slightly overcharacterize it, born of that moment that William Weber calls, in the title of his 2008 monograph, *The Great Transformation of Musical Taste*, where coherent musical forms became audible as parts of larger semi-audible forms. This kind of listening is clearly about training oneself to be conscious of, to retain and recall, surface musical structures and to couple them with other, 'deeper' structures, building the larger framework as the work unfolds. It is a way of listening born both of the concert hall and of close attentive fixation on musical structures, a disciplinary and disciplined listening. As Salzer puts it (1962: xvi): 'Understanding tonal organisms is a problem of hearing; the ear has to be systematically trained to hear not only the succession of tones, melodic lines and chord progressions but also their structural significance and coherence.' This (now) orthodox neo-Schenkerian approach, quite radical in its time, has become central to the musicological construal of listening as 'fixated' (in the manner I am using the term here) on the structural relationships between elements of the 'tonal organism'.

Reduced listening, on the other hand, is a kind of listening, which, though largely coterminous with structural hearing, involves a different kind of discipline, where coherent sound objects are indexed according to raw sonic qualities disassociated from their putative origins and/or cultural meanings. To use Michel Chion's gloss on Schaeffer's term, reduced listening, 'takes the sound—verbal, played on an instrument, noises or whatever—as itself the object to be observed instead of the vehicle for something else' (1994: 29).[3] Whereas structural hearing imagines a process in which the listener communes with the deep 'grammar' of tonal materials with which each work takes up a relation, reduced listening imagines a world in which the wonder of the strange is to be encountered by the listener 'innocently', as it were. Hence, whereas Salzer requires us to develop a set of pattern recognitions which we connect to each other over the period of the 'training' of our listening, Schaeffer imagines a no-less demanding modality of listening in which we learn to detach ourselves from our experience and to attend in a manner that enables the *objet sonore* to speak 'for itself'.

These two models of listening share a need to 'train' the listener, and therefore give rise also to the need for the *regimen*, the *institution*, and a certain *operation of power*. Indeed, while the two modalities are quite distinct from each other, they designate precisely that space I call disciplinary or fixated listening, since it is between these two highly disciplined modalities that most of what musicology considers right listening is deemed to fall. Musicology, an avowedly post-Enlightenment formation, has always been about distinguishing between the amateur and the professional, and about maintaining distance between the worst excesses of what Schenker famously termed 'democratic culture' (1922: xiv) and the self-styled *Gelehrtenstand*; indeed, anyone familiar with Schenker's work will remember his denigration of the masses as a 'rotting humus' (vii). Musicology's own fixation on these two models of listening, then, should be contextualized within the historical moment at which the retreat into the academy is sounded and the vernacular is located firmly 'outside'.

The origins of disciplinary or fixated listening, as I have already intimated, reach back somewhat further than this. Indeed, changes in listening practices can be linked to wider changes in the access to and production of works of art around 1800. Roger Chartier has suggested that around this time a new kind of reading emerges in the so-called 'extensive' reader, who can be juxtaposed with the older 'intensive' reader—the reader faced only with a 'narrow and finite body of texts, which were read and reread, memorized and recited, heard and known by heart, transmitted from generation to generation' (Chartier 1995: 17). By contrast the 'extensive' reader, 'that of the *Lesewut* [reading madness] . . . is an altogether different reader—one who consumes numerous and diverse printed texts, reading them with rapidity and avidity and exercising a critical activity over them that spares no domain from methodological doubt' (17).

A similar process can be traced in the history of listening: just at that moment when listening practices became ever more 'extensive', the *Gelehrtenstand* sought to discipline listening, and to mark right listening (listening that was susceptible to the operation of public discipline) as a symptom of *Bildung*, of refinement, of education. Listening becomes, in this anxious response to the explosion of listening in the early nineteenth century (what we might call a *Hörwut*, a madness for listening, a new *ubiquity* of listening), a site of focused disciplining: over the next 40 years or so listeners would be gradually made to fall silent in the concert halls and perform a kind of possessed fixation. Fixated listening is thus a relatively recent, local, and fragile mode of listening, developed as an overcompensation in the face of listening's ever more rapid democratization and quotidianization. In other words, 'listening', as imagined still by the discipline of musicology, is structurally normalized around a highly exceptional modality of listening that we might term fetishistic and exclusive—in every sense of the word.

Wilhelm Wundt's now famous contribution to psychology is well known, especially in his construction of the regimen of the empirical subject of his experimental tachistoscope. In these experiments a nonsense fragment—a single letter or collection of letters—is exposed to the subjects for milliseconds. These subjects were, as Friedrich Kittler describes it (1990: 222), 'chained so as to hinder or even prohibit movement, facing black viewing boxes out of which for the duration of a flash . . . single letters shone out. This is modernity's allegory of the cave.'[4] The 'subjects' [*Versuchspersonen*] of the experiments are also subjects [*Subjekte*], and it is in this overlap between two typologies—the one articulated as receiver of stimuli, the other as an idealized observer of those stimuli—that the experimental subject is located. It is in this new kind of subject, historically limited, local to the moment of scientific materialism, that modern consciousness studies is incubated, and also, as I have demonstrated elsewhere (Biddle, 2011), where modern musicology itself is also incubated (Schenker himself, for example, imagined his pupils behaving as *Versuchspersonen*). What is striking about Wundt's experimental scenario is its regimen. The inability of the subject to move, his/her similarity to the penal or medical subject in the nineteenth-century imagination, and the close management of the type and degree of stimulus all point to a conception of the human subject as caught in the operation of power—as both subject *to* it and subject *of* it.

Robert Esposito has described modernity as a project focused primarily on 'cutting itself off from every social bond, from every natural link, from every common law' (Esposito 2009: 14). We might add that, in place of those bonds, links, laws, modernity installs the rituals and regimens designed to facilitate a new abstraction of the citizen to symptom, including the ritualization of that regimen of 'freedom' itself which, as Lacan has shown, is the strictest and harshest master of all. What a Lacanian orientation will allow here is an analysis of the implication of discipline and enjoyment in each other: the one is always accompanied by the other, always structurally dependent on the other, always lying in wait for the other. Here in this undergrowth, where enjoyment and discipline play off each other, modernity plays out an experimental scenario. As we shall see, this will help us to understand something of the political consequences of the experimental subject in musicology's fixation on disciplined listening.

Music and consciousness: what it feels *like*

In the account I gave above of listening to Madonna's 'What it feels like', I attempted to find a technical-descriptive idiom that captures both the specific characteristics of the sounds as they present themselves to us (samples, textures, filters, and other production techniques) and the harmonic structure of the opening fragment (dominant anacrusis to tonic structural downbeat). There is at least something of the phenomenological reduction here—the disciplined attention to the details of the sounds themselves—but this is by no means a fully fledged reduced listening. What we have here, at best, as I suggested above, is a hybrid descriptive idiom that attempts to steer a course between music-analytic and music-objective modes of description. If we are to examine the limits of both models of listening as pointing to a conceptual gap in the construction of musical consciousness as an object of study, then we must tarry with Madonna a while longer. Between these two listening modalities (that is, between structural and reduced listening), the complex materiality of the sounds poses a challenge. To put this in the terms that Lacan might have used (had he written anything on music), the sounds do not present themselves as autonomous phenomena, but as something in which we are always already implicated. They tell us something about the manner in which we are stitched in to the world and about the fragility of that stitching. They also tell us something about our manner of being, about the regimen that ties us in place when all other ties have been severed by the project of modernity. Fixated listening, we might say, is the consequence of a historically delimited set of problems, implicated, like Wundt's tachistoscope, in the discipline, of subjecting oneself to a certain ritual or regimen. In other words, what 'modernity's allegory of the cave' brings into focus is precisely that shortfall which modernity has installed: the casting adrift of the experimental subject from the 'common laws' of belonging (to use Esposito's formulation again), and the consequent need for rituals of belonging that fill that gap.

Of course, Madonna's 'What it feels like' is also itself precisely about sketching a particular *Lebensart* or way-of-being-in-the-world. For Lacan, many things can occasion the question of being, that primary question posed by the neurotic: 'What is it to be?' Imagine *this* kind of being, the lyrics incite; imagine what it would feel like to be *like that*, to be in that world in *that* way. Gestures, metonyms, synecdoches, metaphors all jostle for attention in the lyrics—the eye of the narrator falls on the hips, the tears, the hair, finger tips, all ripe with meaning, all membranes, endings, borders, all moist with the humidity of the body. What the song attempts to play out here is a delicious contagion, a disturbing incitement to desire as if to say to (heterosexual) men, 'in woman you think you find your object of desire'.

And yet the question, foregrounded in the title, overrides all else: [can you know] 'What it feels like?' The question, of course, is about gender, or rather about what gender as a socio-cultural construction allows and does not allow. In other words, the 'what it feels like' of the title is an incitement to question the terms on which gender is enacted as a *regimen*. Modernity, it seems, is all about discipline. But what is even more interesting here is the extent to which this incitement draws attention to the complex interdependence of regimen and enjoyment. As Lacan (1989) has eloquently shown, enjoyment, or *jouissance*, is resolutely political. The trick of modernity has been to project a reality in which discipline and enjoyment seem disengaged from each other, as if the one operated without recourse to the other; the one is presented as a restriction, the other as a kind of free play. And yet that projection operates with a certain project in mind: the founding and continuation of the fantasy of the autonomous citizen of what Lacan terms 'the ego's era' (Lacan 1989: 77).

The operation of this fantasy (of what Lacan terms the 'alienation' of man from himself, a 'derealization of others', or more broadly the 'social psychosis' of modernity (31–2)) makes possible a set of key epistemological orientations towards the world that have implications for our understanding of the listening subject. First, this abstraction allows for the listening subject to conceive of her- or himself as 'free' from the constraints of older (pre-modern) allegiances (such as religion, clan, myth, magic) and therefore as absolutely 'free'. Second, it allows for the listening subject to imagine her- or himself as privileged or exemplary, as standing in for all auditors. Third it facilitates a way of thinking about the sonic environment as a site of contagion that must be stilled, hushed, managed, or curtailed such that musicology's peculiarly fixated modality of listening can be installed. Fourth, and following on from the third orientation, it ensures a systematic and protracted institutional disdain for the vernacular more widely. Consciousness, in this reading, thus stands for the moment at which the privileged subject of the ego's era begins to conceive of her- or himself as abstractable, as representative, and, in the final analysis, as distinct from the majority.

There are many objections we could level at Lacan's disdain for what he would term the ego-sciences, not least the fact that he himself is deeply implicated in the structures he seeks to critique. But there is one thing we can take from him in this context that is worth examining further: the notion that modernity constitutes a project that has systematically engineered the demise of belonging. In this sense, Lacan's critique of modernity—which Žižek's every work (and typically Žižek 1989, 2002) intensifies into a critique of late capitalism, and of neoliberalism in particular—has a very persuasive force. The Lacanian project was never about seeking out a nostalgic return to some primordial togetherness or a rose-hued premodern pastoral idyll, but it does represent a very real attempt to understand the horrors of the modern. Lacan allows us to think about fixated listening as ensnared in the machinations of authoritarian modernity, which hold listening in place but which put inordinate pressure on listeners to keep the doors of the concert hall firmly closed.

Conclusion: the idealized scene of listening

The final segment of my argument pertains to precisely this moment at which the doors of the concert hall are closed to the hubbub of the street. In whose name was this territorialization enacted? And for what reason? Territorializations of this kind speak of power play and point to something quite striking in the mechanisms by which boundaries are installed and maintained. The inside/outside distinction is managed not by a simple, out-in-the-open or violent exclusion of the subaltern outsider, but through a complex (and by no means uniform or strictly coherent) set of regimen-oriented practices, which normalize fixated listening through ritualization. The closing of the doors, the hush before the start, the expectation that one fall silent, and the public display of concentration are all set in place in order to maintain precisely the inside/outside distinction that any territorialization requires. These ritualizations are about maintaining what I have here termed 'the charm of the universal', the charm, that is, of what analytical philosophy would call the *sui generis* of fixated listening. Musicology labours under the illusion that this particular mode of listening subsumes all others as their meta-category.

Returning to the two related questions of who installed this territorialization and why, it is useful to keep in mind the linguistic distinction drawn between universal sets and elements within such sets. One clue as to how to answer these questions lies in recognizing something important about the force of the grammatical article in 'consciousness'.[5] Consciousness, without an article, stands for a consciousness *sui generis*, a designation that cannot be included within any larger formulations since it is always the umbrella, the field, the space in which other concepts are allowed to function. With the indefinite article, however, as in 'a consciousness', the term comes to stand for an instance or particularity. In the latter, the charm of the universal is broken by turning the universal set into an element within a larger set. To put it in terms Lacan would recognize, consciousness is susceptible to this kind of specificity effect, beholden to the operation of what it cannot fully discipline. Consciousness *sui generis*, then, is a kind of fantastical territory, a *percipi* or supposition (that is, something brought into being in order to fill in a conceptual 'gap' or to cover over an inconsistency of some kind), which, although available to numerous and varied articulations, is structurally committed to maintaining a close watch on its borders.

Wherever the term consciousness operates in the social sciences and in the arts and humanities, there is a concomitant absence of certain kinds of materials, certain kinds of questions, and certain kinds of actors. In particular, the vernacular is almost universally excluded. Just as the concert halls closed their doors to the street, so 'musical consciousness' tends to enact a selective deafness to the specificity effects of listening as a social and material act.[6] The structural relation between these two territorializations, then, is not coincidental. Nor is it something that can be abstracted out into any number of other disciplinary encounters. *This* encounter has its own history, its own material ground and its own structure. In short, what makes this encounter so remarkable is the fact that both territorializations make recourse to extensive and quite precise filtering processes: like Wundt's experimental *Versuchsperson*, the subject of consciousness and the listening subject are tethered by the demands of a certain quietude. Wundt sought to filter out all extraneous stimuli just as the concert hall is built with the stilling of the outside in mind.

I have often been struck by the manner in which some of the 'harder' (material-scientific) public presentations on musical consciousness I have attended in the last 10 years or so have sought to restage modernity's allegory of the cave all over again. PowerPoint, darkened rooms, and gleaming screen images all no doubt contribute to this effect. In images of coloured lit-up zones of the brain, in visual reductions of the subject to simple on/off stimuli indicators, there seems to be a certain *quietude effect*: the *Versuchsperson* here operates in highly select circumstances, restricted by the 'cap' or subjected (in all senses of the word) to external stimuli in a highly controlled (filtered) manner. Functional magnetic resonance imaging (fMRI) is a case in point, since, as perhaps the most commonly used device in the field of (both clinical and more broadly investigative) neuroimaging, it bears a striking resemblance to the allegory of the cave. The subject is restrained by pads and sometimes by a gag (euphemistically often referred to as the 'bite bar'). The machine is extremely noisy, and the quietude effect here operates by obliterating all other noise, by so overwhelming the subject as to render all other noise mute.[7] In brain images of this kind, whether produced by fMRI, positron emission tomography (PET), or single photon emission computed tomography (SPECT), there resides still the key fantasy of a subject free from the quotidian, as abstractable, as Lacan put it, to the point of a mere *percipi*, construed as a subject *sui generis*, but removed fundamentally from all common laws. The drowning out of the quotidian also, and perhaps especially, extends to those moments when the image is revisited—on the screen, in the conference hall, in the darkened silence of the lab. Just as Esposito marks modernity as a cutting off, so the allegory of the cave closes the doors and brings silence.

Modernity's allegory of the cave, then, is staged with a certain kind of quietude in mind. Stillness attends the analytical moment as a kind of disciplinary (institutional) regimen, which insists on the immobility (in all senses of the word) of the subject, on its abstractability, and on its susceptibility to measurement. As Kittler (1999: 224) puts it, 'man in his unity decomposes into illusions dangled in front of him'. Or, to think this from a Lacanian perspective, the kinds of knowledge-regimens that install this abstraction are themselves implicated in a certain historical moment we have come to call modernity proper: the ego's era, the great disenchantment, the great 'social psychosis' (Lacan 1989: 31–2). Quietude in the end speaks of a certain institutional desire to render the street mute and to hold off its topsy-turvy affray. There is no room for the vernacular *Katzenjammer* and brouhaha, no place for the roar of the outside. No hubbub here.

References

Biddle, I. (2011). *Music, Masculinity and the Claims of History: The Austro-German Tradition from Hegel to Freud* (Aldershot: Ashgate).

Biddle, I. and Iyer, L. (2006). What it feels like for a phenomenologist. . . . Paper presented at the International Conference on Music and Consciousness (University of Sheffield, July 2006).

Brennan, T. (1993). *History after Lacan* (London: Routledge).

Chartier, R. (1995). *Forms and Meanings: Texts, Performances and Audiences from Codex to Computer* (Philadelphia, PA: University of Pennsylvania Press).

Chion, M. (1994). *Audiovision: Sound on Screen* (New York, NY: Columbia University Press).

Crary J. (1999). *Techniques of the Observer: On Vision and Modernity in the Nineteenth Century* (Cambridge, MA: MIT Press).

Dahlhaus, C. (1983). *Foundations of Music History*, trans. J.B. Robinson (Cambridge: Cambridge University Press).

DeNora, T. (2000). *Music in Everyday Life* (Cambridge: Cambridge University Press).

Esposito, R. (2009). *Communitas: Origins and Destiny of Community*, trans. T. Campbell (Stanford CA: Stanford University Press).

Fechner, G.T. (1860). *Elemente der Psychophysik*, 2 vols (Leipzig: Breitkopf und Härtel).

Fortlage, K. (1856). Materialismus und spiritualismus. *Blätter für literarische Unterhaltung*, **30**, 109–76.

Gramsci, A. (1971). *Selection from the Prison Notebooks*, trans. and (ed.) Q. Hoare and G. Nowell-Smith (New York, NY: International Publishers).

Kassabian, A. (forthcoming). *Affective Listening* [working title] (London: University of California Press).

Kittler, F. (1990). *Discourse Networks: 1800/1900*, trans. M. Metteer (Stanford CA.: Stanford University Press).

Kittler, F. (1999). *Gramophone, Film Typewriter*, trans. Geoffrey Winthrope-Young and Michael Wutz. (Stanford CA.: Stanford University Press).

LaBelle, B. (2010). *Acoustic Territories: Sound Culture and Everyday Life* (New York, NY: Continuum).

Lacan, J. (1988). *The Seminar. Book II. The Ego in Freud's Theory and the Technique of Psychoanalysis*, trans. S. Tomaselli (Cambridge: Cambridge University Press).

Lacan, J. (1989). The function and field of speech and language in psychoanalysis, in *Écrits: A Selection*, trans. Alan Sheridan, 33–125 (London: Routledge).

Madonna Ciccone, M.L. and Sigsworth, G. (2000). What it feels like for a girl, *Music*. CD (Warner, B000GW88PQ).

Marx, A.B. (1841). *Die alte Musiklehre im Streit mit unserer Zeit* (Leipzig: Breitkopf and Härtel).

Marx, A.B. (1857). *Ludwig van Beethoven: Leben und Schaffen* (Berlin: Janke).

Marx, A.B. (1867). *Das Ideal und die Gegenwart* (Jena: Kessinger).

Maus, F.E. (2004). The disciplined subject of music analysis, in A. Dell'Antonio (ed.), *Beyond Structural Listening: Postmodern Modes of Hearing*, 13–42 (Berkeley, CA: University of California Press).

Salzer, F. (1962). *Structural Hearing: Tonal Coherence in Music*, 2 vols (New York, NY: Dover Publications).

Schaeffer, P. (1966). *Traité des objets musicaux* (Paris: Le Seuil).

Schenker, H. (1922). *Kontrapunkt*, vol. **2** (Vienna: Universal Edition).

Subotnik, R. (1996). *Deconstructive Variations: Music and Reason in Western Society* (Minneapolis, MI: University of Minnesota Press).

Toop, D. (2010). *Sinister Resonance: The Mediumship of the Listener* (New York, NY: Contiuum).

Weber, W. (2008). *The Great Transformation of Musical Taste* (Cambridge: Cambridge University Press).

Žižek, S. (1989). *The Sublime Object of Ideology* (London: Verso).

Žižek, S. (1991). *Looking Awry: An Introduction to Jacques Lacan through Popular Culture* (Cambridge, MA: MIT Press).

Žižek, S. (2002). *For They Know Not What They Do: Enjoyment as a Political Factor*, 2nd edn (London: Verso).

Notes

1. Lyrics are available in the CD liner notes for Ciccone and Sigsworth (2000).

2. There is a small body of classic work that has dealt critically with this discipline-specific nature of musicology's construal of listening (see, in particular, Subotnik (1996); Maus (2004)). It remains the case, however, that, with the (partial) exception of a handful of very recent texts (e.g. Toop 2010; LaBelle 2010; Chapter 17), Kassabian's is the only work to deal systematically and inclusively with quotidian forms of listening as such, complementing advances in the sociology of music and the everyday made by Tia DeNora (2000).

3. For further discussions (and critiques) of Schaeffer's account see chapters in this volume by Eric Clarke (Chapter 11), Michael Gallope (Chapter 3), Rolf Inge Godøy (Chapter 13), Bennett Hogg (Chapter 5), and Andy McGuiness and Katie Overy (Chapter 14).

4. Kittler's reference is of course to Plato's allegory of the cave in Book VII of *The Republic*.

5. See also Chapter 11, this volume.

6. Clearly, the contents of the present volume present a richer range of views. While some chapters would certainly reflect the tendency described here, others (e.g. those by Eric Clarke (Chapter 11), Richard Elliott (Chapter 19), Ruth Herbert (Chapter 17), Tia DeNora (Chapter 18), and Benny Shanon (Chapter 16)) do indeed include everyday and/or vernacular modalities of listening as their focus. The extent to which this might represent a paradigm shift, however, is still too early to call. Premature announcements of the return of the vernacular often speak more loudly about the entrenchment of the establishment than they do of seismic shifts in the discipline.

7. I am grateful to Eric Clarke for this insight.

Chapter 5

Enactive consciousness, intertextuality, and musical free improvisation: deconstructing mythologies and finding connections

Bennett Hogg

Introduction

The present chapter began as a descriptive account of my own practice as a musical improviser, from a perspective based on my reading of *The Embodied Mind* by Francisco J. Varela, Evan Thompson, and Eleanor Rosch (1993). However, that initial aim changed as I uncovered ideological formations and other 'blind spots' that had framed (and to an extent determined) what it was possible for me to say. In particular, I was drawn towards reconsidering how earlier theorizations of the body by artists working in the 1960s and 1970s had informed the position from which I began. These earlier accounts seemed to be rethinking how the physical and experiential materiality of the body might challenge the apparent dominance of the intellect in Western philosophical formations; further, they appeared to anticipate some of the theories of enactive consciousness that were to emerge some years later. However, in the course of following up these ideas it quickly became clear that such rethinkings themselves invited their own critique. The formulations I started from now appear towards the end of this chapter, where they serve to concretize some of the ideological (and metaphysical) suppositions that have framed them. At the core of my account is the connection proposed by Varela *et al.* between the idea of consciousness understood as *enactive cognition* and the perceptions within philosophy that 'knowledge depends on being in a world that is inseparable from our bodies, our language, and our social history—in short, from our *embodiment*' (1993: 149). Various avatars of these three factors of our knowledge—body, language, and history—reappear over and over in what follows. However, what has become the main theme of the chapter arrived unexpectedly in the connection that emerged between an understanding of consciousness as an enactive phenomenon, and a speculative and specifically musical/sonic interpretation of the idea of intertextuality.[1]

Grotowski's critique of improvisation

Jerzy Grotowski was one of the best known individual voices in a proliferating experimental theatre scene that emerged throughout the 1960s, and whose methodical interrogation of the interrelationships between text, actor, the actor's body and voice, and the audience made a significant contribution to the development of later twentieth-century theatre practice. As will become clear, for me his writings articulate something of a *Zeitgeist* whose resonances were also felt in music, and for this reason I dwell on his ideas here. They are characterized by a shift of focus away from the intellect and rational thought towards the body and (apparently) unpremeditated action, and as such offer a critique of epistemological frames generally considered to have been established through the Enlightenment. Grotowski's approach to theatre, sometimes called 'Poor Theatre', focuses upon the body of the actor, and a specialized conception of the correct training of that body. In Poor Theatre, there is, at its root, the actor and the audience. Everything else, even the underlying literary text, is, in a sense, extra.

In Grotowski's theatre most of the work is in the training and preparation of the actor. His actors would spend much of each day training their bodies, acquiring not only fitness and strength but also a sense of being in their bodies as an expression of a kind of physical *intelligence*, so that rather than thinking and then acting, his actors would strive for the 'total act' defined as the point at which 'consciousness and instinct are united' (Grotowski 1968: 210). This phrase implicitly identifies a binarism between consciousness and instinct, predicated upon a dual association of consciousness with thought and instinct with the body, that to a greater or lesser extent has structured many of the debates about the phenomena of consciousness.[2] Grotowski's training—at least as it is articulated and accounted for in his own writings, and in the documentation of his workshops by participants and observers such as Franz Marijnen—is concerned with bringing to a point of deployability the 'natural' capabilities of each actor: 'The natural physiological processes—respiration, voice, movement—must never be restricted or obstructed by wrongly imposed systems and theories' (Marijnen 1968: 185). In 'The actor's technique' Grotowski underlines this, writing:

> We are not after recipes, the stereotypes which are the prerogative of professionals . . .
> [O]ne must ask the actor: 'What are the obstacles blocking you on your way towards the total act which must engage all your psycho-physical resources, from the most instinctive to the most rational?'. We must find out what it is that hinders him in the way of respiration, movement and—most important of all—human contact. What resistances are there? How can they be eliminated? I want to take away, steal from the actor all that disturbs him. (1968: 209)

While the phrase 'from the most instinctive to the most rational' appears to allow for the inclusion of 'systems and theories' in the 'psycho-physical resources' of the actor, it is nevertheless clear that much of the work towards the elimination of blockages is to be done by putting the mind, and thinking (figured here as something done with the conscious brain) into abeyance, allowing the body to act without hindrance:

> My main principle is: Do not think of the vocal instrument itself, do not think of the words, but react—react with the body. (Marijnen 1968: 185)[3]

> [T]here is one absolute rule. Bodily activity comes first, and then vocal expression . . ..
> First you bang on the table and afterwards you shout! (183)

> It is of the utmost importance . . . that we learn to speak with the body first and then with the voice. (184)

This privileging of the body over the mind runs throughout Grotowski's writings and, on the face of it, offers up a challenge to a culture that, at least in its urban and educated sectors, had historically placed the mind over matter. The traditionally dominant half of the binarism is sidelined, disavowed, and put into suspension in order that the body may come into its full potential as both the place and means for the 'total act' of theatre to be realized. However, even if there is an implicit binary opposition between instinct and consciousness in Grotowski's theorizations, his aim is to 'unite' them. For him the respective figurations of body and mind do not conform to those reductive formations that make intelligence, self-awareness, and consciousness the exclusive prerogatives of 'mind', with the body as little more than the site of mind, its physical home. Despite his Cartesian conceptual framework, in urging the actor to 'think with the whole body' (Marijnen 1968: 204), Grotowski implicitly opens up a possibility for deconstructing this binarism. There is a resonance here with the agenda formulated in the first *Manifesto of Surrealism* where André Breton does not simply advocate the supplanting of the rational, waking conscious mind with the irrational, dreaming unconscious, but hopes for 'the future resolution of these two states, dream and reality, which are seemingly so contradictory, into a kind of absolute reality, a *surreality*' (Breton 2004: 14). Grotowski, then, seeks not to simply reverse an existent binarism, but to suspend its terms; for example, he explicitly acknowledges the impossibility, even the undesirability, of escaping completely from 'consciousness':

> how could I cut myself off from my consciousness even in order to rediscover my spontaneity? I am as I am, as far away from mechanics as from chaos: between the two shores of my precision, I allow the river, which comes out of the authenticity of my experience, to advance, slowly or rapidly. (1969: 174; cited in Kumiega 1985: 139)

'a substitute for work . . .'

It is thus not a simple matter of disconnecting from consciousness for spontaneity to automatically ensue. As indicated in the quotations above, spontaneity, for Grotowski, is only achieved through rigorous training, and so when confronted by experiments with theatre that, as he saw it, avoided training and preparation in the name of a liberatory 'improvisation' he dismisses the notion of improvisation *tout court* as 'a pretentious word serving as a substitute for work' (1969: 173; cited in Kumiega 1985: 133). Although the context of this dismissive definition is specific—a response to some of the 'let it all hang out' elements in 1960s theatre, American experimental theatre in particular (see Kumiega 1985: 133)—Derek Bailey mentions similarly negative connotations in some definitions of musical improvisation—such as 'making it up as you go along'—and as in some senses a lazy, work-shy way of producing music. Bailey records how some musicians are reluctant to use the term 'improvisation', despite its being integral to their practice, because of the 'widely accepted connotations which imply that improvisation is something without preparation and without consideration, a completely ad hoc activity, frivolous and inconsequential, lacking in design and method' (Bailey 1993: xii). He proposes that for some people improvisation is thought of as a 'conjuring trick, a doubtful expedient, or even a vulgar habit' (ix), and suggests that some musicians 'reject the word . . . [recognizing] that, as generally understood, it completely misrepresents the depth and complexity of their work' (xii).

Stockhausen: Intuitive Music

Grotowski's pioneering work with his 'Theatre Laboratory' and the foundations of his conception of theatre were developed around the same time that free improvisation was emerging in the early 1960s (Bailey 1993: 84). Reversals of dominance in the mind–body binarism became something of a trope during this period, perhaps most explicitly manifested in popular culture of the period with its countercultural concatenation of a rejection of law, authority, and rationalism with an (apparently) uninhibited valorization of the hedonistic and experiential corporeality of sex, drugs, and—among other musics—rock and roll. In the case of Karlheinz Stockhausen, who was perhaps less sceptical of the counterculture than some of his Darmstadt colleagues, it is possible to trace another articulation of the same reversed binarism, as well as what we might speculate is an instance of exactly that aversion to the term improvisation noted by Bailey.

By the later 1960s Stockhausen had consolidated a regular group of musicians with whom he worked on a whole series of pieces exploring different degrees of indeterminacy and performer involvement, frequently using his so-called 'Plus–Minus' notation, along with live electronics and, occasionally, recorded extracts of his own works. By 1968, in response to the working methods that had evolved with the Group Stockhausen, he arrived at the text compositions of what he termed his 'Intuitive Music', the 'scores' *Aus den Sieben Tagen* (1968) and *Für Kommende Zeiten* (1968–70). In choosing the term 'Intuitive Music' over that of 'improvisation' he was perhaps distancing himself from the pejorative associations of the word noted by Bailey. That 'intuitive' here carries connotations of authenticity, a lack of artifice, and even an implicitly biological foundation by seeming to be 'natural', is also significant. These texts also carry spiritual connotations, injunctions to meditate, to expand one's consciousness, usually in ways that sideline Western rational thought. Where the term 'consciousness' is used by Stockhausen in this period of his work it is often couched in terms of a spiritual or mystical phenomenon, a 'cosmic consciousness', of which everyday human consciousness is but a pale flickering shadow.[4] Such an everyday consciousness, predominantly concerned with thinking, with the brain, and with the waking mind, is seen as an obstacle to the higher states of consciousness required by Intuitive Music: 'acting, or listening, or doing something *without thinking* is the state of pure intuitive activity, not requiring to use the brain as a control' (Stockhausen 2000: 124; emphasis added).

Sidelining 'thought'

Stockhausen's remarks are strongly reminiscent of some of Grotowski's comments on his approach to theatre. While running a workshop for theatre students in 1966

Grotowski 'points out . . . that thought must be excluded. The pupils are to speak the text without thinking . . . Grotowski therefore interrupts every time he notices that the pupil is thinking during the exercise' (Marijnen 1968: 176). As already indicated, though, those aspects of Grotowski's thought that seem to valorize the body over the mind are only heuristic devices on the way to 'engage all [of the actor's] psycho-physical resources, from the most instinctive to the most rational' (Grotowski 1968: 209).

> If you think, you must think with your body . . . When I tell you not to think, I mean with the head. Of course you must think, but with the body, logically, with precision and responsibility. You must think with the whole body by means of actions. Don't think of the result, and certainly not of how beautiful the result may be. If it grows spontaneously and organically, like live impulses, finally mastered, it will always be beautiful— far more beautiful than any amount of calculated results put together. (Marijnen 1968: 204)

This seems close in spirit, if not exactly in praxis, to Stockhausen, who writes that '[t]he most profound moments in musical interpretation and composition are those which are not the result of mental processes, are not derived from what we already know, nor are they simply deducible from what has happened in the past' (2000: 125). There is a connection here between 'calculated results' and 'what we already know', whose rejection, for Grotowski and Stockhausen, marks a particular modernist moment of renewal at the expense of the culturally already-existent, a particularly modernist insistence on 'the new'. This is partly to be attained by recourse to 'the natural': something identified with the bodily and in (at least partial) opposition to 'the mental'. There is a Western self—a self that Stockhausen rather reductively identifies with the ego—that must be overcome because 'otherwise you only play yourself, and the self is nothing but a big bag full of stored information' (125).

Thought—for Stockhausen 'what we already know', 'what has happened in the past', or 'a big bag full of stored information'—can be equated with the negative connotations in Grotowski's training of 'calculated results', 'wrongly imposed systems and theories', and 'recipes [and] stereotypes which are the prerogative of professionals'. We might associate these different elements under the heading of 'the cultural', against which the body is deployed as 'the natural', believed—naïvely, from current perspectives—to stand beyond the restrictions, controls and predictable outcomes of a conscious thought that is culturally constituted.[5]

Stockhausen, then, avoids the term improvisation, Grotowski is unambiguous in damning it, and yet there are significant elements within their respective practices that are prominently shared with the practice of free improvisation: the notion of naturalness, an attention to the sense of embodiment, and the avoidance of learned actions whose presence can be constituted as an obstacle.[6] If, as I have suggested, recourse to the 'natural' is one strategy by which to effect a sidelining of the obstructions and repressions of the 'cultural', this is also something that has been deployed to answer the critique that there is no 'work' in improvisation. Making a virtue of necessity, as it were, it embraces the critique but neutralizes its effectiveness by figuring improvisation as something that comes 'naturally', and thus needs no 'work'.

The 'naturalness' of improvisation

'Improvisation is a basic instinct, an essential force in sustaining life', writes Bailey (1993: 140). Taken at face value this is an extravagant claim, but such a positioning of improvisation on the—for want of a better term—natural side of things is wide-spread. The motivations for believing in the naturalness of improvisation are diverse. Some see free improvisation as emerging from modernists' (apparent) rejection of established practices, and find in this appeal to instinct an overturning of formalist and music-theoretical conceptualizations.[7] Those with a liberatory political agenda can find a return to 'precultural' basics, a Rousseauesque 'noble savagery' reaching back to a putative time before the dualism of mind and body, objectification, and the commodity (Durant 1989: 269–71). Improvisers who have either never learned an instrument, or who wish, for whatever reasons, to 'unlearn', can 'just do it' (Cornelius Cardew's Scratch Orchestra might exemplify such a position). On the assumption that improvisation is natural, and free improvisation the least culturally constrained of any form of improvisation, it is 'open to use by almost anyone—beginners, children and non-musicians' (Bailey 1993: 83). On this basis the drummer Jon Stevens more or less derived a whole practice and philosophy of community music making, passed down in his community music manual *Search and Reflect* (1985). Whatever the motivating impulse, there is frequently a strong sense that free improvisation taps into the primordial and instinctual capacities of human action, and is celebrated 'because it meets the creative appetite that is a *natural part* of being a performing musician' (Bailey 1993: 142; emphasis added).

Improvisation, for Bailey, is also not only natural but comes historically before all other musics. He writes that '[t]ransient musical fashion . . . is unlikely to have any effect on something as *fundamental* as the nature of improvisation' (xiii; emphasis added) implying that the vagaries and contingencies of culture cannot significantly affect this 'something fundamental'. Later he writes that 'as regards method, the improvisor employs *the oldest* in music-making . . . it *pre-dates* any other music—mankind's *first* musical performance couldn't have been anything other than a free improvisation' (83; emphases added).

This carries a strong implication that there is something originary about improvisation, but from certain perspectives the concept of origins can be problematic. In particular, claims for the cultural and philosophical values of the originary have been brought under extensive critique by Jacques Derrida, who writes in *Limited Inc.* that

> [t]he enterprise of returning 'strategically', 'ideally', to an origin or to a priority thought to be simple, intact, normal, pure, standard, self-identical, in order then to think in terms of derivation, complication, deterioration, accident, etc. . . . is not just one metaphysical gesture among others, it is the metaphysical exigency, that which has been the most constant, most profound and most potent. (1998: 236)

The most potent of the metaphysical consequences of binaristic thinking is the notion that the dominant side of the equation is originary, ideal, and pure, temporally and epistemologically preceding the subordinate element, which is figured in terms of a degeneration, or a fall. In their different ways Grotowski, Stockhausen, and Bailey all play to this agenda. What Derrida (1998) has named 'the metaphysics of presence' presupposes that there is thought—primary and originary—which is then put into words and communicated. Speech, seeming to the speaker to be coterminous with thought, therefore appears closer to the presence of the origin than writing. This implicates speech in a metaphysics of presence with respect to which writing is inferior, subsequent to speech, and distanced from presence. However, as Jonathan Culler comments:

> A word's meaning within the system of a language . . . is a result of the meaning speakers have given it in past acts of communication . . . [T]he structure of a language, its system of norms and regularities, is . . . the result of prior speech acts. However, when we take this argument seriously and . . . look at the events which are said to determine structures, we find that every event is . . . already determined and made possible by prior structures. The possibility of meaning something by an utterance is already inscribed in the structure of the language . . . [H]owever far back we try to push, even when we try to imagine the 'birth' of language . . . we discover that we must assume prior organisation, prior differentiation. (1989: 956)

Hence, no matter how much speech might be claimed—in the name of a metaphysics of presence—to be closer to the truth of thought than writing (with all the latter's ambiguities and distractions), speech remains just as much structured by language as writing is; therefore however close to an originary 'truth' speech might imagine itself to be, this 'truth' cannot be separated from its articulation. The idea that thought comes first and exists independently of a language into which it is then merely translated is seriously challenged; and from such a critical perspective the idea that the improvisation of music can effectively come before 'music' per se, as Bailey seems to suggest, becomes commensurably questionable.

The metaphysics of presence claims a transparency between speech and thought that is obscured in writing; and something akin to this can be discerned in Bailey's reports on how improvisers understand their relationships to their instruments. There is an anti-instrument lobby that sees the instrument as an obstruction between the musician and the music, and so reject techniques and mastery. Bailey offers a hypothetical quotation from such a musician: 'It doesn't matter what sort of instrument you play, a Stradivarius or a tin drum, it's the person behind it that counts'; for such a musician 'the instrument has to be defeated. The aim is to do on the instrument what you could do if you could play without an instrument' (Bailey 1993: 101). The pro-instrument lobby sees total mastery of the instrument as a different means to what amounts, philosophically, to the same end. Complete mastery of the instrument means that the musician's every desire is articulated immediately and perfectly; the instrument has become so much a part of them that it has been effectively eliminated. This is close to Stockhausen's ideal: 'if musicians . . . play in a technically self-conscious way, the intuition can't work well . . . The best intuitive musician is really at one with his instrument, and knows where to touch it and what to do in order to make it resonate so that the inner vibrations that occur in the player can immediately be expressed as material vibrations in the body of the instrument' (Stockhausen 2000: 123). Whether for or against the instrument, the philosophical results are the same—an unapologetic assertion of the metaphysics of presence.

Deconstructing the nature–culture binarism

If the first move in a deconstructive approach is often to reverse the existent binarisms, en route to interrogating the 'text' (in an extended sense of the term), then we
might imagine Grotowski and Stockhausen to have initiated such a deconstructive
move in positioning the body before the mind. Their respective marginalizations of
thinking, for example, appeal to the natural as *prior* and therefore originary with
respect to culture, against which culturally established instances of theatrical or musical
practice are derivations or deteriorations. The emphasis on the non-cerebrating body
as the true site of consciousness in Grotowski, the desire to escape from the 'big bag of
stored information' and to eschew the brain in Stockhausen, and the natural and
primordial claims made in the name of improvisation by Bailey all strive to reclaim a
more fundamental state of being, something closely identified with the natural, and
lost under the dominance of culturally determined works of art and linguistically
ordered thought.

Recent theories of consciousness have, however, not been content to reduce the
body to nature—or to its scientific avatar, biology—and leave culture to the mind.
Nor have they been content merely to reverse the terms of a binarism; rather, like
Derrida in his own field, they have sought to critically dissolve the binaristic ground
upon which much of Western epistemology rests. Varela, Thompson, and Rosch's
'enactive cognition' fundamentally problematizes the validity of binaristic thinking,
in particular, the notions that body and mind are separable, and that an embodied
consciousness is separable from the environment in which it exists. The authors not
only question the idea that consciousness is fundamentally concerned with *mental*
representations, but also challenge three fundamental assumptions that stand behind it:

> The first is that we inhabit a world with particular properties, such as length, color, move-
> ment, sound, etc. The second is that we pick up or recover these properties by internally
> representing them. The third is that there is a separate subjective 'we' who does these
> things. (Varela *et al.* 1993: 9)

Against this they propose an *enactive* cognition,

> to emphasize the growing conviction that cognition is not the representation of a pregiven
> world by a pregiven mind but is rather the enactment of a world *and a mind* on the basis
> of a history of the variety of actions that a being in the world performs. (9)

Consciousness, then, is something we *do*, not something we *have*, and it is possible
to find more or less oblique resonances of this way of thinking in the work of other
writers. Terry Eagleton, for example, finds value in Heidegger's 'insistence that theoretical knowledge always emerges from a context of practical social interests', concluding
that '[k]nowing is deeply related to doing' (Eagleton 1983: 64).[8] Related to this is the
insistence by Heidegger's student, Hans-Georg Gadamer, that understanding
(*Verstehen*)—which can be deployed to inform a non-binaristic conceptualization of
consciousness—must bring together the cognitive, the practical, and the social
(Gadamer 2004; as discussed by Grondin 2002: 36–42). Indeed, there are further arguments that consciousness has emerged through a combination of cognitive, practical,
and social factors. Frank R. Wilson, for example, argues that the unique physiology of

the human hand is a precondition for the possibility of tool manufacture, which, as an emergent cooperative social activity in early humans, may have 'provided the crucial precondition for the evolution of language' (1998: 33).[9] All these perspectives share to some extent the notion that consciousness is active, not something we have but something we do. Though Grotowski comes near to something like this understanding of the interdependence of mind, body, and environment when he talks of 'thinking with the body', he remains nevertheless constrained by a binaristic logic that he can begin to reverse but scarcely move beyond.

My own experience of improvisation at first seems to confirm the claims that it is something instinctive and pre-conscious. I feel myself reacting emotionally and physiologically to the improvisations of others in a group, an experience which I then externalize through playing the violin. When I am improvising well, I am not aware of making decisions, recalling things from memory, or deploying practised techniques. It seems, at first sight, as though the violin is nothing more than a screen onto which I project my instinctive, physical reactions to incoming sounds in directly felt physical gestures. Resonant with Stockhausen's claim that 'the inner vibrations that occur in the player can immediately be expressed as material vibrations in the body of the instrument' (2000: 123), I used to enjoy thinking of the violin as a scientific measuring device, a seismograph of my inner state, something like a weather station tracing the tiny fluctuations in my body's chaotic systems. A lie detector might be just as appropriate an example, particularly when the violin shows that I was faking it, that I didn't really *mean* what I played, or wasn't listening. Tellingly, then, in playing my own game of origins in my early attempts to understand my own improvisation practice, I had introduced a biological–empirical subtext—the notion of bodily action measured with scientific devices.

However, one thing is certain: the violin is saturated with cultural meanings, both as an object and from the standpoint of the sounds it produces. It is not—and cannot be—a neutral screen; nor, arguably, can any scientific device. Although I do not think of myself as a particularly 'trained' violinist, I did take lessons and have *learned* to play the violin, though much of this learning has been relatively unconsciously achieved simply by virtue of growing up in a culture that has violins and violin music. I have played a variety of already existent musics on it, and this, along with my unconscious cultural learnings, shapes what it is possible for me to do with it. The inner states that I imagine being externalized onto the violin are not in themselves originary and instinctive, but have *found their way inside*, as it were, through the enactive nature of my own embodied consciousness and the inescapably culturally mediated condition of every object with which I interact. However extended or experimental or 'original' I might imagine my playing techniques to have become, the meanings they generate come as much from the fact that it is a violin that I am interacting with, as from the sheer physicality of the bodily gestures that the resultant sounds encode. I would go so far as to say that the possible bodily gestures I can deploy are, to a great extent, determined by the violin. Although some might hope that improvisation is a means by which to approach our 'true nature', our own cultural situatedness, and that of the tools, objects, and instruments we use, means that whatever we do is always-already culturally mediated, always-already distanced from any putative natural source. And this leads to the insight that musical sounds, their enactment, the gestures that produce them, and the consciousness associated with them, all have a strongly *intertextual* dimension—a notion which I now turn to explore.

Sonic intertextuality and enactive consciousness

Musical sounds—indeed, all sounds—do not carry meanings in and of themselves, but are the sites of complex and mediated sets of relationships between physical sounds, perceptual systems, personal associations, culturally signifying gestures, bodily and emotional responses, observed actions and reactions, and culturally learned listener expectations. For example, there are what we might call 'residues' of the physical world carried in sounds: Denis Smalley's theory of spectromorphology names one aspect of this physicality in terms of different degrees of 'surrogacy', the varying degrees of distance that a sound may have from a putative causal event (1986: 82–3). And when we respond to an unfamiliar sound (or musical work) with the phrase 'it sounds like', we tap into the same multisensory and experiential sonic intertextuality named by Smalley's term; we make sense of that sound by connecting it with a whole host of related experiences. Gesture, for example, is not something 'out there' that we perceive, but a culturally and experientially encoded phenomenon, something we know and do as embodied and—crucially—social beings. Gesture actively affects our listening and we know it as much from our bodily experiences of motion, touch, and resistance as we do from a purely auditory experience of sound (Norman 2004: 8–11; Smalley 1986: 82). David Borgo suggests that sonic gestures can be meaningful because there are common neurological roots to listening and motion (Borgo 2007: 42),[10] and while I am cautious about using neuroscience to 'explain' cultural phenomena, the existence of such neurological connections does add weight to the idea that sonic intertextuality is a multisensory phenomenon.

When we try to think of music as intertextual there is a temptation to look for stylistic traits, or a polystylism, grounded in an understanding of 'musical material' confined to little more than those elements of pitch and duration that can be rendered in conventional Western music notation. As Trevor Wishart has argued, this fails to account for other equally significant aspects of musical sound—timbre, dynamics, articulation, etc. (Wishart 1985: 7–27). Serge Lacasse (2008) has offered another approach to musical material, theorizing recorded rock music in terms of an intertextuality that includes sonority and production values, under the term 'transphonography'. These theories take us well beyond a reading of musical intertextuality grounded in 'the notes', but remain nevertheless orientated towards considering music in terms of a thing rather than an activity; something we 'have' rather than something we 'do'. In this respect Christopher Small offers an inspiring and thoughtful lead when he makes the distinction between music (noun) and musicking (verb), and illuminates the ways in which our culturally conditioned epistemology has led us to think of music as a thing rather than an activity (Small 1998: 61; *passim*).

If consciousness is something we do, then we do this within limits set not only by our physiology but also by our cultural experience (and, I should add, by our imaginative capabilities). My use of the violin *qua* violin passes through and is formed by personally internalized cultural filters of sonority, history, learning, expectation, listening, watching, and acting. My physical reactions to the sounds coming from my fellow improvisers (and, of course, to my own sounds) are filtered through the violin which, from the point of view of enactive consciousness, is not just a physical object with finite properties but something that is only fully constituted *as* a violin in its interrelationship to my embodied and enculturated consciousness. My ears, right forearm, primary school bowing exercises, and the 'Newcastle Style' of traditional hornpipe playing[11] are as much a part of the violin bow as the wood and horse hair. What I originally thought of, then, as purely physiological gestures are wholly mediated through cultural filters and the filters of my individual memories of the different instances of experiencing these gestures—whether consciously recalled or not.

'Free' improvisation and enactive consciousness

Free improvisation, viewed from this perspective, is not originary, but instead represents a play across memory, history, embodiment, and a culturally situated consciousness. The conditions of possibility of improvisation are the palimpsests of what music *is* or *has been*. In terms of a theory of an enactive consciousness that refuses the separation of the mind from the body, or of the self from its material/cultural environment, these palimpsests must be understood to include the multisensory experiences and actions that come together in our perception of sound. Alan Durant (1989: 273) has observed how our bodies and personal histories can be figured as a form of 'psychical "notation" or "score"'. This suggests that music is culturally and experientially inscribed within us, as it were—an internalization of musical experience that also organizes it. This is an idea that resonates strongly with Culler's interpretation of Derrida cited earlier, that 'however far back we try to push . . . we must assume prior organisation, prior differentiation'. Even if we improvise for the first time, such improvisation is only possible because there is 'prior organisation, prior differentiation'—'music', in other words: music that sets up the possibility of something (an improvisation, for example) to *be* music. Consciousnesses—figured as the attributes of cognizing, acting, social beings that experience, mediate, translate, and transfer information (for want of a more suitable general term)—can be conceptualized as sites where sonic intertextuality is made possible—where transductions occurring across culturally mediated knowledges, experiences, and imaginings efface the boundaries between, and strengthen the interdependences of, practices, bodies, and thoughts. At the same time, what I am calling sonic intertextuality concretizes and records these interdependences in the register of the cultural, negotiating and establishing networked dependencies and interconnections. This is not to claim that enactive cognition and sonic intertextuality are interchangeable modes of thinking, but they do seem productively to touch edges when we deploy them in relation to sound and music. At different conceptual registers, they name and account for the dynamic processes through which musical and sonic meanings are actuated. A musical, or more generally sonic, intertextuality, then, cannot be reduced to the interplay of musical products or actions, but is, rather, an enactive phenomenon, something that is experienced (though not necessarily consciously), something encompassed in Small's concept of 'musicking'.

Investigating improvisation in these terms exposes the workings of a metaphysics of presence that grounds apparently counter-hegemonic claims made in the name of improvisation. This then furthers an understanding of improvisation in terms of enactive cognition as a practice that deploys the intertextual play of the cognitive, the practical, and the social—along lines congruent with Gadamer's formulation of 'understanding', and in ways that further support such a deconstructive turn. Although improvisation has been represented in terms of self-presence and as a site of origin, seen from an angle that takes in consciousness studies and deconstruction it becomes, like all cultural practice, a play across any individual's set of cultural experiences. It takes Bailey until the last page of his book on improvisation finally to acknowledge that 'in spite of earlier arguments . . . [a]ll improvisation takes place in relation to the known whether the known is traditional or newly acquired' (Bailey 1993: 142). I take this statement's position at the end of the book as evidence of the resistances that he had to work through to arrive at that point.

Although Grotowski, Stockhausen, and Bailey might each have grounds to claim that their work challenges the apparent binarisms of Western culture, closer examination from the deconstructive angle shows their practices as uncritical avatars of the metaphysics of presence. However, while free improvisation's implicit or explicit claims to an originary status cannot be upheld, neither can it be dismissed as inconsequential, a 'substitute for work', or 'a conjuring trick'. In the ways that free improvisation engages in an articulation of consciousness (understood in terms of the mutual encounter of the mental, the bodily, and the cultural/historical) even the most inexperienced or naïve improviser is always already trained, bringing complex layers and relays of knowledge, learned capabilities, and a creativity that can emerge from the interplay of these factors. This might be a good place, then, to stop ascribing too much significance to origins and the unprecedented, and to celebrate instead the cognitive virtuosity of any creative act. To think of improvising as a site where texts of all sorts coincide with the embodied and enactive consciousness of the improviser may be uncomfortable for some, insofar as it seems to unseat improvisation from any privileged claims to presence, naturalness, or origins. But returning it to its place as a creative practice that illuminates the workings of the culture of which it is a part—rather than as something that claims a distance from that culture—should be more than adequate compensation.

References

Bailey, D. (1993). *Improvisation: Its Nature and Practice in Music* (New York, NY: Da Capo Press).

Bordo, S. (2003). *Unbearable Weight: Feminism, Western Culture, and the Body* (Berkeley, CA: University of California Press).

Borgo, D. (2007). *Sync or Swarm: Improvising Music in a Complex Age* (New York, NY: Continuum).

Breton, A. (2004). *Manifestoes of Surrealism* (Ann Arbor, MI: University of Michigan Press).

Butler, J. (1990). *Gender Trouble: Feminism and the Subversion of Identity* (New York, NY: Routledge).

Cardew, C. (1971). Towards an ethics of improvisation, in *Treatise Handbook*, xvii–xx (London: Peters Edition).

Culler, J. (1989). *On Deconstruction: Theory and Criticism after Structuralism* (London: Routledge).

Derrida, J. (1998). *Limited Inc.*, Gerald Graff (ed.), trans. Samuel Weber (Evanston, IL: Northwestern University Press).

Durant, A. (1989). Improvisation in the political economy of music, in C. Norris (ed.), *Music and the Politics of Culture*, 252–82 (London: Lawrence and Wishart).

Eagleton, T. (1983). *Literary Theory: An Introduction* (Minneapolis, MN: University of Minnesota Press).

Fink, B. (1995). *The Lacanian Subject: Between Language and Jouissance* (Princeton, NJ: Princeton University Press).

Foucault, M. (1984). *The History of Sexuality Volume I: An Introduction* (Harmondsworth: Peregrine).

Gadamer, HG. (2004). *Truth and Method*, trans. J. Weinsheimer and Donald G. Marshall (London and New York: Continuum).

Grondin, J. (2002). Gadamer's basic understanding of Understanding, in R.J. Dostal (ed.), *The Cambridge Companion to Gadamer*, 36–51 (Cambridge: Cambridge University Press).

Grotowski, J. (1968). The actor's technique, in E. Barba (ed.), *Towards a Poor Theatre*, 205–15 (Holstebro: Odin Teatrets Forlag).

Grotowski, J. (1969). External order, internal intimacy. *The Drama Review*, **45**, 172–7.

Hogg, B. (2010). Embodied consciousness as a site of cultural mediation in thinking about musical free improvisation, in D. Meyer-Dinkgräfe (ed.), *Consciousness, Theatre, Literature and the Arts 2009*, 266–75 (Newcastle upon Tyne: Cambridge Scholars Publishing).

Kumiega, J. (1985). *The Theatre of Grotowski* (London and New York, NY: Methuen).

Lacasse, S. (2008). La musique pop incestueuse: une introduction à la transphonographie. *Circuit, musiques contemporaines*, **18**(2), 11–26.

Lewis, G. E. (1996). Improvised music after 1950: afrological and eurological perspectives. *Black Music Research Journal*, **16**(1), 91–122.

Limb, C. J. and Braun, A. R. (2008). Neural substrates of spontaneous musical performance: an fMRI study of jazz improvisation. *PLoS ONE* **3**(2). Available at: http://www.plosone.org/article/info%3Adoi%2F10.1371%2Fjournal.pone.0001679 (accessed 10 August 2010).

Marijnen, F. (1968). The actor's training, in E. Barba (ed.) *Towards a Poor Theatre*, 175–204 (Holstebro: Odin Teatrets Forlag).

Meelberg, V. (2008). Touched by music: the sonic strokes of *Sur incises*, in C. Birdsall and A. Enns (eds.), *Sonic Mediations: Body, Sound, Technology*, 61–74 (Newcastle upon Tyne: Cambridge Scholars Press).

Norman, K. (2004). *Sounding Art: Eight Literary Excursions through Electronic Music* (Aldershot: Ashgate).

Rizzolatti, G. and Arbib, M. A. (1998). Language within our grasp. *Trends in Neuroscience*, **21**(5), 188–94.

Skipper, I.J., Goldin-Meadow, S., Nusbaum, H.C., and Small, S.L. (2007). Speech-associated gestures, Broca's area, and the human mirror system. *Brain and Language*, **101**, 260–77.

Small, C. (1998). *Musicking: The Meanings of Performing and Listening* (Middletown, CT: Wesleyan University Press).

Smalley, D. (1986). Spectro-morphology and structuring processes, in S. Emmerson (ed.), *The Language of Electroacoustic Music*, 61–93 (Basingstoke: Macmillan).

Stevens, J. (1985). *Search and Reflect* (London: Community Music).

Stockhausen, K. (2000). *Stockhausen on Music: Lectures and Interviews compiled by Robin Maconie* (London: Marion Boyars).

van Schie, H.T., Toni, I., and Bekkering, H. (2006). Comparable mechanisms for action and language: neural systems behind intentions, goals, and means. *Cortex*, **42**, 495–8.

Varela, F.J., Thompson, E., and Rosch, E. (1993). *The Embodied Mind: Cognitive Science and Human Experience* (Cambridge, MA, and London: MIT Press).

Wilson, F.R. (1998). *The Hand: How its Use Shapes the Brain, Language, and Human Culture* (New York, NY: Pantheon Books).

Wishart, T. (1985). *On Sonic Art* (York: Imagineering Press).

Notes

1. For an earlier published version of this chapter, see Hogg (2010).

2. Roughly put, these debates range from 'hard' neuroscience and experimental psychology at one end of the spectrum, to speculative philosophies and spiritual practices at the other.

3. Here and in similar contexts the quoted words are Grotowski's own, as recorded by Marijnen.

4. The inclusion or appropriation of Eastern philosophical elements in Stockhausen's thinking comes from several culturally significant directions: Germanic philosophical and literary traditions deriving from Hermann Hesse, Carl Jung, and others; the influence of Zen Buddhism that was culturally current from the 'Beat' Generation onwards; and the suddenly fashionable 1960s appropriation of Indian mystical traditions, perhaps most publicly exemplified in The Beatles' association with the Maharishi Mahesh Yogi.

5. The body is, of course, also culturally constituted—see Fink (1995: 11–12), Foucault (1984: 47–8, 146–7), and *passim*; Bordo (2003: 33–6); Butler (1990: 124–38), and *passim*. But it is culturally constructed to do the work of being *not* culturally constituted insofar as it is constructed as being on the nature side of the nature–culture binarism. The present chapter moves towards a position where such binarisms are dissolved in an understanding of consciousness that brings together the elements of mind, body, and culture (social, historical, and environmental), otherwise considered to be separate phenomena.

6. Even at the 'hard' end of neuroscience there is evidence from studies of jazz musicians that during improvisation the self-reflective and regulatory functions sited in the frontal lobes of the brain are inhibited; see Limb and Braun (2008).

7. Something of this perspective can be discerned in Cardew (1971). This is also resonant with what George Lewis (1996) has defined as a specifically 'Eurological' stance to improvisation.

8. Though Eagleton also recognizes that 'the other side of [Heidegger's] peasant-like practicality is a contemplative mysticism', and that for Heidegger the interpretation of literature 'is not first of all something we *do*, but something we must let happen' (Eagleton 1983: 64).

9. To cite Wilson at greater length (1998: 32–3):

   > Early tool use and manufacture were associated with a modest increase in brain size in *Homo Habilis*. The increasing refinement and perhaps specialization of manipulative, hunting, and offensive skills, as well as the ramification of social interactions enabled by more structured communication (and migration) by *Homo Erectus*, had a further "kindling" effect on brain operations and structure. Finally, intraspecies cooperation and competition greatly increased the need for an elaborated social structure and communication and for coordinated industry, all of which demanded a more powerful and versatile brain. When he finally had enough brain to be able to guess what the brain itself was doing, *Homo* pronounced himself *sapiens*'.

   Michael Gallope's deconstructionist discussion of 'technicity' (see Chapter 4, this volume) is also relevant here.

10. Although dancing to music or the way that infants seem to instinctively move to rhythmical sounds are perhaps the most obvious expressions of this, the conceptual repercussions are extensive. Consider, for example, the notion that speech may be as much the product of this (apparently) neurological relationship between sound and muscular action. This has been offered as one possible explanation of how infants acquire the capacity to speak through imitation (for a composer such as myself the idea that phonemes are the sonic resultants of muscular gestures contains some strong creative possibilities). A great deal of neuroscientific research has been devoted to exploring the connections between sound perception and human movement (Skipper et al. 2007; van Schie et al. 2006), and, in particular, the controversial theory of 'mirror neurons' (Rizzolatti and Arbib 1998) has excited some musicological interest (Borgo 2007; Meelberg 2008).

11. Fiddle hornpipes are characterized by a dotted quaver–semiquaver rhythm, which in the so-called 'Newcastle Style' is often articulated by changing the direction of the bow on the semiquaver, giving a physically rewarding lilt not obtainable by a 'straighter' bowing style.

Chapter 6

The music of what happens: mind, meditation, and music as movement

Ansuman Biswas

'What is the finest music in the world?' asks Fionn of
his son, Oisin.
'The cuckoo calling from the highest tree', says he.
Those gathered round say, 'The belling of a stag across
the water, the ring of spear against shield, the baying
of a tuneful pack in the distance, the song of a lark, the
laughter of a gleeful girl.'
'Well, they are good sounds all', says Fionn, 'but what is
the finest music of them all?'
Oisin listens.
'The music of what happens, that is the finest music in
the world.'
(Attrib. Fenian Cycle)[1]

Introduction

A significant lacuna in academic and scientific studies of consciousness is a description of how it actually feels to be here. The study of consciousness has proved to be extremely elusive when using the traditional third-person methodology of science. Any description of qualia—by definition lived, subjective experience—seems to necessitate the admission of first-person data, which has hitherto been the province of the arts.

If the problem of consciousness is nothing more than the attempt to capture the mechanism and experience of being a person, then each of us can appeal to only one authority for an answer. In this chapter I want to speak from the personal perspective of a multidisciplinary artist–researcher, drawing on the experience of a praxis that inhabits a space between art, science, and religion.[2] In the camouflage of an artist

I find I can infiltrate and range between disciplines without being restricted by conventional boundaries. I am free to devote myself not to the abstract and theoretical knowledge of an academic discipline but to the embodied and applied wisdom of a beautiful life.

This account, then, will show theory and practice as closely woven together, experiment and experimenter as necessarily indivisible. A key element in this narrative is meditation, specifically the tradition known as *vipassana*, of which I am a longstanding practitioner. Following an account of this practice I will map some connections between it and music, showing how the latter may be understood as a more public aspect of the former. In doing so, I hope to draw out the relevance of both music and meditation to consciousness studies.

Vipassana

Vipassana meditation is the cultivation of continuous mindfulness of the present moment. The distinctive feature of the practice as I have learnt it from the Burmese/Indian teacher S.N. Goenka, is the importance given to conscious awareness of changing bodily sensation. The technique is described in detail in the *Mahāsatipaṭṭhāna Sutta* (Goenka 2000), which was written in the Pali language about 300 years after the death of Siddhārta Gautama, the Buddha.

The purpose of the practice is to clarify the mind, eradicate mental afflictions, and learn to be perfectly happy. The method is to cultivate clear comprehension of the dynamic, changing nature of the world. Attention is directed to every part of the physical structure of the body, from the top of the head to the tips of the toes, inside and out. Every sensation, from the unavoidably apparent to the vanishingly subtle, whether pleasant, unpleasant, or neutral, is consciously identified, examined, and analysed. Attention is trained on the one characteristic shared by every phenomenon: its changing nature. The object of meditation is movement. Over time the clear insight develops that in this flux nothing is permanently graspable or dependable. This is not a conceptual understanding but a moment-by-moment experience. The technique does not aim to foster a theoretical intellectual appreciation, but rather to clarify awareness of actual, physical experience, in as much detail as possible.

In the Burmese/Indian Theravada tradition two complementary meditative techniques support the practice of *vipassana*. The first is a preparatory exercise called *ānāpānasati*, which is designed to settle and focus the mind. It consists of sustained conscious awareness of the natural, unregulated breath as it passes in and out of the nostrils. The second, more extrovert, practice is *metta bhavana*, the cultivation of loving, compassionate, and joyful thoughts towards others. These three meditative disciplines themselves rely on a foundation of ethical action called *silā*, consisting of conscious avoidance of harmful activities in everyday life. As the practitioner progresses with these practices they become evermore tightly intertwined and mutually supportive.

Vipassana meditation, then, is just one part of a network of practices that operate together as a single methodology for understanding the nature of consciousness. The purpose of this understanding is not simply to satisfy curiosity or gain technical skill, but to address the problem of personal unhappiness that seems to be an integral part of experience.

While examining the changing nature of the mind and body, a few categories of phenomena become apparent. There is the body itself, belonging to the field of matter. This is a huge category of course, including the entire physical universe and everything that can be discerned by the organs of sense, but it may be roughly lumped together in order to distinguish it from the mind. The mind is a hazy, nebulous entity, but may be characterized, again roughly, as everything that is not the physical stuff. Mind is the feeling, thinking, knowing, reacting thing. Further subdivisions of it can be made precisely on this broad basis—feeling, thinking, knowing, reacting.

In the *Mahāsatipaṭṭhāna Sutta* these large categories—matter, feeling, thinking, knowing, and acting—are called the five *khanda*, collections or aggregates.[3] Everything that exists can be taken to fall into one or other of these categories:

- *rūpa* (matter): the world of forms, the material universe, composed of the various elements;
- *viññāṇa* (consciousness): the cognizing part of the mind, the feeling of knowing;
- *vedanā* (sensation): the physical feeling arising at any of the sense organs;
- *saññā* (perception): the naming, labelling, evaluating activity;
- *saṅkhāra* (volition): the reactive, formulating part of the mind which generates things.

As Jay Garfield comments, this categorization should be taken as a practical, empirical division, not an ontological fundamental (1995: 142). The categories should be taken not as a credo, but simply as signposts that may or may not be useful. The meditation technique does not rely on them. What is paramount is the practice of training the attention on what actually presents itself.

A key finding expressed in these terms is that all phenomena flow along with sensation, an idea expressed in Pali as 'vedana-samosarana sabbe dhamma' (Hardy *et al.* 1900: 107). The sensation may not always be in conscious awareness, that is to say *viññāṇa* may or may not arise along with *vedanā*, but at some level of the mind sensation is always present, giving rise to further chains of reaction. Sensation, then, is a primal and influential part of the world and it is this sensation which is the object of the meditation regardless of any naming or labelling.

Music

The biological value of music is widely contested. Charles Darwin thought it played a vital role in sexuality but in Steven Pinker's provocative caricature music is just 'auditory cheesecake . . . a cocktail of recreational drugs that we ingest through the ear to stimulate a mass of pleasure circuits at once' (1997: 524, 528). Such a position contrasts sharply with that of Michael Thaut who suggests that music is an 'innate, modular, perceptual language of the brain . . . a part of our basic brain architecture'. According to Thaut, 'Music, driven by the affective-aesthetic responses, is a critical input for appropriate regulation of physiological arousal. To further specify: Music communicates critical time dimensions into our perceptual processes' (2008: 34).

These contrasting positions exemplify the wide-ranging debate on the nature of music, which seems as resistant to scientific analysis as consciousness. One important reason for this continuing mystery is identified by Daniel Levitin in terms of a peculiarly modern blind spot:

> The arguments against music as an adaptation consider music only as disembodied sound, and moreover, as performed by an expert class for an audience. But it is only in the last five hundred years that music has become a spectator activity . . .. And it has only been in the last hundred years or so that the ties between musical sound and human movement have been minimized. (2006: 251)

Clearly embodiment has a political as well as organic dimension. During the industrial revolution, music gradually shifted from something one does to something one consumes. Such an enervated music, floating in an ideal, imaginary space, and piped directly into our ears, might well seem like a rarified luxury, a biologically superfluous ornament. But in thinking only of disembodied music we forget that the ear is not only the organ of hearing but also the organ of balance. The ear measures our place in the world but it is not until we *take* our place that the music is resolved. Sound and movement, reception and action, are intimately connected. A dance watched from the sidelines might lead to partial understanding, but only when enacted, however falteringly, can it lead on to grace. In the pursuit of happiness a disembodied sound is as unhelpful as a disembodied science. When put into practice however, both music and meditation become powerful tools.

Music as meditation: a personal history

My own relationship with music has paralleled my meditation practice. It had been a ubiquitous but only incidental part of my childhood until the middle of one hot summer's night in my early twenties when a pair of drums flew through the open window of my ground floor bedroom and landed on me. I still have no idea where these drums came from, and can only surmise that some revellers had randomly discarded them on their way past. For me they were a godsend. While casually tinkering I gradually became fascinated by the repetitive rhythmic playing they facilitated. It was at around this time that I was first formally learning meditation. I made no deliberate connection but in retrospect my trajectory seems clear. I began to use the drums in the same way as the initial meditative exercises are used, to attain a degree of mental concentration.

According to Buddhist practice, before it can engage in any sustained analysis the attention needs to be made firm and stable to prevent it from being blown away by every passing thought. Any object can be used as a tether. In *ānāpāna* the attention is repeatedly brought back to observe the unceasing rhythm of the breath. This voluntary, repetitive gathering of attention around an object to make out its details concentrates and strengthens the mind. The faculty of *viññāṇa* (consciousness) increases. Deliberate repetition gives way to longer and longer periods of awareness of the involuntary, naturally repetitive rhythm of respiration.

Different objects suit different temperaments. I found repetitive drumming to be an extremely effective focus. My whole body was engaged and yet, once a continuous rhythm had been established, intentional activity was minimized. I was free to observe the complexity of my various sensations, some of which seemed to be under conscious control but many more of which were accidental and involuntary. This method gave access to aspects of the body that had hitherto been below the threshold of consciousness.

As conscious control relaxed, rhythmic processes throughout the psychosomatic structure became progressively more coherent, and over the course of the next few months I spontaneously discovered profound states of absorption and trance. At the time I was not deliberately trying to achieve any particular state, nor did I have a particular terminology for my experiences. It was interesting and fun, and felt therapeutic. Looking for external references the nearest I could find were the trance drumming traditions of Shamanic cultures and African possession rituals. But, searching through various precedents in disparate cultures in an attempt to ground my experience, I gradually homed in on my own cultural identity and embarked on a serious study of Indian classical music. Here, in the physical activity of *riyāz* (daily practice), if not necessarily in all the details of its conceptualization, I found something familiar. Sustained and tightly focused concentration on the basic material, with an underlying attitude of humility seemed like a good approach to the study of the mind.[4]

A key attraction of Indian classical music was the importance given to improvisation. I had already learned theatrical improvisation techniques and now I began to consciously connect these with music. I then came, via Western avant-garde practices, to free improvisation and the approaches represented by Fluxus and the London Musicians' Collective. The openness to irrational bodily impulses and the eschewing of both political hierarchy and performance conventions seemed to connect these musics to meditation. Close mentors such as John Stevens and Paul Burwell introduced me to an exploded notion of drumming which respected the materiality of the instrument without fetishizing it. For a percussionist perhaps more than for other instrumentalists, any object has particular properties to be sounded out, but the music lies in the musician's attitude. This embodied approach militated against any identification with a particular instrument, and the development of associated technical skills in the service of an external composer. The purpose of repetition was to cultivate the quality of listening that exists in free improvisation. As John Stevens says, 'Improvisation is the basis of learning to play a musical instrument' (quoted in Bailey 1992: 98).

Progressing through the practice of free improvisation I have gradually put aside instruments altogether to focus on the musicality that subtends sound. This route is paralleled in a meditation practice that moves from unconscious identification with the body and the myriad particularities of its sensations through to an embodied understanding of the dynamics that underlie all perceptual phenomena regardless of self-identification. In my case, drumming focused the mind enough to enable it to begin to discern the subtler motion of the breath. Even if one begins with prescribed exercises, eventually the mind's conceptual rigidity may relax enough to allow it to perceive the constant stream of changing phenomena. Such exercises progressively establish quiescence, a subsiding of compulsive hyperactivity, until ultimately interference gives way to insight. Or, to put it another way, the initial deliberate restraint of *saṅkhāra* (volition) gives an opportunity to glimpse *vedanā* (sensation) and weaken the rigidity of *saññā* (perception).

The difference between preparation and performance dissolves, and in practice, as in playing, a flow is released, a motion with eddies and currents within it. Areas of blockage or tension appear and disappear. The attention may sometimes focus on variations in the grain of the most minuscule details, and sometimes expand to take in the widest overview. The balance between wilful decision making and choiceless observation gradually shifts. That which was overdeveloped in some parts and weak in others is brought by degrees into a perfect proportion.

Gregory Bateson invokes Aldous Huxley's use of the word 'grace' to describe such a state:

> The problem of grace is fundamentally the problem of integration and that what is to be integrated is the diverse parts of the mind—especially those multiple levels of which one extreme is called 'consciousness' and the other the 'unconscious'. For the attainment of grace, the reasons of the heart must be integrated with the reasons of the reason. (1972: 129)

Meditation is the work of attaining a gracefully integrated consciousness. When the roiling turbulence of *vedanā* can be brought fully into awareness without throwing it off balance, then there is a gracefulness about the movement. Any object may be grasped to steady oneself. It might be a spoken mantra, a beautiful picture, a geometrical figure, a candle flame, or an idea. The object itself has no particular meaning or significance. Like the Pole Star for a mariner, or the lamppost for a drunk, it provides support rather than illumination.

A problem with many objects, however, is that while the mind becomes concentrated and somewhat steady, it can begin to become fascinated with the object itself and ascribe meaning to it. A set of nonsense syllables may be treated as a magic spell, a picture of a god as a real being, or an invented idea as an ultimate truth. This kind of delusional attachment limits flexibility and openness to alternative points of view. Nevertheless, for an extremely unbalanced or agitated mind, a carefully designed handle can be helpful. Music, despite its cultural accretions, can function as such a device.

A musical focus for attention

The focal object in Indian classical music is *swara*. The word might be translated as 'note', but *swara* is certainly not the same thing that a Western musician means by a musical note. In English, a note exists in an idealized space. It is objectively verifiable. The note 'A' is a particular rate of vibration, consensually determined (at least in the West in present times) as 440 Hz. *Swara*, by contrast, exists only when I sound it. When sung it is a function of my particular body and breath, and the space and time in which it occurs. It is the vibration of this embodied moment. When sung perfectly it is not even *my* vibration, but simply resonance in which the notion of me or mine becomes vestigial. The perfection of *swara* consists of this dissolution of the singer.[5]

This delicate distinction between embodiment and identification is of utmost importance. *Swara* happens only here and now. But without any active, creative person, free of ownership, *swara* is part of a much wider music for which this body is simply an instrument. The music continues under its own momentum, effortlessly influenced only by past conditions. It may be appreciated in all its intricacy without judgement. As *swara* manifests, *viññāṇa* and *vedanā* become predominant while *saññā* and *saṅkhāra* dwindle away.

Recognition of this state underlies Rabindranath Tagore's entreaty in the following song, in which some of the complexity of the idea of *swara* may be glimpsed. The word 'shur' is the Bengali cognate of the Sanskrit 'swara', which I have translated here as melody:

> Bajao, amare, bajao
> Bajale je shurey probhato aalore
> Shei shurey more bajao
> Je shuro bhorile bhasha bhola geete
> Shishuro nobino jibono bnasheete

> *Make me your instrument*
> *Just as you play the dawn light,*
> *Play me with that melody*
> *The melody with which you fill the wordless song*
> *In the newborn flute of a child*
> (Tagore 1961: 127; my translation)

From tool as means to tool as object: the passage to awareness

A mind that is not yet sharp enough to appreciate that it is itself an instrument played by a supra-personal musician, or sharp enough even to observe its own singing, may begin, as I did, by relying on external tools. The musical instrument, like the scientific instrument, is not an end in itself but a means. Technical facility is incidental, the natural result of parts of the body falling under the spotlight of conscious intention. *Siddhi*, a Sanskrit term for the seemingly miraculous powers that are a by-product of meditation, are inevitable and spectacular distractions from the goal of understanding consciousness. When *siddhi* becomes the goal, further progress halts. The erection of a dazzling edifice of technique can only obstruct more vital traffic. Instruments can likewise become obstructions if they become ends in themselves. The most appropriate appreciation of a musical instrument is to use it to sensitize the mind to the music of what happens.

Instruments are bequeathed to us socially. Every given instrument has been shaped by other bodies before ours. Its shapes and mechanisms are designed to suit the pressure human lungs can exert, or the surfaces and extensions of human fingers. The structures of human societies too are written into instruments which might be loud enough to be heard by vast crowds or quiet enough for a drawing room, which might have been forged by teams of blacksmiths or whittled by a lone boy. By engaging with a given instrument I accept the proclivities and decisions of all those generations who have contributed to its design. The shapes and balances of their bodies are figured into its size and materials. I echo those bodies and enter a larger social body when I pick up or sit at this trace of them. I become the reification of a social idea.[6] But to examine the mind in itself, all such reifications must eventually be abandoned. This is why in Indian classical music the voice is accorded the highest status. Even if all other instruments are renounced, the voice continues to embody millions of years of accidents between individuals and environments. As an object of meditation the voice is an ideal site at which to observe the interplay of conscious control, cultural conditioning, and biological determination.

Even without the specificity of language, singing may fall into culturally determined patterns that initially draw attention to, but increasingly obfuscate, the nature of the mind. An important aspect of vipassana is to strive to see reality 'as it is', *yatha bhuta*, in itself, without anything added or removed. If singing is treated as a step in the cultivation of a clear view of the world, then its cultural accretions must gradually be dropped. Any words should be downplayed or replaced completely by sounds free of meaning. In forms such as jaap mantra, zikr, or dhrupad the words may be meaningful but, through constant repetition, it is their sound that becomes important. The melodic and rhythmic material may then be simplified in order to minimize distractions from the examination of *swara*.

This process of focusing in on the basic reality of the present manifestation can continue until even vocalization is abandoned completely. All that remains is the breath itself. Any boundary between music and meditation then dissolves. *Ānāpāna* reduces the musical material to pure movement. All that is left as an object of awareness is the varying speed and rhythm of the breath, and even this rhythm is left to be free. Voluntary control is relinquished in order more clearly to discern the underlying patterns of long and short, deep and shallow breaths governed by the brain stem.

So the voice can function initially as a focus for the mind, but then also as an object in which we can examine the nature of the mind itself. As we follow the voice to its essence we approach the origin of consciousness and move from the flowering creations of the neocortex towards the impulses of the primitive hindbrain. Graceful *riyāz* is the retracing of the evolution of voice to arrive at the primal origin, integrating rational awareness with the animal body. Then at the point where vocalization is abandoned there begins the field of *anāhat nād*, the unstruck sound, the vibration that is below the threshold of hearing. Without audible sound, just the attitude of listening remains and the musician becomes aware of the more subtle motions of the mind. Listening is an open space in which the rhythm of arising and passing away of all phenomena becomes apparent.

Close attention to the decaying note of a bell leads the awareness from a loud sound to the continual underlying vibration of what previously seemed inanimate. Similarly the progression from voice to breath hones the mind's sensitivity to quietness until all that remains is an attitude of listening to the music of what happens. Gradual training in this way leads the observer from the deliberate, conscious, surface functions of the brain down to the workings of the autonomic nervous system and the dark zone in which lie the roots of awareness.

Deep listening and meditation

The composer and performer Pauline Oliveros, describing her practice of deep listening, distinguishes between the 'involuntary nature of hearing and the voluntary, selective nature of listening' (Deep Listening Institute: mission statement (n.d.); see also

Oliveros 2005: xxi). While this might be understood as a narrowing of the field of attention, it can also indicate an expansion of awareness. Listening is voluntary because it entails active restraint from habitual, involuntary reactions; and it is selective because it seeks out that which is subtle or obscure, at the fringes of awareness. Listening perseveres with what was at first too loud to bear, and reveals what was at first too quiet to hear.

The practices of meditation and deep listening are analogous. Both send a border patrol out into the landscape of consciousness, whose mission is to bring to light the faintest, subtlest, most tenuous facts. Just as appreciation of music increases with deep listening—revealing the partials and overtones rather than the fundamentals, the reverberation of the space rather than the source, and sensitizing us to echoes and allusions—so the study of one's own mind can proceed by sustained and patient attention to the details which are just beyond the known. Although some phenomena are apparent to consciousness, a great many things happen unconsciously. These two affect one another. To be fully understood, experience must be examined not just at the flower, or thorn, of lucid, conscious awareness, but down to its roots in the dark soil of the body. From a third-person perspective, it is the body that is clearly materially present and the mind that is mysterious. From a first-person perspective, it is the mind that is clearly evident and its autonomous nervous system which is hidden. To arrive at a full understanding from either direction, some expansion is necessary. For a meditator a deliberate expansion of awareness, a mobility of perspective, is the only activity in the radical passivity of listening. It is a voluntary activity only insofar as it is a restraint from the irrational, automatic reactivity of *saññā* and *saṅkhāra*, which locks the mind to a viewpoint. Restraint from ignorant action steadily lessens our susceptibility to the illusion of fixity, definition, and stability.

Meditative listening reveals the seated body, whether singing or just breathing, as wide at its base and tapering to an apex at its fontanelle. Distinct in its parts like the crown, shoulder, waist, and lip of a bell, the body similarly resonates as a whole. It is a sensitive oscillatory system through which even the tiniest forces undulate and ricochet—forces as small as a quantum of light, the glimmer of a thought, or the rippling ion exchange along a single dendrite. Indeed the neural network is a very clear example of a system poised in the most precarious of instabilities, resonating in response to forces so small as to be indiscernible.

Listening is a skill that can be practised. But we get things back-to-front when we practise music in order to perform. For someone interested in fathoming the nature of the mind, performance is practising for listening. A wise musician is first and foremost one who has learned to listen. For this kind of musician, practice is about not the construction or achievement of something—functions of *saññā* and *saṅkhāra*—but the reception of something—functions of *viññāṇa* and *vedanā*.

In this sense listening is the core of vipassana meditation. The Pali phrase 'atapi sampajana na rincati' (Rhys Davids 1925: 425) is an exhortation to the meditator to strive to maintain continuous uninterrupted clear understanding of sensations—'atapi' ('work hard'), because listening, as opposed to hearing, is not an easy skill to learn. For an organism that has evolved to be acutely responsive to pleasure and pain, listening consciously without any reaction may even feel like a revolt against nature.

But it is evolution that has brought us to this juncture. The hyperdevelopment of the cortical layer in the human brain has enabled us to make deliberate choices and thus control our habitual tendencies. For a musical yogi the challenge is to appreciate *swara* continuously. Listening must be deliberately cultivated *at this very moment*, however difficult, rather than as a special framed activity done in ideal conditions.

The ear and the voice are connected in a loop. The voice projects both inwards and outwards. It makes oneself audible to oneself and to others. In the choral antiphony of a formal meditation teaching session, one's commitment to an intention is made audible not only to others but also to oneself. One hears oneself as a deliberate actor in the world rather than as a series of accidental overspills from a private interior. This may begin as a formulation of rational thoughts, an intention then voiced in speech, but the voicing of intention beginning at the surface of the mind is heard by the body and soaks through to its depths. Ultimately the sound knits together—integrates—intention with actuality.

Shared consciousness

Allowing the vocal cords to vibrate brings awareness very firmly into the experience of the present moment, and a resonance that is social, external, and objective as much as it is personal and internal. Positioned at the portal between inside and outside, the vocal folds broker a sympathetic resonance between the body's proprioception and the space of the environment, between the oxygen that sustains a single body and the body of air that moves through the world.

David Abram (1996) examines the etymologies of words for 'air' in various languages. *Prāṇa, psyche, ruach, spiritus, anima,* and *woniya wakan* all attest to the intertwined nature of breath and mind. And the body of air enveloping the planet is suggestive of a mind that is likewise not confined to the single individual. Atmosphere flows through every one. It is not simply the gaseous layer that clings to the earth from troposphere to stratosphere, but also something invisibly shared, something that suffuses mind and body.[7] 'Atmosphere' is recognized in common parlance as that emotional quality which is not confined to a single consciousness, a shared feeling. As this atmosphere flows through the standing reed of my body, the mind cannot help but sculpt it. Between us all mind can be heard, and in this social construction of conscious experience the voice is a central force.

Deep listening makes it clear that every part of the mind is in vibration. There is no fixed point and, in this fluidity, no boundary between listener and sound. Motion, experienced as music, weaves together, soaks through, and connects what might otherwise be sharply demarcated as Self and Other. The saxophonist Evan Parker evokes this space when he describes how his '"ideal music" is played by groups of musicians who choose one another's company and who improvise freely in relation to the precise emotional, acoustic, psychological and other less tangible atmospheric conditions in effect at the time the music is played' (cited in Bailey 1992: 81).

Thought and emotion

Since Darwin, language has seemed to be the last bastion of human superiority over the rest of nature. However, even in this achievement there is far more continuity than discontinuity between humans and other animals. Language is rooted in the ancient reptilian centres of the brain. The sounds of speech arise from the motion and emotion of the body. As David Abram puts it, 'We learn our native language not mentally but bodily' (Abram 1996: 75). Merleau-Ponty (2002), in the *Phenomenology of Perception*, devotes a whole chapter, 'The body as expression, and speech', to the sensational, gestural basis of both emotion and language. Gregory Bateson likewise describes the communication of emotion as being fundamentally a matter of the body: 'If you want to know what the bark of a dog "means", you look at his lips, the hair on the back of his neck, his tail, and so on' (1972: 370).

These notions have their precursors in eighteenth-century philosophers such as Giambattista Vico, Jean-Jacques Rousseau, and Johann Gottfried Herder, who all trace the roots of language to the pre-conceptual, gestural, emotional expression that also gives rise to music and dance. The additional conceptual element of modern speech, abstracted from the particular, embodied instance, might be seen as a thin crust recently grown over a deep and ancient substrate. Leonid Perlovsky (2010) suggests that this thin layer is quite literally the cortex of the brain.[8] Identifying the split between the limbic and cortical systems in the control of vocalization in proto-humans, he argues that music and language evolved from a common ancestor along divergent paths. This divergence allowed the separate hyper-development of the intricate semantic and emotional patternings that we experience today. In a variation of the organically based mental development described by Steven Mithen (1996: 94) as 'cognitive fluidity', Perlovsky considers how the extensive development of the cortex in modern humans now provides the hardware with which to decouple emotional from intellectual utterance.

Attentive vocalization, then, might lead back to an archaic consciousness that prefigures discursive, conceptual thinking. From this perspective 'cogito ergo sum' seems a most misleading formulation. The root of the mind is not thinking. *Saññā* and *saṅkhāra*, based as they are on partial awareness, gradually fade away in the light of sustained attention. At a more fundamental level what remains is feeling. I am not so much a thought as a dance. Consciousness is rooted in a feeling of movement. A body in motion. Emotion.

Motion and emotion

Emotion is fundamentally to do with movement, or more accurately the tendency to move.[9] Any movement is always away from or towards something. In Pāli, *tanha* signifies this potential energy—desire, the urge towards some thing, away from another. Vipassana meditation is the investigation of this movement at the level of immediate bodily experience. In giving attention to *vedanā*, the physical sensation of change, one also inevitably becomes aware of the mental feelings of which they are an aspect. Vipassana meditation is the practice of awareness of the emotional basis of consciousness at the subtlest level. At surface levels the emotions may be describable in words, identified as they often are with external thoughts events and objects. But at deeper levels the conceptual, linguistic faculty diminishes and there is simply awareness of subtle tendencies of movement in the physical sensations and mental feelings. Music too is the investigation of just this motion. In the words of composer Roger Sessions

(1965: 18–19), 'The basic ingredient of music is not so much sound as movement . . . music is significant for us as human beings principally because it embodies movement of a specifically human type that goes to the roots of our being and takes shape in the inner gestures which embody our deepest and most intimate responses.'

William James defined emotion in physical, bodily terms. For James emotion is the mind's response to the physiological conditions that are caused by a stimulus. It is not that we see a bear, fear it, and run. We see a bear and run, and as a consequence we fear it. Our response to the higher adrenaline level, increased heartbeat, shortness of breath, perspiration, etc., *is* the emotion (James 1884: 189–90). This has important implications for aesthetics. Could the feelings aroused by music be a result of the physical movements it engenders? In this passage from James's *Principles of Psychology*, a clear connection is drawn:

> aesthetic emotion, *pure and simple*, the pleasure given us by certain lines and masses, and combinations of colors and sounds, is an absolutely sensational experience . . .. To this simple primary and immediate pleasure in certain pure sensations and harmonious combinations of them, there may, it is true, be *added* secondary pleasures; and in the practical enjoyment of works of art by the masses of mankind these secondary pleasures play a great part. The more *classic* one's taste is, however, the less relatively important are the secondary pleasures felt to be, in comparison with those of the primary sensation as it comes in. Classicism and romanticism have their battles over this point. Complex suggestiveness, the awakening of vistas of memory and association, and the stirring of our flesh with picturesque mystery and gloom, make a work of art *romantic*. The classic taste brands these effects as coarse and tawdry, and prefers the naked beauty of the optical and auditory sensations, unadorned with frippery or foliage. To the romantic mind, on the contrary, the immediate beauty of these sensations seems dry and thin. (James 1901: 468–70)

To try to capture the infinite varieties of emotion in a linguistic net is futile and misleading. The *navarasa,* the gamut of emotions described in the ancient Indian *Nātya Sāstra* treatise (Bharata 2000) or the elaborate emotional schematics of Robert Solomon (1977) or Kate Hevner (1935), all tend towards what James calls romanticism. By contrast scientific studies of music and emotion often find it more useful to reduce the complex designations of emotion down to two or three, such as 'happiness', 'sadness', and 'fear', as used by Johnsen *et al.* (2009).

This 'romantic' tendency is the work of the *saññā* and *saṅkhāra*, naming and labelling, relating one fact to another and making associations. James does not discuss which approach is 'right', but to a vipassana meditator it becomes clear that the *saññā* is always wrong because it never knows the whole truth. The actions generated by *saṅkhāra* on the basis of these valuations proliferate on the basis of a partial truth. Any words or concepts describing emotional experiences are themselves based on this *saññā* and therefore inadequate. Words such as 'fear', 'happiness', 'anger', or 'pride' are like spears thrust into a moving school of fish. The seabed is strewn with these spears while the living schools flash and glint just out of sight.

The perception of change

In vipassana no attempt is made to name or label an object. The focus of meditation is change and movement. The insight to be developed is that everything is in motion.

Even what appears static is part of a stream. In the Western tradition, Lucretius in the first century BCE first wrote of the existence of atoms while watching the glitter and spin of motes of dust in sunbeams (see Lucretius 1921: Book II, 67–9). Their motion is usually hidden from our sight, he said, but in 1827 the Botanist Robert Brown described the jittery motion of particles he saw through a microscope. This Brownian motion hastened the acceptance of atoms in modern science. Nowadays the existence of these invisible corpuscles is generally acknowledged. No rational person denies that everything is made of atoms and that atoms are in constant motion. Yet this knowledge is very difficult to square with our senses. Unconscious *saññā* is quick to evaluate hazy sensory information, to judge it and label it. And then the irrational *saṅkhāra*, behaving as if the world were fixed around us, attempts to move closer to or further from the objects it perceives. This motion is experienced as emotion. But if *vedanā* can be attended to more closely it becomes sharper, like a microscope coming into focus. Then details become clearer. Movement and change can be discerned in what had seemed static. *Saññā* is proved wrong again and again, and the reactions based on it weaken. That is not to say that emotional experience disappears. The movement of life continues, but one is not dragged along by it. Rather one is free to observe calmly, and to appreciate the motion in its subtle detail. In tranquillity one is free to act skilfully and rationally.

Like meditation, music creates a space in which to *practise* this special point of view. As Thaut puts it (2008: 34), 'In music we exercise and express the aesthetic components of our biology, the logic and critical thinking of musical perception and cognition, just as we exercise motor control aspects in sports or cognitive aspects in mathematics or language.' Music is a perfect laboratory for the examination of what David Chalmers (1996) has called 'the hard problem'. It allows the observer to discern fine physical and emotional details, allows experimental manipulation of states of mind, creates a forum for the comparison and verification of otherwise private, subjective experience, and has begun to establish a literature and methodology for just such activity.

Mind in motion

Rhythms reverberate through the entire structure of a body. According to Thaut, the brain is sensitive to rhythmic movement at a deeper level than we can know:

> The motor system is very sensitive to arousal by the auditory system. Neural impulses of auditory rhythm project directly into motor structures. Motor responses become entrained with the timing of rhythmic patterns. The entrainment process can be modeled well via resonant network functions and coupled oscillator models. The motor system has access to temporal information in the auditory system below levels of conscious perception. (2008: 57; see also Chapter 14)

The organic basis of consciousness, then, is in some way musical. In becoming self-aware, humans learn to play with this very musicality. The energy that animates an individual body also affects its environment and other bodies around it, so it may be amplified, shared, and compared. Whereas music arose as intrinsic to the function of the organism, it has evolved to become available to us as an object in itself.

Music abstracts movement for its own ends. There is no danger to escape, enemy to vanquish, or food to ingest. Listening to music allows us to feel emotion without acting on it. In vipassana this way of listening is characterized as *upekkha*—literally 'waiting': waiting with awareness but without interference or expectation, allowing the object to develop in its own way. The word has also been translated as 'detachment' or 'equanimity'. Music allows us to practise this attitude under controlled conditions. In music, since there is no substantive danger or reward, no real-life object of hate or desire, the emotion can be observed in itself, as a bodily fact. Just as mathematics delineates the structure and pattern of logic without its referents, music maps the dynamic of emotion without its content. When desire or hatred can be viewed without personal identification with them, they are reduced to mere movement. Like pressure, magnetism, gravity, or a game of boules, emotion can then be reduced to a simple binary of attraction and repulsion.

Unlike an abstract, theoretical pursuit, however, both music and meditation afford techniques for moving beyond mere analysis to social agency. We might posit that all music makes audible the mind of its creator, whether or not that is the conscious intention. The technique of *metta bhavana* can be compared to a musical practice in which investigators consciously amplify and share only their positive, loving mental states. Some music, according to this view, can act as a kind of extroverted meditation. Whatever qualities of mind have been developed radiate outwards. The practitioner's conscious state does not remain isolated but is promulgated through sound, the vibrations permeating the environment and potentially moving other sentient beings to resonate in sympathy.

Conclusion

Music and meditation are complementary tools in not only the study but also the transformation of consciousness. I have described three distinct mutually supportive phases of meditation practice, *ānāpāna*, vipassana, and *metta bhavana*, and have mapped these onto three aspects of musical activity: practice, the investigation of emotion, and social interaction. These three aspects are interdependent, each effective in its respective field. The overall aim in the case of meditation is wisdom and peace. If there is an analogous goal in music it may be aesthetic beauty.

Music, used as an object of study and a series of training exercises, can have a regulatory, balancing effect on the mind. Like the breath, music can be deliberately used as a bridge between the voluntary and autonomic nervous systems. But as the skill of listening develops, consciousness reveals itself to be fundamentally musical. Music is deeply rooted in the irrational processes of the body. It moves beyond intellectual, conceptual, discursive thinking towards an emotional, sensual realm. An explanation of the emotional and sensual quality of experience is a fundamental problem in consciousness studies. Abstract language leaves out the essential person and ordinary speech is imprecise. Music, supported by a contemplative practice, affords a highly effective means by which to both examine and communicate the nature of consciousness.

Pre-composed music is useful as an object of attention. A composition with a defined structure can be employed to focus the mind, establishing a state of uninterrupted vigilance and clarity. Of all musical forms, however, improvisation seems particularly suited for opening up awareness to the dynamic, irrational, embodied mind. It offers a set of practices for training the attention and directing it to examine the constantly changing, emotional substrate of conscious experience. And emerging from this introverted phase, music also offers a means of sharing and communicating the insights gained. Language can share only fixed concepts and labels, but music communicates the feeling of the constantly flowing and changing world. It is the social pattern of the mind. Music is mind in the environment. Mind is the music of what happens.

References

Abram, D. (1996). *The Spell of the Sensuous: Perception and Language in a More-Than-Human World* (New York, NY: Vintage).

Bailey, D. (1992). *Improvisation: its Nature and Practice in Music* (London: The British Library National Sound Archive).

Bateson, G. (1972). *Steps to an Ecology of Mind*. (Chicago, IL: University of Chicago Press).

Bharata (2000). *The Natya Sastra of Bharatamuni* (Delhi: Satguru).

Biswas, A. *Website of Ansuman Biswas*. Available at: www.ansuman.com/home.html (accessed 19 August 2010).

Chalmers, D. (1996). *The Conscious Mind: In Search of a Fundamental Theory* (New York, NY: Oxford University Press).

Deep Listening Institute. (n.d.) Mission statement. Available at: www.deeplistening.org/site/content/about (accessed 27 September 2010).

Garfield, J.L. (1995). *The Fundamental Wisdom of the Middle Way: Nagarjuna's Mulamadhyamikakarika* (New York, NY: Oxford University Press).

Goenka, S.N. (ed.) (2000). *Mahāsatipaṭṭhāna Sutta: The Great Discourse on the Establishing of Awareness* (Seattle, WA: Vipassana Research Institute).

Hardy, E., Hunt, M., Morris, R., and Rhys Davids, C.A.F. (eds.) (1900). *Anguttara Nikāya* Volume V (London: Pali Text Society).

Hevner, K. (1935). Expression in music: a discussion of experimental studies and theories. *Psychological Review*, **47**, 246–68.

James, W. (1884). What is an emotion? *Mind*, **9**, 188–205. Also available at: http://psychclassics.yorku.ca/James/emotion.htm (accessed 19 August 2010).

James, W. (1901). *The Principles of Psychology*, vol. **2** (London: Macmillan).

Johnsen, E.L., Tranel, D., Lutgendorf, S., and Adolphs, R. (2009). A neuroanatomical dissociation for emotion induced by music. *International Journal of Psychophysiology*, **72**, 24–33.

Levitin, D.J. (2006). *This is Your Brain on Music: The Science of a Human Obsession* (New York, NY: Dutton).

Lucretius (1921). *On The Nature of Things*, trans. C. Bailey (Oxford: Clarendon Press).

Merleau-Ponty, M. (2002). *Phenomenology of Perception*, trans. Colin Smith (London: Routledge).

Mithen, S. (1996). *The Prehistory of the Mind: The Cognitive Origins of Art, Religion, and Science* (London: Thames & Hudson).

Oliveros, P. (2005). *Deep Listening: A Composer's Sound Practice* (Lincoln, NE: iUniverse, Inc.).

Perlovsky, L.I. (2008). Music and consciousness. *Leonardo*, **41**, 420–1.

Perlovsky, L.I. (2010). Musical emotions: functions, origins, evolution. *Physics of Life Reviews*, 7, 2–27.

Pinker, S. (1997). *How the Mind Works* (New York, NY: W.W. Norton).

Rhys Davids, T.W. (ed.) (1925). *Pali–English Dictionary* (London: Pali Text Society).

Sessions, R. (1965). *The Musical Experience of Composer, Performer, Listener* (New York, NY: Atheneum).

Solomon, R.C. (1977). *The Passions* (New York, NY: Anchor Press).

Tagore, R. (1961). *Gitabitan* (Kolkata: Government of West Bengal).

Thaut, M.H. (2008). *Rhythm, Music, and the Brain: Scientific Foundations and Clinical Applications* (New York, NY: Routledge).

Notes

1. The Fenian Cycle is one of the major cycles of Irish mythology. The version of the characteristic passage cited here is my own paraphrase of an orally transmitted rendition.

2. For information on my work see www.ansuman.com.

3. This notion and meditation in Buddhism more generally are also discussed in Chapter 7, this volume.

4. See also the discussion of *riyāz* in Chapter 8, this volume.

5. See also Chapter 8, this volume.

6. A related point is made in Chapter 3 (this volume) by Michael Gallope—see the section entitled 'The history of life and the emergence of the world'.

7. Cf. the Hindu concept of *ākāśa* ('ether'), discussed by David Clarke and Tara Kini in Chapter 8, this volume.

8. See also Perlovsky (2008) for a further account by this author of music and emotion.

9. See also Chapter 14, this volume.

Chapter 7

'In the heard, only the heard . . .': music, consciousness, and Buddhism

Bethany Lowe

An anecdote in the Buddhist Pali canon tells how Sona the monk, previously a delicately raised musician, had been doing walking meditation for so long that his feet had begun to bleed. Discouraged, he wondered whether it would be better to return to lay life and concentrate on doing good deeds. Taking pity on him, the Buddha engaged him in conversation about his mental state with a musical metaphor that would have hit home all too well:

> 'Now what do you think, Sona. Before, when you were a house-dweller, were you skilled at playing the vina [lute]?' 'Yes, lord.'
>
> 'And what do you think: when the strings of your vina were too taut, was your vina in tune and playable?' 'No, lord.'
>
> 'And what do you think: when the strings of your vina were too loose, was your vina in tune and playable?' 'No, lord.'
>
> 'And what do you think: when the strings of your vina were neither too taut nor too loose, but tuned to be right on pitch, was your vina in tune and playable?' 'Yes, lord.'
>
> 'In the same way, Sona, over-aroused persistence leads to restlessness, overly slack persistence leads to laziness. Thus you should determine the right pitch for your persistence, attune the pitch of the faculties, and there pick up your theme.'
> (Ṭhānissaro 1997)[1]

That the Buddha (known also as Siddhārtha Gautama, and active in north-east India during the fifth century BCE) should choose musical practice as an analogy for the development of consciousness tells of his characteristic flexibility of thought and pragmatic skill in teaching.[2] But this type of metaphor only hints at much deeper connections between sound/music and consciousness within Buddhist thought. Within the body of insights attributed to the Buddha and subsequent followers and scholars in this field, there are numerous perspectives that use an awareness of sound to deepen understanding of the mind, and vice versa; the various connections between these areas will be the subject of this chapter.

Before exploring the interaction between music and consciousness in Buddhist thought, some initial understanding of a Buddhist view of consciousness is called for, since it differs from a typical Western understanding in numerous subtle ways. As belief systems and emphases in different Buddhist schools can vary as much as in different Christian denominations, I have focused primarily on the early mainstream sources of the Indian Pali canon (which possesses a clear philosophy of mind and well-developed scholarship) and have introduced ideas and practices from the later Mahāyāna schools where relevant.[3]

Consciousness in Buddhism

Buddhist thought can provide a fresh approach to the understanding of consciousness, since it adopts fundamentally different axioms and situates itself outside the Western philosophical tradition. In particular, the 'hard problem' of Western consciousness studies, neatly summarized by Susan Blackmore as 'How do subjective experiences arise from objective brains?' (Blackmore 2005: 4) and unpacked by its originator David Chalmers as 'Why should physical processing give rise to a rich inner life at all?' (Chalmers 1995: 201), is simply circumvented, or rather does not arise. The reason that this problem has been so notoriously intractable (even Chalmers continues 'It seems objectively unreasonable that it should') is that it makes a materialist assumption that matter is prior to mind, which Buddhism does not support. Admittedly, competing hypotheses in the history of Western thought have had an equally difficult time explaining themselves: of the other two main strands of thought, Berkeley's idealist view held that material objects had no existence independently of a mind perceiving them, but then relied on a postulated omniscient mind to ensure continuing consistency of the objective world (thereby appearing to undercut his own argument); and Descartes, in expounding what has come to be termed substance dualism, was at a loss to explain convincingly how mind and matter could causally interact with each other, proposing the central pineal gland of the brain as the doorway between the two.[4]

In Buddhist thought, consciousness could be seen as arising logically prior to the bodily system, and is a result of prior karma. Figure 7.1 shows the '12 links of conditioned existence' which explain the causative processes of life and death:[5] here the presence of ignorance (i) gives rise to karmic actions motivated by volition (ii), and the results of these actions produce certain types of consciousness (iii); this consciousness acts as a support for the rest of the mind–body system (iv), and with it constitutes the conditions for the sense bases (v), sensory data or contact (vi), feelings about this contact (vii), and emotional reactions (viii–ix, discussed presently), which in turn perpetuate the repeated cycle of unenlightened life (x–xii).[6] Are Buddhists therefore idealists, distant cousins to Berkeley, since, by placing consciousness (iii) prior to physicality (iv–v), they 'make mind fundamental' (Blackmore 2005: 4)? According to Blackmore, idealists 'must then explain why and how there appears to be a consistent physical world' (4). But this assumption too is undercut in Buddhist thinking where our differing karmic qualities cause us to see quite different realities and situations—an observation that is borne out by everyday experience and encounters between distant cultures. That we can agree on any basic truths and observations at all is a function of our relatively similar human biology and culture; though each person operates within their own worldview, 'the similarity in people's karmic "seeds" means that our "worlds" have much in common' (P. Harvey 1990: 110).[7] Still, we must be careful

(i)	ignorance	(*avijjā*)
	↓	
(ii)	volitional formations	(*saṅkhārā*)
	↓	
(iii)	consciousness	(*viññaṇa*)
	↓	
(iv)	name-and-form	(*nāma–rūpa*)
	↓	
(v)	six sense bases	(*saḷāyatana*)
	↓	
(vi)	contact	(*phassa*)
	↓	
(vii)	feeling	(*vedanā*)
	↓	
(viii)	craving	(*taṇhā*)
	↓	
(ix)	clinging	(*upādāna*)
	↓	
(x)	existence	(*bhava*)
	↓	
(xi)	birth	(*jāti*)
	↓	
(xii)	ageing-and-death	(*jarāmaraṇa*)

Fig. 7.1 The 12 links of conditioned existence.

before we classify the Buddhist worldview as an idealist philosophy, for it is not so much that this consciousness creates body (or a perception of body),[8] but that prior karmic actions (i–ii) serve as a condition for the experience of both to unfold (iii–v).[9]

Furthermore, the processes of mind and body are not as separate as the habits of Western philosophy would have us imagine them:

> at any given moment of experience, body–mind represents an intimate organic unity. For though Buddhism recognizes a polarity between mental and physical constituents of sentient beings, it never sharply divides them but on the contrary strongly emphasizes the close relationship of all mental and physical states. (King 1964: 19; quoted in P. Harvey 1993: 29)

The alleged problem of substance dualism is therefore avoided, since 'there is no dualism of a mental "substance" versus a physical "substance": both *nāma* [mind] and *rūpa* [body] each refer to clusters of changing, interacting processes' (P. Harvey 1993: 39). Thus mainstream Buddhism favours instead what Peter Harvey has labelled a 'twin-category process pluralism' (29), through viewing mind and body neither as reducible to one another nor as isolated substances in interaction, since they 'shade off into each other or thoroughly interpenetrate each other' (King 1964: 20). In this way of understanding things, the mind–body system continually makes choices that lead to intentional (karmic) actions, which then affect both mind and body again as established in the twelve links of existence above.

In Buddhist thought, then, living beings are divided not dualistically into mind vs body, but into five aggregates or categories of experience (Sanskrit, *skandhas*, lit. 'heaps').[10] Of these, one is physical and the remaining four are mental: respectively, form or body (*rūpa*), feeling (*vedanā*), discernment (*saṃjñā*), volitional formations (*saṃskāra*), and consciousness (*vijñāna*).[11] The term for this last element consists of a root, *jñāna*, meaning cognition, knowing, or gnosis (and whose semantic essence survives in the *gn-* and *kn-* of these words), together with a prefix, *vi-*, which signifies a separation between the subject and the object of knowledge (Conze 2001: 88). Thus consciousness is a somewhat alienated way of knowing that characterizes ordinary unenlightened beings, while the liberated mind with full insight into reality operates through *jñāna* and the related *prajñā* (wisdom, or higher cognition), which constitute the main goal of spiritual practice (Conze 2001: 100, 109–10; P. Williams 2000: 133–4).[12]

This 'aggregate' of consciousness is further divided according to its source in one of the six senses: eye, ear, nose, tongue, body, and mind (see Figure 7.2)—the mind being treated for these purposes much like the others, as a sense function, albeit one which deals primarily in conceptions rather than direct perceptions (Tsering 2006: 24–6). Each of these six consciousnesses is viewed as a 'main mind', and (perhaps counterintuitively) only one of these can operate at once: thus in order to listen and see (for example) at the same time, we must shuttle repeatedly between these minds, 'so rapidly that we experience the illusion that both are operating together' (24–6).[13] The same, crucially, is true for the mental and any of the sense consciousnesses, so that sensing what is currently present (on the one hand) and reflecting on our internal recollections, projections, and so on (on the other) take energy away from each other (as we must all have experienced when suddenly 'coming round' from an absorbing daydream to realize that we have not been taking in what is in front of us at all—or conversely in completely losing a train of thought due to a compelling sensory stimulus).

Of these six main consciousnesses, the most relevant from a musical standpoint will inevitably be the auditory main mind (the second) and the mental main mind (the sixth), since we commonly construe music as variously that which is heard and that which is mentally imagined—though other sense consciousnesses also contribute, as Christopher Small (1998: 8–10, 19–29), among others, has pointed out. Though the auditory and mental main minds may alternate rapidly, and may interact on a

Form	Feelings	Discernment	Volitional formations	Consciousness
(*rūpa*)	(*vedanā*)	(*saṃjñā*)	(*saṃskāra*)	(*vijñāna*)

Eye	Ear	Nose	Tongue	Body	Mind
Mental factors	Mental factors	Mental factors	Mental factors	Mental factors	Mental factors

Fig. 7.2 The five aggregates and the six consciousnesses.

moment-to-moment basis, one of the provocative implications of this theory of mind is that only one of these, broadly speaking either listening or cogitating, will be to the fore at any moment during a musical experience; thus a person may be primarily aware of a given strand of their current sensory experience, or else primarily withdrawn from sense impressions in order to recall them, relate them to a bigger picture, and/or pursue personal associations. While it may seem obvious that to experience music most directly it is necessary to devote our attention to auditory consciousness and resist going into processing mode until later—and this probably does describe many 'peak listening experiences'[14]—it is not so obvious how we would go about cultivating this approach deliberately (especially for those whose habits and values have come to prioritize reflective thought) or what its potential might be. And although this distinction may seem to replicate the two types of listening summarized by Nicholas Cook (1990) as 'musical' (experiential, direct) and 'musicological' (theorizing, abstract), in fact there is an important underlying distinction. Whereas in Western thinking, sensory perceptions are commonly construed as raw data received by the sense organs, with feelings and interpretations being the property of a later stage of mental activity, in Buddhist thought each of the 'main minds' (including the sensory consciousnesses as well as the mental consciousness) is accompanied by its own range of 'mental factors' that give intensity and emotional depth to the experience (see Figure 7.2). Mental factors constitute the remainder of the (mental) aggregates of a person listed above, and include always-present functions such as discernment (*saṃjñā*), which notes the characteristics of what is perceived and identifies it, and feeling (*vedanā*), which causes us to experience it as pleasant, unpleasant, or neutral, as well as a raft of emotional reactions (*saṃskāras*) which can arise in response to these.[15] Therefore even a 'pure' experience of listening, where the auditory consciousness is far more active than the so-called mental consciousness, can provide a rich and full experience without our having to take leave of our senses, so to speak. From a Buddhist standpoint, it is the mental factors that can cause us suffering when they constitute unhealthy and compulsive emotional response patterns, and that also prevent us from seeing the nature of the mind directly.

The distinctive Buddhist description of the mind includes an important experiential, heuristic dimension which is intended to fundamentally transform one's experience. This soteriological function is somewhat different from the scientistic ontological aspirations typical of later Western philosophy: as Paul Williams explains (2000: 40), 'the "ought" (pragmatic benefit) is never cut adrift from the "is" (cognitive factual truth)', though nonetheless 'the teachings of the Buddha are held by the Buddhist tradition to *work* because they are factually *true* (not true because they work)'.[16] Since the insights into sound and consciousness that Buddhist thought is intended to develop, or reveal, are different from those that seem self-evident from Western culture, the reader is strongly encouraged to try out these perspectives through the reflective exercises that are explored in the next section.

Sound and music in consciousness

The Bahiya Sutta (from which the epigraph of this chapter is taken) is perhaps the Buddha's most pondered teaching on how to tackle the experience of our senses, and is therefore central to the current discussion. Having achieved a good reputation (and livelihood) on the grounds of his spiritual development, Bahiya becomes aware that he is not as spiritually accomplished as he had previously assumed, and not even heading in the right direction. He seeks out the Buddha and, on pressing him for a relevant teaching, is told:

> Then, Bahiya, you should train yourself thus: In reference to the seen, there will be only the seen. In reference to the heard, only the heard. In reference to the sensed, only the sensed. In reference to the cognized, only the cognized. That is how you should train yourself. When for you there will be only the seen in reference to the seen, only the heard in reference to the heard, only the sensed in reference to the sensed, only the cognized in reference to the cognized, then, Bahiya, there is no you in terms of that. When there is no you in terms of that, there is no you there. When there is no you there, you are neither here nor yonder nor between the two. This, just this, is the end of stress. (Ṭhānissaro 1994)[17]

The meditative practice that the Buddha recommends here allows (or encourages) us to engage directly with the contents of our sensory and mental consciousnesses, without accretions, filtering, or distractions. Here the third category of 'the sensed' bundles together the contents of the smell, taste, and touch consciousnesses,[18] and the 'cognized' refers to the contents of the mental consciousness, treating it in exactly the same way as the previous (sensory) consciousnesses. Thus even our thoughts ('the cognized') should be experienced simply as another form of experiential data, without further associative overlay. The verbal function should be allowed to be relatively quiescent (rather than actively pursued) so that it can be recognized as part of what is 'only the cognized'; this is a practical challenge for those who normally construe thought in terms of words, but can be a revelation in terms of mental experience.[19]

Awareness of the sensory consciousnesses and/or the mind is regularly taught as a Buddhist (and indeed non-Buddhist) meditational exercise, when it is generally transmitted orally as an introductory practice. One written version of the practice is given by the Buddhist teacher Lama Surya Das, who outlines our habitual behaviour and the meditational alternative as follows:

> Whether it is through the 'ear gate' (hearing) or the 'eye gate' (seeing) [or any of the other four gates of consciousness], objects or forms enter, and thus our individual experience occurs. A loud sound, for example, enters our ear gate and we respond. Recognition (or not) occurs, and we label it: 'thunder', 'door slam', or even 'What was that noise?' This is almost immediately followed by subjective, karmically conditioned feelings of liking and disliking—all based upon this almost instantaneous labeling and conceptualizing, as in 'nice gurgling brook sounds', or 'awful, loud honking car alarm', or even 'scary, strange, unfamiliar sound' . . .
>
> As you begin this practice, whether you are concentrating on sound or taste or smell, try to practice bare attention, which is also known as naked awareness. Be aware of what is entering the sense gate, but don't stray into the next step of labeling or judging. Keep it very precise and simple, one moment at a time. (Das 2003: 244–5)

Here the straightforward experience of a stimulus belongs to one of the main minds of consciousness, while the recognition/labelling, liking/disliking, and emotional reactions constitute respectively the discernment, feelings, and volitional formations of the mental factors as shown on Figure 7.2. (Note that a mental stimulus in the form of a thought that entered the mind would be divided up in the same way.) Put in terms of the 12 links of existence shown in Figure 7.1, the sound stimulus corresponds to stage (vi), whilst the feelings of liking and disliking equate to stage (vii), and the emotional reactions to stages (viii) and (ix), depending on the intensity of the experience.

What is being proposed in this practice is nothing less than that we allow the habitual conditioned reaction along the chain of the 12 links from contact (vi) to feeling (vii) to craving (or aversion) (viii) to subside. This is a crucial point at which one can choose to perpetuate—or escape—the cycle of suffering described by the 12 links.[20] Craving is not merely the experience of pleasure, or a wish to be happy, but a mental factor (also described as attachment) that grabs onto an experience, *must* have it (or continue to have it), and is disappointed if it cannot.[21] The experience of aversion, pushing away an unpleasant experience or feeling, is merely the other side of the same coin and causes exactly the same problems of suffering (Nhat Hanh 1999: 22–3). According to the Buddha's first and most all-encompassing teaching (known as the Four Noble Truths), this emotion of craving is the most immediate source of suffering (or stress, in the version of the Bahiya Sutta given above),[22] without which we can leave the process of conditioned existence illustrated on Figure 7.1 and become a liberated being. Thus the practice of so-called 'bare attention', developing full awareness of conscious experience without leaping into conceptual labelling or emotive judging, can begin a deep process of transformation of both our state of mind and our awareness of sound and other sensory events. A more equanimous response to sensory perception is just the first stage of the practice, however, and what is excluded from 'only the heard' is just as crucial.

What of the Buddha's comments to Bahiya that 'there is no you there' and 'there is no you in terms of that'? These comments invoke the Buddha's distinctive teachings known as non-self (*anātman*), dependent origination (*pratītya-samutpāda*), and emptiness (*śūnyatā*), philosophical–experiential insights into reality that the practice may deliver if pursued thoroughly. By 'there is no you in terms of that', he is suggesting that Bahiya should not identify himself with any of the six consciousnesses—that none of them is his 'self', either individually or in combination. In the words of Bhikkhu Bodhi, 'The Buddha teaches, contrary to our most cherished beliefs, that our individual being—the five aggregates—cannot be identified as self, as an enduring and substantial ground of personal identity' (Ñāṇamoli and Bodhi 1995: 27–8)—and hence that there is no substantial self as such.[23] Bodhi goes on to reference various suttas where the Buddha forcefully repudiates views that support the existence of a fixed self, among them the Alagaddūpama Sutta:

> 'Bhikkhus [monks], you may well cling to that doctrine of self that would not arouse sorrow, lamentation, pain, grief, and despair in one who clings to it. But do you see any such doctrine of self, bhikkhus?'—'No, venerable sir.'—'Good, bhikkhus. I too do not see any [such] doctrine of self . . .' (Ñāṇamoli and Bodhi 1995: 231)

This carries a perhaps shocking implication for Western notions of consciousness, which seem to have taken for granted that if consciousness can be located and identified, then that is where our selfhood inheres.[24] In addition, the question of self in Western thinking seems habitually to be tied up with the possibility or otherwise of our in some way surviving the death process—whereas the Buddha explicitly refutes the idea that the aggregate of consciousness remains the same beyond the death process, or indeed from moment to moment, insisting that (like everything else) it is dependently arisen, subject to continual change and reconstitution.[25]

The phenomenon of dependent origination is illustrated by the Buddha using another analogy drawn from music:

> Suppose there were a king or king's minister who had never heard the sound of a lute [vina] before. He might hear the sound of a lute and say, 'What, my good men, is that sound—so delightful, so tantalizing, so intoxicating, so ravishing, so enthralling?' They would say, 'That, sire, is called a lute, whose sound is so delightful, so tantalizing, so intoxicating, so ravishing, so enthralling.' Then he would say, 'Go and fetch me that lute.' They would fetch the lute and say, 'Here, sire, is the lute whose sound is so delightful, so tantalizing, so intoxicating, so ravishing, so enthralling.' He would say, 'Enough of your lute. Fetch me just the sound.'
>
> Then they would say, 'This lute, sire, is made of numerous components, a great many components. It is through the activity of numerous components that it sounds: that is, in dependence on the body, the skin, the neck, the frame, the strings, the bridge, and the appropriate human effort. Thus it is that this lute—made of numerous components, a great many components—sounds through the activity of numerous components.'
>
> Then the king would split the lute into ten pieces, a hundred pieces. Having split the lute into ten pieces, a hundred pieces, he would shave it to splinters. Having shaved it to splinters, he would burn it in a fire. Having burned it in a fire, he would reduce it to ashes. Having reduced it to ashes, he would winnow it before a high wind or let it be washed away by a swift-flowing stream. He would then say, 'A sorry thing, this lute—whatever a lute may be—by which people have been so thoroughly tricked and deceived.'[26]

That one cannot find the *sound* of a lute apart from the components of the lute (nor from the conditions of having someone play it and a suitable acoustic context in which it can sound) is evident to anyone with the smallest experience of musical instruments. The metaphorical point of the story—that one's self cannot be found except as a result of our aggregates,[27] and in dependence upon a network of supporting conditions—is worth further pondering once we have gained some initial direct experience with the meditation practice outlined above. Music in fact provides an opportunity to practise reflecting on the broader implications of dependent origination, since any piece of music or music-making event arises from a staggering concatenation of people, circumstances, traditions, recording and/or notation and/or oral transmission practices, instrument functioning, discourses, and so on, each of which even on its own is impressively complex.[28] As Small points out, 'It is in musicking that we experience most directly and intimately the relationships of the pattern that connects' (Small 1998: 143). Thus 'it is closer to the truth to picture ourself as a cell in the vast body of life, distinct yet intimately bound up with all living beings' (Gyatso 2000: 50).

In the Buddhist understanding of dependent origination, how things arise, persist, and cease is thus shown to be dependent on a vast range of interconnected conditions, with nothing being exempt from this process of change and influence. Even the constituents of the self are shown to be empty of inherent or fixed existence: in the Pali canon, the Buddha compares the five aggregates to a blob of foam, a water bubble, a mirage, a tree with no heartwood, and an illusion (Bodhi 2000: 951–2), and this teaching is developed in the later Mahāyāna scriptures such as the Heart Sutra with its claim that each of the aggregates is 'only emptiness' (P. Williams 2000: 140–52). The aim of this teaching is to free us from the mistaken way that our minds tend to grasp and reify objects and ideas as if they existed substantially and permanently (and which causes us confusion and sorrow when these things inevitably cease, change, or otherwise elude us). A deep understanding of emptiness, such that it transforms our perception of reality, is proposed as the ultimate wisdom remedy for the ignorance at the root of the 12 links of conditioned existence.

Music is arguably particularly well suited to getting the beginnings of a glimpse into emptiness, since the way in which it appears to us is not the way in which we know it exists. As a starting point, take the account of Beethoven's Piano Concerto No. 5 provided in a popular textbook on acoustics:

> As the dramatic piano arpeggios well up out of a majestic sustained orchestral chord . . . a curious visitor from outer space sits unobtrusively at the back of the hall observing this fascinating human activity. Focusing his superior vision on the orchestral players in turn, he notes that the majority are scraping tensed horsehair back and forth over metal wires attached to wooden boxes of various sizes. Others are blowing air into or over tubes of wood or metal; one is hammering a plastic sheet stretched on a metal hemisphere. The soloist is operating a complicated system of wooden levers whose purpose is not immediately apparent. The mêlée is controlled, it seems, by hand signals from the conductor. Consulting the dials on a little black box which he is holding, the visitor detects small but rapid fluctuations in the pressure of the air in the hall. These fluctuations have no obvious pattern; he dismisses the speculation that they are perhaps connected with the purpose of the ceremony, which remains obscure to him. (Campbell and Greated 1987: 1)

This imaginary account is an amusing exercise in defamiliarization: although it accords comfortably enough with our scientific understanding of sound, it is certainly not our habitual mode of appreciating orchestral music. Human perception tends to construe vibrations of fewer than 16 beats per second as repeated pulses, those between 16 and 10,000–20,000 beats per second as pitches and/or timbres, and those above that as nothing whatsoever, all using a tiny membrane coupled to a system of differently sized hairs (Campbell and Greated 1987: 111–12, 48–55). As anyone who has had the shock of seeing their first spectrograph of a simple sound recording will attest, the discrete notes we are familiar with from Western music notation are a gross simplification of the mass of frequency information appearing there in chaotic and detailed patterns. This is a particularly good illustration of the lack of self-existence of familiar so-called objects, a case study of 'the world [as] a web of fluxing, inter-dependent, baseless phenomena' (P. Harvey 1990: 99).[29] Everything we seem to perceive, like the coherent concerto movement evident to those familiar with the genre, is thus 'like a magical illusion', and empty of primary, substantial existence (P. Williams 2000: 135, 141).[30] Thus music is culturally mediated on an even deeper level than that anticipated by cultural theory: our karmic propensities as humans predispose us to apply chunking, assumptions, interpretations and meanings to sound that are by no means 'there' in the raw stimulus.[31] Through this exercise we can understand that what we commonly term 'the music' is empty of self-existence, and derives from a variety of sources, inputs, and influences.

In case this all seems too remote, we can (and must) go on to relate this elevated view of music's emptiness to our normal conventional perspectives: this is known in Mahāyāna Buddhist theory as the 'union of the two truths' (where the truths in question are the 'absolute truth' of emptiness and the 'relative truth' of conventional reality), and strongly moves us towards the full enlightenment of a Buddha (Gyatso 1996: 45–72, 2). As it is explained in the poetic English rendering of the Buddhist mind-training text *The Wheel of Sharp Weapons*:

> When musicians are playing a beautiful melody,
> Should we examine the sound they are making
> We would see that it does not exist by itself.
> But when we're not making our formal [i.e. philosophical] analysis
> Still there's a beautiful tune to be heard,
> Which is merely a label on notes and on players;
> That's why lovely music can lighten sad hearts.
> (Dharmarakshita 1973: v. 112)

Music is thus an excellent opportunity to reflect on our perception and see directly the illusoriness of the musical object; if we can grasp the dependently originated, empty nature of music, there is the chance of applying the same insight to other, seemingly more solid or intractable, phenomena.

Finally, a way to come to experience the mind directly using sound is provided by the Mahamudra meditation practice (versions of which can be found in various Tibetan Buddhist traditions), whose initial stages represent a deepening of the six senses practice we have already experienced. Alexander Berzin recommends we begin by experiencing our mind like a flashlight: normally we focus externally on what is illuminated, or sometimes we disengage from experience as if we are the person behind the flashlight, but here 'we are looking from the point of view of the flashlight itself. . . . We look all around us, slowly, just being the flashlight, focusing attentively on the cognitive process that is occurring of the mere arising and engaging with a sight' (Berzin and Dalai Lama 1997: 67). Then:

> After investigating seeing sights, we follow a similar procedure with hearing sounds. What is the [perceptual] difference between hearing the sound of birds or traffic, music or a child's haphazard banging on a drum, soft music or the dentist's drill, a song that we like or one that we hate, a voice or the wind, the voice of a loved one or of someone we cannot stand, words we can understand or those we cannot, a mosquito buzzing around our head or one on the other side of the screened window next to our ear, and so on? (69)

Through practising this method, one may find that the experiential difference between these pairs of stimuli is less than one thought, as the emotional response of craving or aversion begins to abate under close and steady examination.

Once one has developed these initial skills in observing the direction of the mind (while maintaining a circumspect distance from its skittish behaviour), the attention can be turned to observing the mind itself.[32] One may begin by observing the mind that is observing the sensory stimulus, with the perspective that the contents of the experience are simply something that the mind is giving rise to (Berzin and Dalai Lama 1997: 71–3). In the Gelug tradition of Mahamudra practice, mind is provisionally defined as *clarity* and *cognizing* (or awareness); to meditate one seeks a generic image of the mind by contemplating these functions together with the mind's non-spatial nature and (non-paradoxically) its location at one's heart chakra (Gyatso 2005: 100–2, 106). When one has accomplished the ability to stay with this focus of meditation for five minutes or longer without any lapse or distraction, one moves on to further stages of this powerful practice, which involve using ever deeper layers of consciousness to realize the mind directly and mix it with an understanding of emptiness. Once this is achieved we are said to be on the verge of enlightenment (106–14), a state of mind perpetually free from ignorance or suffering which represents the highest possible level of mental development.

Indeed, the Śūraṅgama Sūtra of the Mahāyāna Buddhist tradition describes how Bodhisattva Avalokiteshvara reached full enlightenment through the practice of focusing on sound: 'Mentally detaching hearing from its object and then eliminating both those concepts, he had at first perceived that both disturbance and stillness are illusory and next came to realize the non-existence even of that rarified perception' (as described by Blofield (1977: 43)). Though the practice, along with the others described in the sūtra, is esoteric, the choice of sound as a meditational object out of the 25 possibilities presented is recommended by the gathering of highly developed beings as both easy to engage with and far-reaching in its profundity (Luk 1966: 135–6, 139–50).[33] Overall, then, a practical Buddhist approach offers the potential for deep insight into the nature of sound, and into the very nature of consciousness itself.

Buddhism in music

One question that arises in a consideration of music, consciousness, and Buddhism is whether any music has been or could be composed that would enable, encourage, or support listeners to gain an insight into the perspectives on consciousness that have been outlined above. The place of music in traditional Indian Buddhism is restricted, since it has been considered something of a sensuous luxury, but nonetheless a simple form of chant has had an important role in mnemonically preserving the teachings and in creating a ritual space (Mabbett 1993/4; S. Williams 2006: 170–7). The circular breathing often used to play wind instruments in the more musically elaborate Tibetan Buddhist ceremonies can form a meditative practice in itself, while the skilful alternation of sound cells and silences in the shakuhachi flute playing associated with Japanese traditions of Buddhism evokes the arising and dissolving of conditioned objects into emptiness (S. Williams 2006: 176, 183). As Buddhist ideas have proliferated more broadly through Western culture in the second half of the twentieth century, they have infiltrated and often challenged existing art music practices to produce some stimulating new compositional and aesthetic approaches. Reflecting my own background and specialisms, what follows is a brief exploration of the role and potential of Buddhist ideas in Western art music of the later twentieth century and beyond.

Of those born in the West, one of the cultural figures to have had the greatest—and earliest—effect on the dissemination of Buddhist ideas among musicians was John Cage, whose *Silence* (1961) introduced snippets of Zen to a largely unsuspecting audience of future composers and non-composers alike.[34] Cage's interest in this Japanese form of Buddhism developed out of a general interest in Asian aesthetics and philosophy and, following his own explorations in the literature, deepened with a period of study at Columbia University with D.T. Suzuki between 1950 and 1952 (Patterson 2002). His influential talks from 'Lecture on Nothing' (c. 1950; Cage 1961: 109–26) onwards show the impact of this radically new perspective; while works such as *4′33″*—whose spiritual resonances are suggested by its original working title, *Silent Prayer* (Pritchett and Kuhn 2010: §3)—are probably amongst those he had in mind when he said 'What I do, I do not wish blamed on Zen, though without my engagement with Zen . . . I doubt whether I would have done what I have done' (Cage 1961: xi). The function of this famous piece for non-performing performer is to set a frame around a certain duration of ambient sound, allowing it to be perceived with full attention, and thus revealing that any sound can become music when (and if) the mind of the listener imputes it as such,[35] since the status of 'music' (as already explored) is empty of self-existence from its own side.

Cage's lifelong project to discover means to 'let sounds be themselves' (1961: 10) acquires a new significance in the light of the Buddha's instruction to Bahiya—'In reference to the heard, only the heard . . . That is how you should train yourself'. And the specific practice of staying with the contents of the six consciousnesses directly is echoed in Cage's advice that 'the wisest thing to do is to open one's ears immediately and hear a sound suddenly before one's thinking has a chance to turn it into something logical, abstract, or symbolical' (1969: 98). Cage makes a clear connection between musical and spiritual practice, and references the familiar Buddhist aim of declining to move from experience into craving, when he writes 'And what is the purpose of writing music? . . . Simply a way of waking up to the very life we're living, which is so excellent once one gets one's mind and one's desire out of its way and lets it act of its own accord' (1961: 12). Perhaps Cage's biggest contribution is the way in which his attention to sounds in their own right has become an indispensable approach to art music from the latter part of the twentieth century onwards, creating a fertile context for the development of a variety of styles from electronic music to minimalism. Thus perspectives drawn from Buddhist thought are already woven inextricably into Western contemporary musical culture.

The 'meditative' quality that critics are keen to attribute to the music of Philip Glass (Kostelanetz 1997: 319) probably reflects the way in which its repetition of simple musical materials provides the opportunity to examine these closely without their usual implications of resolution and narrative (Mertens 1983: 16–17). This listening attitude is similar to the target of meditation exercises above, which encourage us to engage perceptually with our experiences without invoking our habitual discriminations, feelings, and volitions. Glass comments on his four-and-a-half-hour minimalist epic, *Music in Twelve Parts* (1974) that

> When it becomes apparent that nothing 'happens' in the usual sense, but that, instead, the gradual accretion of musical material can and does serve as the basis of the listener's

attention, then he can perhaps discover another mode of listening—one in which neither memory nor anticipation . . . have a place in sustaining the texture, quality or reality of the musical experience. It is hoped that one would be able to perceive the music as a . . . pure medium 'of sound'.[36]

Although in theory any sonic stimulus could be perceived as a 'pure medium of sound' (and Glass's music remains stylistically distinctive for many listeners), the construction and content of such a piece may well be conducive to fostering a certain receptivity or clarity of perception in the listener. Jonathan Kramer believes that it is the experience of 'vertical time', where our perception is strongly focused on the present, that creates the special experience of consciousness that is common to meditation and minimalist music. Similar states can also be generated by psychedelic drugs, certain kinds of mental illness, and the experience of the unconscious in dreams (Kramer 1988: 376), but Kramer is careful to note that one need not be prone to mental illness (375) or to taking drugs (381) in order to experience these kinds of states. By similar reasoning, one need not be a Buddhist either to write or to enjoy such music, but if one develops the skills and habit of perceiving 'in the heard, only the heard' through this particularly conducive soundscape, it could fruitfully prepare the ground for such experiences to be developed in meditation practice. Elsewhere, John Richardson has linked Glass's evocation of the lament and chaconne tropes in *Akhnaten* (1984) with the experience of repeated suffering inherent in the Buddhist ideas of *saṃsāra* and rebirth (Richardson 1999: 67)—a connection that draws on Glass's own speculation that the chaconne form, popular in Flamenco, may have had its origins in the East (Glass 1988: 115–16).

Glass himself has been a practising Buddhist in the Tibetan tradition since the late 1960s, having encountered the Tibetan refugee community while visiting India and being impressed by how they put their spiritual teachings into practice (Mackenzie 2003: 234–43). He has contributed a knowledgeable and enthusiastic foreword to a book of teachings on Buddhist tantra (Yeshe 2001: vii–ix) and has 'given performances as a prelude to the [Dalai] Lama's public appearances in New York' (Maycock 2002: 180). Despite this obvious commitment, he prefers to rebuff all questions about his own religious practice and any connections between his beliefs and his music, protesting in the early days of the mid-1970s that 'my music is so very odd already that I see no reason to make myself sound any odder' (Glass 1988: ix) and insisting in a recalcitrant interview given to the Buddhist magazine *Tricycle* in 1992 that 'the real impact of Buddhist practice affects how you live your life on a daily basis, not how you do your art' (Kostelanetz 1997: 322). Some of his more recent works have ventured an explicit Buddhist theme, including his music for the Scorsese film *Kundun* (1997) on the subject of the exodus of the Dalai Lama (Mackenzie 2003: 243–5) and his Symphony No. 5: *Requiem, Bardo, Nirmanakaya* (1999), where the latter two parts of the title refer, respectively, to the intermediate state between death and rebirth, and the manifested body of a Buddha after enlightenment. However, even in this piece Glass refrains from fully pinning his colours to the mast by choosing texts from a variety of world traditions (beginning with the Rig Veda, the Qur'an, Genesis, the Hawaiian Kumulipo, and a Zuñi creation myth) to fill out the overall trajectory. He does not invoke a Buddhist text until the sixth of the 12 movements—claiming that all the texts are 'compatible with Buddhism though they are mostly not Buddhist' (Maycock 2002: 96). A clue to his persistent ambivalence can be found in his experience of the alternative concert scene in the late 1960s, with 'Western musicians dressed in Indian clothes and lighting incense on stage', and his wish to distinguish himself from such practices (Kostelanetz 1997: 321), as also from later self-styled 'meditation music' played in New Age contexts, whose aims and soundworld are entirely different (319).

In contrast, the British composer Jonathan Harvey (b. 1939) is an 'out' practitioner of Tibetan Buddhism whose enthusiasm for explaining the connections between his music and the most transcendent insights about Buddhism and consciousness shines through in all his interviews and writings. Much of the energy of Harvey's youthful interests in Christianity, mysticism, and Rudolf Steiner seems to have become absorbed into his primary spiritual practice, since he admits, 'I have gradually become more Buddhist and that again is a defining moment for me. More and more in recent works I take the ideas of Buddhism, of sutra and tantra, and put them into my music' (Whittall 1999: 18). If spiritual/philosophical content can find its way into a piece of music at the content level, the musical level, and/or the deep constructional level, Harvey uses all three to entertain concepts from Buddhist perspectives with which he himself has deeply engaged.[37] Pieces in the first two of these categories, those with explicit Buddhist content and/or musical references, include *Forms of Emptiness* for three SATB choirs (1986) which references the Heart Sutra, probably the best-known scripture expounding the emptiness of the aggregates and all other possible formations; *Tranquil Abiding* (1998) for chamber orchestra with gongs, bells, and various other eastern instruments, whose title refers to the power of stable concentration that can be achieved after much meditative practice; and two 'Buddhist songs' for mezzo-soprano and piano (2003/4) setting texts from the long Shantideva poem (the *Bodhicaryāvatāra* or *Guide to the Bodhisattva's Way of Life*) which Glass also drew on for his Fifth Symphony. However, perhaps even more interesting are the methods Harvey deploys to reach deeply into the third level of the musical material and create structures that are analogous with certain inspired or revelatory states of mind. These are nicely showcased in his *One Evening* (1994) for two voices, chamber ensemble, and electronics, where the underlying theme of the texts is the calmness, joy, and even shock that can arise from the insight that reality, others, and oneself are empty of independent existence. The first movement is composed symmetrically around a central pitch axis, a device that Harvey first adopted after struggling to find a sufficiently spiritual means of expression for Jesus's resurrection music in his opera *Passion and Resurrection* (1981). For Harvey the pitch axis gives 'a poised, floating stillness to the harmony', enabling listeners to be 'freed from the dark gravity of bass-oriented music', which for the composer had become associated with ideas of individuality and its passions (J. Harvey 1999: 42, 53).[38] The second movement uses electronics to dissolve a shimmering abstract sound into concrete physical dance rhythms and back again, illustrating the union of the two truths of absolute and relative realities discussed earlier (58–9); the use of electronics is crucial throughout Harvey's oeuvre for symbolizing 'vivid metaphysical experiences' which lie beyond everyday rationality (57).

While some of his compositional techniques are shared with composers such as Stockhausen or Bartók, Harvey's distinctive contribution is the deepening of their introspective significance and, therefore, their philosophical/psychological power and potential benefit. Harvey claims that 'it was not until I came to practise (rather than read about) Buddhist philosophy that I understood how music I love works—and, more importantly, *why* I love it' (J. Harvey 2007: 30). This claim is supported by such insights as how ambiguities of thematic or textural identity (as can be found in music of the entire Western common-practice era) effectively demonstrate the principles of non-self and dependent origination (Harvey 1999: 24). His own *Ritual Melodies* (1990) and *Mortuos Plango, Vivos Voco* (1980) go further in morphing electronically between the timbres of well-defined instrumental characters (J. Harvey 1999: 60–2), in order to demonstrate

> the hide-and-seek process where sounds which you took to be individual, highly charac-
> terized sounds, identities, instruments . . . come in and out of identity. They are highly
> individual beings and yet they are also empty, lacking in inherent existence, just part of
> some whole. (Harvey, interviewed in Whittall 1999: 28)

The explicit identification Harvey makes between sound and consciousness is apparent in his instruction to listeners to hear a particular passage from Stockhausen's *Kontakte* as though 'you "are" a line—deconstructed into short impulses, reassembled in transformed guise as meditational, spaced-out self . . . and eventually your self-hood is destroyed in deep crashes of sound' (J. Harvey 1999: 22). This identification with the music is necessary for the heuristic purpose of perceiving our own emptiness through it—hence 'we love some music because it presents us with a *representation* of illusions seen through—we comprehend musical entities as the projections they really are' (J. Harvey 2007: 31). Many more examples of such insights could be presented, but the sources already cited give ample scope for further exploration and reflection. Thus for Harvey, music, mind and Buddhist insights are inextricably connected:

> Music links to meditation in that it is in some sense a picture not of an object but of
> wisdom, an explanation even of how mind works. Forms build in 'mental space', the fine
> forms of a Beethoven or a Boulez; yet these are ultimately emptinesses, kept in memory
> alone, in the mind. (38)

Not only can different types of music, then, arise out of Buddhist perceptions, but even the music with which we are already familiar can appear in new and striking ways when seen from this perspective. Thanks to commentators such as Cage and Harvey, it can be possible to develop insight into the habitual workings of our consciousness by observing the way our mind conceptualizes music—even if this turns out to demand a meditation-like approach to pursue in any depth.

Reflections

The development of insights into consciousness through meditative practice (or merely through music-related introspection) provides an alternative epistemological avenue to that provided by materialistic neuroscience—which arguably cannot observe consciousness itself but at best a physical correlate of its processes in the brain (Wallace 2007). Yet although introspection is the only way that it is possible to experience consciousness or know of its existence, mainstream science and many consciousness theorists have fought shy of engaging with such methods, even rejecting outright that there is anything worth observing. Why is this? Alan Wallace points out that in Western society we generally take on trust the findings of modern experimental science (even though we have not personally verified them) due to its cultural dominance and its assurance that these experiments are repeatable by those with the right equipment, training, and opportunity. Likewise, in cultures where contemplative meditative experience is prized and validated, most people respect and trust the findings of experts in this approach, and are confident that if they were to engage in the same process they would eventually discover the same insights (Wallace 2000: 184). The difference between the two cases is that the scientific method may appear to be objective and public, and the meditative method subjective and private; but in fact a similar process of opportunity, training, enculturation, and application must be followed to achieve authority in either case. Furthermore, quantum physics has undermined the notion that there is an objective world that can be observed directly without the involvement of the senses and the mind which observe it; a little reflection makes it evident that 'the very concept of the "real external world" of everyday thinking rests exclusively on sense impressions' (68)—those of the scientists and other members of the same culture who observe it. Max Velmans has argued this point at length,[39] concluding that 'we each live in our own private, phenomenal world', and that public phenomena can only be agreed upon on the basis of shared similar experiences (Velmans 1999: 302–3). In this sense, reductive scientific approaches provide no greater assurance of rationality or objectivity than any other, and are in no position to dismiss alternative forms of insight that may take a different path towards the study of consciousness. It is for this reason that Wallace has urged the use of experienced contemplatives within a new discipline of consciousness studies:

> What is needed . . . is a discipline, embracing a range of modes of scientific inquiry into the nature of consciousness, that takes firsthand experience seriously and devises means of exploring it with scientific precision. Such a discipline has the potential to be profoundly contemplative as well as rigorously scientific, and I believe it is the most promising, pluralistic mode of inquiry for discovering deep truths concerning consciousness and its role in the natural world. (Wallace 2000: 13)

In distinguishing established meditative methods from more pragmatic approaches to introspection, Varela and Shear (1999a: 7) conclude that 'enough useful results are already at hand to make a case that such first-person methods are not a chimera'.

Buddhism, then, has a rather different epistemology from the mainstream of Western scientific, philosophic, or academic thinking (which is what also makes it challenging to discuss in the present context): it provides meditative experiments to be carried out in one's own experience, the results of which cannot be communicated through linguistic description alone if one does not have the flavour of experience (or 'qualia') to match to it. This experiential approach to knowledge, of course, is not restricted to Buddhism, nor even to the contemplative strands of other religions:[40] the Western philosophical tradition of phenomenology founded by the writings of Edmund Husserl (1859–1938) has some potential resonances with meditational practice.[41] However, apart from the fact that Buddhism pre-dates modern Western philosophical writings by up to 2500 years and may well have had some influence upon them,[42] Buddhism (along with other ancient Indian yogic traditions better described as Hindu) more practically presents several sets of explicit methodologies in a thorough theoretical framework and has an established tradition of practising them which is not a predominant feature of recent secular disciplines in general.[43] Similarly the philosophical notions of non-self and dependent origination, distinctive and central to Buddhist thought, might appear to have some resonances with the views of European poststructuralists and psychoanalytic theorists such as Lacan who emphasize that the subject is neither unified nor the origin of meaning (Belsey 2002: 65–6). However, the outcome of this type of philosophy, being so resolutely wedded to the world as we know it (in Buddhist terms, *saṃsāra*), appears to entirely lack or even forestall any soteriological or transcendent possibilities: whereas in Buddhist theory suffering can be cured by the removal of craving and ignorance, for Lacan desire is a structural part of being human 'and thus a perpetual condition' (Belsey 2002: 59). Perhaps the most happy resonance is with contemporary physics, whose investigations seem to have propelled some towards a partial realization of the lack of inherent existence and the ways in which mind constitutes reality at the quantum level (Ricard and Xuan Thuan 2001), even though matter still constitutes its primary focus of interest.

What, then, can Buddhist perspectives contribute towards our understanding of music or consciousness? At the least, a knowledge of Buddhist thinking on consciousness can illuminate the way that a new approach to sonic materials has radicalized Western art music since the 1950s, and suggest fresh insights into all kinds of music through observing our mental processes in response to it. At its most ambitious, insight and awareness into a Buddhist view of sound, if developed to a high level, has the potential to reveal profound truths about the nature of existence, and even to facilitate significant changes in the structure of consciousness. Such theories and practices that show us new ways to perceive the nature of sound, of consciousness, and of reality itself suggest how the elusiveness of music can be turned to good account.[44]

Acknowledgements

Grateful thanks to Ian Biddle, David Clarke, Eric Clarke, Paul Fleet, Jonathan Harvey, Sean McMenamin, Nagapriya, Jonathan O'Flaherty, Catherine Reding, Sagaramati, and Claire Taylor-Jay for their helpful comments and encouragement.

References

Abelson, P. (1993). Schopenhauer and Buddhism. *Philosophy East and West*, **43**, 255–78.

Adams, J. (2008). *Hallelujah Junction: Composing an American Life* (London: Faber and Faber).

Allison, H.E. (2006). Kant's transcendental idealism, in G. Bird (ed.) *A Companion to Kant*, 111–24 (Oxford: Blackwell).

Baars, B.J. (1997). *In the Theater of Consciousness: The Workspace of the Mind* (Oxford: Oxford University Press).

Belsey, C. (2002). *Poststructuralism: A Very Short Introduction* (Oxford: Oxford University Press).

Berzin, A. and Dalai Lama, H.H. (1997). *The Gelug/Kagyü Tradition of Mahamudra* (Ithaca, NY: Snow Lion Publications).

Blackmore, S. (2003). *Consciousness: An Introduction* (London: Hodder and Stoughton).

Blackmore, S. (2005). *Consciousness: A Very Short Introduction* (Oxford: Oxford University Press).

Blofield, J. (1977). *Bodhisattva of Compassion: The Mystical Tradition of Kuan Yin* (Boston, MA: Shambala Publications).

Bodhi, B. trans. (2000). *The Connected Discourses of the Buddha: A Translation of the Saṃyutta Nikāya* (Somerville, MA: Wisdom Publications).

Brown, D. (2006). *Pointing Out the Great Way: The Stages of Meditation in the Mahamudra Tradition* (Somerville, MA: Wisdom Publications).

Cage, J. (1961). *Silence: Lectures and Writings* (London: Marion Boyars).

Cage, J. (1969). Julliard lecture [1952], in *A Year from Monday*, 95–111 (Middletown, CT: Wesleyan University Press).

Campbell, M. and Greated C. (1987). *The Musician's Guide to Acoustics* (London: J.M. Dent and Sons).

Chalmers, D.J. (1995). Facing up to the problem of consciousness. *Journal of Consciousness Studies 2*, 200–19. Also available at: www.imprint.co.uk/chalmers.html (accessed 18 August 2010).

Chalmers, D.J. (2002). *Philosophy of Mind: Classical and Contemporary Readings* (New York, NY: Oxford University Press).

Conze, E. (2001). *Buddhist Wisdom: The Diamond Sutra and the Heart Sutra* (New York, NY: Vintage Books).

Cook, N. (1990). *Music, Imagination and Culture* (Oxford: Clarendon Press).

Cousins, L.S. (1996). The dating of the historical Buddha: a review article. *Journal of the Royal Asiatic Society*, Third Series, **6**, 57–63. Available at: http://indology.info/papers/cousins/ (accessed 18 August 2010).

Dalai Lama, H.H. and Hopkins, J. (2000). *The Meaning of Life: Buddhist Perspectives on Cause and Effect* (Somerville, MA: Wisdom Publications).

Das, L.S. (2003). *Letting Go of the Person You Used to Be: Lessons on Change, Loss and Spiritual Transformation* (London: Bantam Books).

Dharmarakshita. (1973). *The Wheel of Sharp Weapons*, trans. A. Berzin *et al*. Available at: www.berzinarchives.com/web/x/nav/n.html_1952435027.html (accessed 13 September 2010).

Epstein, D. (1995). A curious moment in Schumann's Fourth Symphony, in J. Rink (ed.) *The Practice of Performance: Studies in Musical Interpretation*, 126–49 (Cambridge: Cambridge University Press).

Glass, P. (1988). *Opera on the Beach: On His New World of Music Theatre* (London: Faber and Faber).

Gyatso, G.K. (1996). *Heart of Wisdom: The Essential Wisdom Teachings of Buddha* (London: Tharpa Publications).

Gyatso, G.K. (2000). *Eight Steps to Happiness: The Buddhist Way of Loving Kindness* (Ulverston: Tharpa Publications).

Gyatso, G.K. (2005). *Mahamudra Tantra: The Supreme Heart Jewel Nectar* (Ulverston: Tharpa Publications).

Harvey, J. (1999). *In Quest of Spirit: Thoughts on Music* (Berkeley, CA: University of California Press).

Harvey, J. (2007). Buddhism and the undecidability of music, in J. Harvey and J.-C. Carrière, *Circles of Silence*, 29–38 (Lewes: Sylph Editions).

Harvey, P. (1990). *An Introduction to Buddhism: Teachings, History and Practices* (Cambridge: Cambridge University Press).

Harvey, P. (1993). The mind–body relationship in Pāli Buddhism: a philosophical investigation. *Asian Philosophy*, **3**, 29–41.

Harvey, P. (1995). *The Selfless Mind: Personality, Consciousness and Nirvāṇa in Early Buddhism* (London: Routledge Curzon).

Hassler, J.F.W. (2010). *Towards Hermeticist Grammars of Music: A Proposal for Systems of Composition based on the Principles of the Hermetic Tradition, with Musical Demonstrations* (PhD. diss.: University of Newcastle upon Tyne).

Husserl, E. (1965). Philosophy and the crisis of European man [1936], in *Phenomenology and the Crisis of Philosophy*, trans. Q. Lauer, 149–92 (New York, NY: Harper and Row).

Ireland, J. (1997). *The Udāna and The Itivuttaka* (Kandy, Sri Lanka: Buddhist Publication Society).

King, W.L. (1964). *In the Hope of Nibbana: The Ethics of Theravada Buddhism* (LaSalle, IL: Open Court).

Kinsley, D.R. (1986). *Hindu Goddesses: Visions of the Divine Feminine in the Hindu Religious Tradition* (Delhi: Motilal Banarsidass).

Kostelanetz, R. (ed.) (1989). *Conversing with Cage* (London: Routledge).

Kostelanetz, R. (1997). *Writings on Glass: Essays, Interviews, Criticism* (Berkeley, CA: University of California Press).

Kramer, J.D. (1988). *The Time of Music: New Meanings, New Temporalities, New Listening Strategies* (New York, NY: Schirmer Books).

Laywine, A. (2006). Kant's laboratory of ideas in the 1770s, in Graham Bird (ed.) *A Companion to Kant*, 63–78 (Oxford: Blackwell Publishing).

Lowe, B. (2003). On the relationship between analysis and performance: the mediatory role of the interpretation. *Indiana Theory Review*, **24**, 47–94.

Luk, C. [Lu K'uan Yü], trans. (1966). *The Śūraṅgama Sūtra (Leng Yen Ching)* (London: Rider). Also available at: www.buddhanet.net/pdf_file/surangama.pdf (pagination altered; accessed 18 August 2010).

Mabbett, I.W. (1993/4). Buddhism and Music. *Asian Music*, **25**, 9–28.

Mackenzie, V. (2003). *Why Buddhism? Westerners in Search of Wisdom* (London: Thorsons).

May, T. (2006). *The John Adams Reader: Essential Writings on an American Composer* (Pompton Plains, NJ: Amadeus Press).

Maycock, R. (2002). *Glass: A Portrait* (London: Sanctuary Publishing).

Mertens, W. (1983). *American Minimal Music: LaMonte Young, Terry Riley, Steve Reich, Philip Glass* (London: Kahn and Averill).

Nagapriya (2004). *Exploring Karma and Rebirth* (Birmingham: Windhorse Publications).

Ñāṇamoli, B. and Bodhi, B. (trans. and ed.) (1995). *The Middle Length Discourses of the Buddha: A Translation of the Majjhima Nikāya* (Somerville, MA: Wisdom Publications).

Nhat Hanh, T. (1999). *The Heart of the Buddha's Teaching: Transforming Suffering into Peace, Joy, and Liberation* (London: Rider).

Nyanaponika T. and Bodhi, B. (trans. and ed.) (1999). *Numerical Discourses of the Buddha: An Anthology of Suttas from the Aṅguttara Nikāya* (Walnut Creek, CA: Altamira Press).

Patel, A.D. (2007). *Music, Language, and the Brain* (New York, NY: Oxford University Press).

Patterson, D.W. (2002). Cage and Asia: history and sources, in D. Nicholls (ed.) *The Cambridge Companion to Cage*, 41–59 (Cambridge: Cambridge University Press).

Pritchett, J. and Kuhn, L. (2010). Cage, John, in *Grove Music Online* (Oxford Music Online). Available at: www.oxfordmusiconline.com/subscriber/article/grove/music/49908 (accessed 8 October 2010).

Rabten, G. (2005). *The Mind and its Functions* (Mont-Pèlerin: Edition Rabten).

Rao, K.R. (1998). Two faces of consciousness: a look at Eastern and Western perspectives. *Journal of Consciousness Studies*, **5**, 309–27.

Rhys Davids, T.W. and Stede, W. (1925/1992). *Pali–English Dictionary* (Oxford: The Pali Text Society).

Ricard, M. and Xuan Thuan, T. (2001). *The Quantum and the Lotus* (New York, NY: Three Rivers Press).

Richardson, J. (1999). *Singing Archaeology: Philip Glass's Akhnaten* (Hanover: Wesleyan University Press).

Sangharakshita (1998). *What is the Dharma? The Essential Teachings of the Buddha* (Birmingham: Windhorse Publications).

Sangharakshita (2004). *Living with Kindness: The Buddha's Teaching on Mettā* (Birmingham: Windhorse Publications).

Skilton, A. (1994). *A Concise History of Buddhism* (Birmingham: Windhorse Publications).

Small, C. (1998). *Musicking: The Meanings of Performing and Listening* (Middletown, CT: Wesleyan University Press).

Ṭhānissaro B. (trans.) (1993). Dhammacakkappavattanna Sutta, *Samyutta Nikaya* 56.11. Available at: www.accesstoinsight.org/tipitaka/sn/sn56/sn56.011.than.html (accessed 19 August 2010).

Ṭhānissaro B. (trans.) (1994). Bahiya Sutta, *Udāna* 1.10. Available at: www.accesstoinsight.org/tipitaka/kn/ud/ud.1.10.than.html (accessed 19 August 2010).

Ṭhānissaro B. (trans.) (1997). Sona Sutta, *Aṅguttara Nikāya* 6.55. Available at: www.accesstoinsight.org/tipitaka/an/an06/an06.055.than.html (accessed 19 August 2010).

Ṭhānissaro B. (trans.) (1998). Vina Sutta, *Samyutta Nikāya* 35.205. Available at: www.accesstoinsight.org/tipitaka/sn/sn35/sn35.205.than.html (accessed 19 August 2010).

Tsering, G.T. (2005). *The Four Noble Truths*, The Foundation of Buddhist Thought, vol. 1 (Somerville, MA: Wisdom Publications).

Tsering, G.T. (2006). *Buddhist Psychology*, The Foundation of Buddhist Thought, vol. 3 (Somerville, MA: Wisdom Publications).

Varela, F.J. and Shear J. (1999a). First-person methodologies: what, why, how? in F.J. Varela and J. Shear (eds.) *The View from Within: First-Person Approaches to the Study of Consciousness*, 1–14 (Bowling Green, OH: Imprint Academic).

Varela, F.J. and Shear J. (eds.) (1999b). *The View from Within: First-Person Approaches to the Study of Consciousness* (Bowling Green, OH: Imprint Academic).

Varela, F.J., Thompson, E., and Rosch, E. (1993). *The Embodied Mind: Cognitive Science and Human Experience* (Cambridge, MA: The MIT Press).

Velmans, M. (1999). Intersubjective science, in F.J. Varela and J. Shear (eds.) *The View from Within: First-Person Approaches to the Study of Consciousness*, 299–306 (Bowling Green, OH: Imprint Academic).

Vessantara (2003). *Meeting the Buddhas: A Guide to Buddhas, Bodhisattvas, and Tantric Deities* (Birmingham: Windhorse Publications).

Wallace, B.A. (2000). *The Taboo of Subjectivity: Toward a New Science of Consciousness* (Oxford: Oxford University Press).

Wallace, B.A. (2007). Materialism of the gaps. *Mandala: A Tibetan Buddhist Journal*, December 2006/January 2007, 8–10.

Whittall, A. (1999). *Jonathan Harvey* (London: Faber and Faber).

Williams, P. (2000). *Buddhist Thought: A Complete Introduction to the Indian Tradition* (London: Routledge).

Williams, S. (2006). Buddhism and Music, in G.L. Beck (ed.) *Sacred Sound: Experiencing Music in World Religions* (Waterlook, Ontario, Canada: Wilfred Laurier University Press).

Woodward, F.L. (trans.) (1948). *The Minor Anthologies of the Pali Canon, Part II. Udāna: Verses of Uplift, and Itivuttaka: As it was Said* (London: Geoffrey Cumberlege, Oxford University Press).

Yeshe, L. (2001). *Introduction to Tantra: The Transformation of Desire* (Somerville, MA: Wisdom Publications).

Notes

1. Ṭhānissaro's translation preserves the musical metaphor for the Buddha's conclusion. A more literal rendering can be found in Nyanaponika and Bodhi (1999: 168).

2. An introduction to the life of the Buddha can be found in P. Harvey (1990: 1–2, 9, 14–27); and in P. Williams (2000: 1–6, 21–30). More scholarly specifics on the dating of the Buddha's life and 50-year teaching career are given in Cousins (1996).

3. An account of the development and nuances of the various Buddhist schools goes beyond the scope of this paper but can be found in Skilton (1994) and P. Williams (2000).

4. Blackmore (2003: 7–14 and *passim*) presents an introduction to these issues, while Chalmers (2002: 1–9 and *passim*) provides further discussion and examples, though neglecting idealist perspectives.

5. Translations of the Pali terms in Figure 7.1 are from Bodhi (2000: 518–19), though Sangharakshita (1998: 41–8) is also instructive (and gives the Sanskrit equivalents).

6. For more on how this process works, see P. Williams (2000: 62–74) (part of a useful introductory chapter on the ideas of mainstream Buddhism), Bodhi (2000: 516–25), and Dalai Lama and Hopkins (2000). The system is generally considered to illustrate salient qualities and their consequences through three cycles of life, with consciousness (iii) and existence (x) being the linking factors.

7. Although we are all resolved that we cannot know exactly 'what it is like to be a bat' (or an ant or a flatfish), we can only imagine that it is rather different—and still more so for beings in other Buddhist 'realms' of existence, due to their rather different karmic seeds and experiences (see P. Harvey 1990: 32–6; P. Williams 2000: 74–81).

8. This view is akin to the understanding of the maverick Cittamatrin school of Buddhism (see P. Harvey 1990: 104–7, 109–10; P. Williams 2000: 154–5). It should be borne in mind that the Cittamatrin view in particular is considered to have an heuristic rather than an ultimately ontological function.

9. *Nāma–rūpa* (iv) includes mental factors (discussed below) as well as physical form, and is sometimes translated 'mind and body' (P. Harvey 1993: 29–33) or 'materiality–mentality' (Ñāṇamoli and Bodhi 1995/2005: 56–7).

10. This scheme is also discussed in by Ansuman Biswas in Chapter 6.

11. I have provided the Sanskrit terms for the aggregates, as their etymology is easier to see and because they are arguably more commonly found (as in Nagapriya 2004: 85, and Conze 2001: 86–8) than the similar Pali terms from which the primary sources have been translated. The Pali equivalents (respectively *rūpa, vedanā, saññā, saṅkhārā*, and *viññāṇa*) and some further definitions can be found in the general introduction to the *Majjhima Nikāya* (Ñāṇamoli and Bodhi 1995/2005: 26–7); note how four of these terms also appear in the causal chain illustrated in Figure 7.1. A useful introduction to the nature and significance of the aggregates can be found in Bhikkhu Bodhi's introduction to 'The Book of the Aggregates' (in Bodhi 2000: 839–48). I have mostly adopted Bodhi's choices of English terms for the aggregates, but have preferred 'discernment' for the third aggregate (as in Tsering 2006: 30–2) rather than 'perception' to avoid confusion with the perceptual function of the fifth aggregate. More details of the aggregates' individual functioning are presented in P. Harvey (1995: 138–54).

12. Although this definition puts the consciousness of human beings on a somewhat lower level of existence than we may be used to imagining from a Western perspective, there is in fact a parallel in the transcendental idealism of Kant, where 'human intellectual finitude manifests itself precisely in the fact that we engage in empirical thought [whereas] God does not have experience' (Laywine 2006: 68). The difference is that in Buddhism one can aspire to the full and direct knowledge of reality that a Buddha has, whereas in Kant's philosophy a God's eye view is considered unattainable (Allison 2006: 114).

13. Contemporary neuropsychology has recognized this issue in the form of the perceptual 'binding problem', namely how we fuse different kinds of sensory input to create a single percept; answers to this puzzle in terms of brain areas, however, remain speculative and hence controversial within the field (see Baars 1997: 71–2).

14. Cook (1990: 66) points out that 'most people can probably recall occasions on which they were so gripped by a piece of music that they listened intently and energetically to the unfolding of the entire work from start to finish', adding that such absorption may be the most rewarding type of engagement with music but is not the most prevalent in practice.

15. The general operation of the mental factors and the main minds is neatly outlined in Tsering (2006: 21–37). A more detailed picture including the types of mental factor that can arise is provided in Rabten (2005: 126–95). The factors typically explored in detail by Buddhist textbooks are those crucial to the success of meditation and ethical practice; however, it seems that the category subsumes any imaginable emotional reaction, since 'generally speaking, there are innumerable mental factors' (Rabten 2005: 129). Such detailed presentation of Buddhist psychology is strongly developed in the Tibetan tradition of which these authors form a part, but their understanding is based on earlier Indian commentaries on the Abhidharma, which is the third principal division of the Pali canon and constitutes a schematic summary of the material found in the canonical Suttas.

16. The same overall point is made in Bodhi (2000: 516–17).

17. An alternative translation of the *Udāna*, from which this passage is taken, is provided by John Ireland. His rendering of the passage quoted here reads: 'In the seen will be merely what is seen; in the heard will be merely what is heard [etc.]. . . . Just this is the end of suffering' (Ireland 1997: 21). The version used in my title, 'in the heard[,] only the heard',

is that commonly used by the Friends of the Western Buddhist Order and seems to have been formulated by their founder Sangharakshita some time in the late 1960s or 70s (it turns up, for instance, in Sangharakshita 2004: 61). The pioneering translation by Woodward—'in the heard just the heard' (1948: 10)—is likely to have been influential.

18. There is a scholarly query over this word *muta* (rendered here as 'the sensed'). Although its proximity to the more etymologically clear *mata* have led some to speculate that it may indicate a mental rather than a sense consciousness, predominant opinion seems clear that its context in a range of sources indicates 'received by other vaguer sense impressions than by sight and hearing' (Rhys Davids and Stede 1992: 536). The meaning of the previous term, *suta*, as 'the heard' is unambiguous.

19. Neurological experiments with music suggest that significant mental processing can take place without focusing primarily on words, since the areas of the brain that are activated by musical experience and verbal input overlap only partially. Epstein (1995: 128–30) summarizes the argument and the literature, while Patel (2007: 72–8) reports on recent scholarly investigations in this area, concluding that 'musical and linguistic sound categories are acoustically distinct and neurally dissociable in the adult brain' (77). This suggests that mental awareness and representation more generally are not necessarily dependent upon verbal functioning.

20. 'A chain is only as strong as its weakest link. So where is the nidana chain [of the twelve links] weakest?. . . . The crucial point is where, in dependence upon *vedana*, feeling, arises *trishna* [Pali: *taṇhā*], craving' (Sangharakshita 1998: 106).

21. Rabten defines attachment as 'a distinct mental factor that, when referring to a contaminated [i.e. everyday] phenomenon overexaggerates [*sic*] its attractiveness and then proceeds to wish for and take a strong interest in it'. Attachment 'develops out of our misconceiving an object to be more attractive and agreeable than it really is' and 'acts as a basis for the continued production of discontent' (2005: 170).

22. The Buddha gave the essence of his main teaching on the ending of suffering many times, but the first and most famous is in the 'Dhammacakkappavattana Sutta', *Samyutta Nikāya* 56.11 (translations in Bodhi 2000: 1843–47 and Ṭhānissaro 1993). Tsering (2005) provides an extensive commentary on the sutta.

23. Bodhi adds that the aggregates 'creat[e] the appearance of selfhood through their causal continuity and interdependent functioning'. But it is not that the Buddha posits a self outside and beyond the five aggregates: 'The notion of selfhood, treated as an ultimate, he regards as a product of ignorance, and all the diverse attempts to substantiate this notion by identifying it with some aspect of the personality he describes as "clinging to a doctrine of self"' (Ñāṇamoli and Bodhi 1995: 28). Other helpful and concise insights into non-self include P. Harvey (1990: 50–3), Dalai Lama and Hopkins (2000: 53–4), and Nagapriya (2004: 84–91).

24. The approaches of various world traditions to the problem of locating and identifying the self are considered in Varela *et al.* (1993: 59–64), along with useful reflections on the idea of non-self.

25. 'Mahātaṇhasankhaya Sutta', *Majjhima Nikāya* 38 (Ñāṇamoli and Bodhi 1995/2005: 349–50). Nonetheless this does not imply a swing to the nihilistic view that death represents the end of our 'mental continuum', since the causal process of rebirth is still in operation in dependence upon intentional actions as already described.

26. 'Vina Sutta', *Samyutta Nikāya* 35.205 (Ṭhānissaro 1998). The sutta can also be found in Bodhi (2000: 1253–4).

27. The sutta continues: 'In the same way, a monk investigates form, however far form may go. He investigates feeling . . . perception . . . fabrications . . . consciousness, however far consciousness may go. As he is investigating form . . . feeling . . . perception . . . fabrications . . . consciousness, however far consciousness may go, any thoughts of "me" or "mine" or "I am" do not occur to him' (Ṭhānissaro 1998).

28. This observation is prefigured in my article on musical 'interpretation' (Lowe 2003: 52–9), where I use this term to mean the notion of a piece that one holds in one's mind and on which one draws to create a performance or analytical account; many past influences have formed such a mental construct which is hence dependently originated.

29. In explaining emptiness here Harvey also compares modern physics with classical physics as a means of beginning to gain an insight into the fluidity of reality, 'with particles not being real separate entities, but provisional conceptual designations' (P. Harvey 1990: 100).

30. Williams' initial account of emptiness (P. Williams 2000: 134–36) veers dangerously close to nihilism, in order, as he admits (261 n. 3), to emphasize its radical, even disturbing import. However, the concept receives a more nuanced reading during his examination of Madhyamaka philosophy (140–52).

31. Alan Wallace (2000: 67) points out that perceptions may be valid for a particular person at a particular time (e.g. personal preferences); for a specific human society/culture (e.g. laws, aesthetics); for certain species (e.g. the pungent taste of ginger, the rough texture of wool cloth); or for all conscious beings (possibly the laws of mathematics) though this category is hard to postulate confidently. The perception of these sounds as some kind of music appears to hover between the second and third of these categories.

32. The trajectory of the overall practice is encapsulated by Rangjung Dorjé (1284–1339): 'Let me understand the mind's clear light and the way the realized mind stays: / By viewing sense objects, but seeing them not as sense objects, but as mind, / By viewing the mind, not as mind, but as an empty entity' ('The Mahamudra Devotional Prayer', quoted in Brown 2006: 478).

33. In the online version of Luk's translation the equivalent page numbers are 191–2 and 197–212. In both versions the section is entitled 'Meditation on the organ of hearing'.

34. Philip Glass insists that it was not yoga that introduced him to Buddhism; rather 'it was through John Cage that I knew anything at all, through his book *Silence*' (Kostelanetz 1997: 316). John Adams was given a copy of the book as a graduation present and recalled that 'I read *Silence* and its sequel, *A Year from Monday*, and I kept going back to them almost as if they were sacred texts' (Adams 2008: 56); in his early career he was 'a devout follower of Cage' partly because 'many of Cage's philosophical interests like Zen and Buckminster Fuller appealed to me' (May 2006: 12, 10). My own first exposure to Buddhist ideas was likewise through Cage's *Silence*.

35. Cage enjoyed ambient sound and argued for the dissolution of any distinction between ambient sound and music: speaking of background drones such as that of the refrigerator, he commented 'I'm beginning to enjoy those sounds, I mean that I now actually listen to them with the kind of enjoyment with which I listen to the traffic', adding that 'the traffic is easy to recognise as beautiful' (Kostelanetz 1989: 97).

36. Kramer (1988: 376), quoting Glass in Mertens (1983: 79).

37. The three levels outlined here are adapted from a schema delineated by Johann Hassler (where they are labelled aesthetic, symbolic, and speculative levels, respectively) in an account of speculative music that expresses occult themes (Hassler 2010: §1.2.3). As a comparison, it seems that Glass's music references mostly the first level, since his musical style generally remains unaffected by the type of texts he is setting, while the impact on Cage's music is entirely on the third, more abstract level of constructional principles.

38. The issue for Harvey here is the predominance of the ideas of the individual and his/her passions that have been thematic for opera since its origins around the year 1600, and the concurrent rise of figured bass as a vehicle to express those passions (see also Chapter 20, this volume). Harvey compares this with earlier and non-Western methods of construction that tend to be 'less centred and emotionally dependent on some tonic' (Harvey, in Whittall 1999: 19).

39. Velmans asks us to imagine a 'subject' observing a lightbulb who is in turn observed by an experimenter. Conventionally these would be assumed to be operating in the subjective and objective modes, respectively. But if they now change places, can the experimenter maintain the same objectivity and (unlike the previous subject) see the light bulb in an objective way? If not, how did this person acquire the ability previously to view the subject in a supposedly objective way? Hence the distinction between these modes is a false one (Velmans 1999: 300–2, paraphrased vividly in Blackmore 2003: 380–1).

40. My focus here is on the philosophies and methods of Buddhism, but these inevitably have much in common with those of Hinduism in particular: see Chapter 8.

41. Various articles and responses in Varela and Shear (1999b) debate the possibility of using the phenomenological *epoché* or reduction as a first-person approach to the study of consciousness.

42. It is commonly accepted that there was dialogue between Indian systems of thought such as Buddhism and the Greek philosophies in which the Western tradition has its roots (due partly to the expansionist activities of rulers such as Alexander the Great and the Indian emperor Aśoka), though it is probably impossible to reconstruct the complicated network of influence. Only much later are the philosophical connections revitalized. For example, Arthur Schopenhauer (1788–1860), who had a pervasive influence on later European philosophy, was actively inspired by the Hindu Upaniṣads but later claimed that the similarity between his philosophy and that of Buddhism was a happy coincidence (Abelson 1993); nonetheless this does make it clear that accounts of Buddhism were entering the Western intellectual world in the mid-nineteenth century.

43. As Rao (1998: 323) points out, 'the *epoché* . . . falls short of reaching its logical end of realizing pure consciousness', partly because phenomenologists follow Husserl in treating his method 'as a logico-epistemological tool rather than a practical method'. Husserl himself distinguished his own basis in the Western tradition, with its origins in Greek philosophy, from 'Indian, Chinese, and other philosophies' which he categorized as mythical–religious rather than theoretical (1965: 164, 164–73).

44. It is customary within Buddhist texts to acknowledge the archetypal Buddha figures who personify the positive qualities invoked there. Thus in the current context one might mention Manjushri, representing wisdom and thus aspects of the mind; Vajrasattva, the manifestation of purified consciousness; and Saraswati, the goddess of intelligence, music, and spiritual practice (see Kinsley 1986: 55–64; Vessantara 2003: 149–58, 229–40, 325 n. 49). The meditative *sādhanā* practice relating to each of these figures (Vessantara 2003: 155–6, *passim*) has been beneficial in the preparation of this chapter.

Chapter 8

North Indian classical music and its links with consciousness: the case of dhrupad

David Clarke and Tara Kini

Introduction

While the seemingly new Western discipline of consciousness studies wrestles with its problems of definition and methodology, it is salutary to note that consciousness has been a near continuous concern—in both theory and practice—in Eastern cultures for much of their history. This is certainly true of India, whose spiritual and religious belief systems have identified the passage from more mundane to higher states of consciousness as a moral aspiration since at least the time of the Upaniṣads. Links between these systems and India's various art forms are often invoked in discussions of aesthetics at large, yet consciousness itself has rarely been an explicit or extensively treated topic in contemporary accounts of Indian music (at least in Western musicology), just as consciousness studies seems to have overlooked this music (as most others) as a source of potential insight; hence in this chapter we seek to redress this neglected connection and pursue its implications. Our contention is that Indian classical music both emanates from and is able to instil deep states of consciousness, and that it is discursively grounded in ideas about consciousness consistent, even if not coterminous, with concepts from longstanding Indian philosophical traditions.[1] Our focus is on North Indian (Hindustani) classical music, since—with our differing levels of experience and expertise—we are ourselves practitioners in this field. While we both practise the khyāl vocal style, and draw on this here, our principal case study is the older style known as dhrupad (in which we also share an interest), since this most powerfully illustrates the cultivation of deeply meditative states. Such states can be most notably located in renditions of ālāp—the improvised opening phase of a rāga performance that is common to dhrupad, khyāl, and other styles, but is especially developed in dhrupad.

Our approach has two main strands, one informally ethnographic, the other broadly philosophical. The first draws on a body of interview and questionnaire material gathered principally by TK, while the second interprets these in the light of philosophical and aesthetic accounts in an analysis constructed primarily by DC (though our roles have inevitably overlapped). Participants in the questionnaires and interviews include both listeners to and professional performers of dhrupad. An important institution in this work has been the Dhrupad Sansthan Gurukul at Bhopal—an institute for the teaching of dhrupad founded by the Gundecha brothers, Umakant and Ramakant, who are regarded as leading dhrupad vocalists of the present day.[2] The Gundechas are among the interviewees consulted, and they have welcomed both of us as participant–observers at their gurukul. While ethnography and philosophy may not be regular companions, our point is that many of the underlying cultural assumptions of dhrupad are indeed philosophical—allowing for a necessarily flexible definition of the term. In other words, it is an anthropological fact that those involved in Indian classical music (as performers or listeners) will tend to relate their deepest experiences of it to a spiritually informed worldview, in which philosophy and religion are not rigidly distinct categories. That this worldview maintains currency within a modernizing society well aware of rationality and materialism may be due to what Richard Lannoy describes as the *hylozoistic* nature of Indian culture: the monistic inclination 'to draw no clear distinction between matter, life, and mind' (1971: 272).

A further ingredient in our account is an outline of certain key features of Indian classical music generally (e.g. the concept of *rāga*) and of dhrupad in particular, as well as a sketch of related historical and contextual issues. While this may sometimes necessitate an apparent divergence from the core topic of consciousness, some minimal description of the processes and practices of our musical object of inquiry is necessary in order to portray the kind of phenomenon in which this consciousness inheres. That said, we are of course not able to generate in words the actual musical experience (the qualia) of dhrupad itself; and for that, readers unfamiliar with the music are directed towards numerous commercially available and streamable recordings.[3]

Dhrupad and the concept of *mārga*

Dhrupad is the most ancient form of Hindustani classical music still practised today. For this reason among others it enjoys particularly elevated status, often regarded as the epitome of classical practice. While many of its exponents have been players of the bīn (also known as vīṇa), a kind of stick zither, it is as a vocal genre that dhrupad is especially significant. Its identity is in part articulated in relation to the historically more recent and more romantic vocal style known as khyāl, which began to overtake dhrupad in popularity after around the eighteenth century, yet which draws many of its principles from it (indeed khyāl performers often look to dhrupad as a kind of taproot of their own practice). The consciousness and sensibilities that we associate here with dhrupad need to be understood historically in the light of these and other generic intertwinings.

Writing of 'dhrupad ideology', Ritwik Sanyal and Richard Widdess note: 'When asked the question: what is the objective (*prayojan*) of dhrupad performance, many musicians use the terms *sādhanā* or *upāsanā*, both of which might be translated "worship" or "praise" . . . A related idea is that dhrupad is essentially a form of private contemplation' (2004: 38). Sanyal and Widdess go on to point out that this relates to longstanding distinctions in Indian culture (going back to *c.* 1000 CE) 'between music performed for spiritual benefit according to strict and ancient rules, and music for pleasure to which the rules need not apply so strictly' (39). One version of this distinction is that between *mārga* (lit. 'path'), a disposition towards spiritual well-being or salvation, and *deśi*, regional styles of music and dance aimed at more worldly aesthetic enjoyment (also discussed by Lewis Rowell (1992: 12–13)). Styles such as dhrupad do not sit immutably or unequivocally at any given pole of such schemes, but mutate and are reimagined in the ebb and flow of their own and other genres' histories. A seventeenth-century treatise, Faqīrullāh's *Rāg-darpan*, describes dhrupad's rise to prominence two centuries earlier in the court of Rājā Mān Singh at Gwālior at a time when the earlier *prabandha* style of singing and *mārga* forms were falling out of favour (Mutatkar 1987: 78; Sanyal and Widdess 2004: 47); here dhrupad is depicted as a synthesis of *deśi* and *mārga* elements. At the sixteenth-century court of Akbar the Great, when the genre was in its heyday and the singer Miyān Tānsen achieved near-mythological status as one of its finest exponents, dhrupad was 'a form of refined but essentially secular musical entertainment. It is only as the newer genres of khyāl and ṭhumrī have taken the stage as secular art forms, during the eighteenth and nineteenth centuries, that dhrupad has become, in effect, the current . . . *mārga*, and has therefore taken on a higher, esoteric, salvific function' (Sanyal and Widdess 2004: 40). Even so, qualitative distinctions between such genres remain somewhat blurred or mediated: light-classical forms such as ṭhumrī can be regarded as endowed 'with a substance and beauty' through the influence of dhrupad (Mutatkar 1987: 82), while dhrupad itself is enjoying a resurgence of popularity on the contemporary concert stage, and khyāl arguably sits at a mid-way point, perhaps not unlike dhrupad's synthesis of *deśi* and *mārga* earlier in its history.

Musical concepts: *ālāp, rāga*

Without too much distortion we might posit that the extent to which Indian musical forms engender consciousness consistent with *mārga* is proportional to their foregrounding of *ālāp*, the unmetred melodic improvisation with which most classical performances begin. The significance acquired by an *ālāp* is also in proportion to the section that follows it, known as *bandiś* (in a vocal performance) or *gat* (in an instrumental one). This latter section is based on a short composition around which the artist extemporizes, and is structured by a rhythmic cycle (*tāl*) sustained by percussion. While in khyāl and light-classical genres an *ālāp* serves, broadly speaking, as a short prelude to the more substantial *bandiś* section, in dhrupad the reverse is the case, with an *ālāp* commonly lasting an hour or more, and the *bandiś* (accompanied by pakhāvaj—a barrel drum) relatively truncated, at times almost seeming like a postlude or coda. We know from documents such as the *Sahas-ras* collection of song texts that *ālāp* has been a prominent feature of dhrupad since at least the seventeenth century (see Sanyal and Widdess 2004: 45–6, 50–1). Its subsequent evolution, with its corresponding potential for enhancing contemplative consciousness, would seem to have placed *ālāp* at its heart—hence the focus of the present study.[4]

One of the chief concerns of *ālāp* is with the exposition of the *rāga* on which a performance is based. *Rāga* (also *rāg, raag*), an essential principle of Indian classical music (and indeed of Indian music more widely), needs definition in both technical and aesthetic terms, the latter being ultimately the more important. As Sengupta (1991: 105–6) puts it:

> A *rāga* is normally understood as the basic melodic pattern whether simple or complex, consisting of several notes, either five or six or seven, ... never less than five, in a fixed ascending and descending order ... The progression of notes has a definite structure exhibiting a specific balance, harmony and proportion of the notes thus used ... This is in keeping with the mood or sentiment of the *rāga* which it tends to depict.

Numbering in their hundreds (some would claim thousands), *rāga*s are distinguished from one another not merely by the scale on which they are based, but by the mood which they instil: two *rāga*s based on the same scale—e.g. *Multānī* and *Miyan ki toḍī*, which both employ sharpened fourth and flattened second, third, and sixth degrees— may have a very different feel. Partly this is because each *rāga* has its own grammar, sustaining some scale degrees more than others, foregrounding certain distinctive turns of phrase, perhaps having a particular style of ornamentation. But a *rāga* cannot be created by merely adhering to the rules. In effect each *rāga* is a particular colouration of consciousness, and a *rāga* is achieved when that mode of consciousness is attained.

Without seeking to raise a spectre that haunts Western consciousness studies, we might suggest in passing that each *rāga* presents a different quale, which, like all qualia, exceeds description in third-person informational terms: it has to be known experientially or phenomenally. It is perhaps for this reason that Indian classical music is largely orally transmitted, from guru (teacher or preceptor) to *śiṣya* (also *shishya*; student or disciple). A *rāga* is taught through the cumulative production and ceaseless variation of phrases by the guru, imitated, and eventually also extemporized upon, by the *śiṣya*. This essentially dialogical process alerts us to the fact that qualia might occupy a place other than in the isolation of first-person experience: a *rāga* is co-created in the exchange between individuals physically present to one another; it is a living process and like all living beings its process is its truth.

So too with the unfolding of a *rāga* in performance—only here the relationship obtains between artist and audience. The process of *ālāp* is the means whereby the performer incrementally generates the shared state of consciousness or being that is the *rāga* in question. Accompanied by tānpurā—a large, resonant lute (sonically akin to the sitār) which provides an open-stringed drone—artists characteristically begin by intoning the tonic note, *sā*, in the middle register, then improvise a gradually more complex series of phrases that introduce successively more notes of the *rāga*. The performer might tarry briefly in the lower register, before climbing through the middle register to upper *sā* and a little beyond. The radical expansion of this process in dhrupad allows time for significant focus on the quality of each note. In vocal performances greater attention is often given to the extreme lower register in the initial stage of an *ālāp* than is the case in other genres; male dhrupadiyas are required to develop a robust bottom octave which typically extends to lower C♮3 or C3. But eventually, over the extended course of the *ālāp*, much of a performer's three-octave range will be explored. Also distinctive to dhrupad (where melisma—*akār*—is discouraged) is the use of so-called *nom tom* syllables: semantically void words, such as *te, ta, ra, na, rī, ra, nūm*; indeed dhrupad *ālāp* sometimes goes under the name of *nom tom ālāp*.

Initially these syllables are voiced in phrases based around sustained notes in free, unmeasured rhythm (a style known as *anibaddh*); but by around the half-way stage these are gradually animated in shorter, regular notes to create pulsing patterns—the phase known as *joṛ*—which go through several increases of tempo and other forms of intensification to take the *ālāp* to climactic closure in the phase called *jhālā*.

Dhrupad *ālāp* and listener consciousness

So much for a discussion of dhrupad and its *ālāp* in the abstract. How does this relate to the testimony of actual subjects regarding their own states of consciousness in relation to it? In this section we consider the commentaries of 12 respondents to a questionnaire devised by TK. All of the participants had some familiarity with dhrupad, and ranged from lay listeners to classical music to those who were trained, and some who were performers.[5] They were asked to consider their responses to dhrupad *ālāp* as *listeners*, recollecting their experience of either live or recorded performances. The written responses provided a rich textual base for qualitative analysis, and displayed a number of pertinent common tropes or themes.[6] While no single respondent described a complete phenomenology of listening to dhrupad, their collective testimony revealed a larger image of the consciousness engendered by it; we will attempt to demonstrate how this is congruent with a philosophico-religious outlook deeply rooted in Indian culture and history.

This last point is most explicitly evident in one of the most poetic statements from the lay respondents. As it happens, GS's description of dhrupad *ālāp* is partly a lyrical version of the more technical account given above, but it also imagines this in a framework rich with associations from Indian (more specifically, Hindu) culture:

> In these as in every other Dhrupad vocal alap I listen to, it feels like each note is being awakened and breathed out for the first time ... Along with the slow uncovering of the note, the essential melodic pattern of the raga is also detailed, the part and the whole fusing together seamlessly ...
>
> There is also the connection it arouses with the basic elements of the universe. I don't know how much of this is emotional, how much is based on its origins in the Vedas, on the rigorous physical 'pranic' discipline it entails on the singers. But the early alap certainly appears to unfurl from the very earth and move upwards until the higher notes appear to be plucked from the empyrean beyond. Air, water, earth, these elements are woven into the texture of the alap, making up as they do, the breath of the singer too ...
>
> Dhrupad alap is always a deep and sombre experience, moving and meditative, powerful, with the force of emotions like sadness, separation, yearning (for higher reaches of existence), submission to a heightened state of awareness, to the irresistible power of heavenly sound, to a Higher Power that has created all this.

We will pick up on the many resonances of this depiction as we proceed, beginning by noting that that several other respondents also told of an evocation of meditative states in performances of *ālāp*.[7] These were linked variously to expressions of peaceful feelings linked to higher states of consciousness—for example:

> It is meditative and by far the only (experienced) form in classical singing which can put someone in a trance-like state. (PS)

> I feel peace, calm. Introspection, a quest to reach within. This music gives me the space to reach beyond this plane. (NB)

A cross-cultural dimension to these impressions is illustrated by the comments of international students at the Dhrupad Sansthan Gurukul in Bhopal; for example, one student from Switzerland said of her earliest responses to dhrupad: 'I felt like it was meditation—a connection with higher things.'[8] Meanwhile, from within the questionnaire, respondent IB describes how such higher states might be one way to manage the contingencies of everyday life:

> Every time a Nom Tom [*ālāp*] starts, I feel like I am shaken out of the situation I am in and taken away. Immediately, I am transported into a dark blue space—sitting cross legged staring at nothing. It is a feeling of immense peace. Sometimes I imagine levitation to be like that. These feelings are more pronounced if times have been terribly stressful. I use this as a calming influence when I'm driving in Bangalore.

To the above statements we should also add the following from VS:

> I have felt the sense of immersion in very primordial sounds. I also associate the experience with centering as in meditation practice.

This last sentence reminds us that meditative associations ascribed to dhrupad *ālāp* are made in more than an informal sense. They relate to actual disciplinary *practices*, such as yoga, in which a harnessing of mind and body through, among other things, concentration on the breath (*prāṇa*), facilitates a search for transformed states of being or consciousness. In other words, there is in the background of these statements the notion of a metaphysical quest pursued as much practically as intellectually.[9]

Together these accounts envision the possibility of a centred state of inwardness that creates an adjustment of one's relationship to the outer world, reaching beyond it; and this reorientation is mobilized around *sound*. In more than one case there are descriptions of a surrendering of self to sound:

> Nom Tom Alap sounds like a call from the innermost depths of a person—sometimes a plea, sometimes an acknowledgement of total surrender. (IB)

> I must get involved and let the music enter me—seek to merge with the music ... [T]he music has to enter me, it has to 'resonate' within me. Only if I am willing to give myself so completely to Dhrupad can I listen to it. (PC)

PC here suggests a loss of self through a merging with the music, through a shared *resonance* (an important metaphor in Indian culture). What is also significant is that this is reported as something beyond words—as AB, another respondent, puts it: 'the Dhrupad style of singing ... is very profound which reflects a deep connection between yourself and infinity. This is something you can't really express very well in words— one has to feel it.' And, perhaps paradoxically, PS states: 'I feel it is secular as it is not bound by language with an enormous text to be understood and explained as the other forms.' We might read this as meaning that the experience of dhrupad goes beyond the experience of engaging intellectually with doctrinal texts, precisely because (in its *ālāp* phase at least) its words are the semantically empty *nom tom* syllables—'the fact that they are meaningless adds to their depth', says AB. Meanwhile, PS (who is a freelance researcher in music therapy) continues:

> I have been in the search for the most primeval sounds in music and I know when I under-stood the method of the nom tom I had hit upon something. So now I have come to the point of seeing that the pre-literate, the non-dual cannot be accessed only through this. This is where the science of music, sound and healing coalesce.

PS is one of several respondents to use the term 'primeval' or 'primordial' to refer to dhrupad sounds (see also VS above), which might suggest something (however prob-lematic to Western cultural theorists) beyond culture or history; indeed, as we shall note later, this is exactly how the highest levels of consciousness in Indian philosophy are understood. Equally, we shall come back to notions underpinning PS's allusion to an overcoming of the duality of subject and object, of self and world, through an accessing of the pre-literate, or pre-linguistic, which dhrupad with its *nom tom* sounds affords.

Swar as a focus (and locus) of consciousness

In the second phase of our informal ethnography we consider statements extracted from transcripts of interviews with professional artists—among them Ramakant and Umakant Gundecha and Uday Bhawalkar—and some of their students. Perhaps non-coincidentally, the accounts of those most deeply immersed in actual musical practice often focus on the seemingly simplest of notions (one entirely continuous with what we have discussed above): the musical note, or *swar*. Yet 'note' is a poor translation of *swar* (also *swara*, *svara*, *sur*): a note can be produced by any mechanical means; all we need is a frequency of vibration within certain limits, and we have a musical note; but *swar* is something more.[10] In the words of Raghava Menon (2000: 36):

> With the opening of the Swara, the single note, which looked so closed and narrow, becomes spacious. We find that in each note there are directions such as up and down, sides and depths, curves and textures of every kind, from grainy rough surfaces to velveteen and to those that shine like shot silk. There are various facets to each note and even moods. It now becomes a fit vehicle to express the musician's inner reaches.

This is intimately connected with the microtones, called *śruti*, found in Hindustani classical music. The term, derived from the root 'śru' (to hear), simply means 'that which is audible'.[11] Fine discrimination between *śruti* is a critical aspect of dhrupad practice. Ramakant Gundecha explains that each *swar* acquires a particular position in the unique context of a *rāga*. He demonstrates how the sixth degree of the scale of two different *rāga*s would sound identical on a keyboard, but sound quite different in the context of either *rāga* when sung or played on a stringed instrument. For example, in *rāg Toḍī*, the flattened sixth degree (*dha*) is placed on a *śruti* very close to the fifth (*pa*); whereas in *rāg Bhairav* the flattened sixth is placed considerably sharper (relatively speaking), often blurring with the seventh above it when approached from the latter via a glide (*mīṇḍ*).

This fine discrimination in the voicing of *swar* permeates the deepest reaches of improvisation in a dhrupad *ālāp*, where it operates at a very subtle level of the space within each note of the given *rāga*. While the *rāga* framework represents a first layer of constraint, the microtonal understanding of each note within this framework forms the next layer, a subtler set of boundaries that demands a correspondingly sophisticated technique to fashion and improvise upon the microtones.[12] The greater the constraints within which the mind is encouraged to create, the greater the demand on the creative thinking process. Hence it is the extremes of concentration demanded by dhrupad's improvisatory exploration of *swar* that foster enhanced levels of consciousness and that connect with meditation.

Congruent with dhrupad's quest for purity of *swar* is the stance its exponents take towards its accompanying instruments. Most decisively, artists such as the Gundecha brothers abjure the harmonium, which in recent years has come to accompany Indian vocal music almost as a matter of convention. Ramakant Gundecha describes the fashionable use of this instrument, tuned in Western equal temperament, as a 'terrorism in Indian music', and (less sensationally but still critically) as a 'comfortable companion which allows you to be mediocre, to be out of tune. It allows [you] to . . . not too much look . . . deep in [the] *rāga*, to *swar*, to the note . . . It doesn't allow you to focus.' But if the harmonium inhibits an accurate realization and deep consciousness of *swar*, the instrument that promotes it is the tānpurā, the chordophone whose tonic drone is the perennial accompaniment to Hindustani classical music performances. 'I consider this instrument is the best instrument in the world', says Gundecha, who also talks of the 'philosophy' of the tānpurā. This may not be unrelated to the fact that the instrument takes apparently little skill to play (merely a repeated, gentle stroking of its four open strings) but requires great concentration in listening (typically, an artist will spend a great deal of time ensuring the accompanying tānpurās are perfectly tuned before a performance). The instrument is so constructed that each string produces a cascade of overtones—reinforced and multiplied by those of the other strings. Gundecha describes how he determines the *swar* of a particular *rāga* by 'appropriating' the microtones of the tānpurā: 'I appropriate them according to the *rāga*'s position, because every pitch has a unique position according to our theory, according to this instrument.'

This view is borne out by statements from students of the Gundechas and also of Uday Bhawalkar, another leading contemporary exponent of dhrupad. ASM, a disciple of the latter, states: 'When I sing, I listen to the tānpurā and my voice, and when the two match perfectly there is a completely different feeling.' And this from AJ, another *śiṣya*: '[What] attracted me [to dhrupad] was listening to your own voice, mixing with the tānpurā, with the same frequency, for a longer time—it creates some sort of resonance for me and then you are lost in that—it is unexplainable in words.' Note here the idea of resonance between self and *swar* and then the loss of self within it (a notion encountered in our earlier discussion of listeners' perceptions). On the one hand, then, concentration on *swar* is an act of mind: 'it is the frequency of the tānpurā and matching it with that of your voice[, t]he travel of frequency [from] one [*swar*] to another . . . that keeps the mind engaged' (AJ). On the other hand this points to what lies beyond *swar* and thus perhaps beyond mind:

> Guruji [Uday Bhawalkar] has explained in lec. dems. [lecture–demonstrations] that when you sing the notes there is a *nād* [sound], a *bhāva* [emotion or feeling], that is beyond just the note. There is freedom in *ālāp*, no words, only [*nom tom*] syllables, like *aa ra ra na*.

How much can you beautify these syllables with these notes? You think beyond the notes—Guruji says do not think about the note at all—go beyond that. (RS)

And Bhawalkar himself states:

> every *swar* . . . has a divine form and it needs no clothing. When we dress it up, it becomes a *rāga*. When we ornament it becomes a *rāga*. The *swar* has a divine soul [*divya ātma*] and when you sing it, it is not emerging superficially. It is coming from deep within.

Here we have an allusion to something profound in an Indian musician's experience. To attribute a 'divine soul' to *swar* is to ascribe to it an essence or ontology of its own (and again to indicate how this is different from a mere 'note').[13] And this in turn emerges from 'deep within' the self of the singer. If we sense that an affinity between two consciousnesses (that imputed to *swar* on the one hand, and that of the singer on the other) is tending towards identity in such accounts, the point is clinched as Bhawalkar continues:

> So we can always try to achieve *dhyān* [meditation]—I am there and the *swar* is there— then you become one with the *swar*: *ātma* [self] and *swar* become one and you are not aware of what you are singing and which *swar* you are singing. So if this oneness can happen with the *swar*, then why not with the *rāga*? So that is what I meant by saying, the concentration is so intense that you become the *rāga*.

Consciousness in Hindu culture and philosophy

It should by now be evident that consciousness in dhrupad *ālāp*, and in Indian classical music more generally, is configured and informed by a wider understanding of being—or ontology—that shades into broader philosophical and religious thought. These last are themselves, typically of Indian culture, much more permeable to one another than is the case in Western thinking, which since its own Age of Reason (the Enlightenment era of the seventeenth and eighteenth centuries) has radically separated its various spheres of knowledge and experience. In highlighting congruences between the preceding musical accounts and Indian thought more widely, our point is not that Indian musicians universally operate with such ideas in the foreground of their activities. Rather, we surmise that ideas and practices in India's long and extensive spiritual, philosophical, and religious heritage offer a hermeneutic (interpretative) resource that may illuminate the deeper implications of a musical practice such as dhrupad.[14]

Fundamental to all this—and a possibly salutary alternative to dualistic mind–body debates in Western consciousness studies—is the notion that 'there is no absolute distinction in India between matter and sprit' (Lannoy 1971: 282). Paradigmatic in this respect are conceptions of *sound* whose history goes back to the Vedic era (first and second millennia BCE), which continue to have importance in India today, and which are of obvious importance in illuminating the significance of more specifically musical concepts such as *swar*. For Brahmins (the priestly caste that arose in the Vedic era) 'sound has in itself a metaphysical power', as W. Norman Brown puts it in an account cited by Lannoy (1971: 274–5). Even though Lannoy's discussion of India's 'culture of sound' is orientated towards 'The Word', the point he makes is that this culture's profound rootedness in orality throws emphasis on the Word's sonic qualities. Hence Brahmins were required to memorize exactly not only the texts of the Vedas but also their requisite chanted intonation. Thus 'Hindus still believe that such precision in the *repetition* of exact intervals, over and over again, permits sounds to act upon the internal personality, transform sensibility, way of thinking, state of soul, and even moral character'; and Brahmins advocate 'a need to study the influence of sound phenomena on human consciousness and physiology by orientating the perceptual centres towards the inner acoustic space of the unseen' (275).

This principle is embodied in the chanting of mantras, where conventional semantics becomes blurred by the sonic properties of the word in repeated incantation. And it is encapsulated in the sacred syllable *oṃ*, in which it is believed, as Rowell puts it, that '[a]udible sound has become a means of knowledge because of its ability to reveal the inaudible' (1992: 38). It is perhaps only a short step from this musicalization of the word to the use of semantically void syllables in a specifically musical form such as the *nom tom ālāp* of dhrupad. Indeed it is commonly held that these syllables are derived from mantras such as 'oṃ ananta nārāyaṇa hari' (an invocation to the immortality of Viṣṇu).[15]

The roots of these conceptions of consciousness and sound lie in the Upaniṣads, a collection of texts probably composed from the seventh to the sixth centuries BCE, and canonic for Hinduism as it began to look beyond the rituals of the Vedic era. It is in the *Māṇḍūkya Upaniṣad* that the metaphysics of the sound *oṃ* are most concisely and classically expressed. The text's opening declares: 'OM—this whole world is in that syllable!' The three phonemes of the syllable—'a', 'u', 'm'—are then considered in turn, each portrayed as representing a different state of consciousness: 'a', the waking state, 'u' the state of dream, 'm' the state of deep sleep. This continuum from intentional to contentless consciousness concludes with a fourth, transcendent state (*turiya*), signified by the silence which follows the first three components: it is held as being 'beyond the reach of ordinary transaction; as ungraspable; as without distinguishing marks; . . . as one whose essence is the perception of itself alone; as the cessation of the visible world . . . That is the self (*ātman*)' (Olivelle, trans. 1996: 289). The self denoted by *ātman* is not the egoic self, but one's inmost, spiritual self; and this relates to a further key Upaniṣadic term (no easier to translate), *brahman*: the fundamental principle or ground of being, 'the basic reality of the world' to which the sound *oṃ* is believed to give access (Olivelle 1996: liv). One of the most fundamental legacies of the Upaniṣads, one very germane to the higher levels of consciousness under discussion here, is the equation of the two concepts of *ātman* and *brahman*.

Upaniṣadic notions of consciousness and its intimate relation with being were subsequently developed in two foundational traditions of Hindu philosophy: on the one hand, Sāṃkhya (also Sāṅkhya, Samkhya), which is intertwined with the philosophy of Yoga (specifically the tradition subsequently termed Rāja Yoga);[16] and, on the other, Advaita Vedānta.[17] Significantly, accounts of these have featured in recent contributions to present-day consciousness studies by Ramakrishna Rao (1998, 2002, 2005), who has argued for a confluence of Western and Eastern thinking as a potentially fruitful line of advance for the discipline (a plausible argument, though perhaps more complex in practice than a simple resolution of a perceived complementarity of positions). For us, an additional challenge is to coax out connections between these discourses on consciousness and our own musical concerns. But first we consider these post-Upaniṣadic philosophies on their own terms, both as a preparatory step for exploring possible linkages with Indian classical music and as an avenue suggestive of an alternative take (at least for Western readers) on constructions of consciousness per se.

Canonical thinkers of these traditions were Patañjali, famed for his epigrammatic *Yoga Sūtras* (Ballantyne and Deva, trans. 1963), which resonate substantially with Sāṃkhya philosophy; and Śaṅkara (also Shankara, Samkara), whose commentaries on the Upaniṣads form the basis for Advaita Vedānta.[18] Vagaries of dating notwithstanding, it is not implausible to suggest Śaṅkara's consolidation of Advaita Vedānta as both a development and critique of ideas in Sāṃkhya philosophy, given both the confluence and crucial distinctions between them. In particular, Advaita Vedānta is a monist philosophy (*advaita* meaning 'non-dualist'): its reading of the Upaniṣadic equation of *ātman* with *brahman* is that there is no distinction between the self and the larger (conscious) principle of Being; empirical reality is but an illusion (*māyā*). By contrast Sāṃkhya–Yoga is a dualist philosophy that attributes reality to matter—*prakṛti* (also *prakriti*)—while nonetheless seeing consciousness—*puruṣa* (also *purusha*)—as occupying a distinct, metaphysical plane.

The latter, dualist tradition is different again from Western Cartesianism, which separates mind from body and generally assumes consciousness to be a facet of mind. In Sāṃkhya–Yoga, *puruṣa*—consciousness-as-such—is distinguished from mind, which is seen as part of the material world (albeit operative on the plane of 'subtle' rather than 'gross' matter). To elaborate: *puruṣa* stands for pure consciousness, consciousness as a transcendent principle (in Western terms, the position here is one of philosophical idealism); while the individual person, or *jīva*, represents a condition of *embodied* consciousness, since his or her consciousness arises from the association of *puruṣa* with the *buddhi* (intellect)—an evolute of matter (see Rao 2005: 12).

This relation is very subtly conceived. As Rao puts it, *puruṣa* is 'inactive', 'inert and formless' (2005: 14, 12)—an unchanging, contentless, non-intentional state of being. Meanwhile, the *buddhi*, which is the principal function of mind (*citta*), is an active faculty that undergoes transformation (*vṛtti* (also *vritti*)) by taking the form of the perceived object, so informing cognition (a process perhaps not unrelated to notions of mental representation or cognitive modelling in Western psychology). However, these transformations do not in themselves lead to consciousness, indeed the *buddhi* is by nature unconscious: its contents only become conscious through the illumination of the *puruṣa*, to which it is proximate. Rao (2002: 202; 2005: 12) reminds us that this is not a question of interaction, more one of association or reflection; and Richard King (1999: 176) writes that the *buddhi* 'represents the mediating point of intersection between consciousness and matter'. Thus, the responsiveness of *buddhi*, which has content without consciousness, to *puruṣa*, which is pure consciousness without content, leads to phenomenal consciousness.

There is more. The *buddhi* comes with a (personal) history. It is shaped by the inherited and acquired tendencies—or, in more culturally precise terms, the *karma*—of the individual whose mind it is. As Rao puts it, '[It] is the storehouse of latent subconscious impressions and tendencies (*samskaras* and *vasanas*) that colour our cognitions and form our dispositions to act' (2005: 14). Because the *buddhi* is in many senses personal property, the individual—*jīva*—mistakenly attributes his experience of consciousness to this, the construction of his personal self, rather than to the transcendent *puruṣa* that is the illuminating source of consciousness, and indeed ground of all being. This state of ignorance, or *avidyā*, is the cause of human suffering and unhappiness.

Sāṃkhya–Yoga and Advaita Vedānta, among various other schools of Indian thought, aim to foster liberation from such a state, through their claims to philosophical descriptions of being as it truly is and through meditative practices designed to overcome mind–body distinctions. Such practices are orientated towards achieving *turiya*, the fourth, transcendent, contentless state of consciousness described in the *Māndūkya Upaniṣad* (discussed above). This is also known as *samādhi*—a state of 'steady one-pointed concentration that results in unwavering absorption in the object of attention . . . [until] the duality of subject and object disappears' (Rao 2002: 208; see also King 1999: 191–4). *Samādhi* states have been variously classified (King 1999: 192–4; Rao 2002: 208), but at their apex is a condition of pure, objectless consciousness in which liberation from empirical existential conditions can be known. The aim of philosophy and spiritual practice such as meditation is the removal of the illusory veil (*māyā*) of empirical reality—in the case of Advaita Vedānta, the illusion that obscures the recognition that the individual self, *ātman*, is the same as the foundation of all being, *brahman*. And all of this is but a translation into practice of the 'great wisdom' (*māhavakyā*) of the *Chandogya Upaniṣad* (6.8–6.16) that declares the identity of *ātman* and *brahman*: '*tat tvam asi*'—'thou art that'.[19]

Consciousness in Hindustani classical music—revisited

Having sketched something of the place of consciousness per se in Indian, specifically, Hindu philosophy, we now need to revisit the question of whether and to what extent these conceptions can be connected with species of Indian classical music such as dhrupad. At first glance, direct connections might seem tenuous. The day-to-day discourse of classical musicians might not in itself provide substantial evidence that many of them practice with an explicit, fully worked out philosophical application of systems such as those we have outlined. For one thing, by no means are all musicians practising Hindus. Indeed, given the historical roots of dhrupad (and later khyāl) in the Mughal courts, it is not surprising that most of its most famous exponents have been Muslims—for example the Ḍāgar family, who over several generations have created one of the most important *gharānās* (clans/schools) for dhrupad (Zia Fariduddin and Zia Mohiuddin Ḍāgar were ustads (gurus) of the Gundecha brothers, Uday Bhawalkar, and other important contemporary dhrupadiyas). And yet, as George Ruckert (2004: 18–19) points out:

> No matter what the practicing faith of a musician might be, most acknowledge the music's origin as a divine manifestation, a gift from God, which is a profound root of its affect. The Hindus will call this aspect of the music *Nād-Brahmā*, 'sound as God', or 'the language of God'. The purpose of serious music, then, is to bring oneself in tune with the

highest planes, and the practice of music is like a prayer. The musician is on a lifelong path (*mārga*) which has spiritual overtones, mixed with the *yoga* ('yoke') of refinement, knowledge, and purification . . . Although these ideas are part of the Hindu tradition, one does not hear them contradicted by musicians of other faiths.

Ruckert's depiction is borne out by the testimony of many classical musicians, who in turn describe the devotional attitude of *Nād–Brahmā upāsanā* as widespread among other musicians. This outlook is congruent with observations noted above (and expanded on below) that sound bears metaphysical import in Indian culture. The principle of the divine with which sound is correlated here need not be read as something radically different from consciousness, since the concept *brahman* allows for considerable conflation of these terms. For example, notwithstanding the fact that Sāṃkhya philosophy couches consciousness in non-theistic, indeed atheistic, terms, Patañjali recommends in his *Yoga Sūtras* (informed, let us recall, by Sāṃkhya) that another route to abstract meditation, less strenuous than the cultivation of transcendent consciousness is 'by profound devotedness to the Lord [*Īśvara*]' (Ballantyne and Deva 1963: 22). And, a little later on in Patañjali's text (and its accompanying commentary attributed to Vyāsa), we see—entirely congruently with notions in the Upaniṣads—the divinity also correlated with sound: 'His name is "Glory" . . . "*Om*"' (24). Thus the *Nād–Brahmā upāsanā* with which musicians express a strong affinity can be seen as homologous with that key theme of the Upaniṣads, the merging of the individual mind, *ātman*, with the universal consciousness, *brahman*, and the metaphysical equation of the latter with sound. In this light the statements made by dhrupad listeners and practitioners from our ethnography bear re-reading. Most quintessential among these—and worth recapitulating here—was that made by Uday Bhawalkar, who stated that: 'the *swar* has a divine soul [*divya ātma*]'; that in a state akin to meditation '*ātma* [self] and *swar* become one'; and as with *swar* so with *rāga*: 'the concentration is so intense that you become the *rāga*'.

Nor would it be incorrect to construe this intense concentration as a form of *samādhi*—a desideratum of philosophical systems and meditative practices of Advaita Vedānta and Sāṃkhya–Yoga. The very improvised nature of forms such as dhrupad requires absolute concentration in the moment on the performer's part—even in the more extravert *bandiś* section, where extemporization must operate within the discipline of the rhythmic time cycle or *tāl*; but especially in the creation of an *ālāp*, where there is acutely focused attention on the *swar*. If these aspects of a (public) performance are not completely defined by the search for states of pure, non-representational consciousness (because there is still musical content), another context in which this might be yet more closely approached is in the (private) experience of *riyāz*, the musician's daily regime of practice. Apart from fostering the practical development of technical and musical expertise, this process (perhaps unlike Western musicians' practice sessions) also has a spiritual dimension. The quintessence of this is the (often extended) intoning of *sā*, the tonic note, which vocalists undertake at the beginning of their *riyāz*. While the motive might be partly to build up strength in the vocal cords and to foster high levels of acuity in pitch discrimination, it is also the case that the reduction of sensory awareness to a single object—in this case a sonic one—resembles standard meditative techniques orientated towards the attainment of *samādhi* states.[20]

It is also worth also considering more fully the word *Nād* (or *Nāda*) in the *Nād–Brahmā* concept. *Nāda* is a particular denotation of sound, with a long historical pedigree and with significant cultural connotations. Rowell summarizes an account in the *Bṛhaddeśī* treatise authored by Mataṅga (dating from c. 800 CE), which uses the term *Nāda* in four distinct (though arguably related) ways. Rowell's paraphrase (1992: 45) merits quotation, as it links these ancient ideas to musical practices that are still current, and culminates with a reference to syllabic intoning which is the very stuff of dhrupad *nom tom ālāp*:

> [*Nāda*] appears to be used in four distinct senses in [the *Bṛhaddeśī* of Mataṅga]: (1) in the special sense of 'primordial sound', the pervading causal sound that animates the universe . . .; (2) as a general word for musical sound . . .; (3) as a technical term for the process of emerging vocal channels; and (4), most specific of all, as a term signifying what eventually became the standard beginning gambit in Indian musical performance— the improvised exposition of a *rāgā*. Once again the line of semantic development is clear: the systematic exploration of the characteristic pathways and tonal landmarks of the chosen *rāgā* is seen as an analogy to the manner in which vocal sound follows the bodily pathways, touching in turn each of the centers of resonance and organs of articulation. It is further interesting to observe that many singers begin their improvisation by vocalizing on the syllable *na*, in preference to an open vowel—conceivably a form of phonetic testimony to their inner experience.

What is significant here is that the several connotations of *Nāda* reflect a continuum from a 'primordial' or transcendental conception of sound to a general musical one, to one in which sound is located in the body of an individual, to one where it is rendered in actual musical practice. Or to look at it the other way around: musical renditions have as their foundation a concept of sound which covers a spectrum of consciousness—entirely consistent with the notion in Hindu philosophy of gradations from gross (bodily) to the most subtle forms of matter, leading eventually to pure consciousness. As Rowell puts it:

> If there is a central core to the idea of sound as developed in the systematic Indian philosophies, it is that sound is a quality, inhering in the substratum of *ākāśa* ['ether'] which pervades both the outer spaces of the world and the inner spaces of the body. It is one, universal, eternal, causal (but not caused), permeating both personal and transpersonal consciousness, and manifested along the human pathway from inner to outer space. Its discharge in the form of vital breath is both an act of worship and an affirmation of universal process. (41)

The notion of *ākāśa* has resonances with pre-modern Western ideas. Rowell tells us that the word is 'translated sometimes as "space" but more often as "ether", the first of the elements evolved from the universal consciousness (once again the *Ātman*)' (40)—once again, in other words, the connection between sound and the notion of uncaused, transpersonal consciousness: *atman/brahman* or *puruṣa*.

We might consider the performance situation of forms of classical Indian music such as dhrupad as reflecting exactly this picture of consciousness. The soloist represents the embodied consciousness of the individual (*jīva*); the ceaseless tānpurā drone— on the one hand integral to the performance, on the other hand unaffected by it, as if uncaused and free from causation—creates the image of the universal, unchanging consciousness (*puruṣa* or *brahman*). The performer seeking to merge his *swar* with the ethereal tānpurā enacts the quest for union between self (*ātman*) and being that represents consciousness in its most elevated sense. Once again we would want to temper our claims with an awareness of actual empirical conditions of performance. We do not assert that every Indian classical music performance is marked throughout by a state of transcendental consciousness on the part of performers and audiences—more often, the modes of enjoyment are quite worldly, in the vein of *deśi* traditions. Yet a fundamental motivation for all involved remains the possibility of momentarily touching a higher state of consciousness—an aspiration that underpins modern-day dhrupad's claims to the status of *mārga*. In these contexts, then, sound (*nāda*), shining forth in the acute attunement of musical tone (*swar*), serves as both metaphor and actual vehicle for consciousness in its most essential sense.

Conclusion

This way of putting it—'metaphor and actual vehicle'—prompts us to dwell finally on the epistemological status and implications of the linkages we have suggested. One of our points is that the performance situation just described both *symbolizes* a culture's metaphysically informed construction of a higher-order consciousness and (at its peak moments) *realizes* it. This is to imply that, on some level, these experiences are *real*: they make a claim to truth. The question is, on which level? An epistemologically 'safe' way to ground such a claim would be to posit it, in the language of anthropologists and ethnomusicologists, at an 'emic' level.[21] In other words, the kinds of consciousness described are acknowledged as real to those subjects who believe they have them—valid in terms of the culture from which the subjects hail. However, attributing 'emic' status to such accounts implies that there must also be an 'etic' version: some universal, objective, or transcultural standpoint from which such claims can be judged as 'really real'—or not.[22] With this we move onto slippery ground, since it is raises the question, as Michael Agar (2007) frames it: 'What is the etic for humanity in general and who decides?' The mode of investigation that might be seen as quintessentially 'etic' would be the techniques of modern science, with its claims to be able to verify or falsify subjective claims through experimental procedures whose methods and results are repeatable any place, any time. But there are at least two problems with this.

First, in relation to our claims for consciousness in Indian classical music, it is hard to know exactly what kind of procedure could be used to make the necessary verification or falsification. This is partly a practical matter: would it be possible, for example, to sing a *rāga* under normal performing conditions while in an fMRI scanner? This is self-evidently contradictory. But even if it were practicable, the resulting data would still need interpretation, and this would necessarily emanate from some cultural—in other words, emic—position. Hence we might ask, would access to the neurological configurations of subjects experiencing some form of heightened consciousness in a *rāga* performance ever enable us categorically to identify this as approaching some ineffable state of *samādhi*? Such questions around the *meaning* of experience clearly represent an order of inquiry beyond that of etic description, yet they are arguably more fundamental, since they concern the very nature of the relationship between consciousness, world, and reality.

Which brings us to the second, paradoxical problem of a putative etic approach: that the very desire for an etic standpoint from which to legitimate an emically located position might itself be emically located. For example, non-Hindus might believe the worldview underpinning the musical states of consciousness we have been discussing to be fascinating on an emic level but illusory at an etic one (if, in other words, the significance attributed to these states does not pass certain empirical tests of verification). However, that Eastern worldview problematizes the whole question of what is real and what is illusory; for an Advaita Vedāntist or Buddhist, it is empirical reality itself that is the source of delusion (the veil of *māyā*).

Thus we may need to embrace the fact that the only external position from which to evaluate an emic position is another emic position. While one implication of this might be a value-neutralizing relativism in which one culture's experiences and knowledge systems are seen as no more (or less) than that, there is a potentially more promising take on the situation, which may after all make it possible to recover some qualified notion of the etic. This alternative, founded on the notion of dialogue, involves seeking the emic experience of another for oneself, that is, making it one's own emic position. The only way to know what it is like to experience a *rāga* is to experience a *rāga*, and that experience, like any music, is in principle available to all of us, regardless of which culture we start from. This availability is arguably due to an etic substrate from which we might approach the music. A dhrupad *ālāp* is potentially intelligible because it is based on core musical notions that are culturally widespread if not universal, involving categories such as note, scale, vocality, performativity, expression, focused listening, and so on. The key here is that these points of similarity are simultaneously points of profound difference: the etic acts as a gateway to an ever deepening experience of the emic.

There is, then, perhaps something in this akin to the principle of repeatability that underpins scientific experimental methodology—only what is repeated by any second party here is repeated as an emic experience.[23] But if this assumes a process of acculturation, it does not mean leaving one's own culture behind. Just as many Hindus might understand and operate an ego-based version of selfhood well known to Westerners while simultaneously believing in the version of the self known as *ātman*,[24] so it might be more generally possible to internalize (or dialogize) more than one cultural perspective on the experience of consciousness. That the Hindu worldview constructs the relationship between self, mind, and world in a radically different way from Western consciousness studies, with a different array of terms—*jīva, ahankara, citta, buddhi, puruṣa, ātman, brahman*—need not be seen as archaic or strange; instead these different standpoints offer a basis for mutually critical and informative interrogation, and so help move debates about consciousness onwards. It is our hope that our account of consciousness in dhrupad—informed by our own respective cultural standpoints—might represent a contribution to just such a venture.

Acknowledgements

We should like to express our gratitude to our interviewees and questionnaire respondents, whose statements we include with their permission. Thanks are also due to Vardan Hovikimyan and Bethany Lowe, who helpfully commented on earlier drafts of this chapter.

References

Agar, M. (2007). Emic/etic, in G. Ritzer (ed.) *Blackwell Encyclopedia of Sociology* (Blackwell Reference Online). Available at: www.blackwellreference.com/subscriber/tocnode?id= g9781405124331_chunk_g978140512433111_ss1-35 (accessed 11 October 2010).

Bagchee, S. (1998). *Nād: Understanding Rāga Music* (Mumbai: Eshwar).

Ballantyne J.R. and Deva, G.S. trans. (1963). *Yoga Sutras of Patañjali*, 4th edn (Calcutta: Susil Gupta).

Bharati, A. (1985). The self in Hindu thought and action, in A. Marsella, G. Devos, and F.L.K Hsu (eds.) *Culture and Self: Asian and Western Perspectives*, 185–230 (New York: Tavistock Publications).

Brown, W.N. (1970). *Man in the Universe; Some Continuities in Indian Thought* (Berkeley, CA: University of California Press).

Daniélou, A. (1995). *Music and the Power of Sound: The Influence of Tuning and Interval on Consciousness* (Rochester, VT: Inner Traditions International).

Daniélou, A. (2003). *The Rāga-s of Northern Indian Music* (Delhi: Munishiram Manpharlal Publishers).

Dasgupta, S.N. (1974). *Yoga Philosophy in Relation to Other Systems of Indian Thought* (Delhi: Motilal Banarsidass).

Dennett, D.C. (1991). *Consciousness Explained* (London: Penguin).

Dhrupad.info. *Mp3 excerpts of dhrupad, rudra veena and pakhawaj maestros.* Available at: www. dhrupad.info/maestros_mp3.htm (accessed 2 October 2010).

Dhrupad.org [website of the Gundecha brothers]. Available at: www.dhrupad.org/index.htm (accessed 2 October 2010).

Gundecha Brothers [Gundecha, R. and U.] (1999). *Ancestral Voices: A Dhrupad Vocal Recital.* CD (London: Navras Records, NRCD 0106).

Hamilton, S. (2001). *Indian Philosophy: A Very Short Introduction* (Oxford: Oxford University Press).

King, R. (1999). *Indian Philosophy: An Introduction to Hindu and Buddhist Thought* (Edinburgh: Edinburgh University Press).

Lannoy R. (1971). *The Speaking Tree: A Study of Indian Culture and Society* (London: Oxford University Press).

Menon, R.R. (2000). *Alaap: A Discovery of Indian Classical Music* (Pondicherry: Times-Aurobindo Ashram).

Menon, R.R. (2001). *The Musical Journey of Kumar Gandharva* (New Delhi: Vision Books).

Music India Online. Available at: www.musicindiaonline.com/#/ (accessed 2 October 2010).

Mutatkar, S. (1987). Dhrupada: its legacy and dynamics, in Mutatkar (ed.) *Aspects of Indian Music: A Collection of Essays*, 76–83 (New Delhi: Sangeet Natak Akademi).

Nercessian, A. (2002). *Postmodernism and Globalization in Ethnomusicology: An Epistemological Problem* (Lanham, MD: Scarecrow Press).

Olivelle, P. trans. (1996). *Upaniṣads* (Oxford: Oxford University Press).

Rao, K.R. (1998). Two faces of consciousness: a look at Eastern and Western perspectives. *Journal of Consciousness Studies*, **5**(3), 309–27.

Rao, K.R. (2002). *Consciousness Studies: Cross-Cultural Perspectives* (Jefferson, NC: McFarland and Co.).

Rao, K.R. (2005). Perception, cognition and consciousness in classical Hindu psychology. *Journal of Consciousness Studies*, **12**(3), 3–30.

Rowell, L. (1992). *Music and Musical Thought in Early India* (Chicago, IL: University of Chicago Press).

Ruckert, G.E. (2004). *Music in North India: Experiencing Music, Expressing Culture* (New York, NY: Oxford University Press).

Sanyal, R. and Widdess, R. (2004). *Dhrupad: Tradition and Performance in Indian Music*. (Aldershot: Ashgate).

Sengupta, P.K. (1991). *Foundations of Indian Musicology* (New Delhi: Abhinav Publications).

Notes

1. The term 'India' (and with it 'Indian') implies not only the geographical area of the present-day nation state, but also the region sometimes termed 'South Asia'—including what is now Pakistan and Bangladesh among other modern-day countries. We have elected not to use a term such as 'South Asian music' since this has little currency among practitioners.

2. For further information see the Gundechas' website, www.dhrupad.org.

3. The CD *Ancestral Voices* (Gundecha Brothers 1999) represents as good as an introduction as any to a complete rendition of a *rāga* by contemporary dhrupad exponents. The accompanying CD to Sanyal and Widdess (2004) provides sound-clips of the elements and techniques of dhrupad by Ritwik Sanyal. Streamable recordings by various artists can be found at Dhrupad.info, as well as at Music India Online—a well-established and comprehensive website for Indian music of all kinds—using the search term 'dhrupad'; URLs for both websites are given in the references. These sources of course represent only a tiny selection of possibilities, among which readily searchable popular websites such as YouTube and MySpace afford many further examples.

4. The topic of *ālāp* indeed receives substantial treatment in Sanyal and Widdess's magisterial monograph (2004: 141–208).

5. Demographically speaking, all respondents were Indian professionals, about half of them involved in education—principally as teachers, but also as researchers and, in one case, as a student.

6. All respondents wrote in English, except for idiomatic Hindi and Sanskrit terms whose orthography we reproduce as originally rendered. Beyond this we have made only minor typographical emendations to respondents' statements.

7. For further discussion of meditative practice and experience see Chapters 6 and 7, this volume.

8. This response comes from a separate set of interviews conducted by TK.

9. An observation by Sue Hamilton (2001: 10) is apposite:

   From the perspective of the Indian worldview . . . the possibility of changing one's cognitive perception is something to be regarded as systematically possible by means of regular disciplinary exercises in a manner not all that different from systematically acquiring the ability to play a musical instrument. Both require long-term perseverance and practice and involve the fine-tuning of various aspects of bodily and mental coordination.

10. See also Biswas (Chapter 6, this volume), for a discussion of *swar*.

11. Cf. Bagchee (1998: 23): 'The number of theoretically possible intervals between notes is limitless but the actual number used in music is comparatively small, as there are limitations imposed by the ear, which cannot differentiate among all of these. In theory, these are supposed to be intervals that lie between each successive note and add up to 22 in number [in an octave].'

12. In this context it is also worth noting the work of Alain Daniélou, which includes an extensive exploration of interval and microtones in Indian music—see, for example, his discussion of *śrutis* in Daniélou (2003: 27–49), as well as his yet more substantial treatment in Daniélou (1995), which also encompasses Chinese and Western pre-modern tuning systems.

13. Menon talks of two faces to a musical sound: an inner face and an outer face. The outer face is what we are accustomed to calling a note. *Swara* is born when the inner face comes into being and shines through the outer note. Or, in Menon's own words (2001: 36):

    > Broken down to its Sanskrit roots, the root Swa refers to the inner self of the student, the resident deity that inhabits all created things, and the root Ra which refers to a shining out of this inner self. In combination the word Swara would mean the radiance of the inner self and this is the essence of the Swara.

14. Perhaps an analogue from European music would be the way in which the philosophy of German early Romanticism and Idealism illuminates—and is culturally of a piece with—music composed in the Austro-German tradition of that period, regardless of whether composers and listeners then (or listeners now) were *au fait* with those bodies of thought.

15. See Sanyal and Widdess (2004: 152–61 (especially 156–7)) for a fuller account, which also includes other putative mantric sources for *nom tom* syllables, including Sufi ones (154).

16. While yoga is probably best known to Westerners as a regime for the promotion of physical well-being, it is more accurately a practice that seeks to bring together bodily and mental control of the self with the aim of achieving an enlightened state of consciousness. Hence, yoga is a philosophical practice.

17. For a concise but detailed introduction to these various philosophical systems see King (1999), especially Chapters 7 and 8.

18. Like much else in early Indian culture, chronologies of these traditions and their exponents are difficult to ascertain conclusively. Rao (2002: 197) recounts how one view of Patañjali's *Yoga Sūtras* dates them at the second century BCE, while more recent scholarship holds that they may belong to the fourth or fifth centuries CE, with Sāṃkhya philosophy emerging round 200 CE. This discrepancy raises the question of the respective direction(s) of influence between Sāṃkhya and Yoga philosophies. In his classic study of the subject, S.N. Dasgupta (1974: 51) claims that Patañjali 'not only collected the different forms of Yoga practices . . . but grafted them all on the Sāṃkhya metaphysics'. But in another take on this chronology and relationship, Richard King (1999: 189) states that Patañjali's *Yoga Sūtra* is older than the key text of Sāṃkhya philosophy, the *Sāṃkhya Karika* of Īśvarakṛṣṇa (350–450 CE, according to King (170)); nonetheless, King also points out that, according to some scholars, 'it may be . . . that the final compilation of the *Sūtra* was precipitated by the appearance of Īśvarakṛṣṇa's work' (189).

    Similarly for Advaita Vedānta philosophy, Śaṅkara was once been assumed to have been active around 200 BCE, although recent scholarship suggests this to have been around the late eighth to early ninth centuries CE (as discussed in King (1999: 153); Rao (2002: 216) also dates Śaṅkara as eighth century).

19. For a discussion of *ātman* and *brahman* in the Upaniṣads see Brown (1970): 33–8.

20. Again, see the account of meditation and music given by Biswas (Chapter 6, this volume).

21. For a discussion of 'emic' and 'etic' see Agar (2007). For an account of this notion specifically in relation to ethnomusicology see Nercessian (2002: 12–13; 24–6).

22. This way of arguing is also akin to Daniel Dennett's notion of 'heterophenomenology', which accepts subjects' first-person accounts of their experiences as an anthropological fact, but rather than ending the matter there attempts to find some third-person, putatively objective standpoint from which to verify them—or otherwise (see Dennett 1991: Ch. 4; also Chapter 11 by E. Clarke, this volume).

23. A similar point is made in the final section of Chapter 7 by Lowe, this volume.

24. For an interesting account of this see Bharati (1985).

Chapter 9

From formalism to experience: a Jamesian perspective on music, computing, and consciousness

Meurig Beynon

Introduction: repudiating dualism

In his essay 'Does consciousness exist?' William James identifies a commonly held (mis)conception: that consciousness is 'one element, moment, factor—call it what you like—of an experience of essentially dualistic inner constitution, from which, if you abstract the content, the consciousness will remain revealed to its own eye' (1912a: 8). In response to this notion, James writes:

> my contention is exactly the reverse of this. *Experience, I believe, has no such inner duplicity; and the separation of it into consciousness and content comes, not by way of subtraction, but way of addition*—the addition, to a given concrete piece of it, of other sets of experiences, in connection with which severally its use or function may be of two different kinds. (9)

The key sentiment in this quotation is expressed in the phrase italicized by James himself. It represents a subtle form of repudiation of a perceived duality between form and content that is also often invoked in relation both to music and computing. It is a useful point of departure for thinking about consciousness in music.

Dualism in music is perhaps most potently represented in the saying colloquially attributed to a certain school of piano teachers: 'Now that we've learnt the notes, it's time to put in some expression.' There is a presumption here that there is such a thing as merely 'playing the notes', and that it would pose no problem to a pianist of the stature of Emil Gilels or Sviatoslav Richter to be asked to play a piece of music without any expression. In this connection, James's point would be that there is but one experience that can be viewed as 'playing the notes' and as 'making music', and, setting aside the issue of how successful the novice pianist may be at doing either, one cannot help but simultaneously attempt to do both. The implications of James's repudiation of such dualism go deeper. They relate to a blurring of distinctions and a problematization of concepts that is endorsed by much contemporary musicology. As illustrated by Giles Hooper's recent account of the discourse of musicology, it is deemed facile to speak without qualification about intra- and extra-musical factors, of high-art and popular music, of classical and romantic compositions, of authentic editions and performances (Hooper 2006: Ch. 1).

In the following account I set out to show how James's thinking, in association with an alternative foundational approach to computing, provides the basis for a treatment of the theme of music and consciousness that can embrace many varieties of musical experience and interpretation without compromising integrity. As an amateur musician with a casual interest in musicology, I am not best placed to justify this claim directly. Instead I shall venture a more oblique justification, drawing on my professional background in computer science to highlight parallels between composing or performing music and *Empirical Modelling* (EM)—a specific way of using computing technology to build artefacts that has been developed under my direction over the past 20 years. The musical illustrations and references I discuss are drawn from the German classical and romantic traditions, which are most salient in my own experience as a pianist and accompanist with a particular interest in chamber music and songs. But while this reflects my area of relative musical competence, it should not necessarily be taken as indicating that the ideas developed apply only to the narrow musical culture of Western score-based tonal music on which I shall focus.

Music, computing, and consciousness: moving beyond formalism

The advent of computing has been closely associated with the rise of consciousness studies. Much of the thinking in the latter field has been inspired by computational theories of mind that originated in the study of artificial intelligence. Though research on music has not had the same prominence as topics such as natural language in this context, it has been the focus for studies that are both linguistic (e.g. Longuet-Higgins 1978, Steedman 1984, Winograd 1968) and connectionist (e.g. Desain and Honing 1992, Gjerdingen 1990, Todd and Loy 1991) in approach. There are obvious reasons why these approaches appeal. Music has already developed notations and conventions for interpretation that closely resemble the formal languages of computing in certain respects. Musical scores and computer programs are both ways of representing rich, state-changing activities in an abstract manner, and both have an associated realization by way of an external behaviour.

Viewing music from a formal perspective, musical structures inferred from the score have primary significance. Composition and performance are understood with reference to established rules and conventions. Musical analysis in this spirit is well represented by work such as William Caplin's *Classical Form* (1998). Here the underlying mathematical model of harmonic relationships, as represented in the well-known cycle of keys, plays a crucial role in framing the rules of classical form. By treating music as a rational activity based on formal representations and transformations it is possible to give an effective account of it in terms of familiar abstractions used in computer science. For instance, Geraint Wiggins and his collaborators have developed an application program interface that can be used to give computer support for musical analysis and reasoning about music (Wiggins *et al.* 1993). This relies on introducing abstract data types to express the mathematical properties of the elements of Western tonal music.

A more ambitious objective inspired by a formal view of music, closely related to the theme of musical consciousness, is the application of artificial intelligence techniques to generate music. David Cope's *Virtual Music* (2001) is one of the best known examples of research of this kind. Cope's approach, challenging his readers to distinguish human compositions from computer-generated pieces solely on the basis of studying the music itself ('The Game'), has stimulated much controversy—see for instance the responses by Hofstadter (2001, n.d.) and the review of Cope (2005) by Wiggins (2008). As Margaret Boden has observed, the idea that mechanical methods of constructing music can produce results of aesthetic value is perceived by some as threatening deeply rooted ideas about the nature of human creativity (Boden 2006a). Boden views computationally inspired approaches to generating music as challenging 'romantic notions' about creativity in composition. The abstract concept of music that this viewpoint endorses is well suited to the way in which computer generation of music is effected. What guides computer-generated composition is an abstract specification based on metrics that are applied to musical constructions, and a process for organizing notes into patterns that is framed as an algorithm. In this respect, it is well matched to the classical view of computer programming, where all negotiation of meaning is preparatory to the process of construction.

The kinds of 'scientific' explanation of musical experience to which some researchers in artificial intelligence aspire are not representative of humanistic conceptions of music. In *Music and the Mind* the psychologist Anthony Storr recognizes the need to take 'the expressive aspects of music' into account, and observes: 'the language used by both philosophers and scientists is neutral and objective. It eschews the personal, the particular, the emotional, the subjective . . . Whilst it is perfectly possible to study music from a purely objective, intellectual point of view, this approach alone is insufficient' (Storr 1993: 38). Storr himself gives far more attention to cultural, physiological, and psychological aspects of musical experience than to formal aspects.

Radical empiricism commends an alternative perspective that is neither formalist and positivist nor as sceptical of theoretical metanarratives as is postmodern musicology. It is based on a reorientation in which the concrete and immediate experience of artefacts is fundamental rather than peripheral, and on interpretation that, while never absolute, is amenable to pragmatic authentication. It addresses the need identified by Storr for a philosophical outlook that does not eschew 'the personal, the particular, the emotional, the subjective'. And while encompassing these characteristics, it also proposes pragmatic criteria for making judgements about the objectivity of interpretation that may help to address Hooper's concerns regarding recent hermeneutic tendencies in musicology (Hooper 2006: 39).

Musicology and computer science: comparisons and analogies

The philosophical shift in perspective to radical empiricism in thinking about music and consciousness is effected by considering a different analogy that relates music and computing: that between a musical artefact as concretely experienced (for instance, in performance or listening), and an artefact based on computer technology viewed from a phenomenological rather than an abstract computational perspective. The principles and practical tools of EM (discussed at greater length below) have been developed with a view to just such a reorientation in thinking about computing.

A computer program, as traditionally conceptualized using Turing's notion of computation, is much more prescriptive of a specific behaviour than a musical score. Putting aside the fact that one computer may outperform another in terms of speed or data storage capacity, and that there are physical limits on the capabilities of any computing resource, there is an abstract notion of a program which can be implemented so as to perform essentially the same function on different computer architectures and with different interfaces. By comparison, the performances of the same musical work by different artists and on different instruments are extremely diverse in character.

Experiential considerations that are peripheral to whether a program meets its abstract specification are typically of the essence in determining whether a piece of music is effective. Music is not intended to be 'used' but to be experienced. Its full appreciation has always relied on broader intelligence about the context in which it was conceived, composed, and performed. Developments in technology that support musical composition through the direct crafting of concrete sound experience, using electronic representations rather than musical scores, detract from the idea that musical artefacts resemble abstract programs expressed in a formal language. The diversification of musical cultures and the advent of new modes of music-making based on unconventional paradigms have had a similar impact.

As Hooper (2006) observes, musicology has negotiated a shift of emphasis from formal to experiential and contextual dimensions. Computer science, as a much younger discipline with strong historical roots in abstract mathematics, has yet to make such a shift. Modern applications of computing meanwhile expose the limitations of the narrow 'classical' conception of a computer program. As new digital technologies for interaction and communication develop, greater emphasis is given to the experiences that the computer can generate. Visual and auditory effects become more significant, and, in mediating these, real-time response and aesthetics are relevant. A more profound impact of these developments in computing culture has been to subvert the naïve idea of computer user, and the notion of systems meeting narrowly specified functional needs. It is inconceivable that computer science could embrace a postmodern framework of interpretation, but the limitations imposed by its current narrow interpretative framework are quite apparent. In establishing an appropriate science for computing in its full generality, the need for a perspective that embraces formal and experiential aspects without enfranchising wholesale deconstruction is endorsed both by computer scientists and researchers in many related disciplines (see for instance Cantwell-Smith 2002, Jackson 2006, Latour 2003, McCarty 2005, Winograd and Flores 1986).

In the early 1970s access to computers was through a corporate culture, and applications were predominantly of a computational data processing variety. The need to make the most efficient and effective use of what were at that time limited and expensive resources focused attention on issues such as the design of algorithms, the structure of programs, and the abstract processes of software construction. The advent of the personal computer, and the technological developments that brought computing into prominence in everyday life, transformed the practice of computing and challenged its epistemological framework. It has become difficult to understand the role that the classical theory of computation is playing—and potentially can play—in a computing culture dominated by rich digital artefacts, where issues of embodiment and human experience come much higher on the agenda.

To make a speculative analogy, the corporate computing culture of the 1970s might be seen to have had a counterpart in the courts of eighteenth-century musical patrons. The context in which music was commissioned and performed influenced its character, tending to promote its formal and decorative aspects. The turn of the nineteenth century saw the rise of the artist as an autonomous subject; this was a period during which instrumentation developed significantly in ways that afforded new potential for orchestral sound. It also saw the development of the pianoforte as a bourgeois domestic instrument that in some respects had a role analogous to that of the personal computer, giving individuals access to effects that had previously required large organized groups of instrumentalists. During this period, it became possible for ambitious musical compositions to be conceived that reflected the greater autonomy of the composer.

Beethoven's innovative treatment of musical forms and meanings serves as a useful illustration. This included elaborations of established forms (as discussed in Caplin 1998); deviation from the traditional organization of the harmonic palette, enabling the organization of tonal canvases on an unprecedentedly large scale (as discussed in Tovey 1944); and the assimilation of narrative elements (as discussed by Seaton (2005) in his commentary on the 'Tempest' Sonata). Significant as these innovations were, it is in emancipating new potential modes of musical meaning that they perhaps had the greatest novelty and impact. Beethoven's own testimony concerning the personal meaning invested in his music—corroborated by his sketch and conversation books, and embellished as his reputation grew—itself helped to stimulate this. The close association of music with the 'great' composers and their personal lives licensed attitudes that for many years inhibited critical analysis of cultural influences on the construction of musical meaning (see Cooke 1959, Garnett 1998, Hatten 1994). Various recent approaches in musicology have derived some of their force from a reaction to such neglect.

It is the parallel between musicology and computer science—rather than that between musical and computing artefacts—that is crucial here. Musical compositions and modern-day computing products are necessarily hybrid, having both formal and experiential characteristics. It is no more appropriate to classify one product of computer technology as strictly a 'program' and another as strictly an 'artefact' than it is to classify one musical composition as 'classical' and another as 'romantic'. But our conceptions of computing and musical artefacts cannot be divorced from the ways in which they come to be constructed and analysed—both must evolve together. In computer science there is topical need for a stance that can justify a more pluralistic interpretation of computing artefacts. What is more, this pluralism has to be consistent with the need in conventional applications for meanings that are sufficiently objective to endorse traditional computational activity. In musicology, there is a topical need for a more principled and discriminating stance on the interpretation of musical artefacts.

What is more, this must take account of the objections that led to earlier musicological outlooks being placed under critical scrutiny.

Conjunction and experience: perspectives from James

Endorsing plurality in interpretation while giving integrity to a pluralistic world is a central concern in James's philosophical outlook (cf. James 1909). I shall develop this theme by first reviewing how James's thinking relates to the shift in perspective on music that can be associated with the classical and romantic musical traditions; I shall then briefly consider how computer science can benefit from a similar shift in perspective.

The philosophical stance behind James's vision of consciousness is that of *radical empiricism*. In an empiricist outlook it is commonplace to think of entities being separated in our direct experience. In listening to a song we hear the sound of the piano and the sound of the voice, and distinguish these. James's contention, as set out in his preface to *The Meaning of Truth*, is that *relations* connecting the entities we perceive as separate are also given in experience: 'The relations between things, conjunctive as well as disjunctive, are just as much matters of experience, neither more nor less so, than the things themselves' (1911a: xii–xiii). The connection that the pianist makes between a note on the stave and a note on the keyboard can be such a relation. Such conjunctions can also relate to less mundane aspects of experience, as in a listener's emotional response to a chord.

James's perspective is well attuned to the sensitivities of contemporary musicologists in key respects. This can be seen in relation to what Jenefer Robinson identifies as 'the most fundamental question' in the introduction to her *Music and Meaning*: 'Can music, without the help of words (as in song, opera, or program music), signify aspects of human life and experience "beyond" the music? And if so, how?' (1997: 4). In the spirit of the quotation from James with which I began this chapter, we can assert that the separation of experience into 'music' and 'beyond the music' is a specious duality. Nor does the idea of a relation directly given in experience decisively endorse or contradict the kinds of rational explanations for musical responses that are proposed by Boden (2006a), are postulated by Cope (2005), or underlie Cooke's attempt to decipher 'the language of music' (Cooke 1959). But, in keeping with James's view that 'the "truth" of our mental operations must always be an intra-experiential affair' (1912b: 202), the claims for each of these possible construals of musical meaning are subject to pragmatic validation, and rest ultimately on matters of personal experience.

James's philosophical stance gives a positive answer to the first of the two questions posed by Robinson ('Can music . . . signify aspects of human life and experience "beyond" the music?'), but not in such a way as to decisively refute the sceptical scientist or formalist. Reliable and immediate associations between abstract music and extra-musical signifiers are commonplace in many musicians' experience, but to what extent these associations can be regarded as objective is much harder to establish. Some associations will be entirely personal, perhaps relating to life events of a totally individual nature. Others will be connected with cultural factors, perhaps derived from a common tradition of musical education. Possibly some associations have deep cognitive or physiological roots. What distinguishes James's epistemologi-cal stance in such matters is his contention that 'subjectivity and objectivity are affairs not of what an experience is aboriginally made of, but of its classification' (James 1912c: 141).

James also offers an explicit answer to Robinson's subsidiary question ('If so, how?'). In his essay 'How two minds can know one thing' he draws attention to the impossi-bility of explaining the origin and nature of relations given in experience:

> Experiences come on an enormous scale, and if we take them all together, they come in a chaos of incommensurable relations that we can not straighten out. We have to abstract different groups of them, and handle these separately if we are to talk of them at all. But how the experiences ever *get themselves made*, or *why* their characters and relations are just such as appear, we can not begin to understand. (James 1912d: 133)

It might be plausible to construe 'we can not begin to understand' in the light of the much more rudimentary knowledge of neuroscience a century ago. However, given the pragmatic nature of James's outlook, and the emphasis he has added to the text, this is surely not his intended meaning. Conjunctive relations in our experience can indeed be established in the most accidental and unpredictable ways. Their empirical and potentially transient nature is entirely in keeping with James's contention that 'radical empiricism . . . refuses to substitute static concepts of the understanding for transitions in our moving life' (1912e: 238–9).

Neither is the substance of James's observations about consciousness undermined by advances in neuroscience. Gerald Edelman, for instance, cites the need for models of consciousness that reflect what he identifies as Jamesian properties: 'Consciousness is a form of awareness, is continuous but continually changing, is private, has inten-tionality, and does not exhaust the properties of its objects' (Edelman 2005: 164). In Edelman's view, 'computer or machine models of the brain and mind do not work' (114). In their place, he proposes an alternative organizing principle—based on the (controversial) notion of a 'phenomenal transform'—in which a conscious process depends upon its underlying neural activity in a fashion that echoes James's notion of conjunctive relation (Edelman 2005: 76–8).

James's view of consciousness is predicated on our capacity to make separations within our immediate experience and yet apprehend these separate components as one. An apposite view of consciousness corroborated by experimental research in neuroscience is again offered by Edelman: 'One extraordinary phenomenal feature of conscious experience is that normally it is all of one piece . . . Any experienced con-scious moment simultaneously includes sensory input, consequences of motor activity, imagery, emotions, fleeting memories, bodily sensations, and a peripheral fringe' (61). This bringing of unity to diversity relies on a complementary phenomenon: the fact that 'consciousness can be modulated by focal attention' (61).

The tension between attending to an experience as a whole or focusing on specific ingredients within it is familiar to every experienced musician. The objective of rehearsal may be to integrate many aspects of a musical experience, but the process may involve the independent exploration of each aspect in detail. Realizing the form of music involves subordinating the details and specific contextual ingredients of musical experience; while appreciating music as an experience entails being responsive to all the relations that are conjured by each momentary sound.

It is the reference here to 'momentary sound', rather than to formalistic musical elements (such as notes or phrases), and to all the relationships to which this can allude through conjunction in direct experience, that opens the Pandora's box of contemporary musicological concerns. To what extent does this sound encompass the tuning of the instrument, the extraneous noises made by the performer, or the coughing of the audience? To what extent does it embrace the contextual factors that are contingent on the situation, such as the acoustics of the hall, the topical life events that might impinge on the imagination of the performer uniquely on this occasion, or the actual thunderstorm that coincidentally accompanied the thunderstorm in a performance of Beethoven's *Pastoral Symphony* I once attended?

The relationship between a formal intellectual stance on experience and an open pluralistic interpretation of experience is the primary concern in James's *A Pluralistic Universe*. With these two perspectives in mind James writes:

> The only way in which to apprehend reality's thickness is either to experience it directly by being a part of reality one's self, or to evoke it in imagination by sympathetically divining some one else's inner life. But what we thus immediately experience or concretely divine is very limited in duration, whereas abstractly we are able to conceive eternities. (James 1909: 250–1)

James promotes a view of experience that goes beyond what, in relation to music, could be conceptualized in conventional musical terms. In particular, he alludes to a distinction between time as *felt* and time as conceptualized (developed at length in his discussion of Zeno's paradox of Achilles and the Tortoise) that would subvert the idea of individual notes as atomic elements of musical experience. In keeping with the Jamesian notion that knowing—rooted as it is in directly experienced conjunctions—is of its essence personal, I shall illustrate the above discussion with reference to my own musical experience.

A personal case study

In the course of preparing this chapter I have in parallel carried out some informal experiments in musical performance to understand better my own musical consciousness. My main access to music is through the score. Within the musical tradition with which I am most familiar I can read and play from the score much of the piano literature to a passable standard. With the score in front of me I am aware of the structure of a composition, can parse complex phrases and chords without difficulty, and appreciate harmonic progressions and tonality. Without the score, despite being able to find great enjoyment as a listener, I have by contrast scarcely any conscious conceptual grasp of this rich musical content. Any kind of reconstruction of the score, or realization of a performance, from the sound alone—whether in playing from memory, or playing by ear—is extremely problematic. With a view to understanding this limitation better, I have been trying to memorize music with which I am very familiar.

My observations have highlighted for me the complexity of the interaction between many aspects of the experience of playing the piano that come together fluently in my experience when I play from the score, but are otherwise for the most part obstinately dislocated. They give practical insight into what it means to say that relationships can be given in personal experience. I recognize that my ability to sight-read music is informed by two component skills that are not specifically concerned with music as an aural experience at all: a facility for identifying visual patterns that has been acquired through long experience of reading conventional chords and harmonic progressions; and dexterity at reconfiguring and moving my hands that is predominantly muscular in nature and does not in general require me to look at the keyboard.

By comparison, when trying to play from memory I am deprived of the visual experience that is quite clearly my primary gateway to musical knowledge and competence. There are figurations and coordination patterns that I can only physically play with the score in front of me. I have difficulty in reliably discerning any coherent disjunctions in my experience. For instance, unused to looking at my hands while playing, I cannot directly apprehend a connection between playing specific notes and hearing the associated sound as confidently and immediately as I connect patterns in the score with configurations of the hands.

These experiments illustrate key characteristics of James's notion of conjunctions-given-in-experience: the significance of connections that are immediately registered rather than laboriously figured out; the relevance of practice and rehearsal; the essential personal character. There is no way in which you can corroborate my account by studying it as a propositional statement. Yet, despite its subjectivity, its authenticity could to some extent be confirmed by a suitably qualified observer inviting me to demonstrate the competences I claim. As for the authenticity of my claims to incompetence, they pose a greater problem, though I know only too well that the absence of certain kinds of directly perceived relationship in my musical experience is genuine.

It is in relation to broader conjunctions, such as those that impute subjective and/or emotional content to music, that the 'romantic turn' in the conception of music discussed above becomes topical. Where composers explicitly testify that their compositions have been conceived with associations drawn from 'external' experience, considerations similar to those raised above pertain. We have no direct or decisive means to authenticate their claims. But, insofar as it makes sense to speak of corroboration, it is to interpreters and performers who realize the musical experience, rather than musical analysts, to whom we must turn. It is only the performer who can venture to make sense of music as an object whose properties cannot be exhausted—in keeping with Mahler's cryptic dictum 'Das Wichtigste steht nicht in den Noten' ('The most important part [of music] is not in the notes') (Nikkels 1999: 327); or with Schumann's paradoxical injunction to play the coda to the final movement of his Piano Sonata Op. 22 *prestissimo* ('as fast as possible') with subsequent indications to play *immer schneller und schneller* ('ever faster and faster').

In assessing claims to musical meaning beyond formal explication, we may posit the performer as an experimenter. In this context the intentional fallacy is a necessary, if entirely speculative, part of the hypothesis, since the music is assumed to have invoked a conjunction in experience in the consciousness of its composer. Consistent with the romantic stance of James articulated in the preceding quotation, the performer's attention is attuned to 'sympathetically divining some one else's inner life'; is focused

Example 9.1 Schumann, 'In der Nacht', *Fantasiestücke*, Op. 12: opening.

on what is 'immediately experienced'; and is 'very limited in duration'. But whereas the formal analysis of music begins with the score as a given, the consciousness of each moment that is demanded of the performer may be fragile and hard-earned.

By way of illustration, consider the pianist's task in performing the opening bars of Schumann's 'In der Nacht' from his *Fantasiestücke*, Op. 12 (Example 9.1). To be able first to juggle the surging arpeggio figurations in groups of eight semiquaver between two hands in such a way as to emphasize the sighing quaver–crochet beats, then to transfer the arpeggio figuration entirely to the left hand and superimpose a triplet figure in the right demands practised skill of the performer, qualities of the instrument, a suitable context for listening, and clarity of mind. Beyond that, the effect will not—in compliance with Schumann's annotations—express fervour (*mit Leidenshaft*) or evoke being 'in the night' without the most careful attention to an elusive balance of touch, dynamic, and rhythm.

By far the most challenging aspect of interpreting 'In der Nacht' is dealing with the associations that are least directly linked to the formal structure. The idea that the notes are intrinsically and objectively associated with being 'in the night' is but a romantic notion. The piano teacher will nevertheless incite the imagination of a pupil by using imagery in ways that unquestionably contribute not merely to mastering a pattern of sound but to achieving a phenomenal effect. Though it may of itself have little to do with the imagery of night, prior experience of watching waves breaking on the shore and hearing the undertow of other waves receding may help in conjuring the state of consciousness to which the pianist aspires in these opening bars.

As the above discussion illustrates, a significant factor in the effective exposure of conjunctions is understanding of an 'extra-musical' nature. This is especially relevant where music has an explicit programme or text. In Schumann's song 'Mondnacht' from his *Liederkreis* Op. 39) the sentiment that the music ostensibly accompanies is explicit in von Eichendorff's eponymous poem. Each of the three verses is a different take on what it is to experience a moonlit night. In verse 1, whose opening is quoted in Example 9.2(a), it is 'as if heaven had laid on earth a kiss' (*als hätt der Himmel die Erde still geküsst*); in verse 2 it is that 'the breeze sighs over the meadows and the waving corn' (*Die Luft ging durch die Felder, die Ähren wogten sacht*); and in verse 3 it is as if 'my soul spreads out its wings . . . and flies home' (*meine Seele spannte weit ihre Flügel aus . . . als flöge sie nach Haus*). The pulse of the song is maintained through some 400 stately semiquavers. Embedded within the texture of the accompaniment, in tension with the melody but in such a way as to accentuate the sense of momentary transitions in experience, a single note is at one point repeated more than 40 times. This invites the performers to enlist or refresh conjunctions in experience repeatedly, setting up a field of possible interpretations to which the words serve as a guide.

Rehearsing the accompaniment to 'Mondnacht' is an exercise in managing consciousness while realizing an experience. In this rehearsal, the words colour the way in which each note is interpreted. The superposition of the three different takes on one experience is suggested in the music by repeating a pattern of simple phrases three times, but leaving the cadence at the end of the first two iterations unresolved (like the semicolons in my textual description). The sentiment of flying home is conveyed by moving decisively towards a closing perfect cadence on the final repetition (see Example 9.2(b)). Rehearsal is the means to discovering what effects are under your control, and how to exercise that control most expressively. Each of the individual semiquavers has its significance in relation to the whole, but their execution is one of many aspects that need to be absorbed into the subconscious for a performance to be effective. The notion of conjunction in experience applies quite as much to matters of detail (such as how the pianist shapes the dynamics of notes within each chord and phrase) as to the overall interpretation. How successful the performance is perceived to be will be highly dependent on matters over which it is hard to gain conscious control, such as what associations come to mind in the particular context of performance.

These discussions of musical performance exemplify the experience-led crafting of an artefact in association with sense-making. Such an activity is nowhere better represented than in music-making, whether in composition or in performance. Conceiving or performing music invokes moment-by-moment experience. The art of the composer or the performer may be to minimize or to conceal the effort invested in crafting each moment. It may also be to draw the focus of attention to a specific moment by placing it in a context that invites reflection and response.

Empirical Modelling and musical phenomenology

An approach to artefacts in which the primary emphasis is phenomenological rather than functional is not only ill-matched to a computational model of mind but also quite unlike any established way of conceiving computing artefacts in certain key respects. Even in processes like agile programming, in which development involves interaction with partially completed prototypes, there is no counterpart to

Example 9.2(a) Schumann, 'Mondnacht', *Liederkreis*, Op. 39. Opening (verse 1).

Example 9.2(b) Closing cadence (verse 3).

the coherent journey through states of mind on which both the composer and performer set out to travel step-by-step. This is unsurprising when we consider Brian Cantwell-Smith's observation concerning the largely mysterious nature of the connection between a piece of software as traditionally conceived and the external world to which its constituent components refer (Cantwell-Smith 1987: 215). By contrast, EM is a body of principles and tools that has been developed with a view to shifting from a functional to a phenomenological perspective on interaction with computer artefacts. I shall focus here on sketching the analogies that EM establishes between musical and computing artefacts.[1]

EM is to be practised and appreciated as an activity that involves tracking states of mind. In this respect it is—at any rate in aspiration—very similar in character to music-making. Its primary focus is on an open-ended process of exploration that involves identifying through rehearsal the stable entities in experience ('observables'); the relationships that express the way in which changes to these observables are perceived to be directly linked ('dependency'); and the means by which these observables are subject to change ('agency'). The artefact and the patterns of interaction that the modeller weaves around it evolve in parallel, and serve as means of exposing tacit understanding (cf. Polanyi 1961, 1983). To echo the Jamesian characteristics of consciousness, as identified by Edelman, such modelling serves to explore—and celebrate—the respects in which the properties of its object cannot be exhausted.

The effect of such activity is to create a network of dependencies between observables, somewhat similar to the defining formulae that relate the cells of a spreadsheet, or to the physical dependencies between keys and vibrating strings in a piano. At any given instant, the network itself metaphorically resembles a single sustained sound, a moment in time, or a state of mind. The most significant feature of a dependency between observables, which is typically expressed by formulating an explicit definition, is that it specifies implicit computational activity to update values (cf. the updating activity in a spreadsheet)—activity that is latent in the model and is hidden from the modeller. As far as the modeller is concerned, such a dependency simply expresses the way in which one change to an observable entails another. And since—on account of the speed at which the update is carried out—this entailment is perceived as an atomic connection, it establishes a form of conjunctive relation such as James identifies in his account of consciousness.

The most significant music-related model that has been built with EM tools to date is a model of Schubert's celebrated song *Erlkönig* (D. 328).[2] The observables in this model correspond quite precisely to the features to which a musician might attend in a performance. They relate to each specific moment in the song, and include display components—as shown in Figure 9.1—to convey (i) the current key, (ii) the current role being played by the singer, (iii) the words being sung, and (iv) some characteristic features of the accompaniment. The principal observables and dependencies that can be found in this model are depicted in the dependency graph in Figure 9.2, where each node corresponds to an observable and each incoming edge at a node emanates from an observable on which its value depends. As can be seen from Figure 9.2, all the components of the visualization are linked by dependency to the current point in the score, as recorded in the observable termed *noofbeats*: the 'number of [triplet quaver] beats' from the beginning of the song. By way of illustration, Figure 9.1 corresponds to the moment at which the Erlkönig makes his final appearance, and the current value of *noofbeats* at this point in the score is 933.

The main novelty in the *Erlkönig* model is the way it visually conveys the harmonic subtlety of Schubert's setting. For this purpose, it exploits an animation of the traditional cycle of keys together with a colour wheel that associates colours with keys according to a mathematical formula (see Figure 9.1). This animation is unconventional in that at certain points in the song there is tonic major–minor ambiguity that is quite characteristic of Schubert, but is especially prominently and unusually expressed in *Erlkönig*. To convey this harmonic effect faithfully visually, it is appropriate to distort the geometric figure that displays the cycle of keys in such a way that the nodes representing major–minor tonalities associated with the same tonic are from time to time dynamically conflated. Such a distortion is in progress in Figure 9.1, where the outer circle representing the minor keys is rotating anticlockwise and contracting in such a way that the nodes representing C major and C minor will coincide. This reflects the tonal ambiguity at the point where the Erlkönig issues his final ultimatum to the child.

The entire *Erlkönig* model was constructed manually by analysing the score—a process that more closely resembled the rehearsal that leads up to a musical performance than conventional computer programming. There was no direct counterpart of the compiling and debugging of a global algorithmic specification of the model behaviour that is characteristic of programming. In musical terms, the mapping of dependency establishes a simultaneous vertical conjunction similar to an aggregation of harmony,

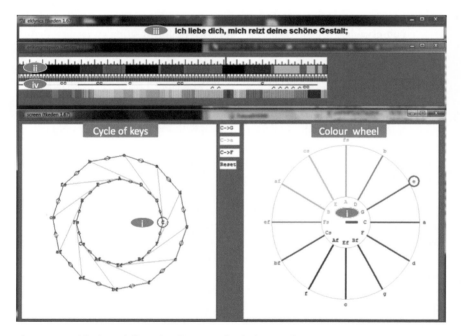

Fig. 9.1 Empirical Modelling visualization of Schubert, *Erlkönig*, D. 328.

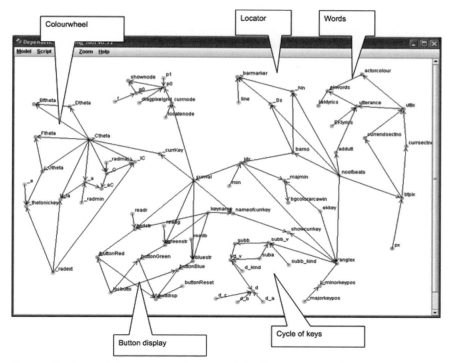

Fig. 9.2 Empirical Modelling dependency graph for Schubert, *Erlkönig*.

texture, and context, while the linear melodic elements are first realized through tracing out manually the changes to the primary observables. Automating the execution of the visualization in the model in conjunction with a recorded performance of the song then requires only a synchronization of the current location in the song with a point in the performance. This can be simply achieved through adapting the digital audio output so that the value of the observable *noofbeats* is incremented on each beat.

In this process of model development, the metaphor of rehearsal is most apt. There is the same sense of gradual building from mastery of momentary state towards gestures extending over time, sometimes developed individually and subsequently integrated. There is a prominent sense of the layering of consciousness. The primitive relationships that are to be expressed by dependency (such as that which determines the current bar number from the number of beats elapsed, or associates a specific colour with the current key—cf. Figure 9.2) are first consciously crafted, then composed in an incremental fashion to establish more complex relationships. At each stage, what has been successfully expressed through dependencies becomes a part of the modeller's subconscious environment. This happens both in the mind of the human modeller, in that attention shifts from the mechanism that was used to establish the dependency to the higher level relationships between observables that the dependency establishes, and in the concrete model itself, where the mechanism is no longer being explicitly observed and invoked but serves to update relationships automatically.

As in rehearsal, an important aspect of the shifting focus of attention during model-building is the manner in which—in Jamesian terms—new conjunctions become topical. This is the kind of phenomenon highlighted earlier, in the discussion of Schumann's 'In der Nacht'. As the rehearsal proceeds, the performer's attention moves—as far as his or her skill allows—from individual notes, to musical figures, to synchronizing and balancing parts, to melodic lines, to musical structures and to affective impact. Although this uplifting of attention can be facilitated by studying the composition as a whole, the experience of conjunction itself has to come from the performance. This mode of acquiring understanding ('understanding forwards') is identified by James as quite characteristic of radical empiricism, in keeping with that '[refusal] to substitute static concepts of the understanding for transitions in our moving life' mentioned above (James 1912e: 238). A parallel can also be drawn with certain styles of composition, whereby—rather than stating themes that are subsequently developed, as in classical sonata form—a composer first presents thematic material in fragmentary form that is only later integrated into a coherent statement (of which an example might be the first movement of Sibelius's Second Symphony).

Perhaps the most important affinity between EM and music is the capacity it affords for live migration and negotiation of meaning. The observables in a network of dependencies need have no specific declared meaning—they represent whatever they can enlist from the modeller's imagination according to the patterns they exhibit when some change to an observable or dependency is introduced. In contrast, the primitive ingredients of a conventional program are themselves behaviours with specific functions optimized to best serve the specific function of the whole. In realizing a behaviour, a conventional program's engagement with the environment is then intentionally similar to that of a musical recording: it plays obliviously, quite possibly immaculately, but not in such a way as to admit ready integration with any other musical recording.

In EM one model can be composed with another simply by combining two or more networks of dependencies. In the first instance, this combination may involve no more than treating several unrelated networks as if they were one. Much more expressive power can be realized by adapting or extending the dependencies within individual networks so that they become interrelated. A simple, if somewhat contrived, example designed to illustrate this principle adapted an EM model originally developed to emulate an educational program called JUGS (Beynon *et al.* 1989). This model featured two containers that held integer quantities of liquid, and incorporated definitions of all the observables and dependencies necessary to express operations such as prescribing the capacities and contents of the containers, filling and emptying containers, and pouring liquid from one to the other. The observables in this model were taken in conjunction with a totally independent model of a standard music keyboard. By adding a small set of dependencies it was possible to relate the content of the containers to locations on the keyboard and to modify the visualization of the containers so that they both had the same 'capacity' but were of very narrow width.[3] In this way, the containers could be viewed as representing the strings of a guitar, and the combined model as depicting how the notes that might be played by selecting frets on a guitar would correspond to notes on the keyboard.

James: further prospects

In this chapter, I have set out in broad terms respects in which James's philosophical stance of radical empiricism holds promise in relation to epistemological problems that currently face both musicology and computer science. The parallels I have drawn between musical compositions and computing artefacts motivate an account that can unify musical and computing perspectives on consciousness. Any such unification must contend with the paradigm that computer science has traditionally endorsed: the computational theory of mind. Boden identifies this theory with the claim that 'mind is explicable by *whatever theory turns out to be the best account of what computers do*' (Boden 2006b: 1428)—which is a paraphrase of Chrisley's characterization of Transparent Computationalism as 'the claim that the best account of cognition will be given by *whatever theory turns out to be the best account of the phenomenon of computation*' (2000: 106). The analogy between computers and musical instruments, the points of convergence between activities such as musical rehearsal and EM, and the modern development of new musical instruments with much greater technological sophistication and scope for autonomous and adaptive behaviour lead me to suggest an alternative thesis: that (to adapt Chrisley's words) 'mind is explicable by *whatever theory turns out to be the best account of the phenomenon of music, or of what musical instruments do*'. Defending this thesis serves to highlight some of the key characteristics of a Jamesian outlook as they relate to Edelman's view of consciousness and to EM.

Edelman's emphatic opposition to the notion of the brain as computer has stimulated fierce criticism (see for example Boden 2006b: 1200–5). I have been no more successful than other—better qualified—reviewers in understanding Edelman's research in point of detail, but my experience of EM comprehensively endorses his contention that investigating how conjunctive relationships between experiences are established in the brain is quite distinct from *devising a new variety of computation*. Computational frameworks are archetypally concerned with prescribing behaviours that achieve functional goals through manipulating inputs and monitoring outputs that have preconceived, abstractly specified interpretations. By contrast, the studies to which EM and Edelman's research relate are essentially concerned with creating dispositions in which the human observer perceives semantic connections. In EM the emphasis is on explicitly crafting artefacts through model-building and managing the contexts for observation in such a way as to recruit conjunctive relations in immediate experience. In Edelman's research, the focus is on determining through experiment how such perceived relations correspond to the organization of neural structures in the brain.

The mind resembles a computer or a musical instrument according to whether we see the brain as performing computation or establishing dispositions. I speculate that Edelman's preference for the latter interpretation stems in part from his experience as a practising musician who might in other circumstances have become a professional violinist.[4] To the musician, making meaning moment-by-moment through the engagement of mind and body with an instrument is quite unlike performing a computation. A computational interpretation relies on being able to invoke causality without ambiguity. As has been illustrated in previous discussions, it is impossible to determine to which of a wealth of factors a musical performance owes its effect.

The principle that we can have no absolute knowledge of causality is one of the fundamental premises of James's pragmatic stance: 'no philosophic knowledge of the general nature and constitution of tendencies, or of the relation of larger to smaller ones, can help us to predict which of all the various competing tendencies that interest us in this universe are likeliest to prevail' (1912f: 180; see also 178–80). This is not to dismiss the importance of the attributions of agency we make when linking the way in which we depress the piano key with the resulting sound, or when—within the context of a particular musical tradition—we associate a certain emotional response with a specific harmonic progression. In respect of musical idioms and compositions, where melodic, harmonic, and rhythmic features that are astonishing in one context are commonplace in another, the musician develops a capacity to entertain different realities, and inhabit each as if it were the sole reality. Different concepts are apposite to each context, and have to be assimilated into the subconscious as if they could not be otherwise. But the essential need for the musician to be alive all the while to new possibilities accords well with James's assertion that 'as reality is created temporally day by day, concepts . . . can never fitly supersede perception . . . The deeper features of reality are found only in perceptual experience' (James 1911b/1996: 100, 97). In this way, construals of music can legitimately represent perspectives that range freely from the formal to the experiential.

It may also be that deeper exploration of the relevance of radical empiricism for music can offer reciprocal support for some of James's thinking. As Taylor and Wozniak (1996) observe, James's philosophical writings have not enjoyed the same degree of respect and influence as his contributions to psychology (most notably James 1890/1950). Marianne Janack (2004) attributes the suspicion with which many later philosophers view James to his failure to acknowledge the epistemological border between philosophy and psychology. In particular, James insists on considering reasons for belief in conjunction with causes for belief, maintaining that we cannot freely elect to believe or disbelieve propositions on the grounds of their rationality alone. Janack's concise interpretation of James's accounts of the relationship between reality and belief (cf. for instance James 1890/1950, vol. 2: 297) is that what carries conviction for a person must have for them the sting of reality (Janack 2004). The confluence of formal and experiential factors in music discussed in this chapter highlights the way in which musical appreciation similarly blurs the duality between our intellectual and our passional natures.

Other objections to a Jamesian stance centre on its treatment of language. In response to James's account of 'pure experience', in which the notion of a conjunctive relation plays a fundamental role, the philosopher Graham Bird writes: 'We are left . . . with a puzzle about the role or sense of "pure experience". It is evidently of great importance in James's account, and yet also totally inarticulate' (1986: 108). Bird goes on to cite Wittgenstein's observation to the effect that 'a nothing would do as well as something about which nothing can be said' (1953: 304). The presumptions about the expressive reach of language implicit in such a criticism may be viewed with some scepticism by musicians. They are unlikely to agree with Boden (1995) when she writes: 'the constraints of music, complex though they are, are more amenable to definition than those involved in literature'.

An alternative perspective on language that is much closer to the spirit of radical empiricism and EM is framed by Don Paterson in an essay expressing his understanding of what it is to be a poet. Having first characterized primal experience as preceding language and being imbued with a sense of 'everything as everything else', he writes:

> When we allow silence to reclaim those objects and things of the world, when we allow the words to fall away from them—they reassume their own genius, and repossess something of their mystery, their infinite possibility. Then we awaken a little to the realm of the symmetries again, and of no-time, eternity . . . [W]hen the things of the world . . . that we have contemplated in this wordless and thoughtless silence reenter the world of assymetrical concept, of discrete definition, of speech and language—they return as strangers; and then they declare wholly unexpected allegiances, reveal wholly unsuspected valencies. We see the nerve in the bare tree; we hear the applause in the rain. These things are, in other words, *redreamt*, they are *reimagined*, they are *remade*. This I think is the deepest meaning of our etymology as maker. (Paterson 2004)

Perhaps it is no coincidence that Paterson is also a performing musician.

References

Beynon, W.M. (2005). Radical Empiricism, Empirical Modelling and the nature of knowing. *Pragmatics and Cognition*, **13**, 615–46.

Beynon, W.M. (2006). *Mathematics and music—models and morals*, in R. Sarhangi and J. Sharp (eds.), *Bridges London: Mathematical Connections in Art, Music, and Science*, Conference Proceedings, 437–44 (St Albans: Tarquin Books). Available at: www2.warwick.ac.uk/fac/sci/dcs/research/em/publications/papers/094/ (accessed 30 March 2010).

Beynon, W.M., Norris, M.T., Russ, S.B., Yung, Y.P., and Yung, Y.W. (1989). *Software construction using definitions: an illustrative example.* Computer Science Research Report No. 147, University of Warwick. Available at: www.dcs.warwick.ac.uk/reports/147.html (accessed 30 March 2010).

Beynon, W.M., Russ, S.B., and McCarty, W. (2006). Human computing: modelling with meaning. *Literary and Linguistic Computing*, **21**, 141–57.

Bird, G. (1986). *William James*. 'The Arguments of the Philosophers' (series) (London: Routledge and Kegan Paul).

Boden, M. (1995). Creativity and unpredictability. *Stanford Humanities Review*, **4**, special issue: *Constructions of the Mind*. Available at: www.stanford.edu/group/SHR/4-2/text/toc.html (accessed 30 March 2010).

Boden, M. (2006a). What can AI teach us about arts and letters? Seminar, Centre for Computing in the Humanities, King's College London, 23 November.

Boden, M. (2006b). *Mind as Machine: a History of Cognitive Science*, vol. 2 (Oxford: Oxford University Press).

Cantwell-Smith, B. (1987). Two lessons of logic. *Computational Intelligence*, **3**, 214–18.

Cantwell-Smith, B. (2002). The foundations of computing, in Scheutz, M. (ed.), *Computationalism: New Directions*, 23–58 (Cambridge, MA: MIT Press).

Caplin, W.E. (1998). *Classical Form: a Theory of Formal Functions for the Instrumental Music of Haydn, Mozart, and Beethoven* (New York, NY: Oxford University Press).

Chrisley, R.L. (2000). Transparent computationalism, in M Scheutz (ed.), *New Computationalism: Conceptus-Studien* **14**, 105–21. Available at: www.cogs.susx.ac.uk/users/ronc/transparent.pdf (accessed 30 March 2010).

Cooke, D. (1959). *The Language of Music* (London: Oxford University Press).

Cope, D. (2001). *Virtual Music: Computer Synthesis of Musical Style* (Cambridge, MA: MIT Press).

Cope, D. (2005). *Computer Models of Musical Creativity* (Cambridge, MA: MIT Press).

Desain, P. and Honing, H. (1992). *Music, Mind and Machine: Studies in Computer Music, Music Cognition and Artificial Intelligence* (Amsterdam: Thesis Publishers).

Edelman, G. (2005). *Wider than the Sky: A Revolutionary View of Consciousness* (London: Penguin Books).

Empirical Modelling Projects Archive. Available at: http://empublic.dcs.warwick.ac.uk/projects (accessed 6 August 2010).

Empirical Modelling Research Group. Available at: www.dcs.warwick.ac.uk/modelling (accessed 6 August 2010).

Empirical Modelling Web Eden. Available at www.warwick.ac.uk/go/webeden (accessed 6 August 2010).

Garnett, L. (1998). Musical meaning revisited: thoughts on an 'epic' critical musicology. *Critical Musicology Journal*. Available at: www.leeds.ac.uk/music/Info/critmus/articles/1998/01/01.html (accessed 30 March 2010).

Gjerdingen, R.O. (1990). Categorisation of musical patterns by self-organising neuron-like networks. *Music Perception*, **7**, 339–70.

Hatten, R. (1994). *Musical Meaning in Beethoven: Markedness, Correlation, and Interpretation* (Bloomington, IN: Indiana University Press).

Hofstadter, D. (2001). Staring EMI straight in the eye—and doing my best not to flinch, in D. Cope (ed.), *Virtual Music: Computer Synthesis of Musical Style*, 33–82 (Cambridge, MA: MIT Press).

Hofstadter, D. (n.d.). *Sounds like Bach*. Available at: www.unc.edu/~mumukshu/gandhi/gandhi/hofstadter.htm (accessed 29 March 2010).

Hooper, G. (2006). *The Discourse of Musicology* (Aldershot: Ashgate).

Jackson, M. (2006). What can we expect from program verification? *IEEE Computer*, **39**(10): 53–9.

James, W. (1890/1950). *The Principles of Psychology*, 2 vols (New York, NY: Dover Publications).

James, W. (1909). *A Pluralistic Universe* (New York, NY: Longmans, Green, and Co.).

James, W. (1911a). *The Meaning of Truth* (New York, NY: Longmans, Green, and Co.).

James, W. (1911b/1996). *Some Problems of Philosophy: A Beginning of an Introduction to Philosophy* (Lincoln, NE: University of Nebraska Press).

James, W. (1912a). Does consciousness exist? in *Essays in Radical Empiricism*, 1–38 (New York, NY: Longmans, Green, and Co.).

James, W. (1912b). The essence of humanism, in *Essays in Radical Empiricism*, 190–205 (New York, NY: Longmans, Green, and Co.).

James, W. (1912c). The place of affectional facts in a world of pure experience, in *Essays in Radical Empiricism*, 137–54 (New York, NY: Longmans, Green, and Co.).

James, W. (1912d). How two minds can know one thing, in *Essays in Radical Empiricism*, 123–36 (New York, NY: Longmans, Green, and Co.).

James, W. (1912e). Is Radical Empiricism solipsistic? in *Essays in Radical Empiricism*, 234–41 (New York, NY: Longmans, Green, and Co.).

James, W. (1912f). The experience of activity, in *Essays in Radical Empiricism*, 155–90 (New York, NY: Longmans, Green, and Co.).

Janack, M. (2004). Changing the epistemological and psychological subject: William James's psychology without borders. *Metaphilosophy*, **35**, 160–77.

Latour, B. (2003). The promises of constructivism, in D. Ihde and E. Selinger (eds.), *Chasing Technoscience: Matrix for Materiality*, 27–46 (Bloomington, IN: University of Indiana Press).

Longuet-Higgins, H.C. (1978). The perception of music. *Interdisciplinary Science Reviews*, **3**, 148–215.

McCarty, W. (2005). *Humanities Computing* (New York, NY: Palgrave MacMillan).

Nikkels, E. (1999). Mahler and Holland, in D. Mitchell and A. Nicholson (eds.), *The Mahler Companion*, 326–37 (Oxford: Oxford University Press).

Paterson, D. (2004). Rhyme and reason, T.S. Eliot Lecture 2004; published in abridged form in *The Guardian Review*, **6**, 34–5. Available at: www.poetrylibrary.org.uk/news/poetryscene/?id=20 (accessed 6 August 2010).

Polanyi, M. (1961). Knowing and being. *Mind*, **70** (new series), 458–70.

Polanyi, M. (1983). *The Tacit Dimension* (Gloucester, MA: Peter Smith).

Robinson, J. (1997). Introduction: new ways of thinking about musical meaning, in J. Robinson (ed.), *Music and Meaning*, 1–22 (Ithaca, NY: Cornell University Press).

Seaton, D. (2005). Narrative in music: the case of Beethoven's 'Tempest' Sonata, in J.C. Meister (ed.), *Narratology beyond Literary Criticism: Mediality, Disciplinarity*, 65–81 (Berlin: Walter de Gruyter).

Steedman, M.J. (1984). A generative grammar for jazz chord sequences. *Music Perception*, **2**, 52–77.

Storr, A. (1993). *Music and the Mind* (New York, NY: Random House).

Taylor, E.I. and Wozniak, R.H. (eds.) (1996). *Pure Experience: The Response to William James* (South Bend, IN: St Augustine's Press).

Todd, P.M. and Loy, D.G. (1991). *Music and connectionism* (Cambridge, MA: MIT Press, Cambridge).

Tovey, D.F. (1944). *Beethoven* (London: Oxford University Press).

Wiggins, G. (2008). Review of D. Cope, *Computer Models of Musical Creativity*. *Literary and Linguistic Computing*, **23**, 109–16.

Wiggins, G., Miranda, E., Smail, A., and Harris, M. (1993). A framework for the evaluation of music representation systems. *Computer Music Journal*, **17**(3), 31–42.

Winograd, T. (1968). Linguistics and the computer analysis of tonal harmony. *Journal of Music Theory*, **12**, 2–49.

Winograd, T. and Flores, F. (1986). *Understanding Computers and Cognition: A New Foundation for Design* (Boston, MA: Addison-Wesley).

Wittgenstein, L. (1953). *Philosophical investigations*, trans. G. Anscombe (Oxford: Blackwell).

Notes

1. Further discussion of EM in its relation to humanities computing and to music in particular can be found in Beynon *et al.* (2006) and Beynon (2006); the association of EM with radical empiricism is the subject of Beynon (2005). See also the website of Warwick University's Empirical Modelling Research Group. (URLs of all websites mentioned in the notes are given in the references).

2. A screenshot from the model similar to that displayed in Figure 9.1 can be seen in context in an online poster (see the directory kaleidoscopeBeynon2005 in the Empirical Modelling Projects Archive), and a variant of the interactive model can also be accessed online via the Empirical Modelling Web Eden webpage.

3. See the online JUGS poster in the directory kaleidoscopeBeynon2005 in the EM archive.

4. For more background, see the biography of Edelman available at: www.notablebiographies.com/supp/Supplement-Ca-Fi/Edelman-Gerald-M.html (accessed 6 July 2010).

Chapter 10

Music, language, and kinds of consciousness

Lawrence M. Zbikowski

Introduction

Let's imagine two situations in which you and I communicate with each other. In the first, I say 'Here is a waltz by Mauro Giuliani.' In the second, I play a waltz by Mauro Giuliani.

One of the first things that may strike you is the way I've stretched the notion of communication. To tell the truth, my use of the word is not very heavily freighted— I intend it simply as a covering term for a sequence of interpersonal exchanges between two people. Running a close second is the question of just who Mauro Giuliani is, something almost certainly outside your knowledge unless you are a guitar aficionado or a student of minor Italian composers of the early nineteenth century. What may never enter the picture are the two very different kinds of consciousness associated with these contrasting situations.

The first kind of consciousness involves a cascade of mental images prompted by the words 'Here is a waltz by Mauro Giuliani' (or 'Hier ist ein Walzer von Mauro Giuliani', or a rendering of the statement in any other natural language; I should emphasize that 'image' in this context is conceived quite broadly, and extends far beyond vision to include any sensory information). Having heard these words, you might well summon a scene in which I present you with a score, a recording, or a performance of the piece; or explain who Mauro Giuliani is; or give some account of why I would want to trouble you with the work and its composer. Your thoughts might also turn to other waltzes that you know, to memories of your first waltz with your aunt, to the last good Italian meal you had, or to reflections on the general state of my sanity.

The second kind of consciousness involves a cascade of mental images prompted by my performance of the work. Although the work that I would play is not a long one (the score is given in Example 10.1), in most cases this cascade will unfold steadily over time, guided by the music and transformed by events like the repetition of the opening material that begins in bar 5 or the introduction of new ideas that begins in bar 9. If you are a dancer, your thoughts may also be informed by the sequence of movements prompted by Giuliani's waltz, by strongly embodied memories of the physical experience of dancing the waltz, and by your attention to the formal articulations of the music (such as the shift from waltz to trio) that would inflect the larger course of your steps. Of course, it is also possible that once you recognize the waltz as a bit of pleasant Biedermeier

Example 10.1 No. 15 (Tempo di Valzer and Trio) from *La Tersicore del Nord, contenente una prescelta raccolta di pezzi ballabilli per chitarra sola* (1828), Op. 147, by Mauro Giuliani (1781–1829).

music your attention will wander, and you will become occupied with technical aspects of my performance of the piece or with memories of similar (and perhaps better) waltzes by other composers of the period. In the last case the mental images that would occupy your thoughts would not be substantially different from those prompted by language, but in the first two cases—in which the cascade of mental images is a direct response to the succession of musical events proper to Giuliani's waltz—the thoughts with which you are occupied will be of rather a different sort than those summoned by language. This would be so not simply because you were occupied with patterned non-linguistic sound, but because the dynamic aspect of these thoughts—the contours of their cascade—would reflect key aspects of musical organization.

In this chapter I would like to explore the idea that the kind of consciousness associated with attending to music is different from the kind of consciousness associated with attending to language. In the first section that follows I shall offer a preliminary view of how music shapes consciousness, with particular attention to the relationship between music and movement epitomized by Giuliani's waltz. In the second section I shall provide a brief sketch of aspects of consciousness that support the distinction that I should like to draw between attending to music and attending to language. This sketch approaches consciousness as a biological phenomenon, one that is also informed in important ways by memory function and by culture. In the third section I shall return to Giuliani's waltz and describe in a bit more detail how music shapes our conscious experience, and how the means it uses are different from those of language.

The early nineteenth-century waltz: content and context

Although writing a waltz would, on first glance, appear to be a fairly straightforward endeavour, it was not something that A.B. Marx took for granted when he introduced the topic in the course of his discussion of free composition in *Die Lehre von der musikalischen Komposition* of 1837–8. From Marx's perspective, the waltz was representative of a genre of music closely associated with actual physical movement, a genre that included marches and that was distinct from genres focused on melody. As such, it was paramount that the composer understand the specific movements of the dance so that the music could be shaped accordingly. Marx thus began with the steps of the dance: 'The waltz has two movements: first each pair of dancers turns itself in a circle around its own centre; second the pair progresses with these continuous turns in a greater circumference until it reaches its starting place and the circle is closed. Each little circle is performed in two-times-three steps and is, as it were, the motive of the dance' (Marx 1837–8, 2: 55). The result of these movements is a distinctive circular path that the dancers describe through successive repetitions of their smaller circles, a path represented diagrammatically in Figure 10.1.

These circular movements are perhaps the most important feature of the dance, and one that Marx believed had to be clearly supported by the music: 'At the very least the waltz must bring into prominence this basic motive of movement. Each bar, or, better, each phrase of two bars, must answer to the dance motive marking the first step firmly, and also the swinging turn of the dance. Where the bars do not point it out they must still favour it, by a melody which spiritedly turns away from the first note' (1837–38, 2: 55).

All of these features are quite evident in Giuliani's waltz from *La Tersicore del Nord*. First and foremost, the two-bar motive of the dance pervades both waltz and trio. In some cases—as in bars 17–20 of the trio—the grouping of the bars is suggested by changes in melody and harmony: bars 17 and 18 have a melody derived from an inverted-turn figure (F♮–E–F♮–G–F♮) over a D3 pedal bass that obscures the change of harmony; bars 19 and 20, by contrast, have an arching melody harmonized in thirds and supported by single bass notes (A3 and D3) that mark a clear change in harmony. In other cases two-bar groupings are suggested by changes in compositional strategy. In the opening of the waltz, for instance, bars 1 and 2 are organized around a brusque statement of the dominant seventh of A major answered by a descending scalar passage over the tonic. Bars 3 and 4, by contrast, are organized around an ascending scalar

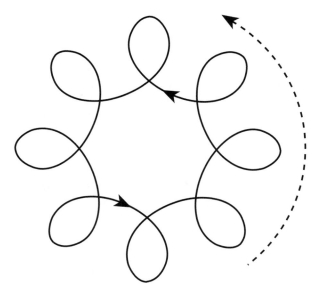

Fig. 10.1 Diagram showing the pattern of the dancers' path while waltzing, as described by A.B. Marx. Figure reproduced from Yaraman, S. (2002) *Revolving Embrace: The Waltz as Sex, Steps, and Sound,* with permission from Pendragon Press.

bass harmonized in tenths, with the topmost voice (on E4) reduced to an accompanying role. In other cases the contrast between two-bar groups may be less pronounced (as in bars 9–16 of the waltz, or bars 25–32 of the trio) but, as Marx recommends, the melody turns away from the first note of the bar through devices such as appoggiaturas (bars 9–10, 13–14), running scalar passages (bars 25–28), or a rest on the first quaver (bars 16 and 32, a device also used in bars 7, 24, and 40). Perhaps most important in this regard, however, is the gesture with which Giuliani opens the waltz: by creating an agogic, harmonic, and registral accent on beat 2 of bar 1 Giuliani thrusts the listener forward into the space that will be filled by the descending passage of bar 2, and thereby suggests the impetus generated by the swirling turn of the dance.

In sum, then, Giuliani's waltz conforms quite well to the compositional design described by Marx, a design predicated on the notion that the main purpose of the waltz was to guide the dancers' steps. It is worth remembering, however, the performance context within which the piece would have been heard during the early nineteenth century. Although works for the guitar were given a place in concert settings (Heck 1995), the instrument was better suited to the bourgeois salon, within which its subdued voice could more easily be heard. In this setting it might be used in small instrumental ensembles, or to accompany song, or to perform short solo pieces. It might also be used to accompany the dancing with which such gatherings often concluded (Hanson 1985: 119). Giuliani's waltz could, of course, have been used to accompany actual dances, but the layout and organization of *La Tersicore del Nord* suggest that the 'choice collection of dance pieces' it offered was intended for listening rather than dancing. Consisting of 16 pieces distributed across three volumes, it is only No. 15 that is identified as a particular genre of dance. Among the rest of the works there are those that could be used as contredanses, but others belong to no specific dance genre. It seems likely, then, that the pieces of *La Tersicore del Nord* were aimed at listeners rather than dancers.[1] As such, the works served to evoke the scene and circumstances of the dance, to summon a reminiscence of the vibrant ballrooms where, amid the circling dancers, a new form of social interaction, predicated on shared experience and physical movement, was developing (Hanson 1985: 150–68).

During the early nineteenth century, then, the waltz as a musical genre was thought of as being in an intimate relationship with the waltz as it was danced in the ballrooms of Vienna and other metropolitan centres. On the floor of the ballroom or within the more modest confines of the bourgeois salon, the music provided a template onto which dancers could map their bodily movements. Even when used only for listening, however, the music of the waltz still invited corporeal engagement, although one imagined rather than enacted.

I would like to propose that the real or imagined corporeal engagement prompted by dance genres in particular and music in general is indicative of a kind of experience that is markedly different from that in which one's thoughts are guided by language, and that these different kinds of experience are associated with different kinds of consciousness. The next section will set out some of the features of consciousness that support this distinction, with particular attention to relationships between consciousness, memory, and culture.

Consciousness, memory, and culture

I should like to start with a slightly obscure but still useful distinction, between *awareness* and *consciousness*. To be aware of something is, in some measure, to take note of it: for instance, you are aware, in some measure, that you are reading a chapter from a book on music and consciousness. Consciousness is quite closely affiliated with awareness—were you unconscious (as the term is typically construed) you would not be aware that there was a book on music and consciousness to be read, much less that you were reading a chapter from it—but complications quickly ensue. Had you started playing David Starobin's recording of Giuliani's *Zwölf Walzer für die Guitare* Op. 57 as an accompaniment to your reading and been lulled to sleep by it, some part of your cognitive faculties would continue to register the presence of music in the room. When the recording came to an end, those same cognitive faculties might signal alarm at this change in your proximate environment and stir you to wakefulness. You might then become aware that you had dozed off, now conscious of a gap in your conscious experience. This points to a special kind of awareness—an awareness that we are aware—that is of the substance of consciousness as it is typically construed.

Let me see if I can tease out the implications of this example in just a little more detail. Awareness is generally thought of as being under cognitive control (Prinz 2005: 364). In the case of the cognitive faculties that kept track of aspects of your environment while you slept, these would not count as awareness for the simple reason that they are not subject to a control mechanism which could direct them elsewhere: you could not shift those faculties from keeping track of Starobin's recording, to noting the surface and resistance of the chair you were slumbering in, and then go back to

Starobin's recording. Awareness, then, involves having various mental images derived from perceptual and proprioceptual cognitive activity, and being able in some fashion to control which images are at the centre of attention. The capacity for such awareness is what Gerald Edelman (1989: Ch. 5, 1992: Ch. 11, 2006: Ch. 2) calls primary consciousness, or what Antonio Damasio (1999: Ch. 3, 2003: Ch. 5) calls core consciousness; the mark of such a capacity is a kind of phenomenological presence that is lacking from unconscious states. In addition to having this capacity, humans also have the rather more remarkable capacity that they are aware *that* they are aware—that is, they have the capacity to reflect on their own thought processes, to realize that they *have* thought processes. This capacity to take thought as an object for awareness is key to what Edelman calls higher-order consciousness, and what Damasio calls extended consciousness. Although there are certainly differences between Edelman's and Damasio's characterizations of different sorts of consciousness, for the sake of simplicity I shall, in what follows, adopt Damasio's terms—core and extended consciousness.

Although any number of writers have explored the issue of consciousness, it is no accident that the two I have just cited both come to the topic from neuroscience. While it is still somewhat exceptional for neuroscientists to concern themselves with consciousness (a topic that is often regarded as an abstruse and unrewarding), among those who do there is now broad agreement that consciousness is biological in nature, and Edelman and Damasio have made significant contributions to the description of the brain structures that contribute to consciousness. The perspective they offer also comes with two important entailments: first, that humans are almost certainly not the only species that is conscious (although other species may be limited to core consciousness); and second, that consciousness is an evolutionary adaptation. That is, having consciousness (and, in the case of humans, extended consciousness) gives a species competitive advantages, not the least of which is the capacity to focus on just those mental images that are most relevant to a given environmental situation.

Sorting out the evolutionary advantages of having extended consciousness is destined to remain a project much more speculative than discovering the brain structures that contribute to having consciousness, if only because the emergence of extended consciousness in our species occurred in remote prehistory. That said, the psychologist Merlin Donald has offered an account of some of the factors that may have influenced the development of extended consciousness, and his approach is useful for thinking about how musical consciousness might differ from other sorts. Among the factors that Donald believes is crucial is the role of culture in human societies—indeed, he argues that culture, construed as knowledge that is shared between members of a social group, provided the means to accelerate the evolutionary development of our species by taking advantage of and then emphasizing adaptations in cognitive structure (Donald 2001: Ch. 7). More specifically, the process of sharing knowledge basic to culture required being able to keep track of both the actions of others and our own actions. It is just this ability to split awareness—between self and other, but also between past and present, between an action and its broader significance—that is one of the prerequisites of extended consciousness.

According to Donald's perspective, being able to keep track of multiple processes required developing much more sophisticated memory systems. In general, the cognitive functions basic to memory systems are regarded as essential to consciousness—indeed, Edelman's catch phrase for core consciousness is 'the remembered present'. Because memory functions will be central to the view of consciousness I want to develop here, I would like to consider briefly three aspects of memory.

First, although it is sometimes convenient to think of memory as a kind of storage system, memories are actually highly dynamic cognitive constructs that are constrained by the biological mechanisms through which they are maintained. Put another way, every time we revisit a memory we change it slightly, strengthening certain of the synaptic connections proper to the memory, weakening others. One of the challenges faced by biological memory systems, then, is to develop means to *stabilize* memories while still allowing them to change as environmental circumstances change. In general, cultural practices—including those associated with language and music—offer our species an additional means to stabilize memories, a point to which I shall return below.

Secondly, for a number of years it has been common to distinguish between three separate types of memory, each with its own temporal frame and cognitive mechanisms. The briefest of these, with a duration of perhaps two to three seconds, comprises various sensory memory systems that function as components of perceptual processing; there is fairly robust evidence, for instance, for a visual memory store often called iconic memory, and for an acoustic storage system that Ulric Neisser called echoic memory (1967: Ch. 8). At the middle level of memory systems is what has come to be called working memory, which provides a buffer around 10–15 seconds long within which information provided by perceptual processing can be evaluated (Baddeley 2007). There are any number of situations where buffers like this are important, but one ready example is provided by the task of comprehending language, which often requires taking in a certain amount of information, evaluating it, and, subsequent to this process, figuring out what to do with it. It is perhaps also good to note that part of Merlin Donald's argument about the evolution of consciousness was that keeping track of the knowledge basic to culture required a further compartmentalization of working memory, allowing us to monitor our own actions and those of others, to keep in mind actions performed in the immediate past as well as those with which we are presently occupied, and to attend to linguistic as well as other modes of communication (Donald 2001: 257–8). Coordination of these multidimensional streams of thought represented a cognitive development that made more involved systems of learning, and thus more complex forms of culture, possible. Finally, the last type of memory is what is typically called long-term storage, although it should be kept in mind that 'long term' is a relative notion, and refers chiefly to the sort of changes to synaptic connections that are the biological basis of memory. These kinds of memory are all, of course, intimately related to one another, but also appear to involve different brain structures for their support.

The third aspect of memory that I would like to consider, one suggested by Donald's argument for multiple kinds of working memory, is that there is good evidence that human cognition makes use of a number of different *memory systems*—these systems being thought of as distinct from the three different types of memory just discussed. In the course of reviewing this evidence the psychologist David Rubin offers six questions to illustrate different sorts of memory systems:

1 *What is your name?*

2 *What is the colour and shape of winter squash?*

3 *How many windows are there in your home?*

4 *Is the first note of your national anthem higher than, lower than, or the same as the second?*

5 *Where is the letter 'a' on your keyboard?*

6 *How do your feelings when you have a manuscript accepted differ from your feelings when you have a manuscript rejected?* (adapted from Rubin 2006: 278)

The first question, which requires the retrieval of linguistic information, seems the paradigm of memory. Note, however, the recall process associated with the second question, which seems very different from the first, not the least because it involves tactile and visual information. Of a different sort is the third question—as Rubin notes, while there is a strong visual component to this question, to answer it many people will take an imaginary walk through their home as a way of making an inventory of the windows therein. The fourth question takes us quite a distance from the first, and of course involves the sort of auditory information with which musicians are well familiar. The fifth question definitely seems to involve motor skills, and when it is asked listeners may well summon an imaginary keyboard on which to enact the solution. The sixth question is of yet a different sort, and engages with a memory for emotion that can be as vivid as it is elusive. Although memory systems connected to audition will clearly be important for music, I would like to propose that systems connected with motor function and emotions are also important. That is, musical practice, especially as a cultural phenomenon, includes sounds, kinaesthetic experiences, and the emotions associated with both.

Again, my interest in touching on various memory functions here is restricted to what these functions can tell us about consciousness. What seems most evident is that, to the extent that consciousness relies on memory, it is not monolithic, and is shaped by both short-term processes such as working memory and long-term processes that allow us to retrieve information from the relatively distant past. Further, the different kinds of memory systems outlined by Rubin's six questions would seem to indicate that there are conscious states that are quite different from one another—as different as remembering the colour and shape of winter squash is from remembering the opening of a national anthem.

One piece remains to complete the sketch of musical consciousness I would like to draw, and that is an account of the function of music within human cultures. This is relevant not least because it provides a way to pull together some of the ideas about consciousness and memory that I have set out. In my recent work on musical grammar (Zbikowski 2008; in press), I have found it useful to contrast the function of music with that of language. Drawing on the work of the developmental psychologist Michael Tomasello, I take the position that the primary function of language within human culture is to direct the attention of another person to objects or concepts within a shared referential frame (Tomasello 1999: Ch. 5). The primary function of music, by contrast, is to represent through patterned sound various dynamic processes that are common in human experience. Chief among these dynamic processes are those associated with the emotions (which, following Damasio, can be construed as sequences of physiological and psychological events that subtend feelings (Damasio 1999: Ch. 2, 2003: Ch. 1)) and the movements of bodies—including our own—through space. The invocation of such movement brings us back to the steps of the waltz, which Marx thought so important to understanding the organization of its music. As I proposed above and have argued elsewhere (Zbikowski 2008), the music for the waltz provides a sonic template onto which dancers map their steps, and thus represents a sonic analogue for the dynamic process of the dance itself.

Let me now see if I can pull these various strands together, and if not create a whole cloth of musical consciousness at least set out a relatively robust network of concepts. Without being overly specific about what consciousness *is*, we can conceive of it as a consequence of biological processes that humans share to some extent with other species, and that give a competitive advantage to those species that have it. One of the chief manifestations of these processes in humans is an expansion of memory function, including a diversification of working memory which made it possible for our species to keep track of a number of different domains of experience simultaneously. These domains include those focused on tactile and visual images, on movement, on emotions, on sound, on the sort of abstract symbolic structures basic to language, and on thought itself. Our awareness of mental images proper to each of these domains, and our memories of these images, can contribute to the sense that each is associated with a somewhat different kind of consciousness. The consciousness of the dancer, for instance, might include an awareness of the motor movements specific to the dance, of the feel of the dance floor and of her partner's body, and of the temporal frame set out by successions of musical sounds. By contrast, the consciousness of the listener who knows the dance might have to rely on memories of motor movements and tactile sensations, but would still take in musical sounds that provide a frame and context for the dance. But what of the listener who has never danced the dance? Here I would like to suggest that the same musical structures that serve as sonic analogues for the movements of the dancer provide the basis for musical understanding *even if one does not know the dance*. To explore this point further, let us now return to Giuliani's waltz from *La Tersicore del Nord* to examine some of the structures through which it shapes musical consciousness.

On structuring consciousness through music

In the following brief sketch I shall focus on aspects of Giuliani's waltz that connect with different memory systems of the sort explored by Rubin, including systems associated with 'musical' relationships (such as pitch structure), motor function, and emotions. The intent here is not to provide an exhaustive account of the memory systems activated by the waltz (which would be a quite different project) but to suggest how they contribute to formation of a kind of consciousness that is specific to music.

Metrical and tonal structure

It is easy enough to look at the notation for Giuliani's waltz and observe that it is in triple metre, but it is perhaps more interesting to think about the musical materials through which such a metre is projected. For instance, although triple metre is typically thought of as consisting of a strong (accented) first beat followed by two weak (unaccented) beats, with each beat marking the initiation of an approximately equal durational span, there are moments in Giuliani's waltz that do not support this way of thinking. In bar 1, for example, beat two is at least as strong as beat one (given the agogic accent on the second chord of the bar); in bar 4, there is little to make the first beat stand out from the surrounding beats (the E4 of the upper voice being not particularly prominent); and in bar 8 there is again an agogic accent on the second note in the bass. What is perhaps much more important for marking off spans of durational units comprising three beats are the regular changes of harmony: harmonies change in an alternating pattern for almost the entirety of the waltz. The two exceptions occur in bars 8–9, when a tonic harmony is followed by a tonic harmony, and in bar 15, which includes both a tonic and a dominant harmony. This compositional strategy is also evident in the trio, with two differences: first, the consistent change of harmony falls into a larger, four-bar pattern (tonic–subdominant–dominant–tonic) which has as its consequence the uncharacteristic repetition of a harmony in bars 20–21, 28–29, and 36–37; and, second, bar 25 begins with contrasting material in what will eventually become the key of the dominant (representing a higher-level change of harmony). In both waltz and trio harmonic changes are often marked by a single note in the bass followed by two beats of rest (as in bars 9–14 of the waltz) which, while typical of the genre, here serves to reinforce the established sense of triple metre.

These features, together with aspects of melodic organization that group bars in pairs (Marx's 'waltz motive'), create a contextual framework relative to which we hear the progress of musical events. Thinking only in terms of eight-bar spans, for instance, when bar 1 follows bar 8 (if the repeat sign is taken) it initiates a reprise; when bar 9 follows bar 8, however, it takes the listener into new musical territory. The point is not simply that bar 1 contrasts with bar 9, but that our appreciation of this relationship—an appreciation that supports ideas about whether the music is 'staying in the same place' or 'moving forward'—is facilitated by the framework provided by the rhythmic structure.

The tonal organization of the waltz supports this framework and adds another layer of relationships. Bar 1, for instance, introduces dissonance (the compound seventh E2–D4, and the augmented fourth D4–G♮4) whose resolution is found in the C♮4 and A4 of bar 2. Bar 9, by contrast, is organized around a consonant harmony, but the melody begins with an appoggiatura F♮4, a pitch foreign to the tonic chord but yielding (as Marx would say) 'a melody which spiritedly turns away from the first note'. Although much has been written about the inherent instability of the dominant, Giuliani leaves nothing to chance: the dominant chord in both the waltz and the trio is consistently destabilized, either through metric placement (as the first bar of a two-bar waltz motive) or by the inclusion of a dissonant seventh. Strategies such as these show that the point of repose represented by tonic harmony is not simply a given, but is established through a careful treatment of musical material.

The metrical and tonal features of Giuliani's waltz thus provide a set of interrelated frameworks according to which a listener can judge the progress of musical events. Bar 16, whether sounding for the first time or the fourth, marks the consummation of metric processes (the completion of a two-bar waltz motive, the conclusion of an eight-bar phrase, and the completion of a sixteen-bar dance form) as well as tonal processes (the last of a sequence of alternating dominants and tonics, preceded by the only disruption of the regular alternation of these harmonies in the entire work). There are, of course, other aspects of metrical and tonal organization that inform these processes (including the way the beat is subdivided, and the contrapuntal relationships between the melody and the bass) that not only help to flesh out the frameworks I have outlined but also help to anchor them in memory. With respect to metrical and tonal structure, then, my proposal is that the memory systems we draw on—which are the same as those we use to answer Rubin's fourth question ('*Is the first note of your national anthem higher than, lower than, or the same as the second?*')—are guided by frameworks specific to musical organization, which are invariably dynamic and relational. Although it may well *seem* that the musical knowledge we keep in memory is static, to the extent that it deals with actual musical events (as distinct from abstract conceptualizations of such events) it is in truth shaped by tonal and metrical frameworks that define and articulate temporal spans. Such spans are one of the defining characteristics of musical practice, and are reflected in our notions of musical departure, return, and progress.

Sonic analogues for physical movement

My preliminary discussion of Giuliani's waltz was guided by Marx's argument that the musical organization of a waltz had to conform to the steps of the dance; as I proposed above, the music thus provides a sonic analogue for the dynamic process of performing the waltz. In truth, the relationship between music and dance is in most cases much looser: some of the gestures or steps of the dance may have no correlate in the music (as in the case of bar 1 of Giuliani's waltz, in which there is no corresponding musical event for the third step of the waltz), and aspects of the music will not be represented in the dance (there is, for instance, no convention through which the dancers would mark the conclusion of an eight-bar unit). What is perhaps more important for the perspective I wish to develop here is that musical materials have the *potential* to serve as analogues for motor movement. Thus listeners who know nothing of the waltz could still map a sequence of bodily movements—which might, of course, have nothing to do with the steps of the dance—onto the template provided by Giuliani's music. Although the metric organization of the music certainly supports such a mapping (providing the listener with a predictable pattern with which movements can be correlated), tonal structure too plays a part: the sense of departure and return that fixed pitch relationships facilitate can also serve as a framework for regulating physical movements. The conclusion of the waltz (marked by the tonal close of bar 16) would thus suggest a conclusion of physical movement, but even the completion of eight-bar phrases delimited by tonal arrivals might suggest ways that physical movements could be articulated (a suggestion which, again, is not necessarily taken up in any explicit way by most who dance the waltz).

Sonic analogues for emotion processes

Any thorough discussion of emotion would, of necessity, take us far afield. My thought here is not to attempt such a discussion, but simply to note a few correspondences between the music of Giuliani's waltz and emotional states. The tempo of the waltz in the early nineteenth century was brisk; this, combined with major-mode harmonies, a relative lack of rhythmic disruptions, and an absence of all but the most conventional of harmonic dissonances make Giuliani's waltz a good match for a positive emotional state—though this match might be almost purely intellectual: were you in a particularly foul mood you could still correlate the waltz with a positive emotional state even if such a state were not for you. The waltz also offers a means to more directly change emotional states: were you to surrender repose, rise to your feet, and dance through Giuliani's waltz and trio, your emotional state would almost assuredly change (one would hope, for the better). A similar change might occur were you to only *imagine* moving to the waltz while listening to it but, lacking a physical component, the effects of such an exercise would almost certainly be less pronounced and of shorter duration than were you actually moving to the music.

Structuring consciousness through music

Although Marx focused on the conformance between the music of the waltz and the steps of the dance, the dynamic processes for which Giuliani's waltz provides sonic analogues are not limited to those proper to the dance floor. The music further offers, through its metrical and tonal structure, analogues for processes such as departure, return, and moving forward. Through its summoning of more abstract processes such as these, as well as more concrete processes associated with physical movement, the music also provides analogues for psychological processes associated with an energized emotional state. In sum, then, attending to Giuliani's waltz activates memory systems connected with musical relationships, motor function, and emotion, all of which give rise to a cascade of mental images—with a strongly kinaesthetic component—that is markedly different from the network of mental images engendered by language. Put another way, were I to play this waltz for you and were you to attend to the succession of musical events it comprises, the result would be a kind of consciousness distinct from that of language, a kind of consciousness occupied with dynamic processes rather than relationships among objects and events.

Conclusions

I have argued that the kind of consciousness associated with attending to music is different from the kind of consciousness associated with attending to language. This difference reflects the different memory systems exploited by music, systems which are for the most part much more focused on the salient features of dynamic processes than on lexical knowledge or relationships between objects and events. That music should exploit such systems is a consequence of its function within human cultures, which is to provide sonic analogues for various dynamic processes that are common in human experience.

An appropriate question—but one whose full answer is outside of the reach of this chapter—is why human cultures would have found a need to analogize such processes. Part of the answer can be found in the ballrooms and salons of nineteenth-century Vienna: dynamic processes such as those associated with the waltz are an integral part of complex forms of social interaction that are key to the construction of culture. That is, the rituals of the dance floor are organized around bodily movements that, in Paul Connerton's term, incorporate social memory:

> Both commemorative ceremonies and bodily practices . . . contain a measure of insurance against the process of cumulative questioning entailed in all discursive practices. This is the source of their importance and persistence as mnemonic systems. Every group, then, will entrust to bodily automatisms the values and categories which they are most anxious to conserve. They will know how well the past can be kept in mind by a habitual memory sedimented in the body. (Connerton 1989: 102)

Music, by providing sonic analogues for the bodily movements of ritual, adds a further layer to this habitual memory, not least because of the unique form of experience it engenders. It is not surprising, then, that Merlin Donald connected this form of experience through what he called kinematic imagination to the species of consciousness that is specific to humans, one intimately connected with the cultural interactions that typify human societies (2001: 271–4).

The kind of consciousness summoned by music, then, is not an epiphenomenon, nor is it a poor substitute for the kind of consciousness summoned by language. It is instead a testament to what it means to be human in the fullest sense of the word.

References

Baddeley, A. (2007). *Working Memory, Thought, and Action.* Oxford psychology series, no. 45 (Oxford: Oxford University Press).

Connerton, P. (1989). *How Societies Remember* (Cambridge: Cambridge University Press).

Damasio, A.R. (1999). *The Feeling of what Happens: Body and Emotion in the Making of Consciousness* (New York, NY: Harcourt Brace & Company).

Damasio, A.R. (2003). *Looking for Spinoza: Joy, Sorrow, and the Feeling Brain* (Orlando, FL: Harcourt Inc.).

Donald, M. (2001). *A Mind so Rare: The Evolution of Human Consciousness* (New York, NY: Norton).

Edelman, G.M. (1989). *The Remembered Present: A Biological Theory of Consciousness* (New York, NY: Basic Books).

Edelman, G.M. (1992). *Bright Air, Brilliant Fire: On the Matter of Mind* (New York, NY: Basic Books).

Edelman, G.M. (2006). *Second Nature: Brain Science and Human Knowledge* (New Haven, CT: Yale University Press).

Hanson, A.M. (1985). *Musical Life in Biedermeier Vienna.* Cambridge Studies in Music (London: Cambridge University Press).

Heck, T.F. (1995). *Mauro Giuliani: Virtuoso Guitarist and Composer* (Columbus: Editions Orphée).

Marx, A.B. (1837–38). *Die Lehre von der musikalischen Komposition, praktisch theoretisch* (Leipzig: Breitkopf & Härtel).

Neisser, U. (1967). *Cognitive Psychology* (New York, NY: Appleton-Century-Crofts).

Prinz, J.J. (2005). Emotions, embodiment, and awareness, in L.F. Barrett, P.M. Niedenthal, and P. Winkielman (eds.), *Emotion and Consciousness*, 363–83 (New York, NY: Guilford Press).

Rubin, D.C. (2006). The basic-systems model of episodic memory. *Perspectives on Psychological Science*, **1**, 277–311.

Tomasello, M. (1999). *The Cultural Origins of Human Cognition* (Cambridge, MA: Harvard University Press).

Zbikowski, L.M. (2008). Dance topoi, sonic analogues, and musical grammar: Communicating with music in the eighteenth century, in V.K. Agawu and D. Mirka (eds.), *Communication in Eighteenth Century Music*, 283–309 (New York, NY: Cambridge University Press).

Zbikowski, L.M. (in press). Musical gesture and musical grammar: A cognitive approach, in A. Gritten and E. King (eds.), *New perspectives on music and gesture* (Aldershot: Ashgate).

Note

1. Thomas Heck notes that as a composer of *Ländler* and waltzes Giuliani was quite prolific, producing over 200 (1995: 185). It is telling that Heck does not include *La Tersicore del Nord* in his comprehensive list of collections of Giuliani's dance music.

Chapter 11

Music perception and musical consciousness

Eric Clarke

Introduction: defining (musical) consciousness

Is there such a thing as 'musical consciousness', what are its defining or characterizing features, when do people experience it, and what is its relationship to other kinds of consciousness? On the one hand, music's complex and changing relationship to the rest of human experience seems to place it in a special realm, where the idea of a distinctively musical consciousness, or a range of musical consciousnesses, seems justified—even necessary. On the other hand, its entanglement with everyday life makes a specialized musical consciousness seem either superfluous, or the pretext for a profusion of other kinds of consciousness: would we also need to identify and investigate a poetic consciousness, a narrative consciousness, a football consciousness, a driving consciousness? If the last of these seems to stretch the point, from another perspective it might seem perfectly reasonable: the experience of driving is quite distinctive (it can be differentiated from cycling, or operating a lathe, for example), even if it also overlaps with a variety of other experiences (flying a plane, watching a grand prix). If there is a resistance to the idea of a driving consciousness, perhaps it is only because driving is thought too mundane to justify such an apparently lofty term—implying that an acceptance of different kinds of consciousness is as much as anything to do with implicit social, cultural, even aesthetic values.

These remarks indicate the way in which 'consciousness' is used in both more generic and more narrowly specific ways.[1] 'Consciousness' (without an article) is used as a broadly inclusive term, to distinguish either between those organisms that do seem to have it, and those that don't (people on the one hand and flatworms on the other); or between people who at different times in their lives are, or are not, possessed of it (awake versus comatose). And 'consciousness' preceded by certain kinds of modifier (e.g. 'visual', 'linguistic', 'somatosensory') is used to identify different kinds, or components of human experience. The *Oxford English Dictionary* (OED) lists a number of definitions of consciousness that highlight these distinctions, with three of them being particularly revealing. The OED's definition 5a is broad and general in its reach, but confined to an individual: 'The totality of the impressions, thoughts, and feelings, which make up a person's conscious being'. 5b restricts this to a particular domain of human experience: 'Limited by a qualifying epithet to a special field, as the moral or religious consciousness'. And 5c opens the term out beyond the domain of private experience: 'Attributed as a collective faculty to an aggregate of men, a people, etc., so far as they think or feel in common' (*Oxford English Dictionary* 2010).

Chris Frith (2008) argues that attempts to define consciousness are premature, and that alongside distinctions between levels of consciousness it is crucial to understand better what aspects of a situation a clearly conscious person is conscious *of*—an enterprise that is closely associated with questions of attention and awareness on the one hand, and of conscious and unconscious processing on the other. More than a century ago, William James (1890: Ch. 11) remarked on the dual character of attention—that in the rich and multi-modal environment we inhabit, we are necessarily selective about what we attend to, and that what is attended to acquires increased perceptual salience. As Gerald Edelman (1989) points out, consciousness is a process not a thing—continuous, changing, object-oriented and intentional, and 'selective in time, not exhausting all aspects of the objects with which it deals' (Edelman 1989: 5). It is therefore fundamental to the study of music and consciousness to investigate those aspects of musical material people can and do attend to—to understand musical consciousness on the basis of principles of music perception.

Kinds of consciousness: primary and higher-order

Is consciousness a single phenomenon, or are there useful distinctions that can be made between generic kinds of consciousness? In closely related ways, both Antonio Damasio (1999) and Edelman (1989) draw a distinction between two kinds of consciousness—*core* and *extended* consciousness for Damasio; and *primary* and *higher-order* consciousness for Edelman. Adopting Edelman's terminology, primary consciousness is roughly equivalent to what is in an organism's current awareness, or the contents of its perceptual present. It is understood as an attribute of many living things—certainly higher mammals as well as humans—and depends upon a three-way relationship between: 1) the manner in which the organism perceives and tacitly categorizes its world, understood as a sensorimotor engagement; 2) the distinction between self and non-self; and 3) a fundamental 'value system' (see Edelman 1989: 95–100) expressed in terms of the hedonic, homeostatic, and adaptive value of an organism's encounter with its environment. 'Primary consciousness may thus be briefly described as the result of the ongoing discrimination of present perceptual categorizations by a value-dominated self-nonself memory' (Edelman 1989: 102). A concrete example might be encapsulated by a person's awareness that 'this food looks good to eat': the identification 'food' denotes a perceptual category with a sensorimotor basis; 'this food' identifies something that is non-self in nature (i.e. is not part of the person's own body); and 'looks good to eat' constitutes the adaptively and hedonically positive experience that eating the food promises. 'I have a sore foot' features the same three components, but in this case they are foot pain (perceptual category), self (my foot), and hedonically negative (soreness).

Two things are important to note. First, the incorporation of a self–non-self distinction as a fundamental component means that all consciousness necessarily has what might be termed a proprioceptive character (see also Chapter 12, this volume). Secondly, while these two examples have been expressed as if they were internal narratives in words, this is only for explanatory purposes, and the direct awareness that the two examples are intended to illustrate is non-verbal in character. The stream of dynamically changing awareness that constitutes primary consciousness has connected, structured, and relational qualities, but there is none of the reflexive character that the term 'narrative' implies in other contexts. It is a kind of consciousness that is as available to a three-month old human infant, or a dog, as to a language-possessing human adult. As Damasio puts it in relation to his equivalent term, 'core consciousness':

> The story contained in the images of core consciousness is not told by some clever homunculus. Nor is the story really told by *you* as a self because the core *you* is only born as the story is told, *within the story itself*. You exist as a mental being when primordial stories are being told, and only then; as long as primordial stories are being told, and only then. (1999: 191)

Edelman and Damasio regard primary (core) consciousness as the basis for, and outcome of, subject–object relations, and as brought into being 'when the brain forms an imaged, non-verbal, second-order account of how the organism is causally affected by the processing of an object' (Damasio 1999: 192). Primary consciousness, as its name implies, is therefore the basis of *all* consciousness, and is the foundation for higher-order consciousness (Damasio's extended consciousness), which is reflexive, dependent on language, and thus characteristic only of human beings. Higher-order consciousness brings with it the capacity to be aware of, and reflect on, a past and a future, and to construct and consider a narrative of events—most specifically the narrative of events that constitutes a person's autobiographical self.

The approach to musical consciousness taken in this chapter is centrally concerned with primary consciousness of music—the kind of consciousness that is associated with immediate perceptual engagement with music, rather than with imagining, remembering, or reflecting upon music.[2] Being pre-linguistic, both developmentally and phylogenetically, primary consciousness is manifest behaviourally rather than in language. A dog, a child, or a human adult demonstrates generic primary consciousness in the ways that it interacts with its environment—engaging with, and actively seeking out certain objects and events, avoiding others, and showing pleasure or distress in those interactions. By analogy therefore, primary musical consciousness is a selective and differentiated engagement with music, demonstrated in a variety of overt behaviours that include foot-tapping, dancing, singing along, applause, changing or repeating a track, rapt attention, fidgety irritation, and a huge array of changes in facial expression and posture. Primary musical consciousness is also manifest in the more covert behavioural changes that are associated with emotional responses, including changes in heart rate, breathing, pilo-erection, sweating, endocrine balance, and muscle tone.

These are the outward manifestations of primary musical consciousness, complemented by the corresponding first-person perspective/experience that might be partially describable in language, but which is not itself linguistic. The paradox that we face is the intuition that there is a level or kind of musical consciousness that is prior to, or other than, language—but which only gains articulacy through language. The nature of this direct (primary) experience is dynamic, auditory, and proprioceptive—a continuous flux of sensorimotor engagement, powerfully, and yet not solely, auditory. It is pre-reflective, a 'saddle-back' of time as William James put it, 'with a certain breadth of its own on which we sit perched, and from which we look in two directions into time' (1890: 609).[3] By analogy with the 'driving consciousness' mentioned at the start of this chapter, primary musical consciousness is like the continuous awareness of, and active engagement with, the total 'driving scene' (road, traffic, surroundings, internal environment of the car, physical engagement and manipulation of the car's controls, sounds of the engine and road noise, etc.) that characterizes the primary consciousness of a skilled and engaged driver.

Edelman argues that there is constant interchange between primary and higher-order consciousness, and that once acquired, higher-order consciousness cannot be suppressed: 'because human beings have higher-order consciousness, they cannot subjectively experience or reconstruct primary consciousness without the intrusion of some additional components of direct awareness and higher-order consciousness' (1989: 104). A number of Eastern philosophical traditions—most notably Buddhism—would take issue with this, and argue that, hard though it may seem to the dominant mode of Western thinking, primary consciousness can be recaptured through the discipline of meditation or meditation-like practices (see Chapters 6–8, this volume). The same might be claimed for those intensely focused and engaged circumstances—of which peak musical performance, 'deep listening' (Becker 2004), and dancing are examples—in which consciousness seems to be entirely taken up with the activities or events at hand, and which has a close relationship to that seamless and unreflective condition that Mihalyi Csikszentmihalyi has termed 'flow' (Csikszentmihalyi and Csikszentmihalyi 1988). While acknowledging the inevitable influence of reflective higher-order consciousness that a written account necessarily engages, the following section explores the characteristics of primary musical consciousness from a listener's perspective.

Ways of listening

What is it like to hear music?[4] The psychology of music is now well over a century old, and yet still offers few attempts to document the direct experience of listening. Dominated as it is by a particular type of analytical scientific model, and suspicious of the introspectionist approaches of the later nineteenth and early twentieth centuries, the psychology of music (in common with auditory psychology more generally) has been preoccupied with controlled empirical investigations of what might be called musical and auditory capacities. The overwhelming majority of research on musical listening has focused on the human capacity to detect and evaluate supposedly 'basic' properties such as pitches, intensities, and durations on the one hand; and more complex attributes such as melodic shapes, harmonic sequences, rhythmic patterns, and structures of tension and release on the other. As Nicholas Cook (1990) has argued, these are attributes of music that listeners *can* be asked about, and *can* make judgements about; but it is much less certain how many of these attributes form an important part of musical experience 'in the wild' (cf. Hutchins 1995). At least some of the empirical evidence (Baily 1996; Dibben 2001) suggests that these are not the basic or primary elements of hearing and listening—or that if people are aware of attributes of this general type, they do not spontaneously describe them, experience them, or think of them in those terms. It is important, on the other hand, not to leap to the conclusion that only those aspects of music of which people seem to be consciously aware, and which they can describe, are of any significance. There may be dramatic differences in what listeners are able, or inclined, to report; and while a great deal of perceptual activity is non-conscious, it may nonetheless have profound significance for our conscious experience of music. For example, many listeners may not be consciously aware during a long symphonic movement that a melody has been repeated with a different harmonization, or they may lack the language to describe such an event;[5] but may nonetheless experience a strong response to it, perhaps through a sense of the familiarity of the material, without being able to pin down where that familiarity comes from. At some level, therefore, such a listener has picked up and responded to the melodic identity without (in this case) being able to describe it in those terms—in other words without higher-order consciousness of it.

So the question remains: What is it like to hear music? Where are the 'data of musical consciousness' from which to develop such an account? The phenomenology of musical listening is still a poorly developed field, for reasons that are both understandable and more arbitrarily disciplinary in nature. The thought that anyone could provide a complete and faithful account of their own listening experience is as illusory for music as it would be for any vivid human experience, undermined by at least three insurmountable factors. First, introspection—on which a phenomenological account depends—is necessarily limited to an account of *conscious* experience, excluding what Edelman (1989) terms both non-conscious and unconscious processes. The former term refers to perceptual and cognitive processes that are necessarily and intrinsically below the level of conscious awareness; the latter to processes that although available to consciousness in principle may be blocked or repressed for a whole range of reasons. The potential significance of both of these cannot be overestimated: as an example of the former, many of the perceptual processes involved in making sense of what Albert Bregman (1990) calls the 'auditory scene' (i.e. the objects and events of the auditory environment) are non-conscious and yet crucial to a person's understanding of what is going on. The phenomenon of auditory streaming (in which rapidly alternating sounds are heard as two parallel perceptual streams) depends on processes of aggregation/integration and segregation that are insuppressible but unavailable to conscious awareness (i.e. are non-conscious), and which nonetheless have a dramatic impact on how the auditory scene is perceived. By contrast, the overwhelming emphasis on a structural account of musical listening in much of twentieth- and twenty-first century musicology at the expense of almost everything else, as discussed in Subotnik (1996) and Dell'Antonio (2004), represents an example of the way in which an ideological process can suppress (i.e. render unconscious) other domains of musical experience (texture, gesture, timbre, space and feel/swing/groove) that are in principle thoroughly available to consciousness.[6]

A second factor that profoundly affects any introspective account is the limit of language. Words about music frequently either run beyond their object—taking on a drama and dynamic of their own—or fall short of a phenomenon whose corporeality, temporality, and multiplicity elude the rational, spatial, and linear character of the written word. A person's description of their listening experience is often either disappointingly lacking in detail, 'grain', and vividness; or can lead to the feeling that the musical experience has disappeared below a flood of associations and connections generated in the writing process, but whose relationship to the original listening is much less certain. Lawrence Kramer's account of hearing Richard Strauss's *Metamorphosen*, for example, illustrates the way in which hearing can be densely overlaid with a complex network of associations and connections. Kramer writes of finding the piece 'moving in its bleakness and resignation' when he first heard it, but that 'a subsequent hearing, the one that has stuck with me, unexpectedly filled me with a rage I could not understand' (2002: 285). Kramer's investigation of this apparently inexplicable rage takes him back to his childhood, and to his family's unwillingness or inability to talk about the holocaust. 'What I heard in the Strauss', he writes in conclusion, 'and especially in its contorted cover of Beethoven's voice, which could not have conceived of this either but at least had been plain spoken within the limits of the tragedies of its age, was the silence of my family, the silence of those who above all should speak' (286). This is undoubtedly a 'hearing' of sorts, but one that is so intertwined or overlaid with a specific family history that the auditory starting point seems almost to disappear behind a web of connections that takes on a life of its own.

Third, and tightly bound up with the language problem, is the myth of unmediated description: the idea (or fantasy) that it might be possible to give some kind of pure and unsullied account of the contents of consciousness—a kind of 'mind dump' (by analogy with the 'screen dump' of a computer). It is doubtful that anyone would really subscribe to such a possibility—though it is arguably the implication of a simplistic introspective method. These concerns and limitations are only a problem if the 'complete and faithful' fantasy is what is sought, but just as valid and interesting is an account of what it is that people are able, or choose, to report. Such a phenomenological account takes the mediated and necessarily partial nature of an individual's account of their own experience as given. It recognizes that the manner in which people report their musical experiences is necessarily a product of the graspability of the musical materials, of individuals' capacities as listeners, of the limitations of language, and of the inaccessibility of unconscious and non-conscious processes.

These may seem like serious limitations, but they actually help to define the very problem that is under investigation: what do we experience when we listen to music, how do we describe it, and—in the end—how do we account for it? Given the inescapably first-person *and* third-person nature of consciousness (we know what it is like both to experience our own consciousness and to witness consciousness in others), Daniel Dennett (1991: Ch. 4) argues for what he calls a heterophenomenological approach to the study of consciousness—a kind of generalized phenomenology that recognizes both the primacy of one's own, first-person experience, and the equal importance of other people's phenomenological accounts. Those accounts (like our own first-person accounts) cannot simply be taken at face value, but there is no more reason to exclude them as legitimate data as there is to exclude our own direct experiences.

Case studies of listening

Narrowly focused empirical studies have tended to dominate research on musical listening, but more recently an increasing number of exceptions to that perspective have started to appear, offering insights into different aspects of musical consciousness. To give some sense of the kinds of listening that this research reveals, consider the following case studies.[7]

William Gaver (1993a, 1993b) presents arguments for studying listening using methods and terms that capture what listening is actually like—rather than from the perspective of supposed 'sonic primitives' (frequency, amplitude, duration, and phase) that properly belong to the domain of physical measuring instruments. He argues for a theory of auditory event perception that identifies events in ecologically appropriate terms (i.e. terms appropriate to the scale, capacities, interests, and 'niches' of the perceiving organism—human listeners in this case), and puts the primary emphasis on systematically investigating the available information, relative to the listener's perceptual capacities, which specifies those events. Gaver (1993b: 285–6) presents a dialogue from an imaginary experiment in auditory perception that dramatizes the conflicting views of a reductionist experimenter and an increasingly puzzled participant. A musical equivalent of such a dialogue might run as follows: imagine that you are a participant in a music perception experiment, in which you have been asked simply to write down what you hear for each of a number of short examples. Having heard the first example three times, with pauses in between, you write down: 'The opening of the Aria of the Goldberg Variations played by Glenn Gould in his 1955 recording, played from the vinyl LP', feeling pleased with the level of detail that you have provided—only to be told by the experimenter that she doesn't want to know what the example *is*; she wants to know what you *heard*: the pitches, melodic profile, rhythmic structures, timbral elements, metre, *rubato*—those kinds of things. But what you have written *is* what you heard, you protest: you don't have any idea what pitches were involved, what metre it was in, or any of those other things that were mentioned. You heard the Goldberg Aria, and Glenn Gould in his 1955 recording, and the characteristic sounds of a vinyl surface—which is what you wrote. As in the more general auditory field, music perception research has made inappropriate assumptions about the perceptual relevance of the elements of physical acoustics—further compounded by assumptions about the perceptual relevance of the elements of standard music theory (see also Cook 1990, 1993).

Dibben (2001) presents a study that tackles these assumptions, and provides empirical evidence for perceptions of the kind that the example imagined above suggests. Her study involved two tasks: one required listeners to group short clips of various everyday sounds and musical extracts into pairs on the basis of their similarity; the other asked them to provide free descriptions of these same extracts. In the categorization task, participants were far more likely to use a strategy of acoustical resemblance (crackly sounds, high-pitched music, dissonances), while in the descriptive task participants overwhelmingly used the language of source, function, or genre (sounds of water, cadence, 'posh music', drum 'n' bass)—in other words 'event'-type descriptions. There might be various explanations for this difference: the more analytical categorization task may itself induce a more analytical type of listening, while the descriptive task encourages a more holistic and situated type of listening. And in a number of cases participants indicated that they were sensitive to both acoustic and source-based similarities, and found themselves having to make a difficult choice between conflicting options. Nonetheless, it is striking that listeners' spontaneous descriptions of these short extracts of sound and music are of a broadly ecological kind, such as 'something large rolling', 'Vietnamese puppet theatre sound', or '1970s movies'.

Using ethnographic methods, Ruth Herbert (2009; also Chapter 17, this volume) has collected interview and diary data to build up a phenomenological description of the musical listening experiences of a small number of case-study participants. Herbert's participants were selected on the basis of their significant involvement with music, as either listeners or players; they had widely varying amounts of formal musical training and between them produced a fascinating body of descriptive accounts of their own everyday listening experiences in a wide variety of circumstances. As an example, here is a diary record by 'Max' of listening in the bath, demonstrating an intense attention to sound itself, coupled with a mixture of stereotyped and autobiographical spatial and location attributes:

> One of his [John Taverner's] masses for a cappella choir comes on next. Utterly transported by never ending rising and falling of long drawn out polyphony, purity of human voices only. Eyes closed moment . . . aware of monochromatic colourless textures—little variation or contrast but beauty in voices in cathedral acoustic—endless phrases washing around. Partly conscious of how Latin words are mostly soft vowel sounds. Totally transported to choirboy days & how it felt to sing in a grand setting. Filmic images of candle light & shadows, monastic/liturgical rituals and so on . . . attention very much inwards. (Herbert 2009: 100–1)

The same directly perceptual engagement, mixed in this case with the incongruous components of a listener's specific circumstances, is demonstrated by the following extracts from diary entries provided by 'Will', who is listening to music in his car on both occasions:

> Borodin *Polovitzian dances*. Only listening to it with half an ear before. Particularly riveted by Eastern European folk music imitation on clarinet—etched over Tonbridge library roundabout, complete with 'Poundstretcher' shop. (110)

> Passing West Malling Air Station noticing a guitar style in a blues copied by John Renbourne . . . noticing a certain grain in the voice combined with a guitar tone in passing Ashdown Forest. As if particular moments of 'greater consciousness' (i.e. when the music is stretching me in some way) automatically include other coincidental impressions. (112)

These extracts, as written statements, are necessarily a reflective manifestation of higher-order consciousness. Nonetheless, they also vividly illustrate—at one remove, as it were—the intertwining of primary (direct, dynamic, unreflective) and higher-order (self-conscious, autobiographical, referential) musical consciousness; and a striking mixture of fine-grained perceptual attention (John Renbourne's guitar style, Latin vowel sounds) coupled with a wry and reflective awareness of the network of connections stretching into and out of the music—some concurrent and contingent (the Poundstretcher shop, Ashdown Forest), others deeply rooted and part of the listener's life history (choral singing, folk styles).

A more extended experiment in what, after Dennett, we might call a heterophe-nomenology of musical listening is Elizabeth Le Guin's account of listening to Debussy's setting for voice and piano of Mallarmé's poem *Soupir* (Le Guin 2004). The underlying theme of Le Guin's essay is the relationship between immediacy and delib-eration in listening, and her starting point is the problem of how to convey listening experiences, and what kinds of listening such attempts seem to endorse. Le Guin's aim is to try to capture a kind of listening that approximates to Debussy's own intimi-datingly confident claim that 'When one really listens to music . . . one hears at once what should be heard' (Debussy 1971: 216; translated and cited in Le Guin 2004: 235). Her approach stops short of limiting herself to a single listening (as implied by Debussy's 'at once'), but heads in the same direction by renouncing any sight of the score, and is based entirely on what she hears.[8] The result is a remarkably honest and clear account.

From her rich description, the following are some prominent features. As a trained musicologist and performer she observes the inevitability (particularly initially) of creating 'score-like' representations in her head—hearing interval patterns and their consequences, and enjoying the exercise of her own competence. Equally, though, she endeavours to avoid a focus on pitch (too burdened with academic conventions) and to pay attention to rhythm, timbre, register, and articulation—the singer's particular vocal sounds eliciting a powerfully embodied pleasure as they subliminally evoke 'the peculiar sensations that arise in my American palate and throat when I try to pro-nounce French' (238).[9] She describes how successive listenings generate increasingly definite expectations, from the fulfilment of which she derives increasing satisfaction,[10] not only for the sounds themselves, 'but also because I crave their momentary qualities of connection, their adherence to an unexpected sequence of events, their participa-tion, perhaps, in a plan' (239)—that sense of preparation, temporally directed atten-tion, and consequent receptiveness. Equally, she describes the intrusions of anxiety at the features that she wants to hear but cannot (the shape of the poem reflected in the music), and those that she hears but would rather not (Debussy's 'irrelevant feint' at closure, as she puts it, when the opening piano gesture of the song reappears at the end); and what she experiences as her own listening limitations and frustrations:

> I am acutely aware of how well I fit the bill of Debussy's 'honorable people who hear but one bar in eight', that awareness (and the chagrin it causes me) becoming, in fact, one of the chief points of continuity between listenings; I worry and worry at certain vague but compelling matters, like timbral recurrence and metamorphosis, like vocal-register-in-relation-to-surrounding-harmony, over successive listenings, and the worry becomes part of my 'score', in the unhappy sense of a score I am trying to settle. (240)

Le Guin also acknowledges the strong tendency for the internal descriptive process to take on a life of it own, and move away from its object of description:

> In this view, the phenomenon—in our case the musical work as heard—is a *clue* to the range of its possible appearances within the hearer, which can be further teased forth by processes such as memory, association, and reflection. (247)

Ironically, the danger that this network of associations will obscure 'the musical work as heard' may be particularly acute for a musicologist, intent on trying to give the most vivid and 'transparent' account of what she hears, but overequipped with technical knowledge and a whole array of possible rationalizations that threaten to take hold and divert. Le Guin concludes that inevitably the experience of expression and meaning in the song comes down to the personal and private networks of memory and association, and that these can never be 'captured' on any occasion—perhaps not even over a whole succession of occasions: 'there can be no denying that I am left, in the end, with an unfinished monument, a descriptional torso' (249). This is no cause for distress, however: the 'partiality' (in both senses of the word) of the description is the possible state of affairs, and corresponds to the necessary selectivity of perceptual and cognitive processes themselves.

> [E]verything valuable about my description hinges on *which bar* (or gesture or timbre or rhythm or personal association) *of the eight* (or eight hundred or eight hundred thousand that inhabit the phenomenal sphere of even a short piece like 'Soupir') *gets described*. As a critic, I have a positive obligation to make the selection, not only accepting but rejoicing in its incompleteness: according to Baudelaire, complete description is not just impossible (and impossibly pedantic), it is fundamentally unsuited to how people think, and remember, and understand. (250)

Like the diary entries of Herbert's participants, Le Guin's account vividly illustrates the shifting relationships between primary and higher-order consciousness. On the one hand there are those sensorimotor and barely articulable qualities of her listening (the sensation in the throat; the 'vague but compelling' sense of timbral change and return, register and harmony) that dynamically shape and constitute consciousness. And on the other there are the explicit narratives, commentaries, and anxieties— verbal, selective, less tied to the temporality of the song itself—that accompany, interpret, and sometimes intrude upon the flow of her listening, like a voice in the head. Described here as if neatly partitioned, Le Guin brings home how thoroughly intertwined the two actually are, how elusive the experience of primary musical consciousness really is.

History, culture, and musical consciousness

There is a danger that a narrowly psychological approach to music perception and the nature of musical consciousness might end up radically ahistorical and focused only on familiar cultural contexts. But musical listening and musical consciousness are profoundly culturally and historically specific, and any attempts to generalize about music perception and musical consciousness come up against the unassailable other- ness of different times and places. In the wake of controversies about how earlier European musical repertories might or should be played (e.g. Kenyon 1988), attention has inevitably turned to how people in other times might have listened—or in some cases whether people were even doing what we might now call listening at all (Johnson 1995; Weber 1997). Shai Burstyn's contribution to a special issue of *Early Music* dedi- cated to listening (Burstyn 1997) lays out some of the considerations in thinking about what listening might have been like at earlier times, and whether such an inquiry was even remotely feasible. The range of factors that might need to be considered is indeed overwhelming, encompassing aesthetic attitudes, the physical circumstances of musical events, people's memory skills and associative networks, the 'cognitive styles' of orality and of literacy, the impact of different kinds of representations of music (scores, paintings and other depictions, recordings), aesthetic ideologies, religious beliefs, conceptual and perceptual categories, relationships between music, dance, and drama— a panoply of biosocial factors as they might relate not only to music, but beyond that to the whole auditory and corporeal context of a historical subject. Burstyn is admirably inclusive in attempting to recognize the bewildering range of factors that would have to be considered to reconstruct the 'period ear', so it is then surprising that he apparently confidently suggests: 'If, however, we wish to understand better the ways past listeners may have perceived their music, we can enlist the combined resources of our historical knowledge and musical sensitivity to construct a hypothetical musical–mental model of listeners in a given place and time' (1997: 695).

If only it were so easy. But equally, is it really *impossible* ever to understand the consciousness—musical or otherwise—of other people at different times and places, and by extension perhaps even the person in the neighbouring seat on a train whose habitus (to use Bourdieu's term)[11] may be as far from your own as her body is near? At the limit the answer must be Yes, because it will always be impossible to take account of all the factors that contribute to another individual's current consciousness. But the solipsism on which this pessimistic analysis is based is as extreme and unreal as the blind and sweeping optimism that would have us believe that we are all one in our common and timeless humanity. Empirical studies (e.g. Deliège 1996; Sloboda 1991; Watt and Ash 1998) demonstrate significant common principles among listeners' affective, structural and semantic responses to music, as well as revealing important differences (e.g. Gregory and Varney 1996). The alternative to both of these is to approach consciousness, and musical consciousness in particular, from a perspective that takes account of the dialectical relationship between human capacities and environmental opportunities—steering a course between biological determinism on the one hand and complete cultural relativism on the other. One framework within which to attempt such an approach is provided by the ecological psychology of James Gibson, in which the mutual adaptation of perceivers and their environments plays a central role.

The ecology of listening

Living organisms are highly adaptable at a variety of timescales. In evolutionary terms, processes of adaptation have given rise to the great diversity of life forms that inhabit the planet. In developmental terms, higher mammals in particular have the ability to acquire and modify a huge range of sensorimotor and cognitive capacities. And on a moment-to-moment basis, human beings are strikingly able to be flexible in the ways that they behave (in the most general sense of the word) in relation to a constantly changing and highly complex environment. Sentient organisms can only be properly understood in relation to their environments, and their remarkable capacities are the consequence of that organism/environment interaction.

As developed at greater length elsewhere (Clarke 2005), music perception can be understood in the context of the adapted and adaptable attunement of listeners to their structured environments. The relatively undifferentiated but powerful sensori-motor capacities of newborn human infants are shaped and differentiated by the infant's immersive contact with, and action upon, a structured and dynamically evolving world. As Eleanor Gibson (1969) argued for perceptual learning and development, this process is largely a question of the differentiation of attention—the capacity to notice and act appropriately upon differences that were in some sense 'always there', but to which the perceiver previously had no sensitivity. Perception is a self-tuning process, in which the pickup of environmental information is intrinsically reinforcing, so that the system self-adjusts so as to optimize its resonance with the environment: 'A system "hunts" until it achieves clarity', wrote James Gibson (1966: 271)—a little like the scanning of a digital radio tuner.

Perception is essentially exploratory, seeking out sources of stimulation in order to discover more about the environment and to act optimally within it. This operates in so many ways and so continuously that it is easy to overlook: we detect a sound and turn to it; or we catch sight of an object, turn our eyes to it, lean forward and reach out to touch it. What a perceiver needs and wants is to know what is going on and what to do about it—what the environment *affords*. In the practical auditory environment of daily life this tangible relationship between perception and action is all around us, but in the socially regulated ways in which music is heard, the dynamic relationship between perception and action is changed or attenuated in important ways and with significant consequences for the type of music-listening consciousness that people experience. Many musical cultures—particularly those that might be loosely classified as art-music cultures, and perhaps all those that identify 'performers' and 'audiences' as distinct categories—introduce a break in the relationship between perception and action. Members of an audience, whether at a rock concert in a stadium, a performance in a concert hall, or a jazz gig in a bar, are placed in a situation in which they are largely prevented from acting on (or acting in relation to) the sounds they hear—even if traces of a more direct engagement can be seen in socially sanctioned patterns ranging from applause, head-nodding and foot-tapping, to dancing and singing along. What this situation affords for listeners is a type of attentive but receptive listening that has come to be regarded as more or less the paradigm of listening in the Western art music tradition—despite its historical and cultural peculiarity (see Dell'Antonio 2004; Johnson 1995).

An even more radical break came with the development of sound recording and broadcasting, which for the first time allowed music to be heard completely removed from the time and place of its production. Placed in the acousmatic realm, sounds that might otherwise specify the tangible, here-and-now realities of an environment to be acted upon come to specify a virtual world that may be populated with broadly the same kinds of objects and events—but in a manner that places them radically 'out of reach'; or by virtual objects and events that have no real counterparts at all.

Consider the start of the track 'Thriller' from Michael Jackson's 1982 album of the same name. The creaking door/coffin lid, footsteps, wind, thunder, and howls at the opening of the track (0:00–0:17) specify recognizable objects and events that in a 'real world' setting might elicit any one of a whole range of orienting responses, many of which might be summarized under the term 'fight-flight-or-freeze' (Cannon 1929). At the same time, many listeners will recognize these sounds as specifying the particular virtual world of Hollywood thrillers, as the famous 14-minute music video for the track makes plain in its narrative and imagery. The appeal of these genre-specifying sounds is that they engage powerful underlying perception–action relationships (the stereotype being wide-eyed audience members with their hands at their mouths) while at the same time keeping them confined within the safety of the film's (or soundtrack's) virtual world. The entry of the drum kit, bass, and synthesizer sounds at 0:17, initiating a ramped intro of increasing dynamic and harmonic tension to the explosive fanfare (0:37) and the subsequent drums and bass groove (0:41), signal the entry of the band, and in some sense the start of the song, with Jackson's vocal entry just before 1:00 marking the first verse. These descriptors of the start of the track represent only a small subset of the events that can be heard in this first minute, but they demonstrate the overlapping and simultaneous auditory environments that complex sound sources such as these afford. Imagine, too, the contrasting affordances of these sounds for a young child on the one hand, or a seasoned dance-music listener on the other, encountered unexpectedly either in a darkened room or in a social context—and the kinds of actions-in-response that might ensue.

This account has so far focused on the ways in which sounds *specify* objects and events in real and virtual worlds, but it is also possible to focus listening attention on sound itself, rather than what it specifies. It is arguably harder to do that when sounds specify clearly identifiable real-world objects and events than when no such object or source makes its presence felt—so at the start of 'Thriller' it is very hard to hear to hear the 'sounds as such' (i.e. to listen to them in the manner of Pierre Schaeffer's *écoute reduite*),[12] rather than as door creaks, footsteps, wind, and howls. But when the instrumental and vocal sounds of the track start, it is more possible to adopt a listening stance that deliberately focuses on the character of the sounds themselves—their sharpness or roundness, graininess or smoothness, the changes in the timbre of the bass groove under Jackson's voice in the first verse, and the constant transformations of timbre, timing, and articulation in his own vocal delivery. Gibson makes the same point about the 'dual character' of paintings when he writes:

> A picture . . . is always a treated surface, and it is always seen in the context of other non-pictorial surfaces. Along with the invariants for the depicted layout of surfaces, there are invariants for the surface as such. It is a plaster wall, or a sheet of canvas, a panel, a screen, or a piece of paper. The glass, texture, edges, or frame of the picture surface are given in the array, and they are perceived. The information displayed is dual. The picture is always both a scene and a surface, and the scene is paradoxically *behind* the surface. This duality of the information is the reason the observer is never quite sure how to answer the question, 'What do you see?' For he can perfectly well answer that he sees a wall or a piece of paper. (J.J. Gibson 1979: 281)

In similar vein, the experimental participant imagined earlier, when asked what she hears, can answer 'vinyl recording', 'Glenn Gould', 'a piano', 'the Aria of the Goldberg variations', 'Bach', 'beautiful touch', and a lot more besides.

Music, then, is an endlessly 'multiple' environment in which to perceive and act; and recordings—the most common way in which many people encounter music now—are fascinatingly paradoxical sources. In the sounds of recordings people hear all kinds of things: people (Michael Jackson), actions (singing, walking, creaking, howling), objects (doors, dogs, drums), spaces (the 'thriller' territory, Jackson's places/spaces in the mix), structures (intro, verse, harmonic sequence, duple metre, bass line), genres (soul/funk/dance, horror/thriller soundtrack), emotions (aroused, excited), and even medium (vinyl, CD, mp3 file). Only the last of these is in the domain of the real, the others all being virtual objects or events of one sort or another—some less removed from physical reality (Michael Jackson and Vincent Price were really there—at one time, though of course not at the time of listening), some more removed (the empty, windy, threatening space of the track's opening—which was never really 'there'). Recordings draw listeners into all kinds of different worlds with their own particular affordances—moving/dancing, structure-following, emotional responding, close listening, reminiscing, visualizing.

The characteristics of music perception can be understood in terms of the variants and invariants of the musical environment—focused on the specific features of the immediately present musical materials, but not confined to them—understood in relation to the orientation, capacities, and experience of the perceiver. For a child in the dark, unfamiliar with the sounds and conventions of the thriller genre, and unexpectedly confronted with the opening, the track may afford fear, distress, and withdrawal. For a young adult at an 80s club night, the same opening may afford excited whoops of recognition and approval, Jackson-style dance moves and singing along. At the centre of both of these, and myriad other possible perceptual engagements, is a primary listening consciousness that is powerfully shaped by the temporal, bodily, spatial, spectral, and dynamic characteristics of the musical-materials-in-context. Primary musical consciousness of 'Thriller' is that creaking, windy, reverberant, groove-based, exciting, auditory-motor state of mind that the track affords, and while the listener is engaged with them, these materials are as much the 'stuff' of the listener's consciousness as is the brain matter that is active at the time. Tia DeNora (2000) and Andy Clark (2008) have argued in different ways that music, among many other external systems, objects, and artefacts (language, moving images, mobile phones, bicycles), constitutes a cognitive extension or prosthesis of the self, externally scaffolded and materially distributed, as integral to our thought, action, and experience as are the neurons and synapses on which cognitive neuroscience is focused.

Selective attention, multiple drafts, and the contents of consciousness

The perceptual account presented here has emphasized the diversity and richness of the environment as a source of information, and the adaptability and multiplicity of perception–action opportunities in principle available to a perceiver. Music is a perceptual environment that is often deliberately extremely richly layered, as Debussy's 'Soupir', Bach's Goldberg variations, and Michael Jackson's 'Thriller' all illustrate in their different ways. How is a listener not engulfed by perceptual overload—and what aspects of this densely populated perceptual field actually appear in consciousness? Albert Bregman's *Auditory Scene Analysis* (Bregman 1990) provides a persuasive account of the auditory principles—distributed between perceptual capacities and environmental opportunities—that result in the broadly stable and meaningful auditory scenes that we experience in all but the most exceptional circumstances. A small number of powerful principles can account for this capacity, which can mostly be understood as the relationship between integration (grouping together those elements that belong together) and segregation (keeping separate those elements that correspond to different sources). In most auditory environments—and this is certainly true of most music—this will result in a number of simultaneous auditory streams, and an important question concerns which and how many of these streams we are conscious of. Direct experience and more than 50 years of experimental investigation show that listeners have a limited capacity to attend to competing sources of information—a predicament sometimes summed up in the engineering metaphor of 'limited channel capacity'. People do indeed find it difficult or impossible to attend to competing sources of information in the same modality (hearing, vision, kinaesthesia), but the apparent filtering out of the unattended information has been shown to have paradoxical features. An experimental participant required to listen to one of two competing auditory streams (e.g. the sound of two different conversations going on simultaneously) appears to have little or no knowledge of what was going on in the unattended stream—until, for instance, the participant's name appears in that stream, when conscious attention suddenly switches to that apparently unattended channel (see Eysenck and Keane 2010: Ch. 5). A variety of models and explanations have been proposed, but the crucial point is that the phenomenon seems to demonstrate that simultaneous streams of information are attended up to some level, but that only one (or at the most a small number, when different modalities are involved) reaches conscious awareness.

These questions about selective attention may seem limited in scope and technical in nature, but they point to a fundamental question about consciousness explored at some length in Dennett (1991): given that a great deal of perceptual information is attended to in some way but never reaches consciousness, what kinds of experiences 'appear in consciousness', when do they do so (in relation to their occurrence in the environment), and what determines whether they do so or not? These same questions seem particularly relevant for music perception and musical consciousness, since music is often a deliberately and significantly multiple phenomenon.[13] What aspects of musical multiplicity make it into consciousness, why those rather than others, and when do they get there?

Dennett's position is to reject the idea that there is a 'Cartesian theatre' (as he puts it) within which the contents of consciousness must appear to be viewed/heard by a central executive. Instead he proposes a *multiple drafts* model in which perceptual and cognitive activity proceeds in constant and overlapping parallelism, with different streams of this parallel processing reaching consciousness at different times. Consciousness is not some singular and unified phenomenon, but is constantly in flux, subject both to the perceptual attractors of the external and internal (bodily) environment, and also to the roving probe that is the subject's own intentionality.

Dennett subscribes to what is in many ways a fairly conventional software/hardware view of mind and brain, but adds to that a significantly enriching view of cognitive extension: tools, cultural artefacts, and conceptual systems engaged by the brain and body massively expand the basic infrastructure of the brain and mind. In a manner that is similar—though not identical—to Clark's (2008) approach to distributed cognition and cognitive extension,[14] Dennett summarizes his view of human consciousness as 'a huge complex of memes (or more exactly, meme-effects in brains) that can best be understood as the operation of a "*von Neumannesque*" virtual machine[15] *implemented* in the *parallel architecture* of a brain that was not designed for any such activities. The powers of the *virtual machine* vastly enhance the underlying powers of the organic *hardware* on which it runs' (1991: 210).

Dennett's model is attractive as a way to think about musical consciousness, specifically focused as it is on that quality of 'streams within flux' that seems so central to the experience of music. Ray Jackendoff (1991) proposed very much the same approach in a model of perceptual parsing and emotional responses to music that appeared in the same year as Dennett's book. The core of Jackendoff's paper revolves around the problem of how it is that listeners make sense of the constantly changing multiple possibilities of musical material in 'online' listening. Music of any degree of complexity offers multiple parsings at almost every stage, and listeners cannot know which of these different possibilities will turn out to be sensible or coherent. How can listeners cope with this combinatorially explosive predicament without either keeping huge numbers of alternatives in play, or finding that they have to backtrack to a previously abandoned interpretation—giving up when an interpretation comes unstuck and starting again? Jackendoff's proposal is that listeners continue to entertain a limited number of parallel possibilities at every stage, with the one that seems to be doing best occupying centre stage, while others progressively fade away as they become less coherent or plausible. What people are aware of as they listen to music is mainly the current 'best contender', though there are always other alternatives also in play, waiting to step into the limelight. The opening groove to a dance track, for example, may be heard in one particular metrical orientation, with one or more alternative orientations lurking beneath the surface waiting for the possibility of that perceptual reorganization that Butler (2001) calls 'turning the beat around'. This is very similar to the more general model of consciousness that Dennett proposes, partially summarized as follows:

> Instead of such a single stream [of consciousness] (however wide), there are multiple channels in which specialist circuits try . . . to do their various things, creating Multiple Drafts as they go. Most of these fragmentary drafts of 'narrative' play short-lived roles in the modulation of current activity but some get promoted to further functional roles, in swift succession, by the activity of a virtual machine in the brain. (1991: 253)

Conclusion: musical consciousnesses and musical subjectivities

The multiple drafts model represents consciousness as dynamic, labile, and provisional. Rather than aspiring to a falsely integrated and unified view, it sees consciousness as intrinsically many-voiced, with (pursuing the vocal analogy) the potential for that state of affairs to occupy a position anywhere between polyphony, heterophony, and cacophony. If standard models of consciousness have tended to emphasize a monodic conception, then that too is certainly possible within the multiple drafts perspective, but might be regarded more as the exception than the rule. And the appropriateness of a musical analogy for consciousness is perhaps not just fortuitous, but suggests why music itself engages consciousness so powerfully: music's own multiplicity and temporal dynamism engage with the general character of consciousness itself, with the consequence that music provides us with a domain in which to explore and experience 'what it is like to be human' in terms that are on the one hand familiar, and on the other transformative. From one perspective, this is not surprising: music is the product of human action, and bears the trace of that action in palpable and manifest ways. Musical sounds, like any sounds, specify their sources—the sounds of the bodies, instruments, and actions that make music—most strikingly, perhaps, in the sound of the voice, but much also more widely and in ways that take in the virtual sources of studio production processes (see Clarke 2001; Doyle 2005; Shove and Repp 1995).

If music were no more than the acoustical trace of human action, it might have little more than documentary interest—the sounds of people going about their everyday lives. It is the aesthetic framing, transformation, and ordering of that material, the mediation of the sounds of human action by musical systems, ideologies, and technologies—the intervention of human imagination and creativity—that distinguishes music from location recordings, and turns 'data' into aesthetic objects and processes. Music has the capacity to convey, extend, express, and transform human subjectivity, and in doing so it becomes for many people one of the most richly fulfilling and psychologically important domains of their subjective and intersubjective experience. Music is found in every human culture, and in the great majority of those cultures it is closely associated with powerful experiences of heightened or transformed subjectivity and intersubjectivity: religious experiences, communal dancing, outpourings of public grief and celebration, 'deep listening' (Becker 2004), and trancing. There is little value in trying to claim that music has a uniquely special significance in this respect, since human beings seem to have a prodigious capacity to engage their consciousnesses in powerful ways across an apparently limitless spectrum of materials and activities. But, as demonstrated by the cultural complexity, time, passion, and cognitive commitment that are devoted to musicking, there does seem to be something particularly rich and far-reaching about the many kinds of musical consciousness with which we all engage.

References

Baily, J. (1996). Using tests of sound perception in fieldwork. *Yearbook for Traditional Music*, **28**, 147–73.

Becker, J. (2004). *Deep Listeners: Music, Emotion, and Trancing* (Bloomington, IN: Indiana University Press).

Bourdieu, P. (1977). *Outline of a Theory of Practice* (Cambridge: Cambridge University Press).

Bharucha, J.J. (1987). Music cognition and perceptual facilitation: a connectionist framework. *Music Perception*, **5**, 1–30.

Bregman, A.S. (1990). *Auditory Scene Analysis: The Perceptual Organization of Sound* (Cambridge, MA: MIT Press).

Burstyn, S. (1997). In quest of the period ear. *Early Music*, **25**, 692–701.

Butler, M.J. (2001). Turning the beat around: reinterpretation, metrical dissonance and asymmetry in electronic dance music. *Music Theory Online*, **7**.

Cannon, W.B. (1929). *Bodily Changes in Pain, Hunger, Fear and Rage: An Account of Recent Researches into the Function of Emotional Excitement* (New York, NY: Appleton).

Clark, A. (2008). *Supersizing the Mind. Embodiment, Action and Cognitive Extension* (Oxford: Oxford University Press).

Clarke, E.F. (2001). Meaning and the specification of motion in music. *Musicae Scientiae*, **5**, 213–34.

Clarke, E.F. (2005). *Ways of Listening: An Ecological Approach to the Perception of Musical Meaning* (New York, NY: Oxford University Press).

'consciousness, *n*.'. *OED Online*. November 2010. Oxford University Press. http://www.oed.com/viewdictionaryentry/Entry/39477 (accessed 2 March 2011).

Cook, N. (1990). *Music, Imagination and Culture* (Oxford: Clarendon Press).

Cook, N. (1993). Perception: a perspective from music theory, in R. Aiello with J. Sloboda (eds.), *Musical Perceptions*, 64–96 (New York, NY: Oxford University Press).

Csikszentmihalyi, M. and Csikszentmihalyi, I.S. (1988) (eds.). *Optimal Experience: Psychological Studies of Flow in Consciousness* (Cambridge: Cambridge University Press).

Damasio, A. (1999). *The Feeling of What Happens. Body, Emotion and the Making of Consciousness* (London: Heinemann).

Deliège, I. (1996). Cue abstraction as a component of categorisation processes in music listening. *Psychology of Music*, **24**, 131–56.

Dell'Antonio, A. (2004) (ed.) *Beyond Structural Listening? Postmodern Models of Hearing* (Berkeley, CA: University of California Press).

Dennett, D. (1991). *Consciousness Explained* (London: Penguin).

DeNora, T. (2000). *Music in Everyday Life* (Cambridge: Cambridge University Press).

DeNora, T. (2003). *After Adorno: Rethinking Music Sociology* (Cambridge: Cambridge University Press).

Dibben, N. (2001). What do we hear when we hear music? Music perception and musical material. *Musicae Scientiae*, **5**, 161–94.

Doyle, P. (2005). *Echo and Reverb: Fabricating Space in Popular Music, 1900–1960* (Middletown, CT: Wesleyan University Press).

Edelman, G. (1989). *The Remembered Present: A Biological Theory of Consciousness* (New York, NY: Basic Books).

Eysenck, M.W. and Keane, M.T. (2010). *Cognitive Psychology: A Student's Handbook*, 6th edn (Hove: Psychology Press).

Frith, C.D. (2008). The social functions of consciousness, in L. Weiskrantz and M. Davies (eds.), *Frontiers of Consciousness. The Chichele Lectures*, 225–44 (Oxford: Oxford University Press).

Gabrielsson, A. (in press). *Strong Experiences with Music*, trans. R. Bradbury (Oxford: Oxford University Press).

Gabrielsson, A. and Lindström Wik, S. (1993). On strong experiences of music. *Musikpsychologie: Jahrbuch der Deutschen Gesellschaft für Musikpsychologie*, **10**, 118–39.

Gabrielsson, A. and Lindström Wik, S. (2003). Strong experiences related to music: a descriptive system. *Musicae Scientiae*, **7**, 157–217.

Gaver, W.W. (1993a). What in the world do we hear? An ecological approach to auditory event perception. *Ecological Psychology*, **5**, 1–29.

Gaver, W.W. (1993b). How do we hear in the world? Explorations in ecological acoustics. *Ecological Psychology*, **5**, 285–313.

Gibson, E.J. (1969). *Principles of Perceptual Learning and Development* (New York, NY: Appleton-Century-Crofts).

Gibson, J.J. (1966). *The Senses Considered as Perceptual Systems* (Boston, MA: Houghton Mifflin).

Gibson, J.J. (1979). *The Ecological Approach to Visual Perception* (Hillsdale, NJ: Lawrence Erlbaum Associates).

Godøy, R.I., Haga, E., and Jensenius, A. (2006). Playing 'air instruments': mimicry of sound-producing gestures by novices and experts, in S. Gibet, N. Courty and J.F. Kamp (eds.), *Gesture in Human–Computer Interaction and Simulation: 6th International Gesture Workshop, GW 2005, Berder Island, France, May 18–20, 2005, Revised Selected Papers, LNAI 3881*, 256–67 (Berlin: Springer-Verlag).

Gregory, A.H. and Varney, N. (1996). Cross-cultural comparisons in the affective response to music. *Psychology of Music*, **24**, 47–52.

Herbert, R. (2009). Range of consciousness within everyday music listening experiences: absorption, dissociation and the trancing process. Unpublished PhD thesis, University of Sheffield.

Huron, D. (1989). Voice denumerability in polyphonic music of homogeneous timbres. *Music Perception*, **6**, 361–82.

Hutchins, E. (1995). *Cognition in the Wild* (Cambridge, MA: Bradford Books).

Jackendoff, R. (1991). Musical parsing and musical affect. *Music Perception*, **9**, 199–230.

Jackson, M. (1982). *Thriller*. CD. (Epic BOOOO2663R).

James, W. (1890). *The Principles of Psychology* (New York, NY: Henry Holt).

Johnson, J.H. (1995). *Listening in Paris: A Cultural History* (Berkeley, CA: University of California Press).

Kane, B. (2007). *L'Objet Sonore Maintenant*: Pierre Schaeffer, sound objects and the phenomenological reduction. *Organised Sound*, **12**, 15–24.

Kenyon, N. (1988) (ed.) *Authenticity and Early Music: A Symposium* (Oxford: Oxford University Press).

Kramer, L. (2002). *Musical Meaning. Toward a Critical History.* (Berkeley, CA: University of California Press).

Le Guin, E. (2004). One bar in eight: Debussy and the death of description, in A. Dell'Antonio (ed.) *Beyond Structural Listening? Postmodern Models of Hearing*, 233–51 (Berkeley, CA: University of California Press).

Meyer, L.B. (1967). *Music, the Arts, and Ideas: Patterns and Predictions in Twentieth-Century Culture* (Chicago, IL: University of Chicago Press).

Nagel, T. (1974). What is it like to be a bat? *The Philosophical Review*, **83**, 435–50.

Schaeffer, P. (1966). *Traité des objets musicaux* (Paris: Éditions du Seuil).

Shove, P. and Repp, B. (1995). Musical motion and performance: theoretical and empirical perspectives, in J. Rink (ed.) *The Practice of Performance. Studies in Musical Interpretation*, 55–83 (Cambridge: Cambridge University Press).

Sloboda, J.A. (1991). Musical structure and emotional response: some empirical findings. *Psychology of Music*, **19**, 110–20.

Subotnik, R.R. (1996). *Deconstructive Variations: Music and Reason in Western Society.* (Minneapolis, MN: University of Minnesota Press).

Watt, R.J. and Ash R. (1998). A psychological investigation of meaning in music. *Musicae Scientiae*, **1**, 33–53.

Weber, W. (1997). Did people listen in the 18th century? *Early Music*, **25**, 678–91.

Notes

1. See also Chapter 4, this volume.

2. A proper consideration of higher-order consciousness of music, encompassing a whole array of linguistically mediated, recollective, and metacognitive functions, is beyond the scope of this chapter. The discussion that follows begins by (artificially) bracketing out higher-order consciousness of music, to place the primary component at centre stage, and subsequently considers some of the ways in which primary and higher-order consciousness are bound up with one another.

3. There are clear similarities here with Husserl's approach to time-consciousness, and with the principles of protention and retention (see Chapters 1–3, this volume).

4. My question adopts and adapts the title of Thomas Nagel's (1974) essay 'What is it like to be a bat?', which is concerned with the subjective character of experience and the limits of understanding a different point of view.

5. Given the relationship between language and higher-order consciousness proposed by Damasio and Edelman, not being conscious of a musical feature, and not having the language to describe it, might amount to the same thing—if 'being conscious of' is taken as shorthand for 'having higher-order consciousness of'.

6. It is also the case that the structural listening perspective arguably helps to *make* conscious (by means of higher-order consciousness) attributes of musical materials that might otherwise remain unconscious—as when a structural analysis reveals a motivic connection that might otherwise have gone unnoticed.

7. Further pertinent accounts can be found in the work of Gabrielsson (in press), and Gabrielsson and Lindström Wik (1993, 2003), who investigated listeners' 'strong experiences of music', including their significant descriptions of what those experiences sounded like; Tia DeNora (2000, 2003), who has taken a more sociological perspective on the ways in which listeners use music in their daily lives, including vivid accounts of how those listening experiences both participate in and are informed by a range of more or less significant life events and states of mind; and Judith Becker (2004), who provides an interdisciplinary treatment of so-called 'deep listening' in a number of different cultural contexts (Indonesia and the southern USA among them), bringing together ethnographic, neuroscientific, religious, and psychological perspectives on trancing behaviour and altered states of musical consciousness.

8. Le Guin does not herself specify the number of listenings, but from the account itself it appears to be of the order of 10–15.

9. Le Guin comments that were she a pianist (she is not), she would have a more powerful kinaesthetic insight into that aspect of the song—which, she claims, illustrates the patchy and contingent character of this kind of embodied listening across the generality of listeners, by comparison with the pervasiveness of the 'visualistic and synoptic' kind of listening that characterizes a listener without specific instrumental empathy. Interestingly, research by Rolf Inge Godøy *et al.* (2006; see also Chapter 13, this volume) on so-called 'air instrument' performance suggests that non-instrumentalists actually have somewhat greater implicit kinaesthetic knowledge or empathy than Le Guin assumes.

10. At first sight, expectation-based theories of emotional responses to music might seem to suggest only diminishing effects, but Meyer (1967: 42–53), Huron (2006: 281–304) and Bharucha (1987: 3–5) provide a variety of ways to understand why this is not the case.

11. Bourdieu (1977) uses the term 'habitus' in preference to 'culture', which has unhelpfully static, reified, and totalizing connotations. Habitus, by comparison, brings together the material conditions of an environment, the regulating effects of customs and practices across a range of formal and informal kinds, and the specific dispositions, habits, and resistant practices of an individual.

12. See Schaeffer (1966), and for a critical appraisal Kane (2007); also Chapters 3 and 5, this volume.

13. Huron (1989), using a combination of empirical and statistical modelling methods, has estimated that listeners cannot keep track of more than about three separate parts in timbrally homogeneous polyphonic music.

14. While Dennett is more committed to the view that external reality (whether of a tangible or symbolic variety) must be internally represented in the brain, Clark proposes a more porous model in which the basis for consciousness is radically distributed between brain, body, and world.

15. In other words a serial, as opposed to parallel, computational architecture.

Chapter 12

Towards a theory of proprioception as a bodily basis for consciousness in music

Alicia Peñalba Acitores

Musical consciousness is a difficult concept to define for a number of reasons. Not only is music a very broad and inclusive term comprising different activities (playing an instrument, listening to performances and recordings, composing, remembering music), but consciousness also presents different levels of awareness. When music is ongoing, consciousness can be defined as the ability to be aware of its elements: melody, rhythm, instrumentation, structure. However, musical consciousness also involves other aspects, such as the ability to evoke images, emotions, and memories—attributes that are closely related to the self.

Classical consciousness studies have proposed two different types of consciousness. According to Edelman, *primary consciousness* refers to 'the state of being mentally aware of things in the world', whereas *higher-order consciousness* includes the 'recognition by a thinking subject of his or her own acts and affections' (Edelman 1989: 112). Higher-order consciousness requires not only the engagement of the body, but also the language and social interaction needed to form a concept of the self. This self-concept entails meta-consciousness rather than just an awareness of the world. From this perspective, primary consciousness takes place in the perception of sensory stimuli while higher-order consciousness is concerned with the perception of the self.

This chapter aims to highlight the importance of the body as a basis for consciousness, and is in three sections. The first addresses primary consciousness as a source of awareness in the perception of ongoing musical material in which the body is involved. The second focuses on higher-order consciousness—our capacity to become self-conscious. It can be argued that both types of consciousness, traditionally studied separately, can be considered as belonging to a continuum, as stated by Merleau-Ponty: 'all thought of something is at the same time self-consciousness' (Merleau-Ponty 1962: 371). Based on this idea of a continuum, it will also be argued that primary and higher-order consciousness are both built on bodily input (Edelman 1989, cited in Wider 1997: 140) and that the feeling of that body is possible through proprioception. The third section will use ideas from O'Regan and Noë's sensorimotor contingency theory (2001a, 2001b) to offer an explanation of how musical consciousness takes place.

Primary consciousness

Primary consciousness involves being aware of the world—being aware of perceptual events such as sounds, colours, odours, etc. Primary musical consciousness implies being aware of music's ongoing elements: instruments, themes, modulations, harmonic progressions, cadences, variations, etc. We are aware of these elements because we have a body engaged in perception which allows us to explore musical stimuli. In order to study primary consciousness in music, we will examine ideas from Mark Johnson's embodied mind theory (1987: xv) in which he suggests that we use bodily metaphors to understand abstract domains.[1] Within this embodied-mind paradigm, the body is considered to play a central role in cognition and perception.

Many common statements about music show evidence of a physical metaphorical understanding at work, such as that 'dissonances produce tension'; 'the tonic restores calm'; a person singing is 'out of tune'; pitches are 'high' or 'low'; an anacrusis is 'suspended'; or chords 'push forward to the cadence'. Although Johnson's theory has its origin in linguistics (Lakoff and Johnson 1980; Kittay 1987), it has subsequently been applied to a number of different disciplines including mathematics (Lakoff and Núñez 2000) and politics (Dirven 1994; Lakoff 1996; Schön 1979)). It has also been used in relation to music by a number of scholars (Brower 2000; Cox 1999, 2001; Echard 1999, 2006; Feld 1981; Marconi 2001; Martínez 2004; Saslaw 1996; Spitzer 2004; Zbikowski 1997), since it provides conceptual tools, called 'image schemata', that can be fruitfully applied to musical events.

Johnson argues that we understand abstract domains—such as psychology, mathematics, economics, and music—in terms of more concrete and better known domains—our body feelings and experiences. Newborn infants' first relationships with the world are sensorimotor (Piaget [1926] 1973). Manipulation and movement allow them to build up what Johnson calls 'image schemata', and these schemata help them to understand abstract domains. An image schema is a 'recurring, dynamic pattern of our perceptual interactions and motor programs that gives coherence and structure to our experience' (Johnson 1987: xiv). Image schemata can convey up–down, balance, front–back, full–empty experiences that can in turn be used in abstract thinking through metaphor. Metaphors function by 'mak[ing] use of patterns that obtain in our physical experience to organize our more abstract understanding' (Johnson 1987: xv), allowing us to comprehend the world in terms of what we already know. For instance, the up–down schema is projected metaphorically onto an understanding of price changes (prices are rising); near–far can be used to understand an emotional relationship with a friend (he is a close friend); and the path metaphor allows us to see life as a journey (I have to keep to, or change my course). Although image schemata are created from many different bodily activities, they share an idiosyncratic internal structure, which is an abstraction of the core of the experiences themselves. Riding a bike, skating, and watching a see-saw in motion all share certain features that go into the formation of the balance schema while abstracting from the particularities of each specific activity, and the schema itself has an internal structure based on the compensating actions of gravity and other forces.

In music, for instance, the cycle schema helps us to understand recapitulation in a sonata, or the cycle of fifths (Brower 2000: 343); and Saslaw (1996: 222–3) shows how path and container metaphors are projected in the understanding of a cadence, how near–far and path have a role in conceptualizing the proximity of harmonies, and how major and minor chords can be understood in terms of balance (a major third being considered an inversion of a minor third). As noted by Zbikowski, the verticality schema is the result of experiences such as 'perceiving a tree, our felt sense of standing upright, the activity of climbing stairs' (1997: 202), and is used to conceptualize pitch relationships in music. Balance plays a role in understanding the attraction of the tonic and the movement to other degrees, and path in understanding the arrival of the dominant (Echard 1999: 140). As these examples illustrate, understanding music in terms of image schemata contributes significantly to our awareness of the role and function of musical elements.

Although Johnson claims that we make metaphorical projections between image schemata and abstract domains, he does not explain how it is possible for us to choose or use these metaphors. In order to project a schema, we must identify certain significant features of the target domain that will enable us to select the right schema. Thus, it seems necessary to set up some sort of connection facilitator mechanism. In the case of music, one of a number of specific questions might be: How do we establish the connection between the up–down schema and musical pitch? Among other possible explanations,[2] Arnie Cox (2001) proposes the 'mimetic hypothesis', in which he stresses that we conceptualize musical sounds through activities that we are able to perform ourselves. Musical sounds are understood as vocal sounds: *cantabile* as singing, *sotto voce* as whispering, jazz trumpets as screaming, and recitative as speaking. We can also mimic the actions of a performer: a violin sound can evoke the motor imitation of the gestures needed to perform it. Cox makes reference to evidence from the field of cognitive neuroscience, and in particular to the role of mirror neurons. Discovered by Rizzolatti,[3] mirror neurons were originally found in the ventral premotor cortex of macaque monkeys. They become activated not only when a monkey executes an action, but also when it sees the same action performed by others (Rizzolatti *et al.* 1996, 2000). Mirror neurons 'allow us to directly understand the meaning of actions . . . of others by internally replicating ("simulating") them' (Gallese *et al.* 2004: 396). Within the field of linguistics, the motor theory of speech perception (Liberman and Mattingly 1985) had already suggested the presence of common cognitive representations underlying both speech production and perception, while Molnar-Szakacs and Overy (2006) consider that mirror neurons must be involved in this process. In music, Haueisen and Knösche (2001) showed that pianists exhibited covert (involuntary) contralateral primary motor cortical activity while listening to pieces in which they were well trained; and Lahav *et al.* (2007) showed that non-musicians can show activation in motor areas of the brain when they listen to previously learned melodies.

The common underlying idea, supported by mirror neuron research and Cox's mimetic hypothesis, highlights the role of bodily feeling in image-schematic understanding in music. The proposal is that, although we may not actually move while listening to music, we mimic internally the actions of the performers (fingering, breathing, balancing, etc.)—this imitation being more accurate in trained musicians. Furthermore, other kinds of simulation may also occur when we identify image schemata, since internal action simulation is more abstract than the concrete actions of the performers. So, in the case of the metaphoric projection of image schemata, simulation of physical actions or feelings is considerably more subtle—for example, when we simulate a vertical displacement in the melody, or the effect of gravity on the strong and weak beat, or tension and release in the resolution from dominant to tonic.

Despite the fact that when we listen to a piece of music we may have the impression of perceiving everything, perception is selective; the simultaneous perception of all attributes of a piece of music is impossible. One reason for this is that the musical events that we metaphorize through image schemata emerge into consciousness and become the dominant ones, conditioning us to miss many other features that are less pertinent in the specific context. In his ecological approach to perception, James Gibson (1979: 141) explains the ability to perceive the world in terms of the relationship between action and perception.[4] He asserts that actions determine the environmental features on which we focus, thus facilitating perception; and he underlines the idea that what we perceive when we look at objects are their *affordances*, not their qualities. When we hear a sound we do not perceive the pitch, the timbre, and the duration as independent properties of the sound, but rather we perceive a glass breaking, a baby crying, or the wind blowing. Affordances are the opportunities for action that an object or event in an environment presents to a perceiver, and they determine the way that he or she perceives that object or event.

Listening to music affords mimicking the performer's gestures and simulating a wide range of physical feelings derived from the projection of image schemata: going up and down with melodies, travelling along a path with themes, and so on. Bodily actions (internal simulations) filter the stimuli that give rise to our perceptions, and those actions cause us to perceive certain aspects of reality and to overlook others. In doing so, we become conscious of music as a result of being aware of the simulated actions we perform when exploring musical features.

Higher-order consciousness

According to Edelman, higher-order consciousness includes the 'recognition by a thinking subject of his own actions and affections' (1989: 112), but in the formulation proposed by Bermúdez (1995: 153), it involves additional layers such as the capacity 'to think of one's body as one's own; to recognize oneself as the bearer for mental states; to master the grammar of the first-person pronoun; to view oneself as one object in the world among others, or as one person in the world among others; to have memories about one's past self; to construct autobiographical narratives; to formulate long-term plans and ambitions'. As already stated, primary and higher-order consciousnesses, although studied separately, belong to a single continuum. Higher-order consciousness refers to self-awareness, but the perception of stimuli in the environment also requires the perception of the self. The subject's actions filter the stimuli that engage our perception, and also provide fundamental information about the perceiver's position in space, and movement. In observing a bird in the sky, information from receptors in our neck complements the visual information and informs us about the exact relative location of the bird. As Gibson argues, perceiving external stimuli entails a reciprocal relationship with the perceiver's own actions—and in that sense involves perception of the self: 'the optical information to specify the self, including the head, body, arms and hands, accompanies the optical information to specify the environment' (Gibson 1979: 116). As a result 'awareness of the persisting and changing environment (perception) is concurrent with the persisting and changing self (proprioception in my extended use of the term)' (Gibson 1987: 418).[5] Wider also considers consciousness and the sense of ourselves to 'require the processing of bodily data' (1997: 143), and Edelman (1989) argues that 'without external stimuli and proprioceptive input, primary consciousness could not arise' (cited in Wider 1997: 144). Both primary and higher-order consciousnesses therefore seem to be based on bodily awareness. Since primary consciousness deals with the perception of things in the world, proprioception is needed in that process, since 'all perceptual systems are propriosensitive as well as exterosensitive' (Gibson 1979: 115).

Proprioception provides us with information about the state of our own bodies and allows us to adapt our actions to sensory information. It works both consciously and subconsciously: subconsciously, it adjusts muscles and joints for global motion, and in a conscious way it allows access to awareness of a particular part of the body at any time. The term 'proprioception' was coined within neurophysiology by Charles Sherrington (1906) who proposed it to refer to the information we obtain from our own bodies.[6] Proprioception gathers information about pressure and temperature from the skin receptors, the relative state of the body segments, balance and posture, skin-stretch, fatigue, and effort as well as information from internal organs (Eilan *et al.* 1995: 12). Proprioceptors are mechanoreceptors of various types, which carry various kinds of information depending on their location: muscle spindles and Golgi tendon organs are sensitive to variations of muscular strength (Kandel *et al.* 2000: 723); Pacinian corpuscles, located in deep layers of the joint capsule, detect the pressure and weight of body segments; and Ruffini corpuscles, situated in the individual joint ligaments, also convey information about muscle strength (López Muñiz 2004: 55). The vestibular apparatus, located in the inner ear, is sensitive to head movements (Escudero 1998; Kahle 1997; Sobotta and Becher 1994).[7]

Let us imagine our proprioceptive consciousness when playing a musical instrument. Actions are monitored by proprioception, so that when playing the piano, we regulate the position of the arms, hands, and fingers by proprioception, and control movements of the torso and head. When we move even a small muscle, the entire body compensates for this movement through proprioception, maintaining balance and stability. In executing actions, our attention is usually diverted away from the body, although we may remain conscious of it. This idea can be explained in terms of what Gallagher calls the *body schema* (1995: 235), which constitutes the capacity of the body to adapt to the environment. When we move, our proprioceptive system, through the body schema, works in real time to allow the body to adjust to its own movements. Although we are not aware of every detail of our body, the body schema provides a holistic representation of the body, providing a feeling of belonging: we do not doubt who it is that is moving, and that the body is ours. This feeling of belonging, and the perception of the whole body, enables us to be conscious of ourselves as integrated entities.

Supplementing the body schema concept is what Gallagher calls the *body image*, which refers to 'the subject's perceptual experience of his body, the subject's conceptual understanding of the body, and the subject's emotional attitude towards his/her own body' (1995: 228). In a more explicit manner, it allows us to focus on certain movements or postures of our bodies, and is intentional. Beginner musicians need to consciously control the position and movements of their bodies (Legrand 2007: 501) whereas experts do not. However, experts need what Gallagher calls 'performative awareness' of the body even while not paying attention to specific parts (2005: 74). When one plays the flute, for instance, specific goal-oriented gestures are performed: flautists control their breathing, tongue articulation, and fingering, controlling timbre and pitch with air pressure and blowing angle. Although they might not be *continuously* aware of all of these movements, they will have access, if they need it, to an awareness of these gestures. As stated by Gallagher and Zahavi (2010, 'Although I may not be aware of certain details about my bodily performance, this does not mean however that I am unconscious of my body'. Flautists typically also make a variety of gestures that are not directly oriented to the production of the sound, such as flexing their knees, moving the flute up and down, twisting their torso, balancing, swinging their weight from one foot to the other, etc. Some of these become deliberate at certain times, but most remain below the level of conscious awareness. Most of the gestures of a skilled performer are below conscious awareness in detail, but within awareness globally, as they 'mov[e] in a way that *feels right*' (Cole and Montero 2007: 303).

When a flautist plays, it is not only perceptual aspects of the body (the knowledge of fingering, phrasing, balancing, weight change, or pressure) that constitute higher-order consciousness, but also stored emotional attitudes towards the piece, his relationship with the instrument, his idea of what it is like to play the flute in front of other people, as well as his bodily feelings in both difficult and easy passages. There are certain movements that are typical of most flautists, and other gestures that are characteristic of the specific musical style, or of the specific performer. All of these, as well as specific bodily feelings (for example, the flautist's attention to one hand, or the shape of the embouchure) contribute to self-consciousness within music performance. With proprioception as a basis, we recognize that our feelings, movements, thoughts, and beliefs are indeed our own. On the one hand, performers will have a feeling of integrated belonging (schema-based), and on the other hand they will have access to awareness of specific aspects of the body or the music as required (image-based).

The process of consciousness

Although primary and higher-order consciousness have classically been studied as separate, I have argued that they are closely related to each other: on the one hand, higher-order consciousness requires knowledge of the world in order to create an idea of the self; and on the other, in primary consciousness, the perception of the body is also involved in the perception of the world. Although Gibson suggested that perceptual information is also proprioceptive, he did not develop this idea in any depth, but rather introduced the concept of affordance to understand the actions that subjects can perform with objects, in turn determining and determined by the way subjects perceive those objects.

By contrast, O'Regan and Noë (2001a, 2001b) have developed what they call the 'sensorimotor contingency theory' (SCT) as a basis on which to understand how the subject actively explores the environment, and how attributes of the environment attract the subject's attention. SCT was developed in relation to vision as a way to explain consciousness in perceptual experience.[8] O'Regan *et al.* pointed out that perceiving 'is not "generated" by a neural mechanism . . ., rather, it is exercising what the neural mechanism allows the organism to do. It is exercising a skill that the organism has mastery of' (2004: 104). SCT stresses that when we move while perceiving, a sensorial change in the visual scene is produced by our movements, and experiments provide empirical evidence that eye movements have a role even in colour perception (Bompas and O'Regan 2005, 2006; O'Regan *et al.* 2001). The theory asserts that visual perception is effective when the following conditions occur: (i) there must be eye movements (or the knowledge of how these movements will influence the stimuli) resulting in changes in the input sensory information; and (ii) the brain must be able to process that information and relate it to the position of the eyes in real time. Extrapolating to tactile perception, when we touch a sponge, we feel its softness by virtue of the movement of our hand as it grasps it, and the feeling that the sponge easily changes its shape. SCT asserts that perceptual knowledge of the world is mediated by knowledge of these sensorimotor contingencies (O'Regan and Noë 2001a: 940), which are laws governing the relationships between sensory changes and motor actions. These laws coordinate our movements and the changes these movements produce in the sensory input. O'Regan *et al.* point out that there are distinct forms of physical exploration for each sensory modality: 'Hearing involves a different quality compared to seeing which has a different quality compared to tactile sensation' (2004: 109).

Although SCT has been challenged as a way to explain consciousness (Clark 2006), it provides two interesting concepts that have a potential application for music. These concepts are *bodiliness* and *grabbiness*, also called corporality and alerting capacity. Bodiliness is the 'fact that when you move your body, incoming sensory information immediately changes' (O'Regan *et al.* 2004: 106)—a movement of your eyes towards a red surface, for example, changing the incoming light and brightness. As O'Regan *et al.* (106) put it: 'bodiliness is one aspect of sensory stimulation which makes it different from other forms of stimulation, and contributes to giving it its particular quality.' If an observer is looking at an object and walks towards it, it will expand in his visual field as he approaches. However, the visual image could also undergo the same expansion if the object itself gets closer to the still observer. Here, bodiliness informs the observer whether he is moving or not, disambiguating the two perceptual possibilities. Grabbiness, on the contrary, is 'the fact that sensory stimulation can grab your attention away from what you were previously doing' (2004: 106): if while we are looking at a black screen a bright light suddenly appears on the right side of the screen, we will direct our head and eyes towards the light source.

SCT was originally developed in relation to vision, and evidence has been found of the importance of eye movements in visual perception. However, O'Regan and Noë do not claim that 'action is necessary for experiencing'. Their claim, rather, 'is that knowledge of the ways movements affect sensory stimulation is necessary for experience' (O'Regan and Noë 2001a: 1055). Within auditory perception, physical movements are not so obviously required, although some of them, such as rotations of the head, change the perception of location, and movements of the head in the direction of the sound source affect amplitude (O'Regan and Noë 2001a: 941). However, while listening to music, we 'do' things internally most of the time. Rizzolatti claims that mirror neurons are activated not only upon performing any goal-oriented action, but also when subjects observe other people's movements or listen to the sounds of such actions. It is for that reason that we can consider movement in music to be not only actual, but also virtual—as proposed by Clarke (2005:199).

Bodiliness and grabbiness are of particular importance because, as explanatory tools, they cater for some unexplored issues in Gibson's theory. Gibson states that we perceive objects in our environment according to what we can do with them (affordances). Depending on these affordances, we perceive certain features of objects rather than others. SCT proposes that we perceive objects in the world because we move towards them (grabbiness) as the environment guides our perceptual system provoking automatic orientation reactions;[9] and that we move differently when exploring different things (bodiliness). These two concepts constitute interrelated sides of the perceptual process: the movements that cause changes in the sensory input alternate with the abrupt changes in environmental stimuli that make our bodies move towards them. Perception and the body form an indissoluble whole.

Turning now to music, during listening our perception roams around different aspects of the material, exploring melodies, instruments, chords, structure, and style; and we are aware of that exploration through bodiliness. Referring back to Johnson's image schemata, we realize that we are experiencing melodies because we are singing virtually with the orchestra; we will know that we are exploring silence because we stop moving (internally) with the music; we will know that we are experiencing a *crescendo* because of increasing tension in the muscles; and we will experience rhythm because of the way that it allows us to synchronize our movements (virtual or actual) with the beat. This constitutes bodiliness: the bodily feeling in one's explorations, related to the sensory input. Grabbiness, by contrast, captures the idea that the environment guides the subject in perception. Certain features in music are more likely to draw our attention—to make us move internally—than other stimuli,[10] although this process may be different for each person. A fugue allows a listener to follow the main theme (subject) when it sounds successively in each voice, by virtue of its imitative relationships. In an orchestral piece, a listener might be more likely to be 'grabbed' by timbre, as in the case of *Klangfarbenmelodie* (tone-colour-melody), the term that Arnold Schönberg gave to the technique of distributing a musical line around several instruments. And sonata form might cause listeners to concentrate on structure, identifying the development when the main musical material starts moving to other keys, and recapitulation when familiar material returns in the tonic. Or we may be 'grabbed' by the unexpected change from minor to major in a *tierce de Picardie*.

Bodiliness and grabbiness are closely related to each other. When a certain pattern in music grabs our attention, we will move according to that pattern. Similarly, if we move internally to explore a stimulus, and sound and movement are correlated, then we will be able to perceive it. For example, the phenomenon known as pseudo-polyphony, found among other places in J.S. Bach's solo violin and cello music, consists of the creation of two or more concurrent contrapuntal lines (or streams) using a sequence of single-sounding tones, produced by the rapid alternation of pitches separated by relatively large musical intervals (see Pandey 2005: 549). According to bodiliness, when we listen to one of these passages we are unable to sing along to the literal succession of pitches, because of its speed and pattern of intervals. As a result, we tend to 'sing' (internally, virtually) a melody consisting of either the higher or the lower pitches. The fact that we sing only certain pitches (a factor of bodiliness) makes us perceive the high pitches as belonging to a single line, even though they are interleaved with lower pitches. High pitches may also constitute grabbers since their salience (grabbiness) makes us focus our attention on them when they appear.

Musical grabbiness and bodiliness can also be facilitated or encouraged. When music students have to learn about the structure of a piece, teachers often use techniques that help them to hear and understand the structure. For example, a dance may allow the students to feel in bodily terms certain parts of the piece (bodiliness is induced). Alternatively, various kinds of graphic representation can help to draw attention to different aspects of the music that the students should listen to during the piece: instruments, phrases, rests, repetitions, etc. As defined by Boal and Wuytack, 'the musicogram is a graphic notation of the music, a visual representation of the dynamic development of a musical work. In the musicogram, conventional music notation is replaced by a symbolic system that is more simple and accessible to non-musicians, and which is intended to help the perception of the total structure of a work' (2006: 1266). Musicograms work as grabbers when listeners have not yet developed the necessary bodiliness for listening to structure in music.

Conclusions

Throughout this chapter I have argued that consciousness is based on the body. Primary consciousness in music, which can be characterized as the awareness of musical material, also depends on proprioceptive information, leading back to bodily awareness. In order to perceive musical events we make use of image schemata as a way to understand more abstract musical attributes: if we understand the pitch structure of a melody in terms of verticality, we simulate this internally by moving up and down in a virtual space, and can become aware of this simulation. Proprioception by means of the body image allows us to focus on specific movements, even if they are internal and never externally manifest. Similarly, higher-order consciousness depends on the ability of humans to be aware of themselves. Body image allows us to be aware of goal-oriented movements while, on the other hand, body schema, with its role in body motion control, provides us with information about the body as a whole, and a body that we perceive as ours. While emotions and concepts are implicated in the creation of self-awareness, proprioception is a key agent in this process: it constitutes the basis on which to determine that the experience of listening or playing is subjective in the sense of being acquired through the self.

Not only is the awareness of environmental stimuli intertwined with the awareness of one's own body—an idea already presented by Gibson—but also both the body and sensory stimuli belong to a feedback continuum in which they depend on each other—as proposed by SCT. Human beings, within the process of perception, switch constantly from bodiliness to grabbiness. Bodiliness implies awareness of our own body—observing how it has an influence on the perception of stimuli—whereas grabbiness relates to the capacity of environmental stimuli to attract our attention—in relation to the bodily responses in us that they elicit. In this perceptual interplay, bodiliness and bodily awareness prove to be fundamental in our sensitivity to the characteristics of perceived stimuli. When a person listens to music, a number of its aspects may produce bodily responses, both overt and covert. Depending on the type of activity or sensation elicited, various features appear in consciousness, such as rhythm, melody, form, instrumentation, tempo, harmony, tonality, and ornamentation. The internal singing of a melody implies a sort of concealed activity rather different from following the pulse or anticipating the *accelerando* and *ritardando* in a musical piece. When a person listens to music, only certain aspects of the material reach consciousness. On the one hand, a listener's body performs virtual actions leading to the perception of particular features; and on the other hand, the awareness of those internal actions helps to achieve an understanding of the nature of the elements explored. Critically, action in music is not random, but is guided by music itself, though a variety of factors makes it more likely for some musical actions to predominate, these factors including the listener's background, experiences, knowledge, context, emotional state, and training. Similarly, the music itself has the capacity to draw the listener's attention, and in this way the concepts of grabbiness and bodiliness allow us to explain how certain features in music make themselves evident to us, while others remain hidden from our consciousness. This was something that Renaissance polyphonists understood very well when they placed the 'grabby' tritone, the so-called *diabolus in musica*, in the middle voices—hidden in order not to be heard.

The constant interchange between bodiliness and grabbiness provides one way to understand individual differences in the experience of music listening. Both bodiliness and grabbiness require a feeling of matching movement and music. Despite the fact that certain pieces of music themselves contain grabbers, at a certain moment a listener may not experience any automatic orientation response. Moreover, although a listener performs internal actions in order to understand what he is hearing, this may have no effect on auditory perception. O'Regan and Noë (2001a: 1012) explain how our movements will affect the vision of an object close to us, but will not affect other objects in next room. People strongly habituated to one particular listening perspective, such as Western classical music, may apply it to significantly different types of music—for example looking for bar structures within Indian classical music, resulting in difficulty in understanding *tāls*. Indian classical music uses a combination of additive and divisive rhythms,[11] by contrast with the exclusively divisive rhythms of Western classical music. For listeners unfamiliar with Indian music, there may be a significant reduction in the music's bodiliness or grabbiness, or a bodiliness or grabbiness that does not correspond to the regularities of the musical material: the internal actions they perform do not have an impact on the stimulus (no bodiliness), or the musically relevant characteristics do not attract their perceptual attention (no grabbiness). There is a failure of what Varela (1988: 109) calls a 'structural coupling' between the music and the listener's actions.

Consciousness can be different depending on the subject's personal context, type of activity, and the nature of the phenomenon. The subject's mood, preferences, and circumstances affect this feedback process, and that is why listening to a piece of music is not always the same. Moreover, music is experienced through many different activities: playing an instrument, dancing, conducting an orchestra, as well as listening, and the relationship between bodiliness and grabbiness varies depending on the type of activity. Consciousness also takes different forms in listening to a piece of music, as opposed to remembering or imagining it. Listening to a live symphony orchestra implies a kind of bodiliness very different from recalling Beethoven's Fifth Symphony, or conducting it. Although it may be true that a conductor has a better knowledge of the piece (including the form, harmony, timbre, phrase structure, and instrumental interplay), a listener might be thought to be more conscious of the music because she does not have to divide her attention between the music itself and directing the orchestra. And, however well we may know a piece, remembering it will have a very different phenomenal character from hearing it. In memory, the awareness we have of it remains global, until we start to reproduce the piece in our heads. This sort of global consciousness contains little bodiliness or grabbiness, by comparison with the equivalent phenomena as triggered by a live performance in a concert hall. In the latter case, music leads us to internal motion simulation, and exploration through motion grants us the perception of aspects of music that otherwise would go unnoticed: composing, remembering, analysing, and writing about music are necessarily associated with different kinds of musical consciousness.

Bodiliness is a source of perceptual information linked to the subject's own exploration and consciousness of the musical elements, but in live musical situations the subject's own bodiliness overlaps with those of others. At times, the musicians' gestures and audience reactions work as grabbers in a way that may provoke orientation responses in us, as when people look at certain instruments, or sing along with the vocalist, or clap in synchrony with the rhythm. All such actions have the capacity to make us perceive a particular timbre, focus on a melody, or be aware of a beat. The gestures of a conductor towards a certain orchestral section or musician, their baton movements, and the gestures of the performers can also become silent grabbers of musical perception, and initiate automatic orientation responses that make us anticipate or focus our listening. Here, other people's bodiliness becomes grabbiness for us, to form an indissoluble unity that also contributes to our musical consciousness.

Musical consciousness is a complex phenomenon to study, due to the abundance of social, emotional, biological, and cultural aspects involved. Nonetheless, I have argued that listening, comprising either the awareness of successive elements in a new piece of music or the more global consciousness that arises in relation to a known piece of music, is strongly influenced by the role and consciousness of our own bodies. Considered as the foundation of perception, our bodies enable us to explore the nature (rhythmic, melodic, structural, harmonic, etc.) of what we perceive, and also provide us with an experience particular to ourselves—the feeling that the musical phenomena we experience through composition, listening, imagination, or memory contain that character or property of being experienced by the self.

Acknowledgement

I would like to thank Rachel and Robert Antony, John Bachenski, and José A. Rey for their time and effort in assisting with the English.

References

Bermúdez, J.L. (1995). Ecological perception and the notion of a nonconceptual point of view, in J.L. Bermúdez, A. Marcel, and N. Eilan (eds), *The Body and the Self*, 153–74 (Cambridge, MA: MIT Press).

Boal Palheiros, G. and Wuytack, J. (2006). Effects of the 'musicogram' on children's musical perception and learning, in M. Baroni, A.R. Addessi, R. Caterina, and M. Costa *Proceedings of the 9th International Conference on Music Perception & Cognition* (ICMPC9), Bologna/Italy, 22–26 August 2006, 1264–71.

Bompas, A. and O'Regan, J.K. (2005). Evidence for a role of action in color perception. *Perception*, **35**, 65–78.

Bompas, A. and O'Regan, J.K. (2006). More evidence for sensorimotor adaptation in color perception. *Journal of Vision*, **6**, 145–53.

Brower, C. (2000). A cognitive theory of musical meaning. *Journal of Music Theory*, **44**, 323–79.

Clark, A. (2006). Vision as dance? Three challenges for sensorimotor contingency theory. *Psyche*, **12**, 1–10. Available at: http://www.theassc.org/vol_12_2006 (accessed 2 March 2011).

Clarke, E. (2005). *Ways of Listening. An Ecological Approach to the Perception of Musical Meaning* (New York, NY: Oxford University Press).

Cole, J. and Montero, B. (2007). Affective proprioception. *Janus Head, Special Issue: The Situated Body*, **9**, 299–317.

Cox, A. (1999). *The Metaphoric Logic of Musical Motion and Space*. Unpublished Ph.D. thesis, University of Oregon.

Cox, A. (2001). The mimetic hypothesis and embodied musical meaning. *Musicae Scientiae*, **5**, 195–212.

Decety J., Grèzes J., Costes N., Perani, D., Procyk, E., Grassi, F., Jeannerod, M., and Fazio F. (1997). Brain activity during observation of actions. Influence of action content and subject's strategy. *Brain*, **120**, 1763–77.

Dirven, R. (1994). *Metaphor and Nation: Metaphors Afrikaners Live By* (Frankfurt: Peter Lang).

Echard, W. (1999). An analysis of Neil Young's powderfinger based on Mark Johnson's image schemata. *Popular Music*, **18**, 133–44.

Echard, W. (2006). Plays guitar without any hands: Musical movement and problems of immanence, in A. Gritten and E. King (eds), *Music and Gesture*, 75–90 (Aldershot: Ashgate).

Edelman, G. (1989). *The Remembered Present: A Biological Theory of Consciousness* (New York, NY: Basic Books).

Eilan, N., Marcel, A., and Bermúdez, J.L. (1995). Self consciousness and the body: An interdisciplinary introduction, in J.L. Bermúdez, A.J. Marcel, and N. Eilan (eds), *The Body and the Self*, 1–28 (Cambridge, MA: MIT Press).

Escudero, M. (1998). Propioceptores y sistema vestibular, in J.M. Delgado, A. Ferrús, F. Mora, and F.J. Rubia (eds), *Manual de neurociencia*, 483–506 (Madrid: Editorial Síntesis).

Fadiga, L., Fogassi, L., Pavesi, G., and Rizzolati, G. (1995). Motor facilitation during action observation: a magnetic stimulation study. *Journal of Neurophysiology*, **73**, 2608–11.

Feld, S. (1981). Flow like a waterfall: the metaphors of Kaluli musical theory. *Yearbook for Traditional Music*, **13**, 22–47.

Gallagher, S. (1995). Body schema and intentionality, in J.L. Bermúdez, A.J. Marcel, and N. Eilan (eds), *The Body and the Self*, 225–44 (Cambridge, MA: MIT Press).

Gallagher, S. (2005). *How the Body Shapes the Mind* (Oxford: Oxford University Press).

Gallagher, S. and Zahavi, D. (2010). Phenomenological approaches to self-consciousness, in E. N. Zalta (ed.), *The Stanford Encyclopedia of Philosophy* (Winter 2010 Edition). Available at: http://plato.stanford.edu/archives/win2010/entries/self-consciousness-phenomenological/ (accessed 2 March 2011).

Gallese, V. (1998). Mirror neurons and mind reading. *Trends in Cognitive Sciences*, **12**, 493–501.

Gallese, V. (2001). The 'shared manifold' hypothesis: from mirror neurons to empathy. *Journal of Consciousness Studies*, **8**, 33–50.

Gallese, V. (2003). The roots of empathy: the shared manifold hypothesis and the neural basis of intersubjectivity. *Psychopathology*, **36**, 171–80.

Gallese, V. and Goldman, A. (1998). Mirror neurons and the simulation theory of mind-reading. *Trends in Cognitive Sciences*, **12**, 493–501.

Gallese, V., Craighero L., Fadiga, L., and Fogassi, L. (1999). Perception through action. *Psyche*, **5**, 1–8. Available at: http://www.theassc.org/vol_5_1999 (accessed 2 March 2011).

Gallese, V., Keysers, C., and Rizzolatti, G. (2004). A unifying view of the basis of social cognition. *Trends in Cognitive Sciences*, **8**, 396–403.

Gibson, J.J. (1987). A note on what exists at the ecological level of reality, in E. Reed and R. Jones (eds), *Reasons for realism: Selected essays of James J. Gibson*, 416–18 (Hillsdale, NJ: Erlbaum).

Gibson, J.J. (1979). *The Ecological Approach to Visual Perception* (Boston, MA: Houghton-Mifflin).

Giordano, B. (2005). Sound source perception in impact sounds. Unpublished Ph.D. thesis, Department of General Psychology, University of Padova (Italy). Available at: www.music.mcgill.ca/ bruno/dissertation.htm (accessed 2 March 2011).

Grafton, S., Fadiga, L., and Rizzolatti, G. (1996). Localization of grasp representations in humans by positron emission tomography. 2. Observation compared with imagination. *Experimental Brain Research*, **112**, 103–11.

Haueisen, J. and Knösche, T.R. (2001). Involuntary motor activity in pianists evoked by music perception. *Journal of Cognitive Neuroscience*, **13**, 786–92.

Huron, D. (2006). *Sweet Anticipation: Music and the Psychology of Expectation* (Cambridge, MA: MIT Press).

Johnson, M. (1987). *The Body in the Mind* (Chicago, IL: University of Chicago Press).

Kahle, W., Leonhardt, H., and Platzer, W. (1997). *Atlas de anatomía* (Barcelona: Omega).

Kandel, E.R., Schwartz J.H., and Jessel T.M. (2000). *Principles of Neural Science* (New York, NY: McGraw-Hill).

Kittay, E.F. (1987). *Metaphor: Its Cognitive Force and Linguistic Structure* (Oxford: Oxford University Press).

Lahav, A., Saltzman, E., and Schlaug, G. (2007). Action representation of sound: audiomotor recognition network while listening to newly acquired actions. *Journal of Neuroscience*, **27**, 308–14.

Lakoff, G. (1996). *Moral Politics* (Chicago, IL: University of Chicago Press).

Lakoff, G. and Johnson, M. (1980). *Metaphors We Live By* (Chicago, IL: University of Chicago Press).

Lakoff, G. and Núñez, R.E. (2000). *Where Mathematics Comes From: How the Embodied Mind Brings Mathematics into Being* (New York, NY: Basic Books).

Legrand D. (2007). Pre-reflective self-consciousness: on being bodily in the world, in *Janus Head, Special Issue: The Situated Body*, **9**, 493–519.

Liberman, A. M. and Mattingly, I. G. (1985). The motor theory of speech perception revised. *Cognition*, **21**, 1–36.

López Muñiz, A. (2004). Organización funcional de la información somatosensorial, gustativa y visceral, in S. Rodríguez García and J.M. Smith-Ágreda (eds), *Anatomía de los órganos del lenguaje, visión y audición*, 53–60 (Madrid: Panamericana).

Marconi, L. (2001). Música, semiótica y expresión: la música y la expresión de las emociones, in M. Vega and C. Villar-Taboada (ed.) *Música, lenguaje y significado*, 163–80 (Valladolid: Glares, Universidad de Valladolid-SITEM).

Martínez, I.C. (2004). La prolongación como metáfora cotidiana. Hacia un modelo cognitivo idealizado de las estructuras prolongacionales en la música (unpublished paper). IV Reunión Anual de SACCoM, realizada los días 14 y 15 de Mayo de 2004 en el Instituto Superior de Música de la Universidad Nacional de Tucumán.

McAdams, S., Chaigne, A., and Roussarie, V. (2004). The psychomechanics of simple sound sources: material properties of impacted bars. *Journal of the Acoustical Society of America*, **115**, 1306–20.

Merleau-Ponty, M. (1962). *Phenomenology of Perception* (London: Routledge and Kegan Paul).

Molnar-Szakacs, I. and Overy K.I. (2006). Music and mirror neurons: from motion to 'e'motion. *Social Cognitive and Affective Neuroscience*, **1**, 235–41.

O'Regan, J.K. and Noë, A. (2001a). A sensorimotor account of vision and visual consciousness. *Behavioral and Brain Sciences*, **24**, 939–73.

O'Regan, J.K. and Noë, A. (2001b). What it is like to see: a sensorimotor theory of perceptual experience. *Synthese*, **129**, 79–103.

O'Regan, J.K., Clark, J., and Bompas, A. (2001). Implications of a sensorimotor theory of vision for scene perception and colour sensation. *Perception*, **30**(suppl.), 94.

O'Regan, J.K., Myin, E., and Noë, A. (2004). Towards an analytic phenomenology: The concepts of bodiliness and grabbiness, in A. Carsetti (ed.), *Seeing Thinking and Knowing*, 103–14. (Dordrecht, Holland: Kluwer Academic Publishers).

Oliveira, A.L.G. and Oliveira F. (2002). Por uma abordagem ecológica do timbre, in I. C. Martínezy and O. Musumeci (eds), *Segundo encontro de la Sociedad Argentina para la Ciencia Cognitiva de la Música*. CD-rom (Buenos Aires: SACCoM).

Pandey, A. (2005). *Encyclopaedic Dictionary of Music*, vol. 2 (New Delhi: Global Printers).

Peñalba, A. (2005). El cuerpo en la música a través de la teoría de la Metáfora de Johnson: análisis crítico y aplicación a la música. *Revista Transcultural de Música, Transcultural Music Review*, **9**. Available at: http://redalyc.uaemex.mx/redalyc/pdf/822/82200912.pdf (accessed 30 July 2008).

Peñalba, A. (2006). Compensation movement hypothesis: A conceptual demonstration of virtual action based on O'Regan and Noë´s sensorimotor contingencies theory.

Proceedings of the Second International Conference on Music and Gesture, 121–33 (Manchester: RNCM).

Peñalba, A. (2008). El cuerpo en la interpretación musical. Un modelo teórico basado en las propiocepciones en la interpretación de instrumentos acústicos, hiperinstrumentos e instrumentos alternativos. Unpublished Ph.D. thesis, Universidad de Valladolid. Available at: http://uvadoc.uva.es/handle/10324/55 (accessed 3 July 2009).

Piaget, J. [1926] (1973). *La representación del mundo en el niño* (Madrid: Morata).

Rizzolatti, G., Fadiga, L., Gallese, V., and Fogassi, L. (1996). Premotor cortex and the recognition of motor actions. *Cognitive Brain Research*, **3**, 131–41.

Rizzolatti, G., Fogassi. L., and Gallese, V. (2000). Cortical mechanisms subserving object grasping and action recognition: a new view on the cortical motor functions, in M.S. Gazzaniga (ed.), *The New Cognitive Neurosciences*, 539–52 (Cambridge, MA: MIT Press).

Saslaw, J. (1996). Forces, containers and paths: the role of the body derived image schematas in the conceptualization of Music. *Journal of Music Theory*, **40**, 217–43.

Schön, D.A. (1979). Generative metaphor: a perspective on problem-setting in social policy, in A. Ortony (ed.), *Metaphor and Thought*, 137–63 (Cambridge: Cambridge University Press).

Sherrington, C.S. (1906). *The Integration of the Neurons Systems* (New Haven, CT: Yale University Press).

Sobotta, J. and Becher, H. (1994). *Atlas de anatomía humana* (Madrid: Editorial Médica Panamericana).

Spitzer, M. (2004). *Metaphor and Musical Thought* (Chicago, IL: University of Chicago Press).

Varela, F. (1988). *Conocer. Las ciencias cognitivas: tendencias y perspectivas. Cartografía de las ideas actuales* (Barcelona: Gedisa).

Wider, K.V. (1997). *The Bodily Nature of Consciousness: Sartre and Contemporary Philosophy of Mind* (Ithaca, NY: Cornell University Press).

Windsor, W.L. (1995). *A Perceptual Approach to the Description and Analysis of Acousmatic Music*. Unpublished Ph.D. thesis, City University, London.

Windsor, W.L. (2004). An ecological approach to semiotics. *Journal for the Theory of Social Behaviour*, **34**, 179–98.

Zbikowski, L. (1997). Conceptual models and cross-domain mapping: new perspectives on theories of music and hierarchy. *Journal of Music Theory*, **41**, 193–225.

Notes

1. For a review of Johnson's embodied mind theory see Peñalba (2005).

2. Zbikowski (1997) states that there are invariant principles between the schemata and the music. Feld points out that schemata and music events must have some connotative or denotative similar features. Marconi (2001), whose approach is very close to Cox's, argues that the metaphorization process is possible through physiognomic perceptions that relate music to schemata.

3. Mirror neurons have also been studied by, among others, Gallese (1998, 2001, 2003); Gallese and Goldman (1998); Gallese *et al.* (1999); Decety *et al.* (1997); Fadiga *et al.* (1995); Grafton *et al.* (1996); Rizzolatti *et al.* (1996).

4. A number of authors have applied Gibson's theory to music (Clarke 2005; Giordano 2005; McAdams *et al.* 2004; Oliveira and Oliveira 2002; Windsor 1995, 2004).

5. Proprioceptive information assembles all the information about the body.

6. See Peñalba (2008) for a discussion of the role of proprioception in music performance.

7. The labyrinth is sometimes excluded from proprioceptive receptors, but since it provides information about the self, Eilan considers it to be proprioceptive (Eilan *et al.* 1995: 13).

8. For an application of some ideas from O´Regan and Noë's sensorimotor contingency theory see Peñalba (2006).

9. Gibson also proposes the term *invariants* to refer to the inherent properties of objects. These properties limit the possible affordances for subjects. The concept of grabbiness is rather different since it guides the subject's actions under certain conditions.

10. It may be that grabbiness also incorporates an expectation component, relating to the role of anticipation in music listening (see Huron 2006).

11. In divisive rhythms, larger units are divided into smaller rhythmic units.

Chapter 13

Sound-action awareness in music

Rolf Inge Godøy

Introduction

People often move to music: they dance, march, gesticulate, or display a variety of other kinds of body movements at concerts or in a range of public or private listening situations—or even when simply imagining music with their 'inner ear'. And of course music is primarily made with body movements: by hitting, stroking, bowing, blowing, shaking, kicking, etc., and by musicians who communicate in performance through body movements such as waving hands, nodding heads, and swaying torsos. These music-related body movements seem to be as familiar to most listeners as the 'music itself', and it seems that most listeners, regardless of their level of musical expertise or training, know more or less what kinds of movements 'fit well' to whatever music they are listening to or imagining.

These links between musical sound and various body movements are so numerous and robust that in the programme of research being carried out in Oslo (see www. fourms.uio.no) we have come to believe that sensations of body movement are integral to musical experience as such, or to put it differently, that the perception and cognition of music is a fusion of auditory and motor sensations. In the context of music and consciousness, one consequence of this auditory-motor fusion is the belief that awareness of musical sound can be understood as an awareness of various sound-related actions. For this reason, the topic of this chapter is *sound-action awareness in music*, and besides presenting a spectrum of research that may shed light on this, I shall also present some ideas on how sound-action awareness might encourage us to revise received ways of thinking in Western music theory.

By using the term 'awareness', I am deliberately making a shortcut in relation to the vast problematic of how human consciousness might be understood. Needless to say, we may encounter the terms 'consciousness' and 'being conscious' used in the sense of states of mind and the innumerable neurophysiological, psychological, behavioural, epistemological, and philosophical issues that this entails. But we may also encounter the expression 'conscious of' used in the sense of 'being aware of something', and although the expression 'awareness' is also entangled in a complex web of significations, it does in my opinion have the advantage of more narrowly designating what I would call a *focus of mental content*.

The expression 'focus of mental content' can be understood as an ontological question in the sense of trying to differentiate what feature or set of features we are talking about at any moment. Whatever we perceive or imagine at any moment may be regarded as composite and multidimensional with several concurrent features and significations. For instance, in listening to someone speaking we may focus on the qualities of that person's voice, deciding whether it is the voice of a female or male, someone young or old, someone healthy or someone ill, someone sad, happy, tired, angry, and so on; or we can focus more on the semantic or declarative attributes of the verbal utterance; or we may sense all these (and more) features simultaneously. Likewise, listening to someone playing a musical instrument, we may focus on certain timbral, and/or expressive features, relegating the musical structure to the background; or, conversely, we may focus on the structure and be almost deaf to timbral and expressive features. However, although such ontological complexity is omnipresent in musical as well as everyday, so-called ecological, listening situations, it has not been well conceptualized in Western music theory or in other domains of Western music research. This is unfortunate, because such a lack of critical reflection on 'what is what' (as this ontological differentiation also could be called), has had as one of its consequences a focus on notation in Western music theory at the expense of most other features (timbre, texture, expression, emotion, etc.) that are of the utmost importance in musical experience for listeners and performers alike. There is much to be said about this (see Godøy 1997), and for now it will suffice to assert that any serious discussion of awareness (and consciousness) in music must somehow deal with the issue of ontological complexity if it is really to tackle questions of mental content in musical experience.

Some remarkable ideas on ontological complexity (as well as on music and consciousness in general) that have been of particular importance for our work on sound-action awareness in music can be found in the theoretical work of Pierre Schaeffer. Given the many aesthetic and conceptual challenges posed by *musique concrète*, and the inability of traditional notation-based music theory to say much about this new music, Schaeffer and co-workers took as their point of departure their subjective impressions of repeated listening to various sound fragments, which came to be called *sonic objects* (Schaeffer 1966, 1998). This led both to an ontological differentiation of the various components and signification levels in the listening process, and to an extensive ontological differentiation of perceptually pertinent features of sonic objects. Briefly stated, by means of the strategy of so-called 'reduced listening', partly inspired by the phenomenological philosopher Edmund Husserl, the listener is encouraged to shift focus away from the everyday or anecdotal significations of sonic objects, for example away from that of a squeaking door as signifying someone entering a room, to the perceptual features of the squeaking sound itself, such as its overall dynamic, timbral, and pitch-related shape, and various sub-features of these overall shapes such as fluctuations in dynamics, timbre, or pitch. This is a top-down differentiation of perceptually pertinent features, taking as a point of departure the seemingly simple question 'what do we hear?' or 'what are the subjectively experienced most salient features of the sound?'; and then by way of such a kind of 'naïve' questioning, progressively differentiating more and more features in the sonic object.

In the course of these feature differentiations, metaphorical labels, such as 'grain' (denoting fast timbral, dynamic, or pitch fluctuations) and 'gait' (denoting slow timbral, dynamic, or pitch fluctuations), are used to designate features that are clearly present in musical sound but have previously not been well conceptualized in Western musical thought. By pointing to a feature and giving it a name, our attention is directed towards it, and the next time we listen to the same sound, we may perceive it differently as a result of this change in awareness. One particularly interesting set of metaphors from Schaeffer's theory are those that depict sound features as action trajectories, such as those that designate the overall shape of sounds as *impulsive, sustained*, or *iterative* (see below, next section). As argued elsewhere (Godøy 2006), Schaeffer's use of action-related metaphors can be understood as referring to basic motor schemas in perception, based on the principle that we tend to relate what we hear (or what we see for that matter) to extensive previous experience of sound-action (or vision-action) sensations.

As a background to our own and others' research, we believe that this link between sound and action is not only a matter of metaphorical verbal labelling, but is actually something intrinsic to auditory perception. When we hear sound, it seems that we tend—to a greater or lesser degree—to simulate (either mentally and covertly, or behaviourally and overtly) the actions that we believe generate the sound; or tend to lock onto, or be entrained by, other prominent features of the sound such as its rhythmical patterns or melodic contours: listening to a ferocious drum passage probably evokes images of energetic hand and mallet movements in most listeners, and listening to a calm string ensemble passage probably evokes images of slow bow movements. The extent of such spontaneous sound-action associations remains to be further explored, but we believe such sound-action associations can be understood in light of what we call *the embodied paradigm*. This embodied paradigm is based on a convergence of various neurocognitive findings with the remarkable introspective insights on awareness by classical phenomenological philosophers from the late nineteenth and early twentieth centuries, as will be discussed below (see 'The embodied paradigm in music theory'). One crucial issue in this embodied paradigm is that of segmenting the continuous stream of action and sound into meaningful entities in our minds—into what could be called *chunks*—and this is discussed in the section 'Chunking sound-actions' later in the chapter. However, before tackling these two topics, it is useful briefly to survey the kinds of actions we are talking about in the context of music and awareness.

Sound-related actions

Given the vast number of sound-related actions that we may observe (see, e.g. Godøy and Leman 2010; Gritten and King 2006; Wanderley and Battier 2000), it is important to have some conceptual framework within which to differentiate what we are talking about. Basically, we can think of sound-related actions as either *sound-producing* or as *sound-accompanying*, although this distinction is by no means absolute.

Sound-producing actions include *excitatory actions* such as hitting, stroking, scraping, bowing, kicking, blowing—actions that basically consist of transferring energy from our bodies to resonating objects such as strings, plates, tubes, and membranes. But sound-producing actions also include what we would call *modulatory actions*—actions that modify the sound, such as vibrato and opening and closing a brass mute, and can even include *selection actions* such as selecting a new register on an organ or a synthesizer or placing a string mute on the bridge. However in some cases the distinction between excitatory and modulatory actions may not be clear, for example when shifting the position of the bow on a string instrument and thus modifying the timbre at the same time as exciting the string. In actual musical performance we may see considerable individual variation in the movements that musicians make when playing similar instruments or even when performing the same work of music. We often see musicians consistently making movements that may not be strictly necessary for sound production, movements that are sometimes referred to as *ancillary movements* (see e.g. Vines *et al.* 2006). For instance, clarinettists' or other woodwind and brass instrument players' movements of the whole instrument, or pianists' movements of their shoulders and whole torso, can be understood as variously helping to avoid fatigue, to position the effectors (fingers, hands) in ergonomically optimal positions, or even as helping in the articulation or expressive shaping of the music. Such movements can also have communicative functions in relation to co-performers or even theatrical functions for the benefit of the audience. Whatever their function, such actions are associated with sound production, and seem to be learned and reproduced by listeners who may have little or no training on the instruments in question (Godøy *et al.* 2006a), as clearly demonstrated by the phenomenon of so-called *air guitar* (www.airguitarworld championships.com/).

The category of sound-accompanying actions can include almost any sound-related action that is not directly involved in sound production—such as dancing, walking, marching, or gesticulating. But this category may also border onto sound-producing actions, as demonstrated by the regular swaying of the torso of a listener to the beat of the drums (as if hitting drums) or in the tracing of pitch contours with the hands (as if playing). Such sound-accompanying actions tend to lock onto some feature or set of features in the sound, typically relating to the overall sense of effort (e.g. calm, agitated, slow, fast), and tend to be synchronized with some level of temporal organization (beat, measure, period). With multiple concurrent features in a sound (e.g. a foreground melodic line on top of an accompanying texture with several concurrent rhythmical strata), we may of course see seemingly divergent movements, which nonetheless upon closer examination demonstrate sound-action correspondences at some level (Haga 2008).

What is important in this context is not so much the exact functionality of the actions as their shape, or geometry, and the sense of effort that they convey, i.e. how these actions are perceived in relation to basic motor images. The geometry of sound-actions here includes the relative position of the effectors (fingers, hands, arms) in relation to imaginary musical instruments (e.g. keyboards, drums), as well as the shape of the movement trajectories. As for effort, this is conveyed by images of overall activity, speed and amplitude of movement (e.g. calm, agitated, slow fast, light, heavy), as well as some more specific sound-action categories that we have derived from Schaeffer's classification (so-called *typology*) of sonic objects:

◆ *impulsive*, meaning a fast and short movement followed by relaxation, such as in hitting, kicking, or making a rapid glissando;

- *sustained*, meaning a more or less continuous energy transfer, such as in continuously bowing or blowing;
- *iterative*, meaning rapidly repeated movements such as in a tremolo or a drum roll.

These categories are quite distinct with regard to effort and motor control, but with changes of tempo we may also observe so-called *phase-transitions* between the categories (Haken *et al.* 1985). For example, when slowing down, actions that in other circumstances are fused may decompose into individual component actions, and conversely, when speeding up, otherwise separate actions may fuse into superordinate composites. This last phenomenon is related to so-called *coarticulation*—the contextual smearing of actions and sounds into higher-level units (Godøy 2008).

Furthermore, the generality and transferability of action images as action schemata is important, since familiar action schemata may also be applied to novel sounds, for example as an anthropomorphic projection onto electroacoustic music. This generality and transferability of action schemata is actually one of the key elements in the embodied paradigm, in the sense that we tend to perceive sounds in relation to previously learned action schemata.

The embodied paradigm in music theory

The fundamental idea of what we could call *the embodied paradigm in music theory* is to understand musical sound as inseparable from body movement (Godøy 2003; Godøy and Leman 2010; Leman 2008), and, more precisely, to understand any sound and/or sound feature as actually included in some sound-producing action trajectory. This means that performers usually make preparatory movements before the sound(s) starts, and continue making movement during the sound(s), and after the end of the sound(s) (Godøy 2008). This also means that the sound-producing action is fundamental to the particular note or group of notes, and that we develop extensive experience of sound-action relationships from seeing musicians perform and from everyday auditory experiences. These musical and everyday experiences cause the development of perceptual schema that include what comes before, during, and after the sounding of a note or group of notes or other sounds: a single note on the piano is embedded within the trajectory of the finger/hand/arm prior to the onset of the tone; and a group of piano notes is not just a collection of pitches but a fused sound-action event in which the individual notes and finger movements are subsumed by coarticulation into a superordinate hand movement.

The idea that images of sound-producing actions are essential for the perception of sound was suggested several decades ago in linguistics with the so-called *motor theory of perception* (Liberman and Mattingly 1985). Often criticized, this theory has now with advances in neuroscience come to gain increasing support (Fadiga *et al.* 2002). In the past decade, we have in fact seen a deluge of publications in support of the close link between motor images and perception, with perception in general seen as a process of mentally simulating whatever it is that we are trying to understand (Berthoz 1997). This has been extended to understanding most domains of human thought as related to action, including even apparently abstract thinking (Gallese and Lakoff 2005), and in particular to understanding the actions of others by way of a covert imitation (Wilson and Knoblich 2005). Stated most simply 'to perceive an action is equivalent to internally simulating it' (Gallese and Metzinger 2003: 383), which 'enables the observer to use her/his own resources to penetrate the world of the other by means of an implicit, automatic, and unconscious process of motor simulation' (383).

More specifically with regard to auditory perception, the coupling of sound and action extends from what could be considered more 'hard wired' (Kohler *et al.* 2002) to more learned and music-related couplings in the case of experts (Haueisen and Knösche 2001), as well as quickly learned relationships in the case of novices (Bangert and Altenmüller 2003). Having observed so many people making sound-producing actions when listening to music, we carried out some studies of *air instrument performance*, asking people to make movements in the air as if they were playing a musical instrument, and it seemed that even listeners with little or no musical training were able to imitate many of the corresponding sound-producing gestures when listening to musical excerpts (Godøy *et al.* 2006a). One recurrent feature of this imitation of sound-producing gestures seemed to be that the subjects would focus on certain salient points in the music such as downbeats and other accents or melodic peaks, and often seemed to be less focused on the details of the music between these salient points. We understood this as a more general phenomenon of imitative behaviour, namely that it is often goal-directed, something that has been called GOADI ('goal-directed imitation'—see Wohlschläger *et al.* 2003). That certain features are more readily rendered than others by listeners was also demonstrated in a different pilot study of what we called 'sound tracing', in which we asked listeners to spontaneously draw the shape of the gesture they associated with sound excerpts that they heard. As long as the sound excerpts contained just one or a few concurrent feature dimensions, there seemed to be a fair amount of agreement in sound-gesture correspondences, but with increasing number of concurrent features, the results varied considerably (Godøy *et al.* 2006b; Haga 2008). Similarly, in a series of what we called 'free dance studies', the participating (mostly professional) dancers seemed to spontaneously render into movement one or more of the features in musical excerpts they heard, with reasonable agreements for the overall sensation of effort and more disagreement about the specific shapes of the gestures (Haga 2008).

Although we are only at the beginning of a more comprehensive understanding of sound-action relationships, it seems quite clear so far that listeners spontaneously relate musical sounds to certain kinds of actions. This can be understood as a *perception-action cycle*: we simulate the actions that we believe go with the sounds that we hear, this simulation of sound-related action then modifying our perception of the sound, leading to new simulation of the sound, with corresponding new perceptions of the sounds, and so on.

Chunking sound-actions

Assuming that perception is a constant process of simulating actions, and that this is integral to whatever we are sensing as suggested by the notion of the perception-action cycle, the next issue becomes that of the temporality of this incessant simulation process.

Is there a continuous updating of percepts or images, or is there a more intermittent or discontinuous updating going on? Put differently: is our awareness continuously changing, or does it proceed more discontinuously, in what we could call a 'chunk-by-chunk' manner? Common sense and the classical work of George A. Miller (1956) on chunking suggests that we would have great difficulty coping in the world if we could not somehow organize complex sensory experience into tractable chunks. Yet a proper consideration of continuity versus discontinuity, or of movement versus discrete image states, is actually one of the most intriguing and difficult issues in our work on music-related actions. Although the relationship between continuity and discontinuity remains profoundly enigmatic to us, we believe that we can see a convergence of some remarkable introspective ideas from phenomenological philosophy with more recent neurocognitive and human motor control research, providing a framework for understanding the emergence of sound-action chunks in musical experience.

The question of continuity versus discontinuity in awareness is one of the core issues in phenomenological philosophy. As summarized by Paul Ricoeur: 'Phenomenology begins when, not content to "live" or "relive", we interrupt lived experience in order to signify it' (1981: 116). From Husserl's early writings on time consciousness in 1893 and the following decades, the idea of having to 'interrupt' the continuous stream of sensations into a series of more or less distinct chunks of experience, by what Husserl often refers to as *now-points*, seems to remain more or less unchanged, but the understanding of this process becomes increasingly subtle in Husserl's subsequent writings. The point of departure for Husserl was an idea advocated by his teacher Franz Brentano, as well as other contemporaries:

> [N]amely, the idea that in order to grasp a succession of representations (a and b, for example), it is necessary that the representations be the absolutely simultaneous objects of a knowing that puts them in relation and that embraces them quite indivisibly in a single and indivisible act. All the representations of a route, of a passage, of a distance—in brief, all the representation that contain a comparison of several elements and express the relation between them—can be conceived only as the products of an act of knowing that embraces its objects timelessly. They would all be impossible if the act of representing were itself entirely dissolved in temporal succession. It appears to be an evident and quite inescapable assumption of this conception that the intuition of an extent of time occurs in a now, in one time-point. It simply appears as a truism that every consciousness aimed at some whole, at some plurality of distinguishable moments (hence every consciousness of relation and combination), encompasses its object in an indivisible time-point. Wherever a consciousness is directed towards a whole whose parts are successive, there can be an intuitive consciousness of this whole only if the parts, in the form of representants, come together in the unity of the momentary intuition. (Husserl 1991: 21–2)

Adopting the Husserl scholar Izchak Miller's terminology, we could call this the *Principle of Simultaneous Awareness*, or PSA for short (Miller 1982). So is this the solution to awareness of successive events—that we simply lump these sequentially occurring events together in one chunk? And if this is the case, what then is the nature of this PSA? Husserl uses the perception of melody as the prime example in his discussion, pointing out that it is in the very nature of a melody that it can only be perceived if we somehow have a cumulative image of several tones in succession, that is, that sensory experience somehow be compressed into one unitary mental image. Yet this is also where Husserl sees the problem with the model of successive events simultaneously present in the mind: are the events superposed as tones in a cluster, or are the events only indirectly present, as memory traces of past events? Rejecting various solutions to this riddle, Husserl then directs his attention to the temporality of the act of perceiving in the first place:

> Let us take the example of a melody or of a cohesive part of a melody. The matter seems very simple at first: we hear the melody, that is, we perceive it, for hearing is indeed perceiving. However, the first tone sounds, then comes the second tone, then the third, and so on. Must we not say: When the second tone sounds, I hear it, but I no longer hear the first tone, etc.? In truth, then, I do not hear the melody but only the single present tone. That the elapsed part of the melody is something objective for me, I owe—or so one will be inclined to say—to memory, and that I do not presuppose, with the appearance of the currently intended tone, that this is all, I owe to anticipatory expectation. But we cannot be content with this explanation, for everything that we have said carries over to the individual tone. Each tone has a temporal extension itself. When it begins to sound, I hear it as now; but while it continues to sound it has an ever new now, and the now that immediately precedes it changes into a past. Therefore at any given time I hear only the actually present phase of the tone, and the objectivity of the whole enduring tone is constituted in an act-continuum that is in part memory, in smallest punctual part perception, and in further part expectation. (1991: 24–5)

With the statement that 'the whole enduring tone is constituted in an act-continuum that is in part memory, in smallest punctual part perception, and in further part expectation' Husserl is actually giving a first presentation of the tripartite model of *retention*, *primal impression*, and *protention*, which dominates the rest of his writings on time consciousness and plays a very important role in his philosophy in general (see, e.g. Husserl 1982). The main idea of this model is that in all perception (and mental imagery) there is always the sensation of a primal impression of the present moment, of the *now-point*, but that this now-point also includes sensations of the just passed (*retention*), and equally the expectation of what is to come (*protention*). In this famous tripartite model of awareness, the idea of protention is in my opinion the most remarkable in that it suggests that what we now might call *anticipatory cognition* (various instances of preparatory planning in motor control—see Rosenbaum *et al.* 2007) is an integral part of our subjective sensations of the present moment.

There is much more to be said about Husserl's writings on time in relation to music perception (see Godøy 2010; Chapters 1 and 2, this volume), but the key element here is that perception and imagery proceed by a series of now-points, where each now-point contains the three elements of retention, primal impression, and protention. What this amounts to is a reconciliation of the continuous stream of sensations (be that in sound, movement, or vision), with some kind of more 'solid' percept, what I here call discontinuous chunks.

Interestingly, several of Husserl's contemporaries were preoccupied with similar issues of continuity and discontinuity in experience, for instance William James (whom Husserl had read and much appreciated) with his ideas of the 'specious present' and his statement that 'the practically cognized present is no knife-edge, but a saddle-back . . .' (James 1890: 609).[1] There have been a number of related approaches to what could be collectively called 'the present' (e.g. Stern 2004; Michon 1978), and it is interesting to see that some recent neurocognitive research seems to suggest that there is a discontinuous 'updating' of our sense of coherence, that is, we in fact experience and understand the world in a moment-by-moment manner, although the underlying brain activity is both continuous and highly complex (see, e.g. Engel *et al.* 2001; Pöppel 1997; Varela 1999).

In human movement and motor control research there has also been considerable discussion of chunking-related issues. At the end of the nineteenth century Robert Woodworth (1899) suggested a basic discontinuity in motor control with his idea of an initial impulse in the generation and control of action—an idea that has been much debated throughout the twentieth century (Elliott *et al.* 2001). Of particular interest in our context is Karl Lashley's discussion of so-called 'serial order' (i.e. event succession) in behaviour, and his claim that there has to be some kind of chunk-by-chunk planning and anticipatory control of action (Lashley 1951), an idea that is supported by more recent research (Rosenbaum *et al.* 2007).

In the field of audition, it is well known that there are various thresholds of duration for perceiving different sound features, such as the minimum duration of a sound in order to perceive pitch and timbre (Moore 1995). But there are also sound features that typically are distributed over time: the so-called attack and sustain segments of a sound, although occurring sequentially, tend to mutually influence each other so as to indicate holistic perception of temporally extended segments. This holistic perception of sound fragments and the integration of sequential features into chunks was actually one of the main points of Schaeffer's (1966, 1998) theory. The sonic object in Schaeffer's theory (a fragment of sound typically in the 0.5–5 seconds range) was made the focus of research both because it allowed for this perceptual integration of sequential features and because the fragment was considered more important than large-scale forms in music. From a wider perspective, there is good reason to support Schaeffer's focus on sonic objects rather than large-scale forms and to be suspicious of the assumed importance of large-scale forms in Western music, as for instance suggested by Eitan and Granot (2008).

In our own research on sound-related actions, we have extended Schaeffer's strategy of studying sound fragments into sound-action chunks, because we believe sound-related actions share very many perceptual and cognitive features with sonic objects (Godøy 2006). Actions in general are typically in the same temporal range as sonic objects (Schleidt and Kien 1997), are conceived and perceived holistically as one chunk, and can be understood as centred around certain *goal-points* or *key-postures*, similar to what are called *keyframes* in animation (Rosenbaum *et al.* 2007). In animation, keyframes are salient moments in time that serve as points of orientation, such as when a gesture reaches its target. The continuous movements between keyframes are connected by means of *interframes*, which constitute a succession of incrementally different frames that produce the sensation of smooth transition between the keyframes.

We are currently trying to understand music-related actions in a similar manner: we call salient moments in the stream of musical sound such as various kinds of accents, melodic peaks, and other prominent sound onsets, *goal-points*. These goal-points in the sound are correlated with the position and posture of the effectors, for example the position and the shape of the hands on a keyboard. We regard the trajectories of the effectors to these goal-points as *prefixes*, and the trajectories from these goal-points as *suffixes*. The note-events within these prefixes and suffixes are hierarchically subsumed, or coarticulated, in relation to the goal-points (see Godøy 2008 for details).

One essential element in this *chunking by goal-points* scheme is that all note-events are embedded in some trajectory context, a context that we believe fits quite well with the Husserlian scheme of *retention*, *primal impression*, and *protention*: correlating the *now* with the salient moment of the goal-point, this goal-point also carries with it the retention sensation of what happened just before and the protention sensation of the anticipated movement. With coarticulation, this is very clear, as has been extensively studied in linguistics (Hardcastle and Hewlett 1999), and as we are presently exploring in our lab: at each moment the effectors and the sound are conditioned by what has just passed as well as by what is just to come. We thus have a contextual smearing of the sound as well as the sound-producing movement, and this contextual smearing of the movement is what we are presently studying with various motion capture technologies (Godøy *et al.* 2010; Jensenius *et al.* 2008).

In summary, we believe there is evidence converging on the idea that these sound-action chunks, typically in the 0.5–5 second range, are very much in accordance with basic constraints on the perception and cognition of music, and that these chunks may hold the key to an enhanced understanding of awareness in music. This means that we could consider three different concurrent timescales in the perception and cognition of music:

- *Sub-chunk level*, meaning continuous sound, with pitch, timbre, and loudness features, but always subsumed by the chunk-level sound-action context.

- *Chunk level*, the prime awareness-level, typically in the 0.5–5 second range, with holistic perception of sonic and movement features. This is in our opinion the most significant timescale in musical experience and encompasses elements such as rhythmical, textural, and melodic patterns, as well as harmonic and modal patterns, and to a large extent, also style-defining features. This seems also to be the prime timescale for expressivity features, as well as for movement patterns in general, including affective features of movement.

- *Supra-chunk level*, meaning the concatenation of several chunks into sections, movements, or whole works. The perception of large-scale works in music is not a well-researched topic, and what evidence there is remains contested (cf. Eitan and Granot 2008), but this does not mean that extended sequences of chunk-level musical sound as such are unimportant for listeners.

With different timescales simultaneously present, we hypothesize that they exert an influence on one another—that the supra-chunk level does have some kind of contextual and long-term memory and/or priming influence on the chunk (Snyder 2000), and that the sub-chunk level provides the basis or the substrate for the chunk. There has been some interesting work on the different timescales in music (Clarke 1987; Levinson 1997), but we believe the challenge now is to supplement our understanding of timescales in music with the sound-action perspective. This means understanding the supra-chunk level as extended scripts of chunk-level sound-actions, keeping in mind that the basis for large-scale forms in music are the chunk-level sound-actions.

Conclusion

In summary, we believe there is good reason to understand awareness in music as an active mental process, in the sense that we are aware of that which we somehow simulate in movements, whether those are sound-producing movements, or other kinds of movements—such as moving our bodies to rhythmic features in the music, or tracing the evolution of sounds with our hands. For much received Western musical thought, and in particular for music theory, this idea of actions as conceptually prior to notes, is a challenge. Indeed, this relegates notation to a secondary position after actions, rather than (as is often the case) regarding movement and the associated expressivity as features that are added to the score.

Needless to say, we have a long way to go in deepening an understanding of these sound-action relationships. Advances in neuroscience seem promising (e.g. Zatore *et al.* 2007), and methods for studying sound-related actions are steadily improving with increasingly sophisticated means for motion capture and the analysis of motion capture data (e.g. Wanderley and Battier 2000; Godøy and Leman 2010), but finding out what people actually feel when listening and moving to music—that is, deducing the covert from the overt—remains a formidable challenge. This will probably also leave room for important contributions from introspective reflection on awareness in music for a long time to come, along the lines that Husserl began more than a hundred years ago.

References

Bangert, M. and Altenmüller, E.O. (2003). Mapping perception to action in piano practice: a longitudinal DC-EEG study. *BMC Neuroscience*, **4**, 26.

Berthoz, A. (1997). *Le sens du mouvement* (Paris: Odile Jacob).

Clarke, E.F. (1987). Levels of structure in the organisation of musical time. *Contemporary Music Review*, **2**, 211–39.

Eitan, Z. and Granot, R.Y. (2008). Growing oranges on Mozart's apple tree: 'inner form' and aesthetic judgment. *Music Perception, 25*, 397–417.

Elliott, D., Helsen, W., and Chua, R. (2001). A century later: Woodworth's (1899) two-component model of goal-directed aiming. *Psychological Bulletin, 127*, 342–57.

Engel A.K., Fries P., and Singer W. (2001). Dynamic predictions: oscillations and synchrony in top-down processing. *Nature Reviews Neuroscience, 10*, 704–16.

Fadiga, L., Craighero, L., Buccino, G., and Rizzolatti, G. (2002). Speech listening specifically modulates the excitability of tongue muscles: a TMS Study. *European Journal of Neuroscience*, **15**, 399–402.

Gallese, V. and Metzinger, T. (2003). Motor ontology: the representational reality of goals, actions and selves. *Philosophical Psychology*, **16**, 365–88.

Gallese, V. and Lakoff, G. (2005). The brain's concepts: the role of the sensory-motor system in conceptual knowledge. *Cognitive Neuropsychology*, **22**, 455–79.

Godøy, R.I. (1997). *Formalization and Epistemology* (Oslo: Scandinavian University Press).

Godøy, R.I. (2003). Motor-mimetic music cognition. *Leonardo*, **36**, 317–19.

Godøy, R.I. (2006). Gestural-sonorous objects: embodied extensions of Schaeffer's conceptual apparatus. *Organised Sound*, **11**, 149–57.

Godøy, R.I. (2008). Reflections on chunking in music, in A. Schneider (**ed.**), *Systematic and Comparative Musicology: Concepts, Methods, Findings. Hamburger Jahrbuch für Musikwissenschaft*, **24**, 117–32 (Vienna: Peter Lang).

Godøy, R.I. (2010). Thinking now-points in music-related movement, in R. Bader, C. Neuhaus, **and** U. Morgenstern (**eds.**), *Concepts, Experiments, and Fieldwork: Studies in Systematic Musicology and Ethnomusicology*, 245–60 (Frankfurt: Peter Lang).

Godøy, R.I. and Leman, M. (eds.) (2010). *Musical Gestures: Sound, Movement, and Meaning* (New York, NY: Routledge).

Godøy, R.I., Haga, E., and Jensenius, A. (2006a). Playing 'air instruments': mimicry of sound-producing gestures by novices and experts, in S. Gibet, N. Courty, **and** J.F. Kamp (**eds.**), *Gesture in Human-Computer Interaction and Simulation: 6th International Gesture Workshop, GW 2005, Berder Island, France, May 18–20, 2005, Revised Selected Papers, LNAI 3881*, 256–67 (Berlin: Springer-Verlag).

Godøy, R.I., Haga, E., and Jensenius, A.R. (2006b). Exploring music-related gestures by sound-tracing: a preliminary study, in K. Ng (ed.), *Proceedings of the COST287-ConGAS 2nd International Symposium on Gesture Interfaces for Multimedia Systems*, 27–33.

Godøy, R.I., Jensenius, A.R., and Nymoen, K. (2010). Chunking in Music by Coarticulation. *Acta Acustica* united with *Acustica*, **96**, 690–700.

Gritten, A. and King, E. (eds.) (2006). *Music and Gesture* (Aldershot: Ashgate).

Haga, E. (2008). *Correspondences between Music and Body Movement*. PhD diss., University of Oslo (Oslo: Unipub).

Haken, H., Kelso, J.A.S., and Bunz, H. (1985). A theoretical model of phase transitions in human hand movements. *Biological Cybernetics*, **51**, 347–56.

Hardcastle, W.J. and Hewlett, N. (1999). *Coarticulation: Theory, Data and Techniques* (Cambridge: Cambridge University Press).

Haueisen, J. and Knösche, T.R. (2001). Involuntary motor activity in pianists evoked by music perception. *Journal of Cognitive Neuroscience*, **13**, 786–92.

Husserl, E. (1982). *Ideas Pertaining to a Pure Phenomenological Philosophy, First Book* (Dordrecht: Kluwer Academic Publishers).

Husserl, E. (1991). *On the Phenomenology of the Consciousness of Internal Time, 1893–1917*. Trans. J. B. Brough (Dordrecht: Kluwer Academic Publishers).

James, W. (1890). *The Principles of Psychology*, vol. 1 (New York, NY: H. Holt and Company).

Jensenius, A.R., Nymoen, K., and Godøy, R.I. (2008). *A Multilayered GDIF-based Setup for Studying Coarticulation in the Movements of Musicians*. Proceedings of the International Computer Music Conference, 24–29 August 2008, Belfast, 743–6 (International Computer Music Association).

Kohler, E., Keysers, C., Umiltà, M.A., Fogassi, L., Gallese, V., and Rizzolatti, G. (2002). Hearing sounds, understanding actions: action representation in mirror neurons. *Science*, **297**, 846–8.

Lashley, K.S. (1951). The problem of serial order in behavior, in L.A. Jeffress (**ed.**), *Cerebral Mechanisms in Behavior*, 112–31 (New York, NY: John Wiley & Sons, Ltd).

Leman, M. (2008). *Embodied Music Cognition and Mediation Technology* (Cambridge, MA: MIT Press).

Levinson, J. (1997). *Music in the Moment* (Ithaca, NY: Cornell University Press).

Liberman, A.M. and Mattingly, I.G. (1985). The motor theory of speech perception revised. *Cognition*, **21**, 1–36.

Michon, J. (1978). The making of the present: a tutorial review, in J. Requin (ed.), *Attention and Performance VII*, 89–111 (Hillsale, NJ: Erlbaum).

Miller, G.A. (1956). The magic number seven, plus or minus two: some limits on our capacity for processing information. *Psychological Review*, **63**, 81–97.

Miller, I. (1982). Husserl's account of our temporal awareness, in H. Dreyfus (ed.), *Husserl, Intentionality, and Cognitive Science*, 125–46 (Cambridge, MA: MIT Press).

Moore, B.C.J. (ed.) (1995). *Hearing* (San Diego, CA: Academic Press).

Pöppel, E. (1997). A hierarchical model of time perception. *Trends in Cognitive Science*, **1**, 56–61.

Ricoeur, P. (1981). *Hermeneutics and the Human Sciences* (Cambridge: Cambridge University Press).

Rosenbaum, D., Cohen, R.G., Jax, S.A., Weiss, D.J., and van der Wel, R. (2007). The problem of serial order in behavior: Lashley's legacy. *Human Movement Science*, **26**, 525–54.

Sacks, O. (2004). In the river of consciousness. *New York Review of Books*, **51**(1), 15 January.

Schaeffer, P. (1966). *Traité des objets musicaux* (Paris: Éditions du Seuil).

Schaeffer, P. (with sound examples by Reibel, G. and Ferreyra, B.) (1998). *Solfège de l'objet sonore* (Paris: INA/GRM).

Schleidt, M. and Kien, J. (1997). Segmentation in behavior and what it can tell us about brain function. *Human Nature*, **8**, 77–111.

Snyder, B. (2000). *Music and Memory: An Introduction* (Cambridge, MA: MIT Press).

Stern, D.N. (2004). *The Present Moment in Psychotherapy and Everyday Life* (New York, NY: W.W. Norton).

Varela, F. (1999). The specious present: the neurophenomenology of time consciousness, in J. Petitot, F.J. Varela, B. Pachoud, and J.M. Roy (eds.), *Naturalizing Phenomenology*, 266–314 (Palo Alto, CA: Stanford University Press).

Vines, B., Dalca, I., and Wanderley, M. (2006). Variation in expressive physical gestures of clarinetists, in M. Baroni, A.R. Addessi, R. Caterina, and M. Costa. *Proceedings of the 9th International Conference on Music Perception and Cognition (ICMPC9), Bologna/Italy, 22–26 August 2006*, 1721–2.

Wanderley, M. and Battier, M. (eds.) (2000). *Trends in Gestural Control of Music* (Paris: IRCAM).

Wilson, M. and Knoblich, G. (2005). The case for motor involvement in perceiving conspecifics. *Psychological Bulletin*, **131**, 460–73.

Wohlschläger, A., Gattis, M., and Bekkering, H. (2003). Action generation and action perception in imitation: an instance of the ideomotor principle. *Philosophical Transactions of the Royal Society of London B*, **358**, 501–15.

Woodworth, R.S. (1899). The accuracy of voluntary movement. *Psychological Review*, **3** (Suppl. 13), 1–119.

Zatorre, R.J., Chen, J.L., and Penhune, V.B. (2007). When the brain plays music: auditory-motor interactions in music perception and production. *Nature Reviews Neuroscience*, **8**, 547–57.

Note

1. For a remarkable presentation of James's, his contemporaries', and more recent researchers' ideas on continuity and discontinuity, see Sacks (2004).

Chapter 14

Music, consciousness, and the brain: music as shared experience of an embodied present

Andy McGuiness and Katie Overy

Introduction

This chapter considers the neural basis of musical experience alongside theories of the embodied nature of consciousness. Drawing on previous theoretical work on the role of the human mirror neuron system in emotional responses to music (Molnar-Szakacs and Overy 2006), we propose that the nature of the musical listening experience is of a shared subjectivity between individual listeners and performers, underpinned by innate bodily responses to musical gestures. Based on an outline of this broad theory, we offer a number of conclusions that include a reassessment of the ideas of 'musical meaning' and 'musical communication'.

We argue that, while communication can be found in music, one of the attributes that distinguishes music from language is that music provides an intimately shared, embodied experience rather than communicating a specific message. As Tia DeNora puts it, music fosters

> a co-subjectivity where two or more individuals may come to exhibit similar modes of feeling and acting, constituted in relation to extra-personal parameters, such as those provided by musical materials. Such co-subjectivity differs in important ways from the more traditional (and modern) notion of 'inter-subjectivity', which presumes interpersonal dialogue and the collaborative production of meaning and cognition. Inter-subjectivity . . . involves a collaborative version of reflexivity. By contrast, co-subjectivity is the result of isolated *individually* reflexive alignments to an environment and its materials. (2000: 153)

What music is capable of providing, rather than communication, is communion—an intimately shared experience between listener and listener and between listener and performer. We suggest that the mechanism of emotional contagion supports an experience of empathy in music listeners, and offer some insights into the relationship between underpinning neural processes and levels of consciousness. This chapter deals only with listeners' experience, but the argument could be extended (with some modifications) to include performers' experience.

We begin with a review of current findings in music neuroscience, including a discussion of the potential role of the 'mirror neuron system' (MNS). A clarification of the distinction between subpersonal and conscious processes, and between pre-reflective and reflective levels of consciousness, then follows. A view of musical performance as a series of individual short motor actions links the notion of the MNS to the perception of gesture in music listening, and a consideration of gesture introduces several ideas that in turn become key points in later sections of the chapter, including the idea of entrainment. Entrainment—keeping time with the beat—has the important function of coordinating listeners' responses temporally.

We suggest that motor responses to gesture contribute to an emotional response to music and depend on subpersonal processes (not available to consciousness) that provide affective outputs to consciousness at the bodily, pre-reflective level. Motor resonance to musical gestures experienced by the listener thus contributes to a highly developed, but still pre-reflective, form of empathy or co-subjectivity. We propose that experience of this kind does not approach communication until the listener's own affective response is actually identified at the reflective level of consciousness. Musical communication is no doubt founded on such shared experience, as Molnar-Szakacs and Overy (2006: 2) have suggested. Gallagher (2001), for instance, argues that the mechanisms of 'primary intersubjectivity' during infancy continue into adult life, supporting more sophisticated and reflective forms of social interaction. However, as both of these sources note, shared representations are a basis for, but do not constitute, communication. Communication depends on agentive understanding of both the sender (in the case of music performance, the performer) and the receiver of a message. If you do not understand that I am an agent, with goals and the means to attain them that may differ from yours, you will have no reason to believe that you can change what is in my mind. On the other hand, if I do not understand that you are an agent, even if you succeed in changing what is in my mind I cannot be said to have received a communication. The question for the listener's experience in relation to the performer then, is whether they have a clear sense of the performer as an agent, separate from themselves.

Accordingly, we review the contribution of representations by the human mirror system to the attribution of intention and agency. Motor intentionality (where goals are expressed in terms of relational structures between body effectors and parts of the environment) underpins agent intentionality (where goals are expressed as intentional relations between agents and the world). We argue that the mechanism of emotional contagion, involving motor resonance experience at the pre-reflective level without involvement of the reflective level of consciousness, will not give rise to a sense of separate agency in the listener. Rather, the listener experiences an *ambiguity* of agency that fosters co-subjectivity.

The neural basis of musical experience

Grappling with ideas of music and consciousness is a difficult enough enterprise without attempting to introduce complex and sometimes contradictory neuroscientific evidence into the discussion. However, the massive expansion and development of brain-imaging techniques over the past 20 years is inescapable—it has led to an explosion of research in cognitive neuroscience, with music becoming increasingly recognized as an important aspect of human intelligence. A strong emphasis in such research is the localization of specific perceptual and cognitive abilities to specific neural regions, leading to the realization that music listening alone can activate more regions of the brain than perhaps any other perceptual or cognitive activity— including the left and right frontal, temporal and parietal lobes, as well as the limbic system, cerebellum, and brain stem (for examples see Dalla Bella *et al.* 2009).

The ability to specify relatively distinct regions of neural localization is achieved by designing studies that isolate individual variables of music perception or cognition, such as beat perception, pitch memory, rhythm discrimination, and emotional response. Thus, each individual study is limited in certain respects: the experimental need to isolate individual variables of interest means that real world, active music-making or listening is deconstructed into narrower and less ecologically valid experimental tasks. In addition, participants in a single study tend to be from relatively limited, homogeneous groups, and must remain immobile in the brain-imaging environment for reasons of accurate data recording. Nonetheless, despite such apparent limitations, the sheer range and quantity of recent research in this area has made it increasingly clear that musical experience is an extraordinarily complex human experience, involving the coordination of a wide variety of perceptual and cognitive abilities and neural regions, and with a number of clear themes emerging.

One striking finding is that musical training can have a powerful effect on the human brain, leading to functional and structural differences after even short periods of exposure. Some of the first studies in this area reported the discovery of structural differences between the brains of professional musicians and non-musicians in motor, auditory, and language regions (Amunts *et al.* 1997; Schlaug *et al.* 1995; Sluming *et al.* 2002). Subsequent work has identified structural differences between pianists and violinists (Bangert and Schlaug 2006) and functional differences before and after a period of musical training (Fujioka *et al.* 2006; Lahav *et al.* 2005), thus suggesting a direct effect of musical training, rather than innate neural differences. Hence, the question of whether or not music can have an effect on neural functioning is no longer hotly debated, but has turned to whether such training effects occur only in the musical domain, or can transfer to other domains, such as language. For example, research by Kraus and colleagues (Wong *et al.* 2007) has demonstrated that, when listening to language stimuli, professional musicians show more accurate neural encoding patterns in the brain stem than do non-musicians. This intriguing finding indicates that musical experience can have a powerful impact even at a very basic level of neurological function.

Another emerging theme is the accumulating evidence to suggest that motor regions of the brain are engaged during perceptual rhythm tasks. For example, Grahn and Brett (2007) have shown that the basal ganglia (involved in initiating movement) are activated while listening to stimuli with a strong sense of pulse, compared with stimuli without a steady pulse. Trainor *et al.* (2009) have shown that activation of the vestibular system (involved in balance) contributes to discrimination between duple and triple metres, while Thaut *et al.* (2009) have shown that particular regions of the cerebellum (involved in balance and fine motor control) are involved in different types of rhythmic task, such as isochronous versus non-isochronous tapping. Further studies have shown that the premotor cortex (a region involved in planning and executing movements) is involved in rhythm discrimination tasks (e.g. Bengtsson *et al.* 2009). Such research findings have important implications for our understanding of the potential role of music in learning and therapy, and also contribute to the important idea that musical perceptual experience is 'embodied'—a concept that been gathering pace since the discovery of so-called 'mirror neurons' (see also Chapters 11–13).

The human 'mirror neuron system' (MNS) is a term used to describe groups of neurons in the frontal and parietal regions of the brain that are activated not only when individuals perform intentional actions themselves, but also when they perceive another individual performing that action (Rizzolati and Craighero 2004), such as watching someone pick up a cup to drink from it (Iacoboni *et al.* 2005), or watching someone execute familiar dance movements (Calvo-Merino *et al.* 2005). Rather than visually analysing the motion of an action, and then deducing the intentions of the agent, the mirror neuron theory proposes that we directly engage our own motor systems at a pre-conscious, perceptual level: we 'feel' what another agent intends by their movement—to a greater extent if we are already familiar with the motor gesture (e.g. Molnar-Szakacs *et al.* 2007). This idea is leading to a notable conceptual shift in cognitive neuroscience, since it suggests that the human brain is not an isolated perception-action system, but is intimately connected with the body, and with the brains of other individuals. This conceptual shift has brought powerful and productive ideas about embodied cognition, social cognition, and social learning to the forefront of current thinking about human intelligence and behaviour.

The discovery of the MNS thus has extremely interesting implications for an understanding of music. For example, Molnar-Szakacs and Overy (2006) have proposed a model of the role of the MNS in emotional responses to music, suggesting that apparently disembodied, abstract musical sounds are actually interpreted by the brain in terms of the physical human movements required to produce such signals (either real or imagined). The hierarchical structures and temporal dynamics of the auditory signal can thus convey the structures and dynamics of sequences of human gestures (vocal or physical) with greater or lesser degrees of emotional valence: the apparent motion of the music can convey the potential emotion of an apparent human organism by means of connections between the auditory cortex, the MNS, the anterior insula, and the limbic system. Group synchronization of musical behaviour can thus lead to powerfully affective, shared experiences (Overy and Molnar-Szakacs 2009).

Neuro-imaging evidence for a role of this kind for the MNS in musical behaviour is limited, but is suggested in a number of different sources. For example, musical listening tasks have been found to activate the anterior insula as well as premotor representations for vocal sound production (Brown and Martinez 2007; Koelsch *et al.* 2006). Bangert and colleagues have shown that pianists exhibit more premotor activations than non-pianists when listening to piano music (Bangert *et al.* 2006; Haslinger *et al.* 2005), while Chapin *et al.* (2010) have shown MNS-consistent activations in relation to emotional arousal in musicians. A striking example of such research is a study conducted by Lahav *et al.* (2007), which showed that after a short period of training during which non-musicians were taught to play a simple melody on the piano, fronto-parietal regions consistent with the MNS were activated while listening to that melody, but were less activated for unfamiliar melodies using the same notes. This finding highlights the extraordinary plasticity of this neural system—the speed with which the brain can adapt so as to associate familiar sounds with known actions.

The role of the MNS in musical experience is relevant to our discussion of music and consciousness because it raises the central ideas of embodiment, temporal organization, and shared experience. Molnar-Szakacs and Overy (2006) propose that the MNS offers a potential neural system by which the representation of a musical structure can be shared and experienced between performers and listeners at the same time. Importantly, this simultaneous and potentially affective experience is facilitated by the organized, predictive, and synchronizing structure of the musical pulse: found across most musical traditions, pulse provides an isochronous temporal framework within which accurate prediction can occur. Such prediction and expectation can occur not only between two individuals, but also across large groups of individuals, with high levels of synchrony strengthening the feeling of a shared experience. Pulse-based music is often used in human rituals to bring about some kind of altered conscious state: alongside drugs, and sometimes in conjunction with them, such music seems to facilitate an altered perception of time, and even a blurring of the distinction between self and other (see Chapters 15 and 16).

The specific topic of music and consciousness has received little attention to date from cognitive neuroscience. Koelsch et al. (2006) conducted a study in which they used electroencephalography (EEG) to examine neural responses to music during and after sedation, and found that a higher level of musical awareness (chord error detection) was not present during or after sedation, while a more basic aspect of auditory awareness (timbre perception) was sustained throughout sedation. This supports the results of previous work with patients in a vegetative state, who have been found to show responses to basic auditory stimuli (for a review, see Griffiths 2002). However, it has also been shown that heart rate variability in patients in a vegetative state can be affected by music (Riganello et al. 2010), while Magee (2005) has shown that music therapy can be used with patients in a vegetative state to stimulate motor function, eye movements, and even to awaken them from coma. Music therapy has thus been proposed as an important means to diagnose a patient's level of consciousness, since music seems to be a particularly far-reaching stimulus: patients previously thought to be in a vegetative state can be re-diagnosed as being in minimally conscious state after showing meaningful responses to music (Magee 2007).

Taken together, this range of cognitive neuroscientific and medical research shows that music not only stimulates the brain at high levels of cognitive and social function, but also at low levels of perceptual awareness and indeed neural function—in other words, at different levels of consciousness and at the subpersonal level. In addition, specific temporal aspects of music (pulse, metre, rhythmic pattern) appear to engage specific motor regions of the brain, including the vestibular system, cerebellum, basal ganglia, and pre-motor cortex. Furthermore, there is evidence to suggest that music for which the motor requirements are familiar, and/or which has an emotional effect, appears to engage the human mirror neuron system, indicating a neural basis for affective, shared, musical experiences. We thus propose that music can be conceived of in terms of shared representations of a musical structure that bring about a shared, embodied experience. At this point our discussion moves from neuroscientific evidence to theoretical and philosophical discussion, drawing on a range of previous work. We do not propose to integrate fully the neuroscientific research with the theoretical work, but rather to bring them alongside each other as we take the ideas forward.

Pre-reflective consciousness, reflective consciousness, and subpersonal processes

Neural mechanisms are, of course, not available directly to consciousness: we do not, for instance, hear the individual vibrations of frequencies above 20 Hz, but rather their synthesis into a pitch and timbre—and the same applies to the functioning of higher auditory centres of the brain. We thus ask two questions about conscious experience in response to music. The first question is: At what level of consciousness is a particular response experienced? This section clarifies the distinction between pre-reflective and reflective levels of consciousness, preparatory to a discussion of the second question: Do the mechanisms which underpin a particular kind of response to music involve only the subpersonal level (with outputs direct to consciousness) or do they also involve higher levels of consciousness? Our argument is that emotional responses to musical gesture depend on subpersonal mechanisms with output directly to (pre-reflective) consciousness.

Dorothée Legrand clarifies the difference between pre-reflective and reflective/observational consciousness of the body with the example of one's left hand touching one's right hand:

> Experience of the touched hand corresponds to an observational consciousness: the touched hand is taken as an intentional object of consciousness. Experience of the touching hand is different. It corresponds to what I call here pre-reflective bodily consciousness. At this level, the body is not an object of experience, it is the subject of experience and it is experienced as such. (2007a: 499)

The difference that Legrand identifies is between a subjective experience of the body (the body in the position of subject), and the experience of the body as an intentional object (object-directedness).

Pre-reflective consciousness underpins reflective consciousness. As Zahavi (2006) argues, the continuity of identity of the object through the different experiences that the subject has of it requires that subject and object are not the same thing. If I observe myself now as happy, now as sad, continuity and unity are not found in the different emotions I observe but in the identity of the subject which observes them. The self observed in introspection must be my own self, since it is available to my introspection; but, Zahavi argues, I cannot identify the introspected self as myself unless I know it is the object of *my* introspection (2006: 6). Therefore:

> [m]y pre-reflective access to my own mental life in first-personal experience is immediate, non-observational and non-objectifying. It is non-objectifying in the sense that I do not occupy the position or perspective of a spectator or in(tro)spector on it. (Zahavi 2006: 6)

Similarly, Legrand sees the pre-reflective self as foundational to reflective consciousness:

> It is important to consider that pre-reflective self-consciousness is not only one possible form of consciousness among others. Rather, it is a foundational state, in the sense that it conditions the very possibility to recognize oneself as such at the observational reflective level. (2007a: 498)

Legrand argues that the pre-reflective dimension of consciousness is 'paradigmatically' (although perhaps not necessarily) 'anchored to the subject's body' (2007b: 577). Her argument springs from the ineligibility of the introspected self for the role of the pre-reflective self. If the pre-reflective self is not the self-as-object but the self-as-subject, then the pre-reflective self must be defined by what Legrand calls 'self-relative' information:

> Self-relative information is not information about the self, but *information about the world relative to the self*. At the sensori-motor level, this self-relativity is given by the reciprocal modulation of perceptual afference and motor efference . . . The present proposal is thus that a foundational bodily experience is pre-reflective and rooted in sensori-motor integration, rather than [based] primarily on afference or primarily on efference. (2007a: 513–14)

The foundational bodily experience of the pre-reflective self includes the outputs of subpersonal mechanisms that underpin sensorimotor integration, such as balance and proprioception. The conscious experience of being on- (or off-) balance should be thought of as distinct from—though of course directly relying on—the subpersonal processes that allow us to keep balance, which include, for instance, the functioning of the vestibular system and the resulting motor commands that are generated to adjust muscular tension in order to maintain balance. The changes in muscular tension required to maintain balance are themselves experienced at a pre-reflective, bodily level (and may become the object of reflective consciousness) but the subpersonal mechanisms that generate them are not available to consciousness.

The same argument applies to entrainment, that is, the mechanisms underlying the ability to keep in time with a musical beat. We may be conscious of where the beat falls in time and of adjusting our movements to be in time with the beat, but processes which give rise to the perception of the beat (which appear to involve at least the basal ganglia and the cerebellum—see above) are not available to consciousness. Like the mechanisms of balance, their operation is automatic and to some extent involuntary: we can choose not to tap in time to a beat, but arguably cannot choose not to perceive the beat at all. Similarly, neural processes such as the involuntary mirroring of motor actions and affective responses to gesture are subpersonal rather than conscious.

Musical events, motor gestures, and entrainment

The notion of gesture in music is central both to Naomi Cumming's approach in *The Sonic Self* and to Wilson Coker's *Music and Meaning*. Gestures, Cumming suggests, are the result of a 'unitary impulse of some kind' (2000: 136). The term gesture 'captures the propensity of listeners to hear in short, directed motions the evidence of a sometimes expressive agency in movement' (165). David Lidov's definition is similar: 'gesture', in its general rather than specifically musical sense, encompasses 'all brief, expressive molar units of motor activity, be they of the limbs, the larynx, the torso, etcetera, units which are whole but not readily subdivisible' (1987: 77, cited in Cumming 2000: 138).

Motor aspects of such unitary motor impulses can be perceived directly in the sound:

> When an element of music is heard as expressively 'gestural,' it suggests the kind of 'energy' or directionality commonly linked with an expressive gesture in a person or animal, without the aid of visual cues . . . The direction, force, and timing of a movement (transformed into musical terms) is now the most important aspect . . . It is not so much the *appearance* of the gesture that is informative . . . as it is the variable attributes of apparent energy and control. It is because the varying qualities of motion do not depend on a visual presentation in order to be recognized that they can be musically presented and transformed in such an effective way. (Cumming 2000: 92)

The direct perception of motor impulse in gesture can usefully be referred to as 'motor resonance'—a term which is neutral as to its underlying neural processes. It is important to note that the conscious experience of the 'direction, force, and timing of a movement' is, at least initially, pre-reflective. Any reflective awareness of the kind of gesture perceived in the sound (for instance, as would be required to label it as 'quick', or 'strong', or something else) is founded on the self-relative information provided by bodily involvement, the signature of the pre-reflective self.

If gestures are 'brief, . . . molar units of motor activity' (Lidov 1987: 77, cited in Cumming 2000: 138), each resulting from a 'unitary impulse' (Cumming 2000: 136), and if we perceive those gestures through involuntary subpersonal brain responses—that is, by covert imitation—then our perception of music is founded on a series of short, simulated motor actions. It is of interest, then, that the musical entrainment involved in beat perception appears to occur at periods of around 200–1000 milliseconds (Repp 2006: 166, 174–5), broadly corresponding to the duration of individual motor actions. Entrainment is central to most types of musical behaviour, and can be expected to figure prominently in accounts of human musical experience. The majority of music across cultures and history has a pulse, to which listeners (and, of course, performers) can normally entrain at one or two temporal levels (Large *et al.* 2002: 15). Of these, one level is normally used as a frame of reference for faster or slower levels of pulsation, and this is usually what listeners will make explicit if they tap to the music (Jones and Boltz 1989: 467). The period of the referent time level (the tactus) has been found by a number of researchers to fall normally somewhere between about 370 and 740 milliseconds—most typically near 700 milliseconds (Parncutt 1994: 419), and since motor actions normally occupy a few hundred milliseconds, a motor action can be matched with a single tactus beat. The rather narrow range within which the tactus falls means that different listeners exposed to the same music are likely to choose the same referent level. Since one of the most common responses to music is bodily movement, entrainment serves to delineate the temporal boundaries of discrete actions (a duration of some hundreds of milliseconds) as perceived by the listener. A given tempo will afford some motor movements more readily than others, but different individuals will tend to entrain at the same tempo (the tempo of the tactus), and will also find a common phase—that is, they will tend to be synchronized and coordinated (Clayton *et al.* 2004: 2; Large *et al.* 2002: 8). As Hommel *et al.* put it, when we move in response to music,

> [t]he perceptual event itself does not specify which movements to perform and which limbs to use. However, once these choices have been made by the listener the timing of the movements is captured by the structure of the sound pattern—provided that it exhibits sufficient regularity to allow for anticipation of temporal structure. (2001: 858)

Of course, a musical gesture can include several individual onsets in a rhythmic pattern, which do not all need to occur precisely on the beat (for example we hear onsets just before a beat as anticipations or anacruses), but they will almost always be referenced to the beat. There is some flexibility in this area, so that in the same way that we can shift our attention between nested beat levels (at, for example, double or half the beat period), so we can expect that performers and listeners will sometimes integrate onsets over two beats into a single motor movement. We suggest that entrainment to the beat thus coordinates MNS responses to musical gestures in the same way that it coordinates motor actions: the temporal boundaries of the action are coordinated (see also Overy and Molnar-Szakacs 2009).

With music, then, there is shared experience among co-listeners in a music audience that is intimately correlated between individuals in at least two senses. First, there is the commonality of emotional response to gesture (addressed in detail in the following section); second there is the temporal coordination resulting from entrainment. Taken together, the temporal coordination through rhythmic entrainment and our emotional responses to gesture provide a firm ground for intimately shared representations and the possibility of co-subjectivity.

Musical gesture and emotion

There are some clarifications to be made at this stage of the argument. The first is that there are several components to the emotional response to music, of which the response to gesture considered here is just one. The components of human emotion include: physiological arousal (including changes to breathing and heart rates); motor expression (gestures, facial and vocal expression, posture); subjective feeling (what subjects can report verbally about their emotional state); action tendencies (including general readiness as well as the determination of alternative courses of action in the face of the emotion-provoking situation); and cognitive appraisal (the subjective evaluation of events in relation to the well-being and goal attainment of the subject) (Scherer 2004: 241–2). Juslin and Västfjäll (2008) identify a similar breakdown of the components of emotional responses to music, also noting that the causal mechanisms that trigger different (and conflicting) components of emotion might be activated simultaneously at different levels, resulting in so-called 'mixed emotions':

> Thus, for example, a piece of music could make the listener happy because of the happy expression of the piece (emotional contagion), but at the same time make the listener sad because the piece reminds him or her of a sad event in the past (episodic memory). (564)

The consideration of emotional responses to music is confined in this chapter to motor expression in response to gesture (referred to in the quotation above as 'emotional contagion'), and our comments relate to this level rather than to any other component of the emotional response. Different components of emotional responses may respond in conflicting ways to cues appropriate to the mechanisms underlying them, and so it is possible to speak of emotional responses to music that are innate and universal, while also recognizing differences in culturally conditioned and idiosyncratic emotional responses. Some of the components of emotion will—in the terminology of this chapter—involve reflective consciousness while others are capable of proceeding at the pre-reflective level. Thus, subjective feeling, which involves self-report, necessarily involves reflective consciousness; while cognitive appraisal, which depends on an evaluation of possible events (rather than self-relative information available to the body in the present), depends on reflective consciousness as a causal mechanism. Action tendencies can be expected to appear in pre-reflective consciousness, although consideration of alternative courses of actions would presumably involve reflective consciousness. Motor expression (with which we are concerned here) and physiological arousal are available to pre-reflective consciousness but not to reflective consciousness.

Emotional contagion—the process by which humans in a social situation appear to 'catch' emotions experienced by others at the motor expression level—is thought to arise from the tendency unconsciously to mimic the facial expressions, gestures, postures, and body sway of others, as well as their vocal expressions (Bharucha *et al.* 2006: 156; Wilson and Knoblich 2005: 460). It is important to note that the concept of motor resonance does not in itself explain the emotional response to gesture, but only the ability—indeed, the apparent compulsion—of subpersonal processes in the brain to imitate motor actions. The output of those subpersonal processes need not be a motor action but may be only a pre-reflective bodily understanding of the type of gesture that was made, in terms of properties such as force and timing. An explanation of the emotional expressivity of gesture, based on motor responses, requires us to postulate an additional process. Such an additional process might be at the reflective level, as encapsulated in the reflective thought: 'That was a quick and forceful gesture—perhaps the person who made it is angry.' It might on the other hand require the active involvement of the pre-reflective level of consciousness, since physically mirroring actions can bring about an emotional effect (making a sad face can make a person sad—Decety and Chaminade 2003: 584). This 'chameleon effect' is, for instance, suggested by Molnar-Szakacs and Overy (2006: 4) as being implicated in emotional responses to music. Finally, the emotional force of gestures might bypass both reflective and pre-reflective levels and be the direct result of subpersonal brain processes—perhaps involving the anterior insula, which has links both to motor regions and to the limbic system.

What is important for both Cumming and Coker about gesture is the pre-reflective immediacy of response. Gesture, Coker writes, 'arises at the most rudimentary level of biological behaviour' (1972: 10), and such an instinctively arising gesture by one member of the species triggers an equally involuntary adjusting behaviour in another.

Cumming seems to support the idea that physically mimicking bodily gestures produces emotion:

> Physiological changes are accepted as part of the etiology of at least some emotions, observable not only in the altered sound of a voice, but in characteristic changes of movement and activity, as well as the flow of thought. (2000: 91–2)

A strong argument exists for the idea that subpersonal mechanisms triggered directly by the perception of a gesture contribute to the emotional response to that gesture—without requiring input from conscious levels. Manfred Clynes was an early investigator of the consistent association of certain patterns of movement with particular emotions. Clynes studied the variation in physiological actions within a period of no more than a few seconds, and found that gestures could be classified by overall length and trajectories of direction and force, proposing that they were neurophysiologically encoded to express basic affective states and were invariant across cultures (Cumming 2000: 139–40). One interesting consequence of Clynes's theory of the universality of gestural meaning is that the form of an individual gesture can be enacted with more or less precision. Similarly, Wilson Coker asserts that types of motion are found in music which are 'universals' and cross-sensory, and which are 'intuitively recognizable properties of gestures' (1972: 155). In support of the universality of gestures within a species, Cumming (2000: 141) notes Konrad Lorenz's observation that natural selection tends to preserve those kinds of signalling movements that most unambiguously convey information to another member of the species. Cumming makes an analogy between gesture-as-signal and the icons on a computer screen which, when clicked, trigger pre-programmed functions in the computer:

> Of course, these icons are already 'interpreted.' They have been programmed to hold a specific place in the system and would have no 'meaning' without it . . . The icon, then, is the content of which [users] are conscious at a particular moment, enabling a quick response. If this is useful to students, it is also ecologically sensible. Organisms wishing to adapt to their environment by carrying out defensive or amorous goals do not need to be delayed by questioning the origin and veridity of their already-interpreted perceptions. A sound reads 'danger' or 'mate,' not 'auditory datum which could be associated with certain possible events, given the former experience of your species.' It comes as a 'sign,' hearing X as Y, not just as the representation of a sound in the mind. (113–14)

In related fashion, Bharucha and colleagues, referring to work by Juslin (2001), have suggested that humans have a physiologically determined disposition to respond to emotion expressed in the human voice, and that such an involuntary response transfers to instrumental music:

> Juslin (2001) suggests that vocal expression of emotion is processed automatically by brain modules that detect certain stimulus features . . . These modules may not differentiate between different classes of acoustic stimuli (such as vocalizations and music), but respond automatically to acoustic features that have emotional relevance. (Bharucha *et al.* 2006: 155–6)

In an emotional contagion response to music, Stephen Davies (forthcoming) argues, 'neither the music nor anything else is the emotional object of the listener's response'.

Musical gesture can elicit emotional responses through emotional contagion without reference to a real-world object, and the contagious response to musical gesture does not require that the emotion concerned be an object of intentionality at the reflective level for the listener.

> What is crucial, as I have noted, is that the mirroring [i.e. emotional contagion] response does not take the initial emotional state, appearance, or condition as its emotional object and does not involve the kinds of beliefs about that state, appearance, or condition that are distinctive to emotions of the kind elicited. (Davies, forthcoming)

Not only do musical gestures not (necessarily) elicit a motor intentional response, but the emotional contagion response to gesture does not require any real-world object of intentionality:

> those who are saddened by sad music are not sad *about* or *for* the music. The music is the perceptual object and cause of the sad reaction. Indeed, the music is the attentional focus of the response, which tracks the expressiveness as it unfolds in the music's progress. However, neither the music nor anything else is the emotional object of the listener's response. (Davies, forthcoming)

Emotional responses to music of this kind, then, are experienced independently of knowledge, reasoning, or beliefs—which involve reflective consciousness—about the intentions of the composer or performer. The possibility of 'mixed emotions', due to the activation of different mechanisms of emotion at the pre-reflective level of consciousness, as well as at subpersonal levels, means that a substrate of co-subjectivity may exist even while responses of various kinds at the reflective level of consciousness are present. In an fMRI study to investigate the neural correlates of emotional contagion, Carr *et al.* (2003) found that imitation and observation of facial expressions activated a largely similar network of brain areas, with pre-motor areas, the insula (which connects to the limbic areas processing emotional content) and the amygdala (important for emotional behaviours) activated in each case. These findings suggest that emotional contagion can occur without the need for overt motor expression. Some details of their results support Davies's (forthcoming) assertion that emotional contagion 'does not involve the kinds of beliefs about that state, appearance, or condition that are distinctive to emotions of the kind elicited':

> A study on conscious and unconscious processing of emotional facial expression has suggested that the left but not the right amygdala is associated with explicit representational content of the observed emotion. Our data, showing a right lateralized activation of the amygdala during imitation of facial emotional expression, suggest that the type of empathic resonance induced by imitation does not require explicit representational content and may be a form of 'mirroring' that grounds empathy via an experiential mechanism. (Carr *et al.* 2003: 5501–2)

In the terms used in this paper, identification of the emotion at the reflective level of consciousness is not necessary for the emotional contagion response:

> Taken together, these data suggest that we understand the feelings of others via a mechanism of action representation shaping emotional content, such that we ground our empathic resonance in the experience of our acting body and the emotions associated with specific movements. (5502)

Koelsch *et al.* (2006) reported an fMRI study of responses to pleasant and unpleasant (artificially manipulated) music, whose results suggested that the perception of 'pleasantness' involves the activation of an auditory sensorimotor system that includes a representation of vocal sound production. Thus, if our emotional responses to gestures perceived in music are innate and universal, and result from subpersonal mechanisms which give their output to pre-reflective consciousness, the implication for co-subjectivity among the members of a musical audience are clear. All members of the group will have a basic level of emotional response to the music which is innate, more or less involuntary, and which varies in a similar way and at the same time for each individual—even if higher-level responses (especially those involving reflective consciousness) may differ radically between individuals, depending on familiarity, cultural differences, and preference.

Music perception and ambiguity of agency

Emotional contagion underlines the difference between co- and inter-subjectivity. Co-subjectivity differs from intersubjectivity and communication by virtue of the absence of reflective identification of the other's agency and intention by both the sender and receiver of the communication. For example, I might sigh simply because I feel sad, and you may experience emotional contagion (a feeling of sadness) without reflective awareness of the cause. However, overhearing me sigh frequently, you may become aware of your emotion and conscious of its cause, and so recognize the sigh as evidence of my sadness. At this point, you will have recognized my agency as distinct from your own, but it is only when I also recognize your separate agency and sigh with the intention of you also recognizing my agency and thus receiving the sigh as a message, that communication is achieved.

Knoblich and Sebanz note that the key dimension of difference between more or less complex and flexible social interactions is the extent to which organisms can represent others' intentions as separate from their own (2008: 363). Decety and Chaminade (2003) make much the same point, observing that while mental states are essentially private, they take on the character of shared representations in intersubjective circumstances, raising significant questions about the complex and fluid ways in which the self-versus-other distinction can operate. Since the self-versus-other distinction is precisely what we claim can be suspended in the experience of co-subjectivity, it is worth investigating the preconditions for this more usual state of affairs. Gallese, arguing for the MNS as foundational to empathy, argues that

> in order to understand the intended goal of an observed action, and to eventually re-enact it, a link must be established between the observed agent and the observer. My proposal is that this link is constituted by the embodiment of the intended goal, shared by the agent and the observer. We can speculate on the mechanisms enabling the embodiment of the intended goal to be shared. My suggestion is that the embodiment of the action goal, shared by agent and observer, depends on the motor schema of the action, and not only on a purely visual description of its agent. When the motor schema of the agent is different from that of the observer—as in the case of the mechanical demonstrator, or for mirror neurons, in the case of grasping achieved by using a tool—the observed action cannot be matched on the observer's motor repertoire, and therefore the intended goal cannot be detected and/or attributed to the mechanical agent. (2001: 36)

There are two aspects identified here by Gallese as contributing to the self–other distinction. One is the (pre-reflective) embodiment of the motor intention of the perceived action by the other person. Note that this is not yet recognition of separate intentionality, but only the experience of the goal of an action, such as the MNS can provide. The other is the attribution of the intended goal to an agency separate from the perceiver—'agentive understanding'. We argue that agentive understanding is not necessary for the emotional contagion response, and separately, that agentive understanding is not essential to the nature of music.

Agentive understanding is considered to be the highest level of interpretation of others' actions. It is present where goals are expressed as intentional relations between agents and the world (Pacherie and Dokic 2006). An agent–world intentional relation, for instance, could potentially be expressed through more than one kind of motor intentionality. Agentive understanding of another's actions is the recognition that an observed motor intention subserves an intentional relation to the world that could have been realized through a different motor intention (Pacherie and Dokic 2006: 106–7):

> Indeed, the way MNs [mirror neurons] encode actions is by representing the goal in terms of the motoric means used to achieve it. Thus, at this level [i.e. motor intentionality] goals and means cannot be represented separately. (107)

Agentive understanding entails intersubjectivity—the perceiver is aware not only of motor intentions but of the agency, separate from the perceiver's own, which chooses them. From the perspective of our argument, agentive understanding clearly belongs to the reflective level of consciousness, and should not be confused with the (pre-reflective) perception of gesture. A perceiver's sense of another's motor intentionality and their agentive understanding of another relate, respectively, to a grasp of the immediate motor goals of a perceived action and to an understanding of the world goals which the agent's motor action subserves. These notions are best explained by contrasting 'collective action' with 'joint action'.

Consider the following example of collective action from Martell (2009: 29): *The audience exits the theatre.* Here, actions are distributive since each audience member performs an action of the same type. Individual audience members leaving a theatre need not be aware of others' intentions as separate from their own, and interaction with other people in this situation will be largely intentionally blind. By contrast, Martell's example of joint action is: *The soldiers surround the building* (2009: 30). In this example, each individual soldier must be aware both of the joint intention (to surround the building), and of the relationship between their actions and the actions of the other soldiers. Thus, they have agentive understanding of the other soldiers' actions, for example that two soldiers are performing complementary motor actions by going in different directions in order to achieve a 'world goal' that cannot be expressed or achieved by a single motor goal. The example also makes it clear that agentive understanding rests on a grasp of others' motor intentionality: unless one soldier grasps that another soldier walking in a particular direction intends to take up a tactical position in relation to the building (a motor goal), the first soldier cannot grasp that the motor goal will serve the world goal. In the terms used in this chapter, motor intentionality is perceived at a pre-reflective level, while the reasoning associated with agentive understanding indicates the reflective level of consciousness.

In some respects, the notion of agentive understanding questions the notion of emotional contagion as empathic resonance experienced at the bodily, pre-reflective level. Specifically, agentive understanding of another's motor expression of emotion (their emotion-related facial or vocal gestures) would require explicit representation of the emotion, against which Carr *et al.* (2003) and Davies (forthcoming), among others, have argued. Agentive understanding as described here is intersubjective: it entails the recognition of an agency separate from the perceiver's.

Conclusions

In this chapter, we have argued for co-subjectivity as characteristic of music listening. There are three main ways in which co-subjectivity is promoted among music listeners and between listeners and performers. First, entrainment processes ensure that both auditory perception in general, and the motor resonances to that auditory information, are temporally coordinated between individuals. Second, music is heard as a series of motor gestures that can trigger a substrate of emotional responses that is innate and universal: at the level of this mechanism, the emotional response of each listener to a particular gesture is similar. These emotional responses to gesture depend on subpersonal processes, including motor responses which may involve the MNS, and which provide their outputs directly to pre-reflective consciousness. They do not require reflective consciousness.

Third, we have argued that intersubjectivity depends on a reflective sense of one's own agency as distinct from others'. Agentive understanding involves reflective consciousness and occurs at a higher level than emotional contagion, which is experienced at the pre-reflective level of consciousness. The empathy generated by emotional contagion via music gestures thus does not necessarily develop to a sense of intersubjectivity—instead listeners and performers can enjoy an experience of co-subjectivity during a musical experience. Put another way, the aesthetic emotions of music do not require a real-world object. Agentive understanding depends not just on the perceiver's mirroring of motor intentions, but on a reflective grasp of the reasons for those intentions in terms of the agent's relation to the world. Without a real-world object, musical emotions do not necessarily generate agentive understanding. Co-subjectivity and communion (at the pre-reflective level of consciousness), rather than intersubjectivity and communication (at the reflective level), remain. Whether or not this type of shared experience is unique to music is a separate question, but it is difficult to think of another human activity that occurs with such temporal synchrony across a group, in such an embodied way, and across so many different kinds of human ritual.

An argument might be made that communion in the intimately shared, embodied experience of music can ultimately support a means of musical communication. The possibility of different mechanisms of emotion causation operating independently and at different levels of consciousness means that a sense of co-subjectivity at the pre-reflective level of consciousness might exist as a substrate to a narrative level of communication at the reflective level of consciousness. The precise mechanisms by which this could occur have not been explored here, although one might look to mother–infant narratives or to the communication of emotional states as possibilities (e.g. Juslin and Vastfjall 2008; Molnar-Szakacs and Overy 2006; Trevarthen and Malloch 2009). However, we argue that what remains essential to music is the shared experience of an embodied present, at the co-subjective, pre-reflective level of consciousness.

References

Amunts, K., Schlaug, G., Jäncke, L., Steinmetz, H., Schleicher, A., Dabringhaus, A., and Zilles, K. (1997). Motor cortex and hand motor skills: structural compliance in the human brain. *Human Brain Mapping*, **5**, 206–15.

Bangert, M. and Schlaug, G. (2006). Form follows function. Specialization within the specialized. *European Journal of Neuroscience*, **24**, 1832–4.

Bangert, M., Peschel, T., Schlaug, G., Rotte, M., Drescher, D., Hinrichs, H., Heinze, H.J., and Altenmuller, E. (2006). Shared networks for auditory and motor processing in professional pianists: evidence from fMRI conjunction. *Neuroimage*, **30**, 917–26.

Bengtsson, S.L., Ullén, F., Ehrsson, H.H., Hashimoto, T., Kito, T., Naito, E., Forssberg, H., and Sadato, N. (2009). Listening to rhythms activates motor and premotor cortices. *Cortex*, **45**, 62–71.

Bharucha, J.J., Curtis, M., and Paroo, K. (2006). Varieties of musical experience. *Cognition*, **100**, 131–72.

Brown, S. and Martinez, M.J. (2007). Activation of premotor vocal areas during musical discrimination. *Brain and Cognition*, **63**, 59–69.

Calvo-Merino, B., Glaser, D.E., Grèzes, J., Passingham, R.E., and Haggard, P. (2005). Action observation and acquired motor skills: an fMRI study with expert dancers. *Cerebral Cortex*, **15**, 1243–9.

Carr, L., Iacoboni, M., Dubeau, M-C., Mazziotta, J.C., and Lenzi, G.L. (2003). Neural mechanisms of empathy in humans: a relay from neural systems for imitation to limbic areas. *Proceedings of the National Academy of Sciences*, **100**, 5497–502.

Chapin, H., Jantzen, K.J., Kelso, J.A.S., Steinberg, F., and Large, E.W. (2010). Dynamic emotional and neural responses to music depend on performance expression and listener experience. *PLoS ONE*, **5**(12). Available at: www.plosone.org/article/info:doi/10.1371/journal.pone.0013812 (accessed 13 May 2011).

Clayton, M., Sager, R., and Will, U. (2004). In time with the music: the concept of entrainment and its significance for ethnomusicology. *ESEM CounterPoint*, **1**, 1–45.

Coker, W. (1972). *Music and Meaning: A Theoretical Introduction to Musical Aesthetics* (New York, NY: Collier-Macmillan).

Cumming, N. (2000). *The Sonic Self* (Bloomington, IN: Indiana University Press).

Dalla Bella S., Kraus, N., Overy, K., Pantev, C., Snyder, J.S., Tervaniemi, M., Tillman, B., and Schlaug, G. (eds.) (2009). *The Neurosciences and Music III: Disorders and Plasticity*. Annals of the New York Academy of Sciences, vol. 1169 (New York, NY: New York Academy of Sciences).

Davies, S. (forthcoming). Infectious music: music-listener emotional contagion, in P. Goldie and A. Coplan (eds.), *Empathy: Philosophical and Psychological Perspectives* (Oxford: Oxford University Press).

Decety, J. and Chaminade, T. (2003). When the self represents the other: a new cognitive neuroscience view on psychological identification. *Consciousness and Cognition*, **12**, 577–96.

DeNora, T. (2000). *Music in Everyday Life* (Cambridge: Cambridge University Press).

Fujioka, T., Ross, B., Kakigi, R., Pantev, C., and Trainor, L. (2006). One year of musical training affects development of auditory cortical-evoked fields in young children. *Brain*, **129**, 2593–608.

Gallagher, S. (2001). The practice of mind: theory, simulation, or primary interaction? *Journal of Consciousness Studies*, **8**, 83–108.

Gallese, V. (2001). The 'shared manifold' hypothesis: from mirror neurons to empathy. *Journal of Consciousness Studies*, **8**, 33–50.

Grahn, M. and Brett. A. (2007). Rhythm and beat perception in motor areas of the brain. *Journal of Cognitive Neuroscience*, **19**, 1–14.

Griffiths, T.D. (2002). Central auditory processing disorders. *Current Opinion in Neurology*, **15**, 31–3.

Haslinger, B., Erhard, P., Altenmuller, E., Schroeder, U., Boecker, H., and Ceballos-Baumann, A.O. (2005). Transmodal sensorimotor networks during action observation in professional pianists. *Journal of Cognitive Neuroscience*, **17**, 282–93.

Hommel, B., Müsseler, J., Aschersleben, G., and Prinz, W. (2001). The Theory of Event Coding (TEC): a framework for perception and action planning. *Behavioral and Brain Sciences*, **24**, 849–937.

Iacoboni, M., Molnar-Szakacs, I., Gallese, V., Buccino, G., Mazziotta, J.C., and Rizzolati, G. (2005). Grasping the intentions of others with one's own mirror neuron system. *PLoS Biology*, **3**, 1–7.

Jones, M.R. and Boltz, M. (1989). Dynamic attending and responses to time. *Psychological Review*, **96**, 459–91.

Juslin, P.N. (2001). Communicating emotion in music performance: a review and a theoretical framework, in P.N. Juslin and J. Sloboda (eds.), *Music and Emotion: Theory and Research*, 309–37 (Oxford: Oxford University Press).

Juslin, P.N. and Västfjäll, D. (2008). Emotional responses to music: the need to consider underlying mechanisms. *Behavioral and Brain Sciences*, **5**, 559–75.

Knoblich, G. and Sebanz, N. (2008). Evolving intentions for social interaction: from entrainment to joint action. *Philosophical Transactions of the Royal Society*, **363**, 2021–31.

Koelsch, S., Fritz, T., Cramon, D.Y., Muller, K., and Friederici, A.D. (2006). Investigating emotion with music: an fMRI study. *Human Brain Mapping*, **27**, 239–50.

Lahav, A., Boulanger, A., Schlaug, G., and Saltzman, E. (2005). The power of listening: auditory-motor interactions in musical training. *Annals of the New York Academy of Sciences*, **1060**, 189–94.

Large, E.W., Fink, P., and Kelso, J.A.S. (2002). Tracking simple and complex sequences. *Psychological Research*, **66**, 3–17.

Legrand, D. (2007a). Pre-reflective self-consciousness: on being bodily in the world. *Janus Head*, **9**, 493–519.

Legrand, D. (2007b). Subjectivity and the body: introducing basic forms of self-consciousness. *Consciousness and Cognition*, **16**, 577–82.

Lidov, D. (1987). Mind and body in music. *Semiotica*, **66**, 69–97.

Magee, W.L. (2005). Music therapy with patients in low awareness states: approaches to assessment and treatment in multidisciplinary care. *Neuropsychological Rehabilitation*, **15**, 522–36.

Magee, W.L. (2007). Music as a diagnostic tool in low awareness states: considering limbic responses. *Brain Injury*, **21**, 593–9.

Martell, T. (2009). Hobbes on the simulation of collective agency. *Minerva—An Internet Journal of Philosophy*, **13**, 28–52.

Molnar-Szakacs, I. and Overy, K. (2006). Music and mirror neurons: from motion to 'e'motion. *Social Cognitive and Affective Neuroscience*, **1**, 235–41.

Molnar-Szakacs, I., Wu, A.D., Robles, F.J., and Iacoboni, M. (2007). Do you see what I mean? corticospinal excitability during observation of culture-specific gestures *PLoS ONE*, **2**, e626.

Overy K. and Molnar-Szakacs I. (2009). Being together in time: musical experience and the mirror neuron system. *Music Perception*, **26**, 489–504.

Pacherie, E. and Dokic, J. (2006). From mirror neurons to joint actions. *Cognitive Systems Research*, **7**, 101–12.

Parncutt, R. (1994). A perceptual model of pulse salience and metrical accent in musical rhythms. *Music Perception*, **11**, 409–64.

Repp, B.H. (2006). Rate limits of sensorimotor synchronization. *Advances in Cognitive Psychology*, **2**, 163–81.

Riganello, F., Candelieri, A., Quintieri, M., Conforti, D. and Dolce, G. (2010). Heart rate variability: an index of brain processing in vegetative state? An artificial intelligence, data mining study. *Clinical Neurophysiology*, **121**, 2024–34.

Rizzolati, G. and Craighero, L. (2004). The mirror-neuron system. *Annual Review of Neuroscience*, **27**, 169–92.

Scherer, K.R. (2004) Which emotions can be induced by music? What are the underlying: mechanisms? And how can we measure them? *Journal of New Music Research*, **33**, 239–51.

Schlaug, G., Jancke, L., Huang, Y., and Steinmetz, H. (1995). In vivo evidence of structural brain asymmetry in musicians. *Science*, **267**, 699–701.

Sluming, V., Barrick, T., Howard, M., Cezayirli, E., Mayes, A., and Roberts, N. (2002). Voxel-based morphometry reveals increased gray matter density in Broca's area in male symphony orchestra musicians. *NeuroImage*, **17**, 1613–22.

Thaut, M. H., Stephan, K. M., Wunderlich, G., Schicks, W., Tellmann, L., Herzog, H., McIntosh, G.C., Seitz, R.J., and Hömberg, V. (2009). Distinct cortico-cerebellar activations in rhythmic auditory motor synchronisation. *Cortex*, **45**, 44–53.

Trainor, L.J., Gao, X., Lei, J., Lehtovarara, K., and Harris, L.R. (2009). The primal role of the vestivular system in determining musical rhythm. *Cortex*, **45**, 35–43.

Trevarhen, C. and Malloch S. (eds.) (2009). *Communicative Musicality* (Oxford: Oxford University Press).

Wilson, M. and Knoblich, G. (2005). The case for motor involvement in perceiving conspecifics. *Psychological Bulletin*, **131**, 460–73.

Wong, P.C.M., Skoe, E., Russo, N.M., Dees, T., and Kraus, N. (2007). Musical experience shapes human brainstem encoding of linguistic pitch patterns. *Nature Neuroscience*, **10**, 420–22.

Zahavi, D. (2006). Two takes on a one-level account of consciousness. *Psyche*, **12**, 1–9.

Chapter 15

Drugs, altered states, and musical consciousness: reframing time and space

Jörg Fachner

Introduction

Discussing the effects of drugs on music and consciousness is a difficult enterprise: on the one hand, drugs have specific effects on physiology; but on the other, the phenomena experienced and reported in drug-induced altered states of consciousness (dASC) cannot simply be reduced to the perceptual consequences of those physiological effects. This was already recognized by Charles Baudelaire in his reflections on his own drug experiences at the Parisian 'Club de Hashishin':

> The ear perceives almost inaudible sounds amidst great turmoil. This is where hallucinations start. External objects start to assume a strange look. Then the ambiguities follow, the misunderstandings and alteration of ideas. Sounds dress up in colours, and colours contain music. Some will tell me that this is quite natural and that every poetic brain easily conceives such correspondences in a healthy and normal state. But I have already pointed out to the reader that a hashish trip does not involve anything really supernatural, although the correspondences are unusually vivid. (Baudelaire 1988: 43; author's translation)

This chapter discusses the psychedelic (from the Greek 'psyche'—mind, and 'delos'— to make manifest, or reveal) effects of drugs (mainly cannabis) on the perception and performance of music, and in particular how such drugs influence time perception in the process of performance. I will focus both on scientific studies and on anecdotal evidence provided by musicians and observers of musicians using drugs. Most of the material relates to developments in American jazz of the 1940s, and to the 1960s psychedelic counterculture of the American West Coast, as particular illustrations of how musical consciousness may change in the process of making or listening to music under the influence of drugs. The literature on music and altered states of consciousness contains very few studies that directly focus on music perception or production in dASC (for a review see Fachner 2006b): these include a transcription of and reflection on songs experienced in an Ayahuasca ritual (Katz and De Rios 1971), and studies of LSD-enhanced imagery accompanying music listening in psychotherapy (Bonny 1980), of cannabis and its influence on music perception and electroencephalography (EEG) (Fachner 2001; Hess 1973), of polyrhythms as part of an Iboga ceremony (Maas and Strubelt 2006), and of the connection between lyrics and drug experiences

(Markert 2001)—but there are essentially no musicological studies of the topic. Nevertheless, there is a body of work on sensory, temporal, and motor processing, as well as studies of brain functions and neuropharmacology, which can be used to attempt an explanation of the phenomena described.

Consciousness and drug action in an aesthetic context

Drugs act on certain physiological processes mostly by mimicking[1] and modulating the activity of various endogenous neurotransmitters on receptor systems that are spread with various degrees of density and function over the central and peripheral nervous systems (Julien *et al.* 2008). Drugs therefore emphasize, amplify, or weaken certain brain functions that—even in extreme form—are also possible without drugs. For example, hallucinations reported under the influence of LSD (acting primarily on serotonergic transmitter functions) can be observed after sleep deprivation, in lucid dreams, or in hyper-aroused states (Hobson 2001).

While medical researchers and pharmacologists stress the more or less objective somatic action of drugs on our senses and central nervous system (CNS) functions, in the context of cultural studies on drug use these approaches have been criticized as being too deterministic and narrow (Manning 2007). When considering drug use within a symbolic frame of reference, as a cultural practice, as an identity template, or as a means for creative inspiration, pharmacological effects are not the only significant factor, since they may be radically affected by what people do, think, experience, and expect. In these circumstances the drug effects have been domesticated—as Eichel and Troiden (1978) have described for marihuana (cannabis)—for particular social or personal intentions: to party, to be cool, hip, bad, far out or inspired, to be different from others, and so on. It is not that the physiological effects are irrelevant, but rather that they may interact significantly with the social and aesthetic contexts.

A classic example is Andrew Weil's (1998) concept of 'inverse tolerance'—the observation that the effects of marihuana can be controlled or even turned off at will by an experienced user. In the early 1970s, this led to polemical debates between those who, from an anthropological perspective, accepted that an experienced user (e.g. a shaman) was able to control drug action for certain purposes; and those who, from a more orthodox natural-science perspective, were not convinced that pharmacological substances and their action profiles could be controlled at will (for a review, see Fachner 2001). Katz and De Rios (1971) explained the function of the 'Icarus' songs, sung and whistled in the Peruvian Ayahuasca ceremonies (see also Chapter 16, this volume), as being to help the shaman and also their clients to control the drug action. They compared music's function to a 'jungle gym', giving a structure to control dASC, and providing 'a series of paths and banisters to help them negotiate their way' (De Rios and Janiger 2003: 161).

A specific example of such contrasting attitudes to notionally the same psychological process relates to the functioning of state-specific memory in laboratory and aesthetic contexts.[2] Neuropsychological assessment procedures may seem to indicate that cannabis alters the cognitive functioning of memory, either temporarily or, as Solowij (1998) has shown, for heavy users as a longer-term residual effect. However there are few experimental or neuroscientific data relating to evoked altered states of consciousness (ASC) when drugs are used in creative, recreational, and aesthetic contexts. In the circumstances of creative and recreational drug use, such as rock music performance and perception (Boyd and George-Warren 1992; De Rios and Janiger 2003; Shapiro 1989; Whiteley 1992), there may be very different considerations by comparison with the criteria of perception, attention, and memory in standard neuropsychological testing (Fachner 2006a; Weil 1998). If cognition is a state-specific process resulting in memory traces that are triggered by associated state-specific cues, then the state of a dASC participant in a neuropsychological test situation is very different from a dASC participant who is musicking or painting, for example. It is possible that the 'negative' results found in neuropsychological test batteries may correspond to more 'positive' abilities in creative circumstances. For example, so-called memory dysfunctions under the influence of cannabis may have unforeseen positive consequences (enforced selectivity, lack of distraction) for a skilled improviser attempting to realize and control a potentially overwhelming rush of creative ideas. This selection and control may only be possible when the passage of time is subjectively perceived as dilated, the so-called 'memory impairments' acting as a compensating factor for the limited capacities of working memory (Dietrich 2003). 'If you smoke a joint, you're much clearer, you realize what your thoughts are, but you got to write it down really quickly before it all goes through your head,' said the singer-songwriter Sinéad O'Connor (in Boyd and George-Warren 1992: 204).

Another example of the apparently inverse relationship between neuropsychological functioning and the creative process is represented by the concept of hypofrontality (reduced frontal brain activity) as proposed by Dietrich (2003). The frontal and pre-central lobes of the brain constitute the explicit system, the 'active part' that organizes top-down processing and structures motor activity and output; while the posterior lobes (post-central, temporal, parietal, and occipital) are the 'receiving parts'—the implicit system of the brain. They are primarily concerned with sensory input, and with processing bottom-up information in the implicit system. The pre-frontal cortex, the highest integrating component in a hierarchy of cognitive functions, is deregulated in ASC (Dietrich 2003), ceasing to function in a 'normal' way. This is the hypofrontal state, which may be compared to the state of flow, in which an effortless information processing seems to take place. It enables the temporary suppression of the analytical and meta-conscious capacities of the explicit system, while being relaxed and absorbed in the flood of sensory input, allowing things to be seen from a different perspective, or to arrive at new creative solutions to problems (Dietrich 2004).

However while Dietrich discusses it as a transient state making ASC possible for healthy subjects, in psychiatry, hypofrontality is regarded as a risk marker for schizophrenia (Wuebben and Winterer 2001) or substance abuse (Struve *et al.* 1999). The difference here is the context: the frequency and the setting in which intended and voluntarily evoked ASCs are experienced. Just as Aldridge (2004) has called for research on aesthetic processes that documents and understands art therapy in the actual context of doing therapy, so also there is a need for research on drug-induced state-specific cognition, perception, and performance that is carried out in the appropriate aesthetic context (Fachner 2006a).

Culture-based drug research, musical metaphors, and experience

Manning's (2007) investigation of drug use in popular culture focuses on the role of the media and pop music in the normalization of drug use. His central thesis can be stated concisely: drug use has a history in Western civilization, has developed as a cultural practice in that context, and utilizes contextualized symbolic frames of reference that identify, represent, and rationalize drug use and its functionality within culture. In his classic sociological deviance study of marihuana use among jazz musicians, Becker (1963) demonstrated that recognizing and enjoying the effects of marihuana has to be learned. This demonstration is consistent with intercultural comparisons of drug use and the differing descriptions of drug effects with the same pharmacological origin (Blätter 1990): drugs can produce many different culture-related effects. Becker stressed the culturally contextual determination of human behaviour, and from a sociological stance he questioned the validity of trying to understand 'pharmacologically determined behaviour': experience and behaviour are matters of socially constructed definitions set by groups that have the power to define what is to be perceived in a dASC. If the frame of reference is set by a peer group of musicians, they may focus on the time dilation effects of cannabis (Lieving et al. 2006; Mathew et al. 1998; Tart 1971) as facilitating improvisation and rhythmic variation, while for a group of medics the possible dangers of an accelerated heart rate may be the focus of attention.

Nonetheless, drugs do undoubtedly have a certain action profile on the body, which is what makes some aspects of the drugs useable for medical purposes. Just as heroin or even cannabis has an effect on pain reduction, there are generalizable action profiles for specific drugs and dosages, with the consequence that the cultural effects of drugs share common experience and cognition profiles that result from their drug-induced origins. The metaphors used in popular music magazines demonstrate an experience-related body of knowledge among journalists of stereotyped drug effects (possibly reinforced by their own experiences); such metaphors are used to describe the sound design, musical materials, and staging of the bands and their music. But to what experience is Keith Richards referring when he talks of 'playing his Junkie-Riffs'? What is typical 'stoner-music'? Or what is 'the lyserg-feeling' in the music of Pink Floyd, as described by Sheila Whiteley (1997)?[3] Such questions point to a fundamental problem for any culture-based drug research: how can drug effects be intersubjectively graspable, if they are not mediated via a shared symbolic frame of reference that presupposes an internal perspective on, and an experience of, the experience discussed? As Jimi Hendrix asked with his first album title in 1967: 'Are you experienced?'

Drugs, set, and setting

There is a well-established body of literature demonstrating that the combination of dose and time course of drug action (see Mathew et al. 2002), set (the current psychological and physiological condition of the drug taker), and setting (the social and physical environment) has an influence on what is recognized and processed during the psychedelic drug experience (Rätsch 2005; Weil 1998; Zinberg 1984). Howard Becker's findings on 'learning to perceive the effects of cannabis', discussed above, suggest that the 'habitus of listening' to music within drug cultures will influence the content of what is perceived. Judith Becker makes use of Bourdieu's (1977) term 'habitus' for the study of music and emotion, describing habitus as an 'embodied pattern of action and reaction' (J. Becker 2010: 130) that may influence the way one perceives music; such patterns are based on a set of personal and social dispositions, and on identification with belief systems of chosen peer groups.[4]

In a similar manner, Shapiro (1989) proposes that every popular music style is inevitably the expression of a certain lifestyle, one component of which are the patterns and preferences of drug use by the artists and by members of the scene around them. He describes how musicians associate the effects of a variety of drugs (amphetamines, heroin, cocaine, alcohol, etc.) with their habitus to produce stylistically differentiated music. In *Really the Blues* Mezzrow (1946) describes how his peer group felt about the difference between musicians who did, and didn't, use alcohol:

> We were on another plane in another sphere compared to the musicians who were bottle babies, always hitting the jug and then coming up brawling after they got loaded. We liked things to be easy and relaxed, mellow and mild, not loud or loutish, and the scowling chin-out tension of the lushbands with their false courage didn't appeal to us. Besides, the lushies didn't even play good music—their tones became hard and evil, not natural, soft and soulful—and anything that messed up the music instead of sending it on its way was out with us. We members of the viper school were for making music that was real foxy, all lit up with inspiration and her mammy. The juice guzzlers went sour fast on their instruments, then turned grimy because it preyed on their minds. (94)

From a socio-pharmacological view, the preference of a subculture for a certain drug has always been to aim for certain physiological conditions in order to experience ordinary or extraordinary events and moods more intensively and from a different perspective (Lyttle and Montagne 1992). In short, drug effects are necessarily situated, and involve complex interactions between their pharmacological components and their psychological and physiological setting within a specific aesthetic context that frames the production, perception, and cognition of music.

Coding experience into sound

In answer to the question of what inspired The Beatles' music at the time of their album *Sgt. Pepper's Lonely Hearts Club Band*, Paul McCartney said:

> Experience with drugs, mostly. But remember that in 1967 our drug habits followed a long-established tradition among musicians. We knew about Louis Armstrong, Duke Ellington, and Count Basie that they had always taken drugs. Now it was time for our musical scene to make the experience. Drugs found their way into everything we did. They coloured our perspective of things. I believe we realized that there were fewer limitations than we had expected. And we understood that we were able to break through barriers. (Davis and Pieper 1993: 7; author's translation)

Curry (1968) interpreted the effects of cannabis, psychedelic substances, and amphetamines on music perception as a change in cognitive style, in the sense of a hyper-focused perception of sound and an inner trip into a virtual space. 'Rather than the experience, the musician spends more time concentrating on the structure and logic of the number, which culminates in a type of hyperfocusing of attention' (240)—by manipulating aspects of the figure–ground relationships. 'Some musicians refer to it as "being stoned" or "locked in" on the music, or the beat, or the lyrics, and will swear that they are helped to stay together' (240). This focus on the manipulation of the virtual space of a recording seems to be a central component of drug-influenced musical experiences, and is therefore significantly bound up with changes in recording technology.

With *Sgt. Pepper's*, The Beatles (1967) produced a type of music in which innovations in recording techniques served to realize multi-layered sound spaces within song structures. This album was a milestone in recording techniques, and many of its sound ideas were developed to become part of the subsequent standard recording techniques. Böhm (1999) argues that the degree of distortion for different sound elements is related to textual and compositional considerations in the music. The new four-track techniques used for the *Sgt. Pepper's* recordings allowed new possibilities for the manipulation of the sonic space of the recording. Artificial spaces were realized using reverb and echo units, modulation effects such phasing, flanging, or chorus, together with sounds played backwards, filtered, or changed in speed that were then mixed with the original studio recordings (Martin and Pearson 1995). Examples are the songs 'A day in the life', 'Good morning good morning', or 'Lucy in the sky with diamonds' (The Beatles 1967), all of which transform sound using studio equipment to 'produce a music that a person influenced by psychedelic drugs prefers to hear' (Böhm 1999: 22; author's translation).

Discussing Pink Floyd's 'Careful with that axe, Eugene', Cotner (2002) analyses the use of echo, wide stereo panning across left and right channels, and the localization of sounds in the stereo space, as, for example, the treatment of the voice with echo, reverb, and stereo panning. Regarding a section taken from near the start of the track, Cotner argues that an echo-delay of about 250–300 ms on the vocal entry at 0:23 produces the effect of a 'ghost image' that 'pulls away from its sustained source at a pulse narrowly ahead of the eighth note' connoting a 'divergent reality: perhaps madness, or the mystical potential of LSD-induced aural/visual hallucinations' (74). Discussing textural properties, he claims that properties of the sound-staging of the echo-treated voice in the stereo-mix 'alter one's perception of phrase grouping in relation to meter' such that the spaces or rests between notes vanish in the overall musical texture, with the consequence that the stereo image 'forms a multidimensional conceptual space within which musical ideas enlarge and diminish' (88). As with other recordings considered by Cotner, the piece displays a 'counter-cultural tendency, exploiting formal open-endedness, and a kind of expanding-present consciousness associated with LSD experimentation' (87).

The example illustrates how the desire to trigger a psychedelic experience for the listener by means of a carefully constructed sound architecture might require insider knowledge of drug-induced effects on music perception; it also illustrates how the experience might be transformed into the composition of appropriate sound structures. Sheila Whiteley (1992) analyses music by Pink Floyd, The Beatles, and other groups of the 1960s and 1970s to develop the concept of a 'psychedelic coding' that describes symbolic and semiotic codings of elements of 'psychedelic culture' in compositional techniques. She discusses the metaphorical links between cultural semantics and drug effects in music, and the relationships between the socio-cultural environments of the groups analysed, and their specific and distinctive sound (Whiteley 1997).

The 'sputnik shock' in the 1950s triggered a search for means to promote creativity and talent in the West, especially in the USA (Barber-Kersovan 1991). Psychedelic drugs were discussed as means of enhancing creativity and intelligence, and hallucino-genic drug action was taken as a model for how the brain could switch to a higher level, processing vast amounts of complex information, and therefore achieving miraculous increases in intelligence (De Rios and Janiger 2003; Fachner 2007; Lee and Shalin 1992). The idea that there are states of heightened or expanded consciousness, in which external and internal sensory information is processed differently by the brain received considerable attention during the early 1960s (Nixon 1999). Psychedelic music referred to this 'expansion of consciousness', and the effect and experience of psychedelic drugs on time perception seemed to be a key to the realization of altered sounds.

Music, altered temporality, and neuro-pharmacological concomitance

That cannabis has an effect on music perception and production was first discussed when jazz stepped on the stage of contemporary music in the 1920s (Leonard 1962; Musto 1999; Sloman 1998). Many musicians and listeners have commented on the role of cannabis in musical experience, and in the popular press stories abound relating to drug use and popular music culture (Manning 2007). Drug-induced altered temporality is an important feature that can be used creatively for musical activities like improvising but can also hinder the control of strictly organized playing, for example from notation and in large ensembles (Behrendt 1956; Fachner 2000).

Piel (1943) reported in *Life* magazine that a swing musician reached new heights of virtuosity under the influence of cannabis (cited in Aldrich 1944: 431), while the phy-sician Walton denied improvement in performance, believing deterioration to be more probable, but nonetheless confirming 'an increasing sensitivity to sound and a keener appreciation of rhythm and timing' (431)—though only in the early stages of marihuana consumption. '[I]t [cannabis] lengthens the sense of time, and therefore they [jazz musicians] could get more grace beats into their music than they could if the simply followed a written copy . . . In other words, if you are a musician you're going to play the thing the way it is printed on a sheet. But if you're using Marihuana, you're going to work in about twice as much music in-between the first note and the second note. That's what made jazz musicians. The idea that they could jazz things up, lighten them up . . .' said James Munch, an agent of the US Drug Enforcement Agency in the 1940s (Sloman 1998: 146/7).

Reduced inhibitions might reveal latent talent or evoke a more intensive emotional performance, but the established opinion was simply that subjective assessment of one's own performance is improved by marihuana, and that individuals taking cannabis simply have more self-confidence (Aldrich 1944). Reduced inhibition certainly may encourage individuals to try things they did not believe themselves capable of, but the blues musician John P. Hammond, for example, complained that marihuana 'played around like hell with time perception' (Shapiro 1989: 39). Howard Becker quotes a musician on his first experience with cannabis: 'We played the first tune for almost two hours—one tune! We got on the stand and played this one tune, we started at nine o'clock. When we got finished I looked at my watch, it's a quarter to eleven. Almost two hours on one tune. And it didn't seem like anything. I mean, you know, it does that to you. It's like you have much more time or something' (H.S. Becker 1966: 74).

The idea that an expanded experience of time might be used creatively for improvisation might hold true for a soloist who can expand and elaborate on his improvisations while the pulse is kept under control by the rhythm section of the band. But there is little or no published research that has investigated the objective truth of claims that such performance enhancements can be perceived by independent observers. Studies comparing pre/post interventions with musicians have, however, been carried out in relation to post-hypnotic suggestion (Mellgren 1979) and neurofeedback (Egner and Gruzelier 2003), and in both cases the intervention (which might be compared with an ASC) increased the positive impact of the performance as rated by independent observers.

Timing

For musical purposes, performance timing is the continuously variable pattern of temporal values that is used to convey various aspects of musical style, structure, and emotion, and the physicality of body–instrument interaction in performance (Clarke 1999). If cannabis changes the inner representation of the passage of time by influencing the neural networks responsible for the cognitive realization of temporal judgements, this must have an effect on realizing timing and expression in music. The research literature on timing reflects the debate on subjective timing effects, particularly when time is estimated after an event has taken place. Pöppel (2000) talks of the 'time paradox'—time periods with a dense event structure are subsequently estimated as prolonged when the events are engaging, even when the physical duration is objectively short. It seems that 'time judgments can distort, recalibrate, reverse, or have a range of resolutions depending on the stimulus and on the state of the viewer' (Eagleman *et al.* 2005: 10370).

Tse has proposed the idea of a simple counter model arguing that the brain 'has access to the approximate constant rate of its own information processing' (in Eagleman *et al.* 2005: 10369). For example, if one bit of information processed is interpreted as one unit of objective time, then, in moments of shifted or increased attention, two or three bits of information would be counted again as one unit of objective time 'creating the illusion that time and motion had slowed down' (ibid.). Our sense of subjective time fluctuates in relation to clock time according to the amount of information we receive per second. Only a specific, individually and situation relevant excerpt of sensory data is accessible to our consciousness (with an upper limit of around 15–20 bits/second), as outlined in an information-based model of the optimization and throttling of sensory input and output during top-down and bottom-up processing of sensory information (Spreng and Keidel 1963).

> Determining what constitutes a bit of information in music is the crux of our problem. Basically, it depends on the individual, how well he knows the given musical style, his ability to codify musical events, and his ability to concentrate during the performance. Ostensibly, a note would be a bit of information. But in an extreme case—e.g., an exceptionally familiar recording—the first bar might be grasped as one gesture, which in turn would identify the entire piece, so it might be listened to in huge chunks (i.e., a minimal number of bits.) At the other extreme, one note might be heard as a composite of onset transients and sine tones with individual envelope shapes. More commonly, a chord, an arpeggio, or even an entire cadential gesture could be heard as one bit of information. Experience and training thus have a direct relation to the amount of 'information' that can be grasped from a musical phrase. (Mountain 1989: 4)

However, the perception of time and music does not only depend on expectation, learning, attention, and memory functions in a dynamic process of chunking units of information. A wide variety of endocrine and neurotransmitter activity changes in ASC interweave with these cognitive processes, enabling altered scaling of auditory events (Globus *et al.* 1978). Studies that offer a physiological explanation are based on drug research, and stress the role of various neurotransmitter processes as, for example serotonergic (Wittmann *et al.* 2007), cannabinoid (Fachner 2009; Mathew *et al.* 2002), dopamine, and cholinergic (Meck 1996; Rammsayer 1999) interactions with altered time perception and (re)production (Shanon 2001). Studies of patient populations and drugs indicate variations in the scaling of musical events due to the deceleration and acceleration of the internal clock, and the internal representation of perceived elements when reproducing or estimating time intervals in the millisecond to second, and the second to minute ranges (Meck 2005).

One part of the brain, the cerebellum is associated with activity in the millisecond range of temporal coordination in motor behaviour, and studies of multiple sclerosis and Tourette syndrome (in both of which disorders of the cerebellum are implicated) have shown that motor behaviour of patients can be improved with cannabis (Iversen 2003; Grotenhermen and Russo 2002; MullerVahl *et al.* 1998). As Mathew has shown (Mathew *et al.* 1998), cannabis increases blood flow in the cerebellum and appears to accelerate the cerebellar clock during self-paced behaviour of normal subjects (O'Leary *et al.* 2003).

Interval timing in the second to minutes range is cognitively processed, and is related to attention and decision making. It is mostly explained with the heuristics of a pacemaker-accumulator model of an internal clock and is task-dependent (as well as state-dependent; see Fachner 2010), corresponding to scalar properties and subjects' expectations during time reproduction tasks. Clock, reference memory, and decision stages can be separated. Clock speed (pacemaker) can be influenced by dopaminergic manipulations, whereas memory processes (reference) can be influenced by cholinergic manipulations. Meck illustrates this by a given oscillation of baseline clock-speed at 100 pulses, which are learned to have a chronological duration of 20 seconds. If clock-speed is accelerated by pharmacological agents, the 100 pulses will be accumulated 'earlier in physical time than during the baseline training' (Meck 1996: 236) while decrease of clock-speed will be accumulated later than physical time. Summarized, this means that a faster clock-speed makes events appear to last shorter while a slower clock-speed makes events appear to last longer.

But this process can be influenced by learning experience and the corresponding reference memory. Reference memory may be state-specifically relearned to represent the duration of 20 seconds as a clock-speed of 75 pulses. Cannabis-induced changes of a temporal experience may be explained as a 'modification of the memory-storage speed', but cannabis seems to act on both systems (memory and clock-speed) in the basal ganglia and the frontal cortex, with the cannabinoid receptor system interacting with the dopamine and cholinergic system, leading to an 'increased clock-speed with decreased memory-storage speed' (Meck 1996: 238). Lieving *et al.* (2006) discuss Meck's elaborations and explain the role of cannabis in timing as an acceleration of clock-speed mediated via an increase in the activity of dopaminergic neurons, while the anticholinergic action of cannabis expands the duration of a remembered event. 'The more acetylcholine is present, the shorter the remembered duration of events' (Lieving *et al.* 2006: 182). A higher clock-rate will improve temporal resolution and subjective estimates of duration will expand. In retrospect it may seem that events were passing much faster than it seemed at the time, as described above by the musician who was surprised to find that a piece of music had lasted two hours.

A changed metric frame of reference

If time perception is changed, the perception of musical elements will change. If time is perceived as prolonged in an improvisation, more musical information might be perceived or focused upon in a changed metric frame of reference (Fachner 2000). The musical elements may occur more distinctly while the space between the elements widens, as Whiteley (1992) describes in her analyses of psychedelic rock. However, the time dilation effect seems to vary across drugs. Reports of LSD experiences (Dawson 2001; De Rios and Janiger 2003), for instance, commonly mention a tremendously expanded 'now' and very detailed and focused perception processes. In one case, a musician listening to a 25-minute piece was surprised by his increased and maintained attention span by comparison with other experiences (De Rios and Janiger 2003: 105–7). An analogy for these kinds of phenomena would be the ability to 'look' at music through a magnifying glass, or to hear it, without a change of tempo, with what might be called a 'time lens'. This is what audio editing software can do, allowing the user to change the scaling of the timeline and its units so as to zoom in and out of a piece of music graphically for the purposes of editing. 'I don't know if I can attribute any effects from it [cannabis] towards the music, unless you want to say it does create a larger vision, and if that's the case, then it would apply to your instrument because the more you see, the more you can do,' states the drummer Robin Horn (Boyd and George-Warren 1992: 205).

A heuristic concept that may help to illustrate what is happening in moments where time and space seems to be expanded is the model of a temporarily extended metric frame of reference. This concept can be illustrated by analogy with an elastic metre displaying normal metric units in a non-stretched mode, and providing expanded metric units when stretched. The analogy is used by Globus *et al.* (1978) in an experiment on loudness perception, reproduction, and rescaling under the influence of cannabis, which demonstrated that subjects under the influence of cannabis showed significant changes in the representation and reproduction of a previously learned criterion loudness of 87 dB. The experiment also demonstrated a state-specific learning effect: one of the three groups of subjects learned to reproduce the criterion loudness under the influence of cannabis. These 'cannabis learners' were stable in their reproduction of the criterion in the reproduction phase of the experiment. The other two groups received either a placebo and then a defined cannabis dose during the reproduction phase, or vice versa. These two groups reproduced a significantly higher loudness level only when receiving cannabis, not with placebo. Globus's experiment reflects the importance of the relationship between the state of consciousness at the time of establishing the reference memory (i.e. the learning phase) and at the time of the experimental task when estimating, reproducing, or producing time intervals (Buhusi and Meck 2005).

Hypofrontality and focused sensory perception

Having discussed the interdependencies of timing, attention, memory, and neuro-transmitter functions in drug-induced altered temporality, the question is now how these elements are integrated in dASC. Dietrich (2003, 2004) describes the functions of memory and hypofrontality in ASC and proposes that hypofrontality is connected to a flooding of information in the dorso-lateral pre-frontal cortex (DLPFC), primarily concerned with working memory. This results in a 'buffer overload' of working memory and, accordingly, a state of consciousness that is primarily concerned with reception and the processing of sensory information; there is less activity in the frontal and more activity in the posterior parts of the brain, namely in the temporal, occipital, and parietal areas. In hypofrontal states, the bottom-up perceptual processing of the brain dominates the limited capacity of the working memory system located in the DLPFC, such that this area—involving working memory, temporal integration, and sustained and directed attention (Dietrich, 2004)—is functionally modified during ASC:

> If the eagerly sought-after 'expansion of consciousness' means anything, it means hearing, feeling, tasting, and 'seeing' things in a more pronounced way than is ordinarily possible. And the almost fanatic preoccupation with involving all the senses at once constitutes an assault on ego consciousness or everyday awareness, that, to my knowledge, is unequalled in our history . . . (Curry 1968: 241)

Two studies have correlated music listening and electrical brain activity before and after cannabis consumption. EEG[5] studies by Hess (1973) and Fachner (2002) illustrate that the process of listening is temporarily intensified and focused and that individual listening strategies change, as confirmed by subjective reports associated with the EEG measures. Hess (1973) detected frontal and parietal increases of alpha power and a decrease in the frequency in correlation to the contemplation phase induced by cannabis.

Fachner (2002) analysed topographic power spectrum changes in the EEG of partici-pants listening to music with cannabis. Cannabis-induced amplitude decreases are known drug signatures in EEG studies (Struve and Straumanis 1990), but over the pari-etal lobe, which coordinates attention and integrates sensory perception in spatiotempo-ral cognition (Kolb and Whishaw 2009; Sack 2009), electrodes revealed a marked increase in alpha amplitudes while listening to music after cannabis consumption.

It is generally accepted that the amount of mental effort is reflected in the alpha amplitude, with higher amplitudes indicating less brain activity. This is a common finding in EEG research, but in studies of EEG and cognitive performance with gifted individuals, alpha increases correlated with increased cognitive performance com-pared with normal controls when processing arithmetical tasks (Jausovec 1997; for discussion see Fachner 2002). This suggests that cannabis-induced alpha increase in the parietal cortex may reflect a focused attention on music in the altered state, with modified processing of spatiotemporal processes in an altered timeframe. Rubia and Smith reviewed the role of the inferior parietal lobe in time processing and discussed its role in sustained attention to time intervals as 'a necessary basis function for time estimation processes . . . The parietal lobes with their connections to fronto-striatal and fronto-cerebellar circuits are thus strategically well placed to support cognitive time management processes by assisting them with sustained attention to time' (Rubia and Smith 2004: 336). If the focus of attention is altered, time processes and their metric frame of reference may result in forms of auditory information processing that temporarily reveal new insights 'into the space between the notes' (Whiteley 1992), 'creating a larger vision' (Boyd and George-Warren 1992: 205) of the processing music of musical materials. Alexander refers to clinical observations of disturbed time sense in lesions or disruptions of the posterior right parietal cortex (Alexander *et al.* 2005). Clients were unable to estimate the passage of time in a medical interview, objects moved too fast, too slow, or jerkily, a phenomenon that Critchley in 1953 entitled the 'Time-grabbing (Zeitraffer) phenomenon' (in Alexander *et al.* 2005: 307). The rather speculative possibility is that drugs and their neurotransmitter targets temporarily induce such effects when listening to music.

However, in Fachner's (2002) study, changes in theta in the right temporal lobe and in the alpha band for the left occipital lobe were also significant. Occipital areas prima-rily process visual stimuli, but Petsche (1994) observed that EEG changes in occipital areas compared with others while listening to music perhaps reflect spatiotemporal auditory processes. However, cannabis-induced EEG changes in the right temporal lobe suggest alterations in auditory and limbic processing of music.

One important function of the cannabinoid system is that it can inhibit processes of inhibition, thus resulting in activation of normally inhibited processes. Depending on where and when this happens it may increase or decrease the firing rates of neurons during functional neurotransmission. Menon and Levitin (2005) demonstrated a sequence of activation for music perception and emotion. They found that, starting from the auditory centre, the cascade of activation initializes changes in parts of the frontal cortex, and from there proceeds to the mesolimbic reward centres, finally reaching the nucleus accumbens, releasing waves of dopamine. As expected, the cere-bellum and the basal ganglia—dopaminergic regions of the brain involved in motor, and timing processes and the analysis of rhythm and meter in music—became active as well. Proportionally stronger concentrations of cannabinoid receptors occur in frontal areas, the parietal cortex, hippocampus, basal ganglia, limbic regions, and cerebellum (Iversen 2008). We may expect that after consuming cannabis—and depending on dosage, personal set, the music, and the habituated listening setting—there will be an interaction with the cascade of music processing activations described by Menon and Levitin (2005), resulting in changes in sensory and spatiotemporal processing. Changes in the topographic EEG have shown that activity in the alpha range for the parietal lobes, the left occipital lobe, and the right temporal lobe were changed during music listening in dASC, indicating the hypofrontality that was described above. The functional expression of these changes in activity may be a temporarily changed metric context of intensity, acoustics, and rhythm (Fachner 2000, 2002). However, these somewhat limited results should be understood as showing some interesting tendencies that are not (yet) backed up by more rigorous and robust studies.

Closing remarks

At the start of this chapter I referred to Baudelaire and his notion that 'nothing supernatural happens' under the influence of drugs, but that reality simply becomes more vivid, and receives more attention. This sense that dASC listening is a kind of 'clearer' or renewed perspective on 'ordinary' listening is reflected in the fact that for some musicians it is part of their evaluative strategy to listen once again to a mix of a newly recorded track under the influence of cannabis—as confirmed by members of The Beatles and Fleetwood Mac (see Boyd and George-Warren 1992). 'It [cannabis] breaks down preconceptions you have about something: it allows you to hear it fresh. If you've been working on something for a few hours and you smoke a joint, it's like hearing it again for the first time' (Lindsay Buckingham in Boyd and George-Warren 1992: 201). Drugs have the capacity to reframe perspectives on musical materials through an altered temporality and a temporarily more intense stimulation and evocation of physiological functions. These changes take place in the context of personal musical preferences, in a habituated set and setting that significantly influence the listener's focus of attention on the musical time-space. If the information revealed in the time course of some music becomes meaningful for the listener or performer, the brain has various strategies available to it to zoom into particular parts of the music in order to process musical elements more distinctly and in a more focused manner, in a hypofrontal state of enhanced sensory perception. While drug effects may be negatively presented in standard neuropsychological paradigms, they are often experienced as positive and stimulating for listeners and performers in an aesthetic context. Musicians seem to be able to encode their drug-induced altered perceptual experiences into sounds which can in turn be decoded by those sharing the same experiences— though the musical product and its implicit state of consciousness can also be shared with a much wider audience, as Pink Floyd and other so-called psychedelic bands have demonstrated. Much of this field still remains under-researched and speculative, and more systematic experimental research is needed to investigate the claims of listeners and musicians that drugs such as cannabis alter consciousness and enhance music perception and production. For example, the literature on spatiotemporal processing, rhythm, and timing using well-known procedures (production and estimation tasks) might be compared with drug-induced ASC in controlled experiments; and musicians performing music in a pre/post design, using recordings given to blind raters, could be used to investigate the claims about performance made earlier in this chapter. Brain imaging studies to investigate some of my own explorations, with larger number of subjects and more sophisticated techniques, are also needed. The material sketched here may offer a base from which to start.

References

Aldrich, C.K. (1944). The effect of synthetic marihuana-like compound on musical talent. *Public Health Report*, **59**, 431–5.

Aldridge, D. (2004). *Health, the Individual and Integrated Medicine—Revisiting an Aesthetic of Health Care* (London: Jessica Kingsley).

Alexander, I., Cowey, A., and Walsh, V. (2005). The right parietal cortex and time perception: back to Critchley and the Zeitraffer phenomenon. *Cognitive Neuropsychology*, **22**, 306–15.

Barber-Kersovan, A. (1991). Turn on, tune in, drop out: Rockmusik zwischen Drogen und Kreativität, in H. Rösing (ed.), *Musik als Droge? Zu Theorie und Praxis bewußtseinsverändernder Wirkungen von Musik*, 89–104 (Mainz: Villa Musica).

Baudelaire, C. (1988). *Die künstlichen Paradiese: Die Dichtung vom Haschisch*, vol. 14 (Zürich: Manesse Verlag).

Becker, H.S. (1963) *Outsiders: Studies in the Sociology of Deviance* (New York: The Free Press).

Becker, H.S. (1966). Marihuana: a sociological overview, in D. Solomon (ed.), *The Marihuana Papers*, 65–102 (Indianapolis, IN: Bobbs-Merrill).

Becker, J. (2010). Exploring the habitus of listening, in P.N. Juslin and J.A. Sloboda (eds.), *Handbook of Music and Emotion : Theory, Research, and Applications*, 127–57 (Oxford: Oxford University Press).

Behrendt, J.E. (1956). *Variationen über Jazz* (München: Nymphenburger Verlagsanstalt).

Blätter, A. (1990). *Kulturelle Ausprägungen und die Funktion des Drogengebrauchs* (Hamburg: Wayasbah Verlag).

Bonny, H. (1980). *GIM Therapy: Past, Present and Future Implications*, vol. 3 (Salina: The Bonny Foundation).

Böhm, T. (1999). Was ist Psychedelic Rock? Zum Einfluß von Drogen auf die Musik am Beispiel der Beatles und LSD, in H. Rösing and T. Phleps (eds.), *Erkenntniszuwachs durch Analyse: Populäre Musik auf dem Prüfstand*, 7–25 (Karben: Coda).

Bourdieu, P. (1977). *Outline of a Theory of Practice* (Cambridge: Cambridge University Press).

Boyd, J. and George-Warren, H. (1992). *Musicians in Tune: Seventy-five Contemporary Musicians Discuss the Creative Process* (New York, NY: Simon and Schuster).

Buhusi, C.V. and Meck, W.H. (2005). What makes us tick? Functional and neural mechanisms of interval timing. *Nature Reviews Neuroscience*, **6**, 755–65.

Clarke, E.F. (1999). Rhythm and timing in music, in D. Deutsch (ed.), *The Psychology of Music*, 2nd edn, 473–500 (New York, NY: Academic Press).

Cotner, J.S. (2002). Pink Floyd's 'Careful with that axe, Eugene': Toward a theory of textural rhythm in early progressive rock, in K. Holm-Hudson (ed.), *Progressive Rock Reconsidered*, 65–90 (New York, NY: Routledge).

Curry, A. (1968). Drugs in rock and jazz music. *Clinical Toxicology*, 1, 235–44.

Davis, A. and Pieper, W. (1993). *Die psychedelischen Beatles* (Löhrbach: Werner Piepers MedienXperimente).

Dawson, K.A. (2001). A case study of space-time distortion during a total lunar eclipse following street use of LSD. *Journal of Psychoactive Drugs*, 33, 301–5.

De Rios, M.D. and Janiger, O. (2003). *LSD, Spirituality, and the Creative Process* (Rochester, Vt.: Park Street Press).

Dietrich, A. (2003). Functional neuroanatomy of altered states of consciousness: the transient hypofrontality hypothesis. *Consciousness and Cognition*, 12, 231–56.

Dietrich, A. (2004). Neurocognitive mechanisms underlying the experience of flow. *Consciousness and Cognition*, 13, 746–61.

Eagleman, D.M., Tse, P.U., Buonomano, D., Janssen, P., Nobre, A.C., and Holcombe, A.O. (2005). Time and the brain: how subjective time relates to neural time. *Journal of Neuroscience*, 25, 10369–71.

Egner, T. and Gruzelier, J.H. (2003). Ecological validity of neurofeedback: modulation of slow wave EEG enhances musical performance. *NeuroReport*, 14, 1221–4.

Eichel, G.R. and Troiden, R.R. (1978). The domestication of drug effects: the case of marihuana. *Journal of Psychedelic Drugs*, 10, 133–6.

Fachner, J. (2000). Cannabis, Musik und ein veränderter metrischer Bezugsrahmen, in H. Rösing and T. Phleps (eds.), *Populäre Musik im kulturwissenschaftlichen Diskurs*, 107–22 (Karben: Coda).

Fachner, J. (2001). *Veränderte Musikwahrnehmung durch Tetra-Hydro-Cannabinol im Hirnstrombild*. MD Thesis (Dr. rer. med.), Faculty of Medicine, University of Witten/Herdecke.

Fachner, J. (2002). Topographic EEG changes accompanying cannabis-induced alteration of music perception—Cannabis as a hearing aid? *Journal of Cannabis Therapeutics*, 2, 3–36.

Fachner, J. (2006a). An ethnomethodological approach to accompany cannabis and music perception with EEG-Brainmapping in a naturalistic setting. *Anthropology of Consciousness*, 17, 78–103.

Fachner, J. (2006b). Music and drug induced altered states, in D. Aldridge and J. Fachner (eds.), *Music and Altered States—Consciousness, Transcendence, Therapy and Addictions*, 82–96 (London: Jessica Kingsley).

Fachner, J. (2007). Takin' it to the Streets ... Psychotherapie, Drogen und Psychedelic Rock. *Samples, Online-Publikationen des Arbeitskreis Studium Populärer Musik e.V.*, 6. Available at: www.aspm-samples.de/ (accessed 2 March 2011).

Fachner, J. (2009). Out of time? Music, consciousness states and neuropharmacological mechanisms of an altered temporality, in J. Louhivuori, T. Eerola, S. Saarikallio, T. Himberg, and P.-S. Eerola (eds.), *7th Triennial Conference of European Society for the Cognitive Sciences of Music*, 103–9 (Jyväskylä, Finland: University of Jyväskylä).

Fachner, J. (2010). Music therapy, drugs and state-dependent recall, in D. Aldridge and J. Fachner (eds.), *Music Therapy and Addictions*, 18–34 (London: Jessica Kingsley).

Globus, G.G., Cohen, H.B., Kramer, J.C., Elliot, H.W., and Sharp, R. (1978). Effects of marihuana induced altered state of consciousness on auditory perception. *Journal of Psychedelic Drugs*, 10, 71–6.

Grotenhermen, F. and Russo, E. (2002). *Cannabis and Cannabinoids: Pharmacology, Toxicology, and Therapeutic Potential* (New York, NY: Haworth Integrative Healing Press).

Hess, P. (1973). *Experimentelle Untersuchung akuter Haschischeinwirkung auf den Menschen*. Inaugural-Dissertation, Fakultät für klinische Medizin Mannheim, Ruprecht-Karl-Universität Heidelberg.

Hobson, J.A. (2001). *The Dream Drugstore: Chemically Altered States of Consciousness* (Cambridge, MA: MIT Press).

Iversen, L.L. (2003). Cannabis and the brain. *Brain*, **126**, 1252–70.

Iversen, L.L. (2008). *The Science of Marijuana* (New York, NY: Oxford University Press).

Jausovec, N. (1997). Differences in EEG alpha activity between gifted and non-identified individuals: insights into problem solving. *Gifted Child Quarterly*, **41**, 26–32.

Julien, R.M., Advokat, C.D., and Comaty, J.E. (2008). *A Primer of Drug Action: A Comprehensive Guide to the Actions, Uses, and Side Effects of Psychoactive Drugs* (New York, NY: Worth Publishers).

Katz, R. and De Rios, M.D. (1971). Hallucinogenic music: an analysis of the role of whistling in Peruvian Ayahuasca healing sessions. *Journal of American Folklore*, **84**, 320–7.

Kolb, B. and Whishaw, I.Q. (2009). *Fundamentals of Human Neuropsychology* (New York, NY: Worth Publishers).

Lee, M.A. and Shalin, B. (1992). *Acid Dreams* (New York, NY: Grove Press).

Leonard, N. (1962). *Jazz and the White Americans: The Acceptance of a New Art Form* (Chicago, IL: University of Chicago Press).

Lieving, L.M., Lane, S.D., Cherek, D.R., and Tcheremissine, O.V. (2006). Effects of marijuana on temporal discriminations in humans. *Behavioural Pharmacology*, **17**, 173–83.

Lyttle, T. and Montagne, M. (1992). Drugs, music, and ideology: a social pharmacological interpretation of the Acid House Movement. *International Journal of the Addictions*, **27**, 1159–77.

Maas, U. and Strubelt, S. (2006). Polyrhythms supporting a pharmacotherapy: music in the Iboga initiation ceremony in Gabon, in D. Aldridge and J. Fachner (eds.), *Music and Altered States: Consciousness, Transcendence, Therapy and Addictions*, 101–24 (London: Jessica Kingsley).

Manning, P. (2007). *Drugs and Popular Culture: Drugs, Media and Identity in Contempory Society* (Cullompton: Willan Publishing).

Markert, J. (2001). Sing a song of drug use-abuse: four decades of drug lyrics in popular music—from the sixties through the nineties. *Sociological Inquiry*, **71**, 194–220.

Martin, G. and Pearson, W. (1995). *Summmer of Love: The Making of Sgt. Pepper* (London: Pan Books–Macmillan).

Mathew, R.J., Wilson, W.H., Turkington, T.G., and Coleman, R.E. (1998). Cerebellar activity and disturbed time sense after THC. *Brain Research*, **797**, 183–9.

Mathew, R.J., Wilson, W.H., Turkington, T.G., Hawk, T.C., Coleman, R.E., DeGrado, T.R., and Provenzale, J. (2002). Time course of tetrahydrocannabinol-induced changes in regional cerebral blood flow measured with positron emission tomography. *Psychiatry Research: Neuroimaging*, **116**, 173–85.

Meck, W.H. (1996). Neuropharmacology of timing and time perception. *Cognitive Brain Research*, **3**, 227–42.

Meck, W.H. (2005). Neuropsychology of timing and time perception. *Brain and Cognition*, **58**, 1–8.

Mellgren, A. (1979). Hypnotherapy and art (vocalists and musicians). *The Journal of the American Society of Psychosomatic Dentistry and Medicine*, **26**, 152–5.

Menon, V. and Levitin, D.J. (2005). The rewards of music listening: response and physiological connectivity of the mesolimbic system. *Neuroimage*, **28**, 175–84.

Mezzrow, M. (1946). *Really the Blues* (London: Flamingo/Harper Collins Publishers).

Mountain, R.S. (1989). *Factors that influence our perception of time in music.* Available at: www.armchair-researcher.com/writings/articles/time89.pdf (accessed 2 March 2011).

MullerVahl, K.R., Kolbe, H., Schneider, U., and Emrich, H.M. (1998). Cannabinoids: possible role in patho-physiology and therapy of Gilles de la Tourette syndrome. *Acta Psychiatrica Scandinavica*, **98**, 502–6.

Musto, D.F. (1999). *The American Disease: Origins of Narcotic Control* (New York, NY: Oxford University Press).

Niedermeyer, E. and Lopes da Silva, F. (1993). *Electroencephalogralographyy: Basic Principles, Clinical Applications, and Related Fields*, 3rd edn (Baltimore, MD: Williams and Wilkins).

Nixon, G.M. (1999). Whatever happened to 'heightened consciousness'? *Journal of Curriculum Studies*, **31**, 625–33.

O'Leary, D.S., Block, R.I., Turner, B.M., Koeppel, J., Magnotta, V.A., Ponto, L.B., Watkins, G.L., Hichwa, R.D., and Andreasen, N.C. (2003). Marijuana alters the human cerebellar clock. *Neuroreport*, **14**, 1145–51.

Petsche, H. (1994). The EEG while listening to music. *EEG-EMG-Zeitung für Elektroenzephalographie und Elektromyografie*, **25**, 130–7.

Piel, G. (1943, July 19). Narcotics. *Life Magazine*, **15**, 15–82.

Pöppel, E. (2000). *Grenzen des Bewusstseins: Wie kommen wir zur Zeit und wie entsteht Wirklichkeit?* (Frankfurt: Insel).

Rammsayer, T.H. (1999). Neuropharmacological evidence for different timing mechanisms in humans. *The Quarterly Journal of Experimental Psychology*, **52B**, 273–86.

Rätsch, C. (2005). *The Encyclopedia of Psychoactive Plants: Ethnopharmacology and its Applications* (Rochester, VT: Park Street Press).

Rubia, K. and Smith, A. (2004). The neural correlates of cognitive time management: a review. *Acta Neurobiologiae Experimentalis*, **64**, 329–40.

Sack, A.T. (2009). Parietal cortex and spatial cognition. *Behavioral and Brain Research*, **202**, 153–61.

Shanon, B. (2001). Altered temporality. *Journal of Consciousness Studies*, **8**, 35–58.

Shapiro H. (1989). *Drugs & Rock´n Roll.* (Wien: Hannibal Verlag) [German] (Engl. orig. Shapiro, H. (1988). *Waiting for the Man: The Story of Drugs and Popular Music* (London: Quartet Books)).

Sloman, L. (1998). *Reefer Madness: The History of Marijuana in America* (New York, NY: St. Martin's Griffin).

Solowij, N. (1998). *Cannabis and Cognitive Functioning* (Cambridge: Cambridge University Press).

Spreng, M. and Keidel, W.D. (1963). Neue Möglichkeiten der Untersuchung menschlicher Informationsverarbeitung. *Biological Cybernetics*, **1**, 243–9.

Struve, F.A. and Straumanis, J.J. (1990). Electroencephalographic and evoked potential methods in human marihuana research: historical review and future trends. *Drug Development Research*, **20**, 369–88.

Struve, F.A., Straumanis, J.J., Patrick, G., Leavitt, J., Manno, J.E., and Manno, B.R. (1999). Topographic quantitative EEG sequelae of chronic marihuana use: a replication using medically and psychiatrically screened normal subjects. *Drug and Alcohol Dependence*, **56**, 167–79.

Tart, C. (1971). *On Being Stoned. A Psychological Study of Marihuana Intoxication* (Palo Alto, CA: Science and Behavior Books).

The Beatles. (1967). *Sgt. Peppers Lonely Hearts Club Band*. LP (Hayes, UK: EMI B003YXDN86).

Weil, A. (1998). *The Natural Mind* (Boston, MA: Houghton Mifflin).

Whiteley, S. (1992). *The Space Between the Notes: Rock and the Counter Culture* (London: Routledge).

Whiteley, S. (1997) Altered sounds, in A. Melechi (ed.), *Psychedelia Britannica*, 120–42 (London: Turnaround).

Wittmann, M., Carter, O., Hasler, F., Cahn, B.R., Grimberg, U., Spring, P., Hell, D., Flohr, H., and Vollenweider, F.X. (2007). Effects of psilocybin on time perception and temporal control of behaviour in humans. *Journal of Psychopharmacology*, **21**, 50–64.

Wuebben, Y. and Winterer, G. (2001). Hypofrontality—a risk-marker related to schizophrenia? *Schizophrenia Research*, **48**, 207–17.

Zinberg, N.E. (1984). *Drug, Set, and Setting: The Basis for Controlled Intoxicant Use* (New Haven, CT: Yale University Press).

Notes

1. For example, the endogenous opioid neurotransmitter binds to the endogenous opioid receptor by travelling through the synaptic gap during signal transmission. This results in a blocking or an activation of signal transmission targeting certain areas of the cortex or deeper brain structures. But opioid receptors also bind to heroin (which mimics the endogenous opioids) when injected, inhaled, etc.

2. The term 'state-specific memory' refers to the idea that memory performance is strongly influenced by context—both internal and external.

3. 'Lyserg-feeling' refers to the hallucinogen LSD (lysergic acid diethylamide).

4. Based on similar anthropological considerations, Fachner (2006a) used a mobile EEG device set up in the living rooms of his participants to study drug-induced music listening experiences.

5. EEG shows different ranges of working frequencies of electrical brain activity, in various parts of the brain, gained from the electrical discharges of neuron ensembles, while processing information. High frequencies (above 14 Hz) represent the activity of many different neuron ensembles, processing different components of the information, while low frequencies indicate the processing of synchronized activations of neuron ensembles. These processes are connected to arousal processes and vigilance states, that is, the ability to be attentive and alert. Low-frequency ranges (delta = 0–4 Hz; theta = 4–8 Hz; alpha = 8–12 Hz) are dominant in low arousal states, and in regenerative and internalized information processing; while high frequencies dominate externalized information processing and elevated arousal states (Niedermeyer and Lopes da Silva 1999).

Chapter 16

Music and ayahuasca

Benny Shanon

This chapter examines the musical facets of the special state of mind induced by ayahuasca, a powerful Amazonian psychoactive brew especially famous for the vivid hallucinations that it induces. The chapter is divided into three parts. The first presents background information concerning ayahuasca and its scientific study, and discusses the use of music in ayahuasca rituals. The second part reviews and analyses the phenomenology of auditory and musical effects encountered in the special state of mind induced by ayahuasca inebriation, the effect of music on the ayahuasca experience and its visions, and musical performance. The third part deals with general issues such as the psychological import of music and its relationship to consciousness and its alteration.

Contexts

Ayahuasca and its scientific study

Ayahuasca is an Amazonian plant-derived concoction whose major psychoactive constituent is dimethyltryptamine (DMT). Information about the botany and pharmacology of ayahuasca can be found in Callaway *et al.* (1999), Ott (1993, 1994), Schultes (1972, 1982), and Schultes and Winkelman (1995). The indigenous Amerindians have used ayahuasca for millennia. In the past, it was used for all major tribal decisions (e.g. the declaration of war and the location of game for hunting), served in initiation rites, and was central in the religious practices, belief systems, and artistic creations of these people. In particular, ayahuasca was said to be the source of language, music, myth, and art. Today, the potion is still the basic instrument of shamans and medicine-men (called ayahuasqueros) throughout the upper Amazonian region. It is said to enable healers to see the inner constitution of their patients, establish diagnosis, and perform treatment. For anthropological literature concerning the use of ayahuasca in the indigenous context, the reader is referred to Reichel-Dolmatoff (1975; 1978), Dobkin de Rios (1972), Langdon (1979, 1992), Luna (1986), as well as the various contributions in Harner (1973a), Langdon and Baer (1992), and Labate and Araújo (2002). In the twentieth century, as a result of inter-racial contacts, several syncretic sects have been established in Brazil in which indigenous ayahuasca traditions have been combined with Christian and other non-indigenous (in particular, African) cultural elements. The most important of these sects are the Church of Santo Daime, the *União do Vegetal* (the plant union; UDV, for short), and the Barquinha. In the last two decades the first two groups have expanded significantly throughout the urban centres of Brazil and recently they have also established communities overseas. For general information regarding these groups, see MacRae (1992) and Polari (1984, 1992) for the first group; the Centro de Memoria e Documentação (1989) and Brissac (1999) for the second; and Sena Araújo (1999) for the third, as well as the various contributions in Labate and Araújo (2002).

The consumption of ayahuasca usually induces powerful visions as well as unusual sensations in all other perceptual modalities (paintings based on ayahuasca visions are presented in Luna and Amaringo (1991)). Pronounced non-perceptual cognitive effects are also manifest, including personal psychological insights, intellectual (notably, metaphysical) ideations, and powerful religious and spiritual experiences. Moreover, ayahuasca introduces those who partake of it to what seem to them to be other realities. Those who partake of the potion may thus feel that they are gaining access to new sources of knowledge and that the mysteries and ultimate truths of the universe are being revealed.

Most of the scientific research on ayahuasca falls into two categories: the natural and medical sciences (botany and ethnobotany, pharmacology, biochemistry, brain physiology, and clinical medicine); and the social sciences (notably cultural anthropology). My prime interest is neither in the brain nor in culture but rather in the human psyche and the phenomenology of human consciousness, and my research programme is the first scientific effort to study the ayahuasca experience from a cognitive-psychological perspective. My work is guided by the appraisal that the alliance of ayahuasca research and the study of mind is beneficial to both. On the one hand, cognitive psychology presents a pertinent perspective for the study of ayahuasca. On the other hand, ayahuasca, with the unusual mental phenomena it generates, opens new vistas for the study of mind in general and of human consciousness in particular. A systematic comprehensive charting of the phenomenology of ayahuasca experiences can be found in Shanon (2002a) and Shanon (1990).

The research is based on several sources of data. The first is the compendium of my own diaries which record accounts of all the ayahuasca sessions in which I have participated. Guided by the belief that the ayahuasca experience cannot be studied without firsthand experience, I have spent long periods in South America partaking of the potion in different locations and in different contexts of use; by now, I have done so about 160 times.[1] Second are interviews in which I asked people about their ayahuasca experience. Overall, I have interviewed more than 300 individuals—indigenous shamans, indigenous lay persons, residents of South America who are members of various syncretic sects using ayahuasca, independents (i.e. individuals with extensive experience who are not members of any sect), as well as Europeans and North Americans with no evidence of prior experience with the potion. For comparative purposes, I have also analysed reports in the anthropological literature.

Music in ayahuasca rituals

As a rule, ayahuasca is consumed within a ritualized setting. The rituals vary in different places and with different socio-cultural groups and traditions, yet some generalizations apply. The rituals are communal, are led by individuals whose role in the society or community is precisely this, take place at particular set dates, are well structured, and involve strict regulations (both prescriptions and prohibitions). Significant to the present discussion is the fact that in all places and contexts music features prominently. As will be described below, the music exerts great influence on people's experiences with ayahuasca, and the following provides general information about music in the various contexts of ayahuasca usage.

The traditional Amerindian ayahuasqueros sing chants of power, *icaros*, which are sung only during ayahuasca ceremonies. These are usually curing sessions, with the singing being the healer's major instrument of cure. The chanting is soft and repetitive, and carried out by the ayahuasquero alone continuously over a number of hours in complete darkness. Bunches of dry leaves or rattles are often used as an accompaniment. The function of the *icaros* is to call upon spirits, help the ayahuasquero in his journeys to other realms, modify the effect of the brew, and impart healing. The participants in the ritual sit in a meditative position or lie supine, and remain silent. For further information see Katz and Dobkin de Rios (1971); Siskind (1973); Dobkin de Rios and Katz (1975); Bellier (1986); Gebhart-Sayer (1986); Luna (1992); Buchillet (1992), and Hill (1992).[2]

In the syncretic Brazilian sects, ayahuasca drinking is the pivot of a religious ritual in which the brew serves as a sacrament and is regarded as divine. In the ceremonies of both the Church of Santo Daime and the Barquinha, the singing is communal and goes on during the entire session, which is conducted in well-illuminated halls. The music consists of a predetermined set of melodious hymns, generally with an instrumental accompaniment (usually guitar), and in some rituals of the Santo Daime simple dancing accompanies the singing. The hymns are said to have been 'received' by the major masters of the Church; they constitute the structure and spiritual core of the session and in their totality and form the 'doctrine of Santo Daime'.[3] The Barquinha rituals are based on the Afro-Brazilian religion Umbanda. In regular sessions, melodious long ballad-like *salmos* (psalms) are sung by a cantor, and the congregation joins in for the refrains, with some sessions incorporating a *gira*—a lively 'merry-go-round' dance.

In the União do Vegetal sessions, music plays a lesser role, and the greater part of the sessions (during which participants remain seated) involves verbal exchanges of teaching and question answering by the presiding Master. At times, set invocations are chanted individually, mostly by the Master, and every now and then music is played on an audio system—the music being drawn from a variety of sources, including Brazilian popular songs and classical music, selected at the discretion of the person directing the specific session. In the urban centres of Brazil there are also 'independent' ayahuasca groups conducted by experienced individuals who have left the various established sects and created their own drinking frameworks, free of institutionalized formalities and religious doctrine of any sort. In these sessions selections from a wide range of musical traditions are played through audio systems. For further information concerning music in the Brazilian ayahuasca religions the reader is referred to Labate and Pacheco (2009).

Musical phenomenology

The experiential import of music

In general, the most notable external stimulation during ayahuasca sessions is musical. As indicated above, the music heard during a session exerts a great influence on what is experienced in a session, and while in the ayahuasca context music has many of the same kinds of effects that it has in other circumstances (enjoyment, peace of mind, and the channelling of emotions and sentiments), under intoxication, all of these are greatly amplified and accentuated. The brew significantly enhances people's aesthetic sensitivity and appreciation, and under intoxication people experience manifestations of beauty they deem to be truly fabulous. This is the case in all sensory modalities, and pertains both to perceptions of stimuli actually existing in the external world and to inner, subjective experiences. Thus, under intoxication music sounds immensely beautiful, and is often felt to be enchanting. It evokes strong emotions and deep sentiments, profound meanings are often discerned in it, and it is likely to be characterized as heavenly and/or divine. In an attenuated form, these feelings usually remain even when one is no longer under the effect of the brew. Furthermore, as attested by Polari (Richman 1990/1991), one of the leaders of the Church of Santo Daime, listening to the Daime music even while in an ordinary state of consciousness brings back recollections of these non-ordinary experiences and with them a renewed flavour of the sentiments of well-being, harmony, and sanctity.

The musical effects are grounded in the non-ordinary perceptions of auditory stimuli. Overall, with ayahuasca, people's audition becomes subtler and more acute, and auditory stimuli sound fuller and stronger. With this, one may have the sense of detecting sounds that are not perceived in ordinary conditions. The spatial location of sounds is also transformed, such that sounds are heard as coming from locations and directions that do not correspond to their real-world locations. One consequence is that the music may also be experienced as engulfing one in a quasi-physical fashion, leading the listener to feel transported to other realities.

In addition to these strictly auditory effects, there are also structural effects involving non-standard parsing (i.e. structural grouping) of perceptual stimuli. For example, once during a UDV ayahuasca preparation ceremony that lasted for two days, I was listening to the sounds of the pounding of wood (of which the potion is made) produced by a group of men sitting at my side. In reality, the beating was not coordinated, each man hitting the wood in his own irregular rhythm. However, under the effect of the brew I heard a magical composition: I did not hear any sound that was not actually emitted by the men who were pounding, and yet it seemed to me that the sounds were miraculously structured and that together they generated a composition. There was nothing in the temporal spacing of the sounds as such that was altered, yet they appeared to me to be wonderfully patterned. What I heard in the pounding was a composition in the style of contemporary music (the composer Ligeti came to mind).[4]

Overall, ayahuasca induces an enhanced conferral of meaningfulness and the feeling of heightened understanding. This is especially marked with music. Listening to pieces of classical music that I had heard many times before, it seemed to me that I was hearing them precisely in the same manner that their composer did. I also felt that I had clear understanding of what the composer was doing in the music, what he wished to convey, and how he had decided to do it. I understood the harmonies, the development of the melodic lines, their modulations and resolutions. Indeed, often I felt I could anticipate what the composer was going to do next, as did several of my informants who reported similar experiences.

The altered sensation of sound may be accompanied by unusual interpretations of the source of the sound and its nature. For instance, on one occasion it rained and I heard this as a commotion taking place on the roof of the hut in which the ayahuasca session was taking place; I thought animals were running around up there and felt rather apprehensive. On another occasion, what I eventually appreciated as being a far away motorcycle sounded as if a great, ill-comprehended cataclysmic event was approaching. Both are examples of a phenomenon I call 'hearing-as', analogous to the phenomenon of 'seeing-as' in the visual modality: just as one may see a figure as (or in) something else (e.g. clouds), so also one may hear a sound as something else. An experience of hearing-as that greatly puzzled me took place during an intimate Daime festive session. Amongst the musicians there was a clarinet player, and what I heard him play were traditional Jewish Hassidic melodies. This person was a Brazilian who could know nothing of this kind of music, nor did he know me or anything about me. Unfortunately, I will never know how the music sounded outside of the hallucinatory effect.

A rather common auditory effect that may be regarded as a rudimentary hallucination (i.e. a sensory perception without corresponding stimulation in the real world) is that of hearing an overall sound or buzz, which Harner (1973b) calls 'the sound of running water'. Some people find this sound annoying whereas others regard it as depicting the very essence of the cosmos and may be fascinated by it.

Cases of fully fledged musical hallucinations—musical visions, so to speak—are rare. Both in the anthropological literature and in my own investigations I have encountered reports of angelic music performed in the heavens, and I too experienced such music in one of my first encounters with ayahuasca. The session was held with indigenous people in the Putumayo region in southern Colombia. I was offered a large dosage of ayahuasca and the effect came quickly—as recounted in my field notes:

> Immediately I felt I was thrown up into a realm high above the planet and found myself in the midst of what I interpreted to be a cosmic lottery. My understanding was that my entire existence, both physical and mental, was at stake: if I played it right, I would be saved, if not—I would lose everything and perish. In order to redeem myself, I began to sing. There was no reflection involved in this decision, nor any recourse to past experience with ayahuasca (as would be the case today). For six or eight hours I continuously sang the praises of God. The words that spontaneously came out of my mouth were (in Spanish) *Gloria a Dios* (Glory to God); the melody was being composed as it was being sung. As I was singing, I found myself to be surrounded by an immense choir of angels—I was taking the leading role and they were accompanying me. The music was exceedingly beautiful. Every now and then the choir was joined by guest groups that came in, performed, and then left. One such group that especially impressed me was one of Black, very sensuous, players. The music they played was very different from that sung by the

angels, but it all fit together very well and the ultimate meaning and purpose of it all was one and the same—*Hallelujah*, that is, the singing of God's praises.

This was one of the most marvellous experiences I have ever had with ayahuasca.

Another musical hallucination occurred during an interval of a Daime session when I was lying in the meadow grass. I found that a mosquito was sitting on the tip of my nose. I was about to brush it off, but changed my mind and decided I might as well let it be and observe. I heard it sing Mozart. Later I discovered that the Cashinahua say that during ayahuasca sessions insects sing enchanted music (Chiappe *et al.* 1985), and one of my informants reported that seeing (real) birds flying he also heard them singing—although others reported that this did not actually take place.

Lastly, let me mention an effect I shall call 'the music of silence', which I have experienced only once. One person to whom I recounted this episode told me he recognized this effect from his own personal experience with ayahuasca:

> The scene was celestial. It was a white place which I interpreted to be up in the High Heavens, where the Divine is praised. Acoustically, there was absolute silence there. Yet, I knew it all was full of what was, in essence, music. The ambiance was most serene and I felt this was the music of the angels.

Music and visions

As noted, ayahuasca is especially famous for the visions it induces. As detailed in Shanon (2002a, 2002b) these are of various structural kinds. In progressive order of increasing richness, complexity, and strength, they may consist of geometrical patterns without any semantics, of simple figurative items that do have semantics, and of entire scenes. In the latter case, various forms of interaction with what is seen in the visions may be experienced; when most powerful, the visions involve full immersion and turn into veritable virtual realities. Paradigmatically, music has great influence on the contents of the visions, their dynamics, and their progression.

As with psychedelics in general (see Ludwig 1969), cross-modal perception, or synaesthesia, is prevalent with ayahuasca. As noted in Shanon (2002a, 2003), of all synaesthetic effects the auditory to visual ones are by far the most common, and in most cases they are associated with music. When music is present, it usually guides the visions, and in particular the tempo and rhythm of the music people hear is often reflected in their visions. Notably, the music determines the pace and movement of figures appearing in the visions as well as the rate of change between images. Some note that their visions last as long as the singing, and when the singing stops, so do the visions.

The following myth told by the Kamsa and Inga of southern Colombia and recounted by Ramírez de Jara and Pinzón Castaño attests to these synaesthetic effects:

> In the beginning earth was obscurity. Men already existed, but they lacked intelligence. They took yagé [ayahuasca] and ... [l]ittle by little the shadows took on shape and form and the silhouettes got details. In the sky, they saw yagé entering an immense flower. It got fecundated and transformed into the sun. And from there came the people of the sun with their distinct music played on flutes and tambors. Each melody transformed into a distinct colour. When they arrived to the earth they gave it colour, and when the

world was illuminated, played the symphony of colour and the music awakened the comprehension of people, creating intelligence and language. This is why yagé is used: With it the world is seen as it is, and the intelligence expands making everything clear and harmonious with the spirit of cure. (1986: 175; author's translation)

Many of the non-indigenous people I interviewed who partook of ayahuasca in a traditional Amerindian setting sensed that the ayahuasquero's chanting was directing the course of their visions and determined their general flavour and colouring. Many felt that specific ayahuasqueros had induced, when they sang, special magical powers. Interestingly, such effects are described in one of the earliest ayahuasca reports furnished by a non-indigenous person—see Kusel (1965).

Music can also feature within the contents of the visions themselves. Specifically, people and other creatures (notably angels) may be seen singing or playing musical instruments. On one occasion, I had a vision in which I saw the music of the spheres governing the motion of the planets.

Musical performance

In almost all discussions in the anthropological literature, music is considered from the perspective of those participants in the ayahuasca session who are listening to it. But obviously, the brew also has its impact on those who produce the music, especially those who sing. First, ayahuasca often makes people sing, and this appears to be a special characteristic of ayahuasca that distinguishes it from other psychoactive agents. Indeed, under the effect of ayahuasca, many people (myself included) sing better and in a much stronger voice than they normally could. I have observed this many times, including once when I myself was not under the effect of the brew. When the power of the brew is strong, the ayahuasca drinker may feel that it is not he or she who is the generator of the song, but that they serve as a vehicle for the music to convey itself through his or her voice. Typically, such singing is an expression of the deep appreciation and gratitude experienced under the intoxication. Recordings of Daime sessions corroborate these observations, with a clear transition between the normal (rather mediocre) singing of non-professional people to a powerful, well-coordinated chant. Similar observations were made by Reichel-Dolmatoff (1990) with respect to a Tukano ayahuasca ceremony.

Here is a report by a Brazilian man of what happened to him the first time he participated in a Daime session:

> Without knowing what to do, I decided to sing. I opened the hymn book and I found myself singing in a voice that for me was extremely high. The voice came out of the depth of my being, without stopping, giving me a sensation of great pleasure. I remember thinking in those moments that this should be the sensation that opera singers have in the most overpowering moments of their arias. (Pellegrini 1994: 46)

I myself have had such experiences numerous times, both in the context of Santo Daime and in other contexts of ayahuasca usage. On many occasions I found myself producing high notes that were definitely way above the normal reach of my voice. To do this, I knew I had to sit up straight, monitor my breathing, and transform my entire body into a vocal apparatus. (Later, I showed what I did to a singing teacher and he indicated to me that, indeed, intuitively I had actually practised what a singer should do.) When I was quite experienced with this kind of singing, I would close my eyes and raise both my voice and my inner gaze, and visions would then unfold. On many occasions I felt that as my voice rose, I too was being lifted up—to the skies, to what seemed to me to be the far reaches of the cosmos, and to superior regions of light and energy. My music seemed to emanate from these celestial realms. On some occasions, I produced sounds that appeared to come from the cranial and nasal cavities, as well as chords in which two sounds were emitted simultaneously, through two different resonance cavities. Very often, the melodies were invented (some would say, received) on the spot: I had never knowingly either sung them before, or heard anyone else sing them, and I could keep on singing them for extended periods of time. On some occasions, I kept on singing for an entire day following the ayahuasca session itself.

Several indigenous ayahuasqueros told me that they sing music that they hear in their visions; and some attribute it to angels or other supernatural beings. As noted above, the hymns of the Santo Daime are said to have been received—neither created nor composed—by prominent leaders when under the effect of the brew.

Like those who listen to the singing, the singing person also needs grounding and guidance. Like them, he too can gain these through music. But there are musical effects that are specific to the person who produces the music. Often, the ayahuasca inebriation makes people wish to express themselves in action (as well as acting out in the psychological sense). Some may engage in overt behaviours that bother other participants in the session: over-exuberant dancing, the production of all sorts of sounds, and inappropriate interpersonal interactions. Singing offers a readily available channel of action and thus provides a solution. As is usually the case in all contexts of ayahuasca use, having at one's disposal a set of songs which are already known beforehand affords a state of affairs that is especially comforting: the singer does not have to invest mental effort to decide what to do under the intoxication. This is especially true in Daime rituals in which the session is guided by pre-established, fixed sets of hymns listed in a booklet.

Singing is also a wonderful outlet for emotions, with the capacity to channel emotions in a positive direction—notably those of praise and joy. Singing is uplifting—quite literally so—and when the voice is raised up, so too is one's soul and with it one's visions. Many times I have felt that music helped me to resist the physical sickness that is a common response to drinking ayahuasca: instead of vomiting, I would pour music out of my mouth.

Singing is not the only non-ordinary production of sound manifested with ayahuasca. On some occasions, when partaking of the brew alone, I found myself emitting sounds that I felt were not mine at all—the grunting of jaguars, the whispering of snakes, the calls of birds of all sorts, the sounds of rushing water and the blowing of the wind. Experientially it seemed that it was not me who generated these sounds, that the sounds took me over, and that my body served as a channel through which the sounds came into being by means of forces that were beyond me. Occasionally, the production of the sounds was coupled with a vision, often of a voyage to other realms. It was the beauty of these realms and the enchanted energies that radiated from them that seemed to enable the unusual vocal performances that I was actually producing.

Musical performance also extends to the instrumental domain, and in general, such performance is of an especially high level. I was often most impressed with those moments during Santo Daime rituals in which guitar players, normally taking the role of accompanists, took liberties and improvised freely. This happened in the short intervals between hymns, always towards the end of festive sessions, when the overall atmosphere was that of universal elation and spiritual triumph. Tape recordings I have made demonstrate some of these extraordinary musical performances. Once during such an intermission, I saw a person pick up a violin and play in a manner that amazed all those present. This was someone who knew how to play the violin, but who, by his own attestation, had never played in this manner before: it seemed that the Muses had descended upon the man. On another occasion, at the end of a Daime session, a large Brazilian drum was passed to me. I had never touched such a drum before, and had not touched any kind of drum since I was a young boy, but in the context I felt I had no choice but to play it. I felt a complete identification with the drum and played it with my entire body and being. Indeed, my feeling was that I was dancing with the drum—that I was in a special and wonderful kind of intercourse with it.

An episode that left a special, long-term mark on me involved piano playing. In an amateurish fashion, I have been playing classical music on the piano since childhood, always from the score, never improvising and very seldom with an audience. Once, during a private ayahuasca session, I saw a piano in front of me and decided to play. The score of a Bach prelude was on the stand, and I played the piece repeatedly and felt I was entering into a trance. Then, I left the score aside and began to improvise. I played for more than an hour, and the manner of my playing was different from anything I had ever experienced. I played in a continuous unfaltering flow, producing an ongoing narration that was composed as it was executed. It appeared that my fingers just knew where to go, and the technical level of my performance astonished me—far above what I am usually capable of. At times, I felt that a force was upon me and that I was following its command—not that I was an automaton or enslaved by any external agent, but rather that the playing was the expression of a wondrous cooperation between my self, and forces that I felt were superior to me. Another person was present and he listened to my playing. Later he told me that he felt the music was a story and he was very moved by it. 'It seemed that the Muses descended upon you,' he said. When the session ended, it occurred to me that I had experienced the most wonderful piano lesson of my life. Since then I have continued to improvise without ayahuasca, and while the quality of this playing does not strike me as being like that under the intoxication, it does exhibit features that my piano playing never did before that ayahuasca session (see Shanon 2000).

General issues

Why music?

Why is it that music affects ayahuasca drinkers in such a powerful and enchanting manner? Why does music have such a central role in ayahuasca rituals? These questions are intimately linked with those concerning the effect music in general has on the human psyche, and with the role of music in culture at large. These are broad topics that extend beyond the scope of this chapter, but let me highlight a number of patterns especially salient in relation to ayahuasca.

In many musical cultures, music is strongly associated with eliciting, enhancing, and shaping a range of powerful moods and emotions, and it is similarly the case that music is closely associated with a wide range of religious practices, and is regarded as particularly effective in eliciting or amplifying spiritual and religious sentiments. These effects are experienced with music even in the ordinary state of consciousness; with ayahuasca they are all greatly accentuated and amplified. Moreover, music has the special quality of being able to create an ambiance of enchantment—a property that is reflected in the close relationship between the English words *chant* and *enchant*, as also between *canto* (song) and *encanto* (charm), and between *cantar/e* (to sing) and *encantar/e* (to enchant).

Music also exhibits internal structure and directionality, which carry over to the ayahuasca experience rendering it less chaotic and more manageable. In a similar vein, Dobkin de Rios and Katz (1975) proposed that music allows what they metaphorically call a jungle gym—mental analogues of the bars, banisters, and slides in a playground providing the intoxicated mind with readily available channels around which to organize experience.

Time is especially important in human experience, and more than any art form music is temporal.[5] Not only is music fully embedded in time, but music actually orders and structures people's experience of time. As described in Shanon (2001, 2002a), with ayahuasca time perception may be greatly modified. Often, a moment seems to last an eternity, and if what one is seeing at that moment is frightening, the experience can be quite terrifying, in which case the music being played or sung can be most helpful. Subjectively, one may feel that the experience will never end, yet at the same time, listening to a familiar song may provide some temporal perspective and security. The particular stanza that is being sung or heard may provide a clue to objective time estimation—both the time that has elapsed since the song's beginning, and how much remains until its end. In addition to providing an anchor in time, music also invests the ayahuasca experience with a global temporal perspective: it marks where one is coming from and where one is going to. When the melody is familiar—from either immediate repetition or accumulated long-term experience— this securing effect is especially pronounced.[6]

Coupled with its grounding effect, music has another, different temporal manifestation—namely, its capacity to generate an otherworldly mode of existence. Even in the ordinary state of consciousness, listening to music can transport people to a different temporal matrix, defined not by the clock but rather by the intrinsic dynamics of the composition. With ayahuasca this effect is greatly magnified and one may indeed feel absorbed and swept into what is experienced as another frame of being, or another reality altogether. Thus, ayahuasca amplifies an effect intrinsic to music, and in turn, music provides extra fuel for ayahuasca's psychoactive effects.

In the context of ayahuasca, music also has an interpersonal significance. There is usually little or no interaction between the participants in ayahuasca sessions, and verbal exchange is strictly prohibited. In most contexts of ayahuasca use the only prescribed interpersonal activity is musical. Native and mestizo (racially mixed) contexts of ayahuasca usually take place in darkness, and in all contexts the drinkers' eyes are often closed, with the consequence that each person is within his or her own world, having their own private experiences. In these conditions, the only percept that is distinctly real, that pertains to the ordinary physical world, that is shared with other participants, and is acknowledged to be so, is the music being sung and/or played.

The poetic stance and human creativity

The significance of music's relationship with ayahuasca may be further appreciated when the meaning of ayahuasca visions and their epistemic status is taken into consideration. Most drinkers of the brew believe that ayahuasca can transport them in a paranormal fashion out of everyday time and space, and the visionary scenes are regarded as depictions of other, independently existing realities. It is also very common for people to believe that ayahuasca conveys messages and information from elsewhere. I do not adhere to such paranormal beliefs or the interpretations associated with them, but instead would argue for a poetic perspective (Shanon 2002a, in press). As I see it, ayahuasca shows neither the past nor the future, nor does it reveal the occult or carry factual information that is otherwise unknown. Rather, I maintain that ayahuasca works in the manner of works of art: it makes one feel and experience in a particular manner, involves one in powerful affective dynamics, and bestows spiritual states of mind. The meanings of ayahuasca visions are not factual in the way scientific or historical accounts are, but rather are evocative like poems, paintings, and pieces of music. In light of its non-denotational semantics, music is especially telling in this respect. Although music can be symbolic, and sometimes narrative, usually it is neither: yet, music does convey meaning. Its meaning pertains to the dynamics of the emotions and states of mind that it invokes. Music makes us experience joy and sadness, hopelessness and the regaining of hope, the open-endedness of possibilities, the quest for freedom and the allure of personal aspiration, solemnity and frivolity, the acceptance of one's lot in life and the tragic dimension of existence; something very similar obtains with ayahuasca visions. For further discussion of the meaning of ayahuasca visions and their epistemic status the reader is referred to Shanon (in press).

The foregoing comments further bear on my view of the psychological processes involved in generating visions. In Shanon (2002a) I proposed that the workings of ayahuasca are akin to those of artistic creation, by contrast with traditional conceptualizations in terms of paranormal journeys to other ontologies, or modern accounts based on the unravelling of the unconscious. The propensity to engage in what some cultures would call 'art', and to create, is a fundamental feature of *Homo sapiens*. Admittedly, not every human being is an artist, but there is no human society that does not have some form of art. The great gift of ayahuasca, I believe, is its capacity to bestow on lay people, for a brief period of time, the grace of the muses. It is as if I were able to experience the presentation of an entire, unknown culture, with its works of art and craft, architectural models, everyday utensils and instruments—a coherent whole, but one that I could not associate with any particular culture I had ever known or heard about. There are two options: one that I am being carried in a paranormal voyage, out of normal time and space; the other that what I have been seeing is the creation of my own mind—not a deliberate creation by me as an individual, but the spontaneous creation of the human mind when put in radically non-ordinary conditions. If an artistically untrained mind can create all this, then far from belittling all the wonder and marvel of the ayahuasca experience, such an account emphasizes how much more amazing, how much more mysterious than practically all contemporary students of cognition seem to assume, the human mind must be.

References

Araújo, S.W. (1999). *Navegando sobre as Ondas do Daime: História, Cosmologia e Ritual da Barquinha* (Campinas: Editoria da Unicamp).

Bellier, I. (1986). Los cantos mai Huna del Yajé (Amazonia Peruana). *America Indígena*, **46**, 129–45.

Brissac, S. (1999). A estrella do norte iluminado ate o sul: uma etnografia da união do vegetal em um contexto urbano. Unpublished master's thesis, Rio de Janeiro: Universidad Federal do Rio de Janeiro.

Buchillet, D. (1992). Nobody is there to hear: Desana therapeutic incantations, in E.J. Langdon and G. Baer (eds.), *Portals of Power: Shamanism in South America*, 211–30 (Albuquerque, NM: University of New Mexico Press).

Callaway, J., McKenna, D., Grob, C.S., Brito, G., Raymon, L., Poland, R., Andrade, E.N., Andrade, E.O., and Mash, E. (1999). Pharmacokinetics of Hoasca alkaloids in healthy humans. *Journal of Ethnopharmacology*, **65**, 243–56.

Centro de Memoria e Documentação. (1989). *União do vegetal Hoasca: fundamentos e objectivos* (Brasilia: Centro Espiritual beneficiente União do Vegetal).

Chiappe, M., Lemlij, M., and Millones, L. (1985). *Allucinógenos y shamanismo en el Peru contemporaneo* (Lima: Ediciones El Virrey).

Dobkin de Rios, M. (1972). *Visionary Vine: Hallucinogenic Healing in the Peruvian Amazon* (San Francisco, LA: Chandler).

Dobkin de Rios, M. and Katz, F. (1975). Some relationships between music and hallucinogenic ritual: the jungle gym in consciousness. *Ethos*, **3**, 64–76.

Gebhart-Sayer, A. (1986). Una terapia estetica: los diseños visionarios del ayahuasca entre los Shipibo-Conibo. *America Indígena*, **46**, 189–218.

Harner, M.J. (ed.) (1973a). *Hallucinogens and Shamanism* (Oxford: Oxford University Press).

Harner, M.J. (1973b). The sound of rushing water, in M.J. Harner (ed.), *Hallucinogens and Shamanism*, 15–27 (Oxford: Oxford University Press).

Hill, J. (1992). A musical aesthetic of ritual curing in the Northwest Amazon, in E.J. Langdon and G. Baer (eds.), *Portals of Power: Shamanism in South America*, 175–210 (Albuquerque, NM: University of New Mexico Press).

Katz, F. and Dobkin de Rios, M. (1971). Hallucinogenic music: an analysis of the role of whistling in Peruvian ayahuasca healing sessions. *Journal of American Folklore*, **84**, 320–7.

Kusel, H. (1965). Ayahuasca drinkers among the Chama Indians of Northeast Peru. *Psychedelic Review*, **6**, 58–66.

Labate, B.C. and Araújo, S.W. (eds.) (2002). *O uso ritual da ayahuasca* (Campinas, Brasil: Editora Mercado de Letras).

Labate, B.C. and Pacheco, G. (2009). *Música Brasileira de ayahuasca* (Campinas, Brasil: Editora Mercado de Letras).

Langdon, E.J. (1979). Yagé among the Siona: cultural patterns in visions, in D. Browman and R. Schwartz (eds.), *Spirits, Shamans and Stars*, 63–82 (Hague: Mouton Publishers).

Langdon, E.J. (1992). Dau: shamanic power in Siona religion and medicine, in E.J. Langdon and G. Baer (eds.), *Portals of Power: Shamanism in South America*, 41–61 (Albuquerque, NM: University of New Mexico Press).

Langdon, E.J. and Baer, G. (eds.) (1992). *Portals of Power: Shamanism in South America* (Albuquerque, NM: University of New Mexico Press).

Ludwig, A.M. (1969). Altered states of consciousness, in C. Tart (ed.), *Altered States of Consciousness*, 9–22 (New York, NY: Wiley and Sons).

Luna, L.E. (1986). *Vegetalismo: Shamanism among the Mestizo Population of the Peruvian Amazon* (Stockholm: Almqvist and Wiksell International).

Luna, L.E. (1992). Icaros: Magic melodies among the Mestizo shamans of the Peruvian Amazo, in E.J. Langdon and G. Baer (eds.), *Portals of Power: Shamanism in South America*, 231–52 (Albuquerque, NM: University of New Mexico Press).

Luna, L.E. and Amaringo, P. (1991). *Ayahuasca Visions: The Religious Iconography of a Peruvian Shaman* (Berkeley, CA: North Atlantic Books).

Luna, L.E. and White, S. (eds.) (2000). *Ayahuasca Reader: Encounters with the Amazon's Sacred Vine* (Santa Fe, NM: Synergetic Press).

MacRae, E. (1992). *Guiado Pela Lua: xamanismo e uso ritual da ayahuasca no culto do Santo Daime* (São Paulo: Editora Brasilense).

Ott, J. (1993). *Pharmacotheon: Entheogenic Drugs, their Plant Sources and History* (Kennewick, WA: Natural Products).

Ott, J. (1994). *Ayahuasca Analogues: Pangean Entheogens* (Kennewick, WA: Natural Products Co.).

Pellegrini, L. (1994). Jornada ao coração do Daime. *Planeta*, **265**, 45–9.

Polari, A. (1984). *O livro das mirações* (Rio de Janeiro: Editora Record).

Polari, A. (1992). *O guia da floresta* (Rio de Janeiro: Nova Era).

Ramírez de Jara, M.C. and Pinzón Castaño, C.E. (1986). Los hijos del bejucos solar y la camapana celeste: el yage y cultura popular Colombiana. *America Indígena*, **46**, 163–88.

Reichel-Dolmatoff, G. (1975). *The Shaman and the Jaguar: A Study of Narcotic Drugs among the Indians in Colombia* (Philadelphia, PA: Temple University Press).

Reichel-Dolmatoff, G. (1978). *Beyond the Milky Way: Hallucinatory Imagery of the Tukano Indians* (Los Angeles, CA: UCLA Latin America Center).

Reichel-Dolmatoff, G. (1990). The cultural context of an aboriginal hallucinogen: Banisteriopsis caapi, in P.T. Furst (ed.), *Flesh of the Gods: The Ritual Use of Hallucinogens*, 84–113 (Prospect Heights, IL: Waveland Press).

Richman, G.D. (1990/1991). The Santo Daime doctrine: an interview with Alex Polari de Alverga. *Shaman's Drum*, **22**, 30–41.

Schultes, R.E. (1972). An overview of hallucigens in the Western hemisphere, in P.T. Furst (ed.), *Flesh of the Gods: The Ritual Use of Hallucigens*, 3–54 (New York, NY: Praeger).

Schultes, R.E. (1982). The beta-carboline hallucinogens of South America. *Journal of Psychoactive Drugs*, **14**, 205–20.

Schultes, R.E. and Winkelman, M. (1995). The principal American hallucigenic plants and their bioactive and therapeutic properties, in M. Winkelman and W. Andritzky (eds.), *Yearbook of Cross-Cultural Medicine and Psychotherapy*, vol. 6, 205–39 (Berlin: Verlag für Wissenschaft und Bildung).

Shanon, B. (1990). Consciousness. *Journal of Mind and Behavior*, **11**, 137–52.

Shanon, B. (2000). Ayahuasca and creativity. *Bulletin of the Multidisciplinary Association for Psychedelic Studies*, **10**, 18–19.

Shanon, B. (2001). Altered temporality. *Journal of Consciousness Studies*, **8**, 35–58.

Shanon, B. (2002a). *The Antipodes of the Mind: Charting the Phenomenology of the Ayahuasca Experience* (Oxford: Oxford University Press).

Shanon, B. (2002b). Ayahuasca visualizations: a structural typology. *Journal of Consciousness Studies*, **9**, 3–30.

Shanon, B. (2003). Three stories concerning synaesthesia: a commentary on synaesthesia by Ramachandran and Hubbard. *Journal of Consciousness Studies*, **10**, 69–74.

Shanon, B. (in press). The epistemics of ayahuasca visions. *Phenomenology and Cognitive Science*.

Siskind, J. (1973). Visions and cures among the Sharanahua, in M.J. Harner (ed.), *Hallucinogens and Shamanism*, 28–39 (Oxford: Oxford University Press).

Notes

1. Would anyone imagine writing about music without ever having heard any? Yet, the state of affairs encountered with ayahuasca is precisely that: many of those who have investigated ayahuasca have had little or no firsthand experience with it.

2. Recordings of icaros are available, for instance at www.singingtotheplants.com/listen-to-the-songs/ (accessed 6 March 2011).

3. Recordings of Santo Daime hymns are available at www.daime.org/site/pages/mestre/mes24set-PThtm (accessed 6 March 2011); English translations of several hymns are found in Luna and White (2000).

4. I have heard similar accounts of music-like structuring of auditory stimuli from other people.

5. Not only music is temporal, of course: it takes time to read a novel or even inspect a painting.

6. Recall that *icaros* are highly repetitive and that the melodic lines of the hymns of the Santo Daime and of the Barquinha repeat themselves across stanzas.

Chapter 17

Consciousness and everyday music listening: trancing, dissociation, and absorption

Ruth Herbert

> Trance is clearly a matter of degree. Its characteristics
> change, just as water can change—solidify into ice or
> evaporate.
> (Griffin and Tyrrell 1998: 23)

Intense, emotional experiences with music tend to be well remembered; everyday experiences of music less so. Strongly emotional experiences of and with music, sometimes involving dramatic changes in external behaviour, have often been identified and studied within ritual and ceremonial contexts of various kinds (e.g. Becker 2004) and the phenomenology of strong experiences of music has been the subject of detailed empirical inquiry in recent times (e.g. Gabrielsson and Lindström Wik 2003; Gabrielsson in press).

By contrast, the main emphasis of most listening studies of music in everyday life has been on *function*—the ways in which music can be used to regulate behaviour and mood in different situations. A limited amount of data relating to the subjective 'feel' and quality of such episodes do exist, but overall, information remains tantalizingly sparse: everyday listening experiences may not be emotionally 'tagged', often take place while doing something else, are not necessarily pre-planned, and therefore commonly pass by unremarked upon. And yet, music has been shown to be a highly valued resource in people's everyday routines, used by listeners to negotiate and cope with the demands of daily life (e.g. DeNora 2000).

This chapter explores the range of consciousness occurring within the everyday music experiences of a small sample of UK listeners, particularly those experiences lying between the extremes of intense, emotional involvement, and apparent inattention when music, though present, seems to be barely perceived. Specifically, I draw on the constructs of trance, absorption, and dissociation as explicatory frames that throw into relief the self-regulating character—in psychological terms—of much everyday listening. By concentrating on the detailed nature of music listening episodes as lived experiences it becomes possible to offer a phenomenology of everyday listening, thus 'reclaiming' it for comparison with the literature on strong experiences.

Defining trance and trancing

As music is a semantically malleable, embedded, portable and—in the case of recorded music—literally invisible medium, it may be particularly able to contribute to shifts of consciousness in 'ordinary' or mundane circumstances. Becker, for example, cites the potentially 'dreamy introspective experience' of driving alone while listening to music as 'perhaps the most common vernacular definition of trance' (2004: 38). Whilst this kind of definition may resonate for many people, there are immediate paradoxes in both the vernacular and academic definitions of trance and attitudes to it. For example, if when listening to music while driving, a person experienced the onset of convulsions, extreme emotion, and subsequent amnesia—or, alternatively a swooning, cataleptic or half-awake condition—we would probably consider such symptoms to be representative of some underlying pathology, rather than constituting a set of behaviours appropriate to the situation. In fact, the two kinds of behaviour just described attach to two ways of conceptualizing trance that are familiar within ethnomusicology and anthropology and in depictions of trance in European films, television, and literature. They appear inappropriate to mundane experience for various reasons: the former, which might be termed the *high arousal* model—sometimes defined as *ergotropic* or 'strong' trance—commonly refers to instances of possession or shamanic trance in ritualistic contexts, and has also been explored with relation to American Pentecostal church services (Becker 2004) and Rave culture in Britain (Hutson 1999). The latter, *low arousal model*—sometimes termed *trophotropic*—is related to mesmeric practices, tending to be associated with somnambulant states, immobility and the handing over of volitional control to large-eyed Svengali-figures (i.e. hypnotists). In the light of such models, it would be easy to conclude that everyday experience and trance experience have little or nothing in common.

In addition, the very use of the word 'trance' can seem difficult to work with when related to everyday contexts. In ethnomusicological and anthropological studies of trance, the way the term is defined is widely accepted perhaps because rituals serve to frame and contextualize it, lending it validity as an observable and real phenomenon supported by the belief systems of those taking part. Applied to more mundane contexts, it is at first sight not clear what specific situations trance could attach to, outside the settings of the stage or therapy room and thus definitions seem fuzzier and more 'folkloric'.

It is obvious that the word 'trance' has more than one meaning, dependent on sociocultural context, and that different disciplines privilege different aspects of the phenomenon. Thus, ethnographic studies focus on a variety of cross-cultural contexts and associated behaviours—that is, they consider trance as *situated*; whereas the emphasis in hypnosis studies, for example has been on isolating elements of the *state itself*, usually as evidenced in the hypnotherapeutic setting in order to offer a psychological explanation of trance.

In this chapter, I explore a more flexible conceptualization of trance as *process*, as opposed to state (represented by the gerund 'trancing', first introduced by Judith Becker in 2004), which encompasses the possibility of different *types* of trancing that privilege different kinds of consciousness. By this I do not mean that only one kind of consciousness attaches to one type of trancing—different kinds of consciousness operate simultaneously—but that particular perceived qualities of listening episodes may reflect the dominance of particular modes of experiencing. For example, a sense of pure awareness, perhaps deriving from fascination with the qualities of sounds themselves may indicate the dominance of phenomenal consciousness (understood here as the raw 'feel' of subjective experience), whereas an involvement that comes from musical reminiscence may highlight an extended self-consciousness (understood here as awareness coloured by memories and previous emotional and physical experiences).[1] Interestingly, Becker has applied neurologist Antonio Damasio's notions of 'core consciousness' (moment-by-moment awareness of self created by interactions between neural mappings of internal processes (e.g. homeostasis) and the external environment), and 'extended consciousness' (autobiographical awareness dependent on memory and experience) to the phenomenon of trance, arguing that extended consciousness is suspended during trancing, to be temporarily replaced by a 'trance consciousness' (Becker 2004: 11). However, her focus—unlike that of the present chapter—has been exclusively on high arousal trancing.

Generically, I define trancing as a process characterized by a diminished orientation to consensual reality, a diminished critical faculty, a selective internal or external focus, together with a changed sensory awareness and—potentially—a changed sense of self. Hypnotic procedures simply formalize and intensify this process, and in daily life the role of a hypnotherapist is replaced by the interaction of self with selected internal and/or external stimuli, which may or may not occur at the level of conscious awareness.

I take trancing-as-process to be an over-arching concept which subsumes absorption (total focus) and dissociation (mentally cutting off from internal or external concerns) within it. Such a conceptualization is a useful way of framing certain instances of everyday experience, enabling the reclamation and theoretical revalidation (Bull and Back 2003) of so-called periods of 'empty' or 'transitory' time, when music may appear to be used simply to fill an 'off-line gap' between the important 'on-line' tasks of the day. I argue that such experiences offer the opportunity for the self-regulation of psychobiological functioning, which may either be [transpose] deliberately and consciously instigated, or appear to be non-volitional—prompted by an unconscious awareness of what 'feels right'. Findings from three sources support the trancing perspective: research into quasi-hypnotic phenomena in daily life; existing studies of everyday listening; and an empirical enquiry I conducted with a small sample of UK listeners between 2005 and 2007, concerning the varieties and qualities of everyday experiences of listening to music. A brief discussion of the first two sources will serve to introduce an exploration of everyday trancing, supported via examples drawn from the qualitative material of my own research.

Quasi-hypnotic phenomena in daily life

For more than half a century a debate has centred around whether trance involves so-called 'special processes' or 'normal' psychological mechanisms. In many ways this debate seems misguided and unnecessary, stemming partly from long-standing categorical divisions between abnormal and normal psychology, and also from research on the neurophysiological mechanisms of trance that has largely focused on one instance of it (the use of hypnosis in a clinical, controlled setting), thereby separating it from, and ignoring or even denying, other instances of trancing.

If instead we accept the anthropological viewpoint that trancing is 'a psychobiological capacity, available to all societies' (Bourguignon 1973: 11), then it is reasonable to suppose that it involves normal psychological mechanisms. If it is a given capacity involving normal psychological mechanisms, then it is logical to expect instances of it in everyday life, even if they are not commonly conceptualized in those terms. And in fact, there seems to be a general consensus in the field of hypnosis research that quasi-hypnotic episodes occur in daily life; it is merely that they are less likely to be termed trance, and more likely to be termed absorption or dissociation.

The first investigation of such phenomena was by Ronald Shor (1960; Shor *et al.* 1962) who compiled a 'personal experiences questionnaire' (PEQ) designed to examine the frequency and intensity of 'hypnotic-like experiences' occurring 'in the normal course of living' (Shor *et al.* 1962: 55). Shor defined trance as 'the extent to which the usual waking orientation to generalized reality has faded into the more distant background of awareness' (1962: 55) and PEQ questionnaire items referenced scenarios such as total involvement in a film or daydream; staring off into space, thinking of nothing; complete immersion in nature or art; the shutting out of surroundings via intense concentration, and automatic completion of a task.

Concurrently with Shor, Josephine Hilgard was also investigating the nature of quasi-hypnotic experiences in everyday life via an extensive interview study (1965, 1970, 1979a, 1979b). Hilgard divided experiences into three categories, the first two of which overlap: imaginative, sensory-affective, and non-imaginative involvements. Reported experiences related to listening to and playing music, aesthetic involvement in nature, reading, acting, taking part in sports or adventures, science, and religion. Hilgard described imaginative and sensory involvements as permitting 'a temporary absorption in satisfying experiences in which fantasy plays a large role', noting that they provided 'one means of coping with the problems of living' (1979b: 483).

Both Shor and Hilgard's findings inspired the subsequent study of absorption by Auke Tellegen, including the construction of a scale to measure trait absorption (Tellegen and Atkinson 1974), and Tellegen's work was in turn to influence the thinking of hypnosis practitioners and scholars, leading to an increasing body of support in the hypnosis literature for the notion of a type of trance that is not confined to hypnotherapeutic settings or institutionalized rituals (Battino and South 1999; Deikman 1982; Green *et al.* 2005; Killeen and Nash 2003; Krippner 2005; Ranville and Price 2003; Spiegel 2005), and which may include involvement in music.

Listening experiences in everyday life

Drawing on Shor's examples of quasi-hypnotic experiences, it is possible to re-frame so-called 'contemplative' listening—evident in the close focused, attentive listening expected at a Western classical concert—as a particular form of trancing. Yet, a substantial body of listening studies (Bull and Back 2003; Clarke 2005; DeNora 2000; Dibben 2001; North and Hargreaves 2004; Sloboda *et al.* 2001) indicates that a concentrated focus on the music itself, sometimes termed 'autonomous' listening is comparatively rare. Instead, such studies point towards a type of listening that might encompass one or more of the following:

- distributed attention 'across a complex situation of which music is only a part' (Sloboda *et al.* 2001: 418);

◆ fluctuating concentration and attentiveness with an external or internal focus wider than the music alone;

◆ a heightened awareness with a potentially multi-sensory nature;

◆ a range of underlying functions/effects apart from that of high arousal and strong emotion.

From a phenomenological perspective, the important (and unresolved) issue here is not that music *may* form 'the undemanding backdrop to some other task' (North and Hargreaves 2004: 72), but whether, in situations where music does not form the main focus of attention, such listening is necessarily 'superficial' and fails to inform total experience in any meaningful way. Alternatively, if it is possible for music to become part of a multi-modal experience (see for example Bull's documentation of listening practices of iPod, Walkman, and car users in Bull (2004, 2007); Bull and Back (2003)), involving selective elements of what is being seen, heard, accomplished, and imagined, can this be usefully conceptualized as a multi-sensory type of trancing?

In the empirical research on everyday listening that I carried out between 2005 and 2007, seven participants aged between 18 and 85, and pre-selected for their high involvement in music as players or listeners were interviewed about their listening habits, and were subsequently asked to keep 'listening diaries' in which they logged their listening experiences as soon as possible after they occurred. A number of themes that emerged were consistent with experiential categories previously identified by Gabrielsson and Lindström Wik as relating to strong experiences with and of music (e.g. intensified, sometimes multi-modal perception, and changes in attentional focus). The themes were also consistent with Vaitl *et al.*'s (2005) four-dimensional descriptive system of consciousness, which was designed to simplify previous phenomenological checklists of characteristics of altered states of consciousness (ASC). The four dimensions that Vaitl *et al.* (2005: 114) describe are: activation (arousal levels), awareness span (narrow and focused or broad and contemplative), self-awareness (potential forgetting of self), and sensory dynamics (heightened, sometimes synaesthetic experience). Interestingly, logged experiences frequently attested to changes of conscious functioning (such as reduction of thought, increased imagery production, changed temporal sense) that appear as items included within Pekala's (1991) Phenomenology of Consciousness Inventory (PCI), which has sometimes been used to predict levels of hypnotic susceptibility in formal contexts (Hand *et al.* 1995). Qualities of everyday listening experiences supported a processual model of consciousness as dynamic, fluctuating, and continuous (as opposed to comprising discrete states). Key factors involved in this flux were changes in attentional focus, arousal, level of absorption, sensory awareness, experience of time, and sense of self. It is to the phenomenological detail of everyday listening experiences that I now turn.

Multiply directed attention and multi-sensory involvement: towards trancing

A commonly reported everyday listening experience is that involving a distributed and fluctuating attentional sense. Within one listening episode, music may at times be the prime object of attentional focus, and at others barely perceived (a common experience while driving). There may also be an alternation between an inward and outward focus of attention—from preoccupation with internal thoughts and images to scanning the external environment—which is dependent on current mood or emotion, as well as arousal and vigilance levels. In fact, even when listening to music is the main activity, music may not be autonomously experienced. Instead, musical sound can become 'the starting point for a "thought-ful" exploration of any one of a huge variety of connected domains . . . highly integrated and intensely concentrated—but not directed solely at musical structure' (Clarke 2005: 135), as the following account, from Max,[2] one of the participants in my study, indicates:

> On train listen to Shostakovich Leningrad symphony. Always loved this for describing war horror—very filmy to me. Really feel hate and pain inside the music. Internal images that I was getting were of horror of war from news footage. Lots of slow motion for some reason. Lots of thoughts and pictures about death and destruction mostly, but include frequent images of Shostakovich's face with square framed bakelite glasses & suit and tie & thinking how his appearance and the music seemed so opposite.

This episode shows a diminishing connection with external reality via a narrowed internal attentional focus and relaxed critical faculty, enabling the production of vivid imagery and emotional involvement. There is a fluctuation between absorption and tangential thought that is almost dream-like, demonstrating listening as performative, not passive, with meaning actively constructed.

Attentional shifts, inwards and outwards can also act together to provide a multi-sensory experience—a filmic narrative that relates to the current surroundings, as in this account by Sophie:

> Listening to My Morning Jacket,[3] bluesy tinges, loads of reverb. In my room looking out of the window. The sun keeps dipping in and out of the clouds, and I'm willing it to stay out. Drifting into daydreams about long straight roads in America, just travelling, avoiding work. Sunlight stays—feeling happiness as the guitar solo kicks in and I'm absorbed into the moving landscape. Thinking the bass on these headphones is really good. Start to notice the wind stirring the trees slightly. Song ends.

Music here enhances sensory awareness, contributing to a pleasant and effortless experience that fluctuates in intensity, with attention distributed between the music, surroundings, inner associations, and tangential thought (appreciating the headphones).

The affordances of the music and the wider environment blend together, suggesting a kind of performativity, in which the perceiver herself informally 'blends' together visual and aural elements to construct multi-sensory listening episodes. The process is reminiscent of that theorized in Cook's (1998) account of the perception of music in multimedia works, an analysis involving notions of congruence, contrast, and conflict between individual media. The incompleteness of sensory information in aesthetic objects encourages an active and performative stance to listening, where interpretation can 'fill in the gaps' (see Windsor 2000). Thinking about other things—including associations, memories, noticing certain elements of the external surroundings—rather than being a negative 'distraction' is then reconceived as an essential part of this sense-making.

It is the multi-faceted nature of such experiences that suggests an affinity with trance—or at least one version of it. Within hypnotherapy, trance inductions commonly seek to mobilize as many modes of experience as possible—visual, aural, kinaesthetic, etc.—in order to prompt engagement with an alternative or virtual reality. In the two accounts above, the fusion of different senses encourages what can be termed an informal induction of trancing. Both could be seen as what Josephine Hilgard (1979a) has identified as 'fantasy involvements'—quasi-hypnotic semi-virtual environments which provide a temporary escape from daily life.

Music and trance

Experiences of music listening in daily life resonate with what the influential twentieth century clinical psychologist Milton Erickson described as the 'common everyday trance' (Rossi and Ryan 1985/1998) and which I here term spontaneous trancing. This is a more inclusive conception of trancing than that discussed by Becker, in that she states that 'before trancing happens, one has expectations as to what is supposed to happen . . . trancing is seldom spontaneous' (2004: 42). Spontaneous trancing attaches to situations in daily life that involve a selective attentional focus such as being absorbed in an activity (e.g. DIY activities, looking at a view, shopping) or being gripped by a strong emotion (e.g. anger). The most fundamental instance of everyday trancing is dreaming (Griffin and Tyrrell 1998), but in terms of everyday activities that involve music, a range of possible types of involvement, or ways of trancing is apparent:

◆ Trancing can focus on acoustic attributes of the music, such as repetitive loops, timbres, a pronounced repetitive beat, slow rate of change, layered/polyphonic texture, that is, overtly 'trancey' features, often leading to a reduction in thought.

◆ Trancing can focus on associations/memories. These might be triggered by extra-musical references in the music (words or non-musical sounds) or the social and cultural sources that the music specifies. This type of trancing often features an inward focus and rich imagery.

◆ Trancing can focus on emotion induced by the music. This mode can also blend with the two scenarios above.

◆ Trancing can focus on a fusion of modalities (aural, visual, kinaesthetic), for example composites of:

  • music and movement (e.g. repetitive activity such as walking/running/dancing/doing craftwork);

  • music and movement of other objects (e.g. blurred, changing views on a train);

  • music and external surroundings (blending, heightened sensory effect).

The music involved in trancing situations is most likely to be familiar, probably because the listener has accumulated ways of responding to it over the course of several hearings, and has acquired a belief in its effect. A comparison with the use of music in more formal, ritualistic contexts may serve to clarify this point. The responses of participants in rituals—particularly, but not exclusively in sacred contexts—may be gradually conditioned by repeated exposure to a limited body of texts, music, and actions, all experienced in a particular setting. Over weeks, months, and years, repetition of ritual procedures means that, in cognitive terms, knowledge pertaining to them becomes stored in implicit, rather than explicit memory, that is, they become processed automatically beneath conscious awareness—'routinized' as part of what Whitehouse has described as a 'doctrinal mode of religiosity' (2004: 66).

Thus, familiarity with the ingredients of ritual encourages an increase in automatic behaviours, a decrease of critical thought and an increase in suggestibility levels. Sounds, sights, and actions are experientially combined to function as an induction to involvement (the equivalent of a formal hypnotic induction), and such involvement is likely to be cumulative over time—dependent on the number of occasions the ritual is repeated and whether an individual possesses a belief (or develops a belief) in the values, quality, or subject matter that the ritual communicates. Automatic behaviours, reduction of critical thought, and increased suggestibility levels are all factors that have been recognized as key characteristics of trance (Brown *et al.* 2001), and are most markedly apparent in the behavioural responses of members of cults which typically demonstrate a sense of non-volitional automaticity (Deikman 1994), suggesting that critical faculties are reduced or suspended. Trancing is less likely to occur in unfamiliar situations, or when listening to unfamiliar music, because unusual events or stimuli tend to be processed at a conscious level (Whitehouse 2004: 72) in the context of rational analytical thought and raised vigilance levels.

Components of everyday trancing: dissociation and absorption

The processes of absorption and dissociation have long been recognized within the hypnotherapeutic literature as central to trance. As terms, they function as useful holistic 'wrappers' or shorthands for the overall subjective 'feel' of certain types of experience arising from the interaction of a number of psychological processes. In the following sections I provide definitions of dissociation and absorption and examine the prevalence of dissociative and absorbed trancing in real-world everyday experiences of listening to music. Whether these processes can be separated is debateable, and I have chosen to group experiences by the apparent weighting of these concepts within individual descriptions. Thus, a music listening episode may appear predominantly dissociative, but may also contain an element of absorption (or vice versa).

Dissociation can be defined as 'the temporary alteration or separation of normally integrated mental processes' (Butler 2004: 5). While dissociation is often associated with pathological conditions such as post-traumatic stress disorder (PTSD), there is an increasing body of evidence pointing towards the presence of non-pathological dissociation in everyday life, functioning to provide temporary escape from internal and external pressures. Unsurprisingly, dissociative experiences may include a strong element of absorption. In fact, absorption is considered to be one of three factors (absorption/imaginative involvement, de-personalization or de-realization, amnesia) that dissociation comprises (Butler and Palesh 2004: 63).

Dissociation from self, surroundings, and activity appears to be a common component of a sizeable proportion of everyday music listening experiences. It often seems to have a therapeutic function, although this may not be the overt intention of the listener, as in the following episode where David types an essay for his wife. He explains that he uses music to maintain a focus on typing accuracy, but the description strongly suggests that the music provides a way of absenting himself from the task:

> I play 'Music for Airports' by Brian Eno. This is a fairly long piece that has a repeated theme. I can hear what my wife is saying and I can type it quickly for her, but *I am not*

actually taking in anything she is dictating . . . I don't have to think about it . . . I do feel relaxed with the music. (Emphasis added)

The ways in which dissociation from self and/or surroundings is described often imply an alteration of a state of consciousness perceived as familiar or 'normal', as in this account by Max:

Translate landscapes from train window into bird's eye perspective—hard to explain really, basically seeing things from above. I'm not 'me' for a while, looking out. It's a combination of things—claustrophobia of a train, staring out of window at blurred, changing views, repetitive movement & recent music memories running through my head altering my perception of reality a bit. Takes me away from humdrum internalized thoughts and worries & gives me a different 'bigger picture' angle on things. Hard to rationalize exactly what's going on—some sort of (slight) out of body experience thing. Mind kind of declutters itself of internalized thoughts and drifts into a more open (vacant) minded outward view. The music running through my mind 'scores' the bird's-eye visual.

This listening episode is informed by an established belief in a state of mind/consciousness possibly unfamiliar to others ('hard to explain') and represented visually ('seeing things from above'), and which involves a changing perception of the world ('alters my perception of reality'). Phrases such as 'out of body experience' indicate Max's sense of a move away from a familiar base-line state of consciousness. The experience is not unpleasant ('takes me away from thoughts and worries') and involves standing outside the 'normal self' to view a 'bigger picture'. There is an emphasis on a selective outward attentional focus, coupled with a sense of balanced detachment or dissociation from what is seen, and music is experienced as a soundtrack to this state ('scores the bird's eye visual'). The multi-sensory combination of music, repetitive train movement, and blurred changing views also suggests a component of low-arousal absorption.

Gary provides a clear example of the use of music to aid an intermittent sense of mental removal from both surroundings and self during a walk into town after a domestic argument:

The sounds consist of very little more than looped string sections, which are layered to allow for slow and quite subtle thematic shifts . . . I have selected well and this allows me to drift into the comfortable non-state . . . I wander around town and pop in and out of the quirky little shops, just browsing and apparently advertising my insularity . . . the whole point is to be as unaware of my physical self as is realistically possible—the music allows for gradual and deeper dislocation. Like a waking dream, where I am the conductor and the real world activity . . . is really just a game in which I am choosing to whimsically dabble. I'm lost in the music—it is feeding my spacelessness . . . this works well until I visit the market and am asked a question as I browse the CD stall . . . I am roused from my reverie and all of a sudden thrust into the 'on-mode' again . . . I wander away—I will remain disconnected and insular.

Informing the listening episode is the underlying belief that music possesses qualities that will facilitate an altered state ('allows me to drift into the comfortable non-state'). A gap opens up between the 'subjective' world he has constructed and the 'objective' world, which, at times, intrudes upon this ('asked a question'). The language of these extracts shows an affinity with ideas drawn from the literature on dissociation as a defence mechanism (e.g. Cardeña 1994), in addition to terminology associated with descriptions of altered states. In the case of other respondents, the sense of dissociation seems implicit in the text, but is not explicitly stated, as when Imogen describes music as 'blocking out thought . . . good for not wanting to think anything'.

Absorption—an effortless, non-volitional, deep involvement with the object of experience (Jamieson 2005: 120)—is often more readily associated with live, often strongly emotional experiences of music, where music is the main focus of attention. In everyday listening, absorption does sometimes centre on the music itself and these may be intensely emotional experiences. However, at other times, a type of low arousal absorption appears to occur that involves both music and surroundings, as Sophie describes:

> 6.30pm. Walking out of the gym. I had to stop at the top of the steps because the skyline was so fascinating. I also had to find the right track on my CD to watch the sky for a moment. I listened for about one minute, whilst noticing the birds fly across the light in the clouds. The music made the experience more like a moment of meditation than simply looking at the skyline . . . I was able to filter out any thoughts and be absorbed in the landscape.

Sophie describes a familiar practice of choreographing her surroundings with music, in which music blends with environment so as to elicit a selective external awareness (birds/light/clouds) and an enhanced visual sense as music blends with environment. The multi-sensory and absorbing nature of the experience is probably enhanced by her heightened physiological arousal, following exercise at the gym. Music appears to unify and make extraordinary an experience that would otherwise be ordinary.

Low arousal absorption can occur in very ordinary experiences—during transitional periods of time such as travelling to work—that would ordinarily be quickly forgotten, as Max describes:

> Today's CD is Earl Hooker playing blues guitar . . . am aware of walking along, playing a few tracks with twelve-bar rhythm in brain, avoiding cracks in the pavement. I think avoiding the cracks was something to do with keeping the rhythm—a sort of regular precise thing. Normally I don't worry about cracks—well not since I was a kid! . . . the mind was chilled out and empty.

A selective awareness (pavement cracks) appears to fuse with a physical entrainment that is linked to both what is heard and seen—the repetitive quality of the music (a cycling, 12-bar structure) and the pattern of the paving stones. Such repetition appears to function in the manner of a mandala (a repetitive, usually concentric circular pattern used in meditation), stilling the mind ('chilled out and empty'). This type of absorption equates well with Kaplan's notion of 'soft fascination', a term he uses to describe the restorative benefits of nature:

> Many of the fascinations afforded by the natural setting qualify as 'soft' fascinations: clouds, sunsets, snow patterns, the motion of leaves in the breeze—these readily hold the attention, but in undramatic fashion. *Attending to these patterns is effortless, and they leave ample opportunity for thinking about other things.* (Kaplan 1995: 174; emphasis added)

Kaplan makes a distinction between 'soft' and 'hard' fascination, giving as examples, walking in a natural setting and watching motor racing respectively. His comments pertaining to nature seem particularly relevant to absorbed everyday trancing.

Absorption also shares similarities with many other conceptualizations of experience, including imaginative involvement (Hilgard 1979a), flow (Csikszentmihalyi 1990, 1997) plateau experience (Maslow 1971) and withdrawal experience (Laski 1980). In addition, listeners also sometimes describe their experiences as 'hypnotic' or 'trance-like'. Indeed, within the literature relating to hypnotherapy, absorption has been equated with what has been defined as 'weak' or 'light' trance:

> This state of mental relaxation, absorption in inner experiences such as imagery, memories and feelings, and the detachment from ongoing events in the external world may be labelled as trance. (Heap and Dryden 1998: 9)

Conclusion

Attaching conceptual labels to aspects of phenomenological experience can be both problematic and revealing. The overlapping concepts of trancing, dissociation, and absorption are in a real sense constructs: imposed definitions that bundle together different threads of experience in culturally determined ways. For example, until recently, dissociation has been linked only to negative, pathological elements of experience (as opposed to the positive connotations of the word 'absorption'). Reified, such terms may easily assume a solidity and clarity that phenomenologically they do not possess. At the same time, it is this very 'bundling together' of interacting variables that allows experiences to be grasped holistically and for cross-comparisons to be made—at micro-level between individuals, and at macro-level between separate academic studies.

At the close of a discussion of their large-scale survey of everyday music listening, North and Hargreaves (2004: 73) ask why people state that they listen to music 'for mundane reasons such as habit and passing the time, rather than [as] an attempt to achieve more profound and rewarding experiences'. The listening experiences that I have documented here and elsewhere (Herbert 2009), and to which I have referred in this chapter may provide some answers. From participant reports there emerges a 'hidden' practice of self-regulation via music that seems often to operate at the level of unconscious perception such that the overt, stated purpose of listening might not match the emergent, underlying need. Because many everyday listening episodes are subtle and evanescent experiences, not necessarily attached to strong emotions, they are easily forgotten, and thus not available to reflect upon consciously or learn from. Retrospective recall may emphasize aspects of behaviour during a listening episode (e.g. 'I find that I read quicker') rather than the subjective 'feel' of the experience, meaning that in some instances dissociation or absorption are inferred from behavioural clues, for example staring at cracks in the pavement.

While a continuous, fluctuating model of consciousness has been presented, where 'states' are not considered as discrete and 'thing-like', this need not rule out the possibility that different individuals, and indeed different cultures, may value and seek to emphasize different points along that continuum. Cultural interpretations of what constitutes 'normal' consciousness vary widely, and people's cultural frameworks impact not only on the way individuals describe their experiences, but also (and perhaps crucially) on the experience itself.

The anthropologist Erika Bourguignon has distinguished between 'private, individual, unpatterned states and those that occur in culturally patterned, institutionalized forms' (1973: 8). As an instance of the first, she cites Ludwig's (1966: 226) identification of a trance state involving increased, selective alertness among radar operators. This she interprets as an 'individual, secular state' and it is unlikely that the radar operators would conceptualize this experience as 'a trance state' of any kind. As an instance of 'culturally patterned institutionalized forms', she identifies the same alertness and involvement as being present in the method of divination known as scrying (e.g. gazing at a crystal ball, or at the surface of water). This she terms an example of a 'culturally patterned sacred trance'. Because this occurs within a particular institutionalized, cultural framework, it is far more likely to be thought of, and thus experienced as trance. Everyday music listening episodes seem to accord most closely with Bourguignon's first category, while identifiable strong experiences of listening may be closer to the second.

Strong experiences of music are often clearly situated within a particular cultural framework, often in a live, institutional context, and in the company of others. Whatever the specific circumstances, such experiences seem to be highly valued, and to have a set of clear, commonly accepted functions (e.g. they can be perceived as emotionally cathartic or life-changing) together with accepted ways of talking about such experiences. Everyday listening episodes, as hidden, mundane experiences, lack an institutional framework, or consensual knowledge of how and why they occur in the way that they do, or what their purpose is. They are often private, individually customized experiences that on the surface may appear to have no other function than to pass the time during a 'transitional period', and are not usually discussed with others. Yet although finding ways of talking about such episodes may be difficult, these everyday listening practices are obviously valued by people as an important part of ordinary life, which suggests that a significant affordance of music is its capacity to effect shifts of consciousness that support an individual's sense of daily psychological balance.

References

Battino, R. and South, T.L. (1999). *Ericksonian Approaches: A Comprehensive Manual* (Wales: Crown House Publishing).

Becker, J. (2004). *Deep Listeners: Music, Emotion and Trancing* (Bloomington, IN: Indiana University Press).

Bourguignon, E. (ed.) (1973). *Religion, Altered States of Consciousness and Social Change* (Columbus, OH: Ohio State University Press).

Brown, R.J., Antonova, E., Langley, A., and Oakley, D. (2001). The effects of absorption and reduced critical thought on suggestibility in an hypnotic context. *Contemporary Hypnosis*, **18**, 62–72.

Bull, M. (2004). Automobility and the power of sound. *Theory, Culture & Society*, **21**, 243–59.

Bull, M. (2007). *Sound Moves: iPod Culture and Urban Experience* (London: Routledge).

Bull, M. and Back, L. (eds.) (2003). *The Auditory Culture Reader* (Oxford: Berg).

Butler, L.D. (2004). The dissociations of everyday life. *Journal of Trauma and Dissociation*, **5**, 1–11.

Butler, L.D. and Palesh, O. (2004). Spellbound: dissociation in the movies. *Journal of Trauma and Dissociation*, **5**, 61–87.

Cardeña, E. (1994). The domain of dissociation, in S.J. Lynn and J.W. Rhue (eds.), *Dissociation: Clinical and Theoretical Perspectives*, 15–31 (New York, NY: Guilford Press).

Clarke, E.F. (2005). *Ways of Listening: An Ecological Approach to the Perception of Musical Meaning* (New York, NY: Oxford University Press).

Cook, N. (1998). *Analysing Musical Multimedia* (Oxford: Oxford University Press).

Csikszentmihalyi, M. (1990). *Flow: The Psychology of Optimal Experience* (New York, NY: Harper Perennial).

Csikszentmihalyi, M. (1997). *Finding Flow* (New York, NY: Basic Books).

Deikman, A.J. (1982). *The Observing Self: Mysticism and Psychotherapy* (Boston, MA: Beacon Press).

Deikman, A.J. (1994). *The Wrong Way Home: Uncovering the Patterns of Cult Behaviour in America* (Boston, MA: Beacon Press).

DeNora, T. (2000). *Music in Everyday Life* (Cambridge: Cambridge University Press).

Dibben, N. (2001). What do we hear, when we hear music? Music perception and musical material. *Musicae Scientiae*, **5**, 161–94.

Gabrielsson, A. (in press). *Strong Experiences with Music*, trans R. Bradbury (Oxford: Oxford University Press).

Gabrielsson, A. and Lindström Wik, S. (2003). Strong experiences related to music: a descriptive system. *Musicae Scientiae*, **7**, 157–217.

Green, J.P., Barabasz, A.F., Barrett, D., and Montgomery, G.H. (2005). Forging ahead: the 2003 APA Division 30 definition of hypnosis. *Journal of Clinical and Experimental Hypnosis*, **53**, 259–64.

Griffin, J. and Tyrrell, I. (1998). *Hypnosis and Trance States: A New Psycho-biological Explanation* (Sussex: European Therapy Studies Institute).

Hand, J., Pekala, R.J., and Kumar, V.K. (1995). Prediction of Harvard and Stanford Scale scores with a phenomenological instrument. *Australian Journal of Clinical and Experimental Hypnosis*, **23**, 124–34.

Heap, M. and Dryden, W. (eds.) (1998). *Hypnotherapy: A Handbook* (Milton Keynes: Open University Press).

Herbert, R. (2009). *Range of Consciousness within Everyday Music Listening Experiences: Absorption, Dissociation and the Trancing Process*. Unpublished PhD thesis, University of Sheffield.

Hilgard, J. (1965). Personality and hypnotizability: inferences from case studies, in E.R. Hilgard, (ed.), *Hypnotic Susceptibility*, 343–74 (New York, NY: Harcourt, Brace and World).

Hilgard, J. (1974). Imaginative involvement: some characteristics of the highly hypnotizable and the non-hypnotizable. *International Journal of Clinical and Experimental Hypnosis*, **22**, 138–56.

Hilgard, J. (1979a). *Personality and Hypnosis: A Study of Imaginative Involvement*, 2nd edn (Chicago, IL: Chicago University Press).

Hilgard, J. (1979b). Imaginative and sensory-affective involvements: in everyday life and in hypnosis, in E. Fromm and R. Shor (eds.), *Hypnosis: Developments in Research and New Perspectives*, 483–517 (New York, NY: Aldine Publishing Company).

Hutson, S.R. (1999). Technoshamanism: spiritual healing in the rave subculture. *Popular Music and Society*, **23**, 53–77.

Jamieson, G.A. (2005). The modified tellegen absorption scale: a clearer window on the structure and meaning of absorption. *Australian Journal of Clinical and Experimental Hypnosis*, **33**, 119–39.

Kaplan, S. (1995). The restorative benefits of nature: toward an integrative framework. *Journal of Environmental Psychology*, **15**, 169–82.

Killeen, P.R. and Nash, M.R. (2003). The four causes of hypnosis. *International Journal of Clinical and Experimental Hypnosis*, **53**, 97–118.

Krippner, S. (2005). Trance and the trickster: hypnosis as a liminal phenomenon. *Journal of Clinical and Experimental Hypnosis*, **53**, 97–118.

Laski, M. (1980). *Everyday Ecstasy* (London: Thames and Hudson).

Ludwig, A. (1966). Altered states of consciousness. *Archives of General Psychiatry*, **15**, 225–34.

Maslow, A.H. (1971). *The Farther Reaches of Human Nature* (New York, NY: Penguin).

North, A.C. and Hargreaves, D.J. (2004). Uses of music in everyday life. *Music Perception*, **22**, 41–77.

Pekala, R.J. (1991). *Quantifying Consciousness: An Empirical Approach* (New York, NY: Plenum Press).

Ranville, P. and Price, D.D. (2003). Hypnosis phenomenology and the neurobiology of consciousness. *International Journal of Clinical and Experimental Hypnosis*, **51**, 105–29.

Rossi, E.L. and Ryan, M.O. (eds.) (1985/1998). *The Seminars, Workshops and Lectures of Milton A. Erickson* (London: Free Association Books).

Shor, R.E. (1960). The frequency of naturally occurring 'hypnotic-like' experiences in the normal college population. *International Journal of Clinical and Experimental Hypnosis*, **8**, 151–63.

Shor, R.E., Orne, M.T., and O'Connell, D.N. (1962). Validation and cross-validation of a scale of self-reported personal experiences which predicts hypnotizability. *Journal of Psychology*, **53**, 55–75.

Sloboda, J.A., O'Neill, S.A., and Ivaldi, A. (2001). Functions of music in everyday life: an exploratory study using the Experience Sampling Method. *Musicae Scientiae*, **5**, 9–32.

Spiegel, D. (2005). Multileveling the playing field: altering our state of consciousness to understand hypnosis. *Contemporary Hypnosis*, **22**, 31–3.

Tellegen, A. and Atkinson, G. (1974). Openness to absorbing and self-altering experiences ('absorption'), a trait related to hypnotic susceptibility. *Journal of Abnormal Psychology*, **83**, 268–77.

Vaitl, D., Birbaumer, N., Gruzelier, J., Jamieson, G.A., Kotchoubey, B., Kübler, A., Lehmann, D., Miltner, W., Ott, U., Pütz, P., Sammer, G., Strauch, I., Strehl, U., Wackermann, J., and Weiss, T. (2005). Psychobiology of altered states of consciousness. *Psychological Bulletin*, **1**, 98–127.

Whitehouse, H. (2004). *Modes of Religiosity: A Cognitive Theory of Religious Transmission* (Walnut Creek, CA: Alta Mira Press).

Windsor, W.L. (2000). Through and around the acousmatic: the interpretation of electroacoustic sounds, in S. Emmerson (ed.), *Music, Electronic Media and Culture*, 7–35 (London: Ashgate).

Young, A.W. and Block, N. (1996). Consciousness, in V. Bruce (ed.), *Unsolved Mysteries of the Mind: Tutorial Essays in Cognition*, 149–79 (Hove: Erlbaum).

Notes

1. I am drawing on conceptualizations of kinds of consciousness by the American philosopher Ned Block and neuropsychologist Andrew Young (1996), which are often cited in consciousness studies literature.

2. All participant names have been changed.

3. An American rock band.

Chapter 18

Practical consciousness and social relation in *MusEcological* perspective

Tia DeNora

Inner consciousness is socially organized by the
importation of the social organization of the outer world.
(Mead 1912: 406)

Practical consciousness and cultural ecology

There is a venerable tradition within social philosophy and sociological theory that understands consciousness as a pragmatic achievement. Consciousness is assembled. And it is manifested as an ability to exhibit perceptual orientation to a shared social world. In this sense, consciousness is part of our acquired and informally studied equipment as communicatively 'competent' modern social beings. Consciousness is thus an important (but not the only) component of personhood. It is a means for agency in the world and a sign of a 'healthy' or 'well-adjusted' self. To the extent it is thought to be within the control of the person who has it, moreover, consciousness is also a moral obligation.

In this chapter, I consider the topic of music's role in consciousness formation understood pragmatically. This pragmatic perspective will consist of a focus on consciousness as a form of creative work. I will suggest that, in common with all creative work, it is a 'systematic function' (Csikszentmihalyi 1997: 23; Sutherland and Acord 2007): it emerges from collaborative social and material–cultural settings. Then, to develop this theme and set it in what I consider to be its proper context, I will define my terms and develop a particular understanding of consciousness as taking shape through reference to things outside of individual minds. I will then turn to the main topic, music as an instrument of consciousness and, as such, as part of the care of self and its connection both to sociability and, more critically, governmentality (DeNora 2000; Foucault, 1988; Rose 1996), which I will explore through examples of embodied consciousness (physical orientation to environment) and musically mediated verbal awareness. From there, I will present the topic of musical consciousness in a mental health context, specifically to consider musical consciousness as a medium for social relation, regulation, and self-presentation. Throughout, I will suggest that consciousness consists of dispositional orientations for forms of action (individual and collective) and identity in the world. My exploration of this topic is part of a larger project I have been conducting with music therapist Gary Ansdell on community music therapy and the concept of aesthetic ecology.[1] In that work we have examined musical activity as it is imbricated in clients' passages away from the places, practices, and identities associated with mental illness and towards their reintegration and functioning in the social environment, as defined both by clients themselves and by health professionals.

Conceptually, within this research, we employ an ecological understanding of health, as a species of identity more generally. This ecological model for us involves a *performative, relational* understanding of health (Ansdell 1995; DeNora 2007), which in turn understands health as *afforded* by ecological settings and materials. To be clear, I intend these terms as follows:

♦ *performative*: acting on an ability to align oneself and be aligned with insignia (indicators) of health identity—that is, discursively constructed categories and images of 'being well';

♦ *relational*: the meaning, status or identity of people and things emerges out of an ecology of people, practices, and things;

♦ *affordance* (a term originating with Gibson (1977)): possibilities offered (and/or found to be offered) by materials, texts, and relations—what can be done with these things and how they lend themselves to those doings (see DeNora 2000: 38–40; E. Clarke 2005: 36–8; Streeck 1996).

Putting performativity and relationality together and understanding both in terms of how affordances are appropriated in action (DeNora 2000; 2003), it is possible to understand 'health' as an identity that is achieved (performed) within an environment or ecological setting. For its accomplishment, performance draws on resources that are to be found distributed within that environment, such as objects, practices, attitudes, and postures. In this sense performance emerges *in relation* to resources within an environment. For example, imagine that if I were identified, back in the small town where I grew up, as being 'good at the high jump'. In this case, my identity and ability stand in relation to whether or not I clear a bar of a certain height (can I, in other words, appropriate that bar as one that affords the measurement of my ability to jump?). In the place I come from, it might be that no one else can 'jump' higher than 12 inches, and I can clear 13. I may hold the identity of 'best' here, in a performed, relational sense within that environment.

In this simple example, my performance can be seen to emerge from my position in relation to materials, technologies, and cultures of interpretation—including roles and rules, or preferred or socially sanctioned forms of practice. Switching now to the example of mental health, we might ask about how that identity is also relationally assessed, and relationally performed. From where might the resources for that performance come?

With regard to mental health (and leading back to the subject of consciousness as social achievement) those 'games' might consists of things such as this: one manages to appear composed rather than agitated, to sustain a conversation, to complete various types of tasks, or to seem 'fit' for a particular task (performance). A crucial task here is being able to perceive and orient to features of an apparently shared world 'outside' of oneself; and the issue of that ability returns us to the core topic of this chapter—consciousness and its link to mental health and how both these matters can be understood to be musically mediated.

Here, consciousness is the capacity for a selective sensitivity and perceptual orientation to the external world. It is thus a vehicle for social contact and coordination. With this framework in mind, I will use two questions to organize my discussion. These are: (1) From where does consciousness originate and how is it acquired? (2) In what ways is it possible to see music as a formative material of consciousness? To address the first question I will draw upon work in philosophy of mind and consciousness that highlights the ways in which the seemingly 'individual' matter of mind is built from interactions with and appropriations of materials outside of individuals. I use this discussion to set the scene for considering the second question—music's role as an active or formative ingredient of consciousness. To address the second question, I will employ a variety of examples of music as it can be seen to contribute actively to our perceptual orientation to the world.

I have explored some of these issues in my earlier work on music 'in action' and musical self-identity (DeNora 2000). In particular, I have considered how orientation to the world, and action within it, including the action of constituting self-identity can be understood simultaneously to take shape from and also in turn shape action's contexts. This focus on the mutual determination of action and environment is respectful of the premise that individual action, experience, subjectivity, and identity are socially conditioned. But it is also respectful of the ways that the set of conditions that affords, structures, enables, or constrains action is itself made meaningful and accessible in relation to action. With respect to music, this means that patterns of distribution, political agendas, markets, technologies, critical discourses, and corporate policies structure what is accessible to the acting subject (on this point, see D. Clarke 2007). It also means that the ways these 'externals' come to be known is mediated through meaningful action. To gloss W.I. Thomas ('If men define situations as real, they are real in their consequences), the reality of 'external' constraints (contexts and their impacts on action and subjectivity) is defined within situations of action and through techniques or deeds (Thomas and Thomas 1928: 572; see also MacKenzie 2006).

So 'context', within this reflexive perspective, is never a pre-existing 'given' (Dore and McDermott 1982). Rather, like actors themselves, it *emerges* in and during the course of meaningful action and according to how it is invoked (DeNora 2003: 37–40). Once we accept the notion of the mutual determination of action and context, it is possible to transcend the micro–macro dichotomy that underpins so much of our thinking in the humanities and social sciences. In place of this dichotomy, as I have suggested elsewhere (DeNora 2000: 4), it is possible to pose a 'meso' approach, one that, in my view, enhances considerably our ability to conceptualize and observe music's dynamic role in relation to the reflexive process of constituting the content of both context and action simultaneously. Through the medium of music, in other words, social worlds can be made and neither musicology nor sociology can collapse one into the other (Hennion 2001, 2007).

As I hope to demonstrate in this chapter, a focus on meso-structures (networks, clusters of actions, and objects, scenes, and events) highlights the integration between actors and environments. It does not by any means emphasize agency at the expense of structure. On the contrary, meso-level studies focus on what emerges *between* actors and conditions of action (and on the processes of this emergence). How, in other words, do scenes, perceptions, situations, and actors get 'composed' in ways that perform both the figure and the ground of action? How are materials mobilized for this process, albeit not necessarily (this is important for critical studies) with deliberation or intent? And how—as one of these 'things' that gets composed—is consciousness, both individual and collective, musically enhanced and musically assembled?

The cultural pragmatics of consciousness in the philosophy of mind

Various philosophers have suggested that consciousness is characterized by degrees or levels (some of which humans share with animals), from pre-reflective awareness, to sentience, reflection, and self-awareness (Zelazo 1999; Zelazo and Sommerville 2001). Some scholars, notably Daniel Dennett (1991), have argued that consciousness should not be equated with perception but reserved as a term referring to 'higher order' forms of reflection that include awareness of self, and of self as a knower. This distinction also resonates with the conventional philosophical categories of first- and second-order consciousness, the former (e.g. tasting an apple) linked less to accounts 'about' experience than the latter (e.g. reflecting on one's taste of the apple—and thus preparatory to communicating, to self and other, about that taste).

In its so-called 'higher' or second-order form consciousness is something more than sentience or awareness. It involves the social organization of perception as a form of representation—as 'consciousness of', 'consciousness for', and (since these are arguably inseparable in practice) 'consciousness in relation to' matters outside the individual. Understood in this sense, consciousness is cultural; in Durkheim's sense it is 'a whole world of sentiments, ideas and images which, once born, obey laws all their own' (1915: 471). This collective, or socially mediated consciousness is, as Durkheim suggests, the means by which realities (including the self as known to self and others) come to be *registered* publicly as objects in the world—objects to which one may be directed by others.

Thus, at least in terms of its outcomes, second- or 'higher'-order consciousness is a practical activity, part of what it takes to live and coordinate with others. Indeed, perception itself (first-order consciousness) is also quasi-social, though it is much more of a challenge to say just how (see Acord and DeNora 2008). It is also the means by which perception is aligned with pre-existing classifications and accounts. In these respects, consciousness is the individual's connection and contribution to what comes to count as 'reality'.

But just *how* does first-order consciousness originate? In what follows, I will suggest that it is put together in relation to things outside it. To invoke the quotation from

Mead used as an epigraph for this chapter, we 'import' features from the external world. But how does this occur and can it be investigated empirically? Some of the ground for considering these issues has been prepared by another philosopher of mind, Giovanna Colombetti (2009), in her work on the links between language (poetics), the plastic arts, and emotional experience.

In work that develops Clark and Chalmers's (1998) focus on language as one of the external materials that provides a scaffolding for cognition, Colombetti suggests that language individuates and scaffolds not only cognition but also emotion. By this she means that words, far from being neutral descriptors, give rise to the emergence of feelings (i.e. they perform or formulate feelings); and she makes specific comparison to music in this regard. Both media, as she puts it, 'enhance patients' emotion experience, and [help] to entrain and thereby structure their expression and physiology' (Colombetti 2009: 13; also referencing DeNora 2000). In other words, Colombetti suggests that verbalization, like music, provides an external medium that socializes or draws out subjects' experience and gives experience its shapes. As she puts it, language is a device that 'pulls the mind "from outside", by signposting and recommending possibilities for experience' (23). Moreover, by labelling these feelings, language makes them conventional and publicly available, and thus contributes to their uptake within populations (to their degree of sharedness and conventionality), sometimes in ways that result in new ecological niches (e.g. the apocryphal idea of numerous words for snow in Inuit culture).

For Colombetti, language is but one expressive modality by which experience comes to be formulated. She also considers how the plastic arts, specifically surrealist practices, were able to 'pull' new experiences into being, shedding 'a particular light' on experience and, eventually, via that light, altering consciousness of reality. In sum, expressive modalities and materials prospectively structure, refine, and channel experience and, in so doing, heighten our awareness (consciousness) of experience and of self. In other words, the arts can enrich our capacity to narrate or, more generally, formulate experience as a conscious 'I', giving it inflection, new categories of experience, and, depending on the materials, affective content. These inflections, affective states, and categorical presumptions are, I suggest, part of a dispositional arrangement of our orientation to the world; thus the shape they take is formative of consciousness, of our selective sensitivity to environment. It is this point that I now wish to develop in relation to music. I will speak of 'warm' and 'cool' musical consciousness to highlight some of the different ways in which music affords consciousness; and will relate this conceit to music's role in the production of both so-called 'higher' and 'lower' levels of consciousness. These types are introduced through the example of music's dynamic role in aerobics exercise classes (DeNora 2000).

'Warm' and 'cool' musical consciousness

By 'warm' musical consciousness I mean that the connections between music and action are tight enough for a seemingly immediate relationship to obtain between them. That action is in turn typically accomplished without recourse to 'higher' consciousness (voices in our heads, meaningful imputations to the music).[2] It is a non-verbal, embodied way of being in and being aware of oneself in the world. I use the term 'warm' but perhaps could equally well use the term 'unconsidered', although my choice of term is meant to highlight how these forms of musical consciousness involve articulations between musicking (Small 1998) and doing at an embodied level, where consideration of the music at some remove as a meaningful object does not occur. By speaking of this as 'warm' musical consciousness, I seek to capture the short temporal interval (instantaneous? split second?) involved in this type of articulation work, its 'heat of the moment' quality. And I wish to make a contrast between it and its opposite, 'cool' musical consciousness, in which music presents itself as something upon which to reflect, or on which to project meanings.

'Cool' musical consciousness takes shape more slowly. Here the music features as an object not only of perception but also of contemplation and an object that offers resources for knowledge production, for example through the ways it may provide a basis for metaphor. In other words, cool musical consciousness involves a relationship between music and action/cognition that is less visceral and more verbal.

My earlier work on aerobics exercise classes (DeNora 2000) highlighted music as a medium that could be used to draw participants in and out of self-conscious reflection (i.e. from cool to warm forms of musical consciousness). Sometimes, music could be seen and experienced as a material that recalibrated the exercising person into a bodily mode of being-without-reflection—a moving-being more than a thinking-being. This is 'warm' musical consciousness. At other times within aerobics activity, music was used to 'recall' participants to a mode of conscious reflection, part of a cool-down and a shift into a highly conscious mode of exercise in which one needed to 'think about' ('be conscious of') what one was doing.

In each of these cases certain musical styles and genres were used to afford different 'temperatures' of consciousness—fast-paced rhythmic dance music for warm, slower-paced, more sentimental ballads for cool. These musical properties were in turn augmented, or harnessed, by adjacent practices that contextualized, framed, and presented them—such as talk about the music. Aerobics teachers were quick to emphasize how too much 'core' music (music associated with the 'mind-less' mode of high energy exercise prior to cool-down) was dangerous, since it distracted exercisers from being conscious of their bodies (pain, fatigue), and thus could lead them on to the point of injury. The music that 'took them back', as it were, to bodily awareness, where participants could again reflect on their bodies-as-objects, was music that took them into 'cool' musical consciousness.

'Warm' consciousness need not necessarily involve 'fast' or 'impulsive' forms of action or bodily action, but rather a more general process in which there is a bodily recalibration that does not involve conscious reflection. Music therapeutic practices in the medical field help to clarify this point. In pain management, for example, pain perception is minimized through the distraction and/or bodily transposition that music affords. Music, in other words, offers a substitute medium of bodily perception: not a medium within which to 'think about' one's body, but a medium within which to 'be' and 'sense' one's body (via, for example, entrainment to some subset of music's properties). It is in this sense that music works as a prosthetic technology. Our consciousness of ourselves and our pain is musically recontextualized in ways that offer different resources for being and for making sense of ourselves as bodies.

In a striking case study that illustrates some of the medical and therapeutic ways in which music can be harnessed, Jane Edwards (1995) has described the case of a 12-year-old boy, 'Ivan', recovering from severe burns. The treatment involved an excruciatingly painful process termed 'debridement' (the removal of the dead skin in a bath). Ivan had continually resisted this therapy (having experienced its pain and thus coming to it primed to expect pain), and each time the treatment was conducted he had screamed and cried. When Edwards (the music therapist) played and sang to him during the process (improvising lyrics to one of his favourite songs, 'I get by with a little help from my friends'), the boy was not only able to endure the treatment, telling her at one stage, 'you are singing beautifully', but also told Edwards afterward that he felt little pain during it. Warm musical consciousness here involved a 'cooling' of embodied response, that is, the quelling of pain perception. This encounter, medical staff later told Edwards, provided a watershed in Ivan's treatment. After it, Ivan slept better, was more willing to submit to the debridement process, and more rapidly began to heal. In this example, as with the example of aerobics, music can be understood to recalibrate consciousness, pointing it in different directions in ways that simultaneously transform perception. This recalibration is, arguably, connected to internal neurological processes. Music therapists typically point at this stage to the 'gate theory' of pain perception and its emphasis on the plasticity of pain's transmission—the ways in which signalling and modulating systems vary according to circumstances (Dickenson 2002). This means that music can be understood to be part of those circumstances, redirecting sensory processing away from attention to pain and toward some other stimulus, which in turn recontextualizes the sensations associated with pain in ways that move them into the background.

More recently, research has explored how people suffering from forms of chronic illness use music as part of their everyday circumstances for managing pain, and to achieve the clusters of activities associated with being 'pain-free'—relaxation, sleep, or other forms of embodied reorientation. In this research, music's power is understood to be connected to the ways it is framed through narrative and expectation (e.g. 'this music always helps me sleep'). The coupling of music and narrative provides health resources or technologies of health in everyday life (Batt-Rawden 2006; Batt-Rawden *et al.* 2005).

Just as music may recalibrate consciousness in ways that elide the perception of pain, so too it can recalibrate consciousness in ways that elide other perceptions. For example, it may deflect perception from situational features and definitions, along lines that might in turn potentially reconfigure actors' orientations and even abilities to act in certain ways. One of the most striking, and publicly available, examples of this type of perceptual deflection and calibration for action can be found in George Gittoes' 2004 documentary, *Sountrack to War*. Gittoes' film features interviews with American soldiers during the Iraq war, who describe how they listen to music while on a mission in an Abrams tank (the technology of the tank can be adapted to enable the soldiers to use their MP3 players). As Gittoes' interviewees described it, their music of choice was heavy metal (e.g. Drowning Pool's 'Let the bodies hit the floor'). In part, the soldiers' selections for music 'at work' reflected a 'fit' between the music's sonic features and sonic features in the environment caused by the task (drums sounding like bombs etc). In equal part, the soldiers described how they found this music to be suited to the destructive business of warfare because it 'psyched them up' in occupationally appropriate ways. In other words, Gittoes shows us how music was one of the materials to which soldiers turned as they prepared to engage in potentially and actually violent conduct.

There are echoes, here of Arlie Hochschild's research on how occupations often require individuals to engage in 'emotional work', that is, to cooperate with an image and a feeling that the task requires (Hochschild 1983; see also DeNora 2000). While Hochschild's research focused on airline flight attendants, the concept of emotional work would seem equally appropriate here. As one soldier commented, when speaking of the heavy metal that he used in his work of soldiering, it 'gets you real fired up'. Gittoes' film shows how the soldiers themselves found the 'right music for the job': their fast-paced, blaring music of choice for battle suppressed a mode of consciousness that would have interfered with their work requirements. Whereas in the context of an aerobic exercise session, slower and more sentimental music was employed at a certain point as part of 'cool-down', so as to avoid injury, here, at work in battle, 'sentimental' consciousness (reflection on current activity; self-awareness) is anathema. As one soldier commented when discussing the music of the jazz crooner Diana Krall, 'we support you [Krall] but we can't listen to you while we roll'.

In short, Gittoes documents twenty-first century 'battle music'. His film shows us soldiers as their consciousness is musically configured so as to afford a high level of arousal and a low level of distanced reflection on the meaning of what they are doing: they are musically pumped up for their work. In a manner not dissimilar from the ways in which music has been seen to work in relation to the tasks of eating and drinking (fast music 'causes' fast eating and drinking), here music can be seen to draw actors into a specific form of 'fast conduct' ('rapid reaction') commensurate with the mode of conduct known as battle.

In these examples of music in medicine and music in war, it is possible to glimpse music's role as a medium in which an existing form of consciousness (understood as orientation to action scenarios and trajectories, and thus experience in time) is transformed. This transformation occurs in part when attention comes to be mediated through music (e.g. attention is diverted in the example of pain management) or structured through music's properties (when action's pace quickens or emotional orientation shifts). In this way music can be said to 'transport' us, removing us from one cognitive and/or sensory domain/orientation and into another, facilitating a dispositional shift, and one that does not entail deliberation about how or when to shift.

By contrast, 'cool' consciousness does involve deliberate, or higher-order, awareness. Here, music can be seen to provide structures for formulating thought and/or talk 'about' features of experience, and for formulating knowledge of the world. I will illustrate these points with a brief discussion of an approach known as Guided Imagery and Music, or GIM.

GIM is a technique of music therapy developed by Helen Bonny (Bonny 2002; Summer 2002). It provides one of the clearest examples of music's role as a tool for thinking, and one that examines that topic in real time as a client's consciousness of her or himself and environment is articulated through ongoing narrative. In a GIM session, the client is given a relaxation technique and an image to begin the music listening experience. While listening to a 30-minute programme of evocative classical music, the client responds with a variety of sensory imagery, feelings, and body sensations which he or she relates to the therapist as they occur.

GIM casts music as a material that can offer structuring properties (such as metaphor) against which extra-musical matters can become known, can be explored, and can be resolved (Summer 2002: 44; see also Bonde 2005: 137). It echoes Claude Lévi-Strauss's view of music as 'myth coded in sounds instead of words [which] offers an interpretive grid, a matrix of relations which filters and organizes lived experience, and acts as a substitute for it and provides the comforting illusion that contradictions can be overcome and differences resolved' (Lévi-Strauss 1981: 659). In this sense, music provides a space in which thought and imagination can be elaborated or developed in relation to various issues, problems, or tasks (see also DeNora 1986). Like a Rorschach inkblot, music offers a template that can be used as a guide for actors' imaginative processes as they set to work on a problem or elaborate meaning (see DeNora 1986). So, as in Colombetti's work on 'scaffolding' for the elaboration of feeling discussed earlier, music may provide structure for the shaping up of issues, concerns, images, or concepts that might otherwise remain repressed or unnoticed. The 'things' that we then elaborate can thus be understood to be musically 'led' to the extent that our projections take on some of music's properties, which in turn help to shape what is then taken away from the process of musical engagement. Thus, for the socio-musical scholar interested in musical consciousness, GIM is an excellent natural laboratory, a place in which to see how agents transfer musical properties to extra-musical properties and how they come to understand those extra-musical matters through the sonic structure of music, and in real time, that is, in direct correlation with the unfolding musical event.

GIM also highlights issues that are relevant to the study of collective consciousness. By no means equivalent to a coincidence of individual consciousnesses, collective consciousness should rather be explored in terms of its emergence in relation to things outside of individuals, in terms of the 'scaffolding' through which it is articulated. Collective consciousness may be understood to be built from public or shared affordances, recursively modified through copious micro-adjustments over time. So, for example, as individuals A, B, C, and D hear Music X, A begins to react to the music with interpretation 1, possibly drawing upon earlier articulation work by herself and/or others—these might be other individuals or other sources of information/ interpretation, including media sources. She may say something like, 'Music X reminds me of a flock of geese in flight'. Next, B, who had been orienting to the music in light of interpretation 2 ('Music X is noble and free') can now, having been exposed to A's reaction, pair geese with 'noble and free' and let these terms refine both each other and the music. B can say as much to A, who in turn might find yet another way of responding. On hearing this conversation (or reading about it, or being told about it, or even imagining it!), C and/or D may join in. The result, constantly subject to further elaboration and revision, is an exponentially expanding set of permutations that depend only on the recognition and uptake of 'new' responses to Music X. And each time a further interpretive moment is added, the more the field of Music X's affordances is expanded, and the richer and thicker becomes the culture or set of meanings and practices anchored by Music X. (Thus it is possible to trace the modulations of a particular piece of music's meanings or connotations over time—for example, as a religious hymn is converted into a protest song or vice versa.) And the richer the culture, the greater the potential connection between actors A, B, C, and D, the more that this 'consciousness of all' becomes more than the sum of the consciousness of each.

Over time, then, a focus back on this music—to the extent that it was initially or retrospectively paired with some experience, event, or thing—can afford collective remembering. In this way, Music X offers itself as a technology of memory (Pacifici 1996; Tota 2005); it is not a material that merely 'aids' recall but actually structures what is recalled. So too, collective action in a present moment may involve orienting to musical 'scaffolding' in ways where music can be seen, coolly, to 'lead' consciousness and motivation.

In short, GIM demonstrates how music and music making can provide *transferable* resources for engagement with the social world. In these cases, music can be seen to provide a template, grid, myth, metaphor, model, or mnemonic for elaborating thought—as when we turn to a musical model to show or lead us to the development of a social arrangement, or as when music is used as a structure/technology of memory. In either of these cases, consciousness is composed *through* reference to music. Music provides materials with which to model the perception and narration of the environment and thus orientation, and—as I will now seek to demonstrate—participation in the world.

Music, consciousness, and mental health: the case of BRIGHT

In their essay on collaborative musicality, Mercédès Pavlicevic and Gary Ansdell (2008) summarize recent developments in music psychology as it has shifted from cognitive (individualized) to ecological (social) perspectives and to a focus on music in naturalistic settings of use. Invoking the work of Charles Keil and Steven Feld, they speak of music as a source of 'participatory consciousness', that is, as having the 'capacity not just to model but maybe to enact some ideal communities' (Keil and Feld 1994: 20, quoted in Pavlicevic and Ansdell 2008: 375). Speaking of participatory consciousness returns the focus to music's role as a resource for the emergence of collective consciousness, as described above. Collective musical consciousness is a process that is articulated in and through the making of a shared cultural space, through inhabiting, making, and remaking cultural resources, among them, music. In the final section of this chapter, I will reflect on this theme, using examples from an ongoing case study in the area of music and mental health. I will highlight mental health as the capacity to adopt and adapt participatory consciousness in daily life.

For the past two years, I have had the opportunity to watch Ansdell in action in his work as a community music therapist in and around a centre for mental health. The project, a collaborative, ethnographic study of community music therapy and mental health, is sited at what I shall call the Borough (Centre for) Re-Integration,

Growth, Habilitation and Training, or 'BRIGHT' (this is a pseudonym for an actual project still ongoing). BRIGHT's mission is to support people in recovery from mental illness, which it delivers through various forms of training and occupational therapy: a café, a holiday scheme, and a music programme, including a mid-week musical afternoon.

These sessions are organized as group sing-along and improvisation, open-mic solos, and small group performance, all convened by a music therapist. There are roughly 25 people attending any given session with a core of about 20 who participate each week. Over time it has been possible to map the emergence of collective musical culture within BRIGHT and with it to see how features of this culture permit partici-patory consciousness or the ability to enact community. Within this collective endeavour, it is also possible to see individuals experiencing consciousness shifts—in particular, forms of broadening out from private to public sensitivities and modes of expression within and beyond the BRIGHT world.

Figure 18.1 shows how BRIGHT may be understood as a musical space. This space is configured through musical genres, instruments, modes of performing, and musical styles; and the predominance of these features is indicated by font size (certain places within this space are further differentiated by being 'off the map'). These features offer conventional musical ways of being expressive—subject positions that are adopted (and adapted) in performance with varying degrees of sincerity, skill, and devotion. The relationship between the different musical features and modalities within BRIGHT's musical space is created according to how the participants themselves engage with these features and draw links between them. So, for example, the blues within the BRIGHT musical space were marginal *circa* 2006 but have since come to be

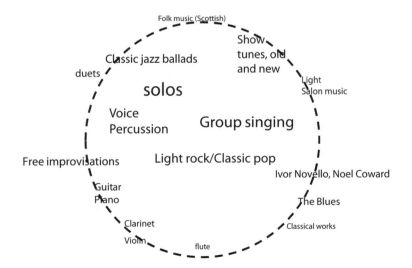

Fig. 18.1 The music space at BRIGHT (genre, instruments, format). Text size indicates relative preponderance.

prominent in the collective music-making. As a genre and style, however, it involves a subset of performers that is clearly distinct from, for example, folk music (discussed below).

So too, BRIGHT's musical features are connected, by participants, to extra-musical matters and these are often used to contextualize (simultaneously) social and musical identities. For example, a participant might announce 'This is *my* song', or might say, 'I'm a Blues man' or 'I'm Noel Coward', and dress the part, adopt an affiliated embodied style and set of gestures, or behave in ways that accord with such a sensibility. Similarly, individuals might simply gravitate to a part of the musical territory, choosing to sing the same song or type of song each time they perform at the open mic. Whatever the strategy, in these acts music becomes a way of holding on to and projecting self, value, and possible lines of action into the BRIGHT space. Equally importantly, music becomes a way of moving outside of BRIGHT to the extent that it can be seen to leave its traces in, or act as a template for, action, thought, and feeling.

Insofar as they are associated with the occupation of varying parts of the musical space at BRIGHT (some participants, for example, tend to stick to some parts of the musical terrain and never venture into others), participants' musical acts can be diagrammed as 'trails' in musical space, patterns of movement across the space that cover portions of the space with varying degrees of frequency and intensity. Trails highlight clients' musical pathways or progressions over time and their traversals of musical forms within a space. For example, the trail depicted in Figure 18.2 is associated with the musical activity of one of the project researchers. It reveals a wide range of musical activity—varied by genre, instrument, and mode of participation.

Within BRIGHT, this inhabitation of a part of the musical space is not unusual. Some members never, as it were, 'touch' some features of the space; indeed, some leave the room for various purposes (to smoke, use the toilet, etc) when certain types of music are performed, while others do not participate in the group singing

Fig. 18.2 One individual's musical trail at BRIGHT.

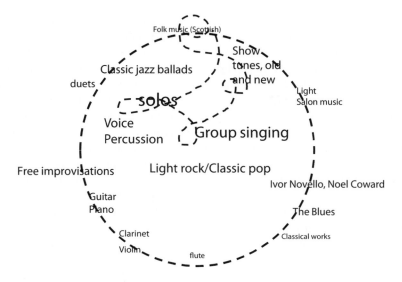

Fig. 18.3 Peter's musical trail at BRIGHT.

of some numbers. Others inhabit only a small part of the whole space. Still others will seek to 'personalize' a part of the space (make it habitable, as it were) through talk about the type of music there, and through attempts to configure, performatively, how the music in that place should sound.

Consider Peter, whose musical trail is depicted in Figure 18.3. (Peter is not an actual client at BRIGHT, though the behaviours and general structure of the musical habitus, or 'incarnation' of history in the form of a system of enduring dispositions (Bourdieu 1984) that I will describe as 'Peter's' do accord with an actual participant. I have altered identifying details so as to preserve his anonymity.) Peter is in his mid-forties, has been in and out of hospital, and is now a regular participant in the BRIGHT music sessions where he routinely brings his favourite songs which he performs at the mic. These are Scottish folk songs, which he cherishes. He is the only one at BRIGHT to perform this repertoire. In the early stages of our research, Peter participated only minimally in the sing-along sessions, and hardly at all in the group improvisations. He typically did not join in when the group sang more 'modern' songs. At that time, Peter described in interview how the songs he sings at the open-mic remind him of his happy holidays in the Scottish Highlands. He also told of how he uses these songs to cope at times when he feels he is beginning to slip into illness again. In common with the respondents in DeNora 2000, he described how these songs provided him with what I have termed a technology of self and health, and a medium for achieving and sustaining focus.

Music, I would suggest, provides Peter with a selective sensitivity to the world, that is, a mode of consciousness. As such, it is a resource for his care of self, for example as a source of ontological security through nostalgia, and a tie to past identity. At the same time, however, this self-care and with it, Peter's musical consciousness, intensifies a gulf between Peter's musical consciousness, his occupation of musical space, and others' musical occupation at BRIGHT where the musical trails of most of the other BRIGHT members do not overlap greatly with Peter's own. In other words, Peter has a musical 'problem' at BRIGHT—how to make connections and thus engage in the remaking of his musical self, becoming more of the 'others' and thus less of what he is musically in relation to them. Peter is thus musically isolated, and the bulk of the work of maintaining the value of his music falls upon his own shoulders. The combination, then, of his music's position in the musical space and his own relative isolation within it limits the resources Peter has to articulate a shared musical world at BRIGHT (though he has other social resources at his disposal, as do other participants). Although Peter's music affords him comfort and pleasure, and a means by which to promote his sense of self identity and 'wellness', it does not simultaneously afford resources with which to align past with present so as to 'be' in the current world, where musically associated sensibilities are only minimally shared. Paradoxically, Peter's music both provides what he needs in order to stay functional, but simultaneously restrains his capacities to function more flexibly over a wider socio-musical territory.

If Peter dwells within his preferred music exclusively, if he continues to function as, in Peterson and Kern's (1996) term, a musical univore, his opportunities for connection to others through music will remain dependent on the degree to which others can be drawn onto his musical territory, his musical sensibility. In other words, Peter's musical habitus removes him from the shared reservoir of tastes and practices, musically speaking, and for this reason it is vulnerable to being ignored or derided (though this is something which does not in fact occur at BRIGHT). Simultaneously, other individuals, perhaps more able to marshal other social resources as well, can more readily inflect the BRIGHT space with their own music, and encourage further uptake of that music, reflexively repositioning themselves more closely in the core of the musical space.

It would be both dangerous and theoretically weak to say that there is anything 'wrong' or pathological about Peter's values and practices, or that there is anything about the music—its connotations and its aesthetic (however configured outside BRIGHT)—that prevent it in principle from taking a more central place in BRIGHT culture. If any custom, taste or practice is fully shared it becomes, in the sociological sense of the term, 'normal'. We can only say that these values are in the minority at present. However, it is correct to acknowledge that Peter's musical values and practices are not able to afford rich participation in the musical world at BRIGHT as currently configured, and that, because of this, his practices reinforce a mode of consciousness that directs him away from the opportunity for a greater shared musical and social world, and from sensibilities and orientations that are constantly emerging and shifting within that world.

More recently, developments instigated by the music therapists at BRIGHT have addressed Peter's musical situation, seeking to broaden his musical opportunities. It is at this stage that it becomes difficult to describe the nature of these changes without potentially compromising Peter's anonymity, and I will not therefore go further with this discussion, except to say that it has resulted in considerable musical development, both of his technical ability and of the repertoire that interests him. He is, at the time of writing, making a shift from a musically anchored preoccupation with private concerns to a musically engendered movement onto a shared terrain characterized by new expressive materials and topics. His horizons—musical and extra-musical—have expanded through his participation in a band, in which repertoire is negotiated and chosen by others. This expansion has not been entirely easy. The process of musical broadening has also involved Peter's attempt to reconcile involvement in a social group and an ever-widening musical terrain with a hitherto devout ploughing of a rather narrow musical furrow. With this widening, Peter's former self (in the form of a musical habitus) was not shed, but took a step back to accommodate new ways of orienting and engaging, new 'outlooks' on his social world.

Conclusion

Peter's musical recalibration, and the changes of consciousness that it wrought, is entirely similar to the ways in which ordinary individuals may turn to music in daily life to 'work through' or alter their outlooks. Music offers us an ally for new or emerging values or action plans. It can foster recalibrations of sensibility and it can hold existing sensibilities in place. In all these examples music is active in the formulation of consciousness. The study of musical consciousness not only helps to elucidate consciousness as an 'extended' and aesthetic phenomenon—something that emerges in relation to social and cultural materials. It also highlights how those materials may be used—at times with deliberation—to heighten, suppress, or alter consciousness, both individual and collective. Considering music's formative role in relation to consciousness elucidates the interpenetration and ecological bases of individual and collective forms of consciousness, which thus helps us to consider music's role in fostering mental health. Finally, considering music in relation to 'warm' and 'cool' consciousness highlights both the ways in which it is possible to 'have' personhood even without language, through orientation in concert with, and in relation to, music's properties. Music is, in sum, often and insidiously part of how, for better and for worse, we are drawn into social relations and made ready, in an aesthetic and pre-cognitive way, for courses of action about which we may be otherwise (i.e. verbally) unaware. As such, the study of music and consciousness highlights the often subtle, often tacit, aesthetic bases of our selective sensitivity to the world.

Acknowledgements

Thanks are due to the editors and to my colleague, Giovanna Colombetti in the Department of Sociology and Philosophy at Exeter University. Thanks too to Trevor Hagen for discussions about collective consciousness and underground culture, and to Lisa Summer for her generous comments on the section on GIM (and for sharing her work on music and consciousness with me).

References

Acord, S.K. and DeNora, T. (2008). Culture and the arts: from art worlds to arts-in-action. *The Annals of the American Academy of Political and Social Science*, **619**, 223–37.

Ansdell, G. (1995). *Music for Life: Aspects of Creative Music Therapy with Adult Clients* (London: Jessica Kingsley Press).

Batt-Rawden, K. (2006). Music—a strategy to promote health in rehabilitation? An evaluation of participation in a 'music and health promotion project'. *International Journal of Rehabilitation Research*, **29**(2), 171–3.

Batt-Rawden, K., DeNora, T., and Ruud, E. (2005). Music listening and empowerment in health promotion; a study of the role and significance of music in everyday life of the long-term ill. *Nordic Journal of Music Therapy*, **14**(2), 120–36.

Bonde, L.O. (2005). 'Finding a new place . . .' metaphor and narrative in one cancer survivor's BMGIM therapy. *Nordic Journal of Music Therapy*, **14**(2), 137–54.

Bonny, H. (2002). *Music and Consciousness: The Evolution of Guided Imagery and Music* (ed.), Lisa Summer (Gilsum, NH: Barcelona Publishers).

Bourdieu, P. (1984). *Distinction: A Social Critique of the Judgement of Taste* (Cambridge: Polity).

Clark, A. and Chalmers A. (1998). The extended mind. *Analysis*, **58**, 10–23.

Clarke, D. (2007). Beyond the global imaginary: decoding BBC Radio 3's *Late Junction, Radical Musicology*, **2**. Available at www.radical-musicology.org.uk/2007/Clarke.htm (accessed 17 July 2010).

Clarke, E. (2005). *Ways of Listening: An Ecological Approach to the Perception of Musical Meaning* (New York, NY: Oxford University Press).

Colombetti, G. (2009). What language does to feeling. *Journal of Consciousness Studies*, **16**(9), 4–26.

Csikszentmihalyi, M. (1997). *Creativity: Flow and the Psychology of Discovery and Invention* (New York, NY: Harper Perennial).

Dennett, D. (1991). *Consciousness Explained* (Boston, MA: Little, Brown, and Co.).

DeNora, T. (1986). How is extra-musical meaning possible? Music as a place and space for 'work'. *Sociological Theory*, **4**(1), 84–94.

DeNora, T. (2000). *Music in Everyday Life* (Cambridge: Cambridge University Press).

DeNora, T. (2003). *After Adorno: Rethinking Music Sociology* (Cambridge: Cambridge University Press).

DeNora, T. (2007). Health and music in everyday life: a theory of practice. *Psyke and Logos* (Dansk Psykologisk Forlag), **1**(28), 271–87.

Dickenson, A.H. (2002). Editorial I: Gate control theory of pain stands the test of time. *British Journal of Anaesthesia*, **88**(6), 755–7.

Dore, J. and McDermott, R.P. (1982). Linguistic indeterminacy and social context in utterance interpretation. *Language*, **58**(2), 374–98.

Durkheim, E. (1915). *The Elementary Forms of the Religious Life* (London: George Allen and Unwin Ltd).

Edwards, J. (1995). 'You are singing beautifully': music therapy and the debridement bath. *The Arts in Psychotherapy*, **22**(11), 53–5.

Foucault, M. (1988). Technologies of the self, in L.H. Martin, H. Gutman, and P.H. Hutton (eds), *Technologies of the Self*, 16–49 (Amherst, MA: University of Massachusetts Press).

Gibson, J. (1977). The theory of affordances, in R. Shaw and J. Bransford (eds), *Perceiving, Acting, and Knowing: Toward an Ecological Psychology*, 67–82 (Hillsdale, NJ: Lawrence Erlbaum).

Gittoes, G. (2004). *Soundtrack to War*. DVD (Beverly Hills, CA: Melee Entertainment LLC).

Hennion, A. (2001). Music lovers: taste as social performance. *Theory, Culture and Society*, **18**(5), 1–22.

Hennion, A. (2007). These things that hold us together. *Cultural Sociology*, **1**(1), 97–144.

Hochschild, A. (1983). *The Managed Heart: Commercialization of Human Feeling* (Berkeley, CA: University of California Press).

Keil, C. and Feld, S. (1994). *Music Grooves: Essays and Dialogues* (Chicago, IL: University of Chicago Press).

Lévi-Strauss, C. (1981). *The Naked Man: Introduction to a Science of Mythology*, vol. 4 (London: Harper and Row).

MacKenzie, D. (2006). *An Engine, Not a Camera: How Financial Models Shape Markets* (Cambridge, MA: MIT Press).

Mead, G.H. (1912). The mechanism of social consciousness. *Journal of Philosophy, Psychology and Scientific Methods*, **9**, 401–6.

Pacifici, R.W. (1996). Memories in the making: the shape of things that went. *Qualitative Sociology*, **19**(3), 301–21.

Pavlicevic, M. and Ansdell, G. (2008). Between communicative musicality and collaborative musicing: perspectives from community music therapy, in S. Malloch and C. Trevarthen (eds), *Communicative Musicality*, 357–76 (Oxford: Oxford University Press).

Peterson, R. and Kern, R.M. (1996). Changing highbrow taste: from snob to omnivore. *American Sociological Review*, **61**(5), 900–7.

Rose, N. (1996). *Inventing Our Selves: Psychology, Power and Personhood* (New York, NY: Cambridge University Press).

Small, C. (1998). *Musicking: The Meanings of Performing and Listening* (Middleton, CT: Wesleyan University Press).

Streeck, J. (1996). How to do things with things. *Human Studies*, **19**(4), 365–84.

Summer, L. (2002). Group music and imagery therapy: an emergent music therapy, in K. Bruscia and D. Grocke (eds), *Guided Imagery and Music: The Bonny Method and Beyond*, 297–306 (Gilsum, NH: Barcelona Publishers).

Sutherland, I. and Acord S. (2007). Thinking with art: from situated knowledge to experiential knowing. *The Journal of Visual Art Practice*, **6**(2), 125–40.

Thomas, W.I. and Thomas, D. (1928). *The Child in America: Behavior Problems and Programs*. (New York, NY: Knopf).

Tota, A.L. (2005). Counter-memories of terror: technologies of remembering and technologies of forgetting, in M.D. Jacobs and N.W. Hanharan (eds), *The Blackwell Companion to the Sociology of Culture*, 272–85 (Oxford: Blackwell).

Zelazo, P.D. (1999). Language, levels of consciousness, and the development of intentional action, in P.D. Zelazo, J.W. Astington, and D.R. Olson (eds), *Developing Theories of Intention: Social Understanding and Self-Control*, 95–117 (Mahwah, NJ: Lawrence Erlbaum Associates).

Zelazo, P.D. and Sommerville, J. (2001). Levels of consciousness of the self in time, in C. Moore and K. Lemmon (eds), *The Self in Time: Developmental Issues*, 229–52 (Mahwah, NJ: Lawrence Erlbaum Associates).

Notes

1. The project, with additional involvement from music therapist Sarah Wilson, has been funded by Nordoff Robbins, and is overseen by the consultant psychiatrist, Dr John Meehan. My role has been as voluntary consultant and participant observer.

2. Cf. Chapter 11, which discusses Edelman's categories of *primary* and *higher-order* consciousness; see also Chapters 1–3, which examine, in some cases critically, Husserl's dichotomy of *primary* and *secondary* memory.

Chapter 19

Public consciousness, political conscience, and memory in Latin American *nueva canción*

Richard Elliott

Introduction

The *nueva canción*, or 'new song', movements that emerged in Latin America in the 1960s and 1970s, and whose beginnings are normally associated with the Chilean Violeta Parra (1917–67) and the Argentinean Atahualpa Yupanqui (Héctor Roberto Chavero 1908–92), have been subject to a significant body of scholarly attention (Benmayor 1981; Fairley 1985; Moore 2003; Moreno 1986; Morris 1986). Much of this literature has focused on the socio-cultural context in which *nueva canción* emerged and on the lives and works of significant figures in the movement, such as Víctor Jara, Inti-Illimani, Quilapayún, Patricio Manns, Silvio Rodríguez, Mercedes Sosa, Chico Buarque, and Daniel Viglietti. The important role played by such performers has consistently been emphasized via collaborations, references, and tributes in a sustained process of memory work, consciousness-raising, and the assertion of a shared history (Elliott 2006, 2008a). In light of the many thousands of people in Latin America and beyond for whom these artists have acted as 'movement intellectuals' (Eyerman and Jamison 1991), it is interesting to consider the role that popular music can play in raising, refining, or otherwise shaping our awareness of a shared world.

This chapter uses the impact of *nueva canción* to explore some of the ways in which consciousness might be thought of as applying to groups as much as individuals. By 'public consciousness', I mean those types of shared consciousness that go under a variety of epithets such as 'collective', 'mass', and 'social'. I use the word 'public' mainly to highlight the ways in which the themes I am interested in are played out in a public sphere connected to politics and what I am calling 'political conscience', where 'conscience' is not always easily distinguishable from 'consciousness'. This interest in public consciousness and conscience emerged from researching issues of music and commitment in Latin America and has been developed as a response to those issues. *Nueva canción* had as one of its guiding themes the quest for identity and renewal in the postcolonial Latin American world, and the musicians associated with *nueva canción* act as movement intellectuals in raising and focusing consciousness of these processes, and in maintaining the relevance of this work in a changing musical world. My case studies here are Víctor Jara and Silvio Rodríguez, but I also discuss

Ricardo Villalobos, a contemporary Chilean disc jockey (DJ) who represents a generation of Chileans at one remove from the traumas of the previous generation and yet
intimately connected to them by inherited memory and shared consciousness. If the
musical agenda of *nueva canción*, much like the political agendas to which it attached
itself, was guided by notions of collectivity, then this essay is written from a belief that
the search for identity inevitably involves a questioning of oneself as an individual
that can only proceed alongside recognition of oneself as definable through one's
relationship to a collective. Along this line of thinking, consciousness can only exist via
recognition of the Other.

The chapter starts with a discussion of the public nature of consciousness and how
one might address consciousness (of any kind) epistemologically, whether through
the brain sciences, psychology, psychoanalysis, or philosophy. This section is followed
by an interpretation of the kinds of consciousness involved in the social and political
world, paying attention to the historical and cultural iterations of consciousness.
Discussion of these modalities inevitably highlights the gaps between them, but it is
not the purpose of this essay to attempt to bridge those gaps. Rather, I suggest, via
reference to the work of Slavoj Žižek, that we should allow these types of inquiry to
resonate with each other. Having set out a general and theoretical contribution
to consciousness studies, the chapter then proceeds to a set of considerations more
clearly located in a specific, ongoing cultural moment, that of the *nueva canción*
movement. This moment, also thought of as an event, is intended to be read not as
an exemplar of ideas in the first part, but rather as part of the ground from which
they emerge.

An epistemological framework

Although I stress the social here, I do not deny the importance of consciousness at
the level of the individual. My point, rather, is to highlight the necessity of thinking
of both together. Consciousness must be thought of as social if it is to mean anything
beyond an organism's response to external stimuli. Furthermore, when music is
brought into relationship with consciousness, then social concerns cannot be ignored;
music too must be thought of as social if it is to mean anything. Defining music provides a challenge in that most dictionary definitions require a notion of organization
that is hard to divorce from the social. A definition such as 'the combination of sounds
with a view to beauty of form' certainly does; 'sounds in melodic or harmonic combination' perhaps less so.[1] It is possible to imagine an isolated experience of these
sounds, such as an individual alone in a forest encountering a pleasing combination of
sounds from an unknown natural source. But because music derives so much of its
meaning from some form of social function, our definitions of it have become similarly socialized. To make this point is to question whether musical affect can be investigated by observing the effects a piece of de-contextualized music has on a similarly
de-contextualized individual, be it my imagined forest dweller or a volunteer taking
part in a scientific experiment. Granted, an individual taking part in an experiment—
whether at home or in a lab—is in *a* context (as is the music he or she is listening to or
playing), but it is highly unlikely that a context organized to map, say, the neurological

responses of the individual will resemble in any manner a normal listening or playing environment. What this discussion highlights is that, traditionally, we seem to be engaging in different activities when we discuss consciousness and when we discuss music.[2] There is a tendency to define the former in terms of the individual and the latter in terms of the collective. What I wish to ask here is whether thinking about music can help us, through recognition of its very powerful socializing processes, to think about consciousness in a manner that reflects the social to a greater extent.

At the same time, we should note that it is also difficult to take account of the seemingly infinite contexts in which music can be listened to, and that a simplistic recourse to *a* 'social context' may do little better than one that relies on the artificially isolated individual. In pursuing the (essentially relativist) logic of the myriad potential social contexts in which a musical performance might be experienced, we arrive at an equally individualizing process in which each individual's listening or playing experience is so distinct as to make the social meaningless again. My response is that the term 'public' designates a position between these extremes that is provisional but sufficiently quilted—to use a term from Lacanian psychoanalysis—to suggest observable phenomena that rely on neither of these individualizing moves.[3]

In a similar fashion, Paul Ricoeur's discussion of collective memory understands the 'tradition of inwardness' inaugurated by St Augustine as a turning away from the collective, the *polis*. Ricoeur follows the development of this tradition through Locke to Husserl, highlighting the emphasis of these thinkers on interiority and reflexivity, but culminating in the problem that 'the entire tradition of inwardness is constructed as an impasse in the direction of collective memory' (2004: 97). This stumbling block anticipates a potential problem in identifying the 'private' and the 'public'. In arguing for an emphasis on the collective in its cultural and political realms, am I endorsing an Augustinian turn away from the universalizing (i.e. public) work of the brain sciences? Or is the paradox already written into the brain sciences and medicine in general— that it is necessary to penetrate the most private parts of the individual's body, including its brain, in order to construct a universal science of medicine? In related fashion, Ricoeur argues against a polarization of phenomenological and neuroscientific methodologies in the study of consciousness:

> This curiosity [about the brain] is one of the dispositions that articulates our relation to the world. The causal dependence in which we find ourselves with respect to cerebral functioning, a dependence whose knowledge we owe to such curiosity, continues to instruct us, even in the absence of suffering due to dysfunction. This instruction helps to warn us about the pretentious *hubris* that would make us the masters and possessors of nature. (2004: 423)

One of the strengths of scientific inquiry into the relationship between the brain and consciousness is that it situates us firmly within the animal world. Science can therefore assist in an even more embracing socializing process than that which we normally associate with the 'social'; beyond our relationship with other humans lies a social as well as a physical relationship with the rest of the natural world. Note the necessity of public consciousness for Ricoeur's point to be thinkable and rhetorically effective: to *be aware* that it is only right to think of humans as animals so as not to have too high an opinion of ourselves is to take part in a complex, unavoidably social and moral train of thought.

In another account that emphasizes the human animal, Slavoj Žižek discusses the 'problem' that cognitive science has with the question of consciousness. Like Ricoeur, Žižek stresses the need for philosophers to take seriously cognitive science's insight that human perception is always already the result of a series of judgements (Žižek and Daly 2004: 54–60). Yet, Žižek states, cognitivism cannot show from where in the human the need to know emerges; there is always an excess maintained by the very act of asking the question. Žižek identifies the central problem of the conflict between philosophy, psychoanalysis, and cognitivism as consciousness itself, and one aspect of the problem resides in asking what consciousness does for us. In evolutionary terms, consciousness may have come about in order to enhance our awareness of the world around us, but this does not mean that consciousness has continued to evolve in response to the increasing complexity of human experience; in its emphasis on the role of judgement in perception, cognitivism suggests that consciousness is actually a process of reducing and abstracting complexity. This being so, it is unclear why aware-ness is needed if consciousness could operate as a blind process guiding our percep-tions. The enigma, for Žižek, is found in Kant's question why it is that 'human beings are destined to ask themselves questions which they cannot answer' (2004: 58). Žižek notes Heidegger's observation that 'what characterizes the human being, in the sense of *Dasein* (being there), is that it's a being that asks questions about its own being, that adopts a self-questioning attitude' (58), and the essential role that philosophy has to play in exploring this self-questioning attitude. Psychoanalysis, meanwhile, asserts that the gap between subject and subject-as-object is an essential part of 'identification and its failure': it attends to the problem encountered when, to use Žižek's example, an objectivizing biological presentation of a genomic formula confronts the subject with the claim that 'this is you' (57). This gap, which presents the cognitive sciences with the challenge of finding a language that could bridge subject and object, is the *raison d'être* of psychoanalysis.

For Žižek, then, there are two temptations that must be avoided. The first is a dismissal of psychoanalysis by a simplistic cognitivist view that sees contemporary neuroscientific advances as having superseded earlier naive claims; psychoanalysis remains important in dealing with those issues for which neuroscience has yet to find a language. The second is a dismissal of cognitivism by a transcendental philoso-phy that would argue that 'even if they find a genetic or neuronal chemical base for neurosis . . . it still remains a fact that we, as speaking human beings, will have some-how to subjectivize it, to symbolize it in a certain way, and that this will always be the domain of psychoanalysis' (60). Symbolization will have to deal with the changes and potential trauma wrought by any such self-objectivization. This trauma may itself be one of the things that drives the maintenance of human self-awareness out into the open, into the conscious mind. Developing his own version of a line of thought explored by evolutionary cognitivists, Žižek suggests that, if we are to think of consciousness in evolutionary terms, we should think of it as a 'mistake' in which 'consciousness developed as an unintended by-product that acquired a kind of second-degree survivalist function' and that it 'originates with something going terribly wrong' (54–9).

More recently, Žižek has developed these issues and provided a more thorough working-through of the relationship between philosophy, psychoanalysis, and the brain sciences (2006: 147–249). In this account we find a return to the notion of a fundamental 'parallax gap' that separates psychoanalytic and cognitivist accounts of consciousness. Žižek is still keen to avoid the temptations of dismissing one account from the viewpoint of the other, but does not believe that the way forward lies in bridging the gap between them. Rather, we need to pay more attention to what constitutes the gap: 'What if the actual problem is not to bridge the gap but, rather, to *formulate* it as such, to conceive it properly?' (214). Žižek draws here on the principle that guides much of his thinking, the notion of a 'parallax view' produced by examining a problem from differing perspectives. Provided these differing perspectives engage thoroughly and effectively with their shared subject matter, the difference between them may be reduced, such that only the slightest shift in perspective allows for the leap from one to the other. This minimal difference does not bring the perspectives together, but marks the unbridgeable gap that separates them from each other and recognizes the gap as a necessity, not an obstacle.

Throughout his work, Žižek (1989, 2002) has shown the fertile ground to be explored by bringing together the work of Hegel, Marx, and Lacan, suggesting that individual and collective psychologies mirror and feed each other. With his continued emphasis on the interaction of consciousness and politics, he keeps open the question as to what constitutes materialism. This is important because it is precisely around a claim to materialism that some cognitivist work attempts to dismiss the tradition of transcendental philosophical reflection on the problem of accessing consciousness. Daniel Dennett (1991), for example, adopts a position that, while seeming to have a superficial correspondence with Žižek's, makes claims for a quite different kind of materialism. Like Žižek, Dennett is suspicious of a too-easy dismissal of cognitivism based on its inability to objectivize consciousness completely. But, rather than opt for a recognition of the gap separating the different perspectives, Dennett claims that anyone who is tempted to look for an account of consciousness in places other than those being explored by materialist science is contributing to a 'defeatist thesis' (1991: 33–42), the word 'defeatist' seemingly utilized to paint a picture of head-in-the-cloud idealists or head-in-the-sand fatalists. I want to stress an equal commitment to a materialist theory, but one that can allow itself to consider the political consciousness of a society coming to terms with cultural trauma (Caruth 1995; Eyerman 2001). Just as science must often put aside questions of faith in order to pursue its goals, certain political situations demand a putting-aside of the scientific in order to address goals of a more urgently materialist nature. Materialism here undergoes a transformation from the realm of scientific experimentation to the more easily and effectively collectivized arena of cultural exploration and dissemination. To look beyond materialist science for explanations of what is happening and what can be done is not to 'wallow . . . in mystery' (Dennett 1991: 37) but to recognize that, in redirecting energy elsewhere, one might have to resort to notions of faith, 'necessary illusion' (Anzieu 1990: 95), or even Dennett's hated 'dualism', to get the job done. As Jeff Coulter states:

> Believing *in* something . . . is usually a matter of conviction (religious, political, etc.).
> What one truly believes is a matter of what one says and does. Contrary to Dennett, we do

not carry our 'beliefs' around in the neural equivalent of a compartment in our heads, but rather what we believe is shown in, displayed by, what we are disposed to say/do and what we actually, in relevant circumstances, say/do. (2008: 31)

Awareness and memory

With the preceding discussion in mind, I suggest a definition of consciousness based on various types of *awareness*: of sensations both immediate and less immediate, of data gathered over a period of time. Inevitably, then, I am also thinking about the processes of *memory* on which such consciousness relies. The kinds of distinctions I wish to make can be broadly mapped onto those found in Walter Benjamin's work, the first of which is between *Gedächtnis* and *Erinnerung*. Benjamin's translator Harry Zohn provides a useful definition of the former term as 'a gathering of unconscious data' and of the latter as 'an isolating of individual "memories" per se' (Zohn 2006: 344). The second distinction is between *Erfahrung*, which refers to 'experience over time', and *Erlebnis*, which refers to 'the isolated experience of the moment' (345). Awareness gathered over time, thought of as experience and memory, can be said to produce consciousness, especially historical, public, or political consciousness: it is not until we have lived among people and played a part in society that we can truly speak of having this kind of consciousness, and it is impossible to imagine being in society without having a sense of public consciousness.

For Jacques Lacan, this awareness of ourselves in society comes about with our entry into the Symbolic Order, the arena of language and the law, of the methods and rules of communicating with others. It is also where we become aware of the imperatives forced upon us by our identification with what Lacan calls the 'big Other', the universe into which we are thrust: 'as soon as the symbol arrives, there is a universe of symbols' (1991: 29). And, being in a universe of symbols, 'the human order is characterised by the fact that the symbolic function intervenes at every moment and at every stage of its existence' (29). While consciousness may not depend on language, our access to it does, with the consequence that we cannot speak of consciousness or the unconscious outside the Symbolic Order:

> If the symbolic function functions, we are inside it. And I would even say—we are so far into it that we can't get out of it . . . [W]hen we try to . . . bring order to a certain number of phenomena, first in line being those of life, in the end it is always the paths of the symbolic function which lead us, much more than any sort of direct apprehension. (31)

The fact that we cannot gain the necessary awareness of ourselves and others until we have become subjects of the Symbolic Order distinguishes the kind of consciousness I wish to discuss here from other understandings of consciousness and awareness: the awareness I am speaking of is one that attaches itself to the signifying community and relies on both memory and politics. Memory, like consciousness, is something that must be thought of at the level of the collective as much as of the individual. As Maurice Halbwachs (1992) observed, memory is most commonly sustained via its social dimension, through the processes of recounting to others, receiving others' memories, or being reminded by others. It is these processes that go to make up collective memory. James Fentress and Chris Wickham develop these ideas in their account of 'social memory':

> Social memory is a source of knowledge. This means that it does more than provide a set of categories through which, in an unselfconscious way, a group experiences its surroundings; it also provides the group with material for conscious reflection. This means that we must situate groups in relation to their own traditions, asking how they interpret their own 'ghosts', and how they use them as a source of knowledge. (1992: 26)

As for the political, we could do worse than remember the post-Hegelian, pre-Lacanian words of Karl Marx: 'It is not the consciousness of men that determines their being, but on the contrary it is their social being that determines their consciousness' (Marx and Engels 1968: 181).

Conscience and consciousness

Since one aim of my chapter is to bring together the terms 'consciousness' and 'conscience', it is necessary to say a little about the relationship between the two. Given the example of Latin American music used below, it is important to note that in both Spanish and Portuguese one word is used for the two English terms (*conciencia* (Spanish), *consciência* (Portuguese)). I want to hold on to this fundamental relationship as sustained in the Romance languages, and additionally to think of conscience as a socially evolved form of consciousness—one that, perhaps taking account of the 'mistake' of consciousness, further removes the human from its animal nature. By this I mean that the possession by humans of something called 'conscience' emphasizes a 'consciousness of being conscious', a condition far removed from consciousness as a blind process functioning alongside other 'blind' biological processes. Conscience distinguishes itself precisely by its appeal to a social contract, which may have its roots in biological necessity, but exceeds biology. Conscience, then, must be part of the Symbolic Order and must be distinguished from another of the Lacanian orders, the Real. The Real is that which cannot be symbolized and which exists beyond our attempts to explain nature; it is 'raw' nature itself, that which always returns to the same place.[4] For our purposes we might distinguish between the Real as the biological system in which we might attempt to locate consciousness and the Symbolic as the governing principles that dictate how we might go about doing so. The Real is that which irrupts into the Symbolic as trauma, the gap between the two orders being only traversed by psychosis or death. Conscience might be thought of as the reminder of that gap, the inner voice that charts the distance between the Real and the Symbolic.

This proposal calls to mind Lacan's theory of the role of language and societal rules in the process of subjectivization (Lacan 2006: 237–68), with subjectivity as the site where the distinction between conscience and 'bare' consciousness is forged. Louis Althusser (1971), drawing on Lacanian notions of identification with the big Other, suggests that subjects identify with ideological state apparatuses via a process of interpellation or 'hailing', which he characterizes 'along the lines of the most commonplace everyday police (or other) hail: "Hey, you there!"' (1971: 163). We are literally called into subjectivity by the voice of the big Other (a voice whose origin we cannot locate). Judith Butler's essay on Althusser, '"Conscience Doth Make Subjects of Us All"' (1995), highlights the ways in which Althusser's theory of interpellation relies on subjects already knowing that they will be called to account (for themselves), Althusser's policeman's hail drawing attention to the guilty consciences we carry around with us in our daily lives.

Mladen Dolar, writing of 'the ethics of the voice' and 'the voice of conscience', asks: 'Given the link between conscience and consciousness (both are modes of *con-scio*), is consciousness about hearing voices?' (2006: 83). Dolar's question leads in turn to the distinction between hearing and listening, analogous to Benjamin's distinction between *Gedächtnis* and *Erinnerung*—one a largely unconscious process, the other an isolated conscious act. When we speak of something 'pricking the conscience', there is a suggestion that conscience, though conscious, is nonetheless subject to the uncontrolled forces of the unconscious. Deciding to listen to the heard voices to which Dolar refers, with the potential then to act on them, designates the site at which conscience leads to agency.

Music of conscience

Greil Marcus writes of hearing Bob Dylan sing 'With God on our side' in 1963, and of being aware of US history being 'brought back to consciousness': the knowledge of that history was already there but had been forgotten. He compares Dylan to someone standing at the edge of a crowd, listening to a politician and spreading a rumour that nothing the politician said was true (Marcus 2005: 20), and writes of a 'kind of common epiphany, a gathering of a collective unconscious' in response to 'Like a rolling stone' in 1965 (33). Both examples demonstrate a recognition that what is revealed in the epiphanic moment is something that somehow was already known but unconscious: it is a becoming-aware in the way that we speak of becoming politically aware.

In a similar manner my own musical example, Latin American *nueva canción*, is deeply engaged with a public consciousness, awareness, and conscience, as developed in the preceding account. Indeed, the term 'example' does a disservice by suggesting something tacked on to a body of theory, acting only to demonstrate the theory's worth. But the opposite is the case: the music anticipates and invites the theory. I write as someone who was interpellated at an early age by the music of Latin America, and in particular by the politically committed songs of the Chilean Víctor Jara and the Cuban Silvio Rodríguez, and by the equally committed literature of Pablo Neruda and Gabriel García Márquez. These artists in turn led me to a fascination with the history, culture, and politics of Latin America, to the academic study of these cultures, and then to firsthand experience. In other words, I can trace a growing awareness of this cultural world, a world to which there was no inevitability that I would be attracted, given my spatial and temporal distance from it and its artefacts. That such a process occurred at all attests to the unpredictable potential of a universe of symbols, to the possibilities of public consciousness across space and time, and to the role played by what Eyerman and Jamison (1991) call movement intellectuals—those artists, critics, and other public figures who disseminate the culture of particular social movements to a wider audience. Víctor Jara personifies a movement intellectual, as do his widow

Joan who told his story to the world (Jara 1983), the Chilean record label owner Ricardo Garcia who distributed Jara's banned recordings, and those who performed his music, such as the exiled *nueva canción* groups Quilapayún and Inti-Illimani. Whatever the process, for me the music came before the need to ask what it was in the music that solicited my identification. Addressing that need by exploring the cultural context in which this music continued to operate meant that a personal response was transformed into the realization of a collectivity. The music connected me as an individual to a network, an imagined community of listeners.

It is a common response to the stimulus provided by a musical epiphany to search for a narrative that will explain the stimulus. The collective dimension of such a phenomenon can involve seeking information in the public domain about those responsible for the music, and this is certainly true of the kind of politicized music associated with the *nueva canción* movements that emerged in Latin America in the late 1960s. A large part of the meaning of the music arguably resides in this publicly disseminated information, in which narratives are woven around the lives of musicians, the significance of song lyrics and musical instruments, and the political potential of musicians and performers to enact change or to assert resistance. Jara, for example, was one of the voices most closely associated with the campaign that brought Salvador Allende's socialist Unidad Popular party to power in the 1970 Chilean elections. Jara played a decisive role in the development of *nueva canción* and in its political manifestation— with the consequence that he was arrested and subsequently murdered by the Chilean army, following the military coup of 11 September 1973 that brought nearly two decades of dictatorship to Chile. Jara became an icon of resistance and his music a form of symbolic exchange among those opposed to the dictatorship—his music and that of the other *nueva canción* musicians representing a beacon of hope, an article of faith that change would come. As I have suggested elsewhere (Elliott 2006), the messianic aspect of music's role in heralding change in Latin America cannot be overestimated.

The Cuban singer–songwriter Silvio Rodríguez has played a somewhat different role from Jara: while he has not always been favoured by the Cuban authorities, his music was at least allied to a revolutionary programme that was not subsequently overthrown. Rodríguez is associated with a type of new song known as *nueva trova*, which arose contemporaneously with other *nueva canción* movements that were emerging in Latin America. Rodríguez's music, mixing explicit political statements with coded, metaphorical pieces, found a receptive audience throughout the Hispanic and Lusophone worlds and, in often brutal times—such as during the military dictatorships which gripped Argentina and Chile during the 1970s—offered messages of hope and remembrance to the victims of oppressive regimes. Rodríguez had visited Chile, where his music was to become enormously popular, prior to the 1973 coup that brought Pinochet to power, and had maintained close links with the *nueva canción* musicians then and subsequently. His return in 1990 for a massive concert in Santiago's National Stadium signified, for many, a return to the promise of the Allende years (1970–3) and an end to the official silencing of his and others' music during the intervening period.

A specific song that connects both men and serves as an example of public consciousness is Jara's 'Te recuerdo Amanda' ('I remember you Amanda'). Jara recorded the song in 1969, and it remained a concert favourite for the rest of the singer's life. The lyric describes the relationship between two working-class Chileans and the rupture of that relationship in some unwanted conflict, making implicit reference to the history of conflicts that had shaped life for many generations in Chile and elsewhere in Latin America. The song survived the singer, going on to enjoy a busy afterlife, appearing on the posthumous collection *Manifiesto* (1974) with an English translation read by Jara's widow Joan over the late singer's original recording. 'Te recuerdo Amanda' was also covered by numerous artists, including Quilapayún, Joan Baez, and Robert Wyatt, and Silvio Rodríguez recorded the song in 1998 on a tribute album to Jara. The Cuban singer's version is 'faithful' to the original in the sense in which we often use the word, meaning that it does not depart from the original musical boundaries. The differences that emerge are subtle: Rodríguez's Cubanizing of Jara's Chilean Spanish; the alternating fragility and grit of his vocal on this paean to persistence in the face of adversity; the sense that Rodríguez is continuing to engage in the event of remembering Jara.

By using the term 'event' in this manner, I deliberately evoke the notion of a revolutionary event, something that breaks with the continuum of being and suggests new possibilities.[5] Such events are both personal and collective and demand of those affected by them a severe kind of loyalty or remembering. In such a manner, something as seemingly slight as a song—a fragile lament such as 'Te recuerdo Amanda'—can grow in stature, becoming a shorthand way to connect people in an act of public consciousness. As with its ghostly appearance on *Manifiesto*, where Jara's voice seems to haunt his wife's reading, 'Te recuerdo Amanda' became a spectral accompaniment to the many performances of opposition to the Chilean dictatorship that took place during the 1970s and 1980s. As arguably Jara's best-known composition, it came to mark both the finality of the singer's death and the necessity for the struggle for democracy to continue. To sing the song was to partake in a performative utterance that asserted fidelity both to a large event—the opposition to authoritarian terror; and to a smaller or more minor musical event—the creation of musical materials and performances associated with that opposition.

The artists associated with the first wave of *nueva canción*, then, have had a significant effect on subsequent musicians and audiences, leading to a continued fidelity to the causes for which the music helped to raise consciousness, and a continued presence in the collective consciousness of listeners around the world. The attachment of this music to very particular historical events has ensured that the story of those events has continued to have a notable presence in the public sphere; in Benjamin's terms, a series of isolated experiences of particular moments (*Erlebnis*) result in a long experiential process (*Erfahrung*). Musicians and other artists have been at the centre of the dissemination of information regarding events in Latin America. Many were among the waves of exiles who fled the most brutal regimes and who brought their stories and music to other parts of the world, helping to form an international network of consciousness about what was occurring back home.

Altered consciousness

If consciousness studies has shown an interest in the effects of drug-induced altered states of consciousness on music (see Chapters 15 and 16), we might ask why such altered states are mostly seen to concern transformations of the immediate perception of individuals, understood from the perspective of chemical changes in their brains. It is equally the case that we never hear any piece of music the same way twice, that we always bring something new and different to it, and that these differences can arise as much from to the impact of history, culture, and politics as of mind-altering drugs. History, culture, and politics are states that are constantly being altered too, even as we attempt to stabilize them, and a different way to think about altered states of consciousness might be as changes wrought by and upon the political state.

Often associated with decadence and hedonism, dance music seems to embody a central tenet of much popular music, where the music and the act of listening emphasize the present. Yet, as much as pop may seem to accept the inevitability of transience, there remain strands of popular music that do not wish to forget and that do not always allow for the easy loss of self. An interesting example of this is offered by Philip Sherburne, who describes watching Chilean techno artist Ricardo Villalobos DJing at the 2005 MUTEK festival in Chile. The effectiveness of the story Sherburne tells relies on recognizing the Chilean folk singer Violeta Parra (the 'mother of *nueva canción*') as an embodiment of the aspirations of the country in the period prior to Pinochet's 1973 coup:

> A few hundred rather messy-looking ravers danced and cavorted while a few dozen Chileans and their families looked down on us from the promenade with a mixture of curiosity and middle-class disdain. And then it happened: out of the matrix of pulses, a voice unfurled like some exotic flower. It was Violeta Parra's song, gently remixed by Villalobos to nestle comfortably with the rest of the mix. As the music fell away, we were left only with her unmistakable voice, which traversed an eerie modal scale that seemed, at least to a foreigner, not Chilean, not Latin American, but simply and terrifyingly otherworldly. Up on the promenade, though, the song's provenance dawned on the passers-by, and their expressions changed. Jaws dropped. Time stopped. A wormhole had appeared— both for the ravers dancing in suspended animation but also, more importantly, for the uninitiated spectators who found themselves transported to a year before the dictatorship, before economic restructuring, before the Internet. Villalobos was working his magic, cheating the clock at 128 bpm. (Sherburne 2007: 33)

Sherburne neglects to mention that the song that Villalobos uses is 'Santiago penando estás' (Parra 1999), notable among other reasons for the instrument on which Parra chose to accompany herself: an Andean bass drum called the *bombo* (she accompanied most of her songs with guitar). The *bombo* provides a dull thudding beat and is the only instrument other than Parra's voice on her recording of the song. In Villalobos's set all sounds are removed at the point where he inserts 'Santiago penando estás'— *except* for Parra's voice and a beat which, while sounding like the generic bass beat of contemporary dance music, echoes the sound of the *bombo* to such an extent that it is impossible to tell how much (if any) of the beat has been sampled from the original, how much has been added in the mix, and whether the purpose was to cover the original sound, evoke Andean tradition, or just keep the beat going at this late stage in a four-hour set.[6] This ambiguity provides another level of connection between the original song and its present incarnation, emphasizing the timelessness that Sherburne finds in this sonic event. Villalobos, it appears, is attempting a strategy of estrangement in which he dislocates his auditors both spatially and temporally while dancing is displaced by remembering. The point may not even be the historical specificity of Parra's music, important as that is—as is borne out by Villalobos's use of Parra's voice in sets that he produces in other parts of the world where his listener/dancers may have no knowledge of the voice's provenance. Even at MUTEK, the specifics of the memory may not be translatable; but the pointer towards an act of remembrance is recognized because the strategy of estrangement has brought about *an* act of remembering, albeit a remembering that is an attempt to figure out just what is going on (when confused, it is to our memory as much as any other 'sense' that we turn). As Pierre Nora writes in regard to official silences, 'the observance of a commemorative minute of silence, which might seem to be a strictly symbolic act, disrupts time, thus concentrating memory' (Nora and Kritzman 1996: 14).

There is no certainty that those observing the silence are remembering the same thing. In Villalobos's time-'cheating', as in officially endorsed public silences, we can expect that 'normal' time will resume: the beat kicks back in, the dancing resumes, and a sort of 'normality' returns. For, while Sherburne's point seems to be that, by keeping the music at 128 bpm throughout his sets, Villalobos is attempting to sustain a 'time out of joint' for as long as possible, it is easy to see how this time becomes a new kind of normality once the DJ's listener/dancers have adjusted their mental clocks. To finish his set with the Parra tribute would be to leave these listeners stranded; it is the silence and uncanniness surrounding Parra's voice emerging from the mix that is the really 'out of joint' aspect of time at work here, not the 'homely' ('housely'?) music with which Villalobos frames it. Perhaps it is not important what is remembered—and yet the point of telling the story (Sherburne's point) is to say that it does matter.

I find Sherburne's narrative convincing precisely because of my own experience of *nueva canción* and because I am engaged in researching these kinds of responses to music and memory. While I can see such responses as highly subjective, I can also determine a loose community of 'believers' (among whom I count myself) who find in this kind of discourse a useful way to account for the effect that music has on them. Music has sent out a call, interpellating listeners who then attempt to account for their identification with music. This inevitably involves telling stories, weaving narratives around the musical materials, creating (auto)biographies and histories that interlace personal and public reminiscences. Public consciousness requires *publicists*—interpreters who will take part in the dissemination of cultural artefacts (Marcus for Dylan, Joan Jara for Víctor, Sherburne for Villalobos). To criticize the use of personal reminiscences by highlighting their subjective specificity is to ignore the fact that memory is a process we share with others and that memory (per se) is nothing without (particular) memories.[7]

Conclusion

I have argued in this chapter for the importance of a sense of public consciousness. Rather than seeing music as merely an example of this, I have argued that music interpellates its audience—issues an invitation to discuss the public dimension of consciousness. My proposal arises from two distinct but related responses. The first is prompted by the absence in cognitivist accounts of consciousness of a convincing exploration of history, politics, or society. The second is my response to the call of a music (*nueva canción*) that demands such an account. Behind both lies the key issue of identification, by which I mean both the construction of identity as one develops subjectivity, and identification with a musical culture—and which in turn suggests that psychoanalysis and phenomenology still have much to say about consciousness.

If *nueva canción* exemplifies the functioning of a public consciousness, the ways in which it is appropriated by subsequent generations may challenge as much as extend the practical uses of its political potential. There would of course be other ways to interpret my use of Sherburne's account of Villalobos's sampling of Violeta Parra (and the abundance of possessives highlights both the fragility and the continuity of the chain). One might focus instead on the role of dance music in altering the consciousness of the individual, and I have already indicated above some of the directions in which such an account might proceed. The question would seem to hinge on the importance we give to interpretation (and to interpreters) when evaluating what 'goes into' consciousness— an issue vividly discussed by Heidegger in his essay 'The origin of the work of art':

> We never really first perceive a throng of sensations, e.g. tones and noises, in the appearance of things . . . rather we hear the storm whistling in the chimney, we hear the three-motored plane, we hear the Mercedes in immediate distinction from the Volkswagen. Much closer to us than all sensations are the things themselves. We hear the door shut in the house and never hear acoustical sensations or even mere sounds. In order to hear a bare sound we have to listen away from things, divert our ear from them, i.e. listen abstractly. (1993: 151–2)

To understand the 'Villalobos narrative' through a cognitivist account of listening in an altered state among consumers of dance music, might be valid—another step in the dialectic, perhaps—but would also be to 'listen away' from the interpretation of this particular music that Sherburne presents. That is something I would want to resist, since it represents an attempt to 'bridge the gap' and solve what may be fundamentally unsolvable differences between philosophy and neuroscience. The gap may be more productively pursued by attending to, but maintaining, that minimal difference that is forced upon the observer by Žižek's parallax view.

References

Althusser, L. (1971). Ideology and ideological state apparatuses (notes towards an investigation), in *Lenin and Philosophy and Other* Essays, trans. B. Brewster, 121–76 (London: New Left Books).

Anzieu, D. (1990). *A Skin for Thought: Interviews with Gilbert Tarrab on Psychology and Psychoanalysis*, trans. D.N. Briggs (London: Karnac).

Benmayor, R. (1981). La '*nueva trova*': New Cuban Song. *Latin American Music Review/Revista de Música Latinoamericana*, **2**, 11–44.

Butler, J. (1995). 'Conscience doth make subjects of us all.' *Yale French Studies*, **88**, 6–26.

Caruth, C. (ed.) (1995). *Trauma: Explorations in Memory* (Baltimore, MD: Johns Hopkins University Press).

Casey, E.S. (2000). *Remembering: A Phenomenological Study*, 2nd edn (Bloomington, IN: Indiana University Press).

The Compact Edition of the Oxford English Dictionary (1971). (Oxford: Clarendon Press.)

Coulter, J. (2008). Twenty-five theses against cognitivism. *Theory, Culture & Society*, **25**, 19–32.

Dennett, D.C. (1991). *Consciousness Explained* (Harmondsworth: Penguin).

Dolar, M. (2006). *A Voice and Nothing More* (Cambridge, MA: MIT Press).

Elliott, R. (2006). Reconstructing the event: spectres of terror in Chilean performance. *British Postgraduate Musicology*, **8**. Available at: www.bpmonline.org.uk/bpm8/Elliott.html (accessed 6 August 2009).

Elliott, R. (2008a). *Loss, Memory and Nostalgia in Popular Song: Thematic Aspects and Theoretical Approaches*. Unpublished PhD thesis, Newcastle University.

Elliott, R. (2008b). Popular music and/as event: subjectivity, love and fidelity in the aftermath of rock 'n' roll. *Radical Musicology*, **3**. Available at: www.radical-musicology.org.uk/2008/ Elliott.htm (accessed 6 March 2011).

Evans, D. (2001). *An Introductory Dictionary of Lacanian Psychoanalysis* (Hove: Brunner-Routledge).

Eyerman, R. (2001). *Cultural Trauma: Slavery and the Formation of African American Identity* (Cambridge: Cambridge University Press).

Eyerman, R. and Jamison, A. (1991). *Social Movements: A Cognitive Approach* (Cambridge: Polity Press).

Fairley, J. (1985). Annotated bibliography of Latin-American popular music with particular reference to Chile and to *Nueva Canción. Popular Music*, **5**, 305–6.

Fentress, J. and Wickham, C. (1992). *Social Memory* (Oxford: Blackwell).

Halbwachs, M. (1992). *On Collective Memory*, ed. and trans. L.A. Coser (Chicago, IL: The University of Chicago Press).

Heidegger, M. (1993). *Basic Writings*, rev. edn, ed. D.F. Krell, trans. D.F. Krell *et al.* (London: Routledge).

Jara, J. (1983). *Victor: An Unfinished Song* (London: Jonathan Cape).

Lacan, J. (1991). *The Seminar of Jacques Lacan. Book II: The Ego in Freud's Theory and in the Technique of Psychoanalysis 1954–1955*, ed. J.-A. Miller, trans. Sylvana Tomaselli (New York, NY: W.W. Norton).

Lacan, J. (1993). *The Seminar of Jacques Lacan. Book III: The Psychoses 1955–1956*, ed. Jacques-Alain Miller, trans. Russell Grigg (New York, NY: W.W. Norton).

Lacan, J. (2006). *Écrits*, trans. B. Fink (New York, NY: W.W. Norton).

Lambek, M. (1996). The past imperfect: remembering as moral practice, in P. Antze and M. Lambek (eds.) *Tense Past: Cultural Essays in Trauma and Memory*, 235–54 (New York, NY: Routledge).

Marcus, G. (2005). *Like A Rolling Stone: Bob Dylan at the Crossroads* (London: Faber and Faber).

Marx, K. and Engels, F. (1968). *Selected Works in One Volume* (London: Lawrence and Wishart).

Moore, R. (2003). Transformations in Cuban *Nueva Trova*, 1965–1995. *Ethnomusicology*, **47**, 1–41.

Moreno, A. (1986). Violeta Parra and 'La nueva Canción Chilena'. *Studies in Latin American Popular Culture*, **5**, 108–25.

Morris, N. (1986). 'Canto porque es neccesario cantar': the New Song movement in Chile. *Latin American Research Review*, **21**, 111–36.

Nora, P. and Kritzman, L.D. (eds.) (1996). *Realms of Memory: Rethinking the French Past, Vol. 1: Conflicts and Divisions*, trans. A. Goldhammer (New York, NY: Columbia University Press).

Parra, V. (1999). *Canciones reencontradas en París*. CD (Warner Music Chile 857380321-2).

Ricoeur, P. (2004). *Memory, History, Forgetting*, trans. K. Blamey and D. Pellauer (Chicago, IL: University of Chicago Press).

Sherburne, P. (2007). Time out of joint. *The Wire*, **282**, 30–5.

Žižek, S. (1989). *The Sublime Object of Ideology*. (London: Verso).

Žižek, S. (2002). *For They Know Not What They Do: Enjoyment As a Political Factor*, 2nd edn (London: Verso).

Žižek, S. (2006). *The Parallax View* (Cambridge, MA: MIT Press).

Žižek, S. and **Daly**, G. (2004). *Conversations with Žižek* (Cambridge: Polity).

Zohn, H. (2006). Translator's notes to W. Benjamin, 'On some motifs in Baudelaire,' in W. Benjamin *Selected Writings*, vol. 4, 1938–1940, ed. H. Eiland and M.W. Jennings, 343–55 (Cambridge, MA: The Belknap Press of Harvard University Press).

Notes

1. These definitions are taken from *The Compact Edition of the Oxford English Dictionary* (1971: 1880–1).

2. This may be less the case when thinking of music in the circumstances of musical analysis, in which there is also the tendency for music to be de-contextualized.

3. I am referring here to what Lacan calls the *point de capiton*, translated as either 'quilting point' or 'anchoring point'. In its literal use this point designates a site where the otherwise shapeless mass of stuffing is fixed in place by an upholsterer's needle; in its metaphorical use it designates a site where an otherwise chaotic mass of meaning can be fixed into an isolated sensible form. For Lacan, it is 'the point of convergence that enables everything that happens in . . . discourse to be situated retroactively and prospectively' (1993: 268).

4. Dylan Evans (2001: 159–60) defines the Real as follows: 'the real emerges as that which is outside language and inassimilable to symbolisation . . . This . . . leads Lacan to link the real with the concept of impossibility. The real is . . . impossible to imagine, impossible to integrate into the symbolic order, and impossible to attain in any way.'

5. I also deliberately evoke the work of Alain Badiou, whose theory of 'event' I have elsewhere connected with the performance of popular music (see Elliott 2006, 2008a: 159–211, 2008b).

6. These observations are based on MP3 versions of Villalobos's sets posted to the internet in 2007, now no longer available.

7. See Coulter (2008: 20) on the 'globalization of Memory' engendered by cognitivism. This is an area provocatively explored in Edward Casey's (2000) attempt to create a 'phenomenology of memory', and also developed by Lambek (1996) and Ricoeur (2004) to account for the ways memory is used to write history. Sherburne's account, when read alongside Ricoeur's interactive process of memory/history/forgetting, is one in which 'memory' and 'state' become historically meaningful.

Chapter 20

The psychic disintegration of a demi-god: conscious and unconscious in Striggio and Monteverdi's *L'Orfeo*

Jeffrey Kurtzman

'Consciousness' is a word used casually in everyday parlance, suggesting that, in the Western world at least, we have an unproblematic understanding of the term, however problematic it may be when examined more closely. Its opposite, 'unconscious', however, is far more vague and manifold in its usage and significance. Both concepts may be studied from many different angles, according to the criteria and practices of many different disciplines. My objective in this chapter is to examine the methods of poetic and musical expression employed by the librettist Alessandro Striggio and the composer Claudio Monteverdi in their first opera, *L'Orfeo* (1607), from a psychological standpoint. Such an approach is particularly fruitful, for the premise of opera from its incipient stages was psychological, leading to a rich musico-dramatic portrayal of both the conscious and unconscious levels of its protagonist's mind.

Monteverdi and the birth of opera

The origins of opera in the late sixteenth century through the efforts of the Florentine Camerata are too well known to require review here. What is worth emphasizing, however, are psychological aspects of the theoretical foundations of opera. Vincenzo Galilei, the principal theorist of the Camerata, argued that the purpose of music was to convey the significance of a textual idea (*concetto*) and to affect an audience emotionally for their moral benefit and improvement, as he believed the Greeks had done in their tragedies. The Camerata had the same objective as contemporaneous oratory: to move an audience the same way a singer had been moved by the ideas contained in the text (Strunk 1950: 302–22).[1] This was an age in which the importance of rhetoric was at its apogee in education, in the Church, in politics and diplomacy, and in poetry (the literature on rhetoric in the Renaissance is vast). Famous preachers, such as San Filippo Neri, had brought untold numbers back into the Church and prayer houses (*oratorii*) by the emotional impact of their rhetoric.

In opera, musical rhetoric combined the magical effects of the word with the magical effects of music.[2] First a *concetto* and its attendant passion were embodied in words by the poet, then realized in music for solo voice and accompaniment by the composer, then projected by the singer functioning as orator, and ultimately received by the listener who was emotionally moved and morally improved. Following Plato, Galilei believed that music had ethical effects upon its listeners, but the more practical musicians of the Camerata, the singer–composers Jacopo Peri and Giulio Caccini, quickly abandoned the moralistic aspect of the recitative and other monodic vocal forms and stressed only the passions—the ability of the singer to move the passions of the listener in accord with the significance of the text and its musical setting. Opera was born as an ideal medium for carrying out this programme.

The Florentine project was profoundly psychological, for its aim was to influence the way people experienced and thought about the world through stimulating their feelings, their affections. This entailed something more than one individual striving to induce a particular psychological state in another; it meant a chain of persons involved in the creation, production, and performance of an opera seeking to affect psychologically a large number of people in an audience.[3]

The first Florentine opera was *La Dafne* of 1598, only fragments of which survive. The tale of Orpheus and Eurydice was the second myth to which these Florentines applied their theories and their practice in the first surviving opera, Peri's and Caccini's *Euridice* of 1600.[4] The story was commissioned again from the Mantuan court poet Alessandro Striggio and court composer Claudio Monteverdi in 1607 by Prince Francesco Gonzaga. Their first effort at the new genre was in obvious emulation of and competition with the Florentines. There had been long-standing Gonzaga interest in this myth, which had previously been dramatized by the Mantuan poet Angelo Poliziano in a court play of 1480 and depicted by the Mantuan painter, Andrea Mantegna, in a series of frescoes in the bridal chamber of the ducal palace in the same period (Scavizzi 1985: 117). Striggio's and Monteverdi's opera, entitled *L'Orfeo*, was first performed in the Gonzaga palace on 24 February 1607 and received another performance on 1 March (Fenlon 1986). Also in emulation and competition with the Florentines, the libretto and music were published: the libretto first in 1607 and the music in 1609, with a second, corrected edition issued in 1615.[5]

The story of Orpheus has long been considered an ideal subject for opera, not just because of its tragic aspects, but because of Orpheus's identity and role as the master musician, the one who could tame wild beasts, make stones weep, stop streams from flowing, and ultimately win the reluctant Eurydice as bride with his music. Orpheus represents the magical power of music, its power to penetrate directly to the soul, as so many sixteenth- and seventeenth-century writers declared.[6] And no one succeeded so well in the early seventeenth century as Monteverdi in accomplishing precisely that: grasping intuitively the psychology of Orpheus as a human-like character and penetrating with his music to the emotional depths of listeners.

Trying to understand just how Monteverdi achieved this is what leads me to an examination of the expression of both consciousness and the unconscious in *L'Orfeo*. Clearly, a psychological approach is required in keeping with the psychological power of the music, but there are many psychological avenues for exploring this matter. I take my point of departure from the writings of Carl Gustav Jung, whose approach I find the richest and most useful in explanatory potential, allowing insight not only into the psychology of Striggio's and Monteverdi's protagonist, but also into their own psychological knowledge and instincts in finding convincing means to express his tragedy. Jung's psychology might be deployed on hermeneutic grounds, but it is also a fact that there are aspects of Jung's psychology that have been widely accepted as valid by the psychological profession, which suggests that these may serve as guides to Striggio's and Monteverdi's own understanding of the psychology of Orpheus. These aspects include Jung's definition of the unconscious in much broader and more inclusive terms than Freud, the idea of psychological growth through self-knowledge (previously emphasized by Friedrich Nietzsche), the identification of psychological types, and the concepts of the 'anima' and 'animus' (the feminine and masculine sides) in men and women.

Jung's conception of consciousness and the unconscious

Jung provided a definition of consciousness in his seminal work *Psychological Types* (1921), whose last chapter constitutes a series of definitions of terms used throughout the book. Jung's definition of consciousness is not easy to grasp apart from the entire complex of ideas contained in this volume. Basing his conception on Paul Natorp's *Einleitung in die Psychologie nach kritischer Methode*, published in Freiburg im Breisgau (1888), Jung begins:

> By consciousness I understand the relation of psychic contents to the *ego*, in so far as this relation is perceived as such by the ego. . . . Relations to the ego that are not perceived as such are *unconscious*. Consciousness is the function or activity which maintains the relation of psychic contents to the ego. (1971: 421–2)[7]

Having grown up with the dialectical intellectual model of Platonic and nineteenth-century German philosophy, Jung defined and understood many of these terms in relation to their opposites. In this case consciousness is understood in relation to the unconscious—and vice versa. Jung's definition of the unconscious begins:

> The concept of the *unconscious* is for me an *exclusively psychological* concept, and not a philosophical concept of a metaphysical nature. In my view the unconscious is a psychological borderline concept, which covers all psychic contents or processes that are not conscious, i.e., not related to the *ego* in any perceptible way. (1971: 483)

Jung later defined the unconscious more concretely:

> Everything of which I know but of which I am not at the moment thinking; everything of which I was once conscious but have now forgotten; everything perceived by my senses but not noted by my conscious mind; everything which involuntarily and without paying attention to it I feel, think, remember, want and do; all future things that are taking shape in me and will sometime come to consciousness—all this is the content of the unconscious. (Segaller 1989)

Key to the definitions of both consciousness and the unconscious in *Psychological Types* are the terms 'psychic contents' and 'ego'. Although Jung offers no definition explicitly of 'psychic contents', it is clear from his definition of the psyche as 'the totality of all psychic processes, conscious as well as unconscious' (C.G. Jung 1971: 463), as well as his use of this term in other discussions, that 'psychic contents' comprehends all mental processes of any kind. Jung's concept of the ego, on the other hand, is specifically dependent on consciousness:

> By ego I understand a complex of ideas which constitutes the centre of my field of consciousness and appears to possess a high degree of continuity and identity. Hence I also speak of an *ego-complex*. The ego-complex is as much a content as a condition of *consciousness*, for a psychic element is conscious to me only in so far as it is related to my ego-complex. (1971: 425)

What Jung means by ego-complex is clearly the individual aware of him or herself, that sense of self-identity that maintains continuity transcending time. 'Psychic contents', or mental processes, therefore, are conscious when the ego, the individual, is aware of them, and unconscious when the ego is unaware of them.

Another way to put this is that consciousness entails the focus of attention on external perceptions or internal thoughts and feelings. As long as we focus sufficient attention on something, we are aware or conscious of it. Those functionings of the mind that go on beneath our level of consciousness, therefore allowing us to focus our conscious attention selectively on just a few things at a time, occupy the realm of the unconscious, that substratum of the mind on which consciousness rests. Jung considered the term unconscious to be a metaphor for all kinds of mental activities that take place without our being aware of them, without entering into consciousness.

Jung divided the unconscious itself into two strata: an underlying *collective* unconscious and a *personal* unconscious. He describes the collective unconscious in this manner:

> in addition to these personal unconscious contents, there are other contents which do not originate in personal acquisitions but in the inherited possibility of psychic functioning in general, i.e., in the inherited structure of the brain. These are the mythological associations, the motifs and images that can spring up anew anytime anywhere, independently of historical tradition or migration. (1971: 485)

The collective unconscious, Jung claimed, is the substratum of the mind whose psychic contents are universal to all humanity. On Jung's view the collective unconscious is the origin of such mythological figures as Orpheus, whose counterpart appears in a number of other mythologies around the globe, resulting from the tendency of the collective unconscious to produce images (archetypes) that embody basic apprehensions and ideas significant to all humankind.

The personal unconscious rests on the collective unconscious and may include the personal aspects of underlying psychic contents from the collective unconscious. The contents of the personal unconscious range from the vast storehouses of memory to the symbolic content of dreams, from the neural networks that generate feeling to suppressed complexes that impinge on behaviour, from instinctive value judgements to imagination and the mysterious ruminations that result in sudden ideas or artistic inspiration. Jung also describes the contents of the unconscious as often in dialectical opposition to the contents of consciousness or as representing the complement or opposite of incomplete or indistinctly focused conscious thoughts, feelings, and experiences. One of the facets of this dialectic Jung explores most deeply is the concept of the *anima* and the *animus*, the gender opposites of the conscious individual—gender images and gender-associated characteristics and behaviours that in their universality originate archetypally in the collective unconscious, but are distinctively shaped in every individual's personal unconscious. These unconscious gender images have profound effects on our attitudes, thinking, feelings, and behaviour, whether positively or negatively. According to Jung, an 'impassioned relationship' between the sexes results from the projection of the unconscious gender opposite, the *anima* or *animus*, onto a real individual. The difficulties in love relationships often result from the failure of that real individual to conform to the unconscious, projected gender image. In Jung's definitions in *Psychological Types*, the concepts of anima and animus—among the most complex and difficult of his ideas to grasp fully—are explained under, and in fact identified with, the term *soul-image*. I give here only part of his explanation:

> The soul-image is a specific *image* among those produced by the unconscious. Just as the *persona*, or outer attitude is represented in dreams by images of definite persons who possess the outstanding qualities of the persona in especially marked form, so in a man the soul, i.e., anima, or inner attitude, is represented in the unconscious by definite persons with the corresponding qualities. Such an image is called a 'soul-image'. . . . With men the anima is usually personified by the unconscious as a woman; with women the animus is personified as a man. . . . In all cases where there is an *identity* with the persona, and the soul accordingly is unconscious, the soul-image is transferred to a real person. This person is the object of intense love or equally intense hate (or fear). The influence of such a person is immediate and absolutely compelling, because it always provokes an affective response. The *affect* is due to the fact that a real, conscious adaptation to the person representing the soul-image is impossible. . . . Affects always occur where there is a failure of adaptation. Conscious adaptation to the person representing the soul-image is impossible precisely because the subject is unconscious of the soul. Were he conscious of it, it could be distinguished from the object, whose immediate effects might then be mitigated, since the potency of the object depends on the *projection* of the soul-image. For a man, a woman is best fitted to be the real bearer of his soul-image, because of the feminine quality of his soul; for a woman it will be a man. Wherever an impassioned, almost magical, relationship exists between the sexes, it is invariably a question of a projected soul-image. (C.G. Jung 1971: 470–1)[8]

As we will see, the projection of Orfeo's *anima* upon Euridice (I will use the Italian forms of Orpheus and Eurydice to refer to the characters in the opera) is a critical factor in a psychological understanding of Striggio's and Monteverdi's work.

The unconscious and its workings are beyond cognition. As Jung wryly observed very late in his life, 'The research comes to the question of the unconscious—there things become necessarily blurred, because the unconscious is something which is *really* unconscious. So you have no object, you see nothing, you only can make inferences'.[9] Nevertheless, it is possible to understand something about the unconscious and its 'psychic contents' through inductive reasoning and other indirect methods, such as dream analysis, hypnosis, or the study of mythology.[10]

In Jung's psychology, the unconscious inevitably holds vastly more 'psychic contents' than does consciousness and is infinitely more complex; indeed, Jung declares,

'The range of what *could* be an unconscious content is simply illimitable' (1971: 485). The unconscious is like an endless sea, ill-formed, deep, unpredictable, uncontrollable and unknowable. But even though the contents of the unconscious are beyond cognition, the boundary between the unconscious and the conscious is permeable. In his definition of the unconscious in *Psychological Types* Jung describes the movement of psychic contents from consciousness to the unconscious through a loss of psychic energy:

> Conscious contents can become unconscious through loss of their energic value. This is the normal process of 'forgetting'. That these contents do not simply get lost below the threshold of consciousness we know from the experience that occasionally, under suitable conditions, they can emerge from their submersion decades later, for instance in dreams, or under hypnosis, or in the form of cryptomnesia, or through the revival of associations with the forgotten content. We also know that conscious contents can fall below the threshold of consciousness through 'intentional forgetting,' or what Freud calls the *repression* of a painful content, with no appreciable loss of value. (1971: 484)[11]

Even more commonly, whenever we change the focus of our attention, whatever had been its previous focus slips into the unconscious. Just as conscious contents may lose sufficient 'energic value' and recede into the unconscious, these and other contents, such as sense perceptions, associations, and judgements whose intensity was originally inadequate to reach the level of consciousness, may gather enough 'psychic energy' to appear in dreams, under hypnosis, or in consciousness under the stimulus of some associated conscious thought, perception, or experience. When a thought, image, or memory suddenly appears in our minds, it has, in Jung's terms, accumulated enough 'energic value' to cross the boundary; it has attained enough psychic energy to bring the 'psychic content' out of the murky and chaotic unconscious into the light and concreteness of consciousness where it can be perceived, subjected to thought, and selectively acted on.

It is through this process of accumulating 'energic value' that the vast contents of the unconscious are productive of contents that reach consciousness. The one such activity Jung cites in his definition of the unconscious is the production of mythological images from the collective unconscious, whereby the image gathers enough psychic energy to become conscious, but its associations and significance remain unconscious. However, Jung's concept of the unconscious, as he describes it in *Psychological Types*, *Two Essays on Analytical Psychology* and in so many other writings, is productive of much more: it is the source of instincts, habits, spontaneous actions, intuitions, creativity, and all new ideas that so often appear abruptly and unexpectedly in consciousness. In Jung's theory, any unconscious contents may at some point be infused with enough psychic energy to come to the surface as conscious thoughts, associations, ideas, images, feelings, judgements, and reactions.

It is fundamental to Jung's psychology and generally accepted in the psychological profession that the unconscious also regularly influences behaviour without its psychic contents gathering enough 'psychic energy' to come to consciousness. Instinctive behaviours, habitual behaviours, emotional reactions that suddenly surface without a known specific cause, most judgements about experiences, people, objects, and situations, come about through the workings of the unconscious, often in response to an external stimulus or some inner rumination. Consciousness too, of course, affects behaviour, for we can deliberately choose to react to something and behave accordingly. On the other hand, many of our reactions and behaviours are unconscious, without our being aware of the relationship between our underlying psychic contents and our response to external stimuli, persons, or events. In such instances, our reaction or behaviour occurs spontaneously, without our thinking about it. Frequently we only become aware of our behaviour or reaction through some outward manifestation commanding attention, or through someone else calling attention to it, while its underlying motivation remains obscure. Indeed, far more of our daily activity and behaviour is governed by the unconscious than by conscious, deliberative planning or judgement.

Beyond this type of interaction between consciousness and the unconscious, Jung considered their overall relationship to be critical to the mental health and well-being of any individual. According to Jung, mental health depends on keeping the conscious and the unconscious in some kind of balance. This requires consciousness to recognize that much of the mind's activity—and much of what motivates our behaviour— is located in the unconscious. Psychic health requires that the individual ego not only rely on the awareness and functions of consciousness, which are quite limited, but also seek to understand something about the unconscious in order to find assistance from that psychic realm in responding to and coping with life. Only by delving indirectly into the unconscious, by descending into its uncharted darkness and chaotic contents, can individuals become aware of their underlying motivations, discover the gender-opposite aspects of their personality, find solutions to the more intractable of life's problems, and grow towards the fullest possible realization of their potential. All broadening of personality, all creative approaches to problems, all wisdom and psychic health depend on a lifelong effort to learn and grow from the unconscious, to bring aspects of the unconscious out of darkness into the light of consciousness where the ego can grapple with them and make effective choices in governing the individual's actions as well as coming to grips with the inevitable frustrations, traumas, and suffering of life.

Jung called this process of learning and growing from the encounter with the unconscious 'individuation'. It is a process not only of defining oneself more specifically by bringing unconscious psychic contents to the light of consciousness, but also of differentiating oneself from others:

> The concept of individuation . . . is the process by which individual beings are formed and differentiated; in particular, it is the development of the psychological *individual* as a being distinct from the general collective psychology. Individuation, therefore is a process of *differentiation*, having for its goal the development of the individual personality. . . . Individuation is practically the same as the development of consciousness out of the original state of *identity*. It is thus an extension of the sphere of consciousness, an enriching of conscious psychological life. (1971: 448–50)

The connection between the process of individuation and the unconscious becomes explicit in Jung's definition of identity—not the unique characteristics of the individual, as the word is often understood in English, but rather the identification of the individual with others, such as the identification of an infant with its parents, or a person with the group of which he or she is a part:

> I use the term *identity* to denote a psychological conformity. It is always an unconscious phenomenon since a conscious conformity would necessarily involve a consciousness of two dissimilar things, and consequently, a separation of subject and object, in which case the identity would already have been abolished. Psychological identity presupposes that it is unconscious. It is a characteristic of the primitive mentality and the real foundation of *participation mystique*, which is nothing but a relic of the original non-differentiation of subject and object, and hence of the primordial unconscious state. (C.G. Jung 1971: 441)

But Jung's definition of individuation in the last chapter of *Psychological Types* only scratches the surface of the process and its importance for the individual in his psychology. The discussions of the subject in this and his subsequent writings repeatedly emphasize not only the separation of the individual from the collective, but the significance of awareness and understanding of the contents of the unconscious, of the individual's underlying attitudes, motivations, feelings, and behaviours, in order to expand consciousness of oneself and bring these matters under the critique and control of consciousness, that is, to integrate the conscious and unconscious. To be unknowingly motivated and moved by the unconscious is to fail to understand or have authority over oneself. Bringing unconscious psychic contents increasingly into consciousness not only achieves greater self-understanding and increased command over one's reactions to life's experiences, but also increasingly differentiates the individual from the collective.

Individuation is a difficult, lifelong effort, resulting in ever-developing maturity and psychological health. Without the aid of the unconscious, ego consciousness is so limited that at times it cannot deal adequately or productively with the hardships and tragedies of life. But because the unconscious contains the potential for everything, not every exploration of the unconscious, every influence of the unconscious, or everything that emerges from the unconscious into consciousness is positive. The unconscious indiscriminately contains the potential for both positive and negative—for both good and evil, creation and destruction—so that delving into and encountering the unconscious can be not only fruitful and energizing but also dangerous and destructive. If the conscious ego becomes confused or overwhelmed by the unconscious, then conscious intentions can fail and psychological chaos can ensue, for the very nature of the unconscious is that it is undifferentiated, untamed, disorganized, fragmented, and beyond conscious control. Such a serious psychic disturbance can, in turn, culminate in psychic disintegration, whereby the conscious ego itself fragments under the pressure of overwhelming unconscious forces or of experiences in a world with which consciousness cannot cope and from which exploration of the unconscious provides no positive relief.

Thus, individuation is a serious matter for the personality, especially in those times of life when the efforts of consciousness to construct one's individuality, orient oneself in the world, and pursue one's goals encounter unexpected difficulties, or fail. That is when it is most crucial to turn one's attention to the unconscious, to seek new understandings, new solutions, and new ways of approaching a world that is no longer manageable by the old conscious means.

These concepts, definitions, and explanations form the investigative and herme-neutic basis for my study and discussion of the psychological aspects of Striggio's and Monteverdi's *L'Orfeo*. What I wish to demonstrate is not that either Striggio or Monteverdi thought about the psychology of their characters and the expression of that psychology in the same terms as Jung, but rather that their own experiential and instinctive knowledge of human psychology and emotions led them to forms of expression which Jung's concepts and formulations can assist in interpreting and explaining. If Jung's understanding and explanation of human psychology is valid irrespective of the fluctuations of history (which Jung himself clearly believed), then this type of investigation should be able to bring to conscious awareness what the librettist and composer understood in many respects only intuitively and instinctively, that is, unconsciously. Such an investigation should also be capable of illuminating how the true-to-life representation of Orfeo's psychology is fundamental to the attraction and power of the opera.

Conscious and unconscious in *L'Orfeo*

The myth of the demi-god Orpheus has proved one of the most popular and enduring tales of ancient Greece. Among several facets of the myth, the one that has fired the imagination of the Western world for well over two thousand years is the story of Orpheus the poet-musician, given his talent by his father, the god Apollo, enabling him to perform the kind of magic typically associated by the Greeks with music. For Orpheus himself, the highest of his musical achievements is to win as wife the nymph Eurydice. In Virgil's and Ovid's versions of the myth, the two principal sources for Striggio's libretto, Orpheus's winning of Eurydice does not last long,[12] for she is soon bitten by a snake, whether in the act of fleeing the unwanted advances of the beekeeper Aristea in Virgil's *Georgics*, or while celebrating her wedding in Ovid's *Metamorphoses*. Orpheus is beside himself with grief and resolves to descend into the Underworld to test the magic of his music in a novel way: to win Eurydice a second time by softening the heart of Pluto. Pluto seems to relent, but he is no fool. He allows Eurydice to follow Orpheus back out of Hades on the condition that Orpheus have complete trust in his word and not look back to be certain. But on the way out of Hades, Orpheus suc-cumbs, according to Ovid, to the fear that Eurydice might not be well; impelled by love, he does turn and look back, thereby losing Eurydice for a second, final time. Emerging from the Underworld, he travels to the plains of Thrace, where he bewails his fate and forswears the company of women forever. In Ovid's story, after a period of mourning, he takes up with young boys. But whether he simply abjures women, as in Virgil, or turns his attention to boys, he meets the same fate. Because he has rejected female company, a savage group of Maenads, female followers of Bacchus, tears him limb from limb and scatters his body parts. There is more to the story, but it goes beyond what Striggio included in his libretto and Monteverdi set to music and need not concern us here.

The psychological picture of Orfeo presented by Striggio and Monteverdi is entire-ly human and individualistic, even though the myth of Orpheus may itself have been a product of what Jung called the collective unconscious. That Monteverdi understood his version of the protagonist as revealing a human psychology imposed on the mythical figure of the demi-god is implicit in a letter to Striggio, dated 9 December 1616. In reference to a proposal for an opera in which the four winds were to be principal characters, the composer writes: 'Ariadne [the heroine of his opera *Arianna* of 1608] moved us because she was a woman, and similarly Orpheus because he was a man, not a wind' (Stevens 1995: 110).[13] Striggio cast the tale in its language and structure in a manner that stimulated and enabled the composer to play upon the human psychological aspects of Orfeo, aspects which may be subsumed under Jung's definitions of the conscious and unconscious, in terms of both dramatic situations and the actions and reactions of the hero. The world in which Orfeo wins Euridice is representative of consciousness itself, for it is a place of light where things can be seen, understood, and enjoyed. The Underworld, on the other hand, is dark, mysterious, frightening, and dangerous—representative of the unconscious, the realm of the unknown and unbounded potential, both positive and negative. Thus, in the myth, the Underworld manifests not only the possibility for Euridice's return to the light of day and the conferral of eternal happiness on Orfeo, as happens in the libretto of Peri's and Caccini's *Euridice* of 1600, mentioned above; but also the potential for the eternal loss of Euridice, as described in Virgil's and Ovid's versions of the myth, in Angelo Poliziano's Mantuan play of 1480, and in Striggio's libretto.

The first act-and-a-half of *L'Orfeo* is all festivity, happiness, and delight. Orfeo and his shepherd companions are celebrating his wedding and his successful wooing of the formerly reluctant Euridice through his music. Dances and closed, strophic musical numbers of the type inherited from the *intermedio* tradition of court entertainment are prominent in this part of the opera. Monteverdi also creates rounded or symmetrical structures on a larger scale by means of repetition of certain numbers, such as the five-part madrigal *Lasciate i monti*, which both precedes and follows the first appearance of Orfeo and Euridice. As is well known, Monteverdi organizes these numbers in a palindromic symmetry in the first act, with the initial appearances of Orfeo and Euridice in the centre. These closed, repetitive, and symmetrical structures are representative of the conscious, rational world of the protagonists themselves and their pastoral companions. The music, whether in the form of recitative, arioso, strophic variations, or strophic song, is an expression of a consistency of feeling of which everyone on stage is fully aware and in which they all share. Moreover, we might assume that these feelings were as clear to Monteverdi's audience as they are to today's.

Yet even in the midst of this conscious revelry, Orfeo's unconscious becomes manifest—in the character of Euridice. Euridice is a shadowy figure in the ancient forms of the myth, in Poliziano's play, in Striggio's libretto, and in Monteverdi's music. She never appears in any of the poetic versions nor in the opera as a well-defined character. Euridice has only one substantive moment in the opera, and even that is brief and indecisively formed.[14] Indeed, in Striggio's libretto, she identifies herself entirely with Orfeo's heart rather than in terms of her own personal affection:

> Io non dirò qual sia
> Nel tuo gioire Orfeo la gioia mia,

Che non ho meco il core,
Ma seco stassi in compagnia d'Amore;
Chiedilo dunque à lui s'intender brami
Quanto lieta gioisca, e quanto t'ami.

I will not say what is
In your joy, Orfeo, my joy,
Since I do not have my heart with me,
But it remains with you in the company of Love;
Ask then of it if you wish to know
How happy it rejoices, and how much I love you.[15]

While this is a typical conceit in sixteenth- and seventeenth-century Italian love poetry, it is nevertheless indicative of the psychological fact that the woman whom Orfeo loves is not, in Jungian terms, an individual separate from himself, but rather his own *anima* projected from his unconscious onto the shadowy figure of Euridice. Monteverdi depicts the insubstantiality of Euridice by giving her music that itself is insubstantial and uncommitted, even ominous. She begins by outlining a dissonant tritone, and the entire brief passage is unstable harmonically, shifting rapidly from cadences on one pitch to another (see Example 20.1).[16] The passage begins on the fourth degree of A, whose cadence in bar 3 is reached melodically through the tritone D–G♮. But motion through F major and C major harmonies (bars 4 and 6) leads hastily to a cadence on G major (bar 7), thence to D minor (bars 10–11), and A minor (bar 13). Once again F major and C major harmonies intervene (bars 14–15) before Euridice concludes on D, whose dominant is preceded by a dissonant melodic B♭ resolved by the supporting G minor harmony (bars 15–16).

The atmosphere of celebration and revelry that characterizes Act I continues at the beginning of Act II; but upon the entrance of Sylvia, the messenger who bears the terrible news of Euridice's death, the musical style shifts radically to a powerful,

Example 20.1 Euridice, *Io non so dirò*.

anguished recitative. Sylvia is barely able to articulate her message because of the oppressive tragedy that overwhelms her:

[Ahi, las]sa,
Ch'ella i languidi lumi alquanto aprendo,
E te chiamando Orfeo, Orfeo,
Dopo un grave sospiro,
Spirò' fra queste braccia, ed io rimansi
Piena il cor di pietade e di spavento.

Ah, alas,
That her languishing eyes [still] somewhat perceiving
And calling you, 'Orfeo, Orfeo',
After a heavy sigh,
She expired in these arms, and I remained
With a heart full of pity and terror.

Her recitative is music of the unconscious, of outpourings of feeling that well up from the depths of the psyche, bursting forth with little sense of control or order (see Example 20.2). Impelled by the powerful emotions underlying the words, the music changes melodic direction and rhythmic configuration abruptly and is infused with dissonance and unexpected shifts of harmony. The excerpt, beginning on a D major triad, the dominant of G major, finally cadences in D, but not before passing through

Example 20.2 Excerpt from messenger's report.

chords or implied chords shifting with erratic and unpredictable chromaticism, a truly irrational succession.[17]

Striggio and Monteverdi's representation of this terrible news, and of Orfeo's reaction to it, is psychologically masterful. It takes some time, after an introduction of anguished lamenting, for Sylvia finally to say unequivocally that Euridice is dead. Orfeo is struck dumb by these words, and can only utter an inarticulate *Ohime, che odo? . . . ohime!* ('Alas, what do I hear? . . . alas'). Sylvia then proceeds to describe at length the circumstances surrounding Euridice's death before reaching the conclusion quoted above. This prolonged passage gives Orfeo time to collect his thoughts, to shape his reaction, both emotionally and intellectually. Even when the messenger has finished, it is a shepherd who first responds with his own anguished outcry, echoing the first outcry of Sylvia herself. When Orfeo finally does react, it is not in the form of an instinctive, unconscious emotional outburst, but rather with emotions couched in the terms of a reasoned, dialectical argument.

> Tu sei morta, mia vita, ed io respiro?
> Tu sei da me partita
> Per mai più non tornare, ed io rimango?
> No, che se i versi alcuna cosa ponno,
> N'andrò sicuro a'più profondi abissi,
> E, intenerito il cor del re de l'ombre,
> Meco trarrotti a riveder le stelle;
> O, se ciò negherammi empio destino,
> Rimarrò teco in compagnia di morte.
> Addio terra, addio cielo e sole, addio.[18]

> *You are dead, my life, and I still breathe?*
> *You have departed from me*
> *Never to return, and I remain?*
> *No, if my verses can do anything at all,*
> *I shall surely descend into the deepest abysses,*
> *And, having softened the heart of the King of Shades,*
> *Lead you back with me to see again the stars;*
> *Or, if cruel destiny will deny me this,*
> *I shall remain with you in the company of death.*
> *Goodbye earth, goodbye sky and sun, goodbye.*

While the text begins with an expression of disbelief that Euridice is dead and Orfeo still alive, this dichotomy serves as the launching point for an emotional, but still rational, dialectical discussion of how to proceed. The opposing conditions of Euridice and Orfeo quickly become a dialectic of spatial separation: Euridice is below in the Underworld and Orfeo remains above in the land of the living. This spatial opposition leads to a decision to act to eliminate the separation by one of two means: Orfeo will descend into the Underworld to retrieve Euridice by softening the heart of Pluto, the King of the Shades, and bring her back to see the stars; or, if that fails, he will remain with her in the Underworld. Once the decision to act is made, Orfeo closes the argument by bidding farewell to the cosmic objects of the space he currently enjoys above in order to descend

Example 20.3 Orfeo, *Tu sei morta*.

below. In contrast to the outpourings of grief by the messenger Sylvia, Orfeo, in a moment of great emotional stress, is composed and capable of conscious deliberation.

Monteverdi's musical representation (Example 20.3) takes its point of departure from Striggio's verbal cues. It is the beginning of the text that is most emotionally charged. Orfeo waits almost two bars before responding with an opening drop of a diminished fourth in *cantus mollis* in G, from B♭ to a very dissonant F♮ followed by an upward resolution (bars 3–4).[19] A chromatic ascent from the G ending Orfeo's first phrase through a dissonant G♮ at the beginning of the second, to A and B♮ at the dissonant high point of the phrase, leads to a half-cadence on an E major triad, remote from the opening G minor (bars 4–8). The dissonance and the remote harmonic juxtaposition underscore the psychological disruption Orfeo has experienced by the sudden loss of his wife. This opening gambit establishes a musical dichotomy paralleling the opposed terms by which Euridice is described: the first phrase ends with *morta* on G, while the second, referring to her as Orfeo's *vita*, concludes on G♮, each representing a radically contrasting harmony and tonality. The expression of dichotomies continues as Orfeo again contrasts his condition to that of Euridice with the words *ed io respiro* (bars 8–10). He begins on G, the pitch of Euridice's death, and moves to B♭, supported by a V–I progression, which sets him, still alive, apart in a different tonality and a different mode from the opening G minor of the deceased Euridice.

The next phrase (bars 11–17) represents an intensification of the first. The bass is repeated, but the opening vocal pitch is a third higher, on D, making the leap down to the dissonant F♮ (also sustained longer) even more striking; and the chromatically inflected ascent, previously to B, is now extended to D and settles on B♮ in contrast to G♮. Whereas the second phrase paused on a dominant E major chord, this variant version continues pressing upward (bars 17–18) to the highest pitch in the piece, E4, on the word *rimango*—musically representing the spatial distance between the living Orfeo, who remains above, and the dead Euridice, whose note of death is the *g* below.

This opening passage is Striggio's and Monteverdi's way of expressing the anguish of Orfeo, but it is not the anguish of a spontaneous, unconscious outburst of pain. Rather, it is a carefully constructed expression of sorrow by someone who has already grasped his circumstance and decided what to do. That decision comes immediately on the heels of the high E4 (bars 19–21) with the word *no*, first on C then repeated and intensified on D, before beginning a stepwise descent. This motion (bars 20–3) articulates Orfeo's intention to descend into the Underworld to return Euridice to life, and the music follows him into the abyss (*più profondi abissi*) to the lowest pitch of the piece, C3. The entire phrase (bars 14–23), beginning with *se' da me partita*, has been one long ascent and descent, with only a couple of momentary pauses for breath, reaching its apogee in citing Orfeo's spatial position and its depth in citing Euridice's. The harmony throughout is much more stable, and far less dissonant, than in the opening phrases, for these are the words not of the distraught Orfeo, but of the Orfeo of decision and action.

Orfeo's purpose in his descent into the abyss is to soften the heart of Pluto (*e intenerito il cor*), and the tritone leap in the bass from F to B♮ is softened by the chromatic descent to B♭, then A (bars 24–6). Similarly, Orfeo's melodic line, which begins with a consonant A, becoming dissonant as the bass moves, is softened by its own resolution to G♮, which itself becomes dissonant in its repetition when the bass moves again, and is in turn softened by its tritone leap down to D and resolution upward to F. But as the phrase continues with the bass descending, the F too becomes dissonant before resolving downwards to the consonant *e* as part of the cadence on D minor (bars 25–8). Thus the entire phrase comprises a succession of consonances and dissonances that concludes on the as-yet-unheard chord of A major as dominant to the new tonic of D, for Orfeo is seeking to change the state of affairs.

By softening the heart of the King of Shades with his verses, he will carry Euridice up again to see the stars, reversing her spatial position. Monteverdi's melodic line (bars 28–30) likewise changes position, from a low tonic D reaching up for a second time to its high point of E4 before settling back to a cadential D an octave above its starting point. But recognizing the possibility of failure, Orfeo presents an alternative solution to his dilemma: he will remain with Euridice in the company of death, that is, he will exchange his spatial position for hers. Once again Monteverdi expresses and reinforces the dialectic with a descent reaching the lowest pitch of the piece, C3, on the word *morte* (bars 31–7). At this point the argument is concluded, and all that remains is for Orfeo to bid farewell to the world and sky above before commencing his descent into the Underworld. As he names earth, sky, and sun, Monteverdi gives him an ascending and intensifying sequence, reaching D4 again as he names the sun (his father Apollo, whom he had already addressed as *Rosa del ciel* in his first musical appearance at the centre of Act I). The final *addio* (bars 38–45) then suddenly drops an octave to D3, as if he had already begun his descent.

Orfeo's decision to descend into the Underworld hinges on his hope that his verses and song can soften the heart of Pluto, repeating with the lord of the Underworld the same kind of success he had previously had with Euridice. When Orfeo reaches the river dividing the living from the dead, he must persuade the ferryman Caronte to carry him across. Here he sings the most famous number in the opera, *Possente spirto*, in which he summons up the most astonishing virtuosity, even verbally and musically thumping his chest in the climactic fourth stanza (see Example 20.4) with Striggio's words, *Orfeo son io*, 'I am Orpheus':

> Orfeo son io che d'Euridice i passi
> Seguo per queste tenebrose arene
> Ove già mai per huom mortal non vassi.
>
> *Orpheus am I who the steps of Euridice*
> *Follow through these dark sands*
> *Where never mortal man has gone.*

An expression of conscious thought, this *tour de force* is cast by Striggio in the poetic form of a *capitolo* of six stanzas and a *commiato*, all in *terza rima*,[20] and by Monteverdi in the closed musical form of strophic variations on a *passamezzo antico* bass (Pryer 2007: 12–14), with each stanza separated by a ritornello. The structure is therefore similar to that of the dance songs of Act I and the first part of Act II before the interruption of the messenger. What is most different about *Possente spirto* is its extraordinary virtuosity. Monteverdi actually published two versions of the vocal line, a simple one and the highly ornamented one illustrated in Example 20.4. It is possible that the embellished version may represent what the first Orfeo, Francesco Rasi, sang at Mantua (Carter 2002: 130–1).[21] In any event, the precisely notated embellishments offer the performer one method of singing the piece, while the simple version furnishes the skeleton on which a skilled singer could improvise his own ornamentation.

But this magnificent vocal display is in vain, and for the first time in his experience, Orfeo utterly fails to achieve his goal by singing. His musical mastery and virtuosity cause a flutter in Caronte's heart but otherwise do not move him. This most forceful possible expression of Orfeo's conscious ego is inadequate to deal with a catastrophe of a kind he has never encountered before, which has completely upset the pattern of his life, and which has taken him to regions beyond his ken. On a musical level, even the most remarkable virtuosity is without power to move the passions, to stir Caronte. Virtuosity may cause one to marvel, but it has no effect on the passions of the soul.[22]

Orfeo recognizes that his virtuosity is ineffectual, and at this point Monteverdi breaks off the regular cycle of ritornellos and stanzas he has pursued up to now. Striggio has not deviated from his *terza rima*, but Monteverdi, recognizing that failure

Example 20.4 Orfeo, *Possente spirto*, verse 4.

Example 20.4 (continued).

has affected Orfeo psychologically, skips the expected ritornello, proceeds directly to the fifth stanza, and turns to recitative, with a more active bass and agitated harmony than before (see Example 20.5).

> O de le luci mie luci serene,
> S'un vostro sguardo può tornarmi in vita,
> Ahi chi niega il conforto a le mie pene?

> *O of my eyes the serene light,*
> *If a glance of yours can return me to life,*
> *Ah, who denies me comfort for my pain?*

At first Orfeo praises the light of Euridice's eyes, which could restore him to light, all in major tonalities; but then, turning to G minor, asks who could deny him comfort for his pain (bars 9–14). This recitative represents the beginning of an important psychological turning point for Orfeo, when, in the face of the unresponsive ferryman, he abandons the conscious pride of his ego-driven virtuosity and begins to pour out his heart in a more spontaneous, intense manner, expressing himself less predictably than the carefully structured preceding stanzas. The fifth stanza turns toward a more unconscious form of utterance, which is given added emotional urgency by repetition

Example 20.5 Orfeo, *Possente spirto*, stanza 5.

of the last line (the first time Monteverdi makes such a gesture in *Possente spirto*). This repetition (bars 15–20) is identical melodically (though slightly altered rhythmically), but its accompaniment is chromatically inflected with more first inversion chords that generate more dissonances with the vocal line.

The final stanza follows directly upon the fifth, again without any intervening ritornello, but with its own harmony and vocal line. This is Orfeo's final plea to Caronte, and even though still in recitative, it assumes a somewhat more formal character than the fifth verse, with more structured melody and harmony. Orfeo tries to win his way across with a conscious argument, still trusting in his familiar ally, the power of his lyre:

Sol tu nobil Dio puoi darmi aita,
Ne temer dei che sopra'un'aurea cetra,
Sol di corde soavi armo le ditta,
Contra cui rigid'alma in van s'impetra.[23]

Only you, noble God, can help me,
Nor need you fear, since upon a golden lyre,
Only with sweet strings arm I my fingers,
Against which a rigid soul in vain hardens itself.

In these fifth and sixth stanzas we hear the authentic voice of Orfeo's emotions, unencumbered by the ego-driven virtuosity and formal structure of the first four strophes, but in the end still controlled enough to make the kind of argument he hopes will persuade the ferryman to transport him across the river.[24] But despite being delighted with Orfeo's singing, Caronte, who is devoid of pity, remains true to character.

In response, Striggio abandons the lengthy 11-syllable lines of *terza rima* of the previous strophes, dissolving into a pair of terzets with 7- and 11-syllable lines followed by a set of 7-syllable lines in paired rhymes. The vocabulary, too, loses its elevated style in favour of simpler words with fewer syllables:

Ahi sventurato amante
Sperar dunque non lice
Ch'odan miei preghi cittadin d'Averno?
Onde qual ombra errante
D'insepolto cadavero e infelice
Privo sarò del Cielo e de l'Inferno?
Cosi vuol empia sorte
Ch'in questi orror di morte
Da te cor mio lontano
Chiami tuo nome invano,
E pregando, e piangendo mi consumi?
Rendetemi il mio ben Tartarei Numi.

Ah, unfortunate lover
To hope is then denied
That the citizens of Averno will hear my prayers?
Whereby as a wandering shade
Of an unburied and unhappy corpse
Deprived will I be of both Heaven and Hell?
Thus does cruel fate wish
That in this horror of death
Far from you, my heart
I call your name in vain,
And pleading and weeping I consume myself?
Return to me my love, Tartarean gods.

This is a very significant shift in tone, for now Orfeo is gushing out his frustration in short words and rapid lines that tumble one after another. Rather than the language of deliberate, conscious planning and argument, this is the spontaneous, instinctive outpouring of despair that comes unpremeditated and unfettered from deep within the heart: the speech of the unconscious.

But even more important and obvious than the poetic change is the musical shift, for now not only virtuosity, but even any sense of melodic shape and harmonic structure have vanished (see Example 20.6). Orfeo, in desperation, spills out his anxiety in declamatory recitative with dissonances at several points of harmonic change (bars 2, 16, 17, 19), no longer singing with the structure of the conscious ego, but in an unconscious, instinctive, nearly staccato effusion of unbridled torment forced to the surface by the strength of its psychic energy. At the end (bars 23–30) his emotional outburst reaches its climax with his demand that Euridice be returned to him, repeated insistently three times in an ascending sequence of chromatic half-steps.[25]

But Caronte has no soul and remains untouched; instead, he is lulled to sleep by Orfeo's music, and Orfeo is able to seize the ferryman's boat and propel himself across the river. When he reaches the opposite shore, he finds that it is Persephone, Pluto's wife, who has been moved—not, I would argue, by his conscious egoistic virtuosity, but by his concluding spontaneous, anguished plea. Significantly, it is Persephone who is

Example 20.6 Orfeo, *Ahi sventurato amante.*

responsive to Orfeo, for she too came from the world above, from the light. She had
been kidnapped by Pluto and brought down into Hades to be his wife, but to keep her
he had to accede to the condition that she return once a year to the upper world and the
light of day. Persephone comes from Orfeo's world, but she has also fallen in love with
her kidnapper and instinctively feels the pain of Orfeo in his plea. It is Persephone, the
feminine aspect of the Underworld, rather than Orfeo, who persuades Pluto to let
Euridice go, not without some seductive musical gestures of her own. But as in Virgil,

Ovid, and Poliziano, Pluto is clever enough to fool both Persephone and Orfeo by setting a condition for Euridice's return that he knows Orfeo cannot fulfil.

This is the crucial moment for Orfeo. He has descended into the Underworld, that realm which in mythologies all over the world represents the unconscious; and by finally letting his heart, his spontaneous feelings, speak instead of his head and lyre, he has gained a measure of success in this dark and dangerous realm. But—and this is the key point—he learns nothing from his encounter with the unconscious. For as soon as Pluto agrees to let Euridice go and states his admonition, Orfeo begins his ascent out of the Underworld, out of the unconscious, singing a rather silly ditty in praise of the lyre he foolishly thinks has won the day (see Example 20.7). In fact, his song in praise of his lyre recalls the strophic celebratory music of Act I and the beginning of Act II. It reflects no change in Orfeo's personality or understanding as a result of his traumatic

Example 20.7 Orfeo, *Qual honor*, stanza 1.

experience and his descent into the Underworld.[26] The unconscious has made no impact on his consciousness:

Qual honor di te sia degno
Mia cetra onnipotente,
S'hai nel Tartareo Regno
Piegar potuto ogn'indurate mente?
Luogo havrai fra le più belle
Imagini celesti,
Ond'al tuo suon le stelle
Danzeranno [con] gir'hor tard'hor presti.[27]
Io per te felice à pieno
Vedrò l'amato volto,
E nel candido seno
De la mia Donna oggi sarò raccolto.

What honour could be worthy of you
My omnipotent lyre
If you, in the Tartarean Realm
Were able to bend every hardened mind?
You will have a place among the most beautiful
Celestial images
Where to your sound the stars
Will dance with turns now slow, now fast.
I, through you, am filled with happiness
I will see her beloved face,
And in the white bosom
Of my lady, today I will be received.

Orfeo thinks it was the magic of his lyre, the result of his conscious virtuosity in the first four stanzas of *Possente spirto*, that won Euridice's release rather than the subsequent spontaneous outpourings of his heart following the failure of his virtuosity. He does not realize that it was Persephone, rather than Pluto, who was the source of his apparent good fortune. He does not appreciate the seriousness of Pluto's warning and the need to constrain his instincts and impulses. He understands nothing about the falsity of appearances and the danger he still faces, nor of the profundity of restoring the dead to life. He perceives nothing new about the world he inhabits, nor about fate and the numinous forces of Hades. Orfeo has gained no new perspective, no new wisdom from his experience in the Underworld, from his plunge into the darkness of the unconscious, and most of all, he understands no more about himself and his unbridled passions than he did before he lost Euridice in the first place.[28]

It is this simple-minded, foolish Orfeo, the singer of the silly ditty to his lyre, who is so easily induced to turn around and look for Euridice by a few noises and taunting from the denizens of Hades. He claims that the god of love is more powerful than the admonition of the god of the Underworld.[29] But he is wrong, because he is unable to place love in a larger context, unable to grasp that conscious understanding of circumstances must hold love within its proper bounds, unable to understand when something else must command his attention in order for love to survive. He is wrong because his love is wholly a manifestation of his unconscious: the love of his own *anima* projection, not the woman Euridice herself.

Orfeo has failed to achieve any growth of consciousness from his experience in the Underworld, any integration of the unconscious with the conscious that would allow him to view himself and respond to his passions differently. In the face of catastrophe followed by an apparently successful outcome to his daring act, he remains the same as he was before, and his failure to achieve any individuation results in a double catastrophe: the permanent loss of both his *anima* and Euridice. The effect of his ineffectual encounter with the Underworld, the unconscious, is immediately devastating, as his psyche, with a crucial part now excised, chaotically disintegrates before our eyes and ears.

Monteverdi's musical interpretation of this disintegration begins already at the moment of Orfeo's uncertainty and fearfulness prompted by the loud noise he hears as he leads Euridice toward the light; it then continues with the shade Euridice herself (see Example 20.8).

> Ahi vista troppo dolce e troppo amara:
> Cosi per troppo amor dunque mi perdi?
> Et io misera perdo
> Il poter più godere
> E di luce e di vita, e perdo insieme
> Te d'ogni ben più caro, o mio consorte.

> *Ah, sight too sweet and too bitter:*
> *Thus for too much love then you lose me?*
> *And I, wretched, lose*
> *The ability to enjoy again*
> *Both light and life, and I lose at the same time*
> *You, more dear than anything, oh my husband.*

Example 20.8 Euridice, *Ahi vista troppo.*

Euridice begins with the same tritone outline with which she had first responded to Orfeo, dissolving into further dissonance (bars 4 and 7) and the tritone again (bars 9–10), as she departs for good. The G minor tonal implication of the opening chord is refuted by the E major triad of the third bar, and the passage remains tonally ambiguous and harmonically unstable, never truly resolving to any tonality until the final cadence on G.[30]

After a spirit orders Euridice back to Hades, Orfeo, bereft of the *anima* part of his psyche, now disintegrates altogether with a series of confused questions accompanied by jolting chromaticism and utter dissolution of harmonic stability and direction (see Example 20.9).

Dove te'n vai mia vita? Ecco i' ti seguo.
Ma chi me'l niegh'ohime: sogno, o vaneggio?
Qual occulto poter di questi orrori,
Da questi amati orrori
Mal mio grado mi tragge e mi conduce
A l'odiosa luce?[31]

Where are you going my love? Here, I'll follow you.
But who denies me, alas: do I dream or rave?
What dark power of these horrid realms,
From these beloved shades,
Despite my wish, drags me and leads me
To the hateful light?

Monteverdi's opening suggests an orientation toward G major (bars 1–4), but this is negated by the B♭ in the bass (bar 5), which in turn suggests a possible D minor (bars 5–6), only to be followed by a tritone leap in the bass to a sudden E major triad

Example 20.9 Orfeo, *Dove te'n vai?*

succeeded by a D major chord implying a dominant of G in keeping with the unanswered question it accompanies. However, not only is resolution to the G minor triad postponed by the C minor triad in bars 8–9, but the ensuing G bass of the minor triad itself immediately thereafter supports an ambiguous major sixth (bars 9–10). At this point the bass suggests A Aeolian for a substantial period, but the melodic line belies it with both sustained and brief dissonances (bars 10–14), and a particularly pungent one in bar 15 at the word *odiosa* ('hateful'). The entire passage then concludes on an unresolved dominant of A, as if suspending Orfeo's entire psyche in mid-air.

The next time we see Orfeo is in Act V on the plains of Thrace lamenting his bitter fate. I find this lament, however brilliantly composed, overly long and therefore ultimately tedious, but I also think that is exactly what Striggio and Monteverdi were trying to achieve psychologically. We witness this poor wretch who no longer seeks solace in the power of his lyre, who pours out his grief to the trees and rocks around him—those entities he used to be able to charm—which now simply echo his words back to him in truncated form. His words and music have no effect but to return amputated with only the final syllables remaining. Such echoes are a clever musical conceit found frequently in Italian music of the late sixteenth and early seventeenth centuries, but Striggio and Monteverdi turn this device to their dramatic ends, for Orfeo's lament is not merely ineffectual; Echo expresses his own frustration with Orfeo by responding in what appears to be a deliberately mocking tone. To Orfeo's *ahi pianto* ('oh tears'), Echo replies *hai pianto* ('you have wept'), in the perfect tense. But Orfeo keeps weeping, to the point of declaring *non ho pianto però tanto che basti* ('I do not have sufficient tears'), to which Echo responds simply *basti*, or, to render the meaning in modern colloquial terms, 'enough, already'. But Orfeo doesn't cease. He continues bewailing his fate for even more time than he had spent lamenting up to this point. A lament, like other forms of weeping, can have a positive psychological effect, discharging a large amount of emotional energy so that the lamenter can redirect his or her energies towards moving onwards, but in Orfeo's case the lament discharges nothing, leading only to more weeping and finally to the rejection of all women, to the denial of any possibility of his *anima* ever returning. To quote the Jungian analyst and scholar James Hollis, 'A reactive depression is . . . pathological when it profoundly disrupts one's normal functioning or when the disabling impact of the experience is prolonged beyond a reasonable period' (1996: 68).

In Striggio's original libretto, as in Virgil's, Ovid's, and Poliziano's versions of the myth, the Bacchic women now appear, though Striggio does not actually show them tearing Orfeo to pieces as the other authors relate—in other words, they do not enact in front of the audience the physical fragmentation symbolic of the psychic fragmentation resulting from Orfeo's failed individuation. Striggio's libretto does refer to Orfeo's fate to come, but leaves it to the audience's imagination and concludes with a dance around Orfeo by the taunting women. This, of course, is not the conclusion we know from Monteverdi's published scores of the opera. There is no proof that Monteverdi ever composed music for this original ending, though an unusual transposition rubric in the score of Act IV suggests that a change in plans had taken place sometime after the composition of the first half of that act, a change that may well have been required by the new text for Act V, and perhaps its music.[32] Prompted by one or more reasons we can only speculate about, Monteverdi either became dissatisfied with the first conclusion or was asked to change it by his patron.[33]

The new ending of Act V has been criticized for its *Deus ex machina* resolution of Orfeo's dilemma, whereby Apollo descends on a cloud from Heaven and carries Orfeo off with him to see Euridice configured eternally in the stars.[34] I have quite a different view of this ending, however, which I think, whatever its shortcomings, rounds out the opera much better than Striggio's original conclusion. In rescuing Orfeo, Apollo criticizes his son for his lack of moderation between emotional extremes (a criticism which represents a fundamental tenet of Platonic philosophy). He had rejoiced too much in his good fortune and now he grieves too much over his bitter fate. He has not learned that all earthly pleasures are only temporary.

Apollo's descent symmetrically balances the paean to the sun (Apollo himself) in Act I (*Rosa del ciel*) where the sun god was witness to Orfeo's excessive outpouring of love; now he is witness to Orfeo's excessive effusion of sorrow. In fact, the chorus had already sung a warning against abandoning oneself to sadness at the end of Act I, and after Orfeo loses Euridice for the second time comments *Degna d'eterna gloria fia sol colui ch'avrà di se vittoria* ('only he who has mastered himself is worthy of eternal glory'—an admonition that meshes well with Jung's theory of individuation); but the thought was left hanging, so to speak, in Striggio's original libretto. Thus the moral to the story can only be brought home by completing the significance of that thought with Apollo's criticism of Orfeo's overbearing grief in Act V. The Act V revision also produces symmetry between Orfeo's earthly experiences in his initial lamentations over Euridice's resistance turned into happiness by her eventual acquiescence, and his otherworldly experiences involving even greater lamentation and a different kind of satisfaction in being transported by Apollo to Heaven to see her configured there.

There is likewise a psychological level on which the new ending of Act V can be considered successful. In Jung's theory, when one is faced with an irresolvable dilemma, one can indeed fragment psychologically as Orfeo does in Striggio's version; but one can also be presented with an unexpected solution produced spontaneously by the unconscious, what Jung calls the 'third way', when caught on the horns of a binary dilemma.[35] The descent of Apollo and his bearing of Orfeo off to Heaven can be viewed as that third way, a solution generated by the unconscious, which is quite different from what Orfeo consciously sought. This unexpected solution enables him to see his relationship to Euridice in an entirely new way, as a constellation in Heaven, rather than as an *anima* projection. In *Tu sei morta*, cited above (see Example 20.3), Orfeo had declared that he would carry Euridice with him out of Hades to see the stars again. Now she herself has become the stars and he is the one transported upwards. Jung's 'third way' is indeed a *deus ex machina*, where the *machina* is the unconscious, the original source of all god images, mythologies, and creative solutions.

Obviously, Striggio, Monteverdi and the author of the revised last act knew nothing of psychoanalytic theory. Jungian psychology, however, provides us with a means of interpreting and understanding the psychological phenomena presented to us by these figures. What I find so remarkable about Monteverdi, taking what his librettist(s) gave him, is the psychological insight with which he responded to Orfeo's circumstances; how clearly he understood psychological principles that Jung later enunciated in his own psychoanalytic terms, and how imaginatively and convincingly Monteverdi presented Orfeo's psychology in his music. Orfeo was a man beset by a typically human problem, the impingement of the unconscious on conscious life and activity. His tragedy, like that of many people, was his failure to recognize that impingement and to come to grips with the subsequent catastrophes of his life by making use of the unconscious to understand, change, and renew himself in the face of these disasters— his failure, in Jung's terminology, to 'individuate', leading inevitably to psychic disintegration.

If there is a moral lesson in Monteverdi's opera, as Galilei thought drama in music should have, it is not only about the need for moderation in balancing the emotional extremes of life and not expecting the permanence of earthly happiness; but also about the need for psychological growth, for individuation, in the face of life's inescapable challenges and tragedies. Perhaps we ourselves instinctively (i.e. unconsciously) recognize this in the story and in Monteverdi's music, and that is why the opera continues to attract, fascinate, and move us over 400 years after its creation.

Acknowledgements

This chapter is expanded from papers read at the University of Toronto, the University of Kentucky, the conference of the International Association for Jungian Studies at the University of Greenwich, and the International Conference on Music and Consciousness at the University of Sheffield. I would like to thank Elizabeth Aurbach, Richard Aurbach, David Clarke, Eric Clarke, Beverly Field, Rose Holt, and Brian Vandenberg for their invaluable comments on and criticism of earlier versions of this essay.

References

Anderson, W.S. (1985). The Orpheus of Virgil and Ovid: *flebile nescio quid*, in J. Warden (ed.), *Orpheus: The Metamorphoses of a Myth*, 25–50 (Toronto: University of Toronto Press).

Carter, T. (1999). Singing *Orfeo*: on the performers of Monteverdi's first opera. *Recercare*, **11**, 75–118.

Carter, T. (2002). *Monteverdi's Musical Theatre* (New Haven, CT: Yale University Press).

Donington, R. (1968). Monteverdi's first opera, in D. Arnold and N. Fortune (eds.), *The Monteverdi Companion*, 257–76 (London: Faber and Faber).

Edinger, E.F. (1999). *The Psyche in Antiquity, Book One: Early Greek Philosophy* (ed.), D.A. Wesley (Toronto: Inner City Books).

Fenlon, I. (1986). The Mantuan *Orfeo*, in J. Whenham (ed.), *Orfeo*, 1–19 (Cambridge: Cambridge University Press).

Hanning, B.R. (2003). The ending of *L'Orfeo*: Father, son, and Rinuccini, in *Journal of Seventeenth-Century Music*, 9/1: In Armonia Favellare. Available at: http://sscm-jscm.press. illinois.edu/v9/no1/hanning.html.

Hill, J.W., (ed.) (2003). In *Armonia Favellare*: Report of the International Conference on Early Opera and Monody to Commemorate the 400th Anniversary of the Italian Music Dramas of 1600, Held at the University of Illinois, Urbana-Champaign, October 5–8, 2000. Available at: http://sscm-jscm.press.illinois.edu/v9no1.html.

Hollis, J. (1996). *Swamplands of the Soul: New Life in Dismal Places* (Toronto: University of Toronto Press).

Jung, C.G. (1953). *Two Essays on Analytical Psychology*, trans. R.F.C. Hull, *Bollingen Series* XX, vol. 7 (Princeton, NJ: Princeton University Press).

Jung, C.G. (1971). *Psychological Types*, trans. H.G. Baynes, rev. R.F.C. Hull, *Bollingen Series* XX, vol. 6 (Princeton, NJ: Princeton University Press).

Jung, E. (1957). *Animus and Anima*, trans. C.F. Baynes and H. Nagel (Dallas, TX: Spring Publications).

Kerman, J. (1956). 'Orpheus: the neoclassic vision', in Kerman, *Opera as Drama*, 25–49 (New York, NY: Vintage Books); reprinted in J. Whenham (ed.) (1986), *Orfeo*, 126–37 (Cambridge: Cambridge University Press).

Kurtzman, J. (2003). Deconstructing gender in Monteverdi's *L'Orfeo*. *Journal of Seventeenth-Century Music*, **9**. Available at http://sscm-jscm.press.illinois.edu/v9/no1/kurtzman.html.

Lax, E. (ed.) (1994). *Claudio Monteverdi: Lettere* (Florence: Leo S. Olschki Editore).

McClary, S. (1989). Constructions of gender in Monteverdi's dramatic music. *Cambridge Opera Journal*, **1**, 203–23.

Mioli, P. (1993). *Claudio Monteverdi: L'Orfeo, Favola in Musica* in *Archivium Musicum, Musica Drammatica, I* (Florence: Studio per Edizioni Scelte).

Palisca, C.V. (1989). *The Florentine Camerata: Documentary Studies and Translations* (New Haven, CT: Yale University Press).

Pryer, A. (2007). Approaching Monteverdi: his cultures and ours, in J. Whenham and R. Wistreich (eds.), *The Cambridge Companion to Monteverdi*, 1–19 (Cambridge: Cambridge University Press).

Robbins, E. (1985). Famous Orpheus, in J. Warden (ed.), *Orpheus: The Metamorphoses of a Myth*, 3–23 (Toronto: University of Toronto Press).

Scavizzi, G. (1985). The myth of Orpheus in Italian renaissance art, 1400–1600, in J. Warden (ed.), *Orpheus: The Metamorphoses of a Myth*, 111–62 (Toronto: University of Toronto Press).

Segaller, S. (director and producer) (c. 1989). *The Wisdom of the Dream: Carl Gustav Jung*, vol. 1 (Wilamette, IL: Public Media Video).

Steinheuer, J. (2007). Orfeo (1607), in J. Whenham and R. Wistreich (eds.), *The Cambridge Companion to Monteverdi*, 119–40 (Cambridge: Cambridge University Press).

Stevens, D. (1972). *Claudio Monteverdi: L'Orfeo, Favola in Musica, Venice 1615* (London: Gregg International Publishers).

Stevens, D. (trans. and ed.) (1995). *The Letters of Claudio Monteverdi*, rev. edn (Oxford: Clarendon Press).

Strunk, O. (1950). *Source Readings in Music History* (New York, NY: W.W. Norton & Co.).

Tomlinson, G. (1993). *Music in Renaissance Magic: Toward a Historiography of Others* (Chicago, IL: The University of Chicago Press).

Warden, J. (1985). Orpheus and Ficino, in J. Warden (ed.), *Orpheus: The Metamorphoses of a Myth*, 85–110 (Toronto: University of Toronto Press).

Notes

1. As Galilei put it (Strunk 1950: 313, 315, 319):

   let men, who have been endowed by nature with all these noble and excellent parts, endeavor to use them not merely to delight, but as imitators of the good ancients, to improve at the same time ... [P]assion and moral character must be simple and natural, or at least appear so, and their sole aim must be to arouse their counterpart in others ... [I]f the musician has not the power to direct the minds of his listeners to their benefit, his science and knowledge are to be reputed null and vain, since the art of music was instituted and numbered among the liberal arts for no other purpose.

For the principal documents relating to the background of opera see Palisca (1989).

2. The Renaissance belief in the magical powers of music is examined extensively in Tomlinson (1993).

3. Galilei's programme is described in his *Dialogo della musica antica et della moderna* (1581). For an English translation of the relevant passages see Strunk (1950), especially pp. 306–7, 312, 317.

4. *Euridice* was first performed in the Pitti Palace on 6 October 1600 as part of the wedding ceremonies of Henry IV and Maria de' Medici. It comprised mostly music by Peri, but with some insertions by Caccini. Both composers published their competing versions in the next few months.

5. A facsimile edition of the 1607 libretto and 1609 score was published with an introduction in Mioli (1993). A facsimile of the 1615 edition was published with an introduction in Stevens (1972).

6. The power of music to penetrate directly to the soul is an important theme in the *Republic* and other writings of Plato, as well as for such diverse Renaissance figures as Ficino and John Calvin.

7. In this and subsequent quotations from this source, I have omitted Jung's original footnotes and cross-references.

8. Jung also explores the significance of the *anima* and the *animus* in many of his other writings, including a chapter in his *Two Essays on Analytical Psychology* (C.G. Jung 1953), first published in 1917, but revised and reissued several times up to 1943. The most focused and comprehensive discussion of this subject was written by his wife: see Emma Jung (1957).

9. Quoted from a London interview in English, featured in Segaller (1989).

10. Dream analysis was a principal focus of Jung's therapeutic practice and many of his writings study mythology and such 'mythological' activities as alchemy.

11. 'Cryptomnesia' is a term Jung coined for the phenomenon of unconsciously appropriating for oneself someone else's thought, writing, or image and later reproducing it as one's own, not recognizing that it had an external source.

12. The myth has a variety of versions. Those of the Roman poets Virgil and Ovid are the best known, but there are several fragments with other, sometimes variant details as well. For an account of the Virgilian and Ovidian versions, see Anderson (1985). On the origins and variant early versions, see Robbins (1985).

13. This oft-quoted letter was sent from Venice, where Monteverdi was employed at the time as *maestro di cappella* at St Mark's. The original Italian may be found in Lax (1994: 19).

14. On Orfeo's Act I song to Euridice and her response see McClary (1989); for my response to McClary see Kurtzman (2003).

15. All translations from Striggio's libretto are mine. I have opted for a literal rendering in order that readers unfamiliar with Italian can, as far as possible, relate each word in the associated music example to its English counterpart.

16. The significance of the tritone as a symbol of the loss of Euridice is penetratingly explored in Donington (1968: 263–4, 272).

17. For a fuller analysis of the tonalities of this passage and their dramatic significance see Steinheuer (2007: 128–9).

18. The version of the text given here is that found in the scores of the opera published in 1609 and 1615 (Mioli 1993; Stevens 1972). The version originally published in Striggio's 1607 libretto differs in a few details.

19. *Cantus mollis* refers to a staff system with a single-flat signature, indicating the soft hexachord.

20. See Steinheuer (2007: 136–9). *Terza rima* is the poetic form of Dante's *La Divina Commedia*. Dante, like Striggio, follows Virgil in describing a descent into the Underworld.

21. Pryer (2007: 12–14) calls attention to a close relationship between Monteverdi's unadorned line and Giulio Caccini's aria *Qual trascorrendo* from *Il Rapimento di Cefalo* of 1600, published in his *Le Nuove Musiche* of 1601—a piece originally sung by Francesco Rasi. Steinheuer (2007: 137) observes that Monteverdi's ornamentation is not merely embellishment of the simple line, but deviates from it 'for purposes of harmonious enrichment of the declamation'.

22. Anderson makes a parallel judgement on Ovid's text at this point in the story:

    > the song he assigns Orpheus is anything but unique: it makes no emotional appeal whatsoever, but works with cheap, flashy, and specious rhetoric to persuade Hades to go against his own nature. As a consequence, Orpheus strikes us as a third-rate poet-orator, assigned the task of creating an inimitable song and trying to regain Eurydice, can only mouth commonplaces or try to devise clever but lifeless points ('colores') and so win applause. . . . Ovid presents it [love] as a chill abstract noun, a calculated point in persuasive discourse that has nothing in the previous narrative or in Orpheus' character to support it. (1985: 40)

23. This line is the *commiato* of the *capitolo*.

24. Steinheuer (2007: 138–9) summarizes the aria as follows: 'In "Possente spirto" . . . Monteverdi paints a singer certain of his abilities at the outset, who is first disturbed and finally overwhelmed by his emotions but then controls them again in the final stanza.'

25. Steinheuer (2007: 139–40) describes this passage as 'rapid, restless declamation soaked with dissonance to give Orfeo's despair free rein, culminating in a refrain section at the end'. Steinheuer continues: 'In this passage Orfeo achieves exactly that affective style, seemingly artless and spontaneous, despite its refined compositional technique'.

26. Kerman (1956: 33, 1986: 131–2) interprets the song egoistically: 'In Act IV, when Eurydice is released, the drama quickens as it reveals Orpheus' rather terrible insufficiency. His reaction is neither gratitude nor real affection, but a hymn of praise to himself and to his lyre'. Steinheuer (2007: 133–4) also notes the parallelism between this strophic song and those of Act II, but in addition outlines its unequal line lengths and strophic variations over a walking bass. Steinheuer considers these strophic songs representatives of a 'low' style in contrast to passages in the 'middle' and 'high' styles.

27. The reading of this line is taken from Striggio's libretto. Both editions of the score substitute *Io* for *con*, which makes no sense.

28. Kerman (1956: 33, 1986: 132) also observes that 'Orpheus learns nothing'. Anderson (1985: 32) likewise comments on Orpheus's failure to come to grips with his passions and to make room for a new future.

29. This idea also echoes Ficino's concept of the power and priority of love, as described in Warden (1985: 101–2).

30. Steinheuer (2007: 129–31) analyses the tonal structure of the entire passage, indicating the dramatic references of the constantly changing tonalities that Orfeo and Euridice pass through.

31. The libretto differs from the text of the published scores in some details: *Dove te'n vai mia vita? ecco i' ti seguo./Ma chi me'l vieta ohime: sogno, o vaneggio?/Qual poter, qual furor da questi orrori,/Da questi amati orrori/Mal mio grado mi tragge, e mi conduce/A l'odiosa luce?*

32. The rubric, in a solo tenor part on p. 76 of the 1609 and 1615 scores, reads 'Un tono più alto', which unequivocally means transposition a tone higher. Such a rubric was a means of avoiding rewriting or reprinting the music at the sounding pitch that had already been notated a step lower. See Carter (1999: 103–5, 2002: 98, 121) for one possible explanation of why this rubric was required.

33. There has been much speculation as to who might have revised the text of the last act as published in 1609 and 1615—whether Striggio, Prince Francesco Gonzaga, or someone else. Recently, however, Hanning (2003), through a close and sophisticated textual analysis, has concluded—quite convincingly in my view—that the new Act V ending was written by Ottavio Rinuccini. Rinuccini was not only the librettist of the Florentine *Euridice* several years earlier, but also the author of the librettos for Monteverdi's second opera, *Arianna*, and for his dramatic ballet, *Il ballo delle ingrate*, both performed as part of the 1608 Mantuan wedding festivities.

34. See, for example, the comments in Kerman (1956: 32, 37, 1986: 132, 135).

35. Jung first introduces this concept in his chapter on Friedrich Schiller's *Letters on the Aesthetic Education of Man* (C.G. Jung 1971: 88–9). The Jungian scholar Edward Edinger explains the 'third way' in this manner: 'If problems on the concrete level of personal human existence are irreconcilable within the usual terms of understanding, then with the help of material from the unconscious such as dreams or fantasies—thus raising the problem to a symbolic level—the dilemma can often be resolved' (1999: 27).

Index